Flea Market Trader

Seventeenth Edition

NOW IN **FULL COLOR!**

THOUSANDS
OF ITEMS
WITH
CURRENT
VALUES

COLLECTOR BOOKS
A Division of Schroeder Publishing Co., Inc.

Editors:
Donna Newnum, Loretta Suiters
Contributing Editor:
Sharon Huxford
Cover Design:
Beth Summers

Editorial Assistants:
Jessica Woodrow, Kim Vincent
Layout:
Terri Hunter

Searching for a Publisher?

We are always looking for people knowledgeable within their fields. If you feel there is a real need for a book on your collectible subject and have a large comprehensive collection, contact Collector Books.

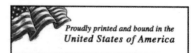

Proudly printed and bound in the
United States of America

Introduction

No level of the collectibles and antiques market offers more fun and diversity than the flea market. This publication is directed specifically toward that venue. With each edition, we scour the malls and markets, check out internet auctions, and dig up as many fresh areas of interest as we possibly can, generally long before the average flea market shopper becomes aware of their potential. We hope you'll enjoy investigating this edition for new categories and that you'll take advantage of being first in the know! Not only will you have the best chance at finding those choice items by learning about them early, but you'll more than likely be able to buy them for much less than when they're in popular demand.

It's the well-informed collector who is the wise shopper. This guide provides everything you'll need to be just that — background narratives with bits of general information, great color illustrations, and current market values. Please bear in mind that the suggested prices in this guide are meant to be just a guide. Many factors determine actual selling prices. Values vary from one region to another; dealers pay various wholesale prices for their wares, and your bargaining skill is important too.

We have organized our listings into general categories for easy use. If you have trouble locating an item, refer to the index. Be sure to read category narratives, as many will explain what condition our suggested values target. When narratives contain no such information, unless noted otherwise, the values we have suggested reflect prices of items in mint condition. NM stands for minimal damage or wear. VG indicates that the items will bring 40% to 60% of its mint price. EX should be somewhere between the two. Glassware is assumed clear unless a color is noted. Only generally accepted abbreviations have been used. When only one dimension is given, it will be height, and height will always be given first in our descriptions.

Abbreviations

dia — diameter	pc — piece
ea — each	pg — page
EX — excellent	pr — pair
gal — gallon	pt — pint
L — long	qt — quart
lb — pound	rnd — round
lg — large	sm — small
M — mint	sq — square
med — medium	VG — very good
MIB — mint in box	(+) — has been reproduced
NRFB — never removed from box	

Action Figures

The first line of action figures Hasbro developed in 1964 was GI Joe. It met with such huge success that Mego, Kenner, Mattel, and a host of other manufacturers soon began producing their own lines. GI Joe, Marx's Best of the West series, and several of Mego's figures were 12", others were 8" or 9" tall, and the most popular size in the last few years has been 3¾". Many lines came with accessory items such as vehicles, clothing, and guns. Original packaging (most now come on cards) is critical when it comes to evaluating your action figures, especially the more recent issues. Values given for MIB or MOC can be reduced by at least 60% when appraising a 'loose' figure in even the best condition — in fact, most are worth only a few dollars. For more information refer to *Schroeder's Collectible Toys, Antique to Modern,* published by Collector Books. See also GI Joe; Star Wars.

Alien, figure, Alien, 18", Kenner, 1980, M, from $175 to...**200.00**

American West, figure, Davy Crockett, Mego, MIB, from $90 to **100.00**

Archies, figure, any, Marx, MOC, from $65 to **75.00**

Batman (Animated), figure, Combat Belt Batman, Kenner, MOC, from $28 to **35.00**

Batman Forever, figure, The Riddler, Kenner, MOC, from $40 to **45.00**

Battlestar Galactica, accessory, Colonial Scarab, Mattel, MIB, from $65 to **70.00**

Battlestar Galactia, figures, Baltar, second series, Mattel, MOC, $75.00; Commander Adama, first series, MOC, $40.00; Imperious Leader, first series, MOC, $30.00. (Photo courtesy Morphy Auctions)

Best of the West, accessory, Buckboard w/Horse & Harness, Marx, MIB.....................**200.00**

Best of the West, figure, Bill Buck, Marx, MIB, from $400 to..**450.00**

Best of the West, figure, Johnny West w/Thunderbolt, Marx, NMIB.....................**125.00**

Best of the West, figure, Sam Cobra, Marx, NMIB, from $75 to.**125.00**

Best of the West, horse, Thunderbolt, Marx, NMIB, from $50 to.**60.00**

Big Jim, accessory, Baja Beast, Mattel, MIB, from $60 to.**70.00**

Big Jim, accessory, Sky Commander, Mattel, MIB, from $60 to.**70.00**

Big Jim, figure, Big Jim (Gold Metal), Mattel, MIB, from $70 to **80.00**

Big Jim, figure, Dr Steel, Mattel, MIB, from $45 to.............**55.00**

Big Jim, outfit, any, Mattel, MIP, ea from $12 to **15.00**

Big Jim's PACK, accessory, Howler, Mattel, MIP, from $55 to.**65.00**

Big Jim's PACK, accessory, LazerVette Blitz-Rig, Mattel, MIP, from $80 to 90.00

Big Jim's PACK, figure, Big Jim (Commander), white pants, Mattel, MIB................125.00

Big Jim's PACK, figure, Dr Steel, Mattel, MIB, from $100 to....................115.00

Big Jim's PACK, figure, The Whip, Mattel, MIB, from $125 to.....................135.00

Big Jim's PACK, figure, Zorack the Enemy, Mattel, MIB, from $125 to...........................135.00

Bionic Woman, accessory, Sports Car, Kenner, MIB, from $90 to.....................110.00

Bionic Woman, figure, Jaime Sommers, Kenner, MIB, from $125 to..........................150.00

Bonanza, figure, Little Joe, American Character, M, from $50 to............................60.00

Bonanza, figure w/horse, any, American Character, MIB, ea from $175 to.................225.00

Bonanza, horse, any, American Character, MIB, ea from $65 to.....................................75.00

Buck Rogers, accessory, Star Fighter Command Center, Mego, MIB, from $50 to......................55.00

Buck Rogers, figure, Buck Rogers, 3¾", Mego, MOC, $60 to.65.00

Buck Rogers, figure, Twiki, 3¾", Mego, MOC, from $40 to.50.00

Captain Action, accessory, Headquarters, Ideal, MIB, from $450 to.................550.00

Captain Action, accessory, Silver Streak Amphibian Car, Ideal, MIB................1,500.00

Captain Action, figure, Action boy (space suit), Ideal, MIB, from $850 to..........................875.00

Captain Action, outfit, Batman (w/ ring), Ideal, MIB, from $700 to....................................725.00

Captain Action, outfit, Super Boy, Ideal, MIB, from $900 to..........................1,000.00

Charlie's Angels (TV Series), figure, any, Hasbro, MOC, from $75 to.............................85.00

CHiPs, accessory, motorcycle (for 8" figures), Mego, MIP, from $75 to.............................80.00

CHiPs, figure, Jon, 3¾", MOC, from $40 to.....................45.00

CHiPs, figure, Ponch, 8", Mego, MOC, from $18 to...........22.00

CHiPs, figure, Sarge, 3¾", Mego, MOC, from $22 to...........28.00

Clash of the Titans, figure, Calibas, Mattel, MOC, from $40 to..45.00

Clash of the Titans, figure, Kraken, Mattel, MOC, rare, from $250 to.....................................275.00

Clash of the Titans, figure, Perseus, Mattel, MOC, from $50 to..55.00

Comic Action Heroes, figure, Spider-Man, M, from $20 to.......25.00

Comic Action Heroes, figure, Wonder Woman, Mego, MIP, from $60 to......................65.00

Evil Knievel, figure, Robby Knievel, Ideal, 1973-74, MIP, from $50 to......................................70.00

Flash Gordon, figure, Dale Arden, Mego, MOC, from $80 to.90.00

Flash Gordon, figure, Dr Zarkov, Mego, MOC, from $100 to.............115.00

Indiana Jones (Adventures of), figure, Belloq, Kenner, MOC, from $60 to.....................70.00

Indiana Jones (Adventures of), figure, Indiana w/whip, 4", Kenner, MOC **250.00**

Indiana Jones (Lost Ark), figure, Indiana, 12", Kenner, MIB, from $200 to **225.00**

Indiana Jones & the Temple of Doom, figure, Indiana, LJN, MOC, from $140 to **150.00**

Johnny Apollo (Astronaut), figure, Jane Apollo, Marx, MIB, from $100 to **125.00**

Johnny Apollo (Astronaut), figure, Johnny Apollo, Marx, MIB, from $150 to **175.00**

Jurassic Park, figure, Tim Murphy (with retracting snare), Kenner, 1993, MOC, $9.00.

Knight Rider, accessory, 2000 Voice Car w/Michael figure, Kenner, MIB **50.00**

Knight Rider, figure, Michael Knight, Kenner, MOC, from $18 to **20.00**

Legend of the Lone Ranger, figure, Buffalo Bill Cody, Gabriel, MOC **28.00**

Legend of the Lone Ranger, figure, Butch Cavendish, Gabriel, MOC, from $24 to **28.00**

Legend of the Lone Ranger, figure w/horse, any, Gabriel, MOC, from $45 to **55.00**

Legend of the Lone Ranger, horse, Silver, Gabriel, MOC, from $28 to **32.00**

Lost in Space, accessory, Bubble Fighter, Trendmasters, MIB, from $75 to **85.00**

Lost in Space, accessory, Jupiter 2, Trendmasters, MIB, from $65 to **85.00**

Lost in Space, accessory, Jupiter 2 (Classic), Trendmasters, MIB **115.00**

Lost in Space, figure, Cyclops, Trendmasters, M, from $25 to................................... **30.00**

Lost in Space, figure, Dr Smith (Classic), 9", Trendmasters, M, from $20 to **25.00**

Lost in Space, figure, Robot B9 (Classic), Trendmasters, MIP, from $45 to **55.00**

Marvel Super Heroes, figure, Daredevil, Toy Biz, MOC, from $34 to **38.00**

Marvel Super Heroes, figure, Dr Doom, Toy Biz, MOC, from $24 to **28.00**

Marvel Super Heroes, figure, Green Goblin (back lever), Toy Biz, MOC................................. **42.00**

Marvel Super Heroes, figure, Invisible Woman (vanishing), Toy Biz, MOC **150.00**

Marvel Super Heroes, figure, Spider-Man, (web-shooting), Toy Biz, MOC **35.00**

Marvel Super Heroes, figure, Venom (Living Skin Slime Pores), Toy Biz, MOC, $20.00.

Marvel Super Heroes (Secret Wars), figure, Hobgoblin, Mattel, MOC............... 60.00

Marvel Super Heroes (Talking), figure, Toy Biz, any, MIP, from $20 to............... 25.00

Masters of the Universe, accessory, Battle Cat, Mattel, MIP, from $45 to............... 55.00

Masters of the Universe, accessory, Mantisaur, Mattel, MIP, from $24 to............... 28.00

Masters of the Universe, figure, He-Man, Mattel, MOC, from $200 to............... 210.00

Masters of the Universe, figure, King Randor, Mattel, MOC, from $80 to............... 85.00

Masters of the Universe, figure, Man-E-Faces, Mattel, MOC, from $60 to............... 65.00

Masters of the Universe, figure, Ninjor, Mattel, MOC, from $75 to... 85.00

Masters of the Universe, figure, Rotar, Mattel, MOC, from $65 to............... 75.00

Masters of the Universe, figure, Saurod, Mattel, MOC, from $40 to............... 50.00

Masters of the Universe, figure, Skeletor, Mattel, MOC, from $175 to............... 200.00

Masters of the Universe, figure, Teela, Mattel, MOC, from $100 to............... 120.00

Masters of the Universe, figure, Twistoid, Mattel, MOC, from $70 to............... 80.00

Micronauts, accessory, Battle Cruiser, Mego, MIB, from $65 to.... 75.00

Micronauts, accessory, Rocket Tubes, Mego, MIB, from $45 to............... 55.00

Micronauts, figure, Centaurus, Mego, MOC, from $200 to......... 210.00

Micronauts, figure, Kronos, Mego, MOC, from $200 to...... 210.00

Micronauts, figure, Repto, MOC, from $90 to............... 100.00

Planet of the Apes, accessory, Action Stallion, Mego, 1970s, MIB, from $75............... 110.00

Planet of the Apes, accessory, Village, Mego, 1970s, MIB, from $175 to............... 225.00

Planet of the Apes, figure, Astronaut, 8", any, Mego, 1970s, MOC, from $100 to...... 130.00

Planet of the Apes, figure, Cornelius, 8", Mego, 1970s, MIB, from $175 to...... 225.00

Planet of the Apes, figure, General Urko, 8", Mego, MOC, from $240 to............... 260.00

Pocket Super Heroes, figure, Spider-Man, Mego, MOC, from $45 to............... 55.00

Robotech, accessory, SDF-1 Playset, Matchbox, MIB, from $425 to............... 475.00

Robotech, accessory, Spartan, Matchbox, MIB, from $35 to............... 45.00

Robotech, accessory, Zentraedi Powered Armor, Matchbox, MIB, from $40 to............ 50.00

Robotech, figure, Lisa Hayes, 12", Matchbox, MIB, from $45 to............... 55.00

Robotech, figure, Miriya (black), Matchbox, 3¾", MOC, from $60 to............... 70.00

Rookies, figure, Chris, LJN, MOC, from $25 to............... 30.00

Rookies, figure, Lt Riker, LJN, MOC, from $30 to............ 35.00

Six Million Dollar Man, accessory, Venus Space Probe, Kenner, MIB.............................**300.00**

Six Million Dollar Man, figure, Steve Austin, bionic arm, Kenner, MIB..................**325.00**

Space: 1999, figure, Zython Alien, Mattel, MOC, from $270 to.......................**280.00**

Starsky & Hutch, accessory, car, Mego, MIB, from $150 to..............**175.00**

Starsky & Hutch, figure, Huggy Bear, Mego, MOC, from $35 to.......................... **45.00**

Super Heroes, figure, Batman, removable cowl, 8", Mego, MOC, from $300 to.......**350.00**

Super Heroes, figure, Captain America, 12½", Mego, MIB, from $175 to..................**200.00**

Super Heroes, figure, Catwoman, 8", Mego, MOC, from $300 to............................... **350.00**

Super Heroes, figure, Conan, 8", Mego, MIB, from $350 to..............**375.00**

Super Heroes, figure, Falcon, 8", Mego, MOC, from $1,200 to......................... **1,600.00**

Super Heroes, figure, Isis, 8", Mego, MIB, from $200 to.........**250.00**

Super Heroes, figure, Joker, 8", Mego, MIB, from $150 to...........**175.00**

Super Heroes, figure, Lex Luthor, 12½", Mego, MIB, from $100 to...................................**150.00**

Super Heroes, figure, Robin, removable mask, 8", Mego, MIB, from $700 to...........................**725.00**

Super Heroes, figure, Supergirl, 8", Mego, MIB, from $450 to **500.00**

Super Heroes, figure, Tarzan, 8", Mego, MOC, from $220 to.............**230.00**

Super Heroes, figure, Thor, 8", Mego, MIB, from $400 to.........**425.00**

Super Heroes, figure, Wonder Woman, 8", Mego, M, from $100 to.........................**115.00**

Super Heroes, figure, Wonder Woman, 8", Mego, MOC, from $475 to..........................**525.00**

Super Naturals, accessory, Ghost Finder, Tonka, 1986, MIB, from $25 to..............................**30.00**

Super Powers, accessory, Batcopter, Kenner, MIB, from $75 to..........................**100.00**

Super Powers, accessory, Darkseid Destroyer, Kenner, MIB, from $45 to..............................**55.00**

Super Powers, accessory, Hall of Justice, Kenner, MIB, from $200 to..........................**225.00**

Super Powers, figure, Cyborg, Kenner, MOC, from $270 to...........**280.00**

Super Powers, figure, Golden Pharaoh, Kenner, MOC, from $75 to..............................**85.00**

Super Powers, figure, Hawkman, Kenner, MOC, from $55 to.**65.00**

Super Powers, figure, Mantis, Kenner, MOC, from $20 to................**30.00**

Super Powers, figure, Martian Manhunter, Kenner, MOC, from $40 to.....................**50.00**

Super Powers, figure, Mister Miracle, Kenner, M, from $125 to...................................**135.00**

Super Powers, figure, Steppenwolf, Kenner, MOC, from $65 to.**75.00**

Super Powers, figure, Tyr, Kenner, MOC, from $45 to...........**55.00**

Teen Titans, figure, Aqualad, Mego, MOC, from $300 to.......**375.00**

Teen Titans, figure, Kid Flash, Mego, M, from $175 to..**200.00**

Teen Titans, figure, Kid Flash, Mego, MOC, from $425.00 to $450.00.

Teen Titans, figure, Speedy, Mego, M, from $300 to **325.00**

Teen Titans, figure, Wondergirl, Mego, MOC, from $500 to **525.00**

Wizard of Oz, accessory, Emerald City (with 7 8" figures), Mego, MIB **375.00**

Wizard of Oz, figure, Dorothy, 8", MIB, from $40 to **50.00**

Wizard of Oz, figure, Munchkin, 4", any, Mego, MIB, ea from $150 to **160.00**

Wizard of Oz, figure, Scarecrow, 8", MIB, from $40 to **50.00**

Wizard of Oz, figure, Wicked Witch, 8", Mego, MIB, from $90 to **115.00**

World's Greatest Super Knights, figure, Black Knight, Mego, MIB, $325 to **375.00**

World's Greatest Super Knights, figure, Ivanhoe, Mego, MIB, from $225 to **275.00**

World's Greatest Super Knights, figure, King Arthur, Mego, MIB, from $175 to **225.00**

World's Greatest Super Knights, figure, Sir Galahad, Mego, MIB, from $275 to **325.00**

World's Greatest Super Knights, figure, Sir Lancelot, Mego, MIB, from $275 to **325.00**

WWF, figure, Akeem, Hasbro, MOC, from $35 to **40.00**

WWF, figure, Dusty Rhodes, Hasbro, M, from $65 to... **70.00**

WWF, figure, Hulk Hogan, Hasbro, MOC, from $15 to **25.00**

WWF, figure, Macho Man, Hasbro, MOC, from $25 to **35.00**

WWF, figure, 1-2-3 Kid, Hasbro, MOC, from $60 to **70.00**

X-Men, figure, Cannonball (pink), Toy Biz, MOC, from $10 to **15.00**

X-Men, figure, Deadpool, Toy Biz, MOC, from $5 to **10.00**

X-Men, figure, Forearm, Toy Biz, MOC, from $5 to **10.00**

X-Men, figure, Gideon, Toy Biz, MOC, from $5 to **10.00**

X-Men, figure, Rogue, Toy Biz, MOC, from $24 to **28.00**

X-Men, figure, Silver Samurai, Toy Biz, MOC, from $5 to **10.00**

Zorro (Cartoon Series), figure, Amigo, Gabriel, MOC, from $25 to **35.00**

Zorro (Cartoon Series), figure, Captain Ramon, Gabriel, MOC, from $20 to **25.00**

Zorro (Cartoon Series), figure, Zorro, MOC, from $25 to **35.00**

Advertising Collectibles

As far back as the turn of the century, manufacturers used characters that identified with their products. They were always personable, endearing, amusing, and usually succeeded in achieving just the effect the producer had in mind, which was to make their product line more visual, more familiar, and therefore one the customer would more often than not choose over the competition. Magazine ads, display signs, product cartons, and commercials provided just the right exposure for these ad characters. Elsie the Cow became so well known that at one point during a random survey, more people recognized her photo than one of the president! There are scores of advertising characters, and many have been promoted on a grand scale. Today's collectors search for the dolls, banks, cookie jars, mugs, plates, and scores of other items modeled after or bearing the likenesses of their favorites, several of which are featured in our listings.

Condition plays a vital role in evaluating vintage advertising pieces. Try to be very objective when you assess wear and damage. Unless noted otherwise, our values are for items in near-mint to mint condition. For more information we recommend *Antique and Contemporary Advertising Memorabilia* by B.J. Summers. See also Ashtrays; Automobilia; Breweriana; Bubble Bath Containers; Character and Promotional Drinking Glasses; Coca-Cola; Gas Station Collectibles; Novelty Radios; Pin-Back Buttons; Soda Pop. See Clubs and Newsletters for information concerning *The Prize Insider* newsletter for Cracker Jack collectors; Peanut Pals, a club for collectors of Planters Peanuts; and the Soup Collector Club (Campbell's Soups).

A&W Root Beer, plush bear, 1997-98, from $15 to **20.00**

Actigall, figure, vinyl, 4", $20.00.

Alka-Seltzer, charm, glass-covered form w/metal frame, 1960s, 1½" 50.00

Alka-Seltzer, vinyl figure, Speedy, 1960s, 5½", EX, from $275 to **300.00**

Allied Van Lines, doll, green uniform, Lion Uniform Inc, 14", MIB **1,200.00**

Alpo, figure, Dan the Dog, walks on front paws, 1970s, 3", EX+.**12.00**

Arden Milk, bank, plastic truck.**60.00**

Aunt Jemima, Breakfast Bear, plush, 13" **175.00**

Aunt Jemima, doll, Aunt Jemima, stuffed oilcloth, 1950s, 12".**50.00**

Aunt Jemima, doll, Uncle Mose, stuffed oilcloth, w/top hat, 1950s, 12" 50.00

Aunt Jemima, doll, Wade, stuffed oilcloth, w/lollipop, 1950s, 9" **50.00**

Baskin-Robbins, bendable vinyl figure, Pinky the Spoon, 1990s, 5" **6.00**

Bazooka Bubble Gum, doll, Bazooka Joe, stuffed cloth, 1970s, 19" **10.00**

Betty Crocker, Doll & Bake Set, stuffed doll w/kit, 1970s, MIB **25.00**

Big Boy, bank, ceramic figure holding hamburger **500.00**

Big Boy, bank, painted vinyl figure, chubby version, 1960s-70s, 9".................. 50.00

Big Boy, comic book, Adventures of Big Boy, #2-#5, ea 50.00

Big Boy, kite, paper w/Big Boy logo, 1960s, MIP 250.00

Borden, bank, Beauregard, red plastic figure, Irwin, 1950s, 5", EX 65.00

Borden, creamer and sugar bowl, Elsie and Elmer, molded plastic, marked TBC The Borden Co., Made in USA, 3½", $65.00. (Photo courtesy Lee Garmon)

Borden, Elsie's Good Food Line punch-out train, 1940s, 25x37".................... 150.00

Borden, game, Elsie the Cow, Jr Edition, EXIB................ 125.00

Borden, milk truck, Keystone #D402, white paint w/red decal, 9", EXIB.............. 385.00

Borden, vinyl figure, Elsie, aqua dress w/white apron, 22". 100.00

Bosco Chocolate, jar pouring top, Bosco the Clown head, plastic, 1950s.............................. 50.00

Bradford House Restaurants, vinyl figure, Bucky Bradford, 1976, 9", EX.............................. 35.00

Burger Chef, pillow figure, Burger Chef, stuffed cloth, 1970s, EX.............................. 12.00

Burger King, doll, Magic King, Knickerbocker, 1980, 20", MIB............................... 20.00

Buster Brown, hobby horse, wood, advertising on saddle, 28x36", VG.............................. 300.00

Buster Brown Shoes, booklet, Playing Movies..., 20 pgs, 1910-20s.............................. 75.00

Buster Brown Shoes, doll, Buster, stuffed cloth, 1974, 14"... 40.00

Buster Brown Shoes, Treasure Hunt Game on shoebox side, 1930s, $50 to.................. 75.00

Campbell's Soup, bank, kids stand side-by-side, gold-painted cast iron.............................. 35.00

Campbell's Soup, bookends, ceramic boy & girl busts, bright colors, pr.............................. 60.00

Campbell's Soup, Campbell Kids Shopping Game, Parker Bros, 1955, NMIB.................... 65.00

Campbell's Soup, clock, 100th Anniversary, kid w/2 cans, 10" dia.............................. 25.00

Campbell's Soup, cookie jar, All Aboard, kids on train, ceramic.............................. 45.00

Campbell's Soup, cookie jar, kids in car, Going Places, 13x10½"........................ 55.00

Campbell's Soup, doll, cheerleader, vinyl, 1967, 8", EX.......... 75.00

Campbell's Soup, doll, chef, cloth outfit, Horsman, 12", MIB.... 250.00

Campbell's Soup, doll, chef, plastic, 10", MIB.......................... 35.00

Campbell's Soup, doll, Clam Digger, porcelain, MIB (soup can). 45.00

Campbell's Soup, doll, compo, Horsman, re-dressed, ca 1910, 14", VG........................ 95.00

11

Campbell's Soup, doll, compo, painted-on shoes, re-dressed, 12", VG **85.00**

Campbell's Soup, doll, pirate, Home Shopper, 1995, 10", EX ... **80.00**

Campbell's Soup, dolls, boy & girl, rag type, 1970s, MIB, pr. **75.00**

Campbell's Soup, dolls, farm kids, denim, 2000, 7", MIB, ea **12.00**

Campbell's Soup, dolls, Kids Bride & Groom, Horsman, '99, 11", pr, MIB **42.50**

Campbell's Soup, shakers, Going Places, kids (shakers) in car, MIB **20.00**

Campbell's Soup, string holder, ceramic kid face, c Campbell, 1950s **210.00**

Campbell's Soup, train car, Campbell Kids 90th Birthday, 0 gauge, MIB **82.50**

Campbell's Soup, wristwatch, 4 different, 1980s, MIB, ea **50.00**

Cheetos, doll, Chester Cheeta, w/ tag, 18" **40.00**

Chevrolet, mask, mascot w/See the New 1940 Chevrolet hat, 12" **600.00**

Chiquita Bananas, doll, uncut printed cloth, framed **50.00**

Chuck-E Cheese Pizza, hand puppet, plush, 1992, 9", EX .. **12.00**

Clark Bar, figure, boy in striped shirt w/Clark bar, vinyl, 1960s, 9" **175.00**

Colonel Sanders, bank, figure w/ cane, round base, Starling, 1965, 13" **30.00**

Colonel Sanders, mask, molded plastic face, 1960s, NM .. **55.00**

Crayola, plush figure, Crayola Ballerina, 7½", EX **10.00**

Crayola, plush figure, Crayola Bear, 7½", EX **15.00**

Dairy Queen, figure, Sweet Nell, plush, 1974, 12", EX **20.00**

Del Monte, figure, Fluffy Lamb, plush, 1980s, EX **20.00**

Dots Candy, beanbag doll, Dots Candy Baby, Hasbro, 1970s, MIB **15.00**

Dubble Bubble Bubble Gum, beanie, suede, round Fleers...logo on front **100.00**

Energizer Batteries, figure, Energizer Bunny, plush, 25", MIP **85.00**

Fanny Farmer Candies, delivery truck, Japan, 1950s, tin, friction, 8" **40.00**

Flinstones Vitamins, figure, Fred, inflatable vinyl w/clothes, 1970s **12.00**

Fruit Stripe Gum, figure, on motorcycle, vinyl, 1967, 7½" **175.00**

Fruit Stripe Gum, figure, Yipes, plush, 15", EX **50.00**

Funny-Face Drink, book, How Freckle Face Got..., Pillsbury, 1965, EX **28.00**

Funny-Face Drink, masks, die-cut paper images, Pillsbury, 1960s, ea **270.00**

Funny-Face Drink, pitcher, Goofy Grape, molded plastic, Pillsbury, 10" **75.00**

General Mills, bank, Twinkles the Elephant, molded plastic, 1960, 10" **350.00**

General Mills, ring, secret compartment; Frankenberry **275.00**

Gerber, bottle, penguin or kitten shape, plastic, 1970s, $10.00 each.

Green Giant, bank, Little Sprout figure, composition, musical, 9", EX **50.00**

Green Giant, figure, Jolly Green Giant, vinyl, 1970s, 10" .. **90.00**

Green Giant, tractor-trailer, Green Giant Brands, 22", G+.. **200.00**

Harley-Davidson, doll, Harley Hog, 9" **25.00**

Hawaiian Punch, doll, Punchy, stuffed cloth, 20" **65.00**

Hawaiian Punch, game, Mattel, 1978, NMIB **50.00**

Heinz, talking alarm clock, plastic, round base, 1980s, 10x6". **125.00**

Icee, bank, Icee Bear, figure, vinyl, 1970s, 8", VG **20.00**

Jell-O, puppet, Mr Wiggle, red vinyl, 1966 .... **125.00**

Jewel Tea, delivery truck, brown & gold paint, 1940s, 10", EX. **350.00**

Keebler, bank, Ernie, ceramic, 10" **50.00**

Keebler, figure, Ernie, vinyl, 1970s, 7" **25.00**

Kellogg's, figure, Tony the Tiger, inflatable vinyl, 1950s, 45", EX **300.00**

Kellogg's, hand puppet, Snap!, 1950, cloth & vinyl, 8", EX.......................... **75.00**

Kellogg's, Magic Color Cards, Rice Krispies, 1930s, complete. **65.00**

Kool-Aid, bank, mascot figure standing, plastic, mechanical, 1970s, 7" **50.00**

Kool-Aid, dispenser, MIB **50.00**

Lifesavers, bank, cardboard & metal cylinder, w/graphics, 1960s, 12" **20.00**

Log Cabin Syrup, pull toy, Log Cabin Express, NMIB... **900.00**

M&M Candy, figure, peanut shape, bendable arms & legs, 7", ea **15.00**

M&M Candy, figure, plain shape, plush, bridal attire, 36", EX **40.00**

M&M Candy, figure, plain shape, plush, 48" from fingertip to fingertip **75.00**

Maypo Oat Cereal, bank, Marky Maypo figure, plastic, 1960s, EX **100.00**

McDonald's, bank, Ronald McDonald bust, plastic, Taiwan, 1993, EX........... **40.00**

McDonald's, doll, Hamburgler, cloth, purple stripes, early 1970s, 15" **200.00**

McDonald's, doll, Ronald, vinyl w/ cloth outfit, Remco, 1976, 7", MIB **30.00**

McDonald's, playset, McDonaldland, Remco, 1976, complete, MIB **125.00**

Michelin Tires, figure, Mr Bib w/ baby, rubber, 7" **125.00**

Michelin Tires, puzzle, forms Mr Bib on motorcycle, MIP .. **55.00**

Mr Clean, figure, white painted vinyl, Proctor & Gamble, 1960s, 8", EX **75.00**

Mr Softee, truck, litho tin, rubber tires, friction, Japan, 1960s, 4" **65.00**

Nabisco, doll, Mr Salty, stuffed cloth, 1983 .... **25.00**

Nalplex Paint, hand puppet, Dutch Boy mascot, vinyl head, 1960s, 16" **60.00**

Nestlé, doll, P Nutty as Morsel Family Clown, Trudy Co, 1984, 10" **18.00**

Nestlé, figure, Quik Bunny, plush, w/Q necklace, 1980s, 21", EX **25.00**

Oscar Mayer, whistle, plastic Wienermobile, 2x1¼" **15.00**

Oscar Mayer, Wienermobile pedal car, EX **125.00**

Ovaltine/Bovril, double-decker bus, windup, Tri-Ang, 1950s, 4x7" **100.00**

Pillsbury, ceramic bank, Poppin' Fresh figure, 1980s **35.00**

Pillsbury, figure, Poppin' Fresh, talker, Mattel, 16" **100.00**

Pillsbury, finger puppet, Biscuit the cat, vinyl, 1974 .... **35.00**

Pillsbury, puppet, Poppin' Fresh, plastic & vinyl, 1971, EX . **25.00**

Pillsbury, radio, Poppin' Fresh, EX, from $65.00 to $75.00. (Photo courtesy Lil West)

Pizza Hut, bank, Pizza Hut Pete, plastic, 1969, 8" **25.00**

Planters, bank, clear plastic Mr Peanut figure, 1950-70s, EX, from $90 to **150.00**

Planters, coloring book, 50 States, 1970s **15.00**

Planters, cookie jar, Mr. Peanut, Nabisco, M, from $50.00 to $65.00. (Photo courtesy Joyce and Fred Roerig)

Planters, figure, Mr Peanut, cloth, Chase Bag Co, 1970, 18" . **25.00**

Planters, game, Planters Peanut Party, lg version, 1930s **100.00**

Planters, hand puppet, Mr Peanut, rubber, 1942, 6", EX, from $750 to **1,000.00**

Planters, yo-yo, Mr Peanut image, Humphrey, 1976............. **12.00**

Popsicle, Music Maker Truck, plastic, Mattel, 11", VG **150.00**

Purina, squeak toy, chuck wagon, vinyl, 1975, 8" **30.00**

Quaker Oats, bank, Quisp figure, ceramic, 1960s............... **100.00**

Quaker Oats, Cap'n Crunch Guppy Sailing Ship, plastic, 1967, 10" L, EX.............................. **200.00**

Quaker Oats, Cavern Helmet, plastic w/headlight, 1967, EX **225.00**

Quaker Oats, coloring book, Cap'n Crunch, Whitman, 1968, EX **25.00**

Quaker Oats, Quisp Space Beanie, pink plastic w/propeller, 1967 .... **300.00**

Raid, figure, Raid Bug, plush, 1980 .... **25.00**

Raid, figure, windup Raid Bug w/ mean expression, 4" **50.00**

RCA, TV Service Truck, plastic, ladder on top, Marx, 8½", NMIB **200.00**

Richfield Gasoline, tank truck, American National, 1920s, rstr, 27" **1,500.00**

Sambo's Restaurant, figure, plush tiger mascot, 7", NMIB **100.00**

Sealtest, rider truck, gray w/decals, Roberts Co, 22", EXIB .. **880.00**

Sears, delivery truck, tin, Shop at Sears... on sides, Marx, 25", VG **225.00**

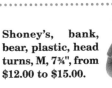

Shoney's, bank, bear, plastic, head turns, M, 7¾", from $12.00 to $15.00.

Snickers Candy bar, doll, w/candy bar-shaped bag, Mars, 1990s, 12", EX **12.00**

Snow Crop Frozen Foods, bear, white plush w/vinyl face, 1950s, 9", EX **50.00**

Snow Crop Frozen Foods, toy van, litho tin, H/Japan, 1960s, 8½", EX **100.00**

Snuggle Fabric Softener, bear, Snuggles, plush, Lever Bros, 1986, 14" **30.00**

Snuggle Fabric Softener, hand puppet, Snuggles, Lever Bros, 1990s, 15" **15.00**

Star-Kist, ceramic bank, Charlie figure on can, 1988, 9½" . **20.00**

Star-Kist, figure, Charlie, Talkin' Patter Pillow, Mattel, 1970s, 15" **25.00**

Star-Kist, lamp base, Charlie figure, painted plaster, 1970s, 12½" **65.00**

Star-Kist, truck, pressed steel w/ red & blue paint, Tonka, 15", VG **500.00**

Star-Kist, Wacky Wobbler, Charlie figure, PVC **15.00**

Taco Bell, dog, beanbag type, w/ tags, 1999 .... **12.00**

Tastee Freeze, figure, Miss Tastee Freeze, plastic, 1950s, 7" . **20.00**

Teddy Grahams, bear, plush w/ purple jacket & shoes, Nabisco, 10" **15.00**

Texaco, bank, red plastic gas pump w/logo, Ideal, 9", EXIB .. **300.00**

Texaco, doll, Cheerleader, 1971, 11", NRFB **20.00**

Texaco, helmet w/speaker on top, plastic, Wen-Mac/USA, EX **75.00**

Texaco, pencil case, red plastic pump form w/hose & hinges, Hasbro, 8" **175.00**

Texaco Service Station, playset, steel w/plastic accessories **250.00**

Tootsie Roll, Train Game, Hasbro, 1969, EXIB **55.00**

Tupperware, figure, Tupper the Seal, plush, Interpur, 1980s, 10", EX **20.00**

Tyson Chicken, figure, Chicken Quick, stuffed cloth, 13", VG **15.00**

US Forest Service, bank, Smokey Bear, red plastic, 1950s, 5", EX 50.00

US Forest Service, bank, Smokey Bear on stump w/shovel, ceramic, 6" 50.00

US Forest Service, bank, Woodsy Owl, ceramic, 1970s, 8½", EX 50.00

US Forest Service, book, Smokey Bear's Story..., 1968, 16 pgs, VG 22.00

US Forest Service, book/stamp kit, Smokey Bear story, Ladybird, 1990s 10.00

US Forest Service, figure, Smokey Bear, ceramic, Ideal, 1950s, 16" 50.00

US Forest Service, figure, Smokey Bear, plush, Knickerbocker, 22" 75.00

US Forest Service, figure, Woodsy Owl w/sad flower, ceramic, 3¾" 35.00

US Forest Service, hand puppet, Smokey Bear, cloth and vinyl, 1959, NM+, $185.00. (Photo courtesy gasoline alleyantiques.com)

US Forest Service, tattoos, Smokey the Bear, any of 6, GordyToys, MIP 8.00

US Postal Service, plastic pull toy, US Mail car, Kusan/USPS, 6x8x12" 85.00

Vlasic Pickles, figure, Vlasic Stork, white fur, Trudy Toys, 1989, 22" 40.00

Ward's Tip Top Cakes, devil face mask, litho on die-cut cardboard 65.00

Wilkins Coffee, hand puppet, painted rubber character, 1950s, 7½" 115.00

Wilrick's Grape Drink, shaker cup, yellow & purple plastic, 7½", EX 35.00

Wrigley's Chewing Gum, Mother Goose booklet, 1915, 28 pgs, EX 60.00

Advertising Tins

Attractive packaging has always been a powerful marketing tool; today those colorful tin containers that once held products ranging from cookies and peanut butter to coffee and tea are popular collectibles. Here is an interesting book on this topic you may want to refer to: *Modern Collectible Tins* by Linda McPherson. It was published by Collector Books.

Our values are for examples in near-mint to mint condition. See also Gas Station Collectibles; Tobacco Collectibles.

Aunt Jemima Pancake Flour, red knob on top, 1983, 6x5" dia, $10 to 20.00

Barnum's Animal Crackers, red pail w/plastic handle, 1991, 5", $10 to 18.00

Bazooka Bubble Gum, bail handle, 1991, 5½x7", from $8 to .. 12.00

Brachs Jelly Beans, cartoon characters, Happy...Bugs, 1989, 6¼" 7.00

Cadbury's Dairy Milk Chocolate, kitchen scene on front, 6¼x4¼" 7.00

Campfire Marshmallows, camping scene, 2nd in limited series, 9" 10.00

Carnation Hot Cocoa Mix, red holiday 3rd, 1997, 5x8x6¼", $5 to 8.00

Chiclets Peppermint Gum, pencil box, Tin Box Co, 4¼x7¾x1" 15.00

Chupa Chups, milk-pail shape, cow w/ lollipop flowers, 3rd, 9½".....20.00

Churchill's Cream Toffee, carousel figures, Made in England, 4½" 12.00

Corn Flakes, made for Kelloggs by Tin Box Co, 1984, 6½x4x3", $10 to 20.00

Crayola, Discovery Series, jungle scene, #1 in 1997, 4x8x2", $5 to 10.00

Crayola, No 8 school crayons on front, 1987, 6x4" dia, from $10 to 20.00

Golden West Coffee, Closset & Devers, Portland, OR, same image on both sides, three-pound, 6x6½", EX+, $250.00. (Photo courtesy Past Tyme Pleasures)

Hershey's Milk Chocolate, pencil box, Tin Box Co, 4¼x7¾x1" 15.00

Iams Cat Food, orange cat & pumpkin on front view, round, 12", $5 to 8.00

Keebler Cookies, elves decorating tree, 1992, 10½x4¼", from $10 to 15.00

Keebler Holiday Cookies, red trim, 4 elves, 1998, 6x8x2½", $5 to 8.00

Life Savers, roll shape, Five Flavor colors, 1995, 3¾x10¼" 15.00

Lipton Tea, red & yellow, Tin by Cheinco, 5½x5½", from $10 to 15.00

M&M's, Fire House, embossed, Christmas Village series #6, 1997, 6" 8.00

Maxwell House Coffee, blue & gold, 1892 100th Anniversary, 7x4x3" 10.00

Milk Bone Dog Biscuits, Boston Terrier, 1996, 7x6x5", from $10 to 15.00

Morton's Salt, black & gold, 5x4½", from $5 to 7.00

Nabisco Ritz Crackers, limited, 1987, 8x4½x4½", from $5 to 15.00

Nestlé Chocolate, girl peeking in nest, 1st in series, 1988, 6x4¼" 5.00

Oreo Cookies, cookie in Christmas wreath, 1990, 6x8x2½", $5 to 7.00

Pillsbury, Doughboy Holiday, 1999, 9½x7¼x2½", from $5 to ... 10.00

Planters Peanuts, holiday fireside scene, 1st in series, 1997, 6x5" 8.00

Quaker Corn Meal, yellow w/red top, Cheinco, 7½x5½", from $10 to 15.00

Quaker Oats, red & blue, replica of 1922 label, 1988, 10x6", $10 to 20.00

Reese's NutRageous, cylindrical, 9x4", from $10 to............. 15.00

Revlon Baby Silicare Powder, from $24.00 to $28.00.

and wear reduce values drastically. The more uncommon forms are especially collectible. For more information refer to *Collectible Aluminum, An Identification and Value Guide*, by Everett Grist. Unless noted otherwise, our values are for examples in mint to near-mint condition.

Russell Stover Candies, Elvis Mother's Day, 1998, 5x12x1½", $5 to **7.00**

See's Candies, Easter eggs & chick on yellow, oval, 1996, 7x9x1½" **13.00**

Sun-Maid Raisins, red w/girl holding grapes, round, 6x4", from $5 to **8.00**

Trix, red, The Tin Box Co, 5¼x3½x2¼", from $4 to **7.00**

Aluminum

From the late 1930s until early in the 1950s, kitchenwares and household items were often crafted of aluminum, usually with relief-molded fruit or flowers on a hammered background. Today many find that these diversified items make an attractive collection. Especially desirable are those examples marked with the manufacturer's backstamp or the designer's signature.

You've probably also seen the anodized (colored) aluminum pitchers, tumblers, sherbet holders, etc., that were popular in the late '50s and early '60s. Interest in these items has exploded, as prices of eBay sales attest. Be sure to check condition, though, as scratching

Ashtray, duck scene, ornate, Wendell August Forge, 6" dia **35.00**

Ashtray, horse head in center, Bruce Fox, 4", $20.00.

Ashtray, Pine Cone, Wendell August Forge, 6" dia **75.00**

Ashtray, sailboat scene, sq, Wendell August Forge, 4½" **25.00**

Basket, fish scene w/hammered bottom, fluted rim, Hand Forged, 12" dia **30.00**

Basket, Morning Glory, china insert, loop handles, Farberware, 7" **65.00**

Basket, sailing ship scene, ruffled edge, Federal Silver Co, 9" dia **40.00**

Basket, Tomato, serrated lip, knot on double handle, Everlast, 11" dia **10.00**

Basket, Tulip, hexagon-shape, floral cut-out handle, Rodney Kent, 4" **35.00**

Beverage set, handled tray holds 8 tumblers, complete, 13" L. **35.00**

Bowl, Bittersweet, notched rim, Wendell August Forge, 5". **35.00**

Bowl, Chrysanthemum, deep center well, Federal Silver, 9"....**15.00**

Bowl, Chrysanthemum, fluted edge, Continental Silver, 5½"...**25.00**

Bowl, Chrysanthemum, handles, beaded rim, Continental Silver, 10"....................................**25.00**

Bowl, Dogwood, plain fluted edge, Wendell August Forge, 7". **45.00**

Bowl, pine scene, oval, gold anodized, Arthur Armour, 11x9"........**35.00**

Bowl, plain spun aluminum, Kensington, 11"..............**15.00**

Bowl, salad; Wheat, Palmer-Smith, 14"..................................**65.00**

Bowl, Tulip, serrated edge, footed, ear handles, Rodney Kent, 10"....................................**45.00**

Bowl, Tulip w/hammered ground, tulip on handles, Rodney Kent, 10"....................................**35.00**

Box, Apple Blossom lid w/handle, pottery base, Wendall A Forge, 3x5"...................................**90.00**

Box, cigarette; Bittersweet, Wendell August Forge, 1½x5x3"...**75.00**

Box, cigarette; duck figure on lid, cast, Laird Argental, 1½x5x3"..........................**75.00**

Buffet server, floral handles & finial, 4-footed, w/lid, Rodney Kent.................................**35.00**

Butter dish, Bamboo, bamboo finial, Everlast, 4x7x4".........**10.00**

Candelabrum, hammered, arms riveted to base, unmarked, 5" dia base.........................**185.00**

Candelabrum, hammered, Art Nouveau style, Langbein, 13"...**135.00**

Candleholders, Oak Leaf & Acorn, cast, Bruce Fox, 10" L, ea. **45.00**

Candleholders, hammered/scalloped base/fluted bobeche, Everlast, 3", pr................**20.00**

Candleholders, removable sockets, beaded saucer w/handle, unmarked, pr.................**20.00**

Candleholders, S-shape w/ tulip, beaded base & socket, Faberware, 8", pr............**45.00**

Candy dish, Butterflies, gold anodized, 2-part, handle, Everlast, 12"....................................**15.00**

Candy dish, Indian Tree, 2-part w/ china inserts, Faber & Sheavin, 12"....................................**45.00**

Candy dish, ship design, leaf shape w/handle, World Hand Forged, 7"....................................**25.00**

Casserole, Dogwood & Butterfly, handles, w/lid, Arthur Armour, 4x10"..................................**50.00**

Casserole, Pea Vine, lid w/pea pod finial, Everlast, 4x7".......**15.00**

Casserole, Wheat, 4-footed, handles, lid w/shell finial, unmarked, 8"....................................**25.00**

Chocolate pot, Chrysanthemum, hinged lid, Continental, 10x5"...............................**85.00**

Coaster, fox hunter on horse, Everlast, 5"........................**5.00**

Coaster, jumping marlin, Wendell August Forge, 5"..............**15.00**

Coaster, sitting Scottie dog, unmarked, 3⅜"...................**3.00**

Coasters, 5-petal flowers, set of 8, in display box, Everlast..**25.00**

Coffee urn, Chrysanthemum, glass finial, handles, Continental, 15x7"...............................**85.00**

Compote, hammered w/tulip & ribbon finial, open pedestal, unmarked.....................**15.00**

Compote, Wild Rose, Continental, 5" dia.................................. **25.00**

Crumber & tray, Grapevine, Lucite brush handle, Everlast... **10.00**

Cup, child's; elephants & other animals, unmarked, 5"......... **10.00**

Dip server, Bamboo, hammered, supporting rods & wheels, Everlast, 11"..................... **45.00**

Double boiler, wood handle & finial, Pyrex liner, Buenilum, 7" dia.. **10.00**

Gravy boat, attached underplate, beaded rim, wire handle, Buenilum, 3"..................... **20.00**

Hurricane lamp, 2 candle sockets, double twisted handle, Buenilum, 10"................. **45.00**

Ice bucket, Chrysanthemum, lid w/mushroom finial, handles, Continental...................... **40.00**

Ice bucket, hammered, barbell handles, fluted top, Everlast, 5x10".................................. **15.00**

Jelly jar, blue pottery insert, w/ ladle, Turnipyard Deerfield Mass, 5"............................ **30.00**

Key chain, teddy bear, rectangular, DeMarsh Forge................ **12.00**

Lazy Susan, Tulip Spray, floral on 2 sides, Rodney Kent, 18".. **15.00**

Magazine rack, duck scene, handles, Wendell August Forge, 9x14x9"........................... **250.00**

Magazine rack, swan, tall handle, Wendell August Forge, 18x14x8"....................... **350.00**

Money clip, lighthouse, DeMarsh Forge................................ **12.00**

Napkin holder, Dogwood, Wendell August Forge, 4½x4x3"... **35.00**

Pitcher, hammered, ice lip, twisted wire handle, Buenilum, 8x6"................................. **35.00**

Pitcher, syrup; hammered, black plastic handle, Stratford-on-Avon, 6"............................ **15.00**

Pitcher, Tulip, ice lip, ear handle, Rodney Kent, 9x5".......... **45.00**

Plate, child's; ABCs on edge, unmarked, 7"................... **30.00**

Plate, Dogwood & Butterfly, Arthur Armour, 10"..................... **45.00**

Plate, river & trout, crimped rim, Wendell August Forge, 8½". **65.00**

Purse, mums, unmarked, 8½" long, from $100.00 to $125.00.

Silent butler, Celtic Knot, Canterbury Arts, 6"........ **10.00**

Tidbit, 2-tier; Tulip Spray, serrated edge & base, unmarked, 10x11"............................. **15.00**

Tray, bread; Chrysanthemum, scalloped edge, Continental, 11x8"............................... **25.00**

Anchor Hocking/Fire-King

From the 1930s until the 1970s, Anchor Hocking (Lancaster, Ohio) produced a wide and varied assortment of glassware including kitchen items such as reamers, mixing bowls, and measuring cups in many lovely colors. Many patterns of dinnerware were made as well. Their Fire-King line was formulated to produce heat-proof glassware so durable that it was guaranteed for two years against breakage caused by heat. Colors included Jade-ite, Azur-ite, Turquoise and Sapphire Blue, Ivory, milk white (often decorated with fired-on patterns), Royal Ruby, and Forest Green. Collectors are beginning to reassemble sets, and for the most part, prices are relatively low, except for some of the rarer items.

Wexford and Early American Prescut are two very popular lines with today's collectors. Both were made in extensive lines that provide an opportunity for building lovely and diverse collections. At least 77 pieces of Wexford have been cataloged; it was in production from 1967 until around 2000. In Early American Prescut, look especially for the oil lamp, tall tumblers, 6¾" plates with the off-center cup ring, small square salt and pepper shakers, the large paneled bowl, and the large relish plate with swirled dividers. These items are some of the most valuable. For more information, we recommend *Anchor Hocking's Fire-King & More, Third Edition,* by Gene and Cathy Florence (Collector Books).

Blue Mosaic, bowl, dessert; white w/decal, 4⅝".......................... 8.00
Blue Mosaic, bowl, vegetable; white w/decal, 8¼"...................... 20.00
Blue Mosaic, platter, white w/decal, 9x12"................................ 18.00
Blue Mosaic, tray, snack; white w/ decal, oval, 10x7½"............. 6.00
Bubble, bowl, berry; Royal Ruby, lg, 8⅜"................................... 20.00

Bubble, bowl, berry; Sapphire Blue, 4".. 18.00
Bubble, bowl, cereal; Forest Green, 5¼"....................................... 20.00
Bubble, bowl, soup; white, flat, 7¾"... 15.00
Bubble, candlesticks, crystal iridescent, pr............................... 16.00
Bubble, creamer, Sapphire Blue. 35.00
Bubble, pitcher, crystal iridescent, ice lip, 64-oz................... 125.00
Bubble, plate, bread & butter; Forest Green, 6¾"........... 18.00
Bubble, sugar, Sapphire Blue. 25.00
Bubble, tumbler, lemonade; Royal Ruby, 16-oz, 5⅞".............. 16.00
Bubble, tumbler, water; Royal Ruby, 9-oz......................... 9.00
Charm, bowl, dessert; ivory, 4¾".............................. 18.00
Charm, bowl, soup; Forest Green, 6".. 15.00
Charm, creamer, Azur-ite White..12.00
Charm, cup, ivory 12.00

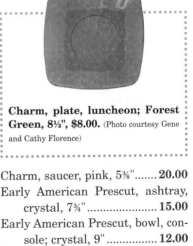

Charm, plate, luncheon; Forest Green, 8½", $8.00. (Photo courtesy Gene and Cathy Florence)

Charm, saucer, pink, 5⅜"....... 20.00
Early American Prescut, ashtray, crystal, 7¾"...................... 15.00
Early American Prescut, bowl, console; crystal, 9"................ 12.00
Early American Prescut, bowl, crystal, paneled, 11¾".......... 145.00

Early American Prescut, bowl, crystal, scalloped rim, 7¼" **18.00**
Early American Prescut, bowl, crystal, 1¼x5¼" **40.00**
Early American Prescut, cake plate, crystal, footed, 13½" **30.50**
Early American Prescut, candy dish, crystal, w/lid, 5¼" ... **10.00**
Early American Prescut, cocktail shaker, crystal, 30-oz, 9" **595.00**
Early American Prescut, lamp, oil; crystal, from $200 to **225.00**
Early American Prescut, plate, crystal, 11" **12.00**
Early American Prescut, plate, crystal, 4-part w/swirl dividers, 11" **90.00**
Early American Prescut, plate, snack; crystal, 10" **25.00**

Early American Prescut, punch bowl, $35.00; Punch cup (not shown), $2.00.
(Photo courtesy Gene and Cathy Florence)

Early American Prescut, punch set, crystal, 15-pc **45.00**
Early American Prescut, relish, crystal, rectangular, 3-part, 11⅞" **25.00**
Early American Prescut, tray, hostess; crystal, 6½x12" **12.50**
Early American Prescut, tumbler, iced tea; crystal, 6" **15.00**
Early American Prescut, vase, crystal, footed, 5" **595.00**
Early American Prescut, vase, crystal, 10" **20.00**

Fish Scale, bowl, soup; ivory, 7½".**18.00**
Fish Scale, bowl, vegetable; pink, 8¾" **35.00**
Fish Scale, cup, ivory w/blue, 8-oz **28.00**
Fish Scale, plate, salad; ivory w/red, 7⅜" **15.00**
Fish Scale, platter, ivory, 11¾".**45.00**
Fish Scale, platter, ivory w/blue, 11¾" **75.00**
Fish Scale, saucer, ivory **3.00**
Fleurette, bowl, chili; white w/decal, 5" **22.00**
Fleurette, cup, snack; white w/decal, 5-oz **3.00**
Fleurette, egg plate, white w/decal **175.00**
Fleurette, mug, white w/decal . **85.00**
Fleurette, plate, bread & butter; white w/decal, 6¼" **10.00**
Fleurette, plate, dinner; white w/decal, 9⅛" **5.00**
Forest Green, ashtray, hexagonal, 5¾" **8.00**
Forest Green, bottle, water; w/glass lid **95.00**
Forest Green, bowl, mixing; 6". **9.00**
Forest Green, bud vase, 9" **10.00**
Forest Green, goblet, 9-oz **10.00**
Forest Green, pitcher, round, 86-oz **40.00**
Forest Green, pitcher, 36-oz .. **25.00**
Forest Green, sherbet, flat **10.00**
Forest Green, tumbler, long boy, 15-oz **11.00**
Forest Green, tumbler, tall, 9½-oz **6.50**
Game Birds, ashtray, white w/decal, 5¼" **15.00**
Game Birds, bowl, cereal; white w/decal, 5" **8.00**
Game Birds, creamer, white w/decal **22.00**

Game Birds, plate, dinner; white w/ decal, 9⅛".............................6.50

Game Birds, sugar, white w/decal, w/lid 27.00

Game Birds, tumbler, juice; white w/decal, 5-oz 38.00

Harvest, bowl, vegetable; white w/ decal, 8¼"......................... 16.00

Harvest, creamer, white w/decal.7.00

Harvest, plate, salad; white w/ decal, 7⅜"............................12.00

Homestead, plate, dinner; white w/ decal, 10" 8.00

Honeysuckle, bowl, soup; white w/ decal, flat, 6⅝"...................9.00

Honeysuckle, cup, white w/decal, 8-oz.....................................4.00

Honeysuckle, mug, $65.00.

Honeysuckle, plate, dinner; white w/decal, 9⅛".........................6.00

Honeysuckle, platter, white w/ decal, 9x12" 16.00

Honeysuckle, relish, white w/decal, 3-part, 9¾".....................125.00

Jane Ray, bowl, dessert; ivory, 4⅞"..20.00

Jane Ray, bowl, oatmeal; Jade-ite, 5⅞" 20.00

Jane Ray, plate, dinner; Vitrock, 9⅛" 20.00

Jane Ray, plate, salad; Jade-ite, hand-painted animals, 7¾"...........25.00

Jane Ray, saucer, Vitrock 2.00

Lace Edge, bowl, milk white w/ Primrose decal, footed, 11".15.00

Lace Edge, compote, milk white, w/ lid, 7x6¼" 13.00

Meadow Green, cake pan, white w/ decal, sq, 8" 6.00

Meadow Green, casserole, white w/ decal, w/crystal lid, 3-qt .10.00

Meadow Green, platter, white w/ decal, 9x12" 8.00

Meadow Green, utility dish, white w/decal, 2-qt 7.00

Prescut (Oatmeal), saucer, crystal, 4⅜" 1.00

Prescut (Oatmeal), soap dish, crystal, 5¼x3¾" 20.00

Prescut (Oatmeal), tumbler, juice; crystal, 4-oz 2.00

Prescut (Pineapple), box, cigarette; crystal, 4¾" 15.00

Prescut (Pineapple), box, dresser; white, 4¾" 12.50

Prescut (Pineapple), butter dish, crystal, round 15.00

Prescut (Pineapple), shakers, crystal, pr..............................10.00

Primrose, bowl, vegetable; white w/ decal, 8¼"........................14.00

Primrose, cake pan, round, white w/decal, 8" 12.00

Primrose, casserole, white w/decal, knob cover, 2-qt..............16.00

Primrose, compote, white w/decal, Lace Edge, 11"...............165.00

Primrose, plate, dinner; white w/ decal, 9⅛"............................7.00

Rainbow, bowl, utilty; primary colors, deep, 5¼" 15.00

Rainbow, creamer, primary colors, footed 12.00

Rainbow, jug, primary colors, 54-oz..60.00

Rainbow, lamp, hurricane; pastel, 7".....................................35.00

Rainbow, plate, dinner; primary colors, 9¼".......................18.00

Rainbow, tumbler, table; pastel, 9-oz..................................15.00

Rainbow, vase, pastel, ruffled top, 9".................................25.00

Restaurant Ware, bowl, Jade-ite, handled, 5"..................450.00

Restaurant Ware, gravy/sauceboat, crystal/white...................30.00

Restaurant Ware, plate, salad; Jade-ite, 6¾"...................14.00

Restaurant Ware, platter, Jade-ite, 9½" L..............................45.00

Royal Ruby, beer bottle, 12-oz, 9½"..................................75.00

Royal Ruby, creamer, flat.......12.00

Royal Ruby, punch bowl........40.00

Royal Ruby, punch bowl base.37.50

Royal Ruby, punch cup, 5-oz....3.00

Royal Ruby, sugar, flat...........12.00

Royal Ruby, tumbler, ice tea; 13-oz.13.00

Sandwich, bowl, pink, scalloped, 8¼".....................................27.50

Sandwich, bowl, smooth, pink, 5¼"..................................7.00

Sandwich, cookie jar, crystal.40.00

Sandwich, cup, custard; Forest Green....................................3.00

Sandwich, plate, dinner; crystal, 9".......................................20.00

Sandwich, plate, dinner; Forest Green, 9"........................135.00

Sandwich, plate, sandwich; Desert Gold, 12"..........................15.00

Sandwich, tumbler, crystal, footed, 9-oz....................................28.00

Sandwich, tumbler, Desert Gold, footed, 9-oz....................265.00

Sheaves of Wheat, bowl, dessert; crystal, 4½".......................8.00

Sheaves of Wheat, bowl, dessert; Jade-ite, 4½"...................75.00

Sheaves of Wheat, plate, dinner; crystal, 9"........................24.00

Shell, bowl, cereal; Jade-ite Shell, 6⅜" 25.00

Shell, creamer, Aurora Shell, footed...............................35.00

Shell, cup, Jade-ite, 8-oz........10.00

Shell, plate, dinner; Golden Shell, 10"......................................6.00

Shell, platter, Lustre Shell, oval, 9".......................................40.00

Shell, saucer, demitasse; Milk White, 4¾".........................12.00

Soreno, ashtray, Aurora, 4¼".15.00

Soreno, bowl, Aquamarine, 4-qt, 11⅜"..................................16.00

Soreno, pitcher, water; Honey Gold, 64-oz....................................7.50

Soreno, tumbler, iced tea; crystal, 15-oz.....................................4.00

Swirl, bowl, cereal; ivory, 5⅞" 24.00

Swirl, bowl, soup; Azur-ite, flanged, 9¼".....................................145.00

Swirl, plate, dinner; ivory, 9⅛".10.00

Swirl, plate, dinner; Lustre Pastel, 9⅛".....................................20.00

Swirl, plate, serving; pink, 11".25.00

Swirl, platter, Jade-ite, 12x9".425.00

Swirl, sherbet, Rose-ite, footed..65.00

Swirl, soup plate, Azur-ite, 7⅝".16.00

Thousand Line, bowl, fruit; crystal, 3-footed, 9¼"...................15.00

Thousand Line, bowl, vegetable; crystal, deep, 8"..............12.00

Thousand Line, bud vase.......12.00

Thousand Line, cake plate, crystal, 12"....................................13.00

Thousand Line, candy dish, crystal, w/lid...............................17.00

Thousand Line, relish, crystal, 6-part, 12"......................15.00

Three Bands, bowl, dessert; burgundy, 4⅞".....................110.00

Three Bands, bowl, vegetable; Jade-ite, 8¼"...........................85.00

Three Bands, cup, burgundy, 8-oz...........................100.00

Three Bands, plate, dinner; ivory, 9⅛".................. 20.00
Turquoise Blue, bowl, soup; 6⅜". 25.00
Turquoise Blue, bowl, vegetable; 8"............................. 23.00
Turquoise Blue, creamer or sugar, ea........................... 8.00
Turquoise Blue, plate, 9"....... 14.00

Turquoise Blue, relish tray, gold trim, 11" long, from $10.00 to $12.00.

Vienna Lace, bowl, vegetable; white w/decal & design............. 18.00
Vienna Lace, cup, white w/decal, no design, 8-oz.................... 4.00
Vienna Lace, plate, dinner; white w/decal & design, 10"........ 7.00
Wexford, ashtray, crystal, 8½". 6.00
Wexford, bowl, fruit; crystal, footed, 10"................................. 14.00
Wexford, bowl, salad; 6"........... 4.00
Wexford, bowl, serving; 14" ... 12.00
Wexford, cake stand w/glass dome.......................... 25.00
Wexford, candleholders, bowl shape w/scalloped rim, 5", pr 40.00
Wexford, cup, 7-oz.................... 2.00
Wexford, decanter, captain's; 32-oz............................. 18.00
Wexford, goblet, 5½-oz............. 4.00
Wexford, ice bucket, w/lid...... 18.00
Wexford, jar, storage; 34-oz 6.00
Wexford, lamp, oil; crystal..... 30.00

Wexford, pitcher, 64-oz.......... 8.00
Wexford, plate, dessert; 6"...... 5.00
Wexford, plate, tidbit; 9½"...... 6.00
Wexford, platter, serving; 12" dia 4.00
Wexford, punch bowl, 11-qt, w/ base........................... 25.00
Wexford, relish tray, 5-part, center circle, 11"....................... 8.00
Wexford, sherbet, stemmed, 7-oz. 2.00
Wexford, tumbler, 11-oz.......... 6.00
Wexford, vase, footed, 10½" ... 12.50
Wheat, bowl, chili; white w/decals, 5"................................. 30.00
Wheat, casserole, white w/decal, knob cover, 1-pt................. 8.00
Wheat, casserole, white w/decal, oval, au gratin lid, 1½-qt. 14.00
Wheat, pan, baking; white w/decal, w/lid, 5x9"..................... 16.00
Wheat, tumbler, juice; white w/ decal, 5-oz...................... 6.00
1700 Line, bowl, cereal; Milk White, 5⅞".................................. 8.00
1700 Line, bowl, soup; Jade-ite, flat, 7½"...................... 45.00
1700 Line, platter, ivory, oval, 9x12"............................ 32.00

Aprons

Vintage aprons evoke nostalgic memories — grandma in her kitchen, gentle heat radiating from the cookstove, a child tugging on her apron strings — and even if collectors can't relate to that scene personally, they still want to cherish and preserve those old aprons. Some are basic and functional, perhaps made of flour sack material, while others are embroidered and trimmed with lace or appliqués.

Commercially made aprons are collectible as well, and those that retain their original tags command the higer prices. Remember, condition is critical, and as a general rule, those that are made by hand are preferred over machine-made or commercially made aprons. Values are for examples in excellent condition unless otherwise noted. For more information we recommend *Ladies' Vintage Accessories* by LaRee Johnson Bruton (Collector Books).

Bib, floral on blue & white, blue trim, pocket, bottom ruffle, M **15.00**

Bib, green organdy w/purple tatting, embroidered, ribbon straps **35.00**

Bib, pink chintz cotton, sweetheart neckline, pocket, red trim. **28.00**

Bib, red cotton w/daisies, blue trim, Dutch figures on pockets . **24.00**

Bib, white cotton Acadiana style, 2-button waistband, pockets **33.00**

Child's bib, bunny print, organdy ruffle trim, 1950s, 16" L . **23.00**

Child's waist, yellow cotton, embroidered spaniel w/green collar. **13.00**

Pinafore, red, green, blue calico patchwork print, 1950-60s **28.00**

Shoulder, cotton percale, green & white gingham print, 2 pockets **20.00**

Waist, baby blue w/moon & black embroidered cats on fence.. **15.00**

Waist, brown gingham w/tulip hem, white trim, short ties **16.00**

Waist, crochet, cream w/3 pink horizontal stripes, late 1940s . **25.00**

Waist, crochet, purple & beige, 19" L **16.00**

Waist, ecru muslin, embroidered Christmas floral, lace trim hem **19.00**

Waist, gold cotton, fall accent pocket & brown rickrack at hem **13.00**

Waist, made from 2 red & white floral handkerchiefs, 1940s **18.00**

Waist, pink & floral stripes, pocket, scalloped edge, M **20.00**

Waist, pink cotton, pocket w/dark pink lace accent, 1950s, 20" L **14.00**

Waist, red w/green waist stripe, 3 green stripes on pocket & hem **12.00**

Waist, sheer jadeite green w/lace & lace applique **11.00**

Waist, white organdy & eyelet, Carmen Lee, 22" L **18.00**

Waist, yellow, embroidered poodle & hydrant, pocket, 18½" L **15.00**

Waist, yellow & white gingham, cross-stitch on hem, 1950s, 22" L **19.00**

Waist, yellow organdy with floral handkerchief trim, ca. 1940s, from $14.00 to $20.00. (Photo courtesy LaRee Johnson Bruton)

Waist, yellow w/tulip applique pocket, reverses to floral **18.00**

Ashtrays

Even though smoking may be frowned upon these days, ashtrays themselves are beginning to be noticed favorably by collectors, who perhaps view them as an 'endangered species'! Some of the more desirable examples are those with embossed or intaglio designs, applied decorations, added figures of animals or people, Art Deco styling, an interesting advertising message, and an easily recognizable manufacturer's mark.

Advertising, Captain Morgan Rum, ceramic boat form, The Right..., 6" L..............................31.00

Advertising, Fairmont Hotels, ceramic, gold & black logo, 4½" dia..............................8.00

Advertising, Howard Johnson, orange glass w/aqua logo, octagon, 5"...........................11.00

Advertising, Jax Beer, milk glass, Jax The Mellow Brew, 5¼" dia................................13.00

Advertising, JC Penney Co, ceramic, white w/yellow & black letters............................25.00

Advertising, Koehler's Beer Distributor, ceramic, red w/ white letters....................25.00

Advertising, Kool Cigarettes, ivory glass w/penguins & jadite letters............................32.00

Advertising, Lucky Strike, clear glass w/white decal & pack image, 4"...........................18.00

Advertising, McDonald's, cream ceramic, center logo, black letters, 7"............................20.00

Advertising, Pizza Hut, glass, red roof logo w/black letters, 5" dia...........................6.00

Advertising, Pyrene Fire Extinguisher, nickel-plated metal, ca. 1930s, 5½x5", $100.00. (Photo courtesy gasolinealleyantiques.com)

Advertising, Sears Paint, ceramic, gold trim, 2 cans in center, 5½"..............................8.00

Advertising, Texaco, clear glass w/ red logo & Vargas girl, 1940-50s.............................28.00

Advertising, Union Pacific Railroad, glass, shield logo, 4¼" dia.19.00

Novelty, couple kissing, ceramic nodder, WELCOME in black, 5"..............................55.00

Novelty, cowboy hat, white pottery, 2¾x6½x5¾"......................17.00

Novelty, Indian w/tepee, ceramic, smoke comes out of tepee top, 4½"..............................25.00

Novelty, log cabin, brass, smoke comes from chimney.......27.00

Novelty, Mexican hat, amber glass, 3 rests, 2½"..........................7.00

Novelty, skeleton nodder, ceramic, gray, Keep on Smoking, 5½" dia..............................17.00

Novelty, snail figure, ceramic, 1950s, 7½x6"...................22.00

Souvenir, California, Rudi's Italian Inn on red ceramic, 2¾x3¼".......28.50

Souvenir, Elvis Presley 1935-1977 in floral circle, white ceramic........................21.00

Souvenir, Green Bay Packers, ceramic, football shape, 5x8" **44.00**

Souvenir, Michigan, House of Ludington, ceramic, 4¾" dia **30.00**

Souvenir, Minnesota, Old Junction Inn, ceramic, Mankato, 4" sq **30.00**

Tire Ashtrays

Tire ashtrays were introduced around 1910 as advertising items. The very early all-glass or glass-and-metal types were replaced in the early 1920s by the more familiar rubber-tired varieties. Hundreds of different examples have been produced over the years. They are still distributed (by the larger tire companies only), but no longer display the detail or color of the pre-World War II tire ashtrays. Although the common ones bring modest prices, rare examples sometimes sell for several hundred dollars. For more information we recommend *Tire Ashtray Collector's Guide* by Jeff McVey; he is listed in the Directory under Idaho.

Dunlop Gold Seal 78 Twin Belt, logo on insert, 1970s, 6" dia **32.00**

Firestone Heavy Duty High Speed **Gum-Dipped** Balloon 6.00-18 Made in USA, glass insert with shield logo, 5½", from $22.00 to $28.00.

(Photo courtesy Jeff McVey)

Firestone, red & black plastic insert w/3 extended rests, 6" dia **24.00**

Firestone Super Sports Wide Oval, clear insert, MIB **29.00**

General Streamline Jumbo, green glass insert, ...Way To Make Friends **65.00**

Gillette, embossed bear standing on tire on clear insert, 7" dia **44.00**

Goodrich Silvertown Lifesaver Radial HR 70-15, clear insert, 6" dia **25.00**

Goodyear Custom Power Cushion Polyglass, clear insert, 3⅝" dia **25.00**

Goodyear Nylon Tubeless Custom Super..., yellow glass insert, 6" dia **30.00**

Goodyear Super SURE GRIP Tractor, glass insert, 1950s, 6" dia **31.00**

Miller Delux Long Safe Mileage, clear insert w/name on bottom **80.00**

Pennsylvania, pink glass insert, 5¼" dia **50.00**

Yokohama, insert decal reads R Radial GT Special, 1970s, 6" dia **37.00**

Automobilia

Many are fascinated with vintage automobiles, but to own one of those 'classy chassis' is a luxury not all can afford! So instead they enjoy collecting related memorabilia such as advertising, owners' manuals, horns, emblems, and hood ornaments. The decade of the 1930s produced the items that are most in demand today, but the 1950s models have their own band of devoted fans as well as do the muscle cars of the 1960s.

Ashtray, Grand Auto Stores, glass, sq, 2⅜x2⅜" **12.00**

Bank, Thunderbird, metal 1955 replica, marked Banthrico Inc..., 7".............................**30.00**

Book, Classic Cars, Peter Roberts, Hamlyn Publishing Group, 1981 ....**12.00**

Book, Dodge Dynasty, Latham & Agresta, Harcourt Brace 1st edition.............................**15.00**

Book, 1947 Floyd Clymer's Historical Motor Scrapbook #4, 1960s...............................**15.00**

Book, 75 Years of Chevrolet, Dammann, Crestline, 1st edition, 1986........................**20.00**

Booklet, Brief Passenger Car Data, Ethyl Corp, 1966, 42-pg, 6½x4" **4.00**

Booklet, Ford Service Technician-Servicing the Falcon Engine, 1960 ....**12.00**

Booklet, Lincoln Quick Facts, 1952, 12-pg, 7¼x4¼"..................**12.00**

Box, cigar; Illinois Automobile Club Cigar, flat, never used **8.00**

Brochure, AMC dealer, 5 cars on cover, 1977, 36-pg, 11x8½"..**14.00**

Brochure, Autocar, 1950s-60s, 4-pg, 8½x11"............................**12.00**

Brochure, Cadillac El Dorado, 1953, unfolds to 24x21¾"..........**65.00**

Brochure, Chevrolet, Let's Get Excited About Power Steering, 1953 ....**15.00**

Brochure, Chrysler Windsor/ Windsor Deluxe, 1953, 12-pg, 11x9½"............................**22.00**

Brochure, dealer's; 1941 Ford Trucks, 11x8½", unfolds to 17x22"............................**20.00**

Brochure, dealer's; 1952 Chrysler's K-310 Experimental Dream Car **12.00**

Can, oiler; Nash General Use Oil, tin w/plastic cap on spout, 4-oz..............................**110.00**

Can, wax; Ford Polishing Wax/M-220-A, round tin w/pry lid, 8-oz................................**30.00**

Catalog, Chevrolet Parts Supplement to Master Parts, 1955 ....**40.00**

Catalog, Pep Boys 1957 Catalog/ New Low Prices/Auto..., 88-pg.............................**30.00**

Clock, Ford, sq wood frame w/ paper face, V-8 Sales/Service, 15x15" **65.00**

Clock, Nash, octagonal w/metal frame, painted tin face, 18x18" **75.00**

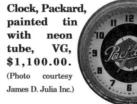

Clock, Packard, painted tin with neon tube, VG, $1,100.00. (Photo courtesy James D. Julia Inc.)

Emblem, hubcap; Porsche, 1960s **40.00**

Emblem, radiator; Chevrolet logo, metal w/blue & white enamel, ca 1940............................**30.00**

Emblem, radiator; Hudson Super Six, triangular, 2½".......**120.00**

Emblem, radiator; Hupmobile 8, worn enamel, 1⅛"...........**70.00**

Handbook, Ford Service 6004, for the 221 V-8 engine, 30-pg . **10.00**

Hubcap, Oldsmobile, 1954-55, 15" **12.00**

Hubcap, Whippet, screw-on, 2½" **20.00**

Magazine, Antique Automobile, March-April, 1977 .... **3.00**

Magazine, Ford Times, 1955 ... **4.00**

Magazine, Speed Age, October 1949, 36-pg **12.00**

Manual, accessories; 1968 Pontiac, 32-pg, 10½x8¼" **15.00**

Manual, Ford Shop for Galaxie, Galaxie 500 & station wagons, 1952 .... **40.00**

Manual, owner's; Chevrolet, 1957 .... **40.00**

Manual, owner's; Ford, 1959. **20.00**

Manual, owner's; Ford Mustang, 1967 .... **20.00**

Manual, owner's; Ford Pinto, 1973 .... **12.00**

Manual, owner's; Hillman Minx, 1958, 84-pg **20.00**

Manual, owner's; Jaguar XK 150, 1950s, 20x27" **20.00**

Manual, service; Chevrolet Power Glide Transmission, 1950. **20.00**

Manual, service; Chevrolet Steering Gear, 1949 .... **15.00**

Matchbook, Spencer Buick, red convertible, 1958 .... **12.00**

Padlock, Ford script oval logo, plate covers keyhole, w/Ford key, 3" **55.00**

Paperweight, Model T, brass, open windows, 5" **25.00**

Photo, dealer's; 1948 Mack Dump truck being loaded at work site, 8x10" **30.00**

Pin, lapel; Ford logo, cloisonné style, 1½" L **4.00**

Pin, Lincoln-Mercury Registered Mechanic, 10k gold-filled, marked LGB **30.00**

Postcard, Corvette, real photo of 3 cars, 1978 .... **7.00**

Postcard, 1967 Marlin & Ambassador **8.00**

Postcard, 1967 Marlin color photo **8.00**

Postcard, 1977 Chevrolet Corvette. **7.00**

Poster, Maxwell Truck, Be Cold Blooded..., 1920, 23x17".. **85.00**

Sign, Automotive Maintenance Association, porcelain, 18x20", **$300.00.** (Photo courtesy B.J. Summers and Wayne Priddy)

Steering wheel, Ford F250, XLT, 1959 .... **110.00**

Stock certificate, General Motors, 100 shares, orange, 1957, cancelled **18.00**

Token, 1954 General Motors Motorama **18.00**

Wrench, open-end; Maxwell #4 . **10.00**

Autumn Leaf

Autumn Leaf dinnerware was a product of the Hall China Company, who produced this extensive line from 1933 until 1978 for exclusive distribution by the Jewell Tea Company. The Libbey Glass Company made co-ordinating pitchers, tumblers, and stemware. Metal, cloth, plastic, and paper items were also available. Today, though, very rare pieces are expensive and a challenge to acquire. New collectors may easily reassemble an attractive, usable set at a reasonable price. Hall has produced special club pieces (for the NALCC) as well as some limited editions for an Ohio company, but these are well marked and easily identified as such. Refer to *Collector's Encyclopedia of Hall China* by Margaret and Kenn Whitmyer (Collector Books) for more information. See Clubs and Newsletters for information concerning the *Autumn Leaf* newsletter.

Baker, cake; Heatflow, clear glass, 1½-qt 85.00
Baker, souffle; 1978, 4½" 75.00
Bean pot, 2 handles, 1960-76, 2½-qt 250.00
Blanket, Vellux, blue, 1979+, twin size, from $100 to 175.00
Book, Autumn Leaf Story 60.00
Bowl, cereal; 1938-76, 6", from $8 to 12.00
Bowl, mixing; New Metal, 3-pc set, 1980+ 325.00
Bowl, mixing; 3-pc set 85.00
Bowl, salad; 9" 30.00
Bowl, vegetable; round, 9" ... 175.00
Cake safe, metal, side motif, 1950-53, from $25 to 50.00
Calendar, 1920s-3Os 200.00
Candlesticks, metal, pr from $70 to 100.00
Candy dish, metal base 600.00
Cleanser can, from $750 to . 1,500.00
Coaster, metal, 3⅛" 12.00

Coffee dispenser, 1941 .... 400.00
Cookbook, NALCC; 1984 .... 45.00
Cooker, waterless, Mary Dunbar, metal, from $50 to 75.00
Cup, coffee; Jewels Best 30.00
Cup, St Denis, 1942-76 .... 40.00
Dutch oven, porcelain, w/lid, 1979+, 5-qt 200.00
Fork, pickle; Jewel Tea 75.00
Hot pad, metal, oval, 10¾", from $12 to 15.00
Lamp, hurricane; Douglas, 1960-62, pr 500.00
Mug, Irish coffee; 1966-76 ... 110.00
Newsletter, Jewel News 20.00
Percolator, 1960-62 .... 350.00
Pie plate, Dunbar, Heatflow, clear glass 55.00
Plate, dinner; Melmac, 10" 20.00
Platter, oval, 1938-76, 13½", from $20 to 28.00
Pressure cooker, Dunbar, metal . 225.00
Salt & pepper shakers, Casper, ruffled, regular, 1939-76, pr. 30.00
Saucepan, w/lid, 1979, 2-qt . 110.00
Saucer, St Denis, 1974-76 .... 8.00
Sifter, metal 400.00

Stack set, four-piece, from $75.00 to $90.00.

Teacup, Ruffled-D, regular, 1936-76 .... 10.00
Teapot, Aladdin, 1942-76 .... 75.00

Avon

Originally founded in 1886

under the title California Perfume Company, the firm became officially known as Avon Products Inc. in 1939. Avon offers something for almost everyone such as cross-collectibles including jewelry, Fostoria, Wedgwood, commerative plates, Ceramarte steins, and hundreds of other quality items. Among the most popular items are the Mrs. P.F.E. Albee figurines. Mrs. Albee was the first Avon lady, ringing doorbells and selling their products in the very early years of the company's history. The figurines are issued each year and awarded only to Avon's most successful representatives. Each are elegantly attired in magnificent period fashions. The workmanship is remarkable. Also sought are product samples, magazine ads, jewelry, and catalogs. Their Cape Cod glassware has been sold in vast quantities since the '70s and is becoming a common sight at flea markets and antique malls. For more information we recommend *Bud Hastin's Avon Collector's Encyclopedia* by Bud Hastin. See also Cape Cod. For information concerning the National Association of Avon Collectors and the newsletter *Avon Times*, see Clubs and Newsletters. Values are for mint-condition examples unless noted otherwise. Mint-in-box items bring much higher prices than those without their original boxes.

Bottle, scent; blue glass, gold filigree on front, handle, 9¼"........ **10.00**

Cake plate, Hummingbird, clear/frosted lead crystal, MIB . **50.00**

Chess/Checkerboard, brown plastic, marked ...NAAC 1976, 21½" sq........................... **45.00**

Figurine, John Wayne, in Dark Command movie attire, 1985, 7½" **42.00**

Figurine, Mrs Albee, dressed in yellow & holding bottle, 1980 .**45.00**

Figurine, Mrs Albee, holding parasol & sample case, 1978, from $65 to.............................. **85.00**

Figurine, Mrs. Albee, with satchel and Scottie dog, 1983, 9", $50.00.

Figurine, Mrs Albee, working at desk, 1985, from $35 to .. **50.00**

Figurine, Mrs Albee, 2002, MIB. **100.00**

Figurine, nativity; Gabriel, white porcelain, w/trumpet, 1992......**50.00**

Figurine, nativity; Shepherd w/lamb, white porcelain, 1985........ **60.00**

Figurine, nativity; The Angel, white porcelain, 1985, 4½", MIB. **60.00**

Figurine, nativity; The Poorman, white porcelain, 1985 ..... **50.00**

Figurine, Rhett Butler, 1984, 6" **45.00**

Plate, Cherished Teddies, A Mother's Love Is..., Enesco, 2002, 6" dia..................... **60.00**

Soap on a Rope, Marvin the Martian, green w/white rope, MIB.................................. **27.00**

Stein, A Christmas Carol, made in Brazil, 1996, 9"................. **10.00**

Stein, Country & Western, #00907, cowboy hat pull-down handle, 1996 .... 30.00

Stein, Legend of the Century Babe Ruth, #62677, 1999, MIB. 35.00

Banks

After the Depression, everyone was aware that saving 'for a rainy day' would help during bad times. Children of the '40s, '50s, and '60s were given piggy banks in forms of favorite characters to reinforce the idea of saving. They were made to realize that by saving money they could buy that expensive bicycle or a toy they were particularly longing for.

Today on the flea market circuit, figural banks are popular collectibles, especially those that are character-related — advertising characters and Disney in particular.

Interest has recently developed in glass banks, and you may be surprised at the prices some of the harder-to-find examples are bringing. Charlie Reynolds has written the glass bank 'bible,' called *Collector's Guide to Glass Banks*, which you'll want to read if you think you'd like to collect them. Unless otherwise noted, our values are for items in near-mint to mint condition.

Ceramic

Boston Terrier Academy, dogs in bus, white, blue & black, 6½" L 135.00

Chicken Feed, rooster, multicolor, Vic Moran, ca 1950, 8" .. 115.00

Corky Pig, green w/bull's-eye backside, Hull, 1957 .... 120.00

Leprechaun on pig's back, multicolor, England, 1960s, 6x4" 55.00

Lobster, red-orange, Atlantic City NJ, Germany, 3⅛" 70.00

Piggy, yellow ware, swirling earth tones, 2½x4x2¼" 125.00

Purse, Pin Money, floral decor w/ gold, Norcrest foil sticker, 4x5" 68.00

Scottie dog, head & body separate, held by padlock, 6½x8" ... 70.00

St Bernards (3 joined), kegs at throats/holds nickels/dimes/ quarters 110.00

Character

AFLAC Duck in lg blue mailbox, 6", MIB 68.00

Batman, ceramic, National Periodical, 7" 42.50

Big Aggie, oversize lady on tractor, painted composition, 1940s, EX 60.00

Boston Braves batter, rare 'cap-on' version, Stanford Pottery . 115.00

Clown head w/smiling face, Empire Savings, Coors 135.00

Court jester's face, brown wash, Bennington-like, mouth slot, 3¼" 110.00

Dale Earnhardt #3 gray Monte Carlo, Winston Cup, 1995, 8" L, MIB 48.00

Dick Tracy Sunnydel Acres, multicolor, Nouvelle Pottery, 6x3x3" 215.00

Donald Duck on chest, plastic, Knickerbocker/Disney, 9". 50.00

Hamm's Beer Bear, ceramic, unmarked Red Wing, 1960s 415.00

Hedwig (owl from Harry Potter), embossed metal, mechanical, 2001, MIB **55.00**

Howdy Doody, ceramic, Puritan, 1952, 9", EX **50.00**

King Royal, Royal Gelatin, vinyl, 1960s, 10" **45.00**

Leprechaun w/red hat, Wade limited edition **85.00**

Linus w/baseball glove, ceramic, UFS, 1971, Made in Japan, 7" **50.00**

Little Lulu, plastic, Play Pal Plastics, 7½", $25.00.

Mighty Joe Young (gorilla), Universal Statuary Co, 1952, 12x8", VG **65.00**

Milwaukee Braves baseball player, papier-maché, 1960s, 6" **88.00**

Mr Zip bendy figure mailbox, hard plastic & rubber, 7½" **42.50**

Old Lady in the Shoe, tin litho biscuit box, 1950s, 4¾x8" **75.00**

Robot, Mr Quasar, Dakin, 1970s, 9" w/arms up, MIP **70.00**

Sad-Eye Joe, Knott's Berry Farm souvenir, multicolor, ceramic, 6¼" **50.00**

Schmoo, pink glass w/blue non-punched slotted, 7⅛" **295.00**

Sinclair Oil brontosaurus, coppertone pot metal, 1930s, 9" L, VG **55.00**

Snoopy on lg red apple, ceramic, United Feature Syndicate, 1966 .... **85.00**

Snow White at wishing well, Disney, Enesco, 1960s **50.00**

Three Little Pigs, tin litho, Chein, 3x3¼", VG w/key **70.00**

Uncle Sam's hat, tin litho, Chein. **75.00**

Glass

Baseball, Knoxville Smokies, blue base, Mobile Oil giveaway, 1950s **95.00**

Goebel Baby Pig, Kristahglas, 4¾", $75.00.
(Photo courtesy Charles Reynolds)

Piano, amethyst, upright, ca 1973, 2⅞" **65.00**

Piggy, Corning Ware w/blue flowers on white, 4¼x6¼" **60.00**

Piggy, This Little Piggy... on clear, cork stopper, Libbey, 20" L **98.00**

Save for the Kids, goats decal on clear bubble, Vic Moran. **130.00**

Save for the New Car, car & family decal on clear bubble, Vic Moran **115.00**

Miscellaneous

Barrel, Start w/a Coin, End w/a Barrel, metal, Chicago Thrift Co, 1923 .... **50.00**

Boy Scout book form, insignia on leather 'cover,' Patented 1923, VG **90.00**

Brinks car, painted cast metal, rubber wheels turn, 1948, 8½" L 85.00

Chest of drawers, brown Bakelite, open drawer for deposit, 6".45.00

Cowboy boot & spur, brown-tone metal, 5¼x5" 50.00

DeSoto promo car, Banthrico, 1949, minor chips/scratches ... 220.00

Ferret, painted composition, Ferret Association of CT, 8½", MIB 65.00

Flop-Earred Rabbit, lead, 6", $600.00. (Photo courtesy Morphy Auctions)

Flying saucer, Save 'n Space, Chicago bank promotional pc, 3½" 170.00

Grocery Store Super Market, tin litho, US Metal Toy, lollipop bank 70.00

Harley-Davidson Horse & Buggy, die-cast, Ertl, 1991, MIB 105.00

Harley-Davidson 1933 motorcyle w/side car, limited edition, MIB 110.00

Haunted House, tin & plastic, mechanical, Brumberger, 1960s, MIB 100.00

Hess 1986 firetruck, working lights, MIB 60.00

John Deere Centennial 1937-1937, oil can, green & yellow paint, 3½" 250.00

Liberty bell, cast metal, realistic paint, dated 1919, 4x3¾". 70.00

Mercury 1953 4-door sedan promo, Banthrico, worn paint/scratches 195.00

Organ grinder monkey tipping hat, tin litho, Chein, VG 60.00

Pennsylvania National...Trust...PA, celluloid, 1920s, 2½x2".. 100.00

Rhinoceros, cast iron, Moore #721, 2½", VG, $500.00. (Photo courtesy Morphy Auctions)

Rocket/spaceship, painted metal, mechanical, Tallahassee FL, 11" 110.00

Singer sewing machine, tin, Germany, EX 335.00

Speedway State Bank, race car, copper-tone metal, 2¾x6x3¼" 330.00

Super Slots Flying Sevens slot machine, battery operated, 18", MIB 72.50

Telephone, painted tin, TH Stough, 1¼x2⅛x2¾" 110.00

Texaco 1913 Model T, 1st in Service Station series 210.00

United States Coast Guard Flyer (airplane), die-cast, Ertl, 1980s, MIB 80.00

Wizard, Insty-prints on base, red & white costume, hard vinyl, 8½" 85.00

Barbie® Dolls

Barbie doll was first introduced

in 1959, and soon Mattel found themselves producing not only dolls but tiny garments, fashion accessories, houses, cars, horses, books, and games as well. Today's Barbie doll collectors want them all. Though the early Barbie dolls are very hard to find, there are many of her successors still around. The trend today is toward Barbie exclusives — Holiday Barbie dolls and Bob Mackie Barbie dolls are very 'hot' items. So are special-event Barbie dolls.

When buying the older dolls, you'll need to do lots of studying and comparisons to learn to distinguish one Barbie doll from another, but this is the key to making sound buys and good investments. Remember, though, collectors are sticklers concerning condition (even the condition of the original packaging is critical). Compared to one mint-in-box, they'll often give an additional 20% if that box has never been opened! As a general rule, a mint-in-box doll is worth twice as much as one mint, no box. The same doll, played with and in only good condition at best is worth only approximately 25% of one in mint condition, often even less.

If you want a good source for study, refer to one of these fine books: *Barbie Doll Fashion, Volumes I, II,* and *III,* by Sarah Sink Eames; *Collector's Encyclopedia of Barbie Doll Exclusives, Collector's Encyclopedia of Barbie Doll Collector's Editions,* and *Barbie Doll around the World* by J. Michael Augustyniak; *Barbie, The First 30 Years,* by Stefanie Deutsch; *The Barbie Doll Years,* by Patrick C. and Joyce L. Olds; and *Schroeder's Collectible Toys, Antique to Modern* (Collector Books).

Allan, 1965, bendable legs, MIB............................**300.00**
Barbie, #4, 1960, blond or brunette, MIB, from $425 to.........**450.00**
Barbie, #6, blond, brunette or titian, MIB........................**425.00**
Barbie, American Girl, 1964, platinum hair, original swimsuit.............................**650.00**
Barbie, American Girl, 1964, red hair, replica swimsuit, NM......**600.00**
Barbie, Army Desert Storm, 1993, Stars & Stripes, NRFB...**30.00**
Barbie, Avon Representative (White or Hispanic), 1999, NRFB............................**50.00**
Barbie, Barbie Sign Language (Black or White), 1999, NRFB............................**20.00**
Barbie, Chinese, 1993, Dolls of the World, NRFB..................**30.00**
Barbie, Color-Magic, 1966, blond, MIB............................**1,200.00**
Barbie, Dream Glow (Black), 1986, MIB..................................**30.00**
Barbie, Dream Glow (Hispanic), 1986, MIB.......................**40.00**
Barbie, Dream Glow (White), 1986, MIB................................**35.00**
Barbie, Easter Party, 1995, NRFB............................**20.00**
Barbie, Enchanted Evening, 1991, JC Penney, NRFB..........**50.00**
Barbie, Enchanted Princess, 1993, Sears, NRFB..................**75.00**
Barbie, Evening Sparkle, 1990, Hill's, NRFB...................**35.00**

Barbie, Fabulous Fur, 1986, NRFB 65.00

Barbie, Fantasy Goddess of Asia, 1998, Bob Mackie, NRFB .150.00

Barbie, Fire Fighter, 1995, Toys R Us, NRFB 50.00

Barbie, Flower Seller (My Fair Lady), 1995, Hollywood Legends, NRFB 70.00

Barbie, French Lady, 1997, Great Eras Collection, NRFB ... 50.00

Barbie, Goddess of the Sun, 1995, Bob Mackie, NRFB 175.00

Barbie, Grand Premier, 1997, Barbie Collectors Club, NRFB 225.00

Barbie, Great Shapes (w/Walkman), 1984, NRFB 30.00

Barbie, Growin' Pretty Hair, 1971, NRFB 475.00

Barbie, Hawaiian Superstar, 1977, MIB 75.00

Barbie, Holiday, 1988, NRFB . 275.00

Barbie, Holiday, 1989, NRFB . 100.00

Barbie, Holiday, 1995, NRFB . 40.00

Barbie, Holiday, 1998, NRFB . 25.00

Barbie, Island Fun, 1988, NRFB .20.00

Barbie, Jamaican, 1992, Dolls of the World, NRFB 50.00

Barbie, Jewel Essence, 1996, Bob Mackie, NRFB 125.00

Barbie, Kenyan, 1994, Dolls of the World, NRFB 40.00

Barbie, Knitting Pretty (pink), 1964, NRFB 1,265.00

Barbie, Live Action on Stage, 1970, MIB 225.00

Barbie, Malibu (Sunset), 1971, NRFB 65.00

Barbie, Medival Lady, 1995, Great Eras Collection, NRFB ... 60.00

Barbie, Moon Goddess, 1996, Bob Mackie, NRFB 175.00

Barbie, Native American #2, 1994, Dolls of the World, NRFB. 40.00

Barbie, Nifty Fifties, 2000, Great Fashions of the 20th Century, NRFB 50.00

Barbie, Opening Night, 1993, Classique Collection, NRFB 75.00

Barbie, Party Sensation, 1990, NRFB 55.00

Barbie, Peach Pretty, 1989, K-Mart, MIB 35.00

Barbie, Perfume Party, 1988, NRFB 30.00

Barbie, Phantom of the Opera, 1998, FAO Schwarz, NRFB 125.00

Barbie, Picnic Party, 1992, Osco, NRFB 30.00

Barbie, Picnic Pretty, 1992, MIB, $25.00. (Photo courtesy Margo Rana)

Barbie, Pink & Pretty, 1982, MIB 60.00

Barbie, Queen of Sapphires, 2000, Royal Jewels, NRFB 125.00

Barbie, Quick Curl (Deluxe), 1976, Jergens, NRFB 100.00

Barbie, Quick Curl Miss America, 1974, MIB 80.00

Barbie, Rockettes, 1993, FAO Schwarz, NRFB 120.00

Barbie, Romantic Wedding 2001, 2000, Bridal Collection, NRFB 50.00

Barbie, Russian, 1988, Dolls of the World, NRFB 35.00

Barbie, Savvy Shopper, 1994, Bloomingdale's, NRFB.... 50.00

Barbie, School Spirit Barbie, 1993, Toys R Us, NRFB 30.00

Barbie, Scottish, 1981, Dolls of the World, NRFB 80.00

Barbie, Sea Princess, 1996, Service Merchandise, NRFB 45.00

Barbie, Serenade in Satin, 1997, Barbie Couture Collection, MIB 100.00

Barbie, Sheer Illusion #1, 1998, Designer Collection, NRFB, ea 80.00

Barbie, Snow Princess, 1994, Enchanted Seasons, blond hair, NRFB 130.00

Barbie, Snow Princess, 1994, Mattel Festival, brunette hair, NRFB 1,100.00

Barbie, Southern Belle, 1994, Great Eras Collection, NRFB ... 75.00

Barbie, Starlight Dance, 1996, Classique Collection, NRFB 45.00

Barbie, Steppin' Out Barbie 1930s, 1999, Great Fashions of the 20th Century 55.00

Barbie, Swan Lake Ballerina, 1991, NRFB 200.00

Barbie, Swirl Ponytail, 1964, blond or brunette hair, NRFB . 650.00

Barbie, Swirl Ponytail, 1964, brunette, NRFB 650.00

Barbie, Talking, 1970, blond, brunette or red hair, NRFB . 300.00

Barbie, Twist 'n Turn, 1969, flipped hairdo, blond or brunette, NRFB 475.00

Barbie, Winter Fantasy, 1990, FAO Schwarz, NRFB............. 200.00

Barbie, Yuletide Romance, 1996, Hallmark, NRFB............ 30.00

Chris, 1967, any hair color, MIB. 200.00

Christie, Beauty Secrets, 1980, MIB 60.00

Christie, Golden Dream, 1980, MIB 50.00

Christie, Talking, 1969, brunette or red hair, NRFB 350.00

Christie, Twist 'n Turn, 1968, red hair, MIB 300.00

Francie, Malibu, 1971, NRFB. 75.00

Francie, Twist 'n Turn, 1969, blond or brunette, long hair, bangs, MIB 425.00

Francie, 30th Anniversary, 1996, NRFB.............................. 65.00

Jamie, New & Wonderful Walking, 1970, blond hair, MIB... 225.00

Kelly, Quick Curl, 1972, NRFB. 175.00

Kelly, Yellowstone, 1974, brunette hair, NRFB 575.00

Ken, Air Force, 1994, Stars 'n Stripes, NRFB................ 30.00

Ken, Beach Blast, 1989, NRFB.15.00

Ken, Crystal, 1984, NRFB..... 40.00

Ken, Dream Date, 1983, NRFB.30.00

Ken, Fashion Jeans, 1982, NRFB 35.00

Ken, Gold Medal Skier, 1975, NRFB.............................. 75.00

Ken, Henry Higgins, 1996, Hollywood Legends Series, NRFB.............................. 65.00

Ken, Jewel Secrets, 1987, NRFB.30.00

Ken, Mod Hair, 1972, MIB 70.00

Ken, Rocker, 1986, MIB......... 40.00

Ken, Sport & Shave, 1980, MIB. 40.00

Ken, Sun Charm, 1989, MIB. 25.00

Ken, Sun Lovin' Malibu, 1979, NRFB.............................. 30.00

Ken, Talking, 1960s, NRFB. 150.00

Ken, Walk Lively, 1972, MIB. 150.00

Midge, Cool Times, 1989, $25.00. (Photo courtesy Kitturah B. Westenhouser)

Midge, Ski Fun, 1991, MIB ... **30.00**

Midge, Winter Sports, 1995, Toys R Us, MIB **40.00**

Midge, 1963, brunette hair, straight legs, MIB **150.00**

Midge, 30th Anniversary, 1992, porcelain, MIB **175.00**

PJ, Fashion Photo, 1978, MIB. **95.00**

PJ, Gold Medal Gymnast, 1975, NRFB **120.00**

PJ, Sun Lovin' Malibu, 1979, MIB **50.00**

PJ, Sunsational Malibu, 1982, MIB **40.00**

PJ, Talking, 1970, MIB **250.00**

Skipper, Deluxe Quick Curl, 1975, NRFB **65.00**

Skipper, Dramatic New Living, 1970, MIB **130.00**

Skipper, Homecoming Queen, 1989, NRFB **20.00**

Skipper, Music Lovin', 1985, NRFB **30.00**

Skipper, Super Teen, 1980, NRFB **30.00**

Skipper, Workout Teen Fun, 1988, NRFB **25.00**

Skipper, 1965, any hair color, MIB **175.00**

Skooter, 1966, any hair color, bendable legs, MIB **275.00**

Stacey, Talking, any hair color, MIB **400.00**

Teresa, California Dream, 1988, MIB **30.00**

Teresa, Rappin' Rockin', 1992, NRFB **45.00**

Tutti, Night Night Sleep Tight, 1966, NRFB **275.00**

Tutti, 1966, brunette hair, original outfit, EX **60.00**

Tutti, 1967, blond hair, MIB. **165.00**

Whitney, Nurse, 1987, NRFB. **80.00**

Miscellaneous

Accessory, Go-Together Ottoman & End Tables, MIB **100.00**

Accessory, Skipper & Skooter Double Bunk Beds & Ladder, MIB **100.00**

Case, Barbie, Francie, Casey & Tutti, hard plastic, EX, from $50 to **75.00**

Case, Barbie & Stacy, vinyl, 1967, NM from $65 to **75.00**

Case, Barbie Goes Travelin', vinyl, rare, NM **100.00**

Case, Barbie pictured in 4 different outfits, red vinyl, 1961, EX. **35.00**

Case, Barbie wearing All That Jazz, vinyl, 1967, from $30 to .. **40.00**

Case, Fashion Queen Barbie, w/ mirror & wig stand, red vinyl, 1963, EX **100.00**

Case, Midge wearing Movie Date, blue vinyl, 1963, rare, NM, $100 to **125.00**

Clothing, Barbie, Disco Dazzle, #1011, 1979, NRFP **15.00**

Clothing, Barbie, Gold 'n Glamour, #1647, NRFP **475.00**

Clothing, Barbie, Groovin' Gauchos, #1057, 1971, NRFP **300.00**

Clothing, Barbie, Lunch on the Terrace, #1649, 1966, NRFP **350.00**

Clothing, Barbie, Movie Groovie, #1866, 1969, NRFP **125.00**

Clothing, Barbie, Overall Denim, #3488, 1972, NRFP **110.00**

Clothing, Barbie, Pajama Party, #1601, 1964, NRFP **75.00**

Clothing, Barbie, Silver Sparkle, #1885, 1969, MIP **200.00**

Clothing, Barbie, White Delight, #3799, 1982, NRFP **15.00**

Clothing, Barbie, Yellow Go, #1816, 1967, NRFP **800.00**

Clothing, Barbie Busy Morning, #981, 1960, NRFP **325.00**

Clothing, Barbie in Hawaii, #1605, 1964, NRFP **300.00**

Clothing, Francie, Clam Diggers, #1258, 1966, NRFP **275.00**

Clothing, Francie, Fur-Out, #1262, 1966 – 1967, complete, M, $225.00. (Photo courtesy Sarah Sink Eames)

Clothing, Francie, Totally Terrific, #3280, 1972, MIP **225.00**

Clothing, Ken, Baseball, #9168, 1976, NRFP **70.00**

Clothing, Ken, Fountain Boy, #1407, 1964, NRFP **150.00**

Clothing, Ken, Western Winner, #3378, 1972, NRFP **60.00**

Clothing, Skipper, Confetti Cutie, #1952, 1968, NRFP **250.00**

Gift set, Ballerina Barbie on Tour, 1976, MIB **175.00**

Gift set, Barbie's Wedding Party, 1964, MIB **700.00**

House, Barbie Deluxe Family House, 1966, complete, VG **135.00**

House, Jamie's Penthouse, Sears Exclusive, 1971, MIB.... **475.00**

Paper dolls, Barbie, Whitman #4601, 1963, uncut, M **85.00**

Puzzle, jigsaw; Barbie & Ken, Whitman, 1963, 100-pc, MIB **40.00**

Vehicle, Barbie, '57 Chevy convertible, 1988, 25" long, MIB, $125.00.

Vehicle, Beach Bus, 1974, MIB .**45.00**

Vehicle, Ken's Hot Rod, red, Sears Exclusive, 1964, MIB.... **900.00**

Vehicle, Star 'Vette, red, 1977, MIB **100.00**

Bauer

The Bauer Company moved from Kentucky to California in 1909, producing crocks, gardenware, and vases until after the Depression when they introduced their first line of dinnerware. From 1932 until the early 1960s, they successfully marketed several lines of solid-color wares that are today very collectible. Some of their most popular lines are Ring, Plain Ware, and Monterey Modern.

Bauer Atlanta, vase, Lotus, pink, 14".....................................**100.00**

Brusche Al Fresco, bowl, covered soup; brown, 5½"..............**20.00**

Brusche Al Fresco, coffeepot..**30.00**

Brusche Al Fresco, plate, bread & butter; pink, 6"...................**6.00**

Brusche Al Fresco, plate, dinner; lime, 11½".........................**12.00**

Cal-Art, jardiniere, Swirl #12, speckeled pink, 12".......**125.00**

Cal-Art, pitcher, yellow matt, 10"................................**120.00**

Cal-Art, vase, bud; blue matt, 7"...................................**75.00**

Contempo, teapot, beige........**65.00**

El Chico, cup & saucer, burgundy...................................**65.00**

Gloss Pastel Kitchenware, bowl, mixing; #24, all colors.....**35.00**

Gloss Pastel Kitchenware, cookie jar (aka Beehive), all colors..**125.00**

Gloss Pastel Kitchenware, ramekin, light blue..................**10.00**

Gloss Pastel Kitchenware, teapot, Aladdin style, all colors, 8-cup...........................**175.00**

High Fire, pitcher, red-brown, Fred Johnson, 11½", minimum value, $450.00. (Photo courtesy Jack Chipman)

High Fire, rose bowl, Monterey Blue, 4"............................**55.00**

High Fire, vase, turquoise, #213, 7"......................................**85.00**

Matt Carlton, bowl, jade green, ruffled rim, 3½x7"........**150.00**

Matt Carlton, vase, carnation; jade green, 10"......................**350.00**

Plainware, bean pot, individual..**135.00**

Plainware, butter pat, black, 4½"..**125.00**

Plainware, creamer, yellow, individual, handmade by Matt Carlton............................**95.00**

Plainware, mug, 4"..............**125.00**

Ring, butter dish, quarter-pound, from $250.00 to $375.00. (Photo courtesy Jack Chipman)

Ringware, ashtray, 4"............**75.00**

Ringware, bowl, batter; 2-qt.**150.00**

Ringware, bowl, pedestal foot, 14".**750.00**

Ringware, casserole, w/lid, in holder, 8½"...........................**200.00**

Ringware, mug, beer............**350.00**

Ringware, plate, chop; 14"...**150.00**

Ringware, plate, dinner; 10½"..**125.00**

Ringware, plate, luncheon; 9".**40.00**

Ringware, platter, 15".........**125.00**

Ringware, tumbler, cobalt, no handle, 12-oz.........................**50.00**

Speckled Kitchenware, baker, pink, 1½-qt................................**40.00**

Speckled Kitchenware, casserole, pink, w/lid, 1½-qt............**40.00**

Speckled Kitchenware, coffee server, green, w/brass-finished holder..............................**45.00**

Speckled Kitchenware, lazy Suzan, 14", $150.00. (Photo courtesy Jack Chipman)

Speckled Kitchenware, mug, green, 8-oz.................................... **15.00**

Speckled Kitchenware, pelican, yellow, 20-oz **35.00**

Speckled Kitchenware, teapot, green, Monterey Modern style............................... **45.00**

Speckled Kitchenware, teapot, white, 4-cup..................... **50.00**

Beanie Babies

Beanie Babies first came on the scene in 1994, and from 1996 until 2000, they were highly collectible. Since then the 'collecting frenzy' has cooled considerably, and you can find Beanie Babies by the score at most large flea markets. Values given are for some of the more desirable Beanie Babies with all tags in mint to near mint condition.

Ally the Alligator, #4032, $20.00.

Baldy the Eagle, #4074, from $5 to **10.00**

Beak the Wiwi, #4211 .... **10.00**

Blackie the Bear, #4011 .... **10.00**

Blizzard the Tiger, #4163 ...... **10.00**

Bones the Dog, #4001, brown . **10.00**

Bronty the Brontosaurus, #4085, blue, minimum value.... **100.00**

Brownie the Bear, #4010, w/swing tag, minimum value **200.00**

Bubbles the Fish, #4078, yellow & black **10.00**

Bumble the Bee, #4045, minimum value **50.00**

Caw the Crow, #4071, $50.00.

Chilly the Polar Bear, #4012, minimum value..................... **200.00**

Chops the Lamb, #4019 .... **20.00**

Curly the Bear, #4052, brown, from $5 to **10.00**

Daisy the Cow, #4006, black & white **15.00**

Derby the Horse, #4008, 2nd issue, coarse mane & tail.......... **10.00**

Digger the Crab, #4027, 1st issue, orange, minimum value.. **50.00**

Digger the Crab, #4027, 2nd issue, red, minimum value **10.00**

Flash the Dolphin, #4021, minimum value..................... **15.00**

Flashy the Peacock, #4339 .... **10.00**

Flip the Cat, #4012, white..... **10.00**

Floppity the Bunny, lavender, from $7 to 10.00

Flutter the Butterfly, #4043, minimum value 50.00

Garcia the Bear, #4051, tie-died, minimum value 20.00

Goldie the Goldfish, #4023 .... 10.00

Grunt the Razorback Pig, #4092, red, minimum value 20.00

Happy the Hippo, #4061, gray, minimum value 50.00

Hippity the Bunny, #4119, mint green, from $7 to 9.00

Holiday Teddy (1997), #4200, from $8 to 10.00

Holiday Teddy (1999), #4257. 10.00

Holiday Teddy (2002), #4564. 10.00

Humphrey the Camel, #4060, minimum value 100.00

Inch the Worm, #4044, felt antennae .20.00

Inch the Worm, #4044, yarn antennae, from $7 to 10.00

Inky the Octopus, #4028, 3rd issue, pink, $6 to 15.00

Kiwi the Tucan, #4070, minimum value 30.00

Lefty the Donkey, #4087, gray. 20.00

Legs the Frog, #4020 .... 10.00

Liberty the Bear, #4057, minimum value 50.00

Lizzy the Lizard, #4033, tie-dyed, minimum value 50.00

Lizzy the Lizzard, #4033, 2nd issue, blue, from $10 to 20.00

Lucky the Ladybug, #4040, 11 spots, 3rd issue, from $10 to 15.00

Lucky the Ladybug, #4040, 3rd issue, 11 spots, from $10 to 15.00

Magic the Dragon, #4088, from $10 to 20.00

Manny the Manatee, #4081, minimum value..................... 20.00

Millennium the Bear, #4226, from $10 to 12.00

Nectar the Hummingbird, #4361, from $10 to 20.00

Patti the Platypus, #4025, 2nd issue, purple, from $10 to 20.00

Peanut the Elephant, #4062, light blue, from $7 to 15.00

Peking the Panda Bear, #4013, minimum value 100.00

Pinchers the Lobster, #4026.. 15.00

Quackers the Duck, #4024, 1st issue, no wings 450.00

Quackers the Duck, #4024, 2nd issue, w/wings, from $10 to 20.00

Radar the Bat, #4019, black, minimum value 30.00

Rex the Tyrannosaurus, #4086, minimum value 100.00

Righty the Elephant, #4085, gray 20.00

Ringo the Raccoon, #4014, from $10 to 15.00

Rover the Dog, #4101, red, from $10 to 15.00

Sammy the Bear, #4215, tie-dyed .10.00

Shamrock the Bear, #4338, from $6 to 10.00

Slither the Snake, #4031, minimum value..................... 200.00

Sly the fox, #4115, brown w/white belly, 2nd issue, from $5 to.10.00

Sly the fox, all brown, 1st issue, minimum value 30.00

Snowball the Snowman, #4201, from $10 to 12.00

Snowgirl the Snowgirl, #4333, from $10 to 12.00

Sparky the Dalmatian, #4100, minimum value 15.00

Splash the Wale, #4022, minimum value 15.00

Spot the Dog, #4000, w/spot .. 30.00

43

Squealer the Pig, #4005......... **10.00**
Tabasco the Bull, #4002, red feet, minimum value............... **30.00**
Teddy Bear, #4050, brown, new face, from $15 to **30.00**
Trap the Mouse, #4042, minimum value **100.00**
Weenie the dashund, #4013, from $10 to **15.00**

Birthday Angels

Here's a collection that's a lot of fun, inexpensive, and takes relatively little space to display. They're not at all hard to find, but there are several series, so completing 12-month sets of them all can provide a bit of a challenge. Generally speaking, angels are priced by the following factors: 1) company — look for Lefton, Napco, Norcrest, and Enesco marks or labels (unmarked or unknown sets are of less value); 2) application of flowers, bows, gold trim, etc. (the more detail, the more valuable); 3) use of rhinestones, which will also increase price; 4) age; and 5) quality of the workmanship involved, detail, and accuracy of painting.

Arnet, Kewpies in choir robes, rhinestone trim, 4½", each from $12.00 to $15.00.

Japan, J-6736, June bride w/veil & rose bouquet, 1950s, 5¼". **32.00**
Japan, months or days of the week, 4½", ea from $20 to **25.00**
Japan (unmarked), girl musician, 1950s, 5¾"...................... **28.00**
Kelvin, C-250, holding flower of the month, 4½", ea from $15 to................................... **20.00**
Lefton, #489, holding basket of flowers, 4", ea from $25 to....... **30.00**
Lefton, #574, day of the week series, ea from $25 to **28.00**
Lefton, #985, flower of the month, 5", ea from $30 to............ **35.00**
Lefton, #1323, bisque, ea from $18 to **22.00**
Lefton, #1987, ea from $30 to. **35.00**
Lefton, #1987J, w/rhinestones, 4½", ea from $30 to **40.00**
Lefton, #3332, w/basket of flowers, bisque, 4", ea from $25 to. **30.00**
Lefton, #6224, applied flower/ birthstone on skirt, 4½", ea $20 to............................ **30.00**
Lefton, #6883, sq frame, day of the week & months, 3¼x4", ea $28 to **32.00**
Lefton, #6985, musical, sm, ea from $40 to **45.00**
Lefton, #8281, day of the week series, applied roses, ea from $30 to **35.00**
Mahana Importing, #1194, white hair, 5", ea **20.00**
Mahana Importing, #1294, white hair, 5", ea **20.00**
Mahana Importing, #1600, Pal Angel, girl or boy, ea....... **18.00**
Napco, A1360-1372, ea from $20 to **30.00**
Napco, A1917-1929, boy, ea from $20 to.............................. **25.00**

Napco, C1361-1373, ea from $20 to **25.00**

Napco, C1921-1933, boy, ea from $20 to **25.00**

Norcrest, F-120, 4½", ea from $18 to **22.00**

Norcrest, F-210, day of the week, 4½", ea from $18 to **22.00**

Norcrest, F-535, 4½", ea from $20 to **25.00**

Schmid, boy sitting w/gift, label, 1950s, 3½" **29.00**

SR, w/birthstone & trait (ie April-innocence), ea **22.00**

TMJ, w/flower, ea from $20 to **25.00**

Wales, long white gloves, white hair, Made in Japan, 6½", ea $25 to **28.00**

Black Americana

This is a wide and varied field of collector interest. Advertising, toys, banks, sheet music, kitchenware items, movie items, and even the fine arts are areas that offer Black Americana buffs many opportunities to add to their collections. Caution! Because some pieces have become so valuable, reproductions abound. Watch for lots of new ceramic items, less detailed in both the modeling and the painting. In the following listings, values are for items in at least near-mint condition, unless otherwise noted.

Ashtray, nude child on bedpan, For Old Butts & Ashes, ceramic, 3½" **20.00**

Bell, girl praying on knees, stamped Japan, 3¾" **35.00**

Book, Billy Oates, Mabel Garrett Wagner, 2nd printing, 1950, 54-pg **32.00**

Book, Gentlemen Be Seated, Preston Powell, 1934, 126-pg, soft cover **30.00**

Book, His Eye Is on the Sparrow, Ethel Williams, 1951, 278-pg, EX **35.00**

Book, Railroad to Freedom, Hildegard Hoyt Swift, 2nd printing, 1960 .... **30.00**

Book, Sambo's Restaurant Family Funbook, premuim, 1978, 12-pg, EX **30.00**

Book, You Funny Little Noddy, Enid Blyton, 1950, hardbound, EX **30.00**

Bottle, scent; glass body, black head w/gold dunce cap, German, 2¼" **75.00**

Bowl, child's; white w/boy & flute, Brownie Downing China, 1962, 6" **45.00**

Cake topper, plastic bride & groom figures, 1970s, Hong Kong, 4½" **55.00**

Canister, man on sugar cane, reads Sugar, Made in England, 1950s, 10" **175.00**

Card, birthday; banjo player on paddleboat, 1950s, 6x4".. **22.00**

Condiment set, Japan label, five pieces, $300.00.

Cookbook, Dainty Desserts for Dainty People, Knox Gelatine, 1914, VG+ 50.00

Corkscrew, boy figure w/steel corkscrew appendage, brass, 4¾" 35.00

Cup, coffee; white w/boy & hat, Brownie Downing China, 1960s, 3x3" 35.00

Doll, chimp, cloth body w/vinyl head, open mouth, Hazelle, 1960s, MIP 45.00

Doll, cloth, pink calico dress, yarn hair, holds baby, 1950s, 12", EX 65.00

Doll, cloth w/wood arms & legs, all original, 1940-50s, 16" .. 215.00

Dolls, brown cloth with stitched features and black yarn hair, unknown maker, ca. 1935 – 1946, 17½" male and 19" female, G, from $175.00 to $225.00 for the pair. (Photo courtesy the M. Davern collection)

Doorstop, Mammy, cloth over weighted glass jar, 1940-50s, 16" 125.00

Drip jar, girl's head, red clay, pink bow on lid, pink lips, Japan 50.00

Figurine, baby girl, heavy pottery, hollow bottom, 1950s, 4½" 35.00

Figurine, golliwog, red vest w/tails, handcrafted, 1950-60s, 13", EX 40.00

Figurine, minstrel w/cane by palm tree, chenille, Japan, 1940-50s, 4" 18.00

Film, Our Gang in Mickey's Pals, 8mm, 1950s, EX (EX 5x5" box) 300.00

Game, Little Black Sambo, Cadaco-Ellis, 1940s, complete, EXIB 100.00

Magazine, Jet, Inside March on Washington cover, 1963, EX 14.00

Matchbook, M&M Cafeterias, front logo, Black waiters on back, unused 22.00

Mechanical toy, Boy Drummer, celluloid, 8" 125.00

Mechanical toy, Dancing Dan, plastic, battery operated, 13½" 100.00

Memo board, Mammy, painted wood, 1950s, 6x8½", EX .. 60.00

Mug, Sambo's Restaurant, pottery, USA, 1970s, 3¼" 24.00

Mug, woman's face w/red lips & side-glancing eyes, Japan, 1940s, 5" 85.00

Paper dolls, Oh Susanna, w/punch-outs/coloring book/record, 1950 .... 55.00

Picture, hand colored, #7218, Don't See Nuthin', Don't Hear..., VG 145.00

Pin-back button, Black Is Beautiful, black & white, 1960s, 1½". 20.00

Place mat, Aunt Jemima's Restaurant at Disneyland, 1955, 14x10", EX 45.00

Plaque, boy w/watermelon, painted chalkware, 1949, 5½x6¾", EX 40.00

Plaque, girl on knees in front of umbrella, painted chalkware, 5x5" 25.00

Plaques, young chef & girl w/hair bow, painted chalkware, 6", pr 60.00

Poster, Uncle Tom's Cabin scene, paper litho, 1970s, 21x28", EX 3,200.00

Potholder, Mammy, painted die-cut wood, wall hanging, 1950s, 4½" 30.00

Program, Louis Armstrong & All His Stars, mid-1960s, 22-pg, EX 48.00

Recipe box, red plastic w/molded Mammy face on front, 1950s, 4x5x3" 185.00

Shakers, Aunt Jemima & Uncle Mose, plastic, F&F, 3½", EX, pr 45.00

Shakers, Aunt Jemima & Uncle Mose, plastic, F&F, 5", EX, pr 75.00

Stereocard, After the Banquet, 3 children rest after a meal, EX 22.00

String holder, butler, string comes out of head, Japan, 1930s, 6¼" 325.00

Table card, die-cut, Aunt Jemima Restaurant, 1953, 4¾x3" 35.00

Tablecloth, caricatures on printed cotton, yellow border, 1950s, 51" 225.00

Teapot, Mammy, Gone w/the Wind Anniversary, MGM/Turner, 1990, 7½" 125.00

Token, Green River Whiskey, man & horse, 1¼" 35.00

Token, Sambo's Restaurant 10¢ Coffee, wooden, 1½", EX . 10.00

Towel, Mammy w/applied bandana & face color, embroidered, 28" L 38.00

Towel, Mammy w/cake & spoon embroidered on white, 1950s, 24x15", EX 35.00

Wall pocket, lady's head, metal coil necklace, Horton, 1950s . 35.00

Black Cats

This line of fancy felines was marketed mainly by the Shafford (importing) Company, although black cat lovers accept similarly modeled, shiny glazed kitties of other importing firms into their collections as well. Because eBay offers an over supply of mid-century collectibles, the value structure for these cats has widened, with prices for common items showing a marked decline. At the same time, items that are truely rare, such as the triangle spice set and the wireware cat face spice set have shot upwards. Values that follow are for examples in mint (or nearly mint) paint, an important consideration in determining a fair market price. Shafford items are often minus their white whiskers and eyebrows, and this type of loss should be reflected in your evaluation. An item in poor paint may be worth even less than half of given estimates. Note: Unless 'Shafford' is included in the descriptions, values are for cats that were imported by other companies.

Ashtray, flat face, Shafford, hard-to-find size, 3¾" 30.00

Ashtray, head shape, not Shafford, several variants, ea from $15 to 20.00

Bank, upright, Shafford features, marked Tommy, 2-part, minimum value.................... **100.00**

Cigarette lighter, sm cat stands on book by table lamp.......... **30.00**

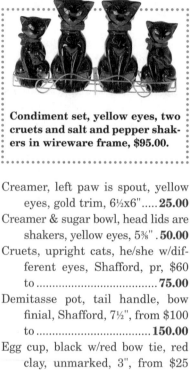

Condiment set, yellow eyes, two cruets and salt and pepper shakers in wireware frame, $95.00.

Creamer, left paw is spout, yellow eyes, gold trim, 6½x6"..... **25.00**

Creamer & sugar bowl, head lids are shakers, yellow eyes, 5⅜" . **50.00**

Cruets, upright cats, he/she w/different eyes, Shafford, pr, $60 to **75.00**

Demitasse pot, tail handle, bow finial, Shafford, 7½", from $100 to **150.00**

Egg cup, black w/red bow tie, red clay, unmarked, 3", from $25 to **35.00**

Mugs, 4", from $65.00 to $75.00; 3½", from $50.00 to $60.00.

Paperweight, head on stepped chrome base, open mouth, yellow eyes **75.00**

Pitcher, milk; seated upright cat, ear forms spout, Shafford, 6½"............................... **150.00**

Pitcher, squatting cat, pour through mouth, Shafford, rare, 5" **90.00**

Pot holder caddy, 'teapot' cat, 3 hooks, Shafford, minimum value **150.00**

Shaker, long & crouching (shaker ea end), Shafford, 10", from $30 to **50.00**

Spice set, 4 cat shakers on wireware cat-face, Shafford, from $450 to **600.00**

Stacking tea set, mama pot w/kitty creamer & sugar bowl, yellow eyes **85.00**

Teapot, cat face w/double spout, Shafford, scarce, 5", from $150 to **250.00**

Teapot, cat's face, yellow hat, blue & white eyes, pink ears.. **40.00**

Thermometer, cat w/yellow eyes stands w/paw on round thermometer face................... **25.00**

Toothpick holder, cat by vase atop book, Occupied Japan..... **12.00**

Tray, flat face, wicker handle, Shafford, scarce, from $75 to **100.00**

Utensil rack, flat-back cat, +3 utensils, Shafford, from $300 to................................ **500.00**

Blade Banks

In 1903 the safety razor was invented, making it easier for men to shave at home. But the old, used razor blades were troublesome, because for the next 22 years, nobody knew what to do with them. In 1925 the first patent was filed for a razor blade bank, a container designed to hold old blades until it became full, in which event it was to be thrown away. Most razor blade banks are 3" or 4" tall, similar to a coin bank with a slot in the top but no outlet in the bottom to remove the old blades. These banks were produced from 1925 to 1950. Some were issued by men's toiletry companies and were often filled with shaving soap or cream. Many were made of tin and printed with an advertising message. An assortment of blade banks made from a variety of materials — ceramic, wood, plastic, or metal — could also be purchased at five-and-dime stores.

For information on blade banks as well as many other types of interesting figural items from the same era, we recommend *Collectibles for the Kitchen, Bath & Beyond* (featuring napkin dolls, egg timers, string holders, children's whistle cups, baby feeder dishes, pie birds, and laundry sprinkler bottles) by Ellen Bercovici, Bobbie Zucker Bryson, and Deborah Gillham (available through Antique Trader Books).

Barber, wood w/Gay Blade on bottom, unscrews, Woodcraft, 1950s, 6".......................**75.00**
Barber chair, For Bald Headed men, Hair Today..., w/original tag....................................**65.00**
Barber chair, lg or sm, from $100 to...................................**125.00**

Barber pole, Old Razor Blades on finial, white ceramic w/red stripes.............................**72.50**
Barber pole w/face, red & white, from $30 to.......................**40.00**
Barber pole w/head & derby hat, white w/red & black, #558.**30.00**
Barbershop quartet, 4 singing barber heads, from $95 to..**125.00**
Bell, white w/man shaving, Cleminson, 3½"...............**25.00**
Friar Tuck Razor Blade Holder (on back), Goebel................**300.00**
Frog, green, For Used Blades, from $60 to..............................**70.00**
Grinding stone, For Dull Ones, from $80 to.....................**100.00**
Listerine, elephant, from $25 to.**35.00**
Listerine donkey, from $20 to.**30.00**
Looie, right- or left-handed version, from $85 to....................**110.00**
Man shaving, mushroom shape, Cleminson, from $25 to..**35.00**
Outhouse, white ceramic w/black roof..................................**30.00**
Razor Bum, from $85 to......**100.00**
Safe, green, marked Razor on front, from $40 to.....................**65.00**
Shaving brush, wide style w/decal, from $45 to.....................**65.00**

Blair Dinnerware

American dinnerware has been a popular field of collecting for several years, and the uniquely styled lines of Blair are very appealing, though not often seen except in the Midwest (and it's there that prices are the strongest). Blair was located in Ozark, Missouri, manufacturing dinnerware from the mid-1940s until the early 1950s. Gay Plaid, recognized by its squared-off shapes and brush-stroke design (in lime green, brown, and dark green on white), is the pattern you'll find most often. Several other lines were made as well. You'll be able to recognize all of them easily enough, since most pieces (except for the smaller items) are marked.

Beer mug, Primitive Bird, from $90 to **100.00**
Bowl, cereal; Spiced Pear, from $15 to **20.00**
Casserole, Gay Plaid, individual, w/ lid **30.00**
Cookie jar, Gay Plaid, round, wooden lid, from $100 to **125.00**
Creamer & sugar bowl, Gay Plaid, mini, from $40 to **50.00**
Cup & saucer, Brick, from $9 to. **12.00**
Cup & saucer, Gay Plaid, from $9 to **12.00**

Gravy boat, Gay Plaid, $35.00.

Pitcher, Spiced Pear, ice lip, from $125 to **150.00**

Plate, dessert; Brick, 6½".........**8.00**

Plate, dinner; Bamboo, from $9.00 to $12.00.

Plate, dinner; Primitive Bird, from $40 to **50.00**
Plate, dinner; Spiced Pear, from $20 to **25.00**
Platter, Gray Plaid, sq, 10", from $15 to **18.00**
Relish dish, Gay Plaid, oblong. **20.00**
Salt & pepper shakers, Gay Plaid, conical, tall, pr from $50 to.**60.00**
Salt & pepper shakers, Yellow & Gay Plaid, short, pr **12.00**
Sugar bowl, Yellow & Gay Plaid, w/ lid, from $18 to................ **22.00**
Tumbler; Spiced Pear, from $20 to.................................. **25.00**

Blue Garland

This lovely line of dinnerware was offered as premiums through grocery store chains during the decades of the '60s and '70s. It has delicate garlands of tiny blue flowers on a white background trimmed in platinum. Rims are scalloped and handles are gracefully curved. Though the 'Haviland' backstamp might suggest otherwise, this china has no connection with the famous Haviland company of Limoges. 'Johann Haviland' (as contained in the mark) was actually the founding company that later became Philip Rosenthal & Co., the German manufacturer who produced chinaware for export to the USA from the mid-1930s until as late as the 1980s.

This line may also be found with the Thailand Johann Haviland backstamp, a later issue. Our values are for the line with the Bavarian mark; expect to pay at least 30% less for the Thailand issue.

Bell, 5½x3¼" **40.00**
Bowl, coupe soup; 7⅞" **12.00**
Bowl, oval, 11¼", from $60 to . **75.00**
Butter dish, ¼-lb, from $35 to . **50.00**
Butter pat/coaster, 3½" **5.00**
Candleholder, 2½x6", ea **35.00**
Candlesticks, 1-light, 4", pr from $35 to **45.00**
Casserole, metal, stick handle, w/lid, 3-qt, 8¼", from $35 to **50.00**
Casserole, metal, tab handle, w/lid, 3-qt, from $20 to **28.00**
Casserole, metal, w/lid, 4-qt, 9¾", from $40 to **50.00**

: **Casserole/soup tureen, 11" wide, $50.00.**

Clock plate **25.00**
Coffeepot/beverage server, w/lid, 11" **45.00**
Cup & saucer, flat or footed **5.00**
Fondue pot, w/lid, from $50 to **65.00**

Goblet, glass, 6¾", set of 6 ..... **40.00**
Gravy boat, w/attached underplate, 10" L, from $20 to **30.00**
Gravy boat, w/separate underplate, 10" L, from $20 to **30.00**
Nut dish, footed, w/handles ... **30.00**
Plate, dinner; 10" **7.00**
Platter, serving; 14½" L **40.00**
Roaster, metal, 13" L, from $50 to **75.00**
Salt & pepper shakers, marked Thailand, pr **20.00**
Salt & pepper shakers, pr from $30 to **40.00**
Saucepan, metal, w/lid, 2 styles, 1½-qt, ea from $30 to **40.00**
Sugar bowl, w/lid, marked Thailand, 3¼" **14.00**
Sugar bowl, w/lid, 5½x7" **18.00**
Teapot, marked Thailand, 7", from $40 to **50.00**
Teapot, 7¾" **60.00**
Tray, tid-bit; 2-tier **35.00**
Tray, tid-bit; 3-tier **40.00**

Blue Ridge

Some of the most attractive American dinnerware made in the twentieth century is Blue Ridge, produced by Southern Potteries of Erwin, Tennessee, from the late 1930s until 1956. More than 400 patterns were hand painted on eight basic shapes. Elaborate or appealing lines are represented by the high end of our range; use the lower side to evaluate simple patterns. The Quimper-like peasant-decorated line is one of the most treasured and should be priced at double the amounts recommended for the higher-end patterns.

Ashtray, mallard box shape, from $55 to **65.00**

Ashtray, railroad advertising, from $55 to **65.00**

Bonbon, Charm House, china, from $175 to **225.00**

Bowl, flat soup; Premium, from $25 to **35.00**

Bowl, fruit; 5¼", from $7 to ... **10.00**

Bowl, vegetable; w/lid **60.00**

Box, powder; round, w/lid, from $100 to **150.00**

Box, Seaside, china, from $125 to **150.00**

Breakfast set, from $350 to . **400.00**

Casserole, w/lid, from $45 to . **50.00**

Chocolate tray, from $450 to . **500.00**

Mug, child's; from $150 to ... **175.00**

Pitcher, Antique, 3½", from $150 to **175.00**

Pitcher, Chick, china, from $100 to **125.00**

Pitcher, Spiral, earthenware, 7", from $45 to **55.00**

Plate, dinner; 10½", from $20 to. **25.00**

Plate, sq, 8", from $20 to **25.00**

Plate, 11½-12", from $50 to ... **65.00**

Relish, Loop Handle, china, from $65 to **75.00**

Salt & pepper shakers, Skyline, pr from $35 to **40.00**

Sugar bowl, Waffle, w/lid, from $15 to **20.00**

Teapot, Palisades, from $125 to.. **150.00**

Coffeepot, Grandmother's Garden, from $150.00 to $175.00. (Photo courtesy Betty and Bill Newbound)

Creamer, Charm House, from $70 to **85.00**

Creamer, Colonial, open, sm, from $15 to **20.00**

Cup & saucer, demitasse; Premium, from $100 to **150.00**

Cup & saucer, Premium, from $40 to **65.00**

Custard cup, from $18 to **22.00**

Dish, baking; divided, 8x13", from $25 to **30.00**

Jug, character; Daniel Boone, from $400 to **500.00**

Lamp, china, from $125 to .. **150.00**

Leftover, w/lid, sm, from $35 to.. **45.00**

Tray, gravy; Chintz, from $60.00 to $70.00. (Photo courtesy Betty and Bill Newbound)

Tumbler, juice; glass, from $12 to **15.00**

Vase, boot, 8", from $80 to **90.00**

Wall sconce, from $70 to **75.00**

Blue Willow

Inspired by the lovely blue and white Chinese exports, the Willow pattern has been made by many English, American, and Japanese firms from 1950 until the present. Many variations of the pattern have been noted — mauve, black, green, and multicolor Willow ware can be found in limited amounts. The design has been applied to tinware, linens, glassware, and paper goods, all of which are treasured by today's collectors. Refer to *Gaston's Blue Willow, 3rd Edition*, by Mary Frank Gaston (Collector Books) for more information. See also Royal China. See Clubs and Newsletters for information concerning *The Willow Review* newsletter.

Ashtray, oval, Exclusively for Your Ashes in center, 6", from $45 to **55.00**

Ashtray, Schweppes Table Waters, English, 4" dia, from $40 to. **50.00**

Biscuit jar, cane handle, octagonal, Gibson & Sons, 6½", $250 to **275.00**

Biscuit jar, Two Temples II pattern, w/cane handle, English, 4½" **175.00**

Bowl, console; glass, Traditional in green enamel, American, 11x3½" **250.00**

Bowl, oval w/pierced sides, scalloped rim, English, 10¼", $800 to **1,000.00**

Bowl, reversed Traditional center, Japan, 15", from $220 to. **240.00**

Bowl, rice; Two Temples II reversed w/Butterfly border, English **35.00**

Bowl, salad; sq, Ridgways, 9x4", from $80 to **90.00**

Bowl, vegetable; footed, w/handles, no mark, English, 12¼x9½".. **130.00**

Bowl, vegetable; porcelain, Traditional center, borderless, English **220.00**

Bowl, vegetable; round w/scalloped edge, English, 8", from $80 to.......................... **100.00**

Bowl, vegetable; variant center, pictorial border, no mark, 10"................................**20.00**

Butter dish, quarter-pound, Japan, from $75.00 to $100.00.
(Photo courtesy Mary Frank Gaston)

Butter dish, Two Temples II on base, silver lid w/cow finial, English **350.00**

Candleholder, ship's light, brass w/ ceramic backplate, no mark, ea.................................... **100.00**

Canisters, barrel shape, Japan, 4-pc set, from $450 to ... **550.00**

Carafe, w/warmer, Japan, from $250 to **300.00**

Coaster, Yorkshire Relish advertisement, no mark, English, 4", $35 to **45.00**

Coffeepot, Japan, 7", from $100 to **120.00**

Creamer, porcelain, pictorial rim, Traditional w/gold trim, Willow, 3" **50.00**

Creamer & sugar bowl, Canton pattern, English, 5", from $80 to **100.00**

Cup, mug; no mark, Japan, 3½", from $10 to **15.00**

Cup, punch; Two Temples II w/ Butterfly rim, no mark, English, 3" **55.00**

Gravy boat, Traditional w/border variation, English, 8¾", $75 to **85.00**

Gravy dish, spout on either side, Gravy & Lean on inside, 6", $80 to **90.00**

Ladle, Traditional center, no mark, 8", from $140 to **165.00**

Mustard pot, flared neck, handled, no mark, 2½", from $80 to **90.00**

Pitcher, Simplified Traditional on body w/pictorial border, 8", $60 to **80.00**

Pitcher, Two Temples II w/ Butterfly border, rope-style handle, 9¼" **150.00**

Plate, cake; Mandarin center w/ Dagger border, Shore & Coggins, 9½" **70.00**

Plate, Canton pattern, GL Ashworth, 9", from $30 to **35.00**

Plate, octagonal, Booths Variant center, Bow Knot rim w/gold trim, 9" **50.00**

Salt & pepper shakers, Japan, 3", pr from $30 to **40.00**

Teapot, musical, Japan, from $130.00 to $150.00. (Photo courtesy Mary Frank Gaston)

Trivet, ceramic in wrought-iron frame, Japan, from $40 to **50.00**

Vase, porcelain, unmarked, Japan, 5", $60 to **70.00**

Bone China Bouquets

Many china companies in England have produced these lovely miniature flower bouquets made of bone china. Each flower petal is individually sculpted by hand and painted in true-to-nature colors. Together they make a beautiful collection, and right now they're very affordable. Though the thin bone china flower petals are unbelievably break resistant, do be careful to check for damage and adjust their values accordingly. In our listings, those rated excellent will have minor chips; all others are priced as if in mint condition.

Adderley, roses, pansies & carnations, 3½x4", EX............. **32.00**

Adderley, swan filled w/7 sm assorted flowers, 2¼x3¼" **16.00**

Adderley, 2 pink roses & 5 flowers in white pot w/handles, 2½", EX **18.00**

Aynsley, red berries & white flowers in white pot, 2¼x3¼". **22.00**

Aynsley, salt & pepper shaker w/1 flower atop ea, 2" **20.00**

Coalport, log section w/assorted flowers, 1½x3¼" **28.00**

Coalport, miniature white pot w/1 blue flower & green leaves. **15.00**

Coalport, wheelbarrow w/assorted flowers, 3x5" **35.00**

Crown Royal, 3 assorted flowers in white base w/handles, 3x3". **18.00**

Crown Staffordshire, 3 tulips in white flowerpot, 3x2¾", EX, pr **20.00**

Denton, brooch & earrings, assorted white flowers, 1½", 1". **15.00**

Denton, brooch w/blue bouquet, 1¼"
dia 16.00
England (Coalport), violets in white
dish, 2½x3", EX 22.00
Lefton, magnolia bloom & bud
on wood slab, Royal Dover,
6x6" 18.00
Radnor, shoe filled w/3 lg flowers,
4" L 16.00
Royal Adderley, basket w/arched
handle, assorted flowers,
3½x4½" 24.00
Royal Adderley, napkin rings, assorted flowers, set of 10 .... 150.00
Royal Adderley, 3-color roses in
pale green bowl, 2x3" 16.00
Staffordshire, assorted flowers, green
swirl bowl, 6x6", EX 30.00

Bookends

Bookends have come into their
own as a separate category of collectibles. They are so diversified in
styling, it's easy to find some that
appeal to you, no matter what your
personal tastes and preferences.
Metal examples seem to be the
most popular, especially those with
the mark of their manufacturer,
and can still be had at reasonable
prices. Glass and ceramic bookends
by noted makers, however, may be
more costly — for example, those
made by Roseville or Cambridge,
which have a cross-over collector
appeal.

Louis Kuritzky and Charles
DeCosta has written an informative
book titled *Collector's Encyclopedia
of Bookends* (Collector Books); they
are listed in the Directory under
Florida. See Clubs and Newsletters

for information concerning the
Bookend Collectors Club.

Anchor, gray metal, attributed to
Dodge, ca 1947, 5¾" 45.00
Angelfish, clear glass, American
Glass Co, 1940s, 8¼" 135.00
Atlas, painted chalk on polished
stone base, JB Hirsch, 1940s,
7¾" 135.00
Capitol Building, gray metal,
Russell...Curtis...CA, ca 1940,
7½" 195.00

**Cherubs and garlands, gray
metal, K&O, 1925, 5", $150.00 for
the pair.** (Photo courtesy Louis Kuritzky)

Crane, gray metal, ca 1946, 6¾". 75.00
Dog at Fence, gray metal, PM
Craftsman, ca 1965, paper tag,
6½" 95.00
Flamingos, cast iron, unmarked
Everstyle, 1948, 5¼" 125.00
Galleon, gray metal, Made in Occupied
Japan, 1946, 6¾" 75.00

**German shepherd at gate, paint-
ed cast iron, EX, $175.00.** (Photo
courtesy Morphy Auctions)

Grazing Pony, painted gray metal, ca 1930, 5¼"................... **110.00**

Horse on Arc, gray metal, Dodge, ca 1947, 5½"........................ **60.00**

Lamp & Book, gray metal, Ronson, 1942, 5"........................... **100.00**

Linden Hall, painted gray metal, ca 1960, 3"............................ **25.00**

Lion on Base, dark amber glass, Imperial Glass Co, 1978, 6"................. **125.00**

Listening to the Wind, horse, bronze clad, Armor Bronze, 1930s, 6¼"...................... **125.00**

Maiden, gray metal, Frankart shop mark, ca 1930, 6"......... **225.00**

Mayo Tunnel, iron, Mine Equipment, Lancaster PA, 1940, 5" ... **75.00**

Oaken Door, wood w/metal ring, ca 1975 .... **15.00**

Pensive Hound, painted gray metal, Ronson, Company Tag #16031, ca 1930............................ **95.00**

Pirate Couple, painted gray metal, K&O, ca 1932, 10½"...... **175.00**

Sailfish, gray metal, PM Craftsman, ca 1965, 8" **65.00**

Sailfish, head up, gray metal, PM Craftsman, ca 1965, 8" ... **65.00**

Ski Queen, gray metal w/enameling, K&O, ca 1932......... **175.00**

Sphinx, bronze clad, Marion Bronze, ca 1956, 6" **150.00**

Up to My Neck (horse head), clear glass, ca 1940, 5"............. **75.00**

Whale, gray metal, PM Craftsman, ca 1965, 7½".................... **50.00**

Woman on Couch, gray metal & celluloid, marked JBH, ca 1930, 5"................................. **300.00**

Bottle Openers

Bottle openers by companies such as Wilton, John Wright, L&L, and Gadzik are fun to collect and come in a wide assortment of amusing figurals ranging from animals of all varieties to drunks and nude ladies. They are rated by rarity and condition — the amount of original paint remaining on the cast iron openers is a very important worth-assessing factor to consider. Watch for reproductions, there are many of them on the market. For more information read *Figural Bottle Openers, Identification and Value Guide*, by the Figural Bottle Openers Collectors. Many of our listings have number codes that refer to this book. Unless noted otherwise, our values are for examples in near-mint to mint condition.

Anchor chain, steel, F-228, 6⅞" L................................... **70.00**

Bear head, multicolor paint on cast iron, wall mount, F-426, VG **135.00**

Billy goat, white paint on cast iron, John Wright, 1940s, F-74, 2¾"...................... **115.00**

Cat, brass, F-95, 2¼x3".......... **40.00**

Cocker spaniel, multicolor paint on cast iron, F-80, 2¾x3¾"... **90.00**

Dragon, green paint on cast iron, F-145, 5", EX................ **225.00**

Elephant, painted cast iron, F-49, 3", VG **40.00**

Geisha, black paint on cast iron, F-186............................. **180.00**

Lady by lamppost w/rolling pin, painted cast iron, F-7, 4". **40.00**

Nude, brass, Russwood c 1946, F-171, 4½"...................... **35.00**

Nude atop globe, chrome, F-179, 4½" **75.00**

Parrot, painted cast iron, plain stand, Wright, F-108, 5½" **45.00**

Pelican, multicolor paint on cast iron, 1930s-40s, F-129 .... **75.00**

Rooster, painted cast iron, Wilton, 1947, F-97, 3⅛x2⅝" **60.00**

Sailor, multicolor on aluminum, F-18, VG **235.00**

Stumbling drunk, painted cast iron, wall mount, 6", from $55.00 to $65.00.

Washer woman standing by lamppost, metal w/copper patina, 1950s, 4" **120.00**

Woman's shoe, aluminum, 1982 club pc, F-209 .... **180.00**

Bottles

Bottles have been used as containers for commercial products since the late 1800s. Specimens from as early as 1845 may still be occasionally found today (watch for a rough pontil to indicate this early production date). Some of the most collectible are bitters bottles, used for 'medicine' that was mostly alcohol, a ploy to avoid paying the stiff tax levied on liquor sales. Spirit flasks from the 1800s were blown in the mold and were often designed to convey a historic, political, or symbolic message. Refer to *Bottle Pricing Guide, Third Edition,* by Hugh Cleveland (Collector Books) for more information.

Dairy Bottles

The storage and distribution of fluid milk in glass bottles became commonplace around the turn of the century. They were replaced by paper and plastic containers in the mid-1950s. Perhaps 5% of all US dairies are still using some glass, and glass bottles are still widely used in Mexico and some Canadian provinces.

Milk-packaging and distribution plants hauled trailer loads of glass bottles to dumping grounds during the conversion to the throw-away cartons now in general use. Because of this practice, milk bottles and jars are scarce today. Most collectors search for bottles from hometown dairies; some have completed a 50-state collection in the three popular sizes.

Bottles from 1900 to 1920 had the name of the dairy, town, and state embossed in the glass. Nearly all of the bottles produced after this period had the copy painted and then pyro-glazed onto the surface of the bottle. This enabled the dairyman to use colors and pictures of his dairy farm or cows on the bottles. Collectors have been fortunate that there have been no serious attempts at this point to reproduce a particularly rare bottle!

Ayrshire Dairy, M. H. Williams, Jr., 5¢ store banner, standing cow, maroon pyro, one-quart, $40.00. (Photo courtesy milkman)

B&A Parkdale Dairy, Washington NJ, embossed letters, sq, 1-pt **195.00**

Barton's Dairy Farm, Davison MI, embossed letters, round, 1-pt................................**30.00**

Benn's Dairy, Medford WI, blue pyro, round & tall, 1-qt...**60.00**

Boulton Dairy, Salt Lake City UT, embossed letters, sq, 1-qt..............................**50.00**

Crenshaw Dairy, Charleston MO, blue pyro, 1914, round & tall, 1-qt..................................**135.00**

Dekalb Dairy Company, Dekalb, IL, red & yellow pyro, 1-gal.**365.00**

Dietrich's Dairy, Danville PA, red pyro, cream top, sq & tall, 1-qt....................................**40.00**

Fisher Dairy, Salt Lake City UT, embossed letters, sq, 1-qt.**55.00**

Golden Heart Creamery, Fairbanks AK, red pyro, pinched, ½-gal..............**55.00**

Griffith Dairy, Kalamazoo MI, orange & black pyro, round & tall, 1-qt.........................**170.00**

Lincoln Hill Dairy, Washington PA, embossed letters, round, 1-qt **35.00**

Luick Dairy, Nature's Best Bood, red pyro, round, 1-qt.......**35.00**

Maple Lawn Dairy, Keokuk IA, orange pyro, round & tall, 1-qt..................................**38.00**

Mountain Dairy Farms, Rye CO, green pyro, round, ½-pt..**35.00**

Murphy's Dairy, Chestnut Hill CT, orange pyro, cream top, ½-pt **90.00**

Paxtang Farms w/owl, Harrisburg PA, red pyro, round & tall, 1-qt...................................**70.00**

Red Canon Dairy, Canon City CO, blue pyro, round, ½-pt **34.00**

Redford Farm, D. Cardillo, Stockbridge, Mass., same front and back, orange pyro, $25.00. (Photo courtesy milkman)

Rehoboth Dairy, Rehoboth Beach, DE, red pyro, cream top, 1-pt............................**175.00**

Sanitary Dairy, Bucyrus OH, red pyro, round & tall, 1-qt...**60.00**

Shamrock Dairy & leprechaun, Tucson AZ, green pyro, cream top, ½-pt..........................**52.50**

Vonderhaar's Dairy, Fort Madison IA, green pyro, sq, w/cap, 1-qt **110.00**

Wapello Dairies, Ottumwa IA, red pyro, cream top, ½-pt......**52.50**

Perfume and Scent Bottles

In the following listings, all bottles are made of glass unless otherwise noted.

Bimini, jockey on horse painted on clear, blown, 1930s, 4½"..**75.00**

Bourjois, Mai Oui, clear fan shape w/blue Bakelite cap w/tassle, 2" 50.00

De Vilbiss, gold mercury w/push-down gold-tone top, #400-25, 3½" 65.00

Fenton, Feathered Swirl, satin & white, scalloped, satin top, 5½" 160.00

Fenton, Hobnail, cranberry opal, footed, w/stopper, 5" 90.00

Germany, lady w/plumed hat, painted porcelain, glass dauber, 4½" 70.00

Guerlain, Chamade, clear teardrop w/stopper, 1969, 1-oz (sealed), MIB 135.00

Hattie Carnegie, clear bust of lady, lt wear to gold, 4" 65.00

Irice, green opaque panels w/gold, glass flower stopper, w/spray pump 155.00

Lalique for Worth, Dans La Nuite, cobalt, globular, 6½" 135.00

Lucien LeLong, Jabot, clear & frosted draped bow, ca 1940s, 2⅝x4x3" 90.00

Murano, enamel swirls on brown w/mica, cap attached by chain, 1½" 130.00

Murano Lavorazione, cased triangle w/multicolor swirls, w/top, 7¼" 60.00

Napco, lady w/pearls, painted porcelain, #C3201C, 1958, 4½" . 60.00

Perthshire, concentric millefiori paperweight base, w/stopper, 1979 .... 140.00

Pressed glass, vaseline w/embossed diamonds, lid w/chain, 2½" . 110.00

Prince Matchabelli, Beloved, blue & gold crown, cross stopper, 2" 95.00

Prince Matchabelli, Wind Song, green & gold crown, 2" ... 58.00

Schneider, lady w/flowers figure, porcelain, crown top, #4468, 3" 75.00

Schneider, man figure, porcelain, sprinkler crown top, #446, 3" 75.00

Venetian, latticinio ribbon w/gold mica, wand stopper, 2½x1¾" 75.00

Waterford, Ballet, clear lay down, MIB 90.00

Waterford, Lismore, cut crystal, w/ stopper, 4¾x2⅝" 82.50

Wedgwood, classical women, white on blue, pump top, 1940s, 4" ... 75.00

Soda Bottles With Applied Color Labels

This is a specialized area of advertising collectibles that holds the interest of bottle collectors as well as those who search for soda pop items; both fields attract a good number of followers, so the market for these bottles is fairly strong right now. See also Coca-Cola; Soda Pop.

Black Kow, dark amber with three-color label, $8.00. (Photo courtesy B.J. Summers)

Dad's Root Beer, brown w/yellow & red label, 1948, 32-oz **22.00**

Dr Nut Soda, clear w/red & white label w/squirrel, 7-oz **16.00**

Gold Medal Beverages, clear w/ red & white label, dated 1951, 8½"...................................**15.00**

Hill Billy Brew, green w/red & white label, 10-oz............ **35.00**

Kist Soda, clear w/red & white label, Kauai Beverage..., 7-oz........................... **220.00**

La Vida Beverages, clear w/red & white label, embossed swirls, 10-oz............................... **40.00**

Red Rock Cola, clear w/red & white label, 1945, 1-qt.............. **85.00**

Sky High Beverages, clear w/airplane on red & white label, 12-oz................................**20.00**

Smile, clear w/smiling citrus figure on blue & white label, 8-oz......**50.00**

Tops, clear w/cityscape blue & white label, Dr Pepper Bottling Co **30.00**

Uppity Up, green w/red & white label, 12-oz **195.00**

Vegas Vic Beverages, clear w/blue & white label, 10-oz........ **42.00**

White Rose, clear w/green & white label, Coca-Cola, 6½-oz... **17.50**

Wolf Soda, clear w/wolf red & white label, 1956, 12-oz **20.00**

Wyoming Beverages, clear w/red & white cowboy-theme label, 10-oz............................... **70.00**

7-Up, Kauai Soda Co., Lihue, Hawaii, $25.00.

Boyd's Crystal Art Glass

Since it was established in 1978, this small glasshouse located in Cambridge, Ohio, has bought molds from other companies as they went out of business, and they have designed many of their own as well. They may produce several limited runs of a particular shape in a number of the lovely colors of glass they themselves formulate, none of which are ever reissued. Of course, all of the glass is handmade, and each piece is marked with their 'B-in-diamond' logo. See Clubs and Newsletters for information concerning a Boyd's Crystal Art Glass newsletter.

Bow Slipper, Crystal Carnival, 1996 .... **12.00**

Chick Salt, Peridot, 1984....... **25.00**

Debbie Duck, Mauve, 1989.... **10.00**

Freddie the Hobo Clown, Orange Spice, 1990 .... **10.00**

Heart Jewel Box, Alpine Blue, 1998 .... 14.00
Heart Toothpick Holder, Aqua, 1978 .... 10.00
Hen on Nest Covered Dish, Misty Vale, #78, 1986 .... 25.00
Jeremy the Frog, Vaseline, #1, 1992 .... 15.00
Kitten on Pillow, Snow, #41, 1982 .... 15.00
Lamb Salt, Windsor Blue, #1, 1989 .... 15.00
Little Luck the Unicorn, Cambridge Blue, #7, 1999 .... 12.00
Mable the Cow, Alpine Blue, #2, 1998 .... 15.00
Miss Cotton the Kitten, Smoke, 1979 .... 12.00
Owl, Black Walnut, 1979 ...... 20.00
Owl, Ice Green, 1979 .... 20.00
Owl Bell, Mountain Haze, #13, 1983 .... 8.00
Rex Dinosaur, Crystal Carnival, 1996 .... 18.00
Robin Covered Dish, Buckeye Satin, 1991 .... 22.00
Skate Shoe, Harvest Gold, 1999 .... 10.00
Skippy the Dog, Golden Delight, #3, 1982 .... 15.00
Sly the Fox, Alpine Blue, decorated, 1999 .... 15.00
Sports Car, Nightwatch Black, #15, 2001 .... 15.00
Swan, Aqua Diamond, 1993, 3" .15.00
Taffy the Carousel Horse, Lemon Custard, #10, 1997 .... 20.00
Teddy Tugboat, Cornsilk, 1983 ..12.00
Texas Creamer & Sugar Bowl, Heather, #1, 1980, pr 20.00
Tractor, Spinnaker Blue, #1, 1990 .... 20.00
Turkey Salt, Jade, 2000 .... 10.00

West Highland Terrier, light lavender blue opaque, diamond mark with R, 2½", $32.00.

Wildflower Candy Dish, Deep Purple, #2, 1979 .... 25.00
Wildflower Candy Dish, Willow Blue, #12, 1980 .... 20.00
Willie the Mouse, Peach, #11, 1991 .... 10.00
Woodsie Owl, Heliotrope, #18, 1986 .... 10.00
Zack the Elephant, Delphinium, 1981 .... 20.00

Breweriana

Beer can collectors and antique advertising buffs alike enjoy looking for beer-related memorabilia such as tap knobs, beer trays, coasters, signs, and such. While the smaller items of a more recent vintage are quite affordable, signs and trays from defunct breweries often bring three-digit prices. Condition is important in evaluating early advertising items of any type. Our values respresent the worth of items in near-mint to mint condition, unless otherwise noted.

Ashtray, Beck's Beer on white ceramic, Germany, 4¼" sq, EX 35.00

Ashtray, Bud Light, Spuds MacMenzie in beach chair, painted milk glass **35.00**

Ashtray, Carlsberg Biere, raised C & crown, tan pottery, Eslan Denmark.......................... **23.00**

Ashtray, Dutch Club Beer, Dutch man w/tray of beer, glass, 4½" dia **60.00**

Ashtray, Schweppes, cobalt blue glass w/white enamel, 1950s, 2x9x6".............................. **125.00**

Ashtray, Stag's Head Lager, red w/white letters, ceramic, Bradings **23.00**

Beer can, Ballantine Export, olive drab, Newark NJ, WWII era, flat top **137.50**

Beer can, Du Bois Light, Du Bois Brewing, Buffalo NY, cone top, EX **185.00**

Beer can, Excell Lager Beer, Maier Brewery, flat top............. **225.00**

Beer can, Haas, Haas Brewing Company, Houghton, Michigan, cone top, VG+, from $125.00 to $145.00. (Photo courtesy Thomas Hopper)

Beer can, Koenig Brau Premium, Prima-Bismark, Chicago, cone top, qt............................. **170.00**

Beer can, Stoney's, Jones Brewing, Smithton PA, cone top **125.00**

Beer tray, Ballantine ale & beer, blue, Ballantine & Sons, 1950s, 12".................................. **24.00**

Beer tray, Blatz Beer, logo on gold paint, Blatz Brewing Co..., 1952 .... **25.00**

Beer tray, Budwieser, all-over labels on white plastic, 13" dia **12.00**

Beer tray, Knickerbocker Beer, red letters on white, Canco, 1950s, 12"................................... **28.00**

Beer tray, Light Lager Piels Beer, white w/red rim, 1963, 12" dia **18.00**

Beer tray, Schiltz Light, sun image, blue letters, 1976, 13"..... **23.00**

Beer tray, Schlitz, white letters on red w/cream background, 1960s............................... **30.00**

Clock, Budweiser, metal w/ glass front, light-up, DuBois Brewing, 15".................. **225.00**

Clock, Busch Beer, Western scene, light-up, 15x15".............. **55.00**

Clock, Miller High Life, plastic front, battery-operated, ca 1988, 12".......................... **48.00**

Clock, Piels Beer, w/Bert & Harry, blue, white, & gold, 1959, 14x11" **95.00**

Coaster, Premium Kato Beer, Mankato Brewing Co Minnesota, 3½".............. **20.00**

Coaster, Sunshine Beer, w/English setter, Buy US War..., 1940s, 3⅜" **25.00**

Corkscrew, Anheuser-Busch & A w/ eagle logo on side of wooden handle............................. **55.00**

Lighter, Coor's Beer, enamel logo on silver, Hi Lite Korea, ca 1950s............................... **17.00**

Mirror, Budweiser, Clydesdale horse & wagon, plastic frame, 14x27"............................. **75.00**

Mirror, Miller High Life, Wisconsin Bass, Sportsmen Series, 1990s, 20".....................85.00

Mirror, Old Milwaukee, winter wolf scene, 5th in series, wood frame.....................90.00

Opener, Frank Fehr's Brewing Co, bottle shape, wood, 4¼"..28.00

Opener, JAX Beer, metal, 4½x¾".10.00

Opener, Schlitz, bottle shape, wood, 1930s, 3⅝".....................32.00

Opener, Schlitz in cursive, enclosed in rectangle, brass, 5¼x2½"....35.00

Opener, Yoerg's Beer, Cave Aged, Vaughan Chicago, 3½x1½".55.00

Pitcher, Budweiser, nickel silver, The Budweiser, Wallace Bros, 9¼".....................85.00

Pitcher, Budweiser King of Beers, clear hard plastic w/ red logo.....................10.00

Pitcher, Falstaff Beer, red pyro on clear glass, 8¼".....................20.00

Plaque, Rolling Rock Beer, plaster, Latrobe Brewing Co, 1960s, 11x10".....................160.00

Playing cards, Lone Star Beer, letters on red shield w/star, 1960s.....................18.50

Playing cards, Schlitz Malt Liquor, pinochle deck, 1970, Jos Schlitz.....................20.00

Shaker, cocktail; Gay Nineties enamel, vivid colors, Hazel Atlas, 1950.....................30.00

Sign, Augustine Beer, painted tin, 20x14".....................65.00

Sign, Berghoff Beer, tin over cardboard, dogs in field scene, 21x13".....................95.00

Sign, Budweiser, embossed cardboard, Anheuser-Busch, 16x11".....................95.00

Sign, Consumer's Beer, tin, Ask Father, man w/glass, 1940s, 28x10".....................275.00

Sign, Gettelman Beer, standup metal, duck scene, 1950s, 16x10".....................65.00

Sign, Michelob Draught, plastic & wood, oval, Anheuser-Busch, 23x15".....................55.00

Sign, Miller High Life on Tap, neon, GHN Neon, 1984.........115.00

Sign, Pabst, neon, red letters on blue ribbon shape, 1960s-70s.....................120.00

Sign, Rhiengold Beer, light-up counter type, 1940s, 10x12"..250.00

Sign, Schlitz, plastic, lights up, red/black/white, 1983, 13x20".28.00

Statue, bust of girl, What'll you have?..., chalkware, 10x12".....................125.00

Statue, Early Times Whiskey, plaster, man in car, 1950s, 14x12".....................95.00

Statue, Labatt's Pilsener Beer, man by barrel, vinyl, 1960s, 10".....................100.00

Statue, Miller High Life Beer, Miller girl w/glass, plastic.........65.00

Statue, Pabst Blue Ribbon at Popular Prices, boxer w/bottle, 15x12x7".....................70.00

Tap handle, Blatz, metal, white w/red letters, 3x2", 1½" handle.........................**30.00**

Tap handle, Michelob Light, bottle shape, wood w/plastic coat, 8".................................. **18.00**

Tap handle, Michelob Light, Lucite, gold Anheuser-Busch symbol on end.............................**15.00**

Tap handle, Murphy's Irish Stout...........................**55.00**

Tap handle, Shiner Bock Beer Brewed w/an Attitude, ram's head finial.......................**55.00**

Tap knob, Coors, cowboy boot w/ spur.................................**70.00**

Tap knob, Utica Club XXX Pale Cream Ale, red, white & black enamel.............................**60.00**

Thermometer, Stegmaier Gold Medal, ...Wilkes-Barre PA, ca 1953, 9" dia......................**30.00**

Tip tray, Miller High Life, duck scene w/red border, 6½x4"..........**18.00**

Tip tray, Pinup Girls, 6 girls, maroon, blue & gold, 1950s, 10"....................................**52.00**

Tip tray, Schaefer, white w/gold & red logo, raised edge.......**37.00**

Umbrella, Budweiser, fabric w/ label logo, wooden shaft & handle **12.50**

Breyer Horses

Breyer collecting has grown in popularity over the past several years. Though horses dominate the market, cattle and other farm animals, dogs, cats, and wildlife have also been produced, all with exacting details and lifelike coloration. They've been made since the early 1950s in both glossy and matt finishes. (Earlier models were glossy, but from 1968 until the 1990s when both glossy and semigloss colors were revived for special runs, matt colors were preferred.) Breyer also manufactures dolls, tack, and accessories such as barns for their animals.

In the following listings, all are of the Classic scale unless noted Traditional. For more information we recommend *Schroeder's Collectible Toys, Antique to Modern*, and *Breyer Animal Collector's Guide* by Felicia Browell, Kelly Korber-Wermer, and Kelly Kesicki (Collector Books).

Andalusian Mare (#3060MA), bay w/black points, stripe, 3 socks, 2003 ....**12.00**

Andalusian Stallion, Classic, chestnut pinto, $15.00. (Photo courtesy Felicia Browell)

Andalusian Stallion (#3060ST), white w/gray-shaded points, 1979-93 ....**11.00**

Arabian Foal (#3055FO), white w/gray mane, tail & hooves, 1973-82 ....**12.00**

Black Stallion (#3030), Arabian, seal bay w/black points, star, 2002 ....**12.00**

Brown Sunshine (#484), sorrel w/ white mane, Traditional, 1996-97 .... **23.00**

Bucking Bronco (#190), gray w/ darker mane & tail, bald face, 1961-67 .... **43.00**

Bucking Bronco (#190), palomino w/white mane & tail, dappling, 1995-96 .... **16.00**

Buckshot (#415), Spanish Barb, chestnut pinto, Traditional, 1988-89 .... **26.00**

Cutting Horse, chestnut w/darker mane & tail, hind socks, 2004 .... **31.00**

Family Arabian Mare, #5, Traditional, 1967 – 1987, $15.00; Fighting Stallion, alabaster, #180, Traditional, 1978 – 1986, $29.00.

Fighting Mesteno (#4811), bay roan w/black points, shading, 2001 .... **13.00**

Ginger (#3040), chestnut w/darker mane, tail & hooves, 1980-93 .... **12.00**

Halla (#63), dapple gray w/black points, Traditional, 1990-91 .... **29.00**

Hobo (#625), buckskin w/black mane & tail, shading, 1975-80 .... **32.00**

Johar (#3030), white w/gray mane, tail & hooves, 1983-93 .... **12.00**

Keen (#3035), gray w/lighter lower legs, Sears Wish Book, 1987 .... **16.00**

Kelso (#601), red chesnut w/blaze, left front sock, QVC, 2002. **20.00**

Lipizzan Stallion (#620), white w/ pink hooves, wings on back, 1984-87 .... **29.00**

Man O' War (#602), red chestnut w/ darker mane & tail, star, 1975-90 .... **17.00**

Merry Legs (#3040), dapple gray w/white mane & tail, 1980-83 .... **12.00**

Mesteno (#480), chestnut pinto w/ white face, Wal-Mart, 2001. **13.00**

Might Tango (3035), bay w/black points, Sears Wish Book, 1987 .... **15.00**

Mustang Mare (#3065), chestnut pinto, gray hooves, Sears Book, 1976-90 .... **12.00**

Mustang Stallion (#3065), buckskin w/black points, Sears Book, 1985 .... **15.00**

Old Timer (#200), alabaster w/gray mane, yellow hat, Traditional, 1966 .... **33.00**

Polo Pony (#626), bay w/black points, early ones w/socks, 1976-82 .... **29.00**

Quarter Horse Foal (#3045), palomino w/white mane & tail, 1975-82 .... **11.00**

Rearing Stallion (#180), bay w/ black mane & tail, bald face, 1965-80 .... **17.00**

Ruffian (#606), dark bay w/black points, star, left hind sock, 1977-90 .... **16.00**

Sagr (#3030), bay Arabian w/ black points, left front sock, 1998 .... **12.00**

Silky Sullivan (#603), black roan w/black points, speckles, 1991-92 .... **13.00**

Swaps (#604), chestnut w/darker mane & tail, star, hind sock, 1975-90 .... **17.00**

Terrang (#605), brown w/darker mane & tail, light hind leg, 1975-90 .... **17.00**

Wahoo King (#466), bay w/black points, hind socks, 2000 . **16.00**

Bubble Bath Containers

Figural bubble bath containers were popular in the 1960s and have become highly collectible today. The Colgate-Palmolive Company produced the widest variety called Soakies. Purex's Bubble Club characters were also popular. Most Soaky bottles came with detachable heads made of brittle plastic which cracked easily. Purex bottles were made of a softer plastic but lost their paint easier. Condition affects price considerably.

The interest collectors displayed in the old bottles prompted many to notice foreign-made products. Some of the same characters have been licensed by companies in Canada, Italy, the UK, Germany, and Japan, and the bottles they've designed have excellent detail. They're usually a little larger than domestic bottles and though fairly recent are often reminiscent of those made in the US during the 1960s. For more information, we recommend *Schroeder's Collectible Toys, Antique to Modern*, published by Collector Books.

Alvin, Colgate-Palmolive, 1960s, 8½", NM, $20.00. (Photo courtesy whatacharacter.com)

Astroniks Robot, buck-toothed, gold w/red base, DuCair Bioescence, EX+ **15.00**

Baloo Bear, Colgate-Palmolive, 1966, NM **20.00**

Bambi sitting & smiling, Colgate-Palmolive, NM **25.00**

Bamm-Bamm, Purex, black or green suspenders, NM, ea **35.00**

Barney Rubble, blue outfit w/yellow accents, Milvern (Purex), NM **35.00**

Batmobile, Avon, 1978, blue & silver w/decals, EX.............. **20.00**

Beatles, any character, Colgate-Palmolive, EX, ea from $100 to **150.00**

Beauty & the Beast, original tag, Cosrich, M, ea from $5 to . **8.00**

Big Bad Wolf, Tubby Time, cap head, EX **35.00**

Bozo the Clown, Colgate-Palmolive, 1960s, NM **30.00**

Brutus (Popeye), Colgate-Palmolive, red shorts & striped shirt, 1965 .... **40.00**

Bugs Bunny, Colgate-Palmolive, light blue & white, NM .. **25.00**

Bullwinkle, several color variations, Colgate-Palmolive, NM, ea **45.00**

Butterfly Princess Barbie, original
tag, Kid Care, M **5.00**
Cement Truck, Colgate-Palmolive,
blue & gray w/movable wheels,
EX+ **35.00**
Charlie Brown, Avon, red baseball
outfit, NM **20.00**
Dick Tracy, Colgate-Palmolive,
1965, NM **50.00**
Dopey, Colgate-Palmolive, purple,
yellow & red, 1960s, NM . **20.00**
Ernie (Sesame Street) holding duck-
ie, original tag, Minnetonka,
M **8.00**
Felix the Cat, Colgate-Palmolive, blue,
red or black, 1960s, EX **30.00**
Garfield lying in tub, Kid Care,
NM **10.00**
GI Joe (Drill Instructor), DuCair
Bioescence, 1980s, NM ... **15.00**
Harriet Hippo in party hat, Merle
Norman, NM **10.00**
Holly Hobbie, several variations,
Benjamin Anshel, 1980s, M, ea
$15 to **20.00**
Incredible Hulk standing on rock,
Benjamin Ansehl, M **25.00**
Jiminy Cricket, green, black &
red, Colgate-Palmolive, 1960s,
EX+ **30.00**
Lucy (Peanuts), red dress w/top
hat, Avon, 1970, MIB **20.00**
Mickey Mouse as band leader,
Colgate-Palmolive, 1960s,
NM **25.00**
Morocco Mole, Purex, 1966, EX,
from $75 to **100.00**
Mr Magoo, red or blue outfit,
Colgate-Palmolive, 1960s,
EX **25.00**
Pebbles Flintstone, several color
variations, Purex, 1960s, EX,
ea **35.00**

Pinocchio, 9¾",
NM, $25.00.

Porky Pig, red tuxedo, Colgate-
Palmolive, 1960s, EX+ **25.00**
Quick Draw McGraw, Purex, 1960s,
NM **30.00**
Red Power Ranger, Centura
(Canada), 1994 .... **20.00**
Robin, Colgate-Palmolive, 1966,
EX, from $75 to **100.00**
Simon (Chipmunks), w/tag & pup-
pet, Colgate-Palmolive, 1960s,
M **50.00**
Skeletor (Masters of the Universe),
DuCair Bioescence, NM .. **15.00**
Snaggle Puss, pink w/green hat,
Purex, 1960s, NM **50.00**
Snoopy in tub of bubbles, Avon,
1971, MIB **20.00**
Speedy Gonzales, Colgate-
Palmolive, 1960s, EX **25.00**
Spouty Whale, blue, original card,
Roclar (Purex), M **20.00**
Sylvester the Cat & Tweety
Bird, DuCair Bioescence,
1988, M **30.00**
Sylvester the Cat w/microphone,
Colgate-Palmolive, 1960s,
EX **30.00**
Three Little Pigs, any character,
Tubby Time, 1960s, M, ea. **40.00**
Tweety on Cage, Colgate-Palmolive,
NM **25.00**

Wally Gator, Purex, 1963, NM, from
$45 to **60.00**
Winkie Blink Clock, yellow w/
blue hands & hat, Avon, 1975,
MIB **15.00**
Winnie the Pooh, Johnson &
Johnson, 1997, NM **6.00**
Wolfman, red pants, Colgate-
Palmolive, 1963, NM, from
$100 to **125.00**
Woody Woodpecker, Colgate-
Palmolive, 1977, NM **45.00**
Yaaky Doodle Duck, w/contents
& neck card, Roclar (Purex),
M **20.00**
Yoda, Omni, 1981, NM **20.00**
101 Dalmatians, red & black dog-
house w/2 pups, Kid Care,
M **5.00**

Cake Toppers

The first cake toppers appeared
on wedding cakes in the 1880s and
were made almost entirely of sugar.
The early 1900s saw toppers carved
from wood and affixed to ornate
plaster pedestal bases and backgrounds. A few single-mold toppers were even made from poured
lead. From the 1920s to the 1950s
bisque, porcelain, and chalkware
figures reigned supreme. The faces
and features on many of these
were very realistic and lifelike. The
beautiful Art Deco era was also in
evidence.

Celluloid Kewpie types made
a brief appearance from the late
1930s to the 1940s. These were
quite fragile because the celluloid they were made of could be
easily dented and cracked. The

true Rose O'Neill Kewpie look-
alike also appeared for awhile
during this period. During and
after World War II and into the
Korean Conflict of the 1950s,
groom figures in military dress
appeared. Only a limited amount
was ever produced; they are quite
rare. From the 1950s into the
1970s, plastics were used almost
exclusively. Toppers took on a
vacant, assembly-line appearance
with no specific attention to detail
or fashion.

In the 1970s, bisque returned
and plastic disappeared. Toppers
were again more lifelike. For the
most part, they remain that way
today. Wedding cakes now often
display elegant and elaborate toppers such as those made by Royal
Doulton and Lladro.

Toppers should not be confused
with the bride and groom doll sets
of the same earlier periods. While
some smaller dolls could and did
serve as toppers, they were usually
too unbalanced to stay upright on a
cake. The true topper consisted of
a small bride and groom anchored
to (or a part of) a round flat base
which made it extremely stable
for resting on a soft, frosted cake
surface. Cake toppers never did
double-duty as play items.

1915 Kewpie couple, bisque figures
on molded plaster base . **135.00**
1920s couple, bisque, no base or
pedestal, marked Germany w/
number, 6" **85.00**
1920s couple, gumpaste, bride
wears wide collar **120.00**

1930s couple, bisque, chalkware base & pedestal conceal music box, 11" **175.00**

1930s couple, crepe-paper & pipe cleaner, 5" **45.00**

1930s Kewpie-type couple, celluloid w/crepe-paper clothes, 3" figures **50.00**

1940s couple, all plastic, three large bells provide backdrop, cloth flowers and green velvet leaves with metallic silver paper in each bell, $40.00. (Photo courtesy Jeannie Greenfield)

1940s couple, chalkware on base, silver metal bell hanging from bower **45.00**

1940s couple, saltware, molded in 1-pc, 3½" **45.00**

1940s military couple, chalkware, stand arm-in-arm, no base, 3¾" **60.00**

1950s couple, chalkware, single mold, no base or pedestal, 4½" **25.00**

1970s military couple, bisque, no base or pedestal, 3½" **50.00**

California Potteries

In recent years, pottery designed by many of the artists who worked in their own small studios in California during the 1940s through the 1960s has become highly sought after. Values continue to be impressive, though slightly compromised by the influence of the internet. Among the more popular studios are Kay Finch, Florence Ceramics, Brayton, Howard Pierce, and Sascha Brastoff; but Matthew Adams, Marc Bellair, and deLee are attracting their share of attention as well, and there are others.

It's a fascinating field, one covered very well in Jack Chipman's *Collector's Encyclopedia of California Pottery,* and *California Pottery Scrapbook,* both published by Collector Books. Mike Nickel and Cynthia Horvath have written *Kay Finch Ceramics, Her Enchanted World* (Schiffer), a must for collectors interested in Kay Finch ceramics; and to learn more about Florence ceramics, you'll want to read *The Complete Book of Florence Ceramics: A Labor of Love,* written by Margaret Wehrspaun and Sue and Jerry Kline. They are listed in the Directory under Tennessee. See also Bauer; Cookie Jars; Franciscan; Metlox.

Adams, Matthew

Ashtray, walrus, star shape, 10x12" **95.00**

Box, glacier on blue, 12" **95.00**

Cookie jar, cabin, elliptical shape, #23, 7x5" **100.00**

Mug, husky dog, #112A, 4½x4¾"..**40.00**

Plate, Eskimo girl, #162, 7½". **40.00**

Salt & pepper shakers, rams on green, 4", pr..................... **40.00**

Tray, polar bear & iceberg, #910, 13x10"............................ **75.00**

Vase, house on yellow, 11½"... **70.00**

Vase, mountain & glacier on black, #114, 12"......................... **80.00**

Vase, polar bear on green, 10"..**100.00**

Bellaire, Marc

Ashtray, Still Life, matt fruits & leaves, 10x15".................. **80.00**

Bowl, Jungle Dancer, 11½x5½".**150.00**

Candlestick, Jamaica Man, 10½", ea.................................... **125.00**

Coaster, Mardi Gras, 4½"...... **15.00**

Dish, Balinese Dancer, 8x10".**55.00**

Figurine, bull, 9".................. **145.00**

Platter, Hawaiian, 3 figures on orange, 7x13".................. **55.00**

Vase, Black Cats, hourglass shape, 8".................................... **100.00**

Brastoff, Sascha

Ashtray, Rooftops, freeform, 10½x7¾".......................... **60.00**

Box, Jeweled Bird, 7¾x5"...... **85.00**

Dish, peacock on cream, freeform, #F40, 9¼x8¼".................. **65.00**

Figurine, bear, amber resin, 7½"............................. **135.00**

Jar, horizontal stripes, 3-footed, egg shape, #044A, w/lid, 7".... **75.00**

Plate, Star Steed, gray background w/black border, 11¾"....... **75.00**

Tray, tile design, gold trim, #052, 15x15"........................... **100.00**

Vase, Rooftops, cylindrical, #47, 8½"................................... **90.00**

Wine flask, mosiac design, footed, signed on lip.................. **165.00**

Brayton Laguna

Bowl, brown w/white & yellow flowers, yellow interior, 3x9". **35.00**

Candleholder, kneeling woman holding bowl, Deco style, 6", ea................................... **100.00**

Cookie jar, Matilda, from $350 to **400.00**

Figurine, bar scene, bartender & 2 customers, #H104, 9x8½", $85 to **100.00**

Figurine, boy playing concertina w/ dog, multicolored, 6½"..... **60.00**

Figurine, cowboy bull rider, wood-tone w/painted clothing, 11x11" **125.00**

Figurine, Dorothy, Childhood series, 4x4" **150.00**

Figurine, egret, wood stain w/HP details, 10"..................... **85.00**

Figurine, rearing horse, textured gold, 16x16", minimum value, $600.00.

Figurine, Gay '90s, Honeymoon, 9", from $100.00 to $135.00.

Figurine, little girl w/fairy wings, index finger to mouth, 3¾".**85.00**
Figurine, man playing bongo drum, white crackle & brown bisque, 9".................................. **85.00**
Figurine, penguin, white crackle & brown bisque, #T-10, 7".. **40.00**
Planter, circus elephant, standing, blue jacket, white pants, 7".**80.00**
Plate, pink, early, handmade, 7". **80.00**
Sugar bowl, brown w/white & yellow flowers, w/lid, 4x2½x4"...... **30.00**
Tray, bird & lily, white, yellow, & green on brown bisque, 7" sq......... **15.00**
Wall pocket, bowl-shaped w/floral decoration, Webton-Ware, 3½x6" **35.00**

Brock of California

Bowl, California Farmhouse, rectangular, 2x11x7½"........... **30.00**
Carafe, Forever Yours, white w/ blue top & lid, 8", from $25 to.................................. **30.00**
Coal bucket, California Farmhouse, 1¾x3" **20.00**
Cruets, oil & vinegar; California Farmhouse, white & brown, pr...................................... **20.00**
Egg plate, California Farmhouse, girl & cow on white, yellow trim, 13"............................ **30.00**
Plate, California Wildflower, 11".**8.00**
Salt & pepper shakers, Forever Yours, w/handles, 2⅝", pr.**12.00**
Server, California Wildflower, 2-part, 11" L, w/metal stand......... **25.00**

Cleminson Pottery

Ashtray, stylized flower in center, leaf in each corner, 6" sq.**16.00**

Bowl, Galagray, 4x11x9"........ **55.00**
Butter dish, Distlefink, bird form.............................**35.00**
Cookie jar, Cook Stove........... **75.00**
Cookie jar, Cookie Book........ **75.00**
Cookie jar, Distlefink, cylinder. **75.00**
Cookie jar, Potbellied Stove. **130.00**
Covered dish, floral lid, base w/ attached scalloped saucer, 5" dia................................... **28.00**
Creamer & sugar bowl, Distlefink.....................**25.00**
Darner, little girl, Darn It, original ribbon, 5" **50.00**
Jar, clown face, lid is tall conical hat, 6x4x8" **40.00**
Match holder, flowers/leaves, wall hanging, rectangular, 6½". **25.00**
Mug, boy on white, Make Mine Black, polka-dot tie, 3¼".**32.00**

Plaque, No Matter Where I Place My Guests..., 1940s – 1960s, $25.00.

Plaque, 2 applied pink roses, scalloped oval, 6¾x5¾".......... **22.00**
Salt & pepper shakers, Galagray, rhumba lady, 6½", pr....... **52.50**
Soap dish, claw-foot bathtub, lg flowers w/white interior, 7½" L..................................... **22.00**
Vitamin jar, Daily Dose, w/lid, 5".**65.00**
Wall pocket, puppy in basket, 7x7"............................... **28.00**

Wall pocket, spinning wheel, Busy Hands..., 9x9"................ **45.00**

DeForest of California

Cookie jar, Elephant Sailor Girl.**100.00**
Cookie jar, Henny (Dandee Hen)........................**185.00**
Cookie jar, Pig w/Goodies on tummy, 1956 .... **85.00**
Cookie jar, Rabbit in Hat, brown w/ multicolored details **35.00**
Cookie jar, Ranger Bear **40.00**
Figurine, bunny, white w/pink accents, black eyes & whiskers, 4⅛" **14.00**
Mayonnaise jar, comical male face w/blue eyes, May N Naise hat, 1957 .... **45.00**
Platter, pig face, Go Ahead & Make a Pig of Yourself, 13x13".**35.00**

deLee

Figurine, Amigo, donkey, white w/black features, marked, 5"............................... **37.50**
Figurine, Daisy, rose on bodice, white skirt w/red trim, sticker, 8".................................... **20.00**
Figurine, Happy, elephant, pink & white w/pink & blue flowers, $40 to.............................. **50.00**
Figurine, June, seated w/open book, 4", from $65 to................. **85.00**
Figurine, Oswald, bunny, white w/ blue overalls, sticker on chest, 5"..................................... **70.00**
Figurine, Sadie & Cy, pigs, 3", 2½", pr..................................... **60.00**
Figurine, Siamese cat, white w/ brown markings, blue eyes, 12"................................... **60.00**

Flower holders, Katrina and Hans, with name labels and round deLee labels, 6½", 7", from $70.00 to $90.00 for the pair.

Planter, Annabelle, wide-brimmed hat, white dress w/trim, 7½".**35.00**
Planter, Mr Chips, chipmunk, opening in acorn he holds, 4½", $25 to **35.00**
Planter, Panchita, Mexican girl holding dress w/eyes closed, 6¾" **40.00**
Planter, Sonny, green jacket, lg planter behind, 8", $50 to. **65.00**
Wall pockets, P & U skunks, incised mark, pr from $50 to **75.00**

Finch, Kay

Bank, lion, #5921, 8"............ **350.00**
Canister, embossed raspberry vines, purple & green on white, 9½" **75.00**
Covered dish, swan, #4957, 6".**75.00**
Figurine, angel, #144a, #144b or #144c, ea.......................... **40.00**
Figurine, cherub's, head, #212, 2¼"..................................... **40.00**
Figurine, choir boy, kneeling, #211, 5½" **40.00**
Figurine, Grumpy, pig, #165, 6x7½" **175.00**
Figurine, Guppy, fish, #173, 2½".**95.00**
Figurine, Jezebel, contented cat, #179, 6x9".....................**175.00**

Figurine, Littlest Angel, #4803, 2½" 95.00

Figurine, Mumbo, sitting elephant, #4840, 4½" 100.00

Figurine, Pekingese, #154, 14" L 300.00

Figurine, Polly Penguin, #467, 4¾" 100.00

Plate, Santa face, 6½" 50.00

Shaker, kitchen; Puss, cat, #4616, 6" 275.00

String holder, dog w/bow over left ear, wall mount, 4½x4" . 400.00

Vase, elephant, #B5155, 6" 75.00

Florence Ceramics

Note: The amount of applied decoration — lace, flowers, etc. — has a great deal of influence on values. Our ranges reflect this factor.

Abigail, 8" 175.00

Adeline, fancy, 8¼", from $250 to 300.00

Amber, 9¼" 700.00

Bea, flower holder, 6¼", from $50 to 60.00

Bride, rare, 8¾", from $1,800 to 2,000.00

Butch, 5½", from $175 to . 200.00

Camille, plain, 8½" 185.00

Choir Boy, 6" 115.00

David, 7½", from $125 to 140.00

Douglas, 8¼" 175.00

Gesille 750.00

Irene, pink dress, 6", from $60 to 70.00

Joy, child, 6", from $125.00 to . 150.00

Louise, 7½", from $125 to . 140.00

Marilyn, carrying hat box, violet, 8", from $500 to 550.00

Mermaid, from $175 to 200.00

Oriental couple, in aqua & wht, 7¾", pr from $125 to 140.00

Patrice, white w/gold trim, 7¼", from $200 to 225.00

Polly, pink & white, flower holder, 6", from $50 to 60.00

Rebecca, aqua dress w/violet trim, 7", from $200 to 250.00

Shirley, 8", from $200 to 225.00

Suzanne, wht dress w/gold trim, matching hat, 9¼", from $550 to 600.00

Suzette, 6", from $140 to 160.00

Victoria, from $300.00 to $350.00.

Winkin & Blynkin, fancy, 5½", pr, from $400 to 450.00

Yvonne, plain, 8¾", from $425 to 500.00

Josef

Basket Pet, 6 in series, bsk finish, Japan, 3½", ea 15.00

Birthday Girls, 1-16, Japan, 7", ea 25.00

Buggy Bugs series, various poses, wire antenna, Japan, 3¼", ea................................. 12.00

Christmas angel praying by decorated tree nightlight, 7".. 50.00

Christmas Choir Boys, 2 different sets of 3, Japan, 5½", ea set 60.00

Dalmatian, Kennel Club series, Japan, 3½".......................20.00

Doll of the Month (tilt head), California, 3¼", ea..........35.00

Ecology Girls, 6 in series, Japan, 4¼", ea.............................40.00

Elephant, sitting, Japan, 3¾", from $25 to...............................30.00

Farmer's Daughter, girl w/hen & basket of eggs, Japan, 5".45.00

First Date, young lady in gr gown holding fan, Japan, 9".....95.00

Girl cutting cake, Japan, 6", from $45 to................................50.00

Hunter, beautiful horse standing, Japan, 6"..........................25.00

It's a Wonderful World series, Japan, 3½", ea.................45.00

Jeanne, Colonial Days series, Japan, 9"......................125.00

Kennel Club, 6 in series, Japan, 4", ea..15.00

Love Makes the World Go Round, 6 in series, Japan, 9", ea ...95.00

Make Believe series, Japan, 4½", ea....................................40.00

Mary Ann & Mama, California, 4", 7", pr..............................135.00

Persian Cat Family, set of 4, Japan, mini, 1½-2", complete set.20.00

Santa, kiss on forehead, Japan, 4¾"....................................45.00

Three Kings, Japan, 8½-11", set of 3.......................................70.00

White Colonial Days, 6 in series, Japan, 9", ea....................75.00

Zodiac Girls series, Japan, 4¾", ea.................................45.00

Kaye of Hollywood

Figurine, lady singer w/book in hand, unmarked, 10"......40.00

Flower holder, boy in blue jacket w/ pink bow tie, #112, 9¼"...35.00

Flower holder, girl carrying parasol tip down, #305/2143, 10".85.00

Flower holder, little girl, hands to chin, wearing dustcap, 9".45.00

Vase, Hawaiian hula girl w/lei covering breast, cala lily bud holders.....................................165.00

Wall pocket, lady figure, #201.25.00

Keeler, Brad

Cookie jar, bass, turquoise w/ white belly, black eyes, #130, 7x13½"...........................150.00

Dish, red lobster on green leaf, divided, 12x7".................80.00

Figurine, bluebird, tail down, 8".40.00

Figurine, cockatoo, #26, 10½", from $70 to.............................95.00

Figurine, female pheasant, 7½".45.00

Figurine, flamingo, wings tucked in, head down, #3, 7¼"....70.00

Figurine, kitten w/ball, Mitzi on silver label, 5x7"............30.00

Figurine, rooster, #744, 6½"...25.00

Plate, serving; trout shape, 13¼x5½"..........................65.00

Tray, Tomato Ware, with lid, from $50.00 to $65.00.

Pierce, Howard

Ashtray, brown on white, unmarked, 2x4", from $20 to.............35.00

Bowl, fluted, blue metallic, w/black ink stamp, 4½x7" 125.00

Figurine, angelfish, multicolored, black stamp, 4½x5" & 3x4", pr 135.00

Figurine, bird, gold, unmarked, 2½x5½", from $35 to 50.00

Flowerpot, salmon-colored matt, #81P, 4¼x4¼", from $50 to .75.00

Planter, white owl, black ink stamp, 6x6¾", from $50 to 75.00

Schoop, Hedi

Chip 'n dip, lady w/skirt forming bowl holds bowl in ea hand, 10x13" 95.00

Figurine, Dutch boy w/opening in back, 10" 85.00

Figurine, lady w/basket on head, opening in skirt at right, 12" 75.00

Figurine, nun standing in prayer, brown habit 65.00

Planter, stylized bird, tan w/yellow, white & black, 6¼x12x4½".75.00

Vase, rooster crowing, dark green, rose, & white, 14x11" 75.00

Twin Winton

Ashtray, Bambi, TW-205, 6x8".100.00

Ashtray, kitten, TW-201, 6x8"..100.00

Bank, Hotei, TW-411, 8" 50.00

Bank, lamb, TW-402, 8" 40.00

Bank, rabbit, 10", from $40.00 to $60.00.

Bookends, poodle, Expanimal, TW-125, 7½" 125.00

Candleholder, Aladdin, TW-510, 6½x9½", ea 45.00

Candleholder, Verdi, TW-501L, 9½x4", ea........................ 15.00

Candy jar, elephant, TW-356, 6x9" 65.00

Canister, Coffee Coop, Canister Farm, TW-113, 4x6" 40.00

Canister, Tea House, Canisterville, TW-104, 3x7" 50.00

Cookie jar, Cow, TW-69, 8½x13½"..75.00

Cookie jar, Elf Bakery, 8¾x12". 90.00

Figurine, ballerina in blue, 3¾".12.00

Figurine, cowboy w/white hat, 12½" 25.00

Figurine, kitten in shoe, 4x6¾"..15.00

Figurine, skunk sitting, mini, #203,¾" 5.00

Ice bucket, Men of the Mountain, Bottoms Up, TW-32, 7½x14".250.00

Mug, Wood Grain Line, rope & spur handle, 4" 40.00

Planter, rabbit crouching beside basket, 5x8" 85.00

Plate, dinner; Wood Grain Line, 10" 40.00

Plate, steak; Artist Palette Line, 7½x12" 60.00

Salt & pepper shakers, bear, TW-184, pr...................... 40.00

Salt & pepper shakers, dinosaur, TW-172, pr.................... 100.00

Salt & pepper shakers, pear, TW-136, pr...................... 75.00

Salt & pepper shakers, sheriff, TW-155, pr...................... 50.00

Salt & pepper shakers, shoe, TW-182, pr...................... 50.00

Spoon rest, cow, TW-23, 5x10" . 40.00

Spoon rest, lamb, TW-10, 5x10".40.00

Tumbler, Artist Palette Line, 4½". 35.00

Vase, bud; Snoopy Bear, 3x4" . **65.00**
Wall pocket, rabbit (head), TW-302,
5½" **100.00**

Wallace China

Bowl, fruit; Boots & Saddle, 4⅞"..**50.00**
Bowl, vegetable; Rodeo, oval, 11⅞".**220.00**
Creamer, Southwest Desert .. **65.00**
Cup, Boots & Saddle, flat **65.00**
Cup & saucer, Dahlia............. **35.00**
Cup & saucer, demitasse; Chuck
Wagon........................... **110.00**
Pitcher, Rodeo, disk type, 7x7½" . **200.00**
Plate, bread & butter; Boots &
Saddle, 7⅛" **60.00**
Plate, chop; Pioneer Trails, 13½". **270.00**
Plate, dinner; Rodeo, bronco rider,
10¾" **85.00**
Plate, Shadowleaf, 11¼"......... **65.00**
Platter, Dahlia, oval, 11½"..... **40.00**
Salt & pepper shakers, Longhorn,
5", pr **130.00**
Sugar bowl, El Rancho **50.00**

Weil Ware

Bowl, divided; Bambu, rectangu-
lar................................... **28.00**
Bowl, sherbet; Malay Blossom,
footed, sq top, 2½x3⅞"..... **20.00**
Candleholder, angel girl w/brown
hair, silver label, 6x5½" .. **35.00**
Casserole, Bambu, w/lid **45.00**

Dish, Malay
B a m b u ,
2 x 9 x 8 ",
$35.00.

Flower holder, boy in short pants
holding flowers, vase behind,
11" **35.00**
Flower holder, girl in teal w/pink
scarf holds 2 baskets, 9½". **45.00**
Flower holder, girl w/Dutch-like cap
holds lg pink bowl, 7¾" ... **30.00**
Flower holder, girl w/lg baskets, lay-
ers of skirts, pigtails, 7¾". **60.00**
Flower holder, lady in pink w/apron
holds 2 white baskets, 10"..**55.00**
Plate, Bambu, sq, 9¾"........... **13.00**
Plate, Malay Blossom, sq, 9⅝". **12.00**
Salt & pepper shakers, Malay
Blossom, flower-form cylinder,
2½", pr............................ **28.00**
Sauceboat, Malay Blossom,
attached undertray **18.00**
Tray, Malay Blossom, center
handle............................ **35.00**
Tumbler, Malay Blossom, 4¼". **38.00**
Vase, Ming Tree, sq sides, incur-
vate rim, 8x4".................. **45.00**
Vase, pink nautilus shell, #720,
6⅛x9½x4" **48.00**

Will-George

Boat, 20" L, separate Oriental w/
oar will attach, NM......... **75.00**
Candleholders, petal shape, green
w/pink interior, 6½", pr. **125.00**
Figurine, Baltimore oriole ... **150.00**
Figurine, flamingo, seated, wings
raised, 3½x3" **95.00**
Figurine, monk, brown bisque,
4½" **50.00**
Figurine, rooster, 4½"............. **50.00**
Leaf dish, green, signed, 10x11". **40.00**
Planter, leaves embossed on green,
pink interior, 10x3½x3" .. **75.00**
Tumbler, chicken figure, multicol-
ored, 4½" **50.00**

Tureen, onion form, w/lid, ladle &
underplate, lg **70.00**

Winfield

Bamboo, bowl, soup; 2x6" **20.00**
Bamboo, creamer & sugar bowl. **55.00**
Casserole, Bird of Paradise, oblong,
w/lid, 8x11" **30.00**
Casserole, Passion Flower, w/lid,
5x9" **15.00**
Egg cup, Dragon Flower, 3½". **40.00**
Platter, Bamboo, rectangular,
15x10½" **30.00**
Salt & pepper shakers, Desert
Dawn, cube form, 2", pr.. **12.00**

Yona

Ash bucket, Country Club, red &
white striped, w/wire grill,
3⅝x4" **30.00**
Figurine, lady w/pot on right shoulder, long dress & apron, #19,
9" **25.00**
Salt & pepper shakers, clown, feet
raised, fan in right hand, 3",
pr **25.00**
Wall pocket, clown w/neck ruffle stands behind receptacle,
6x4" **42.00**

Cameras

Whether buying a camera for personal use, adding to a collection, or for resale, use caution. Complex usable late-model cameras are difficult to check out at sales, and you should be familiar with the camera model or have confidence in the seller's claims before purchasing one for your personal use. If you are just beginning a camera collection, there are a multitude of different types and models and special features to select from in building your collection; you should have on hand some of the available guide books listing various models and types. Camera collecting can be a very enjoyable hobby and can be done within your particular funding ability.

Buying for resale can be a very profitable experience if you are careful in your selection and have made arrangements with buyers who have made their requirements known to you. Generally, buying low-cost, mass-produced cameras is not advisable; you may have a difficult time finding a buyer for such cameras. Of these low-cost types, only those that are mint or new in the original box have any appreciable appeal to collectors. Very old cameras are not necessarily valuable — it all depends on availability. The major criterion is quality; prices offered for mint-condition cameras may be double or triple those of average-wear items. You can expect to find that foreign-made cameras are preferred by most buyers because of the general perception that their lenses and shutters are superior. The German- and Japanese-made cameras dominate the 'classic' camera market. Polaroid cameras and movie cameras have yet to gain a significant collector's market.

The cameras listed here represent only a very small cross section of thousands of cameras available.

Values are given for examples with average wear and in good working order; they represent average retail prices with limited guarantees. It is very important to note that purchase prices at flea markets, garage sales, or estate sales would have to be far less for them to be profitable to a resaler who has the significant expense of servicing the camera, testing it, and guaranteeing it to a user or a collector.

Agfa, box type, 1930-50, from $5 to 20.00
Agfa, Karat-35, 1940.............. 35.00
Aires, 35III, 1958, from $15 to. 35.00
Alpa, Standard, 1946-52, Swiss, from $700 to 1,500.00
Anesco, Folding, Nr 1 to Nr 10, ea from $5 to 30.00
Argus A2F, 1940, from $10 to. 20.00
Asahi Pentax, Original, 1957. 200.00
Bell & Howell Foton, 1948, from $500 to 700.00
Braun Paxette I, 1952, from $20 to 30.00
Canon A-1, from $70 to........ 130.00
Canon IIB, 1949-53.............. 225.00
Canon L-1, 1956-57.............. 400.00
Canon Rangefinder IIF, ca 1954, from $200 to 300.00
Canon S-II, 1947-49.............. 375.00
Canon T-50, from $30 to 50.00
Canon TL, from $30 to........... 50.00
Canon 7, 1961-64, from $200 to..400.00
Canonet QL1, from $25 to..... 40.00
Contax II or III, 1936, from $200 to 400.00
Detrola Model D, Detroit Corp, 1938-40 .... 20.00
Eastman, Premo, many models, ea from $30 to 200.00

Eastman Kodak Baby Brownie, Bakelite, from $5 to 10.00
Eastman Kodak Medalist, 1941-48, from $100 to 175.00
Eastman Kodak Retina IIIC, from $250 to 325.00
Eastman Kodak Retinette, various models, ea from $15 to ... 40.00
Eastman Kodak Signet 35..... 35.00
Eastman Kodak 35, 1940-51, from $20 to 40.00
Exakta II, 1949-50, from $100 to 130.00
Fujica AX-5.......................... 115.00
Graflex Speed Graphic, various sizes, ea from $60 to 200.00
Konica Autoreflex TC, various models, ea from $40 to.......... 70.00
Konica III Rangefinder, 1956-59, from $90 to 110.00
Leica II, 1963-67, from $200 to.400.00
Leica IIIF, 1950-56, from $200 to .400.00
Mamiyaflex TLR, 1951, from $70 to 100.00
Minolta Autocord, TLR, from $75 to 100.00
Minolta HiMatic Series, various models, ea from $10 to ... 25.00
Minolta X-700, from $75 to . 135.00
Minolta-16, mini, various models, ea from $15 to 30.00
Miranda Automex II, 1963 .... 70.00
Nikon F, various finders & meters, ea from $125 to 225.00
Nikon FM 150.00
Nikon SP Rangefinder, 1958-60, from $1500 to 2,000.00
Olympus OM-1, from $90 to.. 120.00
Olympus Pen EE, compact half-frame................................ 35.00
Pentax K-1000, from $50 to .. 90.00
Pentax Spotmatic, many models, ea from $40 to 100.00

Perfex Speed Candid, 35mm, Bakelite body, ca. 1938, from $60.00 to $70.00. (Photo courtesy C. E. Cataldo)

Petri FT, FT-1000, FT-EE & similar models, ea from $35 to ... **70.00**
Polaroid, most models, ea from $5 to **10.00**
Polaroid 110, 110A, 110B, ea from $20 to **40.00**
Polaroid 180, 185, 190, 195, ea from $100 to **250.00**
Praktica Super TL **40.00**
Regula, King, fixed lens, various models, ea **25.00**
Regula, King, interchangeable lens, various models, ea **60.00**
Ricoh Diacord 1, TLR, built-in meter, 1958 .... **65.00**
Rollei 35, mini, Germany, 1966-70, from $150 to **250.00**
Rolleicord II, 1936-50, from $70 to **90.00**
Rolleiflex SL35M, 1978, from $75 to **100.00**
Samoca 35, 1950s **25.00**
Taron 35, 1955 .... **25.00**
Topcon Uni **35.00**
Tower 50, Sears, w/Cassar lens.**20.00**
Voigtlander Vitessa T, 1957, from $150 to **200.00**
Yashica A, TLR **35.00**
Yashica FX-70 .... **60.00**
Zeiss Baldur Box Tengor, Frontar lens, 1935, from $35 to . **150.00**

Zeiss Ikon Nettar, Folding Roll Film, various sizes, ea $25 to **35.00**
Zenit A, USSR, from $20 to ... **35.00**
Zorki, USSR, 1950-56, from $20 to **40.00**
Zorki-4, USSR, Rangefinder, 1957-73 .... **50.00**

Candlewick

Candlewick was one of the all-time bestselling lines of The Imperial Glass Company of Bellaire, Ohio. It was produced from 1936 until the company closed in 1982. More than 741 items were made over the years; and though many are still easy to find today, some (such as the desk calendar, the chip and dip set, and the dresser set) are a challenge to collect. Candlewick is easily identified by its beaded stems, handles, and rims characteristic of the tufted needlework of our pioneer women for which it was named. For a complete listing of the Candlewick line, we recommend *Elegant Glassware of the Depression Era* by Gene and Cathy Florence (Collector Books).

Ashtray, matchbook holder center, #400/60, 6" **165.00**
Ashtray, round, #400/133, 5" . **12.00**
Ashtray, sq, #400/653, 5¾" **40.00**
Basket, beaded handle, #400/273, 5" **225.00**
Bell, #400/179, 4" **85.00**
Bottle, scent, 4-bead, E408 .... **75.00**
Bowl, centerpiece; flared, #400/13B, 11" **55.00**
Bowl, finger; footed, #3400 .... **35.00**
Bowl, relish; 2-part, #400/84, 6½".**25.00**

Bowl, round, #400/92B, 12" ... **45.00**

Bowl, round, 2-handle, #400/42B, 4¾" **12.50**

Bowl, sq, #400/231, 5" **95.00**

Butter dish, round, #400/144, 5½".**35.00**

Cake stand, high foot, #400/103D, 11" **75.00**

Candleholder, 2-light, #400/100 .**24.00**

Candleholder, 3-bead stems, tall, #400/175, 6½" **175.00**

Candy box, round, #400/59, 5½".**50.00**

Candy box, round, 3-section, w/lid, #400/158 .... **250.00**

Compote, #400/63B, 4½" **40.00**

Condiment set, 4-pc, #400/1769.**80.00**

Creamer, domed foot, 400/18.**125.00**

Creamer, plain, footed, #400/31. **9.00**

Cruet, w/stopper, #400/70, 4-oz..**55.00**

Ladle, marmalade; 3-bead stem, #400/130 .... **12.00**

Lamp shade **85.00**

Mustard jar, w/spoon, #400/156.**40.00**

Pitcher, no foot, #400/16, 16-oz.**200.00**

Pitcher, plain, #400/424, 64-oz. **60.00**

Plate, luncheon; #400/7D, 9". **15.00**

Plate, 2-handle, #400/42D, 5½"..**12.00**

Plate, 2-handle, crimped, #400/52C, 6¾" **30.00**

Platter, #400/124D, 13" **110.00**

Relish, oval, #400/256, 10½"..**30.00**

Salt & pepper shakers, beaded foot, chrome top, #400/247, pr.**20.00**

Stem, water; #400/190, 10-oz.**22.00**

Stem, wine; #4000, 5-oz **28.00**

Sugar bowl and creamer, individual bridge; $9.00 each; Tray, 6½", $18.00.

Teacup, #400/35 .... **7.00**

Tray, oval, #400/159, 9" **40.00**

Tray, upturned handles, #400/42E, 5½" **25.00**

Tumbler, #400/19, 10-oz **12.00**

Tumbler, tea; #400/18, 12-oz.. **80.00**

Vase, flat, crimped edge, #400/287C, 6" **50.00**

Vase, fluted rim, beaded handles, #400/87C, 8" **40.00**

Cape Cod by Avon

Though now discontinued, the Avon company sold this dark ruby red glassware through their catalogs since the '70s, and there seems to be a good supply of it around today. In addition to the place settings (there are plates in three sizes, soup and dessert bowls, a cup and saucer, tumblers in two sizes, three different goblets, a mug, and a wine glass), there are many lovely accessory items as well. Among them you'll find a cake plate, a pitcher, a platter, a hurricane-type candle lamp, a butter dish, napkin rings, and a pie plate server. Note: Mint-in-box items are worth about 20% more than the same piece with no box.

Bell, Hostess; unmarked, 1979-80, 6½" **18.50**

Bowl, dessert; 1978-90, 6½"... **10.00**

Bowl, rimmed soup; 1991, 7½". **22.00**

Bowl, vegetable; marked Centennial Edition 1886-1986, 8¾" ... **30.00**

Box, trinket; heart form, w/lid, 1989-90, 4" **15.00**

Butter dish, 1983-84, ¼-lb, 7", from $20 to **22.00**

Candleholder, hurricane type w/ clear chimney, 1985, ea .. **40.00**

Candlestick, 1975-80, 8¾", ea. **12.50**

Candlestick, 1983-84, 2½", ea.. **9.00**

Candy dish, 1987-90, 3½x6" dia. **19.50**

Christmas ornament, 6-sided, marked Christmas 1990, 3¼".......... **12.50**

Creamer, footed, 1981-84, 4" ... **9.50**

Cruet, oil; w/stopper, 1975-80, 5-oz................................. **12.50**

Cup & saucer, 1990-93, 7-oz.. **15.00**

Decanter, w/stopper, 1977-80, 16-oz, 10½" **18.00**

Goblet, claret; 1992, 5-oz, 5¼", from $10 to **14.00**

Goblet, saucer champagne; 1991, 8-oz, 5¼".......................... **15.00**

Goblet, water; 1976-90, 9-oz.... **9.50**

Mug, pedestal foot, 1982-84, 5-oz, 5", from $8 to................... **12.00**

Napkin ring, 1989-90, 1¾"....... **9.50**

Pie/plate server, 1992-93, 10¾" dia, from $20 to **25.00**

Pitcher, water; footed, 1984 – 1985, 60-ounce, from $40.00 to $45.00.

Plate, cake; pedestal foot, 1991, 3½x10¾" dia.................... **50.00**

Plate, dessert; 1980-90, 7½" **8.00**

Platter, oval, 1986, 13", from $45 to **55.00**

Relish, rectangular, 2-part, 1985-96, 9½" **15.00**

Salt shaker, marked May 1978, ea **9.50**

Salt shaker, unmarked, 1978-80, ea.................................... **6.00**

Tidbit tray, 2-tiere (7" & 10" plates), 1987, 9¾" **56.50**

Tumbler, straight sides, footed, 1988, 8-oz, 3½" **12.00**

Tumbler, straight sides, 1990, 12-oz, 5½"......................... **14.00**

Vase, footed, 1985, 8" **20.00**

Carnival Chalkware

Chalkware statues of Kewpies, glamour girls, assorted dogs, horses, etc., were given to winners of carnival games from about 1910 until the 1950s. Today's collectors especially value those representing well-known personalities such as Disney characters and comic book heroes. Refer to *The Carnival Chalk Prize* by Tom Morris. Our values are for examples in near-mint to mint condition; be sure to reduce these figures accordingly if there is damage or the paint loss is more than minimal.

Beach bather, 1940-50, 7½x9". **60.00**

Black boy eating watermelon, marked Buelah, ca 1930-40, 7½" **95.00**

Bulldog sitting, ca 1935-40, 8x7½" **40.00**

Bulldog sitting, Illinois State Fair, 1939, 16x12", $65.00.
(Photo courtesy Tom Harris Auctions)

Cowboy, w/ashtray at base, ca 1930-40, 8¼".............. **45.00**

Dead End Kid, ca 1935-45, rare, 15"............................ **165.00**

Donald Duck's Uncle Scrooge holding bag of money, Disney, 1940-50, 8"............................ **50.00**

Dopey standing w/hands on tummy, 1937-50, 13".................. **100.00**

Fat Kewpie, w/both hands on tummy, ca 1935-45, 7½".. **20.00**

Girl kneeling w/hands covering chest, nude, ca 1940-50, 12"........ **70.00**

Horse, sad face, ca 1945-50, 5". **20.00**

Lighthouse, 3-dimensional, ca 1935-45, 11"..................... **45.00**

Lion standing & growling, ca 1940-50, 9¼x12" **45.00**

May West, marked Al Venice Dolls, ca 1935-45, 14".............. **185.00**

Paul Revere standing, holding rifle, ca 1935-45, 14½" **45.00**

Sailor at ease holding rifle, 1935-45, 13½" **120.00**

Scotty dog sitting w/ears pointed, ca 1940, 7"...................... **20.00**

Shirley Temple standing in short skirt, bows on dress/in hair, 16½" **320.00**

Wimpy standing & holding mug of beer, Jenkins Studio, 1946, 9½" **80.00**

Young girl holding fan, ca 1925-35, 11"................................... **55.00**

Cat-Tail Dinnerware

Cat-Tail was a dinnerware pattern popular during the late 1920s until sometime in the 1940s. So popular, in fact, that ovenware, glassware, tinware, and even a kitchen table were made to coordinate with it. The dinnerware was made primarily by Universal potteries of Cambridge, Ohio, though a catalog from Hall China Co. circa 1927 shows a three-piece coffee service, and there may have been other pieces made by Hall as well. Cattail was sold for years by Sears Roebuck and Company, and some items bear a mark with their name.

The pattern is unmistakable — a cluster of red cattails (usually six but sometimes only one or two) with black stems on creamy white. Shapes certainly vary; Universal used a minimum of three of their standard mold designs — Camwood, Old Holland, Laurella — and there were possibly others. Some pieces are marked 'Wheelock' on the bottom. Wheelock was a department store in Peoria, Illinois.

If you are trying to decorate a '40s vintage kitchen, no other design could afford you more to work with.

Note: Assume that suggested prices for tinware items are for examples in excellent condition. For ceramic items, assume that they are at least near mint.

Bowl, footed, 9½"................... **20.00**

Bowl, mixing; 8".................... **23.00**

Bowl, Old Holland shape, Wheelock, 6".. **7.00**

Bowl, salad; lg....................... **25.00**

Bowl, soup; flat rim, 7¾"........ **15.00**

Bowl, soup; tab handles, 8" ... **17.50**

Bowl, straight sides, 6¼" **12.00**

Bowl, vegetable; Universal, 8¾".**25.00**

Bowl, w/lid, part of ice box set, 4"...................................**20.00**

Bowl, w/lid, part of ice box set, 6"................28.00

Bowl, 3x4"................15.00

Bread box, tinware, 12x13½", VG.50.00

Butter dish, ¼-lb, 3½x6x3¼"..55.00

Cake plate, Mt Vernon..........25.00

Canister set, tin, 4-pc...........60.00

Casserole, paneled sides & lid, 6½x8½"................35.00

Casserole, w/lid, 3¾x7", from $25 to................30.00

Casserole, w/lid, 4¼x8¼"........55.00

Coffeepot, 3-pc........................70.00

Creamer, from $18 to.............25.00

Creamer & sugar bowl, w/lid, Camwood Ivory, 3¾x5¼".45.00

Jug, ball; ceramic-topped cork stopper....................37.50

Jug, 1-qt, 6"............................25.00

Match holder, tinware............45.00

Pickle dish/gravy boat liner...20.00

Pie plate, $30.00.

Pie server, hole in handle for hanging, marked.....................25.00

Pitcher, clear glass w/Cat-Tail pattern, ribbed neck & base, 9".........20.00

Pitcher, ice lip, ball shape, 8", from $45 to................60.00

Pitcher, milk; 7½"...................35.00

Pitcher, milk/utility; straight sides, 5x6"................35.00

Pitcher, utility; straight paneled sides, w/lid, 6½"..............35.00

Plate, dinner; Laurella shape, from $15 to................20.00

Plate, luncheon; 9", from $7 to.8.50

Plate, salad or dessert; round, from $5 to................6.50

Plate, sq, 7¾"............................7.00

Plate, tab handles, 11"..........30.00

Platter, tab handles, Camwood Ivory, 14½" L....................35.00

Platter, tab handles, 13⅜" L..30.00

Platter, 11½" L, from $15 to..20.00

Relish tray, Cat-Tail pattern repeated 4 times at rim, oval, 9x5"...50.00

Salad set (fork, spoon & bowl), from $50 to................60.00

Salt & pepper shakers, Salt or Pepper, glass, 4", pr........35.00

Salt & pepper shakers, wider at ribbed bottom, 4½", pr....50.00

Saucer, Old Holland shape, marked Wheelock, from $4 to........6.00

Scale, metal................45.00

Stack set, 3-pc, w/lid, from $40 to...................50.00

Sugar bowl, w/lid, from $20 to.25.00

Syrup, red top........................70.00

Teapot, 7x8"............................40.00

Tray, for batter set.................75.00

Tumbler, marked Universal Potteries, scarce, from $65 to...........70.00

Tumbler, water; glass.............35.00

Waste can, step-on, tinware ..45.00

Ceramic Arts Studio

Whether you're a collector of American pottery or not, chances are you'll like the distinctive styling of the figurines, salt and pepper shakers, and other novelty items made by the Ceramic Arts Studio of Madison, Wisconsin, from about 1938 until approximately 1952. They're not especially hard to find — a trip to any good flea market will usually produce at least one good buy from among their vast array of products. They're easily spotted, once you've seen a few examples; but if you're not sure, check for the trademark — most are marked. For more information we recommend *Ceramic Arts Studio, The Legacy of Betty Harrington,* by Donald-Brian Johnson, Timothy J. Holthaus, and James E. Petzold (Schiffer). See the Directory for information concerning the CAS Collector's Association, listed under Clubs and Newsletters.

Bank, Skunky, 4", from $260 to **280.00**

Bank, Tony the Barber (blade bank), 4¾", from $75 to **100.00**

Bell, Winter Belle, 5¼", from $75 to **85.00**

Candleholders, Triad Grils, left/ right: 7", center: 5", 3-pc set **300.00**

Figurine, Alice & March Hare (white rabbit), 4½", 6", pr, $350 to **450.00**

Figurine, Alice in Wonderland kneeling, 4¼", from $175 to **225.00**

Figurine, Blythe & Pensive, 6½", 6", pr from $300 to **350.00**

Figurine, boy w/towel, 5", from $300 to **350.00**

Figurine, Butch & Billy (boxer dogs), snugglers, 3", pr from $120 to **160.00**

Figurine, Calico Cat, 3" **45.00**

Figurine, chipmunk, 2" **45.00**

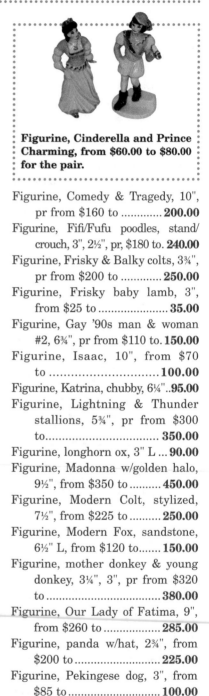

Figurine, Comedy & Tragedy, 10", pr from $160 to **200.00**

Figurine, Fifi/Fufu poodles, stand/ crouch, 3", 2½", pr, $180 to. **240.00**

Figurine, Frisky & Balky colts, 3¾", pr from $200 to **250.00**

Figurine, Frisky baby lamb, 3", from $25 to **35.00**

Figurine, Gay '90s man & woman #2, 6¾", pr from $110 to. **150.00**

Figurine, Isaac, 10", from $70 to **100.00**

Figurine, Katrina, chubby, 6¼"..**95.00**

Figurine, Lightning & Thunder stallions, 5¾", pr from $300 to.................................. **350.00**

Figurine, longhorn ox, 3" L ...**90.00**

Figurine, Madonna w/golden halo, 9½", from $350 to **450.00**

Figurine, Modern Colt, stylized, 7½", from $225 to **250.00**

Figurine, Modern Fox, sandstone, 6½" L, from $120 to....... **150.00**

Figurine, mother donkey & young donkey, 3¼", 3", pr from $320 to **380.00**

Figurine, Our Lady of Fatima, 9", from $260 to **285.00**

Figurine, panda w/hat, 2¾", from $200 to **225.00**

Figurine, Pekingese dog, 3", from $85 to **100.00**

Figurine, Petrov & Petrushka, 5½", 5", pr from $120 to **150.00**

Figurine, Pioneer Sam & Suzie, 5½", 5", pr from $80 to..**100.00**

Figurine, realistic mother bear & cub, 3¼", 2¼", pr from $320 to.............................. **380.00**

Figurine, Saucy Squirrel w/jacket, 2¼", from $175 to **200.00**

Figurine, shepherd & shepherdess, 8½", 8", pr from $180 to.**220.00**

Figurine, Smi-Li & Mo-Pi, chubby man & woman, 6", pr from $50 to **80.00**

Figurine, square dance boy & girl, 6½", 6", pr from $200 to.**250.00**

Figurine, St Agnes w/lamb, 6", from $260 to **285.00**

Figurine, St Francis w/extended arms, 7", from $175 to..**225.00**

Figurine, temple dance man & woman, 7", 6¾", pr from $900 to **1,000.00**

Figurine, tortoise w/hat crawling, 2½" L, from $150 to.......**175.00**

Figurine, Wee Piggy boy & girl, 3¼", 3½", pr from $50 to .**70.00**

Figurine, Zulu man & woman #1, 5½", 7", pr from $1,100 to......**1,400.00**

Head vase, Bonnie, 7", from $125 to **150.00**

Metal accessory, parakeet cage, 13", from $125 to **150.00**

Miniature, Aladdin's Lamp, 2" L, from $65 to **85.00**

Miniature, Flying Ducks (vase), 2½", from $75 to **85.00**

Miniature, Grapes (teapot), 2".**75.00**

Mug, Barber Shop Quartet, 3½".**150.00**

Planter, Lorelei on Shell, 6", from $250 to **300.00**

Plaque, Jack Be Nimble, 5", from $400 to **450.00**

Plaque, Zor, 9" **75.00**

Salt & pepper shakers, bear mother & cub, snugglers, pr from $40 to **60.00**

Salt & pepper shakers, chihuahua & doghouse, snugglers, 1½", 2" L **140.00**

Salt & pepper shakers, elf & mushroom, pr **65.00**

Salt & pepper shakers, monkey mother & baby, snugglers, 4", 2½", pr **50.00**

Salt & pepper shakers, sea horse & coral, snugglers, pr from $100 to **140.00**

Shelf sitter, cowboy, 4¾" **85.00**

Shelf sitters, Budgie & Pudgie parakeets, 6", pr from $100 to..**120.00**

Shelf sitters, Chinese boy & girl, 3½", pr from $30 to **40.00**

Shelf sitters, Pete & Polly parrots, chartreuse, 7½", pr, $170 to **200.00**

Tray, kneeling pixie girl, 4½", from $125 to **150.00**

Character and Promotional Glassware

Once routinely given away by fast-food restaurants and soft-drink companies, these glasses have become very collectible; and though they're being snapped up by avid collectors everywhere, you'll still find there are bargains to be had. The more expensive are those with Disney or Walter Lantz cartoon characters, super-heroes, sports greats, or personalities from Star Trek or the old movies. For more information refer to *The Collector's Guide to Cartoon and Promotional Drinking Glasses* by John Hervey (L-W Book

Sales) and *McDonald's Drinkware* by Michael J. Kelley (Collector Books). See Clubs and Newsletters for information on *Collector Glass News.*

Al Capp, 1975, flat bottom, Mammy or Pappy, ea from $35 to. **50.00**

Animal Crackers, Chicago Tribune/ NY News Syndicate, 1978, Louis **25.00**

Battlestar Galactica, 1979, Universal Studios, 4 different, ea $7 to **10.00**

Burger Chef, Friendly Monster Series, 1977, 6 different, ea $15 to **25.00**

Burger King, Collector Series, 1979, 5 different characters, ea $3 to **5.00**

California Raisins, Applause, 1989, 32-oz, from $6 to **8.00**

Children's Classics, Libbey Glass Co, Alice in Wonderland, from $10 to **15.00**

Children's Classics, Libbey Glass Co, Robin Hood, Moby Dick, ea $10 to **15.00**

Chipmunks, Hardee's (no logo on glass), 1985, Alvin, from $1 to **3.00**

Disney Characters, 1936, Donald, Mickey, Minnie, 4½", ea $30 to **50.00**

Disney's All-Star Parade, 1939, 10 different, ea $25 to **50.00**

Flinstones, Welch's, 1962, 6 different, ea from $4 to **6.00**

Hanna-Barbera, 1960s, jam glasses, 5 different, rare, ea from $60 to **90.00**

Harvey Cartoon Characters, Pepsi, 1970s, action pose, 3 different, ea.. **8.00**

Harvey Cartoon Characters, Pepsi, 1970s, static pose, Richie Rich **15.00**

Harvey Cartoon Characters, Pepsi, 1970s, static pose, Sad Sack, scarce **26.00**

Howdy Doody, Welch's/Kagran, 1950s, 6 different, embossed bottom, ea **10.00**

Jungle Book, Disney/Canada, 1966, 6 different, numbered, 6½", ea **40.00**

Jungle Book, Disney/Pepsi, 1970s, Mowgli, unmarked, from $15 to **20.00**

Jungle Book, Disney/Pepsi, 1970s, Rama, unmarked, from $25 to **35.00**

Leonardo TTV Collector Series, Pepsi, Simon Bar Sinister, 5", $6 to **10.00**

Leonardo TTV Collector Series, Pepsi, 4 different, 6", ea from $10 to **15.00**

Masters of the Universe, Mattel, 1993, 4 different, ea from $5 to **10.00**

Mickey Mouse, Happy Birthday, Pepsi, 1978, 2 different, ea from $5 to **10.00**

Mickey Mouse, Mickey's Christmas Carol, Coca-Cola, 1982, 3 different **7.00**

Pac-Man, Bally Midway MFG/ AAFES/Libbey, 1980, 4 different, ea $4 to **6.00**

Pac-Man, Bally Midway Mfg/ Libbey, 1982, 6" flare top, from $2 to **4.00**

PAT Ward, Pepsi, late 1970s, static pose, Boris or Natasha, 5", ea.........**15.00**

PAT Ward, Pepsi, late 1970s, static pose, Bullwinkle, 6", from $10 to **15.00**

Peanuts Characters, McDonald's, 1983, Camp Snoopy, white plastic 8.00

Peanuts Characters, milk glass mug, Snoopy for President, 4 different 8.00

Peanuts Characters, Smuckers, 1994, 3 different, ea from $2 to 4.00

Popeye, Popeye's Famous Fried Chicken, 1978, Sports Scenes, Popeye............................. 10.00

Popeye, Popeye's Famous Fried Chicken, 1979, Pals, 4 different, ea 15.00

Raggedy Ann & Andy, 4 different, ea from $5 to 10.00

Rescuers, Pepsi, 1977, Brockway tumbler, 7 different, ea from $5 to 10.00

Snow White & the Seven Dwarfs, Bosco, 1938, ea from $20 to. 30.00

Star Trek II, The Search for Spock, Taco Bell, 1984, 4 different, ea 5.00

Star Wars, Empire Strikes Back, Burger King/Coca Cola, 1980, 4 designs............................ 7.00

Sunday Funnies, 1976, Brenda Star, Orphan Annie, Smilin' Jack, $5 to 7.00

Super Heroes, DC Comics, NPP/ Pepsi Super (Moon) Series, 1976, Penguin 60.00

Super Heroes, DC Comics or NPP/ Pepsi Super (Moon) Series, 1976, ea 15.00

Super Heroes, Marvel, 1978, Federal, flat bottom, Spider-Man, $40 to 75.00

Super Heroes, Marvel, 1978, Federal, flat bottom, Spider-Woman......................... 150.00

Super Heroes, Marvel/7 Eleven, 1977, footed, Incredible Hulk, $10 to 15.00

Universal Monsters, Universal Studio, 1980, footed, 6 different, ea 150.00

Walter Lantz, Pepsi, 1970-80s, Anty/Miranda, Chilly/Smelly, ea, $20 to 30.00

Walter Lantz, Pepsi, 1970-80s, Cuddles/Oswald, Wally/Homer, ea $20 to 30.00

Walter Lantz, Pepsi, 1970s, Cuddles, from $40 to....... 60.00

Warner Bros, Acme Cola, 1993, bell shape, 4 different, ea from $4 to 8.00

Warner Bros, Marriott's Great America, 1975, 6 different, 12-oz, ea.......................... 30.00

Warner Bros, Pepsi, 1973, Brockway 12-oz tumbler, 5 different, ea.................. 10.00

Warner Bros, Pepsi, 1973, Federal 16-oz tumbler, Henry Hawk, from $25 to 40.00

Warner Bros., Pepsi, 1976, Federal, Slow Poke Rodriguez, black lettering, 6¼", 16-ounce, from $25.00 to $40.00.

Warner Bros, Pepsi, 1976, Interaction, all others, ea from $5 to 10.00

Warner Bros, Pepsi, 1976, Interaction, Bugs & Yosemite w/cannon......................... 15.00

Warner Bros, Pepsi, 1976, Interaction, Foghorn Leghorn & Henry Hawk.............. **15.00**

Warner Bros, Pepsi, 1976, Interaction, Taz & Porky w/fishing pole. **10.00**

Warner Bros, Pepsi, 1976, Interaction, Yosemite & Speedy Gonzales......................... **15.00**

Warner Bros, Pepsi, 1980, Collector Series, various heads on stars, ea....................................... **10.00**

Warner Bros, Six Flags, 1991, clear, 4 different, ea from $5 to. **10.00**

Warner Bros, Welch's, 1974, action poses, phrases at top, any . **4.00**

Warner Bros., Welch's, 1976 – 1978, Tweety Bird, from $5.00 to $7.00.

Warner Bros, 1998, 6 different, vertically striped background, ea. **6.00**

Western Heroes, A Oakley, Buffalo Bill, W Earp, Wild Bill Hickok, ea....................................... **12.00**

Western Heroes, Lone Ranger, from $10 to.............................. **15.00**

Western Heroes, Wyatt Earp, fight scene or OK Corral gunfight, from $12 to **22.00**

Wizard of Oz, Coca-Cola/Krystal, '89, 6 in 50th Anniversary Series, ea **10.00**

Wizard of Oz, Swift's, 1950-60s, fluted bottom, Emerald City, from $8 to **15.00**

Wonderful World of Disney, Pepsi, 1980s, Alice, Bambi, Pinocchio, ea.................................... **20.00**

Wonderful World of Disney, Pepsi, 1980s, Lady & the Tramp, from from $15 to **20.00**

Wonderful World of Disney, Pepsi, 1980s, Snow White/101 Dalmatians, ea................ **20.00**

Character Collectibles

One of the most active areas of collecting today is the field of character collectibles. Flea markets usually yield some of the more common items. Toys, books, lunch boxes, children's dishes, and games of all types are for the most part quite readily found. Disney characters, television personalities, and comic book heroes are among the most sought after.

For more information, refer to *Schroeder's Collectible Toys, Antique to Modern*, published by Collector Books.

In the listings that follow, values are for items in at least excellent condition unless noted otherwise. See also Advertising; Banks; Bubble Bath Containers; Character and Promotional Glassware; Children's Books; Cookie Jars; Games; Lunch Boxes; Novelty Telephones; Puzzles; Radios; Star Trek; Star Wars; Western Heroes.

Alice in Wonderland, board game, Cadaco, 1984, complete .. **20.00**

Alice in Wonderland, makeup kit, cardboard box w/metal closure, 11x6".............................. **50.00**

Bambi, Colorforms, 1966, complete **20.00**

Bambi, figure, celluloid, attached to metal stand, 1940s, 4" **75.00**

Bambi, mirror, plastic frame, w/ friends, 1970s, 24x21"..**175.00**

Big Bird, doll, talker, Playskool, 1970s, 22", VG................**25.00**

Big Bird, hand puppet, plush, Child Guidance, 1980..............**18.00**

Big Bird, jack-in-the-box, 1980s.**15.00**

Bionic Woman, Paint-By-Number Set, Craftmaster, 1970s, MIB................**30.00**

Bionic Woman, See-A-Show Viewer, Kenner, 1970s, MOC........**15.00**

Bozo the Clown, record player, Transogram....................**65.00**

Bozo the Clown, wristwatch, image & name in red, vinyl band, 1960s.............................**50.00**

Bugs Bunny, doll, plush, Mighty Star, 1970s, 20"..............**18.00**

Bugs Bunny, toothbrush holder, pink plastic wall hanger, 1950s, 9x5"........................**65.00**

Bugs Bunny, wall clock, Seth Thomas, 1970, plastic case, electric, 10"......................**85.00**

Bullwinkle, doll, plush, Ideal, 1960, 20", NM...............**75.00**

Bullwinkle, playing cards, complete, 1962, VGIB..........**10.00**

Bullwinkle, stamp set, Larami, 1970, EXIB.................**25.00**

Captain Hook, figure, plastic, 8".**20.00**

Captain Kangaroo, doll, Captain Kangaroo, Mattel, 1960s, MIB................**150.00**

Captain Kangaroo, doll, Mr Green Jeans, stuffed cloth, 1960s, 13", M...........................**30.00**

Captain Kangaroo, TV Eras-O-Board Set, Hasbro, 1950s, EXIB..............................**60.00**

Captain Marvel, Magic Lightning Box, Fawcett, 1940s........**75.00**

Casper the Friendly Ghost, cloth doll, 1960s, 15", EX+.......**50.00**

Casper the Friendly Ghost, push-button puppet, Casper, Kohner...........................**25.00**

Charlie Chaplin, wristwatch, Bradley, Oldies Series, 1985, MIB...............................**50.00**

Charlie's Angels, Target Set, Placo Toys, 1977, MIB, from $60.00 to $80.00.

Charlie's Angels, wallet, vinyl w/ circular image of stars, 1977, MOC...............................**35.00**

Chilly Willy, figure, plush, 1980s.**30.00**

Cinderella, cookie cutter, red plastic, marked HRM, set of 6......**30.00**

Curious George, doll, plush w/ sweater & red hat, Eden Toys, 1980s, 15"......................**15.00**

Dennis the Menace, pinball machine, 5x8".................**10.00**

Dick Tracy, Candid Camera, complete w/film & case, Seymour Sales, 1955.....................**75.00**

Dick Tracy, Sparkle Paints, Kenner, 1963, complete & unused, NMIB.............................**75.00**

Disney, embroidery set, features characters, complete.......**50.00**

Disneyland, Color-By-Number Oil Set, Hasbro #2195, 1950s.**65.00**

Doctor Dolittle, Colorforms Cartoon Kit, 1967, NMIB.............**30.00**

Doctor Dolittle, Stitch-a-Story, Hasbro, NMIP **25.00**

Donald Duck, cookie cutter, red plastic, Loma, 3¾" **7.50**

Donald Duck, egg cup, ceramic, embossed painted image, footed, 4" **65.00**

Donald Duck, handkerchief, sailing w/3 nephews, 1950s, 8¼" sq **28.00**

Donald Duck, magic slate, Whitman, 1970s **25.00**

Donald Duck, nodder, round green base, 1970s **75.00**

Dr Suess, doll, Cat in the Hat, plush, talker, Mattel, 1970s **75.00**

Dr Suess, doll, Thidwick the Moose, plush, Coleco, 1980s **25.00**

Dr Suess, wristwatch, Cat in the Hat, 1972 .... **150.00**

Dumbo the Elephant, cookie cutter, red plastic, Hallmark, 1977, 4" **20.00**

Emmett Kelly Jr, ventriloquist doll, Horsman, 1978, MIB **50.00**

ET, figure, cloth, Showtime, 1980s, 8" **15.00**

Felix the Cat, figure, composition w/jointed arms, 13", VG. **150.00**

Felix the Cat, flashlight, w/whistle, 1960s **75.00**

Flintstones, Give-A-Show Projector, Kenner, 1964, NMIB **100.00**

Flintstones, paint box, Transogram, 1960s **25.00**

Flintstones, Tricky Trapeze, w/Fred figure, Kohner, 1960s, 5". **30.00**

Flipper, magic slate, Lowe, 1960s **25.00**

Flying Nun, doll, vinyl, cloth habit attire, Hasbro, 1967, 12", MIB **350.00**

Freddie Kruger, doll, w/outfits & body parts, Matchbox, 1989, 8½" **50.00**

Garfield, bubble bath container, lying in tub, Kid Care **10.00**

Garfield, figure, golfer, plush, Dakin, 1980s, 10" **15.00**

Garfield, figure, Halloween witch, plush, Dakin, 1980s, 10½"..**15.00**

Garfield, figure, w/bunny ears, plush, Dakin, 1980s, 4½". **12.00**

Garfield, figurine, Nurses Call the Shots, porcelain, 1981, 3". **23.00**

Garfield, gumball machine, I'll Share But..., plastic, Superior Toy **32.00**

Garfield, lunch box, plastic, 1980s **20.00**

Garfield, music box, Swingin' in the Rain, plastic, Enesco, 7½". **38.00**

Garfield, salt and pepper shakers, Enesco, c 1978 – 1981 United Feature Syndicate Inc., from $35.00 to $45.00. (Photo courtesy Joyce and Fred Roerig)

Garfield, snow dome, as Santa pointing, Enesco, 1980s .. **15.00**

Garfield, teapot, crouching w/mouse finial, ceramic, 29-oz, 6½". **25.00**

Garfield, teapot, holding fish (spout), ceramic, 6" **25.00**

Garfield, tote bag, gray canvas w/red trim, Thermos, 1980s **15.00**

Garfield, tumbler, drink coming out of ears, glass, Goosh, 1978, 5x2" **15.00**

Garfield, wristwatch, face image, Armitron, MIB **25.00**

Goofy, doll, Schuco, 1950s, 14". **350.00**

Gremlins, doll, Gizmo, plush, Hasbro Softies, 1980s, scarce, 12" **25.00**

Gumby & Pokey, bendable figure, Gumby, Applause, 1980s, 5½" **15.00**

Gumby & Pokey, jeep, lithographed tin, Lakeside, 1960s **150.00**

Happy Days, doll, Fonz, stuffed cloth, Samet & Wells, 1976, 16", M **50.00**

Heckle & Jeckle, figures, soft foam, 7", pr **75.00**

Heckle & Jeckle, 3-D Target Game, Aldon Ind/Terrytoons/CBS, 1955, EXIB **50.00**

Honeymooners, dolls, any character, Exclusive Premiere, 9", MIB **25.00**

Howdy Doody, bank, Mr Bluster, plastic w/flocking, Strauss, 1970s, 9" **65.00**

Howdy Doody, earmuffs, furry w/ molded head images, 1950s, VG **50.00**

Howdy Doody, rings, Action (flasher), 8 characters, Nabisco, 1960, ea **20.00**

Howdy Doody, swim ring, inflatable plastic, Ideal, 1950s, 21". **50.00**

Huckleberry Hound, ED-U-Cards, 1961, VGIB **15.00**

Huckleberry Hound, squeeze rubber figure, w/cane & hat, Dell, 1965, 6" **50.00**

Hulk Hogan, Colorforms Sparkle Art, 1991, MIB **15.00**

Hulk Hogan, doll, vinyl with cloth outfit & cape, 1980s, 18", MIB **100.00**

Humpty Dumpty, rubber squeak toy, seated on wall, 1960s, 7" **35.00**

Incredible Hulk, metal TV tray, Hulk walking street, retangular, 1979 .... **25.00**

James Bond 007, Electric Drawing Set, Lakeside, 1960s, MIB **200.00**

James Bond 007, wall clock, 1981, Roger Moore image **50.00**

Jetsons, Slate & Chalk Set, 1960s, unused, MIB **100.00**

Jiminy Cricket, figure, ceramic, tipping hat, Walt Disney, 1960s, 3" **30.00**

Joker, wristwatch, Fossil, 1980s, NMIP **75.00**

Josie & the Pussycats, Slicker Ticker Play Watch, Larami, 1973, MOC **25.00**

Jungle Book, doll, Baloo, plush, 12" **20.00**

Jungle Book, doll, Mowgli, vinyl, Holland Hill, 1960s, 8" ... **25.00**

King Kong, doll, talker, Mattel, 1966, 12" **150.00**

King Kong, Jungle Set w/Magnetic Action Hand, Multiple, 1967, NMIB **250.00**

King Leonardo, doll, stuffed cloth w/royal attire, Holiday Fair, 1960s **75.00**

Kliban, apron, Love To Eat Them Mousies, bib style, cat on stool **40.00**

Kliban, bank, cat in red shoes, Sigma, 1970s, 6", from $45 to **60.00**

Kliban, box, sitting on top hat, Sigma, from $75 to **85.00**

Kliban, brooch, walking cat, enameled, 1½" L **25.00**

Kliban, bud vase, cat climbing tree to reach owl, Japan, 8" ... **75.00**

Kliban, cookie jar, in top hat, paw on brim, red kiss on cheek, 8". **100.00**

Kliban, cookie jar, Momcat w/baby in pouch, Sigma, 11" **250.00**

Kliban, covered dish, white tub as base, cat, mouse & blue water lid **110.00**

Kliban, ice bucket, plastic, all-over cats, Sigma, 1970s, 16x8½".**45.00**

Kliban, jar, cat w/guitar sits on red stool, Sigma **90.00**

Kliban, mug, cat in Santa hat as handle, Sigma **40.00**

Kliban, mug, I (heart) LA, MIB.**22.50**

Kliban, mug, Love To Eat Them Mousies, cat w/guitar **28.00**

Kliban, napkins, cloth, cat w/red roses, 18x18", set of 4 ..... **50.00**

Kliban, ornament, Santa cat as engineer, white train, 2¼x3" ... **32.00**

Kliban, paperweight, Aloha Cat, steel.................................. **8.00**

Kliban, picture frame, clinging from upper corner, Sigma, 9¼x7¼" **60.00**

Kliban, pillow, Momcat shape, mom w/baby in pouch, 18x11", NM................................. **35.00**

Kliban, pillow, walking cat shape, 17x10" **28.00**

Kliban, poster, Momcat, 1977, 24x18" **15.00**

Kliban, puzzle, chef w/fry pan, Great American Puzzle, 100-pc . **20.00**

Kliban, rubber stamp, leapfrogging cats, discontinued **35.00**

Kliban, salt & pepper shakers, walking cats in red shoes, 2", pr.................................... **50.00**

Kliban, T-shirt, Florida Yacht Cats, SS Feliner....................... **35.00**

Kliban, T-shirt, Santa cat on front, reindeer on back **65.00**

Kliban, teapot, Red Baron flying prop airplane, tail is handle, Sigma............................ **495.00**

Kliban, wall clock, Super Cat flies over city, plastic, non-working................................... **45.00**

Kliban, wall plaque, rectangular w/ embossed cat **80.00**

Kliban, wastebasket, walking cat on white plastic, 12x9" ... **22.00**

Koko the Clown, hand puppet, Gund/Out of the Inkwell, 1962, rare, 11" **100.00**

Land of Lost, Secret Look Out, Larami, 1975, MOC **40.00**

Lassie, doll, plush w/vinyl face, metal collar, Knickerbocker, 1966, 24" **50.00**

Laurel & Hardy, doll, Oliver, vinyl, 1950s, 13", VG................. **70.00**

Laurel and Hardy, figures, hand-painted hard plastic, 1971, 16", from $125.00 to $150.00 for the pair.

Laurel & Hardy, TV set, w/filmstrips, 1970s **30.00**

Linus as Baseball Catcher, nodder, ceramic, Japan **60.00**

Little House on the Prairie, Colorforms Playset, 1978, MIB **35.00**

Little House on the Prairie, doll, Laura, Knickerbocker, 1978, MIB **35.00**

Little Orphan Annie, cloth doll, Knickerbocker, 1982, 16".**15.00**

Little Orphan Annie, Colorforms, 1968, NMIB....................**30.00**

Little Red Riding Hood, tea set, litho tin, Ohio Art, 1960s, 11 pcs, M............................**100.00**

Magilla Gorilla, doll, cloth w/plastic head, 1960s, 11".........**75.00**

Man From UNCLE, flicker ring, silver plastic, w/photos, 1960s............................**20.00**

Man From UNCLE, Secret Print Putty, Colorforms, 1965, MOC............................**50.00**

Mary Poppins, figure, bendable, Gund, 12"........................**60.00**

Mary Poppins, nodder, wood, w/ umbrella & satchel, Disneyland, 1960, 6"........................**125.00**

Mickey & Minnie Mouse, candy dish, lustreware, figures on white, 6"........................**110.00**

Mickey Mouse, baby rattle, celluloid beads, bells for feet, 3½"...**50.00**

Mickey Mouse, bank, ceramic head, 1950s, 6", EX+..................**50.00**

Mickey Mouse, Candy Factory, Remco, 1973....................**75.00**

Mickey Mouse, Cut-Out Scissors, Walt Disney Enterprises, 1930s............................**250.00**

Mickey Mouse, figure, ceramic, standing, Enesco, 1960s, 5", EX....................................**35.00**

Mickey Mouse, figure, stuffed, button eyes, Dean's/England, 6".**300.00**

Mickey Mouse, figure, stuffed talker, Hasbro, 1970s, 8", NM+ ..**50.00**

Mickey Mouse, marionette, Pelham, 11"................................**150.00**

Mickey Mouse, nodder, yellow & red outfit, round green base...**75.00**

Mighty Mouse, flashlight, figural, Dyno, 1970s, 3½"............**30.00**

Mighty Mouse, Picture Play Lite, Janex, 1980s....................**10.00**

Minnie Mouse, wall pocket, head form, Disneyland, 1970s.**100.00**

Miss Piggy, figure, bendable, Just Toys, 5"............................**5.00**

Miss Piggy, plush doll, black gown, w/gloves, Applause, 1988, 12", MIP....................................**15.00**

Mork & Mindy, doll, Mindy, jeans & red sweater, Mattel, 1979, 9", MIB....................................**50.00**

Mork & Mindy, doll, Mork, red spacesuit, Mattel, 1979, 9", MIB....................................**50.00**

Mousketeer, figure, Horsman, 1960s, 8"........................**150.00**

Mousketeer, figure, vinyl, blond girl, all original, Horseman.....**45.00**

Mr Magoo, doll, cloth w/vinyl head, Ideal, 1960s, 5"..............**75.00**

Munsters, doll, any character, Presents, 1980s, 10" to 13", MIB..........**65.00**

Munsters, doll, Herman, talker, Mattel, 1964, rare, 20", MIB...........**450.00**

Munsters, flicker ring, Lily's name/ photo, chrome band, 1960s.**20.00**

Mutt & Jeff, figure set, celluloid, Stasco, 5¾" & 4½", VG ..**100.00**

My Favorite Martian, felt beanie, antennae w/bells, Benay Albee, 1960s............................**75.00**

New Zoo Revue, figure, any character, Rushton, 1970s, ea from $25 to **30.00**

Partridge Family, wristwatch, family image on face, 1970s, from $150 to **200.00**

Peanuts, animation cel, Snoopy under the stars, double matted, 14x11"......................**50.00**

Peanuts, bank, Charlie Brown standing, ceramic, Italy, c 1968, 7"................. **165.00**

Peanuts, bank, Snoopy atop lg red strawberry, ceramic, 4¾".............................**35.00**

Peanuts, camera, Snoopy Matic (on doghouse), plastic, Helm Toy, VGIB.............. **55.00**

Peanuts, charm, Snoopy opening presents, Aviva............... **25.00**

Peanuts, chest, w/gang, particle board w/metal overlay, 20" L, VG................................. **65.00**

Peanuts, cookie jar, Snoopy seated, ceramic, 1950s, 12"......... **42.00**

Peanuts, coverlet, the gang in multicolor on yellow, cotton, 1971.............................. **30.00**

Peanuts, cuff links, Charlie Brown w/catcher's mit, Aviva, c 1965............................**18.00**

Peanuts, doll, Linus, Hungerford, c 1958, 8½"........................ **45.00**

Peanuts, doll, Linus, vinyl, jointed, 1966, 7", VG+.................. **25.00**

Peanuts, doll, Peppermint Patty, foam-stuffed, Determined, 1970s, MIP..................... **35.00**

Peanuts, doll, Snoopy seated, painted vinyl, Made in Mexico, 7"....................................**24.00**

Peanuts, earring tree, Snoopy/ Woodstock/doghouse, enameled metal, 5"................. **20.00**

Peanuts, jack-in-the-box, Snoopy, Mattel, 1976.................... **40.00**

Peanuts, magnets, rubber, 2 ea of 12 character poses, MOC......................... **72.00**

Peanuts, mug, Charlie Brown dancing, Snoopy watching, Fire-King.............................. **25.00**

Peanuts, mug, Snoopy dreams of ice cream, suckers, etc, Fire-King, 4"...........................**28.00**

Peanuts, music box, Easter Beagle Snoopy w/basket of eggs, Schmid, 7"...................... **85.00**

Peanuts, ornament, Snoopy w/ drum, ceramic, Made in Japan label, 2½"........................ **60.00**

Peanuts, pennant, Charlie Brown, I Need All..., c 1967, 35x14"..**15.00**

Peanuts, piano, Schroeder's, Child Guidance, 1970s............ **100.00**

Peanuts, pin, Soopy holding Woodstock & 2 Rah, Rah flags, Aviva, 1"........................ **100.00**

Peanuts, pocket doll, Lucy, vinyl, Boucher, c 1966, 7"......... **18.00**

Peanuts, rug, w/the gang, rubber-backed nylon, Jay Fanco, 1900, 20x30"............................. **42.00**

Peanuts, Snoopy Snippers Scissors, plastic, Mattel #7410, 1970s **50.00**

Peanuts, Snoopy/Lucy kiss in round reserve on yellow, ceramic..**25.00**

Peanuts, sweatshirt, Charlie Brown, yellow, I Need All Friends **135.00**

Peanuts, tea set, lithographed tin, Chein, 1970s, complete... **75.00**

Peanuts, telephone, Snoopy Joe Cool/Woodstock, brick wall, Seika, 1972..................... **38.00**

Peanuts, vase, Snoopy, ceramic, Determined, 1970s – 1980s, 4½", from $20.00 to $30.00. (Photo courtesy whatacharacter.com)

Peanuts, telephone, Snoopy/ Woodstock stand on red base, yellow earpiece **65.00**

Peanuts, wastebasket, tin, Charlie Brown/Snoopy on red **20.00**

Peanuts, watch, Snoopy w/tennis racket, Schulz '58, stainless steel bk **22.50**

Peanuts, wristwatch, dancing Snoopy, Determined, various bands, 1969 .... **100.00**

Phantom, camera, Larami, 1970s **75.00**

Pink Panther, plush doll, Mighty Star, 1984, 12" **25.00**

Pink Panther, toothbrush holder, ceramic, figure seated, 1970s, 5" **55.00**

Pinky Lee, serving tray, tin w/photo image, 1950s, 10x14" **30.00**

Pinocchio, figure, bisque, Japan, 1940s, 4" **100.00**

Pinocchio, hand puppet, Knickerbocker, 1962 ...... **50.00**

Popeye, figure, bendy type, Jesco, 1980s **12.00**

Popeye, push-button puppet, Kohner, 1960s, 4" **50.00**

Popeye, tambourine, Larami, 1980s. **8.00**

Popeye, tugboat, inflatable vinyl, Ideal, 1960s, MIP **50.00**

Popeye, wallet, Offical, KFS, 1950s... **20.00**

Popeye, wristwatch, Unique, digital, 1987, NMIB **50.00**

Porky Pig, doll, cloth w/vinyl head, Mattel, 1960s, 17" **25.00**

Porky Pig, jack-in-the-box, Mattel, 1960s **100.00**

Rocky, plush doll, Rocky & Friends, Wallace Berrie, 1982, w/tag, 12" **25.00**

Rocky & Friends, Colorforms Cartoon Kit, 1960s, EXIB **75.00**

Roy Rogers, nodder, compo, sq green base, Japan, 1960s, M, $150 to **200.00**

Ruff & Reddy, Karbon Kopee, Wonder Kit, 1960, EXIB. **75.00**

Scooby Doo, gumball machine, plastic head, Hasbro, 1968.... **25.00**

Scooby Doo, plush doll, seated on haunches, Sutton, 1970, 8".**32.00**

Simpons, doll, any character, stuffed cloth, Dan-Dee, 11" **18.00**

Six Million Dollar Man, waste can, metal w/lithoed images, 1976 ....**25.00**

Smurfs, Colorforms, EXIB **25.00**

Smurfs, pail, plastic, 1-qt, 1981, VG+ **15.00**

Smurfs, record player, Vanity Fair, 1982, EXIB **75.00**

Smurfs, sewing cards, MIB (sealed) **25.00**

Snow White, figure, chalkware, w/glitter accents, 1940-50s, 15" **75.00**

Snow White & the Seven Dwarfs, figure set, bisque, Geo Borgfeldt/Japan............. **440.00**

Speedy Gonzales, figure, vinyl w/cloth outfit, Dakin, 1970, 8"........**30.00**

Spider-Man, finger puppet, 1970 .... **15.00**

Spider-Man, plastic squirt gun, head shape, 1974 .... **25.00**

Spider-Man, walkie-talkies, plastic, battery-op, Nasta, 1984, MIB **50.00**

Starsky & Hutch, dashboard set, 1976 .... **40.00**

Starsky & Hutch, Shoot-Out Target Set, Berwick, 1977, MIB. **75.00**

Steve Urkle, doll, talker, Hasbro, 1991, 18", MIB **50.00**

Super Mario, doll, beanbag type, scarce, 7".......................... **12.00**

Superman, horseshoe set, Super Swim Inc, 1950s, EXIB. **100.00**

Superman, pencil box, Mattel, 1966 .... **35.00**

Superman, plastic water pistol, Multiple Toys, 1960s, MIP. **175.00**

Superman, plush doll, Acme, 1988, 11" **10.00**

Superman, record player, suitcase type w/latch, illustrated, 1970s **75.00**

Superman, stamp set, 6 character stamps, 1960s, EXIP **30.00**

Superman, toothbrush, battery-op, Janex, 1970s **25.00**

Superman, wristwatch, chrome, w/flying Superman, Bradley, 1959, EXIB **700.00**

Superman, wristwatch, Dabbs. **100.00**

Superman & Supergirl, push-button puppet set, Kohner, 1960s, EXIB **175.00**

Sword & the Stone, party decorations, Disney, 1963, unopened **18.00**

Tasmanian Devil (Looney Tunes), plush doll, Mighty Star, 1970s, 13", M **50.00**

Teenage Mutant Ninja Turtles, doll, cloth, ACE, 1989, 8", M **8.00**

The Nanny (TV Series), doll, talker, Street Players, 12", MIB. **65.00**

Three Stooges, dolls, any character, Presents, 1988, 14", M.... **65.00**

Three Stooges, nodder, bisque, set of 3, from $100 to **150.00**

Timon, spoon rest, Lion King, Treasure Craft................ **20.00**

Tom & Jerry, figures, stuffed cloth w/linen faces, 17" & 7½", pr **150.00**

Tom & Jerry, mug, ceramic, shows Jerry tying bomb to Tom, MGM, 3¼" **30.00**

Tom & Jerry, Musical Guitar, Mattel Toys, MGM, 1960s **150.00**

Tom Corbett Space Cadet, Model-Craft Molding & Coloring Set, EXIB **100.00**

Topo Gigio, nodder, w/fruit or w/o fruit, ea **75.00**

Tweety Bird, hand puppet, Zany, 1940s **75.00**

Tweety Bird, ring, plastic, flashes 2 different Tweety poses **15.00**

Umbriago, hand puppet, cloth & ceramic, American Merchandise, 1940s, M... **75.00**

Uncle Scrooge, bank, ceramic, head figure, Cuernavaca/Walt Disney, 11" **950.00**

Underdog, bank, vinyl figure, Play Pal, 1973, 11" **85.00**

Universal Monsters, nightlights, set of 4 different monsters **50.00**

Universal Monsters, pencil sharpener, Wolfman, plastic, UP Co, 3" **25.00**

V (TV Series), Bop Bag, vinyl, 1970s, MIB **30.00**

Vincent Van Gopher, doll, plush w/ vinyl head, felt hands, Ideal, 1961 .... **35.00**

Wally Walrus, wall plaque, figure w/cane, Napco, 1958, 7".. **75.00**

Waltons, Farmhouse Playset, w/ cardboard figures, Amsco, 1975, MIB **75.00**

Welcome Back Kotter, Classroom Playset, for 10" dolls, Mattel, 1976 .... **50.00**

Welcome Back Kotter, magic slate, 2 different, Whitman, 1977, M, ea..................................... **20.00**

Winnie the Pooh, bank, Pooh's Honey Bank on pot, Enesco, 1964, 6"............................ **85.00**

Winnie the Pooh, cookie cutter, yellow plastic, 4¼" **20.00**

Winnie the Pooh, pencil sharpener, ceramic Enesco/Walt Disney, 5" **60.00**

Wizard of Oz, doll, Dorothy, Effanbee (Legend Series), 1984, 15", NMIB **125.00**

Wizard of Oz, Paint w/Crayons Set, w/4 pictures, Art Award, 1989, NMIB **15.00**

Wizard of Oz, pocket watch, dial w/4 characters, Westclock, 1980s, MIB **75.00**

Wizard of Oz, soap figures, 4 different, Kerk Guild, 1939, set **150.00**

Wonder Woman, place mat, vinyl face shape w/color image, 1977................................. **15.00**

Woody Woodpecker, hand puppet, talker, Mattel, 1963 .... **45.00**

Woody Woodpecker, Mattel Music Maker, lithographed tin, 1960s, VG.................................... **50.00**

Yogi Bear, bubble pipe, plastic figure, 1965, MIP **35.00**

Children's Books

Books were popular gifts for children in the latter 1800s; many were beautifully illustrated, some by notable artists such as Frances Brundage and Maxfield Parrish. From this century tales of Tarzan by Burroughs are very collectible, as are those familiar childhood series books — for example, The Bobbsey Twins and Nancy Drew.

Big Little Books

Probably everyone who is now 60 and over owned a few Big Little Books as a child. Today these thick hand-sized adventures bring prices from $10.00 to $75.00 and upwards. The first was published in 1933 by Whitman Publishing Company. Dick Tracy was the featured character. Kids of the early '50s preferred the format of the comic book, and the Big Little Books were gradually phased out. Stories about super heroes and Disney characters bring the highest prices, especially those with an early copyright.

Ace Drummond, Whitman #1177, 1935, EX **18.00**

Adventures of Huckleberry Finn, Whitman #1422, NM **40.00**

Alice in Wonderland, Whitman #759, 1933, NM............. **100.00**

Big Chief Wahoo & the Magic Lamp, Whitman #1483,1940, NM **35.00**

Billy the Kid, Whitman #773, 1935, EX **35.00**

Buck Jones in Ride 'Em Cowboy, **1937, EX+, $75.00.** (Photo courtesy gasolinealleyantiques. com)

Bugs Bunny All Pictures Comics, Whitman #1435, 1944, EX.**30.00**

Convoy Patrol, Whitman #1446, NM **20.00**

Dick Tracy & the Stolen Bonds, 1934, EX **65.00**

Don Winslow & the Giant Girl Spy, Whitman #1408, EX **30.00**

Freckles & the Lost Diamond Mine, Whitman #1164, EX **35.00**

Gene Autry & the Land Grab Mystery, Whitman #1439, NM **40.00**

Ghost Avenger, 1943, VG **18.00**

Goofy in Giant Trouble, Whitman, 1968, NM **10.00**

Ken Maynard in Gun Justice, 1934, VG **40.00**

Mutt & Jeff, Whitman #1113, NM **75.00**

Nancy & Sluggo, 1946, EX+ .. **45.00**

Og Son of Fire, Whitman #1115, NM **50.00**

Porky Pig & Petunia, 1942, EX+ . **60.00**

Tarzan & the Golden Lion, Whitman #1448, NM **75.00**

Tim McCoy in the Prescot Kid, 1935, EX+ **75.00**

Treasure Island, Whitman #720, 1933, G- **20.00**

Zip Sanders King of the Speedway, Whitman #1465, EX **20.00**

Little Golden Books

Little Golden Books (a registered trademark of Western Publishing Company Inc.), introduced in October of 1942, were an overnight success. First published with a blue paper spine, the later spines were of gold foil. Parents and grandparents born in the '40s, '50s, and '60s are now trying to find the titles they had as children. From 1942 to the early 1970s, the books were numbered from 1 to 600, while books published later had no numerical order. Depending on where you find the book, prices can vary from 25¢ to $30.00 plus. The most expensive are those with dust jackets from the early '40s or books with paper dolls and activities. The three primary series of books are the Regular (1 – 600), Disney (1 – 140), and Activity (1 – 52).

Television's influence became apparent in the '50s with stories like the Lone Ranger, Howdy Doody, Hopalong Cassidy, Gene Autry, and Rootie Kazootie. The '60s brought us Yogi Bear, Huckleberry Hound, Magilla Gorilla, and Quick Draw McGraw, to name but a few. Condition is very important when purchasing a book. You normally don't want to purchase a book with large tears, crayon or ink marks, or missing pages.

As with any collectible book, a first edition is always going to bring the higher price. To determine what edition you have on the 25¢ and 29¢ cover price books, look on the title page or the last page of the book. If it is not on the title page, there will be a code of 1/(a letter of the alphabet) on the bottom right corner of the last page. A is for 1st edition, Z would refer to the twenty-sixth printing.

There isn't an easy way of determining the condition of a book. What is 'good' to one might be 'fair' to another. A played-with book in average condition is generally worth only half as much as one in mint, like-new condition. To find out more about Little Golden Books, we recommend *Collecting Little Golden Books* (published by Books Americana) by Steve Santi.

All Aboard!, #152, A edition, 1952, 28 pgs, VG+ **15.00**

Baby's Book, #10, 1st edition, 1942, 42 pgs, VG+ **35.00**

Dale Evans & the Lost Gold Mine, #213, A edition, 1954, 28 pgs, NM **25.00**

Emerald City of Oz, #151, A edition, 1952, 28 pgs, EX **40.00**

Golden Book of Fairy Tales, #9, A edition, 1942, 42 pgs, EX+ . **42.00**

Hansel & Gretel, #17, A edition, 1943, 42 pgs, EX **25.00**

House That Jack Built, #218, A edition, 1954, 28 pgs, EX+ .. **12.00**

How Big, #83, A edition, 1948, 28 pgs, VG **15.00**

Little Yip-Yip, #73, A edition, 1950, 42 pgs, EX+ **18.00**

Lively Little Rabbit, **Ariane, limited edition, twelfth printing, first cover, 1943, VG, $18.00.** (Photo courtesy gaso linealleyantiques.com)

Lone Ranger & Tonto, #297, A edition, 1957, 24 pgs, VG **18.00**

Night Before Christmas #20, A edition, 1946, 42 pgs, EX..... **20.00**

Party Pig, #191, A edition, 1954, 28 pgs, VG **20.00**

Road to Oz, #144, A edition, 1951, 28 pgs, VG **22.00**

Sailor Dog, #156, A edition, 1953, 28 pgs, VG **20.00**

Steve Canyon, #356, A edition, 1959, 24 pgs, EX+ **20.00**

Uncle Wiggily, #148, A edition, 1953, 28 pgs, VG+ **18.00**

Where Jesus Lived, #147, A edition, 1977, 24 pgs, NM+ **8.00**

Wild Kingdom, #151, A edition, 1976, 24 pgs, NM+ **8.00**

Series Books

Bargain for Frances, R Hoban, I Can Read Book, Harper & Row, 1970, EX **25.00**

Black Stallion Returns, W Farley, Random House, hardback, 1983, EX **15.00**

Bobbsey Twins & Their Schoolmates, LL Hope, Grosset & Dunlap, 1928, G+ **10.00**

Bobbsey Twins Merry Days Indoors & Out, LL Hope, Whitman, 1950, VG **6.00**

Cherry Ames Army Nurse, Tatham, Grosset & Dunlap, 1959, EX w/ jacket **25.00**

Cherry Ames Flight Nurse, Tatham, Grosset & Dunlap, 1955, G w/ jacket **15.00**

Chip Hilton Strike 3!, Bee, Grosset & Dunlap, picture cover, 1963, VG **25.00**

Dana Girls Clue in Cobweb, Keene, Grosset & Dunlap, picture cover, VG **20.00**

Dana Girls Clue in Ivy, Keene, Grosset & Dunlap, picture cover, EX.......................... **45.00**

Hardy Boss Tower Treasure, Stratemeyer Syndicate, 1959, G, no jacket **30.00**

Hardy Boys Figure in Hiding, #16, F Dixon, picture cover, 1978, EX **8.00**

Jim Forest & the Flood, Rambeau, Harr Wagner, hardback, 1959, EX **10.00**

Judy Bolton Mystic Ball, M Sutton, Grosset & Dunlap, 1943, EX w/ jacket **40.00**

Ken Holt Clue of Coiled Cobra, Grosset & Dunlap, 1956, EX w/ jacket **55.00**

Lassie & the Fire Fighters, F Michelson, Whitman, 1968, EX **12.50**

Little Men, LM Alcott, World Publishing, hardback, 1950, EX w/jacket **10.00**

Little Women, LM Alcott, Modern Abridged Edition, Whitman, 1955, EX **8.00**

Mary Jane, Her Visit; CI Judson, green cloth hardback cover, 1918, G **20.00**

Nancy Drew Clue in Old Album, #24, Grosset & Dunlap, 1947, EX w/jacket **30.00**

Nancy Drew Haunted Showboat, #35, Grosset & Dunlap, 1958, EX w/jacket **85.00**

Rick Brant Sea Gold, Blaine, Grosset & Dunlap, picture cover, 1963, EX...............**15.00**

Ruth Felding on Cliff Island, Emerson, Cupples & Leon, 1929, VG..........................**20.00**

Tom Swift Black Lagoon, Sormanti cover, Archway, paperback, 1991, VG...........................**5.00**

Trixie Belden Black Jacket Mystery, Kenny, Whitman, picture cover, EX **30.00**

Trixie Belden Gatehouse Mystery, J Campbell, Golden Press, 1985, EX **15.00**

Whitman

The Whitman Company pro-duced several series of children's books, many of which centered around radio, TV, and comic strips. Among them were Tell-A-Tales, Tiny-Tot-Tales, Top-Tot-Tales, and Big Little Books (which are in their own sub category.)

ABC, #80815, 1950s, EX........**25.00**

Baby's First Book, Evelyn Swetnam, #2422, 1970s, VG...........**20.00**

Bingo, D Hogstrom, #2576, 1975, EX...................................**20.00**

Child's Ten Commandments, Jo B Regan, #2624, 1960s, G....**8.00**

Fluffy & Tuffy the Twin Ducklings, McKean, #87215, 1950s, EX **30.00**

Gene Autry & the Lost Dogie, #932, 1950s, EX **20.00**

I Like to See, Tymms, #2422, 1980s, G.....................................**10.00**

Little Gray Rabbit, #2463, F print-ing, EX...............................**8.00**

Little Joe's Puppy, Haas, #2622, 1980s, VG **12.00**

My Little Book of Cats, #2626, 1970s, EX **12.00**

Nursery Rhymes, #2605, 1960s, G **4.00**

Peter Pan & the Tiger, #2616, 1970s, G-............................**2.50**

Rainy Day Story: On the Farm, #858, 1940s, VG **15.00**

Rowdy, Jane Wyatt, #861, 1940s, EX **30.00**

Too Many Kittens, #2452, 1960s, VG...................................**5.00**

Wonder Books

Though the first were a little larger, the Wonder Books printed since 1948 have all measured 6½" x 8". They've been distributed by Random House, Grosset Dunlap, and Wonder Books Inc. They're becoming very collectible, especially those based on favorite TV and cartoon characters. Steve Santi's book *Collecting Little Golden Books* includes a section on Wonder Books as well.

Baby's First Christmas, #738, 1960s, EX+ 25.00

Christmas Puppy, #819, 1980, EX. 15.00

Hide & Seek Duck, #568, 1970s, EX 20.00

Mighty Mouse & the Scared Scarecrow, #678, 1950s, EX+ 25.00

Romper Room Laughing Book, 1970s, VG 20.00

Surprise for Mrs Bunny, Steiner, #601, 1953, EX 25.00

Ten Little Fingers, P Pointer, #714, VG 20.00

Wonder Book of Fireman & Fire Engines, #687, 1977, VG .. 8.00

Miscellaneous

ABC for the Library, Little, Antheneum, hardcover, 1975, EX 10.00

Book of Cowboys, Holling, Platt & Munk, cloth hardcover, 1936, EX 18.50

Born To Trot, M Henry, Rand McNally, hardcover, 1950, 1st edition, G- 20.00

Chuck Squirrel, Goldsmith Publishing, die-cut hardcover, 1922, EX 30.00

Fight of the Pueblo, CJ Cannon, Houghton, hardcover, 1934, EX 25.00

Here's to You Charlie Brown, Schulz, hardcover, 1970, EX+ 8.00

Home Is North, W Morey, EP Dutton, hardcover, 1st edition, 1967, VG 20.00

I Am a Bunny, Scarry, Golden Sturdy Book, hardcover, 1963, EX 25.00

Mickey Mouse Fire Brigade, Disney, hardcover, 1930s, EX 75.00

Mr Putterbee's Jungle, R Helm, Oxford University, hardcover, 1953, VG 15.00

My Picture Story Book, Platt & Munk, hardcover, 1941, EX 40.00

Pooh Story Book, Milne, Shepard, EP Dutton, hardcover, 1965, VG+ 25.00

Riley Fairy Tales, JW Riley, Bobbs Merrill, 1923, EX 30.00

Shifting Winds, L Ware, McGraw-Hill, hardcover, 1948, G.. 10.00

Stuart Little, EB White, Williams, hardcover, 1945, VG w/ jacket 28.00

The Tidy Hen, **Antony Groves-Raines, Harcourt Brace, first edition, 1961, $20.00 (with dust jacket, $35.00).** (Photo courtesy Diane McClure Jones and Rosemary Jones)

Tubby the Tuba, Treasure Books, 1950s, EX 22.00

Uncle Remus Stories, JC Harris, Saalfield, trade paperback, 1934, G- 35.00

Your Friend the Policeman, Miss Frances, Ding Dong School, 1953, EX+ **8.00**

Christmas Collectibles

No other holiday season is celebrated to such an extravagant extent as Christmas, and vintage decorations provide a warmth and charm that none from today can match. Ornaments from before 1870 were imported from Dresden, Germany. They were usually made of cardboard and sparkled with tinsel trim. Later, blown glass ornaments were made there in literally thousands of shapes such as fruits and vegetables, clowns, Santas, angels, and animals. Kugles, heavy glass balls (though you'll sometimes find fruit and vegetable forms as well) were made from about 1820 to late in the century in sizes up to 14". Early Santa figures are treasured, especially those in robes other than red. Figural bulbs from the '20s and '30s are popular, those that are character related in particular. Refer to *Pictorial Guide to Christmas Ornaments & Collectibles* by George Johnson, published by Collector Books. Unless otherwise noted, our values are for examples in excellent to near mint condition.

Bubble light, Noma 8-Tube Snap Over, Noma of England, 1956 .... **150.00**
Bulb, baby in stocking, clear glass, mini, Japan, 1¾" **30.00**

Bulb, bell w/trees, clear glass, 3". **15.00**
Bulb, cat in evening gown, milk glass, Japan, ca 1950, 3". **175.00**
Bulb, cottage on hillside, milk glass, Japan, ca 1950, 2¼" **60.00**
Bulb, dog in basket frowning, clear glass, ca 1950, 2¾" **40.00**
Bulb, fish in fishbowl, milk glass, Japan, 1¾" **35.00**
Bulb, Jiminy Cricket, milk glass, Diamond Brite, Japan, ca 1970, 2" **16.00**
Bulb, lion w/tennis racket, milk glass, Japan, ca 1935-55, 2¾" **30.00**
Bulb, log cabin w/snow, clear glass, ca 1950, 2" **18.00**
Bulb, ocean liner, milk glass, many details, Japan, ca 1950 . **100.00**
Bulb, owl in vest & top hat, clear glass, Japan, 2¼" **110.00**
Bulb, pig in suit, lg head, milk glass, Japan, ca 1950, 2¾" **60.00**
Bulb, pig playing tuba, clear glass, ca 1950, 2¾" **200.00**
Bulb, seashell, milk glass, ca 1945, 2" **40.00**
Bulb, soccer player, milk glass, Japan, ca 1950, 2½" **85.00**
Candle set, Kandle Lamps, NY Merchandising Co, 8-light, 1955, MIB **50.00**
Candle set, 9 bubble-light candles on base, Royal Electric #790, 1948 .... **150.00**
Candle tree, brush type, revolves, Glolite, ca 1955, 14" **50.00**
Candle tree, Bubble Glo, Glolite #601, ca 1949, 16" **75.00**
Candy container, boot, red plastic, 1950s, 2¾" **10.00**
Candy container, clock, printed paper, 4" **125.00**

Candy container, hatbox, printed paper, sm, 1¾"................**40.00**

Candy container, Santa in sleigh, red & white plastic, 1950s, 4x4"....................**35.00**

Candy container, suitcase, pressed paper, 4"........................**65.00**

Decoration, angel child, plastic, late 1940s-50s, 1¾x2¼".....**5.00**

Decoration, choir girl w/candle light, Japan, 1960, 9½"...**15.00**

Decoration, nativity scene, Paylite #577M, ca 1954, 15" L..**150.00**

Jack-in-the-box Santa in a boot, plastic and fabric, 7", from $35.00 to $45.00. (Photo courtesy George Johnson)

Light cover, Santa w/hands on stomach, plastic, ca 1950, 4¾"...................**18.00**

Light display, 8 mini socket stars on streaming stems, Microstar, '50s....................**30.00**

Lighting set, Noma Sno-Ball, #3437, 1959, MIB...........**25.00**

Nightlight, Rudolph, EMC Art, 12" L.........................**50.00**

Ornament, comet, painted glass, 3¼".....................**45.00**

Ornament, dove, spun cotton w/ paper wings, Japan, 5½".**30.00**

Ornament, gingerbread house, porcelain, 3".........................**50.00**

Ornament, heart on heart, gold on silver, 2"........................**20.00**

Ornament, lyre, free-blown, annealed, 1950-60s, 2¾".**30.00**

Ornament, rabbit w/umbrella, mold-blown, embossed on 6-sided house, 3"............**65.00**

Ornament, rosebud, mold-blown generic style, 1980s-90s, 1¾"............................**12.00**

Socket set, Clemco Twin 4 #708, 8-socket, ca 1955, MIB...**60.00**

Socket set, Glamour Lites, 10-socket, World Wide, ca 1955, MIB.....................**20.00**

Socket set, Glolite Do-It-Yourself Lites, 5-socket, ca 1955, MIB............................**35.00**

Socket set, Noma Safety Plug #3020SF, 20-socket, 1952, MIB.............................**20.00**

Tree topper, angel w/star wand, Noma Electic #701, 1950.**20.00**

Tree topper, Metal Star, white w/red borders, Glolite #426, 1941.**15.00**

Tree topper, Noma Star, metal & plastic, ca 1957, 9½"........**20.00**

Tree topper, Sparkling Tree Top Star, Noma #431, 1959...**15.00**

Tree topper, star, gold & silver foil, by National Tinsel, 9".......**2.00**

Wall hanger, Santa face, plastic, Noma #551, ca 1948, 15".**15.00**

Wall hanger, Santa head, Vinylite, Miller Electric #306, 1960s.**20.00**

Wall hanger, 20-light star, Raylite Electric Corp #790, ca 1954, 20"....................**45.00**

Cigarette Lighters

Pocket lighters were invented sometime after 1908 and were at their peak from about 1925 to the 1930s. Dunhill, Zippo, Colibri, Ronson, Dupont, and Evans are some of the major manufacturers.

An early Dunhill Unique model if found in its original box would be valued at hundreds of dollars. Quality metal and metal-plated lighters were made from the 1950s to about 1960. Around that time disposable lighters never needing a flint were introduced, causing a decline in sales of figurals, novelties, and high-quality lighters.

What makes a lighter collectible? — Novelty of design, type of mechanism (flint and fuel, flint and gas, battery, etc.), and manufacturer (and whether or not the company is still in business). In the listings that follow, assume that all lighters are metal unless otherwise noted and pocket lighters unless noted table lighter.

Advertising, AO Smith Harvestore System, raised silo on blue, 2¼" **83.00**
Advertising, FA Motor Sales & Service, VW Beetle Bug on blue front **90.00**

Advertising, Joe's Diner, Camel promotional, gold-tone, 1992, 2¾x1½", from $15.00 to $22.00.
(Photo courtesy James Flanagan)

Advertising, Pepsi, w/painted Pepsi cap, marked Rosen Nesor, 2" **40.00**
Advertising, Planters, peanut shape, painted, 1930s, 2½" **55.00**

Advertising, Raleigh Cigarettes, tube shape, white & red w/ black, 3" **190.00**
Advertising, Scweppes, logo on yellow, marked Penguin No 18250, 1¾" **27.00**
ASR Corp, table lighter, brass top & footed bottom, plastic center **30.00**
Continental, brass w/rhinestone decoration on side, ca 1945, 2x1⅛" **40.00**
Dunhill, silver-plated lift arm lighter w/flared base, 1930-40s, 4" **195.00**
Evans, Aladdin's lamp form, sterling silver, beaded on base, 3x4½" **48.00**
Evans, crystal table lighter, hinged cover, 2 gold bands, 3½".. **35.00**
Evans, egg form, hinged, filigree bands, leaf-design foot, 4½". **27.00**
Evans, Pirate Toby mug-style table lighter, ceramic & metal, 4½" **28.00**
Evans, Queen figure, table lighter, ivory, detailed, footed base . **35.00**
Florenza, owl figure, gold w/green eyes, detailed, 2" **25.00**
Germany, golf caddie figure, red top, WW B MFG CO, 3½" **95.00**
Hamilton, airplane form, Made in USA Pat Pend, 6" L **85.00**
Japan, Baroque-style table lighter, gold metal & frosted glass, 4" dia **50.00**
Japan, butane, touring car form, blue metal w/white tires, 3x8x3" **25.00**
Japan, cut glass, base sits at an angle, pull-out wand, 5x3½" **30.00**
Japan, elephant figure, table lighter, metal, MIJ, 1950s, 2½" **16.00**

Match King Falcon, camera form **135.00**

Occupied Japan, rose Bakelite & chrome, 2¾" **90.00**

Partner, pistol form, marked Japan on trigger, 1½x2" **22.00**

Phinney Walker, windup clock & lighter, chrome, 4¼x3⅝x1½" **80.00**

Ronson Mastercase, Deco tortoiseshell enamel, ivory & chrome, 4½" **92.00**

Ronson Varaflame 600, chrome w/ tan alligator-effect leather, 2½" **135.00**

Sascha Brastoff, rust, tan, white & gold stripe, ca 1953, 4" ... **12.00**

USA, army grenade form, marked MK 2 US, 3¼" **63.00**

USA, oil lamp form, black plastic table lighter, brass top, 4¼" **12.00**

USA, 20mm cannon shell form, brass, steel & copper, 1940s, 7¾" **30.00**

Willis & Geiger, butane, gray metal w/brass inserts on ea side. **65.00**

Zippo, Colt decal on white, on pedestal, early 1980s, 3½" .. **310.00**

Zippo, monogramed gray metal, late 1940s **60.00**

Clothes Sprinkler Bottles

From the time we first had irons, clothes were sprinkled with water before ironing for the best results. During the 1930s and until the 1950s when the steam iron became a home staple, some of us merely took sprinkler tops and stuck them into old glass bottles to accomplish this task, while the more imaginative bought and enjoyed bottles made in figural shapes.

The most popular, of course, were the Chinese men marked 'Sprinkle Plenty.' Some bottles were made by American Bisque, Cleminson of California, and other famous figural pottery makers. Many were made in Japan for the export market.

Cat, marble eyes, ceramic, Cardinal USA, 8½" **255.00**

Cat, variety of designs & colors, handmade ceramic, from $75 to **125.00**

Chinese man, Sprinkle Plenty, yellow & green ceramic, Cardinal **85.00**

Chinese man, white & aqua, w/shirt tag, ceramic, Cleminson **75.00**

Clothespin, face w/stenciled eyes, ceramic, Cardinal **400.00**

Clothespin, yellow w/face, ceramic, 1940s-50s, 7¾" **275.00**

Dearie Is Weary, ceramic, Enesco, from $350 to **500.00**

Dutch girl, white w/green & pink trim, wetter-downer, ceramic, from $175 to **250.00**

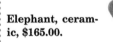

Emperor, variety of designs & colors, handmade ceramic, from $150 to **200.00**

Fireman, California Cleminsons, ceramic, very rare, 6¼".**3,000.00**

Iron, lady ironing, ceramic **95.00**

Iron, souvenir of Aquarena Springs, San Marcos TX, ceramic, $200 to **300.00**

Iron, souvenir of Florida, pink flamingo, ceramic **300.00**

Lady w/embossed apron, cobalt glass, metal sprinkler cap, 7" **60.00**

Mary Maid, all colors, plastic, Reliance, from $20 to **35.00**

Mary Poppins, ceramic, Cleminson, from $300 to **450.00**

Myrtle (Black), ceramic, Pfaltzgraff, from $275 to **375.00**

Myrtle (white), ceramic, Pfaltzgraff, from $250 to **350.00**

Peasant woman, w/laundry poem on label, ceramic, from $200 to **300.00**

Rooster, green, tan & red detailing on white, ceramic, Sierra Vista **125.00**

Coca-Cola

Introduced in 1886, Coca-Cola advertising has literally saturated our lives with a never-ending variety of items. Some of the earlier calendars and trays have been known to bring prices well into the four figures. Because of these heady prices and extreme collector demand for good Coke items, reproductions are everywhere, so beware! In addition to reproductions, 'fantasy' items have also been made, the difference being that a 'fantasy' never existed as an original. Don't be deceived. Belt buckles are 'fantasies.' So are glass doorknobs with an etched trademark, bottle-shaped knives, pocketknives,

and there are others.

When the company celebrated its 100th anniversary in 1986, many 'centennial' items were issued. They all carry the '100th Anniversary' logo. Many of them are collectible in their own right, and some are already high priced.

If you'd really like to study this subject, we recommend these books: *Goldstein's Coca-Cola Collectibles* by Sheldon Goldstein; *Collectors's Guide to Coca-Cola Items, Vols. I* and *II*, by Al Wilson; *Petretti's Coca-Cola Collectibles Price Guide* by Allan Petretti; and *B.J. Summers' Guide to Coca-Cola,* and *B.J. Summers Pocket Guide to Coca-Cola.*

Unless noted otherwise, values in the listings that follow are for examples in near-mint to mint condition.

Ashtray, ceramic & plastic, Drink Coca-Cola logo in bowl, 1950s, EX **250.00**

Bank, dispenser form, red w/single glass **375.00**

Banner, vinyl & canvas, Drink Coca-Cola..., fishtail logo, '60s, 8x14" **200.00**

Border, Enjoy Coco-Cola Classic, corrugated paper, EX...... **35.00**

Bottle, amber, 75th anniversary, 1974, G **55.00**

Bottle, green, block print embossed on shoulder, 32-oz, EX **75.00**

Bottle carrier, cardboard, 24-bottle case, 1950s, EX **50.00**

Bottle carrier, metal & wire w/wire handles, red/white, 1950s-60s, G **45.00**

Bottle carrier, polished aluminum, Coca-Cola embossed, holds 24, 1950s **140.00**

Bottle topper, cardboard, Coca-Cola...Good w/Food, 1950s, 8x7" **550.00**

Bottle topper, cardboard, King Size Ice Cold..., bottle in snow, 1960s **100.00**

Bumper sticker, Don't Say the P Word/Max Headroom, 1980s, EX **15.00**

Button, metal, hand holding bottle, 1950s, 16" **25.00**

Calender, pocket; 1943, Here's to Our GI Joes, 2 girls w/bottles, EX **70.00**

Calender, 1949, girl in red hat drinking from bottle, double month **400.00**

Calender, 1962, Enjoy...New Feeling, young couple dancing **95.00**

Calender, 1968, complete **75.00**

Clock, Drink CC red fishtail, metal & glass, 1960s, 15x15", VG. **150.00**

Clock, regulator, oak, key wind, 1980s, 23" **225.00**

Cooler, picnic; metal, Drink... in Bottles, lg logo, handles, hinged, G **135.00**

Decal, Drink Coca-Cola Ice Cold, 1960, G **30.00**

Display, cardboard, Bartender on Duty..., 1950-60s, 14x12". **375.00**

Fan, bamboo, Keep Cool Drink Coca-Cola, Oriental scene on other side **235.00**

Festoon, Know Your State Tree, 3-pc, 1950s, w/original envelope, EX **800.00**

Frisbee, plastic w/wave logo, 1960s, EX **15.00**

Game, Safety & Danger, 1938, complete **100.00**

Lighter, metal, hobble-skirt bottle, pocket size, 1950s **45.00**

Lighter, metal, logo in white diamond on red can shape, 1960s, EX **50.00**

Match holder, metal wall mount, white w/red trim, CC Bottling, 1940s **400.00**

Matchbook dispenser, metal tabletop, vertical, 1959, EX.. **225.00**

Opener, metal & plastic, 50th Anniversary Coca-Cola in Bottles, EX **60.00**

Pencil holder, ceramic, 1896 dispenser form, 1960s, 7", EX..... **150.00**

Plate, sandwich; white, Coca-Cola...w/Food, Wellsville China, 7½" **750.00**

Playing cards, Welcome Friend!, 1958, MIB **175.00**

Poster, cardboard, America's Favorite Moment, couple dining, 36x20" **395.00**

Poster, cardboard, Coke...Friendly Circle, people in pool, '55, 36x20".... **375.00**

Radio, plastic, hobble-skirt style, AM-FM, 1970s, EX **45.00**

Sign, cardboard, Things Go Better..., skaters, framed, 1960s, 24x40" **200.00**

Sign, neon, Coke w/Ice, 3-color, 1980s, EX **400.00**

Sign, tin, Cold Drinks, fishtail center, 1960s, 15x24" **300.00**

Syrup jug, paper label w/Coke glass, 1950s, EX **20.00**

Thermometer, tin bottle shape, 1950s, 17", EX **125.00**

Toy truck, Buddy L, metal, yellow, 2-tier bay, whitewall tires, 1960s **325.00**

Tray, birdhouse, 1957, 10½x13¼". **125.00**
Tray, girl w/wind in hair, screen background, 1950s, 10½x13¼" **100.00**

Tray, Ice Skating, 1941, NM, $450.00.

Tray, pansy garden, 1961, 10½x13¼", NM **30.00**
Tray, springboard girl, 1939, 10½x13¼" **375.00**
Tray, swimmer, 1930, 10½x13¼", EX **425.00**
Tray, umbrella girl, 10½x13¼"..**375.00**

Coin Glass

Made by the Fostoria company, Coin glass has always been a popular pattern, both at the retail level and on the collector market. It's very easy to find at any of today's flea markets. From 1958 until 1982 Fostoria produced it in many colors — amber, blue, green (called 'emerald' by collectors), Olive (or avocado), and red, as well as crystal. Then in the late 1950s, Lancaster Colony used the original molds to reproduce virtually the whole line in many of the original colors. Although the amber, blue, and green are not a true match with Fostoria's, there is no way to determine the manufacturer of an item in red or crystal. On much, but not all, of the later glassware, the coins were not frosted.

However, adding frost to the coins has proven to be a relatively simple procedure for unscrupulous dealers, so using that factor for identification purposes isn't as foolproof as we once thought. For more information we recommend *Collectible Glassware from the 40s, 50s, and 60s,* by Gene and Cathy Florence (Collector Books).

Ashtray, amber, round, #1372/114, 7½" **20.00**
Ashtray, green, #1372/123, 5". **30.00**
Ashtray, olive, oblong, #1372/115..**25.00**
Bowl, blue, footed, #1372/199, 8½" **90.00**
Bowl, crystal, oval, #1372/189, 9" **30.00**
Bowl, ruby, round, #1372/179, 8" **45.00**
Bowl, wedding; ruby, w/lid, #1372/162 .... **87.50**
Candleholders, blue, #1372/316, 4½", pr............................. **55.00**
Candleholders, crystal, 1372/326, 8", pr **50.00**
Candy jar, green, w/lid, #1372/347, 6¼" **125.00**
Cigarette box, amber, w/lid, #1372/374, 5¾x4½" **50.00**
Cigarette holder w/ashtray lid, green, #1372/372............. **90.00**
Condiment set, blue, #1372/737, tray/2 shakers/cruet...... **335.00**
Creamer, ruby, #1372/680...... **16.00**
Cruet, green, w/stopper, #1372/531, 7-oz................................ **210.00**
Decanter, blue, w/stopper, #1372/400, 1-pt, 10¼"....**265.00**
Lamp, coach; amber, #1372/461.**50.00**
Lamp, coach; amber, oil, #1372/320, 13½" **145.00**

Lamp, coach; crystal, electric, #1372/321, 13½" **100.00**

Lamp, courting; blue, #1372/311, handled, electric, 10⅛" .. **210.00**

Lamp, patio; blue, oil, #1372/459, 16½" **295.00**

Nappy, blue, w/handle, #1372/499, 5⅜" **28.00**

Pitcher, ruby, #1372/453, 32-oz, 6¼" **150.00**

Plate, olive, #1372/550, 8" **20.00**

Salt & pepper shakers, green, #1372/652, w/chrome tops, 3¼", pr **90.00**

Stem, goblet; ruby, #1372/2, 10½-oz **70.00**

Stem, wine; crystal, #1372/26, 5-oz, 4" **33.00**

Sugar bowl, amber, w/lid, #1372/673 .... **35.00**

Tumbler, double old-fashioned; crystal, #1372/23, 10-oz, 5½" . **22.00**

Tumbler, iced tea; ruby, #1372/58, 14-oz, 5¼" **75.00**

Tumbler, water, scotch & soda; crystal, #1372/73, 9-oz, 4¼" ... **22.00**

Urn, amber, footed, w/lid, #1372/829, 12¾" **80.00**

Urn, blue, footed, w/lid, #1372/829, 12¾" **140.00**

Vase, bud; amber, #1372/799, 8" **22.00**

Vase, bud; crystal, #1372/799, 8" **20.00**

Coloring Books

Throughout the 1950s and even into the 1970s, coloring and activity books were produced by the thousands. Whitman, Saalfield, and Watkins-Strathmore were some of the largest publishers. The most popular were those that pictured well-known TV, movie, and comic book characters, and these are the ones that are bringing top dollar today. Condition is also an important worth-accessing factor. Compared to a coloring book that was never used, one that's only partially colored is worth from 50% to 70% less. Unless noted otherwise, values are for unused books.

A-Team Storybook/Coloring Book, Peter Pan, 1984, NM **5.00**

Ann Sheridan Coloring Book, Whitman, 1940s, some coloring, EX+ **50.00**

Batman, Robin Strikes for Batman, 1966, some coloring, EX+. **24.00**

Bewitched, Treasure Books, 1965, M **125.00**

Bing Crosby, #2440, Saalfield, 1954, some coloring, NM **50.00**

Bullwinkle, Golden Books, 1968, some coloring, NM+ **25.00**

Charlie Chaplin, #198, Saalfield, 1941, all pgs colored, EX. **100.00**

Chitty Chitty Bang Bang, 1968, some coloring, EX+ **18.00**

Dennis the Menace, Whitman, 1960, some coloring, EX . **13.00**

Dolly Parton, Dolly Parton Enterprises, 1976, M **42.00**

Donna Reed, Saalfield, 1964, M **30.00**

Donny & Marie, Whitman, 1977, M.................................... **25.00**

Fame, Playmore Publishing, 1983, some coloring, VG **6.00**

Flash Gordon, Whitman, 1952, some coloring, VG **30.00**

Gabby Hayes, Abbott Publishing, rare, 1954, M **100.00**

Greer Garson, Merrill, 1940s, some coloring, EX+ **50.00**

Gunsmoke, Whitman Publishing, 1959, some coloring, EX . **20.00**

Haley Mills in Search of the Castaways, Whitman #1138, 1962, EX **30.00**

Hopalong Cassidy, Pirates on Horseback, Lowe, 1950s, some coloring, EX **25.00**

HR Pufnstuf, Whitman, 1970, M **75.00**

Jack Webb's Safety Squad Dragnet, Abbott, 1957, some coloring, EX+ **35.00**

Jackie Gleason's Dan Dan Dandy, Lowe #2370, 1950s, some coloring, EX+ **50.00**

Lassie, Whitman #115-2, 1982, EX **15.00**

Little Orphan Annie, Junior Commandos, Saalfield #2437, 1943, EX **45.00**

Lone Ranger, Tonto, Whitman Publishing, 1957, some coloring, EX+ **20.00**

Lucille Ball & Desi Arnez, Whitman #2079, 1953, some coloring, EX+ **75.00**

Mr Ed, Whitman #1135, 1963, some coloring, EX **50.00**

Ozzie & Harriet Nelson, Ozzie's Girls, Saalfield, 1973, EX. **15.00**

Peanuts Trace & Color Set, #6122, 1960s, 5-book set, NM+ .. **75.00**

Pink Panther, Whitman, 1976, NM+ **15.00**

Rambo Coloring & Activity Book, Modern Pub, 1985, some coloring, EX **6.00**

Rocky the Flying Squirrel, Golden Books, 1960, NM+ **33.00**

Sergeant Preston, Whitman, 1957, some coloring, NM **25.00**

Sesame Street, Whitman, 1975, EX **10.00**

Shirley Temple's Blue Bird, Saalfield, 1939, some coloring, EX+ **40.00**

Shirley Temple's Busy Book, Saalfield #5326, 1958, some coloring, EX+ **45.00**

Smokey Bear, Whitman, 1958, NM+ **25.00**

Spider-Man, The Arms of Dr Octopus, Marvel, 1983, some coloring, EX+ **15.00**

Star Wars, Kenner, 1977, M .. **68.00**

Straight Arrow Indian, Stephens, 1949, some coloring, EX+. **50.00**

Superman, Saalfield #4583, 1958, some coloring, EX **50.00**

Three Little Pigs, Playmore, 1984, NM **8.00**

Three Stooges, Whitman #1135, 1964, some coloring, EX . **35.00**

Three Stooges Funny Coloring Book, Lowe #2855, 1959, VG **50.00**

Tom Corbett Space Cadet, Saalfield, 1950s, some coloring, VG **25.00**

Toy Story, Golden Books, M **6.00**

Wild Bill Hickok & Jingles, Saalfield, 1957, some coloring, EX **14.00**

Raggedy Ann and Andy, Bobbs-Merrill Co. by Hallmark #75PF1440-1, 1974, 6", from $8.00 to $12.00.

Winnie the Pooh & the Blustery Day, Whitman, 1965, EX. **15.00**

Winnie the Pooh Coloring Book & Follow the Dots, Whitman, 1976, EX **12.00**

Winnie the Pooh Trace & Color, Whitman, 1973, EX **12.00**

Wizard of Oz, from cartoon TV show, Whitman, 1962, NM+...... **25.00**

Comic Books

Factors that make a comic book valuable are condition, content, and rarity, not necessarily age. In fact, comics printed between 1950 and the late 1970s are most in demand by collectors who prefer those they had as children to the earlier comics. Issues where the hero is first introduced are treasured. While some may go for hundreds, even thousands of dollars, many are worth very little; so if you plan to collect, you'll need a good comic book price guide such as *Overstreet's* to assess your holdings. Condition is extremely important. Compared to a book in excellent condition, a mint issue might be worth six to eight times as much, while one in only good condition should be priced at less than half the price of the excellent example. For more information see *Schroeder's Collectible Toys, Antique to Modern* (Collector Books).

Airboy, #1, 1952...................... **24.00**

Alvin & His Pals Merry Christmas, 1963, EX+........................ **55.00**

Amazing Spider-Man, #43, 1966, G.................................... **35.00**

Andy Panda, Walter Lantz Productions, 1976 .... **25.00**

Beatles Yellow Subamarine, w/ poster, 1968, NM, from $150 to **200.00**

Bionic Woman, #1, 1977, NM. **15.00**

Brady Bunch, #2, 1970, NM.. **75.00**

Captain Marvel, #1, 1968, NM. **150.00**

Captain Midnight, #37, NM. **170.00**

Cisco Kid, #17, VG................ **20.00**

Dark Shadows, #5, 1970, NM. **50.00**

David Cassidy, #1, 1972......... **12.00**

Dennis the Menace, #1, 1981, NM+................................ **15.00**

Dick Tracy, #4, NM **120.00**

Elmer Fudd, #689, NM......... **25.00**

Family Affair, #1, with Buffy pull-out poster, from $40.00 to $50.00; #2, #3, and #4, from $2.00 to $4.00. (Photo courtesy Greg Davis and Bill Morgan)

Felix the Cat, #61, 1946, VG. **40.00**

Flintstones, #2, NM **75.00**

Flipper, #1, 1966 .... **15.00**

Get Smart, #1, 1966, NM **65.00**

Hogan's Heroes, #4, 1966, NM. **25.00**

I Dream of Jeannie, #1, 1966, NM............................. **100.00**

I Love Lucy, #5, 1955, EX+.... **85.00**

John Carter Mars, #1, 1964, VG.. **20.00**

Justice League of America, #6, VG **50.00**

Lassie, #27, NM **25.00**

Lil' Abner, #61, 1947, NM.... **190.00**

Little Lulu, #239, 1977 .... **10.00**

Lone Ranger, #37, EX+.......... **45.00**

Mary Poppins, 1964, EX........ **15.00**

Mod Squad, #1, 1969, NM+...**50.00**

Munsters, #4, 1965, EX........**20.00**

Mysterious Adventures, #8, 1952, VG..................**75.00**

Nancy & Sluggo, #100, 1953, VG.**15.00**

Raggedy Ann & Andy, #2, 1946, VG..................**35.00**

Rawhide Kid, #12, EX...........**50.00**

Red Ryder, #69, 1949, NM.....**45.00**

Rifleman, #5, photo cover, 1960, EX.....................**35.00**

Robin Hood, #1, 1963, EX+...**15.00**

Scooby Doo, #1, 1977, NM+...**25.00**

Six Million Dollar Man, #1, 1976, NM....................**15.00**

Space Busters, #2, 1952, EX.**210.00**

Star Trek, #2, 1968, M........**150.00**

Superman, #25, 1941, VG....**225.00**

Tales To Astonish, #22, 1961, VG...................**35.00**

Tarzan's Jungle Annual, #2, 1953, EX.....................**40.00**

Tex Ritter Western, #2, 1954, EX.**60.00**

Tom & Jerry, #115, EX...........**20.00**

Top Cat, #5, 1963, NM...........**45.00**

Tweety & Sylvester, #11, NM.**25.00**

Underworld Crime, #3, 1952, EX+..................**60.00**

Voyage to the Bottom of the Sea, #6, 1966, EX...................**15.00**

Voyage to the Deep, #1, 1962, EX....................**15.00**

Western Tales, #32, 1956, EX+..**80.00**

Wonder Woman, #100, 1958, EX.**45.00**

Wyatt Earp, #860, NM...........**75.00**

X-Men, #13, 1965, VG...........**45.00**

Zane Grey's Stories of the West, #511, 1954, EX..............**25.00**

Compacts

Prior to World War I, the use of cosmetics was frowned upon. It was not until after the war when women became liberated and entered the work force that makeup became acceptable. A compact became a necessity as a portable container for cosmetics and usually contained a puff and mirror. They were made in many different styles, shapes, and motifs and from every type of natural and man-made material. The fine jewelry houses made compacts in all of the precious metals — some studded with precious stones. The most sought-after compacts today are those made of plastic, Art Deco styles, figural styles, and any that incorporate gadgets. Compacts that are combined with other accessories are also very desirable. See Clubs and Newsletters for information concerning the *Powder Puff.*

Book, red leather w/gold trim, green & ivory Deco floral, Mondaine.....................**75.00**

Carryall, gold-tone mesh w/pink rose on round blue enamel case, EX.......................**115.00**

Carryall, silver plated, guilloche glass enamel work on green, chain..........................**135.00**

Fan, gold-tone w/mother-of-pearl floral inlay, 1950s, MIB.**160.00**

Guitar, black plastic w/plastic strings, unmarked, 2x5½"............**200.00**

Half moon, light blue/green enamel, diagonal gold-tone band, Rex, 5"..................**100.00**

Hat, silver-tone w/raised dome center w/bow & flowers, 4".**140.00**

Heart, gold-tone w/engraved lid, from $40 to.....................**60.00**

Lion's head, green w/gold-tone, solid perfume, Estée Lauder, 2".................250.00

Oblong, sterling/gold wash, multicolored Deco enamel, Austria....................125.00

Octagon, blue enamel w/pink rose on white, silver-tone chain & trim...........................130.00

Octagon, sterling, lake scene on blue enamel, concave corners, chain...........................125.00

Oval, harlequin mask decoration on brushed gold-tone, Dorothy Gray, 4"......................100.00

Roulette wheel, gold-tone w/rhinestones, pearl on #7, Estée Lauder, 3"......................75.00

Round, carved mother-of-pearl rose, painted trim, Blue Rose . 65.00

Round, gold-tone, centered green stone on lid w/fish, Max Factor, 2".............................75.00

Round, gold-tone, w/etched flowers on enameled lid, 3".........50.00

Round, silver w/pink shell-design enamel, Birmingham, 1941, 3".............................65.00

Round, silver-tone, Deco lady/rose/ star on blue & black enamel, Karess...........................150.00

Round, sterling w/etched Siamese dancers on both sides, 1940s, 3".............................300.00

Round with gold scalloped edge, enameled flowers on blue, Stratton, Made in England, 2⅞", from $40.00 to $50.00.

Round, w/lipstick, gold-tone w/Mod enamel design, Estée Lauder, 1970s...........................115.00

Square, beige sunburst enamel w/delicate gold-tone trim, 2½"......75.00

Square, brass, enameled Deco bird on nest w/flowers, Vogue, 2½".130.00

Square, brushed gold-tone w/lg green stones, mirror & well inside, 3"......................200.00

Square, gold-tone, multicolored cartouche on ivory, 3½".150.00

Square, gold/silver diamond decoration w/flowers on enameled corners...........................125.00

Square, silver ribbed Deco w/14k gold/rubies, Black Star & Frost, '30s......................150.00

Square, silver-tone, lid decorated w/9 charms, Evans, 2½"..95.00

Suitcase, tan leather w/gold-tone trim, Atomette, 3".........125.00

Triangle, silver-tone w/inlayed enamel decoration, bowed sides, chain....................115.00

Triangle, white figure on pink enameled gold-tone, Schiaparelli, 2"..............................80.00

Trunk, watch/compact, gold-tone, w/straps, Evans, 1940s.175.00

Vanity, flapjack, gold-tone, chased Deco floral design, Rex, 4"..67.00

Vanity, gold-tone, Deco brown & tan leather, Mondaine, 1950s, 3" sq...........................40.00

Vanity, keystone, black silhouette of lady on ivory, 3¼".....100.00

Vanity, pyramidal, fraternal emblem, red/black stripes, Fillwik, 2"......................85.00

Vanity, saddlebag w/tube sleeve & comb pocket, metallic fabric, 4"...........................150.00

Vanity book, embossed leather, Raquel, 2x3".................. **100.00**

Cookbooks

Cookbook collecting can be traced back to the turn of the century. Good food and recipes on how to prepare it are timeless. Cookbooks fall into many subclassifications with emphasis on various aspects of cooking. Some specialize in regional or ethnic food; during the World Wars, conservation and cost-cutting measures were popular themes. Because this field is so varied, you may want to decide what field is most interesting and specialize. Hardcover or softcover, Betty Crocker or Julia Childs, Pillsbury or Gold Medal — the choice is yours!

Cookbooks featuring specific food items are plentiful. Some are die-cut to represent the product — for instance, a pickle or a slice of bread. Some feature a famous personality, perhaps from a radio show sponsored by the food company. Appliance companies often published their own cookbooks, and these appeal to advertising buffs and cookbook collectors alike, especially if they illustrate pre-1970s kitchen appliances.

Perhaps no single event in the 1950s attracted more favorable attention for the Pillsbury Flour Company than the one first staged in 1949. Early in the year, company officials took the proposal to its advertising agency. Together they came up with a plan that would become an American institution, the Pillsbury Bake-Off contest. For more information, we recommend *Collector's Guide to Cookbooks* by Frank Daniels, published by Collector Books. When no condition is noted, our values are for examples in near-mint condition.

Adventures in Good Cooking, Duncan Hines, 1955, soft cover................................. **30.00**

Alice B Toklas Cook Book, Harper & Brothers, 1954, 228 pgs, hardcover........................ **45.00**

Alpha Xi Delta Cook Book, Marion IA, ca 1927, 100 pgs, hardcover.............................. **100.00**

Aunt Chick's Pies, The Chicadees, 1949, 39 pgs, soft cover **5.00**

Ballet Cookbook, Stein & Day, 1966, 416 pgs, w/dust jacket....................... **175.00**

Bel Canto Cook Book, Doubleday, 1964, 219 pgs, hardcover. **33.00**

Better Homes & Gardens New Cook Book, 1953, 416 pgs, ring binder............................. **25.00**

Betty Crocker's Picture Cook Book, 1950, M, $40.00. (Photo courtesy Frank Daniels)

Bible Cook Book, Bethany Press, 1958, hardcover............... **10.00**

Blondie's Cook Book, Bell Publishing, 1946, 142 pgs, w/ dust jacket....................... **45.00**

Book of Hors d'Oeuvre, Bramhall House, 1941, 141 pgs, w/dust jacket **12.00**

Boston Cooking School, Little, Brown & Company, 1930, hardcover **100.00**

Brer Rabbit's New Orleans Molasses Recipes, 1948, 48 pgs, softcover **12.00**

Brown Derby Cook Book, Doubleday, 1949, 272 pgs, w/dust jacket **75.00**

Cake Secrets, General Foods, 1953, 64 pgs, softcover **3.00**

Carnation Cook Book, Carnation, 1948, 91 pgs, softcover **6.00**

Christmas Cookie Book, Little, Brown & Company, 1949, w/dust jacket **15.00**

Clementine in the Kitchen, Hastings House, 1943, hardcover .. **15.00**

Congressional Cook Book, Congressional Club, 1933, hardcover **60.00**

Cookbook of the United States Navy, 1945, 456 pgs, hardcover **25.00**

Cookie-Craft, Kraft, 1946, pamphlet **3.00**

Cooking, Menus, Service; Doubleday, 1935, 977+16 pgs, hardcover **50.00**

Cooking Out-of-Doors, Girl Scouts of America, 1960, 212 pgs, spiral **12.00**

Crisco Recipes for the Jewish Housewife, Proctor & Gamble, 1935 .... **50.00**

Dark Shadows Cookbook, Ace Books, 1970, softcover **50.00**

Deep South Cookbook, Favorite Recipes Press, 1972, 192 pgs, hardcover **6.00**

Democrats' Cook Book, NY Democratic Committee, 1976, spiral bound **60.00**

Dishes Men Like, Lea & Perrins, 1952, 62 pgs, softcover.... **10.00**

Down on the Farm Cook Book, 1943, 322 pgs, w/dust jacket **25.00**

Ebony Cookbook, A Date With a Dish; Johnson, 1962, 390 pgs, hardcover **40.00**

Elsie's Cook Book, Bond Wheelwright, 1952, 374 pgs, w/dust jacket **50.00**

Encyclopedia of Cookery, William H Wise Company, 1948, hardcover **30.00**

Family Circle Dessert & Fruit Cookbook, 1954, 144 pgs, hardcover **4.00**

Farm Journal's Country Cookbook, Doubleday, 1959, 420 pgs, hardcover **25.00**

Good Housekeeping Cookbook, 1962, 760 pgs, hardcover. **30.00**

Home Comfort Cook Book, Wrought Iron Range, 1938, 134 pgs, spiral **40.00**

How America Eats, Scribner's, 1960, 479 pgs, hardcover **50.00**

How to Cook Your Catch, Great Outdoors, 1963, 80 pgs, softcover **3.00**

Jolly Times Cook Book, Rand McNally, 1934, 64 pgs, hardcover **15.00**

Liberace Cooks, Doubleday, 1970, 225 pgs, w/dust jacket **60.00**

Magical Desserts With Whip 'n Chill, General Foods, 1966, softcover **1.00**

Mary Poppins Cook Book, Walt Disney, 1963, 25 pgs, softcover **40.00**

Picture Cook Book, Time Inc, 1958, 292 pgs, spiral bound...... **15.00**

Pyrex Prize Recipes, Greystone Press, 1953, 128 pgs, hardcover................... **20.00**

Shaker Cookbook, Crown Publishing, 1953, 283 pgs, w/ dust jacket......................... **8.00**

Walton Family Cook Book, Bantam Books, 1975, 148 pgs, softcover.................. **50.00**

What Shall I Cook Today?, Lever Brothers Company, 1940, softcover..................... **3.00**

White House Chef Cookbook, Doubleday, 1967, 287 pgs, hardcover......................... **10.00**

World Famous Chef's Cook Book, Otto Naylor, 1941, 637 pgs, hardcover......................... **50.00**

Young Folks' Cookbook, Citadel Press, 1946, 27 pages, w/dust jacket................................ **50.00**

Cookie Cutters

Cookie cutters have come into their own in recent years as worthy kitchen collectibles. Prices on many have risen astronomically, but a practiced eye can still sort out a good bargain. Advertising cutters and product premiums, especially in plastic, can still be found without too much effort. Aluminum cutters with painted wooden handles are usually worth several dollars each if in good condition. Red and green are the usual handle colors, but other colors are more highly prized by many. Hallmark plastic cookie cutters, especially those with painted backs, are always worth considering, if in good condition.

Be wary of modern tin cutters being sold for antique. Many present-day tinsmiths chemically antique their cutters, especially those done in a primitive style. These are often sold by others as 'very old.' Look closely, because most tinsmiths today sign and date these cutters. Tin cutters listed below are circa 1940s except for those noted 'early.' Early cutters usually have wider cutting strips, while those from the '20s and beyond will have strips that are only about ½" deep. Soldering on the older cutters will be spotty, while the later examples will have a thin line. The shape of the backplate on the older cutters tends to follow the outline of the pattern instead of being oval, rectangular, or square as the later cutters are. See also Disney.

Acorn, tin, flat back, early, 4¾x4⅛", EX................................ **110.00**

Airplane, tin, 3½x3½x1"......... **17.00**

Amish lady, flat back, 5½x2½". **47.50**

Angel, aluminum, flat back, 13x8"............................. **25.00**

Barnaby Bunny, light blue plastic, Hallmark, 1975, 5"......... **12.00**

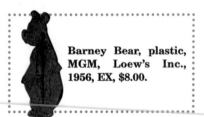

Barney Bear, plastic, MGM, Loew's Inc., 1956, EX, $8.00.

Butterfly, tin, flat back, 4⅜x3½". **30.00**

Cat w/tail up, flat back, 2¾x3½"...................... **45.00**

Cinderella, red plastic, marked HRM, set of 6 .... **30.00**

Davis Baking Powder, horse shape, tin, 2¾x3⅞" **25.00**

Dog, flat back, 3¾x5" **32.50**

Dove, plastic, Hallmark VKK-47-9, MIP **15.00**

Gingerbread man, aluminum, green strap handle, 6x2" **15.00**

Gingerbread man, green plastic, Jolly Miller #127026 .... **25.00**

Girl, aluminum, fashioned after paper doll, McCall Publishing, 8" **23.00**

Goose, tin, early, 3x5" **125.00**

Hansel & Gretel, red plastic, w/ tree, witch & house, HRM, MIB **15.00**

Holly Hobbie set, plastic, American Greetings, 1967, 7-pc **45.00**

Kermit the Frog, green plastic, Hallmark, 1979 .... **32.50**

Linus (Peanuts), red plastic, Hallmark, 1971, 5" **30.00**

Lucy (Peanuts), green plastic, Hallmark, 1971, 5" **30.00**

Man, tin, wearing hat, handle on back, early, 8½x4½" **125.00**

Pink Panther, head only, pink plastic, Hallmark, 1970s, 3" .. **15.00**

Rabbit, tin, handle on back, 1930s, 2x2½" **14.00**

Reddy Kilowatt, red plastic, 3", MIB **20.00**

Santa, tin, Made in Germany #45, 8" **45.00**

Scooby Doo, yellow plastic, Hallmark, 4" **20.00**

Sheep, tin, flatback, 5½x4½".. **26.00**

Snoopy, blue plastic, Hallmark, 1971, 4¾" **30.00**

Soldier, tin, colonial-style high boots & hat, 5¼x1¾" **56.00**

Star, aluminum, red painted handle, 1950s, 3x3" **24.00**

Sunburst, tin, early, 3½" dia.. **95.00**

Swan's Cake Flour, heart shape, aluminum **15.00**

Teddy bear, copper, Nordstrom, 7" **20.00**

Woman, colonial; tin, early, 11x6" **110.00**

Cookie Jars

McCoy, Metlox, Twin Winton, Robinson Ransbottom, Brush, and American Bisque were among the largest producers of cookie jars in the country. Many firms made them to a lesser extent. Figural jars are the most common (and the most valuable), made in an endless variety of subjects. Early jars from the 1920s and 1930s were often decorated in 'cold paint' over the glaze. This type of color is easily removed — take care that you use very gentle cleaning methods. A damp cloth and a light touch is the safest approach. For further information, *The Ultimate Collector's Encyclopedia of Cookie Jars* by Fred and Joyce Roerig (published by Collector Books). Values are for jars in mint condition unless otherwise noted. Beware of modern reproductions!

A Little Company, Blanket Couple, c 87, 12" **150.00**

Abingdon, Daisy, #677 .... **45.00**

Abingdon, Pumpkin, #674, minimum value.................... **300.00**

Abingdon, Windmill, #678, from $200 to **225.00**

Alfano Art Pottery, The Jazz Player, Experimental #1-92 ...... **150.00**

American Bisque, Jack-in-the-Box, USA, from $125 to **150.00**

American Bisque, Mug of Hot Chocolate, USA **50.00**

American Greetings Corp, Strawberry Shortcake .. **450.00**

Appleman, Buick Convertible . **1,000.00**

Brush, Cinderella Pumpkin, #W32. **225.00**

Brush, Davy Crockett, no gold, USA (+) **300.00**

Brush, Elephant w/Ice Cream Cone **500.00**

Brush, Happy Bunny, white, #W25 .... **200.00**

Brush, Hillbilly Frog, minimum value (+) **4,500.00**

Brush, Laughing Hippo, #W27 (+). **750.00**

Brush, Little Red Riding Hood, no gold, #K24, sm **500.00**

Brush, Peter Pan, no gold, sm . **500.00**

Brush, Raggedy Ann, #W16, from $450 to **500.00**

Brush, Squirrel on Log, #W26 . **100.00**

Brush, Teddy Bear, feet apart .. **250.00**

California Originals, Coffee Grinder, USA #861 .... **35.00**

California Originals, Dog on Stump, #2620 .... **32.00**

California Originals, Donald Duck, cylinder, Walt Disney **50.00**

California Originals, Lemon, no mark **35.00**

California Originals, Lion w/ Lollipop, USA #866 .... **45.00**

California Originals, Potbellied Stove, USA #743 .... **40.00**

California Originals, Upside Down Turtle, USA #2627, from $40 to **50.00**

Clay Art, Catfish, 1990, from $35 to **45.00**

Clay Art, Humpty Dumpty .. **125.00**

Deforest of California, Dachshund, #518, from $50 to **60.00**

Deforest of California, Owl, green w/black glass, cap, #5537-5545 .... **25.00**

Deforest of California, Pig, Goodies printed on tummy **85.00**

Deforest of California, Ranger Bear **45.00**

Deforest of California, Snappy Gingerbread Boy, #6 USA, from $100 to **125.00**

Department 56, Mirage Cactus. **45.00**

Department 56, Someone's in the Kitchen,...Handpainted Japan c Dept 56 .... **150.00**

Department 56, Ugly Stepsisters, Tea Time Ugly Stepsister. **65.00**

Doranne of California, Cow on Moon, #J 2 USA, late 1950s, from $275 to **325.00**

Doranne of California, Dragon, USA, from $225 to **250.00**

Doranne of California, Hound Dog, #J 1 USA, from $35 to **45.00**

Doranne of California, Las Vegas Jackpot Machine **50.00**

Doranne of California, Lunch Box, dark & light blue **45.00**

Doranne of California, Shoe House, USA mark, from $30 to .. **35.00**

Enesco, Lucy 'n Me Bear **150.00**

Enesco/Jim Henson Productions, Cookie Monster 45.00

Hirsch, Planet, w/rocket finial, from $75 to 85.00

Hirsch, Smiling Bear w/Badge, unmarked, from $40 to ... 50.00

Hirsch, Treasure Chest 80.00

Lane, Rocking Horse 125.00

Lefton, Bossie Cow, #6594, from $125 to 150.00

Lefton, Chef Boy, #396, from $200 to 225.00

Lefton, Dutch Girl, #2697, from $35 to 40.00

Lefton, Pear 'n Apple, #4335, from $35 to 45.00

Lotus International, Cowboy, Made in China 1991 .... 35.00

Lotus International, Halloween Witch, Made in China 1991 .... 60.00

Maddux of California, Cat, from $75 to 85.00

Maddux of California, Squirrel Hiker, #2110, from $175 to 200.00

Marsh Ceramics, Marsh Pig w/ Apple, no mark 95.00

McCoy, Animal Crackers 100.00

McCoy, Apple, 1967 .... 50.00

McCoy, Blue Willow Pitcher .. 75.00

McCoy, Burlap Bag, red bird on lid 50.00

McCoy, Chilly Willy 65.00

McCoy, Christmas Tree 450.00

McCoy, Clown in Barrel, yellow, blue or green 85.00

McCoy, Coffee Grinder 45.00

McCoy, Colonial Fireplace 85.00

McCoy, Cookie Log, squirrel finial 45.00

McCoy, Corn, single ear 150.00

McCoy, Dalmatians in Rocking Chair (+) 150.00

McCoy, Dog on Basketweave. 75.00

McCoy, Flowerpot, plastic flower on top 350.00

McCoy, Freddy Gleep (+), minimum value 350.00

McCoy, Globe 195.00

McCoy, Happy Face 80.00

McCoy, Hot Air Balloon 40.00

McCoy, Jack-O'-Lantern 500.00

McCoy, Kittens (2) on Low Basket 600.00

McCoy, Koala Bear 85.00

McCoy, Lemon 75.00

McCoy, Mammy w/Cauliflower, good paint, minimum value (+). 1,100.00

McCoy, Mother Goose 95.00

McCoy, Pears on Basketweave. 70.00

McCoy, Pig, winking 250.00

McCoy, Pirate's Chest 95.00

McCoy, Red Barn, cow in door, rare, minimum value 150.00

McCoy, Snow Bear 75.00

McCoy, Touring Car 75.00

McCoy, Turkey, natural colors..250.00

McCoy, Wedding Jar 90.00

McCoy, Wishing Well 40.00

Metlox, Basket, natural, w/cookie lid 50.00

Metlox, Bucky Beaver, from $125 to 150.00

Metlox, Children of the World, 2-qt, from $125 to 150.00

Metlox, Daisy Cookie Canister..55.00

Metlox, Debutante, blue or pink dress, minimum value .. 400.00

Metlox, Egg Basket, from $175 to 200.00

Metlox, Flamingo, minimum value 350.00

Metlox, Grape, from $200 to. 250.00

Metlox, Happy the Clown, minimum value 35.00

Metlox, Lamb, white, from $275 to 300.00

Metlox, Rabbit on Cabbage, 3-qt, 10", from $125 to **150.00**

Metlox, Salty Pelican, from $200 to **225.00**

Napco, Spaceship, spaceman finial **900.00**

North American Ceramics, Airplane, movable propeller. **300.00**

Regal, Churn Boy **250.00**

Regal, Quaker Oats, from $100 to **125.00**

Robinson Ransbottom, Brown Chicken **125.00**

Robinson Ransbottom, Crock . **30.00**

Robinson Ransbottom, Dutch Girl **200.00**

Shawnee, Drum Major, gold trim, #10 USA, from $575 to . **600.00**

Shawnee, Little Chef, caramel, USA, 8½", from $175 to. **200.00**

Sierra Vista, Pig **150.00**

Treasure Craft, Cowboy, from $40 to **45.00**

Treasure Craft, Hobby Horse, from $35.00 to $40.00. (Photo courtesy Joyce Roerig)

Treasure Craft, Jack Skelington's Tombstone, from $150 to. **200.00**

Treasure Craft, Noah's Ark, marked Winton, from $30 to **35.00**

Treasure Craft, Radio, Made in USA, from $35 to **45.00**

Treasure Craft, Soccer Ball, from $25 to **35.00**

Treasure Craft, Tug Boat, from $60 to **70.00**

Twin Winton, Cow, gray **75.00**

Twin Winton, Pear, orange **75.00**

Twin Winton, Poodle, TW-64, 7½x13" **85.00**

Warner Brothers, Bugs Bunny Head, Made in China **75.00**

Warner Brothers, Olympic Torch. **95.00**

Warner Brothers, Porky Pig, in green chair, Made in China, 1975 .... **110.00**

Coppercraft Guild

Sold during the 1960s and 1970s through the home party plan, these decorative items are once again finding favor with the buying public. The Coppercraft Guild of Taunton, Massachusetts, made a wonderful variety of wall plaques, bowls, pitchers, trays, etc. Not all were made of copper, some were of molded plastic. Glass, cloth, mirror, and brass accents added to the texture. When uncompromised by chemical damage or abuse, the finish they used on their copper items has proven remarkably enduring. Collectors are beginning to take notice, but prices are still remarkably low. If you enjoy the look, now is the time to begin your collection.

Bank, bell shape, slot on side, wooden handle, 8½x3⅛".. **20.00**

Basket, display; footed, w/handle, 4½x9x6" **20.00**

Bowl, embossed w/floral on sides, 1½x11" **35.00**

Bowl, serving; shallow, 6¾" ... **15.00**

Bread tray, 12x6¾" **20.00**

Butter dish, rectangular w/scalloped base, ¼-lb **27.50**

Candleholders, hurricane lamp shape w/glass globes, 9½", pr................................. **30.00**

Fondue pot, w/lid & metal warming stand, 5½" dia.................. **30.00**

Gravy boat, w/stand.............. **27.50**

Mirror, copper paint on pressed molded plastic, 22x9½" ... **35.00**

Mug, 4¾x4⅛"........................... **18.00**

Necklace & earring set, leaf design, adjustable to 16".............. **38.00**

Pendant, cross, 3½x2½"......... **13.50**

Piggy bank, all brass, including ears, feet & tail, 5", MIB. **25.00**

Pitcher, water; footed, 9x6" ... **20.00**

Planter, applied brass figure of lady at spinning wheel, 10" L. **10.00**

Plate, hunting scene, 6½" **10.00**

Punch set, 12" bowl & 3 3" cups on 18" dia tray...................... **60.00**

Salad servers, 12½", 12¼"...... **25.00**

Salt & pepper shakers, tapered bottoms, S & P shape in holes, 3", pr.................................... **15.00**

Tray, octagonal, glass 3-compartment insert, 9" **17.00**

Tray, serving; 1½" rim, black leatherette interior, 13" dia **23.50**

Vase, plastic with copper finish, 7¾", from $12.00 to $15.00.

Wall hanging, Raggedy Ann & Andy by well, copper paint, 13x14¾"........................... **15.00**

Wall hanging, The Last Supper in relief, 10x21" **19.00**

Wall hanging, Traveler's Rest, stagecoach before Riverside Inn, 10x14".................... **20.00**

Corning Ware and Visions Cookware

In late 1957, Corning Glass Works introduced a new line of cookware called Corning Ware. This new line of very durable cookware consisted of a skillet, three saucepans, and lids. A metal cradle and detachable handle were included for easy handling of the dishes. Blue Cornflower was the first design, and to the collector's delight, many new designs have since been added.

Visions Cookware first appeared in the United States in 1981. It was imported from France, and 'France' is marked on the top part of the handle. Eventually, it was made in the U.S. in Martinsburg, West Virginia. In 1989 a non-stick surface was added to Visions, because food had a tendency to stick during cooking. In 1992 the Cranberry color was added. The addition of the Healthy Basics line was seen in 1993, then in 1994, the Healthy Basics Versa-Pots were added. This new version of Visions was not very popular and is now extremely rare. For more in-depth information and listings, see *The Complete Guide to Corning Ware & Visions Cookware* by Kyle Coroneos (Collector Books).

Baking dish, Wildflower, w/lid, 1½-qt **15.00**

Bread pan, Floral Bouquet, 2-qt. **12.00**

Bread pan, Nature's Bounty, yellow plastic lid, 2-qt **12.00**

Cake/utility dish, Country Festival, 8" sq **15.00**

Cake/utility dish, Spice O' Life, 8" sq **15.00**

Casserole, Blue Heather, oval, 2 handles, w/clear lid, 1½-qt **10.00**

Casserole, French, black, oval, clear lid, 2½-qt **25.00**

Casserole, French, round, clear lid, 2½-qt **10.00**

Casserole, French, white, oval, clear lid, 2½-qt **15.00**

Casserole, Pastel Bouquet, 2 tab handles, w/clear lid, 5-qt . **50.00**

Casserole, Sculptured Visions, round, w/lid, 24-oz **10.00**

Chafing dish, Black Trefoil, 2½-qt **12.00**

Chicken fryer, Cornflower Blue, 2 tab handles, clear lid, 10". **20.00**

Coffeemaker, Nature's Bounty, black handle & lid, 8-cup........... **25.00**

Container, storage; Country Festival, plastic lid, 2½-qt. **7.00**

Container, storage; Spice O' Life, plastic lid, 1½-qt................ **5.00**

Double boiler, Amber Visions, handle, w/lid, 1½-qt **20.00**

Dutch oven, All White, 2 tab handles, Pyroceram lid w/black knob, 4-qt......................... **15.00**

Dutch oven, Amber Visions, 2 handles, w/lid, 5-qt................ **40.00**

Dutch oven w/rack, Cornflower Blue, clear lid w/knob, 4-qt........ **20.00**

Percolator, electric, Black Trefoil, black handle, 6-cup......... **25.00**

Percolator, electric; Blue Cornflower, black handle, 10-cup....... **30.00**

Percolator, Spice O' Life, black handle, 10-cup **20.00**

Pie plate, All White, 9" **6.00**

Pie plate, French, 8½" **10.00**

Roaster, Amber Visions, w/lid, 4-qt **25.00**

Roaster, open; Blue Cornflower, 13" **20.00**

Roaster, open; Spice O' Life, 13". **15.00**

Roaster, open; Wildflower, 10¼x8½" **15.00**

Royal Buffet w/candle warmer, Avocado Round, clear lid, 2½-qt **15.00**

Royal Buffet w/candle warmer, Floral Bouquet, clear lid, 2½-qt **12.00**

Salt & pepper shakers, Country Festival, pr **8.00**

Sauce maker, Blue Cornflower, tab handle, 2 sm spouts, 1-qt. **15.00**

Saucepan, All White, 2 handles, Pyroceram lid w/black knob, 2½-qt **6.00**

Saucepan, Amber Visions, handle, spout on side, w/lid, 1-qt. **20.00**

Saucepan, Avocado Round, 2 handles, Pyroceram lid w/green knob, 1-qt........................... **5.00**

Saucepan, Blue Cornflower, 2 tab handles, clear lid w/fin handle............................. **8.00**

Saucepan, Blue Cornflower, 2 tab handles, clear lid w/knob, 2½-qt **15.00**

Saucepan, Floral Bouquet, handle, clear lid, 1-pt **7.00**

Saucepan, Sculptured Visions, handle, w/lid, 1½-qt............... **20.00**

Saucepan, Spice O' Life, 2 tab handles, clear lid w/knob, 1½-qt **12.00**

Saucepan, Spice O' Life, 2 tab handles, clear lid w/knob, 3-qt .**20.00**

Skillet, All White, w/clear lid, 10" **10.00**

Skillet, Cornflower Blue, 2 tab handles, Pyroceram lid, 10".. **20.00**
Skillet, electric; Blue Cornflower, w/clear lid, 10" **40.00**
Skillet, Wildflower, handle, w/clear lid, 6½" **7.00**

Stock pot, Cranberry, non-stick, 1992 – ?, 3½-quart, from $30.00 to $40.00. (Photo courtesy Kyle Coroneos)

Teakettle, Blue Cornflower, black handle, 2-qt **15.00**
Teapot, Floral Bouquet, black handle & lid, 6-cup **12.00**
Teapot, Spice O' Life, black handle & lid, 6-cup **15.00**
Tray, serving, Floral Bouquet, 14½" **12.00**
Tray, serving; Renaissance, w/serving cradle, 16" **25.00**
Trivet, Floral Bouquet, 6" sq ... **4.00**

Cracker Jack

The name Cracker Jack was first used in 1896. The trademark as well as the slogan 'The more you eat, the more you want' were registered at that time. Prizes first appeared in Cracker Jack boxes in 1912. Prior to then, prizes or gifts could be ordered through catalogs. In 1910, coupons that could be redeemed for many gifts were inserted in the boxes.

The Cracker Jack boy and his dog Bingo came on the scene in 1916 and have remained one of the world's most well-known trademarks. Prizes themselves came in a variety of materials, from paper and tin to pot metal and plastic. The beauty of Cracker Jack prizes is that they depict what was happening in the world at the time they were made.

To learn more about the subject, you'll want to read *Cracker Jack Toys, The Complete Unofficial Guide for Collectors*, and *Cracker Jack Advertising Collectibles,* both by Larry White, who is listed in the Directory under Massachusetts.

Note: Words in capital letters actually appear on the prize.

Button, US ARMY QUARTERMASTER, gold or silver wash on metal **12.50**
Charm, horse, cat, rabbit, etc, pot metal, ea **5.50**
Charm, man eating watermelon, white metal **8.75**
Clicker/screamer, CRACKER JACK **55.00**
Comb, plastic, marked, thick, Canadian **12.50**
CRACKER JACK FORTUNE TELLER, paper.............. **95.00**
Eyeglasses, CRACKER JACK WHEREVER YOU LOOK, paper w/celluloid inert.... **72.50**
FROG CHIRPER, metal, copyright 1946 Cloudcrest **40.00**
Game, SEND A MESSAGE BY DOT & DASH, paper...... **19.50**
GLOBE, metal........................ **60.00**
GLOW IN THE DARK STICKERS, paper, 1972 copyright **5.50**

Hat, ME FOR CRACKER JACK, paper.............................. **425.00**

JIG-SAW PUZZLE, Akron blimp, paper.............................. **135.00**

License plate card, paper, any of 50, ea...................................... **17.50**

Man, figure, made of wooden beads & wire.............................. **27.50**

Movie Star card, WRITE MOVIE STAR'S NAME HERE, paper........................... **27.50**

Paint books, BIRDS TO COLOR, paper, ea......................... **75.00**

Palm puzzle, cow over the moon, etc, paper & celluloid, ea. **95.00**

PHONEY PENNY 1¢, metal w/gold wash.................................. **30.00**

PICTURE PANORAMA, any of 14, ea...................................... **15.50**

Pipe, lion head, Germany...... **20.00**

RIDDLE BOOK, paper, series 1335, any of 18............................ **3.50**

Scale, metal gold bottom, red pans.............................. **35.50**

Spinner, CRACKER JACK GOLF, paper & wood................ **125.00**

SQUEEZE FACES, paper, any of 9...................................... **15.00**

Standup, motorcyclist, metal, various colors, ea.................. **27.50**

Standup, OFFICER, tin litho metal, about 3".......................... **19.50**

Tennis racquet, metal, Dowst.. **6.50**

SUNDIAL, metal, **$27.00**. (Photo courtesy Mary and Larry White)

TINY TATTOOS, paper, various colors, any of 16................ **1.50**

Top, ALWAYS ON TOP, tin.... **60.00**

TRICK MUSTACHE, paper punch-out card........................... **13.50**

Truck, Express, litho tin........ **74.50**

Whistle, BLOW FOR MORE w/PRIZE box pictured, paper.............. **49.50**

Whistle, CLOSE END WITH FINGERS, metal............. **15.00**

ZEPHYR, TOOTSIETOY, metal, about 2½".......................... **20.00**

Crackle Glass

Most of the crackle glass you see on the market today was made from about 1930 until the 1970s. At the height of its popularity, almost 500 glasshouses produced it; today it is still being made by Blenko, and a few pieces are coming in from Taiwan and China. It's hard to date, since many pieces were made for years. Some colors, such as red, amberina, cobalt, and cranberry, were more expensive to produce; so today these are scarce and therefore more expensive. Smoke gray was made for only a short time, and you can expect to pay a premium for that color as well.

Basket, tangerine w/crystal handle, ruffled rim, Kanawha, 1957-87, 6"............................... **85.00**

Candy dish, tangerine, footed, ruffled rim, Pilgrim, 1949-69, 5½".............................. **150.00**

Creamer, emerald green, drop-over handle, Pilgrim, 1949-69, 3". **45.00**

Decanter, captain's; crystal w/ amethyst stopper, 14" base, Hamon, 10".................... **400.00**

Decanter, crystal, footed, lg stopper, Bonita, 1931-53, 6¼" **200.00**

Pitcher, Blenko, 1940s, from $75.00 to $100.00. (Photo courtesy Stan and Arlene Weitman)

Pitcher, green, pulled-back handle, w/label, Kanawha, 1966-70s, 3¼" **60.00**

Pitcher, olive green, pulled-back handle, Rainbow, 1940s-60s, 3¾" **50.00**

Pitcher, ruby, drop-over handle, pear shape, Pilgrim, 1949-69, 3¾" **50.00**

Pitcher, tangerine, drop-over handle, waisted, Pilgrim, 3½" **55.00**

Pitcher, topaz, drop-over handle, waisted, Pilgrim, 1949-69, 3¾" **45.00**

Pitcher, topaz, pulled-back handle, flared neck, Harmon, 1966-70s, 3" **45.00**

Tumbler, sea green, Blenko, late 1940s-50s, 5¾" **75.00**

Vase, amethyst, low waisted, scalloped top, Bischoff, 1940-63, 7½" **175.00**

Vase, amethyst, waisted, Blenko, 1960s, 4¾" **85.00**

Vase, blue, pinched, Pilgrim, 1949-69, 4½" **55.00**

Vase, cobalt satin, bulbous w/high neck, maker unknown, 6".**110.00**

Vase, cranberry, trumpet neck w/ ruffled rim, Rainbow, 1940-50s, 5" **70.00**

Vase, crystal, block shape, Gillinder Brothers, 1930-50s, 8"..**125.00**

Vase, crystal, cylinder, flared ruffled rim, Bischoff, 1942-63, 5½".**60.00**

Vase, crystal, flared, ribbed sides, Gillinder, 1930-50s, 10".**100.00**

Vase, crystal w/green vaseline base, flared rim, 5" **100.00**

Vase, crystal w/sea green trim at neck, Blenko, 1950s, 5¼".**75.00**

Vase, emerald green, double-neck, Blenko, 1940-50s, 4" **80.00**

Vase, green, 3-ruffle top, trumpet neck, w/label, Jamestown, 1960s, 5" **45.00**

Vase, orange, footed, scalloped ruffles at rim, Blenko, 1940-50s, 7" **145.00**

Vase, smoke gray, waisted w/ruffled rim, Rainbow, 1940-60s, 4¾" **75.00**

Vase, tangerine, slim cylinder, maker unknown, 13" **125.00**

Vase, yellow, high waisted w/ruffled rim, Kanawha, 1957-87, 5¼" **50.00**

Czechoslovakian Glass

Czechoslovakia was established as a country in 1918. It was an area rich in the natural resources needed to produce both pottery and glassware. Wonderful cut and pressed scent bottles were made in a variety of colors with unbelievably well-detailed intaglio stoppers. Vases in vivid hues were decorated with contrasting applications or enamel work. See Clubs and Newsletters for information concerning the Czechoslovakian Collectors Guild International.

Basket, multicolored spatter w/ aventurine, crystal thorn handle, 6x5"............................ 85.00

Basket, pink varicolored, matching handle, 8"........................ 190.00

Basket, pink w/applied clear floral, black rim & handle, 7½x6".95.00

Basket, white cased w/millefiori canes, ruffled rim, blue handle, 9x5".................................. 325.00

Basket, white opaque w/arched orange handle, ruffled rim, 6¾x6¾"............................ 200.00

Bottle, dancing ladies intaglio in stopper, base cut w/4 feet, signed............................. 485.00

Bottle, pressed, topaz tinted w/ jewel ornaments, 2¼".... 100.00

Bowl, cased pink over white, rolled rim, pedestal foot, 3⅛x7½"..48.00

Bowl, crystal, geometric cuttings, facets w/stars, scalloped rim, 3x7"................................. 50.00

Box, crystal, geometric cuttings, sq, etched mark, 2½x3"........ 15.00

Candlesticks, multicolored swirl, white interior, triple-cased, 7", pr..................................... 155.00

Candy jar, orange/red/yellow canes floating in clear, footed, 8½".225.00

Jar, dresser; yellow w/reverse-painted cottage scene, label, 3x2¾"............................... 35.00

Perfume, black opaque w/cuttings, stepped, crystal faceted stopper, 6"............................... 250.00

Perfume, clear w/applied brass filigree & red jewels, ornate lid, 2"..................................... 135.00

Perfume, cut, black transparent w/ jewels, plain stopper, 4½"..750.00

Perfume, green, pyramidal w/faceted corners, ball stopper, 2½".. 75.00

Perfume, Hobnail, cranberry opal, bulbous, 5½"................. 225.00

Perfume, pink, conical w/jeweled stopper, 7¼".................. 115.00

Perfume, white satin w/red spiral, green stem, red finial/foot, 7¾"...................................... 40.00

Pitcher, gold & blue lustre diamond pattern outlined on white, 4½"...................... 20.00

Pitcher, parrot, multicolor, #30, Made in Czechoslovakia, 5x4"................................... 35.00

Vase, autumn-colored mottle w/ white flowers, gold accents, cased, 4"............................ 25.00

Vase, bud; orange w/silver overlay bird & flowers, 8⅜x2⅜"... 50.00

Vase, bud; red w/silver floral, 6x2"................................... 32.00

Vase, green, Mary Gregory boy, footed, 8½", pr 160.00

Vase, green w/multicolored spatter, fan form, 7¼".................. 70.00

Vase, lavender-blue, putti among flower garlands in relief, 3⅛x2"............................... 175.00

Vase, multicolor spatter, marked, 8", $70.00.

Vase, pale blue w/amethyst swirls, bulbous, 7x5½" 55.00

Vase, red w/amethyst spider webs, sm neck, bulbous, 11½x8" 295.00

Vase, red-orange w/black overlay foot, 9½x5" 135.00

Vase, white w/pink interior, ruffled rim, ball form, etched mark, 6".................................**50.00**

Decanters

The James Beam Distilling Company produced its first ceramic whiskey decanter in 1953 and remained the only major producer of these decanters throughout the decade. By the late 1960s, other companies such as Ezra Brooks, Lionstone, and Cyrus Noble were also becoming involved in their production. Today these fancy liquor containers are attracting many collectors. See also Elvis Presley.

Beam, '57 Bel Air, convertible, red, 1990................................**95.00**
Beam, '57 Bel Air Hot Rod, yellow, 1987................................**95.00**
Beam, '63 Stingray Corvette, silver, 1987................................**95.00**
Beam, American Cowboy, 1981..**20.00**
Beam, Chevy Trooper Car, gray & white, 1992......................**75.00**
Beam, Harley Davidson Eagle, 1983..............................**225.00**
Beam, Indianapolis 500, 1970..**14.00**
Beam, Marine Bulldog, 1979.**45.00**
Beam, St Bernard, 1979........**35.00**
Beam, Statue of Liberty Centennial, 1985................................**32.00**
Beam, Volkswagon, red, 1973.**75.00**
Beam, 1903 Model A Ford, red w/ black trim.......................**50.00**
Beam, 1928-35 Model A Ford Pickup, dark green, no markings, 1984..............................**250.00**
Beam, 1930 Ford Model A Fire Truck, 1983...................**225.00**

Beam, 1964 Mustang, red, 1985.......................**125.00**
Brooks, Clown w/Balloons, 1973..**27.00**
Brooks, Clydesdale Horse, 1974.**25.00**
Brooks, Fireman, 1975.........**32.00**
Brooks, Indian Maiden, Kachina #4, 1975............................**38.00**
Brooks, Indy Racer #21, 1970.**45.00**
Brooks, Slot Machine, 1971...**25.00**
Brooks, Snowy Owl #3, 1979.**35.00**
Brooks, 1957 Corvette, blue, 1976...........................**120.00**
Collectors Art, Brahma Bull, 1973.............................. **33.00**
Collectors Art, Dalmatian, mini, 1976............................**25.00**
Cyrus Noble, Carousel, white charger, 1979.........................**55.00**
Cyrus Noble, Deer, white-tailed buck, 1979....................**125.00**
Cyrus Noble, Landlady, 1977.**35.00**
Dugs Nevada, Moonlight Ranch, mini, 1977....................**235.00**
Dugs Nevada, Shamrock, mini, 1978............................**140.00**
Famous First, Bugatti Royal, 1973............................**350.00**
Famous First, Ferrari, red, 1983............................. **75.00**
Famous First, Sewing Machine, 1970..............................**45.00**
Grenadier, American Thoroughbred, 1978......................**60.00**
Grenadier, Napoleon, 1969....**32.00**
Hoffman, Bartender, series #3, 1975 ....**36.00**
Hoffman, Coon Dog, 1979......**56.00**
Hoffman, Doctor, 1974..........**40.00**
Hoffman, Doe & Fawn, 1975.**45.00**
Hoffman, Drummer, mini, 1979.**16.00**
Hoffman, Hare & the Tortoise, 1978 ....**22.00**
Hoffman, Penguins, 1979 ......**50.00**

Kontinental, Dentist, 1978 .... **30.00**

Kontinental, John Lennon bust, silver, 1981 .... **42.00**

Laurel & Hardy, Oliver Hardy, 1971 .... **60.00**

Laurel & Hardy, Stan Laurel, mini, 1971 .... **25.00**

Lewis & Clark (Alpha), Pioneer Family, 1978, pr **115.00**

Lewis & Clark (Alpha), Sitting Bull, 1976 .... **110.00**

Lionstone, Baseball Players, 1974 .... **75.00**

Lionstone, British Pointer, mini, 1975 .... **25.00**

Lionstone, Cardinal, 1972 ..... **29.00**

Lionstone, Fish, large-mouth bass, 1983 .... **65.00**

Lionstone, Hummingbird, mini, 1973 .... **45.00**

Lionstone, Indian Tribal Chief, 1973 .... **30.00**

Lionstone, Paul Revere, 1975. **25.00**

Lionstone, Snake Charmer, mini, 1973 .... **25.00**

MBC, Hacienda Hotel, mini, 1974 .... **53.00**

MBC, MGM Grand, mini, 1975. **38.00**

McCormick, Iwo Jima, 1983. **140.00**

McCormick, Mark Twain, 1977.. **26.00**

McCormick, Patrick Henry, 1975 .... **25.00**

McCormick, Pheasant, 1982.. **45.00**

McCormick, Tom T Hall, 1980. **85.00**

McCormick, Yacht America 13", 1970 .... **69.00**

Michters, Christmas Tree, 1978. **50.00**

Michters, King Tut Death Mask, 1978 .... **50.00**

Mike Wayne, John Wayne Bust, 1980 .... **55.00**

Old Commonwealth, Good Boy #3, 1981 .... **45.00**

Old Commonwealth, Lifesaver #5, 1983 .... **75.00**

Old Commonwealth, LSU Tiger, 1979 .... **47.00**

Old Commonwealth, Octoberfest, 1983 .... **46.00**

Old Commonwealth, Princeton, 1976 .... **23.00**

Old Fitzgerald, Irish Luck, 1972 .... **26.00**

Old Fitzgerald, Rip Van Winkle, 1971 .... **28.00**

Old Mr Boston, Miss Madison Boat, 1973 .... **35.00**

Old Mr Boston, Rocking Chair, 1965 .... **5.00**

Pacesetter, Big Blue Ford Tractor #4, 1983 .... **110.00**

Pacesetter, Case Tractor, mini . **35.00**

Potters, Dog Sled, 1977 .... **265.00**

Potters, Totem Pole, 1971...... **32.00**

Ski Country, Bull Moose, 1982...................... **115.00**

Ski Country, Fox & Butterfly, 1984............................... **82.00**

Ski Country, Red Shoulder Hawk, 1973 .... **66.00**

Ski Country, Scrooge, 1979.... **58.00**

Ski Country, Whooping Crane, 1984, $55.00.

Wild Turkey, Male #1, standing, 1971 .... **155.00**

Wild Turkey, Turkey in Flight #1, 1983 .... **100.00**

Degenhart

Elizabeth Degenhart and her husband John produced glassware in their studio at Cambridge, Ohio, from 1947 until John died in 1964. Elizabeth restructured the company and hired Zack Boyd who had previously worked for the Cambridge Glass Company, to help her formulate almost 150 unique and original colors which they used to press small-scale bird and animal figures, boxes, wines, covered dishes, and toothpick holders. Degenhart glass is marked with a 'D in heart' trademark. After her death and at her request, this mark was removed from the molds, some of which were bequeathed to the Degenhart museum. The remaining molds were acquired by Boyd, who added his own logo to them and continued to press glassware very similar to Mrs. Degenhart's.

Bicentennial Bell, Charcoal... **12.00**
Bird Toothpick Holder, Caramel Slag **25.00**
Buzz Saw Wine, Crystal **20.00**
Elephant Toothpick Holder, Cobalt Carnival, signed Terry Crider, rare **60.00**
Forget-Me-Not Toothpick Holder, Amberina **15.00**
Gypsy Pot, Amethyst **15.00**
Hand Ashtray/Pin Dish, Amethyst **10.00**
Heart Jewel Box, Vaseline **20.00**
Hen Covered Dish, Heliotrope, 2" **40.00**
Hen Covered Dish, Sapphire Blue **25.00**

Hobo Baby Shoe, Caramel Custard Slag **20.00**
Owl, Apple Green **20.00**
Owl, Bernard Boyd's Ebony .. **55.00**
Owl, Elizabeth's Lime Ice #1. **25.00**
Owl, Light Heliotrope **100.00**
Owl, Old Lavender **18.00**
Owl, Peach Blo **20.00**
Paperweight, The Lord Is My Shepherd..., 2¼x3" **88.00**
Pooch, April Green **15.00**
Pooch, Dark Toffee Slag **25.00**

Pooch, Emerald Green, $22.00.

Pooch, Tomato Gray-Ivory Slag Mix **30.00**
Priscilla, Bernard Boyd's Ebony. **22.00**
Priscilla, Bluebell **55.00**
Priscilla, Powder Blue Slag ... **17.50**
Robin Covered Dish, Amethyst, 5" **40.00**
Robin Covered Dish, Fawn Pink, 5" **50.00**
Turkey Covered Dish, Sapphire Blue, 5" **30.00**

Department 56

In 1976, this company introduced their original line of six handcrafted ceramic buildings. The Original Snow Village quickly won the hearts of young and old alike, and the light that sparkled from their windows added charm and warmth to Christmas celebrations everywhere. Accessories followed, and the line was expanded. Over the years, new villages have been developed — the Dickens Series, New England, Alpine, Christmas in the City, and Bethlehem. Offerings in the '90s included the North Pole, Disney Parks, and Seasons Bay. Their popular Snowbabies assortment was introduced in 1986, and today they're collectible as well. Our values are for mint condtion items; mint in box examples will be so noted in the lines. See also Cookie Jars.

Christmas Story, Ralphie's House, MIB 85.00

Dickens Village, Chesterton Manor House, 1987, MIB, $300.00.

Dickens Village, Ramsford Palace 95.00
Dickens Village, Tower of London, MIB 120.00
Halloween, Creepy's Pet Store, MIB 100.00
Halloween, Ghostly Carousel, retired, MIB 185.00
Halloween, Haunted Barn, MIB, from $135 to 175.00

New England Village, Smythe Woolen Mill, 1987, MIB . 385.00
Snow Village, Jingle Bell Houseboat, 1991, MIB, from $150 to. 175.00
Snow Village, Manchester Square, #58301, MIB 115.00
Snow Village, Mansion, w/green roof, MIB 350.00
Snow Village, McDonald's, MIB, from $100 to 135.00
Snow Village, Shelly's Diner, MIB 90.00
Snow Village, Starbucks Coffee Shop, #54859, MIB 300.00
Snow Village, Stardust Drive-In Theatre, MIB, from $100 to 125.00
Snowbaby, And Toto Too?, 1991, MIB 90.00
Snowbaby, Cinderella, baby w/slipper & 2 on pumpkin coach, set of 3 .... 125.00
Snowbaby, Falling for You, 1999 .... 13.00
Snowbaby, Jack Frost Through the Frosty Forest, MIB 185.00
Snowbaby, Polar Express, 2 on polar bear, retired, 6" L.. 65.00
Snowbaby, Wishing on a Star, #7943-0, 4", MIB 9.00

Depression Glass

Depression glass, named for the era when it sold through dime stores or was given away as premiums, can be found in such varied colors as amber, green, pink, blue, red, yellow, white, and crystal. Mass produced by many different companies in hundreds of patterns, Depression glass is one of the most sought-after collectibles in the United States today. For more information, refer to *Pocket Guide to Depression Glass and More*; *Collector's Encyclopedia of Depression Glass, 18th Edition;* and *Elegant Glassware of the Depression Era*; and *Glass Candlesticks of the Depression Era;* all are by Gene and Cathy Florence (Collector Books). See also Anchor Hocking/Fire-King. See Clubs and Newsletters for information concerning the National Depression Glass Association.

Adam, bowl, green, w/lid, 9".. **95.00**
Adam, butter dish, pink, w/lid .**100.00**
Adam, creamer, green............ **28.00**
Adam, plate, grill; pink, 9".... **27.00**
Adam, tumbler, green or pink, 4½"................................. **30.00**
Amelia, candlestick, crystal .. **25.00**
Amelia, plate, blue, 9½"........ **25.00**
American Pioneer, candy jar, crystal or pink, w/lid, 1-lb..... **95.00**
American Pioneer, goblet, water; green, 8-oz, 6"................. **60.00**
American Pioneer, sherbet, crystal or pink, 3½"..................... **16.00**
American Pioneer, vase, round, green, 9"........................ **250.00**
American Sweetheart, bowl, soup; flat, Monax, 9½".............. **87.50**
American Sweetheart, plate, ruby, 8"................................... **115.00**
American Sweetheart, tidbit, 2-tier, pink, 8" & 12"................. **60.00**
American Sweetheart, tumbler, pink, 10-oz, 4¾"............. **135.00**
Ardith, bowl, sq, all colors, 10" ..**80.00**
Ardith, cake stand, pedestal foot, all colors, 9¼"................. **75.00**
Ardith, cup, crystal................ **50.00**

Ardith, tray, sq, center handle, crystal, 10".................... **90.00**
Avocado, bowl, salad; crystal, 7½".**13.00**
Avocado, creamer, footed, pink or green................................. **35.00**
Avocado, pitcher, crystal, 64-oz.**350.00**
Avocado, plate, cake; handles, pink, 10¼"................................. **50.00**
Beaded Block, plate, crystal, green or pink, 8¾".................... **30.00**
Beaded Block, vase, bouquet; amber, 6"........................ **22.00**
Block Optic, bowl, cereal; pink, 5¼"................................. **30.00**
Block Optic, goblet, wine; green or pink, 4½"......................... **45.00**
Block Optic, ice bucket, green. **42.50**
Block Optic, plate, pink, 9".... **38.00**
Cameo, butter dish, green... **140.00**
Cameo, cookie jar, green........ **65.00**
Cameo, plate, grill; yellow, 10½".**10.00**
Cameo, plate, sandwich; pink, 10"................................. **55.00**
Cameo, sherbet, pink, 4⅞"... **125.00**
Cameo, tumbler, footed, yellow, 9-oz, 5"........................... **18.00**
Cherry Blossom, butter dish, pink............................. **100.00**
Cherry Blossom, plate, pink or green, 9"........................ **24.00**

Cherry Blossom, platter, green, 13", $80.00.

Cherry Blossom, salt & pepper shakers, scalloped bottom, green, pr **1,100.00**

Cherryberry, compote, crystal, 5¾" **18.00**

Cherryberry, olive dish, w/handle, pink or green, 5" **20.00**

Cherryberry, pitcher, crystal, 7¾" **185.00**

Chinex Classic, bowl, vegetable; Browntone, 7" **14.00**

Chinex Classic, sugar bowl, castle decal **20.00**

Circle, bowl, deep, green, 4½" . **17.50**

Circle, plate, pink, 8¼" **10.00**

Circle, tumbler, flat, green, 15-oz **30.00**

Cloverleaf, creamer, footed, black or green, 3⅝" **16.00**

Cloverleaf, plate, grill; green or yellow, 10¼" **30.00**

Cloverleaf, salt & pepper shakers, green, pr **42.00**

Columbia, bowl, ruffled rim, crystal, 10½" **20.00**

Columbia, cup, pink **25.00**

Columbia, plate, snack; crystal .**25.00**

Crackle, candlestick, sq base, crystal, ea **15.00**

Crackle, pitcher, bulbous, crystal, w/lid, 64-oz **45.00**

Cupid, cake plate, pink, 11¾". **200.00**

Cupid, candy dish, flat, 3-part, pink, w/lid **295.00**

Daisy & Button w/Narcissus, decanter w/stopper, crystal, 12½" **38.00**

Diana, bowl, cream soup; crystal, 5½" **12.00**

Diana, plate, sandwich; pink, 11¾" **25.00**

Diana, tumbler, crystal, 9-oz, 4⅛" **35.00**

Dogwood, bowl, berry; pink, 8½". **60.00**

Dogwood, plate, bread & butter; green or pink, 6" **9.00**

Dogwood, platter, 12" L **695.00**

Dogwood, saucer, green **7.00**

Doric, creamer, green, 4" **15.00**

Doric, relish tray, pink, 4x8" . **25.00**

Doric, salt & pepper shakers, green, pr **40.00**

Doric, tray, serving; green or pink, 8x8" **40.00**

Ellipse, bowl, w/handle, crystal, 4½" **12.00**

Ellipse, jug, crystal, 61-oz, 7½". **55.00**

English Hobnail, bowl, footed, pink or green, 8" **60.00**

English Hobnail, box, cigarette; turquoise, w/lid, 4½x2½". **55.00**

English Hobnail, lamp, electric, green or pink, 9¼" **150.00**

English Hobnail, plate, turquoise, 10" **85.00**

English Hobnail, vase, flared top, green or pink, 8½" **145.00**

Fancy Colonial, bonbon, w/handle, pink, 5½" **25.00**

Fancy Colonial, compote, footed, green, 6¼" **35.00**

Fancy Colonial, tumbler, iced-tea; pink, 14-oz **25.00**

Fancy Colonial, tumbler, whiskey; green, 2-oz **22.00**

Floragold, pitcher with ice lip, 64-ounce, $37.50.

Floral, butter dish, pink **100.00**

Floral, compote, ruffled or plain rim, pink, 9" **1,000.00**

Floral, pitcher, cone-shaped, footed, green, 32-oz, 8" **48.00**

Floral, platter, green, 10¾" L . **27.50**

Floral, salt & pepper shakers, footed, green, 4", pr **55.00**

Floral, tray, sq, closed handles, pink, 6" **27.50**

Florentine No 1, creamer, yellow .**22.00**

Florentine No 1, sugar bowl, pink or yellow **12.00**

Florentine No 2, gravy boat, yellow **55.00**

Florentine No 2, plate, green, 8½" **9.00**

Florentine No 2, tumbler, footed, green, 5-oz, 4" **15.00**

Flower Garden With Butterflies, candy dish, flat, pink, w/lid, 6" **130.00**

Flower Garden With Butterflies, plate, indented, black, 10" **100.00**

Georgian, bowl, cereal; green, 5¾" **25.00**

Georgian, plate, green, 9¼" ... **25.00**

Glades, candlestick, 2-light, crystal, 5", ea **35.00**

Glades, relish dish, 4-part, tab handle, crystal **32.50**

Hex Optic, bowl, mixing; pink or green, 10" **30.00**

Hex Optic, refrigerator dish, pink or green, 4x4" **18.00**

Hex Optic, tumbler, footed, pink or green, 7" **10.00**

Hobnail, bowl, crimped rim, handled, 6½" **17.50**

Hobnail, pitcher, milk; crystal, 18-oz **20.00**

Hobnail, sherbet, pink **7.00**

Iris, bowl, salad; ruffled rim, green or pink, 9½" **200.00**

Iris, cup, demitasse; crystal .. **45.00**

Iris, goblet, cocktail; crystal, 4-oz, 4½" **22.00**

Iris, plate, sandwich; crystal, 11¾" .**38.00**

Jubilee, cheese & cracker, pink or yellow **195.00**

Jubilee, mayonnaise w/plate & ladle, yellow **195.00**

Jubilee, vase, pink, 12" **195.00**

Laced Edge, tumbler, opalescent, footed, nine-ounce, $50.00. (Photo courtesy Gene and Cathy Florence)

Largo, ashtray, rectangle, amber or crystal, 3" L **16.00**

Largo, cake plate, pedestal foot, blue or red **95.00**

Largo, plate, w/cheese indent, amber or crystal, 10¾" **20.00**

Largo, tray, serving; 3-footed, blue or red, 13¾" **75.00**

Laurel, bowl, vegetable; oval, jade, 9¾" **55.00**

Laurel, creamer, tall, Poudre Blue **40.00**

Laurel, plate, grill; scalloped edge, French Ivory, 9" **15.00**

Laurel, salt & pepper shakers, jade, pr **90.00**

Laurel, tea set, children's; 14-pc, French Ivory **235.00**

Lincoln Inn, bonbon, oval, handles, red **16.00**

Lincoln Inn, bowl, olive; handles, green **9.50**

Lincoln Inn, plate, crystal, 12". **15.00**

Lincoln Inn, vase, footed, cobalt blue, 12-oz **165.00**

Little Jewel, bowl, berry; crystal, 7½" **15.00**

Little Jewel, jelly dish, footed, crystal, 5" **10.00**

Lois, bowl, fruit; pedestal foot, any color, 10" **50.00**

Lois, box, candy; w/octagonal lid, all colors **70.00**

Lois, stem, wine; any color **30.00**

Lotus, bottle, scent; pink, ½-oz.**110.00**

Lotus, bowl, belled, crystal, 11".**60.00**

Lotus, compote, high twisted stem, pink, 8½" **88.00**

Lotus, lamp, crystal **195.00**

Madrid, bowl, cream soup; amber, 4¾" **15.00**

Madrid, cake plate, amber, 11¼" dia **20.00**

Madrid, pitcher, sq, green, 60-oz, 8" **140.00**

Madrid, tumbler, footed, green, 5-oz, 4" **40.00**

Maya, candy dish, 3-part, footed, w/ lid, crystal......................... **42.50**

Maya, mayonnaise dish, crimped rim, 3-footed, red............. **45.00**

Maya, tray, tab-handled, crystal.**25.00**

Maya, tray, tab-handled, red.**60.00**

Mayfair, cookie jar with lid, green, $600.00; pink, $60.00. (Photo courtesy Gene and Cathy Florence)

Miss America, celery dish, pink, 10½" L.............................. **40.00**

Miss America, plate, grill; crystal, 10¼" **11.00**

Miss America, salt & pepper shakers, crystal, pr **35.00**

Miss America, tumbler, iced tea; pink, 14-oz, 5¾"............. **120.00**

Monticello, basket, crystal..... **22.00**

Monticello, bowl, lily; crystal, 5".**20.00**

Monticello, bowl, shallow, crystal, 10" **25.00**

Monticello, cupsidor, crystal.. **65.00**

Monticello, plate, crystal, 16½"..**55.00**

Monticello, vase, crystal, 6"... **22.00**

Moondrops, bowl, casserole; blue or red, w/lid, 9¾"............... **250.00**

Moondrops, butter dish, blue or red.................................. **60.00**

Moondrops, cup, blue or red.. **18.00**

Moondrops, decanter, blue or red, 8½" **70.00**

Moondrops, platter, blue or red, 12" L.. **45.00**

Mt Pleasant, bowl, scalloped rim, handles, pink or green, 8". **19.00**

Mt Pleasant, mint dish, center handle, amethyst or black, 6". **25.00**

Mt Pleasant, plate, w/indent for cup, sq, amethyst or black, 8¼" **16.00**

Mt Pleasant, sherbet, 2 styles, pink or green........................... **10.00**

Mt Vernon, cup, punch; crystal. **5.00**

Mt Vernon, pitcher, 54-oz, crystal................................... **35.00**

Mt Vernon, plate, torte; crystal, 13¼" **27.00**

Mt Vernon, punch bowl, crystal.**35.00**

New Century, bowl, cream soup; green, 4¾"........................ **22.00**

New Century, decanter w/stopper, crystal **75.00**

New Century, sugar bowl, green, w/
lid 28.00
New Century, tumbler, footed, crystal, 5-oz, 4" 22.00
Normandie, plate, grill; pink, 11".25.00
Normandie, plate, iridescent,
9¼" 15.00
Normandie, saucer, amber or iridescent 2.00
Old Cafe, candy jar, crystal w/Royal
Ruby lid, 5½" 28.00
Old Cafe, lamp, crystal 100.00
Old Cafe, vase, Royal Ruby, 7¼".55.00
Old Colony, cookie jar, pink ... 85.00
Old Colony, plate, pink, 7¼" .. 31.00
Old Colony, relish dish, deep,
3-part, pink, 7½" 88.00
Old Colony, vase, frosted pink,
7" 90.00
Olive, bowl, rose; cupped, emerald
or pink, 7" 22.00
Olive, cup, blue or red............ 12.00
Olive, saucer, emerald or pink. 3.00
Orchid, candlesticks, crystal, 5¾",
pr..................................... 125.00
Orchid, vase, crystal, 8"....... 110.00
Parrot, bowl, soup; amber, 7".38.00
Parrot, creamer, footed, green. 55.00
Parrot, platter, amber, 11¼" L. 75.00
Parrot, salt & pepper shakers,
green, pr 295.00
Patrick, bowl, console; yellow,
11" 125.00
Patrick, tray, center handle, pink,
11" 125.00
Radiance, bowl, flared, red, 12".65.00
Radiance, honey jar, cobalt blue, w/
lid 125.00
Radiance, tumbler, red, 9-oz.. 34.00
Rock Crystal, candy dish, crystal,
w/lid 75.00
Rock Crystal, pitcher, crystal, ½-gal,
7½" 195.00

Sandwich (Indiana), celery dish,
crystal, 10½" 16.00
Sandwich (Indiana), plate, green,
10½" 20.00

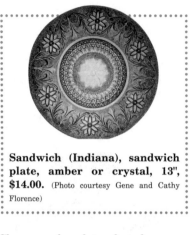

Sandwich (Indiana), sandwich
plate, amber or crystal, 13",
$14.00. (Photo courtesy Gene and Cathy
Florence)

Sharon, cake plate, footed, green,
11½" 65.00
Sharon, platter, pink, 12½" L. 30.00
Twisted Optic, plate, buffet; green,
14" 25.00
Twisted Optic, sugar bowl, blue.18.00
Windsor, bowl, handles, pink, 9". 22.00
Windsor, relish plate, divided, crystal, 11½" 15.00
Windsor, tray, w/handle, pink,
8½x9¾" 24.00

Dollhouse Furnishings

Collecting antique dollhouses
and building new ones is a popular
hobby with many today, and all who
collect houses delight in furnishing
them right down to the vase on the
table and the scarf on the piano! Flea
markets are a good source of dollhouse furnishings, especially those
from the 1940s through the 1960s
made by Strombecker, Tootsietoy,

Renwal, or the Petite Princess line by Ideal. For an expanded listing, see *Schroeder's Collectible Toys, Antique to Modern*.

Armoire, w/hangers, Tomy-Smaller Homes 15.00
Baby crib, pink, Renwal 10.00
Bathroom set, in original box w/insert & floor plan, Plasco 50.00
Bathtub, ivory w/blue trim, Reliable 15.00
Bed, w/blue spread, Jaydon... 15.00

Bedroom set, ½" scale, Allied, MIB, $80.00. (Photo courtesy Marcie Tubbs)

Breakfast nook set, white painted cast iron, table & 2 benches, Arcade 100.00
Cabinet w/television, high, Tomy-Smaller Homes 55.00
Carpet sweeper, 2 rollers w/red & blue handle, Ideal Young Decorator 30.00
Carriage, w/doll, blue, stenciled, Renwal 35.00
Chair, barrel; blue stenciled on brown base, Renwal 15.00
Chair, bedroom occasional; ivory w/hot pink seat, Marx Little Hostess 8.00
Chair, dining; tan w/paper seat cover, Plasco 4.00
Chair, living room; w/base, green or mauve, Plasco 15.00

China closet, dark marbleized maroon, Ideal Young Decorator 25.00
Fireplace, ivory, Marx Little Hostess 20.00
Grandfather clock, #4423-0, Ideal Petite Princess 20.00
Highboy, black, opening drawers, Renwal 22.00
Highboy, tan, Plasco 8.00
Juke box, hard plastic, ½" scale, bright yellow or red, Marx 20.00
Kiddie car, blue w/red & yellow, Renwal 55.00
Kitchen sink, ivory w/black, Jaydon 15.00
Lamp, table; blue, Tootsietoy . 45.00
Lamp, table; ivory w/red shade or red w/red shade, Jaydon. 15.00
Lawn mower, any color combination, Commonwealth 30.00
Medicine cabinet, ivory, Tootsietoy 25.00
Piano w/stool, Blue Box 8.00
Planter, #4440-4, Ideal Petite Princess 15.00
Playground slide, blue w/red steps or yellow w/blue steps, Renwal 22.00
Playpen, pink, Ideal Young Decorator 45.00
Radio, floor; rust, Reliable 15.00
Refigerator, avocado, Marx Little Hostess 25.00
Refigerator, white w/black, opening door, cardboard backing, Deluxe 30.00
Scale, ivory or red, Renwal.... 10.00
Server, red, opening drawer, Renwal 15.00
Sewing machine, tabletop; red w/ blue base, Renwal 85.00

Shopping cart, blue w/white baskets or white w/blue baskets, Ideal **40.00**

Sofa, biege/gold, #4407-3, Ideal Petite Princess **25.00**

Sofa, green flocked, Strombecker, 1950s, 1" scale **25.00**

Stove, opening door, ivory w/red door, Renwal **18.00**

Stove, white w/ivory trim, Strombecker, 1961, ¾" scale **18.00**

Table, coffee; walnut, Kage **3.00**

Table, dining room; #4421-4, Ideal Petite Princess **15.00**

Table, umbrella; blue w/ivory, Plasco **15.00**

Table & chair set, folding; gold table, 4 red & gold chairs, Renwal **120.00**

Table set, occasional; #4437-0, Ideal Petite Princess **27.00**

Television, dog picture, yellow detail, Ideal **45.00**

Toilet, ivory w/black handle, Ideal **20.00**

Washing machine, blue w/pink, bear decal, Renwal **30.00**

Watering can, orange, Irwin .. **10.00**

Dollhouses

Flea markets are a great place to find those old toys of your childhood, including dollhouses. Many are mansions in miniature, finished out with great care and detail. Our listings represent a sampling of dollhouses from the 1930s through the 1980s made by many different manufacturers.

Fisher-Price, 3-story, 5 rooms, #250, spiral staircase, 1978-80, M **40.00**

Fisher-Price, 3-story, 5 rooms, #280, b/o, 1981-84, M **30.00**

Jayline, 2-story, 5 rooms, litho tin, 14½x18½", 1949, VG **50.00**

Marx, Colonial, 2-story, litho tin, breezeway, clapboard over brick, 1960s, NM **75.00**

Marx, split-level, litho tin, patio above garage, red w/gray roof, VG **65.00**

Marx, 2-story w/2 side single rooms, litho tin, 15x43", EX **40.00**

Marx, 2-story w/flat-roofed side room, litho tin, bay window, 13x8x25", EX **50.00**

T Cohn, litho tin, blue shutters, furnished, 16x24", 1951, VG..**200.00**

Wolverine, colonial mansion, no garage, ½" scale, EX **50.00**

Wolverine, country cottage, #800, ½" scale, 1986, EX **50.00**

W. P., Maker of Little Houses, Mamaroneck, N. Y. stencilled on base, seven rooms, central staircase, furnished, 23x45", $675.00.
(Photo courtesy Bertoia Auctions)

Dolls

Doll collecting is no doubt one of the most active fields today. Antique as well as modern dolls are treasured, and limited edition or artists' dolls often bring prices in excess of several hundred dollars. Investment potential is considered excellent in all areas. Dolls have been made from many materials — early to middle nineteenth-century dolls were carved of wood, poured in wax, and molded in bisque or china. Primitive cloth dolls were sewn at home for the enjoyment of little girls when fancier dolls were unavailable. In this century from 1925 to about 1945, composition was used. Made of a mixture of sawdust, clay, fiber, and a binding agent, it was tough and durable. Modern dolls are usually made of vinyl or molded plastic.

Learn to check your intended purchases for damage which could jeopardize your investment. In the listings, values are for dolls in excellent to near mint condition unless another condition is noted in the line or in the subcategory narrative. Played-with, soiled dolls are worth from 50% to 75% less, depending on wear. Many are worthless.

For more information we recommend *Collector Dolls of the 1960s & 1970s* by Cindy Sabulis and *Doll Values* by Linda Edward, and *Collector's Encyclopedia of American Composition Dolls Vol. I* and *II* by Ursula R. Mertz, all published by Collector Books. See also Action Figures; Advertising Collectibles; Character Collectibles; Holly Hobbie and Friends. See Clubs and Newsletters for information on *Doll Castle News* Magazine.

American Character

In business by 1918, this company made both composition and plastic dolls, all of excellent quality. Many collectors count them among the most desirable American dolls ever made. The company closed in 1968, and all of their molds were sold to other companies. The hard plastic dolls of the 1950s are much in demand today. See also Betsy McCall. For more information we recommend *American Character Dolls* by Judith Izen (Collector Books).

Annie Oakley, hard plastic, walker, 1953, 14".........................**400.00**
Cartwright, Ben; Bonanza character, 1966, 9"...................**100.00**
Eloise, cloth w/molded mask face, yarn hair, 1955, 22"......**475.00**
Little Miss Echo, vinyl, recorder in torso, 1964, 30".............**250.00**
Puggy, composition, molded hair, frowning, w/tag, 1928, 13".**475.00**
Sally-Joy, composition/cloth, 1930s, 24"..................................**350.00**
Tiny Tears, hard plastic & vinyl, 1950s, 16".......................**325.00**
Toni, vinyl head w/rooted hair, 1958, 10½"......................**175.00**
Toodles, hard rubber, 1956, 29".**325.00**

Annalee

Annalee Davis Thorndike made her first commercially sold dolls in the late 1950s. They're characterized by their painted felt faces and the meticulous workmanship involved in their manufacture.

Most are made entirely of felt, though Santas and rabbits may have flannel bodies. All are constructed around a wire framework that allows them to be positioned in imaginative poses. Depending on rarity, appeal, and condition, some of the older dolls have increased in value more than 10 times their original price. Dolls from the 1950s carried a long white red-embroidered tag with no date. The same tag was in use from 1959 until 1964, but there was a copyright date in the upper right-hand corner. In 1970 a transition period began. The company changed its tag to a white satiny tag with a date preceded by a copyright symbol in the upper right-hand corner. In 1975 they made another change to a long white cotton strip with a copyright date. In 1982 the white tag was folded over, making it shorter. Many people mistake the copyright date as the date the doll was made — not so! It wasn't until 1986 that they finally began to date the tags with the year of manufacture, making it much easier for collectors to identify their dolls. Besides the red-lettered white Annalee tags, numerous others were used in the 1990s, but all reflect the year the doll was actually made. For more information refer to *Garage Sale and Flea Market Annual,* published by Collector Books. Values are given for dolls in clean, near-mint condition.

Abraham Lincoln, Folk Hero, 1989, 10".....................................**150.00**

Back to School, Logo Kid, 1992, 10".....................................**35.00**

Bear with honey pot and bee, 1986, 18", from $110.00 to $125.00. (Photo courtesy Margart Fox Mandel)

Goin' Fishin', Logo Kid, 1995, 10"...............................**35.00**
Golfer, 1966, 10½"...............**200.00**
Mark Twain, Folk Hero, 1986, 10"...............................**150.00**
Mending My Teddy, Logo Kid, 1999, 10"...................................**18.00**
Naughty, Logo Kid, 1987, 10".**75.00**
Pocahontas, Folk Hero, 1995, 10"...............................**150.00**
Reading, Logo Kid, 1990, 10".**75.00**
Robin Hood, Folk Hero, 1983, 10"...............................**150.00**
Uncle Sam, Folk Hero, 1990, 10"...........................**150.00**

Betsy McCall

Tiny 8" Betsy McCall was manufactured by the American Character Doll Company from 1957 until 1963. She was made from fine quality hard plastic with a bisque-like finish and had hand-painted features. Betsy came with four hair colors — tosca, blond, red, and brown. She has blue sleep eyes, molded lashes, a winsome smile, and a fully jointed body with bendable knees. On her back is an identification circle which reads ©McCall Corp. The basic doll could be purchased for $2.25 and wore a sheer chemise, white taffeta panties, nylon socks, and Maryjane-style shoes.

There were two different materials used for tiny Betsy's hair. The first was soft mohair sewn onto mesh. Later the rubber skullcap was rooted with saran which was more suitable for washing and combing.

Betsy McCall had an extensive wardrobe with nearly 100 outfits, each of which could be purchased separately. They were made from wonderful fabrics such as velvet, felt, taffeta, and even real mink fur. Each ensemble came with the appropriate footware and was priced under $3.00. Since none of Betsy's clothing is tagged, it is often difficult to identify other than by its square snap closures (although these were used by other companies as well).

Betsy McCall is a highly collectible doll today but is still fairly easy to find at doll shows. The prices remain reasonable for this beautiful clothes horse and her many accessories, some of which we've included below. For further information we recommend *Betsy McCall, A Collector's Guide* by Marci Van Ausdall. See Clubs and Newsletters for information concerning the *Betsy McCall's Fan Club*.

American Character, hard plastic, jointed, sleep eyes, 1960, 8"........**225.00**
Horsman, vinyl & hard plastic, sleep eyes, 1974, 12½" **50.00**
Ideal Toy Corp, vinyl, rooted hair, 1961, 22"....................... **175.00**

Ideal Toy Corp, vinyl & hard plastic, saran wig, 1952, 14".......**275.00**
Rothchild, hard plastic, sleep eyes, 1986, 8"...........................**25.00**

Celebrity Dolls

Dolls that represent movie or TV personalities, fictional characters, or famous sports figures are very popular collectibles and can usually be found for well under $100.00. Mego, Horsman, Ideal, and Mattel are among the largest producers. Condition is vital. To price a doll in mint condition but without the box, deduct about 65% from the value of one mint in the box. Dolls in only good or poorer condition drop at a very rapid pace. For more information see *Schroeder's Collectible Toys, Antique to Modern*, published by Collector Books.

Brooke Shields, LJN, 1982, rare, 11½", MIB **150.00**

Debby Boone, © Resi Inc./Taiwan, Mattel, 1966, MIB, from $65.00 to $75.00. (Photo courtesy Cindy Sabulis)

Dolly Parton, Goldberger, 1978, 11½", MIB **100.00**

Elvis Presley, Eugene, 1984, 12", MIB **75.00**

George Burns, Effanbee, 1996, 17", MIB **150.00**

Ginger Rogers, World Doll, limited edition, 1976, MIB **100.00**

Jaclyn Smith, Mego, 1977, 12½", MIB **200.00**

James Cagney, Effanbee, 1987, 16", MIB **125.00**

Kiss, Mego, any from group, 1978, 12½", MIB **350.00**

Lucille Ball, Effanbee, 1985, 15", MIB **175.00**

Marilyn Monroe, Tri-Star, 1982, 11½", MIB **75.00**

Monkees, Davy Jones, Remco Ind. Inc./Harrison N.J., 1970, NM, from $20.00 to $30.00. (Photo courtesy Cindy Sabulis)

Princess Diana, Goldberg, 1983, 11½", MIB **100.00**

Eegee

The Goldberger company made these dolls, Eegee (E.G.) being the initials of the company's founder. Dolls marked 'Made in China' were made in 1986.

Babette, hard plastic & vinyl, rooted hair, 1970, 15" **30.00**

Baby Carrie, hard plastic & vinyl, 1970, 24", w/carriage or carry seat **50.00**

Barbara Cartland, hard plastic & vinyl, painted face, adult, 15" **45.00**

Miss Charming, composition, Shirley Temple look-alike, 1936, 19" **400.00**

My Fair Lady, vinyl, fashion type, jointed, 1958, 20" **65.00**

Susan Stroller, hard plastic & vinyl, rooted hair, 1955, 26" **90.00**

Effanbee

This company has been in business since 1910, continually producing high quality dolls, some of all composition, some composition and cloth, and a few in plastic and vinyl. Our dolls are for those in excellent condition and in their original clothing.

Baby Evelyn, composition & cloth, 1925, 17" **250.00**

Babyette, composition, molded closed eyes, 1943, 13" ... **325.00**

Candy Kid, compositon, sleep eyes, toddler, 1946, 13" **375.00**

Honey, composition, jointed, human hair wig, sleep eyes, 1948, 18-21" **300.00**

Lamkin, composition & cloth, molded gold ring on finger, 1930, 16" **450.00**

Lovums, composition & cloth, sleep eyes, 1928, 16-18" **350.00**

Patsy Ruth, cloth body, crier, sleep eyes, 1934, 26" **1,600.00**

Suzanne, composition, jointed, sleep eyes, wigged, 1940, 14" **350.00**

Fisher-Price

Since the mid-1970s, this well-known American toy company has been making a variety of dolls. Many have vinyl heads, rooted hair, and cloth bodies. Most are marked and dated.

Baby Ann, #204, 1974-76, EX. **25.00**
Elizabeth, Black, #205, 1974-76, EX **25.00**
Jenny, #201, 1974-76, EX **25.00**
Muffy, #241, 1979-80, EX **10.00**
My Friend Christie, #8120, 1990, EX, from $40 to **75.00**
My Friend Nicky, #206, 1985, EX **30.00**

My Sister Mary, vinyl head, cloth body, #200 on body tag, missing skirt, otherwise NM, $28.00.

Horsman

During the 1930s, this company produced composition dolls of the highest quality. Today many of their dolls are vinyl. Hard plastic dolls marked '170' are also Horsmans. Our values are for dolls in excellent condition and in their original clothing. For more information we recommend *Horseman Dolls: The Vinyl Era, 1950 to Present*, by Don Jensen (Collector Books).

Ballerina, vinyl, jointed elbows, 1957, 18" **50.00**
Bright Star, composition, 1930, 14" **200.00**
Cindy, hard plastic, child, 1950s, 15" **125.00**
Dimples, composition & cloth, molded dimples, 1927-37, 13-14". **225.00**
Flying Nun, TV character, 1965, 12" **100.00**
Jackie, vinyl, rooted hair, blue sleep eyes, 1961, 25" **150.00**
Jo Jo, bisque, blue sleep eyes, toddler, 1937, 13" **325.00**
Naughty Sue, bisque, jointed, 1937, 16" **400.00**

Ideal

For more than 80 years, this company produced quality dolls that were easily affordable by the average American family. Their Shirley Temple and Toni dolls were highly successful. They're also the company who made Miss Revlon, Betsy Wetsy, and Tiny Tears. For more information see *Collector's Guide to Ideal Dolls* by Judith Izen. Our values are for dolls in good condition with their original clothes if made prior to 1950; those made after that time are priced as in excellent condition with their original clothing and tags. See also Dolls, Shirley Temple and Tammy.

Captain Action, vinyl, 1966-68, 12" **250.00**
Cinderella, composition, flirty eyes, human hair wig, 1938-39, 22" **375.00**

Clarabelle (Howdy Doody), cloth w/ mask face, 1954, 16", w/accessories **200.00**

Flatsy, Black, vinyl, wire armature, rooted hair, 1969, 5" **30.00**

Flossie Flirt, composition & cloth, flirty eyes, 1924-31, 14". **225.00**

Me So Glad, Belly Button Babies; hard plastic & vinyl, 1971, 9½" **30.00**

Pinocchio, composition & wood, 1940+, 11" **450.00**

Princess Beatrix, composition & cloth, flirty eyes, 1938-43, 14" **175.00**

Snow White, cloth w/mask face, mohair wig, dwarfs on skirt, 1939, 16" **500.00**

: **Tony, hard plastic head, blue sleep eyes, closed mouth, original wig and clothes, 14", EX, $250.00.**
: (Photo courtesy McMasters Harris Auction Co.)

Jem

Accessory, Rock 'n Curl, 1986, MIB **70.00**

Doll, Aja, original outfit, 1986, M **35.00**

Doll, Aja, original outfit, 1986, MIB **80.00**

Doll, Banee, original outfit, MIB . **55.00**

Doll, Clash, original outfit, MIB .. **50.00**

Doll, Danse, original outfit, MIB .. **80.00**

Doll, Jerrica, star earrings & 2 outfits, 1985, MIB **92.00**

Doll, Kimber, original outfit, 1985, MIB **80.00**

Doll, Rio, original outfit, 1985, MIB **40.00**

Liddle Kiddles

Produced by Mattel between 1966 and 1971, Liddle Kiddle dolls and accessories were designed to suggest the typical 'little kid' in the typical neighborhood. These dolls can be found in sizes ranging from ¾" to 4", all with poseable bodies and rooted hair that can be restyled. Later, two more series were designed that represented storybook and nursery rhyme characters. The animal kingdom was represented by the Animiddles and Zoolery Jewelry Kiddles. There was even a set of extraterrestrials. And lastly, in 1979 Sweet Treets dolls were marketed.

Items mint on card or mint in box are worth about 50% more than one in mint condition but with none of the original packaging. Based on mint value, deduct 50% for dolls that are dressed but lack accessories. For further information we recommend *Dolls of the 1960s and 1970s,* by Cindy Sabulis, and *Schroeder's Collectible Toys, Antique to Modern*; both are published by Collector Books.

Animiddle, Kiddles, MIP, ea. **125.00**

Baby Rockaway, #3819, MIP . **75.00**

Chitty-Chitty Bang-Bang Kiddles, #3597, MOC **150.00**

Florence Niddle, #3507, complete, M..................................75.00

Frosty Mint Kone, #3653, complete, M..................................60.00

Heart Charm Bracelet Kiddle, #3747, MIP.....................50.00

Kampy Kiddle, #3753, complete, M..................................150.00

Lenore Limousine, #3743, complete, M............................50.00

Lorelei Locket, #3717, 1967, MIP.............................75.00

Tiny Tiger, #3636, MIP........125.00

Violet Kologne in cologne bottle (part of nine-doll set), 1968 – 1969, M, $25.00 (MIP, $75.00). (Photo courtesy Kathy Tvdik)

Madame Alexander

Founded in 1923, Beatrice Alexander began her company by producing an Alice in Wonderland doll which was all cloth with an oil-painted face. By the 1950s, there were over 600 employees making dolls of various materials. The company is still producing lovely dolls today. For further information, we recommend *Collector's Encyclopedia of Madame Alexander Dolls, 1948 – 1965,* and *Madame Alexander Collector's Doll Price Guide*; both are by Linda Crowsey and published by Collector Books. Our values are for dolls in mint condition with original clothing and tags.

Alice in Wonderland, cloth, flat face, 1930-50s, 16".........775.00

Baby Jane, composition & cloth, 1935, 16".........................900.00

Bride, Alexander-kins, composition, straight leg, 1973-75, 8".75.00

Bridesmaid, plastic & vinyl, 1966-87, 17"............................125.00

Cissette, Coral and Leopard, made for Bloomingdale's Department Stores, 1997, 10", MIB, $125.00. (Photo courtesy Linda Crowsey)

Darlene, cloth & vinyl, 1991-92, 18"....................................85.00

Dutch, hard plastic, straight leg, 1972-73, 8".......................75.00

Emily, cloth, black & white dress, 2002-2003, 14"................90.00

Fairy Queen, composition & cloth, child, 1939-46, 14".........650.00

Gibson Girl, hard plastic, wig, 7-pc adult body, 1957-1963, 10".800.00

Gretel, hard plastic, straight legs, 1976-86, 8"......................60.00

Happy, vinyl, 1970 only, 20".175.00

Karen Ballerina, composition, blue sleep eyes, 1940, 15".....900.00

Little Shaver, cloth, yarn hair, 1940-44, 10"...................275.00

Littlest Kitten, vinyl, 1965, 8"..175.00

Sugar Tears, vinyl, 1964, 12".100.00

Sweet Tears, vinyl, 1965-74, 9".85.00

Baby's Hungry, battery-operated, 1967-68, 17"....................20.00

Baby Say 'n See, eyes & lips move while talking, 1967-68, 17" **100.00**

Chatty Cathy, hard plastic & vinyl, blond pigtail, 1960-68, 20", MIB **610.00**

Grizzly Adams, vinyl, 1971, 10".**40.00**

Mrs Beasley, vinyl & cloth, 1965, 16" **275.00**

Shrinkin' Violette, cloth, yarn hair, pull-string talker, 1964, 16" **175.00**

Tiny Chatty Baby, Black, talker, 1963-64, 15½" **100.00**

Mattel

Though most famous, of course, for Barbie and her friends, the Mattel company also made celebrity dolls, Liddle Kiddles, Chatty Cathy, talking dolls, lots of action figures (the Major Matt Mason line and She-Ra, Princess of Power, for example), and in more recent years, Baby Tenderlove and P.J. Sparkles. Our values are for dolls in excellent condition with original clothing and accessories. See also Barbie; Dolls, Liddle Kiddles.

Baby Beans, talking, 12", M.. **40.00**

Baby First Step, 1964, M **95.00**

Baby Fun, 1968, 7", complete, EX **35.00**

Baby Love Light, battery-op, 16", M **18.00**

Baby See 'n Say, 1967-68, 17", M **35.00**

Baby Tender Love, 1971, 16", EX **45.00**

Chatty Cathy, 1960s, 20", EX.**275.00**

Chatty Cathy, 1970 reissue, MIB **100.00**

Dancerella, 1976, 15", MIB ... **75.00**

Tearful Tender Love, 1971, 16", EX **50.00**

Tiny Chatty Brother, vinyl with sleep eyes, two teeth, rooted hair, 1963, 15½", NM, $50.00. (Photo courtesy Patsy Moyer)

Nancy Ann Storybook Dolls

Nancy Ann Abbott was a multifaceted, multitalented Californian who seemed to excel at whatever was her passion at the moment. Eventually she settled on designing costumes for dolls. This burgeoned into a full-fledged and very successful doll company which she founded in 1937. Early on, her 5" dolls were imported from Japan, but very soon she was making her own dolls, the first of which had jointed legs, while those made in the early '40s had legs molded as part of the body (frozen). But it was their costumes that made the dolls so popular. Many series were designed around various themes — storybook characters; the flower series; Around the World Dolls of every ethnic persuasion; the American girls; sports and family series; and dolls representing seasons, days of the week, and the months of the year. Ms. Abbott died in 1964, and within a year the company closed. Unless otherwise noted, our values are for dolls in good condition with original clothing and wrist tags.

American Girl series, Western Miss, bisque, MIB **900.00**
Around the World series, Chinese, bisque, MIB **1,200.00**
Baby, Storybook Dolls; bisque & hard plastic, painted eyes, 1948, 4" **75.00**
Baby Sue Sue, vinyl, nude, 1960s, EX **150.00**
Margie Ann series, Margie Ann, bisque, MIB **175.00**
Masquerade series, Cowboy, bisque **700.00**
Muffie, hard plastic, wig, sleep eyes, non-walker, 1953-56, 8" **300.00**
Nancy Ann Style Show, hard plastic, sleep eyes, ca 1954, 18", NMIB **850.00**
Topsy, Black, bisque, jointed legs, 1947-48, 5" **450.00**

Raggedy Ann and Andy

Designed by Johnny Gruelle in 1915, Raggedy Ann was named by combining two James Whitcomb Riley poem titles, *The Raggedy Man* and *Orphan Annie*. The early cloth dolls he made were dated and had painted-on features. Though these dolls are practically nonexistent, they're easily identified by the mark, 'Patented Sept. 7, 1915.' P.F. Volland made these dolls from 1920 to 1934; theirs were very similar in appearance to the originals. The Mollye Doll Outfitters were the

first to print the now-familiar red heart on her chest, and they added a black outline around her nose. These dolls carry the handwritten inscription 'Raggedy Ann and Andy Doll/Manufactured by Mollye Doll Outfitters.' Georgene Averill made them ca 1938 to 1950, sewing their label into the seam of the dolls. Knickerbocker dolls (1963 to 1982) also carry a company label. The Applause Toy Company made these dolls for two years in the early 1980s, and they were finally taken over by Hasbro, the current producer, in 1983.

Besides the dolls, scores of other Raggedy Ann and Andy items have been marketed, including books, radios, games, clocks, bedspreads, and clothing. Our values are for dolls in clean, unfaded condition and in appropriate clothing, unless noted otherwise.

Applause, Sleepytime, 17" **30.00**
Applause, 1985, 8" **10.00**
Applause, 20" **50.00**
Georgene Novelties, long nose w/ curved nose edges, 1950s, 15", NM **325.00**
Georgene Novelties, long-nose face, 1944-46, 19" **1,000.00**
Georgene Novelties, nose outlined w/ black, 1938-44, 15-17" **850.00**
Knickerbocker, Korea, 15" **35.00**
Knickerbocker, Musical Ann, 1970s, 15" **100.00**
Knickerbocker, Taiwan, 19", ea .**40.00**
Knickerbocker, Teach & Dress, 1970s, 20" **50.00**
Knickerbocker, 1960s, 19" ... **175.00**
Mollye Goldman, 1935-37, 15".**900.00**

Remco

The plastic and vinyl dolls, made by Remco during the 1960s and 1970s, are gaining popularity with collectors today. Many have mechanical features that were activated either by a button on their back or batteries. The Littlechap Family of dolls (1964), Dr. John, his wife Lisa, and their two children, Judy and Libby, came with clothing and fashion accessories of the highest quality. Children found the family less interesting than the more glamorous fashion dolls on the market at that time, and as a result, production was limited. These dolls in excellent condition are valued at about $15.00 to $20.00 each, while their outfits range from about $30.00 (loose and complete) to a minimum of $50.00 (MIB). Our values are for dolls in good condtion with original clothing and accessories.

Baby Glad 'n Sad, hard plastic & vinyl, 1967, 14", MIB......**18.00**
Baby Laugh A Lot, vinyl w/plush body, battery-operated, 1970, 16"......................................**15.00**
Beatles, vinyl & plastic, 1964, 4½", MIB, ea............................**95.00**
Heidi, vinyl, press button & doll waves, 1967, 5½".............**45.00**
Jeannie, I Dream of; vinyl, 1968, 6", MIB............................**55.00**
Judy Littlechap, 1963+, 12"..**50.00**
Laurie Partridge, vinyl, 1973, 19"................................**95.00**
Lily Munster, vinyl, 1-pc body, #1822, 1964, 4¾".............**90.00**
Orphan Annie, 1967, 15", NMIB.**110.00**

Shirley Temple

The public's fascination with Shirley was more than enough reason for toy companies to literally deluge the market with merchandise of all types decorated with her likeness. Dolls were a big part of that market, and the earlier composition dolls in excellent condition are often priced at a minimum of $600.00 on today's market. Many were made by the Ideal Company, who in the 1950s also issued a line of dolls made of vinyl. For more information we recommend *The Complete Guide to Shirley Temple Dolls and Collectibles* by Tonya Bervaldi-Camaratta (Collector Books). Our values are for dolls in excellent condition with original clothing and shoes.

Bisque, Japan, 1930-40, 6"..**195.00**
Composition, Ideal, jointed, mohair wig, 1934-40s, 11".........**850.00**

Composition, wig, sleep eyes, button, 17", NM, from $875.00 to $950.00.

Plastic, Ideal, white dress w/red dots, 17", MIB.................**40.00**
Porcelain, Danbury Mint, 1987, 16"....................................**65.00**

Vinyl, Ideal, rooted hair, w/plastic scrip pin, ST/12, 1957, 12", MIB **375.00**

Strawberry Shortcake and Friends

Strawberry Shortcake and friends came onto the market around 1980 and quickly captured the hearts of little girls everywhere. A line of accessories and related merchandise were soon added. Strawberry Shortcake vanished from the scene in the mid-1980s but has currently reappeared. The originals have become highly collectible.

Doll, Almond Tea, 6", MIB **30.00**
Doll, Angel Cake & Souffle, 6", NRFB **40.00**
Doll, Apple Dumpling, cloth w/yarn hair, 12" **25.00**
Doll, Apple Dumpling & Tea Time Turtle, 6", MIB **75.00**
Doll, Apricot, 15" **35.00**
Doll, Baby Needs a Name, 15". **35.00**
Doll, Berry Baby Orange Blossom, 6", MIB **35.00**
Doll, Butter Cookie, 6", MIB . **25.00**
Doll, Cafe Ole, 6", MIB **45.00**
Doll, Cherry Cuddler, 6", NRFB. **45.00**
Doll, Huckleberry Pie, flat hands, 6", MIB **45.00**
Doll, Lemon Meringue, cloth w/ yarn hair, 15" **25.00**
Doll, Lemon Meringue, 6", MIB. **45.00**
Doll, Lime Chiffon, 6", MIB... **45.00**
Doll, Mint Tulip, 6", MIB **50.00**
Doll, Orange Blossom & Marmalade, MIB **45.00**
Doll, Orange Blossom & Marmalade, 1984 .... **25.00**

Doll, Peach Blush & Melonie Belle, 6", MIB **115.00**
Doll, pillow; Huckleberry Pie, 9". **10.00**
Doll, Purple Pieman w/Berry Bird, poseable, MIB................. **35.00**
Doll, Strawberry Shortcake & Custard, 6", NRFB........ **150.00**

Doll, Raspberry Tart, plastic hat, 1980, came with bear-like animal called Rhubarb, EX, $15.00.

Figure, Cherry Cuddler w/ Gooseberry, Strawberryland Miniatures, MIP............. **20.00**
Figure, Lime Chiffon w/balloons, PVC, 1", MOC **15.00**
Figure, Merry Berry Worm, MIB.. **35.00**
Figure, Mint Tulip w/March Mallard, PVC, MOC **15.00**
Figure, Raspberry Tart w/bowl of cherries, MOC **15.00**
Figure, Strawberry Shortcake, ceramic, 5"........................ **8.00**

Tammy

In 1962, the Ideal Novelty & Toy Company introduced their teenage Tammy doll. Slightly pudgy and not quite as sophisticated as some of the teen fashion dolls on the market at the time, Tammy's innocent charm captivated consumers. Her extensive wardrobe and numerous accessories added to her popularity with children. Tammy had everything including a car, a house, and a catamaran. In addition, a large number of companies obtained licenses to issue products using the 'Tammy' name. Everything from paper dolls to nurse's kits were made with Tammy's image on them. Tammy's success was not confined to the United States. She was also successful in Canada and in several European countries.

Accessory Pak, luggage case, airline ticket & camera, #9183-0, NRFP **25.00**
Case, Dodi, green background. **30.00**
Doll, All Grown Up Tammy, vinyl & plastic, 1962+, MIB **85.00**
Doll, Misty, Black, vinyl & plastic, 1962+, MIB **100.00**
Doll, Patti, vinyl & plastic, 1962+, MIB **200.00**

Doll, Pepper, vinyl and plastic, carrot-colored hair, MIB, $70.00.
(Photo courtesy Cindy Sabulis)

Doll, Tammy, Black, vinyl & plastic, marked, 1962+, 12", MIB **75.00**

Doll, Tammy's Mom, vinyl & plastic, marked, 1962+, 12½", MIB **45.00**
Outfit, Dad & Ted, blazer & slacks, #9477-1, NRFP **20.00**
Outfit, Pepper, Happy Holiday, #9317-9, M **40.00**
Outfit, Tammy, Cutie Coed, #9132-2 or 9932-5, M **45.00**
Pepper's Treehouse, MIB **150.00**
Tammy's Car, MIB **75.00**
Tammy's Jukebox, M **50.00**

Vogue

This is the company that made the Ginny doll famous. She was first made in composition during the late 1940s, and if you could find her in mint condition, she'd bring about $450.00 on today's market. (Played with and in relatively sad condition, she's still worth about $90.00.) Ginny dolls from the 1950s were made of rigid vinyl. The last Ginny came out in 1969. Tonka bought the rights in 1973, but the dolls they produced sold poorly. After a series of other owners, Dakin purchased the rights in 1986 and began producing a vinyl doll that resembled the 1950-style Ginny very closely. For more information, we recommend *Collector's Encyclopedia of Vogue Dolls* by Judith Izen and Carol Stover (Collector Books). Our values are for dolls in good condition with original clothing unless otherwise noted.

Davy Crockett, hard plastic, w/ coonskin cap & rifle, 1955, 8", MIB **935.00**

Ginnette, vinyl, jointed, sleep eyes, 1956-69, 8", MIB **250.00**

Ginny, hard plastic, strung joints, w/tag, 1948-50, 8" **375.00**

Ginny, rigid vinyl, on roller skates, ca. 1950s, complete, M, $500.00.

Ginny, vinyl, jointed, non-walker, 1977-82, 8" **25.00**

Jeff, vinyl, 5-pc body, 1958-60, 11" **85.00**

Toddles, composition, jointed, 1937-48, 8" **450.00**

Toddles, composition, Red Riding Hood outfit, 1937-48, 8", M **625.00**

Doorstops

Doorstops, once called door porters, were popular from the Civil War period until after 1930. They were used to prop the doors open during the hot summer months so that the cooler air could circulate. Though some were made of brass, wood, and chalk, cast iron was by far the most preferred material, usually molded in amusing figurals — dogs, flower baskets, frogs, etc. Hubley was one of the largest producers. Beware of reproductions! Unless another material is mentioned in the description, our values are for painted cast-iron doorstops. Prices are for examples in exceptional condition unless otherwise noted and should be reduced equivalent to the amount of wear apparent. See Clubs and Newsletters for information concerning the Doorstop Collectors of America.

Apple blossoms in woven basket, Hubley #329, 7⅞x5⅜", $100 to **150.00**

Bellhop, blue uniform, #1244, 8⅞x4⅝", from $275 to **350.00**

Black Golfer, 8½", VG, $385.00. (Photo courtesy Bertoia Auctions)

Bobby Blake w/teddy bear, Grace Dayton design, Hubley, 9½" .**250.00**

Cape Cod, cottage w/flowers, Albany Foundry, 5¾x9", from $125 to **200.00**

Colonial Dame, pink & blue dress, blue shawl, Hubley #37, 8x4½" **250.00**

Cottage w/fence, flowers by door & wall, National Foundry, 7¼", EX **140.00**

Cricket (narrower antennas than bootjack), 2x9" **85.00**

Deco nude stands before elevated circle, 9¼", from $200 to .**275.00**

Delphiniums, roses & forget-me-nots in vase w/blue ribbon, Hubley, 9" **415.00**

Dutch girl, head bowed, full figured, 6x3¾", from $150 to **225.00**

Elephant on stair base, B&H #7798, 10½" **330.00**

Fawn, green on dark green base, Taylor Cook #6, 1930, 10x6" **300.00**

Frog, open mouth, 6½x4½", from $100 to **150.00**

German shepherd, embossed harness, heavy green base, 7⅞x9", EX **140.00**

Grapes & leaves, Albany Foundry, 7¾x6½", from $125 to **200.00**

Hunchback cat, startled look, 10⅝x7½", EX **385.00**

Lighthouse, Light of the World, 9½x6½", from $100 to **175.00**

Nasturtiums in striped vase, Hubley #221, 7¼x6½", from $125 to **175.00**

Peasant girl, fruit basket on head, Hubley #5, 8¾x5" **225.00**

Persian kitten w/tail curled around body, Hubley, 8½x6½" **275.00**

Poppies, CHF Co. #110, 11x9", EX, $600.00.
(Photo courtesy Morphy Auctions)

Rabbit eating carrot, green base w/ cast bushes, 5½" **440.00**

Rose basket, Hubley #121, 11x8" **200.00**

Squirrel, eating nut, 6x6", from $150 to **225.00**

Stagecoach w/driver & 2 horses, 7½x12¼", from $75 to **125.00**

Stork, stylized, comic pose, wedge back, 5x3¾" **415.00**

Tulips in pot, National Foundry, 8¼x7" **550.00**

Welsh Corgi, tilted head, B&H, 8¼x5⅞", from $200 to **275.00**

Windmill in field, National Foundry #10, 6¾x6⅞", EX **195.00**

Woman w/ruffled skirt, unmarked, 6⅜x4⅞", from $150 to **225.00**

Dragon Ware

Dragon ware is fairly accessible and still being made today. The new Dragon ware is distinguishable by the lack of detail in the dragon, which will appear flat.

Colors are primary, referring to background color, not the color of the dragon. New pieces are shinier than old. New colors include green, lavender, yellow, pink, blue, pearlized, and orange as well as the classic blue/black. Many cups have lithophanes in the bottom. Nude lithophanes are found but are scarce. New pieces may have lithophanes; but again, these tend to be without detail and flat.

Items listed below are unmarked unless noted otherwise. Ranges are given for pieces that are currently being produced. Be sure to examine unmarked items well; in particular, look for good detail. Newer pieces lack the quality of workmanship evident in earlier items and should not command the prices of the older ware. Use the low end to evaluate any item you feel may be new.

Candlesticks, black, Made in Japan, pr from $50 to **125.00**

Condiment set, black, salt & pepper shakers, mustard w/spoon & tray **75.00**

Creamer & sugar bowl, orange & white, 3½", from $25 to ... **40.00**

Cup & saucer, child's, green, D China, from $10 to **20.00**

Cup & saucer, coffee; black cloud, HP Bensons, from $30 to. **45.00**

Cup & saucer, demi; double nude lithophane, Niknoiko China, $75 to **125.00**

Cup & saucer, demi; goggly eyes, red & black, Castle mark, $30 to **35.00**

Cup & saucer, demi; googly eyes, red/black swirl, Castle mark, $30 to **35.00**

Cup & saucer, demi; nude lithophane, gray traditional, from $45 to **75.00**

Ginger jar, blue cloud, Lego Made in Japan, 5", from $35 to **50.00**

Lamp, gray, jewel eyes, Nippon quality, 7¾", from $150 to **225.00**

Mustard jar, gray, w/lid & spoon, 3-pc, 3½", from $15 to **40.00**

Nappy, gray, hand painted, w/spoon, Made in Japan, 5½", from $20 to **35.00**

Saki cups, yellow cloud, whistling, set of 6, from $30 to **50.00**

Saki set, blue cloud, whistling, kitten on decanter/plate, 8-pc **175.00**

Salt & pepper shakers, orange, pagoda style, Japan, 4", pr from $15 to **40.00**

Salt & pepper shakers, pink, pearlized, Florida souvenir, pr, $5 to **20.00**

Tea set, gray, sq, Noritake, teapot, creamer & sugar bowl, w/lid **125.00**

Teapot, creamer and sugar bowl with lid, $65.00.

Vase, blue cloud, wide mouth, 5", from $20 to **30.00**

Vase, blue w/gold, Made in Occupied Japan, 2⅜", from $5 to **15.00**

Vase, gray, glass eyes, footed, Nippon quality, 4⅜", from $125 to **275.00**

Vase, orange, Made in Japan, 7½", from $30 to **75.00**

Vase, yellow, Made in Japan, 5", from $7.50 to **20.00**

Watering can, green, Made in Japan, 2½", from $7.50 to **20.00**

Dreamsicles

The sweet-faced cherubs known as Dreamsicles are often found on the secondary market at the flea market and garage sale levels. Many will carry the ink-stamped name 'Kristin' for Kristin Haynes, the artist that created them in 1991, and often a paper label with the name of the particular subject that is depicted. To keep up with growing demands for her products, Haynes turned to Cast Art Industries of Mexico to make her designs. Today they are being the Willits company.

Anticipation, #ASP002	**30.00**
Bunny Love, #10062	**22.00**
Cutout Cutie, #B	**22.00**
Finishing Touches, #DX248	**175.00**
Free Spirit, Angel Hugs, #CD005	**40.00**
Golden Forever Friends, #10658	**18.00**
Hand in Hand, #DC431, 1996	**25.00**
Little Dickens & Long Fellow, bookends, #DC127 & #DC126	**90.00**
Mom's Little Honey, #12205, 2002	**14.00**
Morning Glory Birdhouse Box, 1999	**22.00**
Peace Keeper, musical water globe, #11966D	**15.00**
Relay for Life, American Cancer Society	**15.00**
Spilt Milk, 1996	**50.00**
Star Performer, #1134D	**18.00**
When I Was Two, picture frame, #32383	**16.00**
Yankee Doodle Dandy, #10793, 2002	**15.00**

Egg Timers

The origin of the figural egg timer appears to be Germany, circa 1920s or 1930s, with Japan following their lead in the 1940s. Some American companies may have begun producing figural timers at about the same time, but evidence is scarce in terms of pottery marks or company logos.

Figural timers can be found in a wide range of storybook characters (Oliver Twist), animals (pigs, ducks, rabbits), career and vocational uniformed people (chef, London Bobby, housemaid), or people in native costume.

All types of timers were a fairly uniform height of 3" to 4". If a figural timer no longer has its sand tube, it can be recognized by the hole which usually goes through the back of the figure or the stub of a hand. Most timers were made of ceramic (china or bisque), but a few are of cast iron and carved wood. They can be detailed or quite plain. Listings below are for timers with their sand tubes completely intact.

Black chef standing with frying pan, chalkware, Japan, $95.00. (Photo courtesy Ellen Bercovici)

Bunny standing on hind quarters, timer in right paw, left ear bent, 3"	**55.00**
Chef, towel under right arm w/ timer in left, Occupied Japan, 3½"	**75.00**
Coffeepot, long spout & wooden handle, black finial, 8½"	**35.00**
Duck, yellow w/green hat, red umbrella under right wing, timer in left	**85.00**
Dutch boy & girl kissing in front of windmill, E-6101, 4¾"	**75.00**

Elf stands beside stump w/recipe holder atop, timer by stump, 5½" **55.00**

Friar Tucks (2) in brown, timer between figures, Goebel, 3¼" **125.00**

Girl in black hat & pants, red shoes, timer in hand, Germany, 4¾" **125.00**

Lighthouse, blue, cream & orange lustre, Germany, 4½" **85.00**

Mickey Mouse, seated & holding timer, Hertwig & Co #1417, 3" **125.00**

Newspaper boy, Japan, 3¾" ... **40.00**

Panda bear holding green leaves, timer on back, 2½" **45.00**

Penguin, chalkware, England, 3¾", from $25 to **40.00**

Sailor w/sailboat, Germany, 4". **50.00**

Telephone, black glaze on red clay, Japan, 2" **35.00**

Veggi man or woman, bisque, Japan, 4½", ea **95.00**

Welsh woman, Germany, 4½". **50.00**

Elegant Glass

To quote Gene and Cathy Florence, Elegant glassware 'refers mostly to hand-worked, acid-etched glassware that was sold by better departmant and jewelry stores during the Depression era through the 1950s, differentiating it from dime store and give-away glass that has become known as Depression glass.' Cambridge, Duncan & Miller, Fostoria, Heisey, Imperial, Morgantown, New Martinsville, Paden City, Tiffin, U.S. Glass, and Westmoreland were major producers. For further information we recommend *Elegant Glassware of the Depression Era*, by Gene and Cathy Florence (Collector Books). For the later glassware lines of these companies, see '40s, '50s, and '60s Glassware.

Cambridge

Achilles, plate, cake; crystal, w/ handles, #3900/35, 13½". **85.00**

Adonis, bonbon, crystal, footed, w/ handles, #3900/130, 7½". **45.00**

Apple Blossom, ashtray, yellow or amber, heavy, 6" **100.00**

Apple Blossom, plate, pink, 8½". **30.00**

Apple Blossom, salt & pepper shakers, amber, #3400/77, pr. **95.00**

Apple Blossom, water, crystal, stemmed, #3135, 8-oz **22.00**

Candlelight, bowl, crystal, flared, 4-footed, #3400/4, 12" **85.00**

Candlelight, candlestick, crystal, #646, 5" **65.00**

Candlelight, relish, crystal, 3-part, #3400/91, 8" **65.00**

Caprice, bowl, fruit; blue or pink, #18, 5" **70.00**

Caprice, candy dish, crystal, 3-footed, w/lid, #165, 6" **42.50**

Caprice, nut dish, blue or pink, divided, #94, 2½" **40.00**

Caprice, pitcher, crystal, ball shape, #183, 80-oz **125.00**

Caprice, vase, blue or pink, ball shape, #241, 4¼" **95.00**

Chantilly, butter dish, crystal, round, w/lid **195.00**

Chantilly, cocktail icer, crystal, 2-pc **60.00**

Chantilly, tumbler, ice tea; footed, #3625, 12-oz **24.00**

Chantilly, wine, crystal, #3779, 2½-oz **30.00**

Cleo, bowl, pink, oval, 11½" ... **70.00**

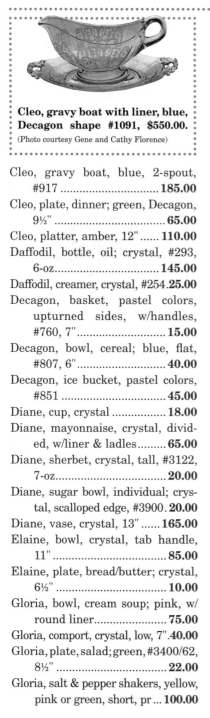

Cleo, gravy boat with liner, blue, Decagon shape #1091, $550.00.
(Photo courtesy Gene and Cathy Florence)

Cleo, gravy boat, blue, 2-spout, #917 .... 185.00
Cleo, plate, dinner; green, Decagon, 9½" 65.00
Cleo, platter, amber, 12" 110.00
Daffodil, bottle, oil; crystal, #293, 6-oz................ 145.00
Daffodil, creamer, crystal, #254.25.00
Decagon, basket, pastel colors, upturned sides, w/handles, #760, 7" 15.00
Decagon, bowl, cereal; blue, flat, #807, 6" 40.00
Decagon, ice bucket, pastel colors, #851 .... 45.00
Diane, cup, crystal 18.00
Diane, mayonnaise, crystal, divided, w/liner & ladles 65.00
Diane, sherbet, crystal, tall, #3122, 7-oz................................ 20.00
Diane, sugar bowl, individual; crystal, scalloped edge, #3900. 20.00
Diane, vase, crystal, 13" 165.00
Elaine, bowl, crystal, tab handle, 11" 85.00
Elaine, plate, bread/butter; crystal, 6½" 10.00
Gloria, bowl, cream soup; pink, w/ round liner...................... 75.00
Gloria, comport, crystal, low, 7".40.00
Gloria, plate, salad; green, #3400/62, 8½" 22.00
Gloria, salt & pepper shakers, yellow, pink or green, short, pr ... 100.00

Marjorie, finger bowl, crystal, #7606 .... 40.00
Marjorie, marmalade, crystal, w/ lid, #145 .... 95.00
Marjorie, nappie, crystal, #4111, 8" 90.00
Marjorie, water, crystal, stemmed, #3750, 10-oz..................... 22.00
Mt Vernon, cake stand, amber or crystal, footed, #150, 10½" 35.00
Mt Vernon, rose bowl, amber or crystal, #106, 6½" 18.00
Mt Vernon, vase, amber or crystal, footed, #54, 7" 35.00
Number 520, bowl, oval, #914, 12" 45.00
Number 520, gravy boat, amber or green, double spout, #917. 95.00
Number 520, platter, oval, Peach Blo, #903, 14½" 75.00
Number 703, candlestick, green, #625 .... 30.00
Number 703, creamer, green, #138................. 15.00
Number 704, cigarette box, all colors, #616 .... 50.00
Number 704, decanter, all colors, #0315 .... 195.00
Portia, cup, crystal, round, #3400/54 .... 16.00
Portia, goblet, crystal, #3124, 10-oz................................ 28.00
Portia, plate, crystal, w/handle, 6".................... 15.00
Rosalie, platter, amber or crystal, 12" 50.00
Rosalie, tray, celery; pink or green, 11" 40.00
Rosalie, vase, blue or pink, footed, 5½" 85.00
Rose Point, ashtray, crystal, #721, 2½" sq............... 30.00

Rose Point, candelabrum, crystal, 2-light, #1338 .... **75.00**

Rose Point, tray, crystal, #3500/67, 12" dia............................ **195.00**

Tally Ho, cup, punch; Carmen or Royal, flat **25.00**

Tally Ho, plate, salad; amber or crystal, 7½" **12.50**

Tally Ho, tumbler, tall, Forest Green, 10-oz **35.00**

Valencia, relish, crystal, 4-compartment, #3500/65, 10" **60.00**

Valencia, tumbler, crystal, footed, #3500 10-oz..................... **20.00**

Wildflower, candy dish, crystal, round, w/lid, #3900/165 .... **115.00**

Wildflower, salt & pepper shakers, crystal, #3400/77, pr **45.00**

Wildflower, vase, crystal, footed, #6004, 6" **65.00**

Duncan and Miller

Canterbury No 115, ashtray, crystal, 5" **12.00**

Canterbury No 115, basket, crystal, oval, 1-handle, 3½" **26.00**

Canterbury No 115, plate, cake; crystal, 14"....................... **25.00**

Canterbury No 115, plate, dinner; crystal, 11¼" **25.00**

Canterbury No 115, vase, crystal, crimped, 5" **17.50**

Caribbean, bowl, vegetable; blue, flared edge, 9¼" **75.00**

Caribbean, creamer, blue....... **22.00**

Caribbean, cruet, crystal **40.00**

Caribbean, wine, crystal, egg cup shape, 2½-oz, 3⅜" **20.00**

First Love, cup, crystal, #115. **12.50**

First Love, honey dish, crystal, #91, 5x3" **30.00**

First Love, sugar bowl, crystal, #111, 10-oz, 3" **15.00**

Lily of the Valley, bowl, crystal, 12".................................... **60.00**

Lily of the Valley, mayonnaise, crystal **30.00**

Lily of the Valley, tumbler, water; crystal, footed.................. **25.00**

Nautical, decanter, blue....... **550.00**

Nautical, ice bucket, opalescent **300.00**

Nautical, plate, blue, 10", $100.00.
(Photo courtesy Gene and Cathy Florence)

Nautical, plate, crystal, 6"..... **10.00**

Puritan, vase, all colors **65.00**

Sandwich, bottle, oil; crystal, 5¾" **30.00**

Sandwich, cake stand, crystal, footed, rolled edge, 11½" **75.00**

Sandwich, champagne, crystal, 5-oz, 5¼".......................... **15.00**

Sandwich, tray, crystal, oval, 18" **18.00**

Tear Drop, candlestick, crystal, 4"................................... **12.50**

Tear Drop, flower basket, loop handle, 12"........................... **100.00**

Tear Drop, plate, torte; crystal, 14" **38.00**

Terrace, cocktail shaker, crystal or amber, w/metal lid **85.00**

Terrace, plate, cobalt or red, 11"
sq **125.00**

Terrace, tumbler, shot; crystal or
amber, 2-oz **15.00**

Fostoria

For more information we recommend *The Fostoria Value Guide*
by Milbra Long and Emily Seate,
published by Collector Books. See
also Coin Glass.

**Alexis, creamer, short hotel;
crystal, $55.00.** (Photo courtesy Gene and
Cathy Florence)

American, ashtray, crystal, 5" sq..**45.00**
American, basket, crystal, 10". **40.00**
American, bottle, scent; crystal, w/
stopper, 6-oz, 5¼" **65.00**
American, bowl, lemon; crystal, w/
lid, 5½" **55.00**
American, butter dish, crystal, w/
lid, ¼-lb **22.00**
American, cup, crystal, footed,
7-oz **7.00**
American, plate, crystal, 8½". **12.00**
Baroque, bowl, celery; yellow,
11" **35.00**
Baroque, candelabrum, crystal,
2-light, 16 lustres, 8¼".. **100.00**
Baroque, sherbet, blue, 5-oz,
3¾" **25.00**
Brocade, candy dish, blue, w/lid,
#2331, 3-pt **185.00**

Brocade, comport, Orchid, twist
stem, tall, #2327, 7" **75.00**
Brocade, finger bowl, crystal,
#869 .... **60.00**
Colony, bowl, salad; crystal, 7¾".**22.00**
Colony, cheese & cracker, crystal.**50.00**
Colony, pitcher, milk; crystal,
16-oz **58.00**
Colony, vase, bud; crystal, flared,
6" **14.00**
Fairfax, bonbon, rose or blue .**12.50**
Fairfax, creamer, topaz or green,
flat **14.00**
Fairfax, gravy boat, amber **20.00**
Fairfax, salt & pepper shakers,
Orchid, footed, pr **60.00**
Fuchsia, bowl, crystal, #2395,
10" **95.00**
Fuchsia, plate, luncheon; #2440,
8" **20.00**
Fuchsia, wine, Wisteria, #6004,
2½-oz **50.00**
Hermitage, mustard, crystal, w/lid
& spoon, #2449 .... **17.50**
Hermitage, relish, pickle; amber or
green, #2449, 8" **11.00**
Hermitage, tumbler, Wisteria,
#2449½, 2-oz, 2½" **35.00**
June, bowl, cereal; topaz, 6½".**45.00**
June, bowl, cream soup; rose or
blue, footed **60.00**
June, tray, crystal, center handle,
11" **25.00**
June, whiskey, yellow or green,
footed, 2-oz **28.00**
Kashmir, bowl, baker; blue, 9". **85.00**
Kashmir, candlestick, yellow or
green, 3" **22.00**
Lafayette, platter, Wisteria, 12".**110.00**
New Garland, platter, amber or
topaz, 15" **50.00**
New Garland, tray, celery; rose,
11" **30.00**

New Garland, water goblet, rose, #4120 .... **28.00**

Rogene, cordial, crystal, #5082, ¾-oz **40.00**

Rogene, marmalade, crystal, #1968, w/lid **45.00**

Rogene, vase, crystal, rolled edge, 8½" **100.00**

Royal, almond dish, amber or green, #4095 .... **28.00**

Royal, egg cup, amber or green, #2350 .... **30.00**

Royal, plate, dinner; amber or green, #2350, 9½" **12.00**

Royal, sherbet, amber or green, low, #869, 6-oz **10.00**

Seville, stem, cocktail; green, #870 .... **14.00**

Seville, tumbler, amber, footed, #5084, 9-oz **14.00**

Seville, urn, amber, sm, #2324. **75.00**

Sunray, bonbon, crystal, handled, 6½" **16.00**

Sunray, coaster, crystal, 4" **8.00**

Sunray, plate, sandwich; crystal, 12" **32.00**

Trojan, bowl, lemon; rose, #2375 ....**24.00**

Trojan, plate, cake; handled, #2375, 10" **45.00**

Trojan, plate, chop; topaz, #2375, 13" **55.00**

Versailles, bowl, fruit; pink or yellow, #2375, 5" **30.00**

Versailles, creamer, green, footed, #2375½ **25.00**

Versailles, plate, bread; blue, #2375, 6" **10.00**

Vesper, candlestick, blue, #2324, 4", ea **50.00**

Vesper, platter, amber, #2350, 15". **95.00**

Vesper, sugar bowl, green, footed, #2350½ **14.00**

Heisey

For more information we recommend *Heisey Glass, 1896 – 1957,* by Neila and Tom Bredehoft, published by Collector Books.

Charter Oak, candlestick, crystal, #116, 3", ea **25.00**

Charter Oak, coaster, crystal, #10 .... **10.00**

Charter Oak, coaster, Flamingo, #10 .... **20.00**

Charter Oak, coaster, Hawthorne, #10 .... **35.00**

Charter Oak, compote, Marigold, low, footed, #3362, 6" **100.00**

Charter Oak, oyster cocktail, crystal, footed, #3362, 3½-oz ... **8.00**

Charter Oak, oyster cocktail, Hawthorne, footed, #3362, 3½-oz **40.00**

Charter Oak, parfait, crystal, #3362, 4½-oz **15.00**

Charter Oak, parfait, Moongleam, #3362, 4½-oz **35.00**

Charter Oak, pitcher, Moongleam, flat, #3362 .... **180.00**

Charter Oak, plate, dinner; crystal, #1246, 10½" **30.00**

Charter Oak, plate, luncheon; Flamingo, #1246, 8" **15.00**

Charter Oak, tumbler, Flamingo, #3362, 12-oz **20.00**

Charter Oak, tumbler, Hawthorne, #3362, 12-oz **40.00**

Chintz, bowl, vegetable; oval, Sahara, 10" **35.00**

Chintz, ice bucket, crystal, footed **85.00**

Chintz, plate, crystal, w/handles, 12" **25.00**

Chintz, tray, celery; Sahara, 10". **30.00**

Chintz, vase, crystal, dolphin foot, 9" **95.00**

Crystolite, bowl, salad; crystal, 10" **50.00**

Crystolite, creamer, crystal, round **40.00**

Crystolite, pitcher, syrup; crystal, Drip Cut **135.00**

Ipswich, finger bowl, pink, w/underplate **80.00**

Ipswich, goblet, crystal, knob in stem, 10-oz **35.00**

Ipswich, tumbler, yellow, footed, 12-oz **70.00**

Lariat, bowl, nut; crystal, individual **28.00**

Lariat, platter, crystal, oval, 15" **60.00**

Lariat, salt & pepper shakers, crystal, pr **200.00**

Lariat, vase, crystal, fan, footed, 7" **25.00**

Minuet, bell, dinner; crystal, #3408 .... **75.00**

Minuet, mayonnaise, crystal, dolphin foot, 5½" **50.00**

Minuet, plate, sandwich; crystal, #1511 Toujours, 15" **55.00**

Minuet, salt & pepper shakers, crystal, #10, pr **75.00**

Narcissus, cup, crystal, #1519 . **30.00**

Narcissus, tumbler, ice tea; crystal, footed, #3408, 12-oz **26.00**

New Era, champagne, crystal, 6-oz **11.00**

New Era, creamer, crystal **37.50**

New Era, relish, crystal, 3-part, 13" **35.00**

Octagon, bowl, soup; yellow, flat, 9" **20.00**

Octagon, plate, green, 14" **35.00**

Octagon, tray, crystal, oblong, #500, 6" **8.00**

Old Colony, bottle, oil; yellow, footed, 4-oz........................ **105.00**

Old Colony, bowl, vegetable; yellow, oval, 10" **65.00**

Old Colony, tray, hors d'oeuvres; yellow, w/handles, 13"..... **75.00**

Old Colony, wine, pink, #3390, 2½-oz **27.00**

Old Sandwich, finger bowl, green **60.00**

Old Sandwich, mug, beer; pink, 12-oz............................. **400.00**

Old Sandwich, pitcher, yellow, ice lip, ½-gal **165.00**

Old Sandwich, tumbler, juice; crystal, 5-oz **7.00**

Pleat & Panel, bowl, cereal; green, 6½" **17.50**

Pleat and Panel, pitcher, Moongleam, three-pint, $165.00.
(Photo courtesy Gene and Cathy Florence)

Pleat & Panel, plate, bread; pink, 7" **8.00**

Pleat & Panel, sugar bowl, crystal, w/lid **10.00**

Provincial, bowl, nut; Limelight Green, individual **40.00**

Provincial, butter dish, crystal ..**80.00**

Queen Ann, jug, crystal, 1-pt.**120.00**

Queen Ann, nappy, crystal, 8".**75.00**

Ridgeleigh, bowl, centerpiece; crystal, 8" **55.00**

Ridgeleigh, box, cigarette; crystal, w/lid, 6"............. **35.00**

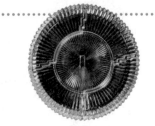

Ridgleigh, divided relish, crystal, 11", $50.00. (Photo courtesy Gene and Cathy Florence)

Ridgeleigh, vase, crystal, 8" .. **75.00**
Saturn, bowl, pickle; crystal, 7"..............................**35.00**
Saturn, marmalade, Zircon or Limelight, w/lid.............**500.00**
Saturn, sugar shaker, crystal. **70.00**
Stanhope, bowl, mint; crystal, w/handles, round knobs, 6".**35.00**
Stanhope, goblet, Limelight, #4083, 10-oz..............................**125.00**
Stanhope, saucer, crystal....... **10.00**
Twist, bonbon, amber, w/handles, 6"..**30.00**
Twist, bottle, dressing; crystal . **50.00**
Twist, bowl, pink, low, footed, 8"................................**80.00**
Twist, tray, celery; yellow, 10".**40.00**
Victorian, decanter, crystal, w/stopper, 32-oz **70.00**
Victorian, rose bowl, crystal.. **90.00**
Victorian, tray, condiment; salt/pepper shakers/mustard, crystal................................**140.00**

Imperial

Cape Cod, ashtray, crystal, #160/134/1 .... **14.00**

Cape Cod, bottle, scent; crystal, w/ stopper, #1601 .... **60.00**
Cape Cod, bowl, crystal, heart-shaped, handle, #160/40H, 6"....................................**25.00**
Cape Cod, bowl, flower; crystal, 1605N, 5".........................**25.00**
Cape Cod, bowl, jelly; crystal, #160/33, 3".......................**12.00**
Cape Cod, cake stand, crystal, #160/67D, 10½"...............**50.00**
Cape Cod, candy dish, crystal, w/ lid, #160/110 ....**85.00**

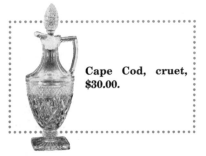

Cape Cod, cruet, $30.00.

Cape Cod, cup, coffee; crystal, #160/37 .... **6.00**
Cape Cod, decanter, crystal, #160/244, 26-oz.............. **135.00**
Cape Cod, goblet, crystal, #3600, 11-oz.................................**20.00**
Cape Cod, pitcher, crystal, #160/24, 2-qt....................................**85.00**
Cape Cod, plate, crystal, #160/7D, 9".......................................**20.00**
Cape Cod, tray, pastry; crystal, center handle, #160/68D, 11".**65.00**
Cape Cod, vase, crystal, cylindrical, #160/192, 10"..................**75.00**

Morgantown

Golf Ball, bell, dinner; red or blue............................ **125.00**

Golf Ball, cocktail, Smoke, 4⅛", $14.00; water, Smoke, 6¾", $20.00. (Photo courtesy Gene and Cathy Florence)

Golf Ball, tumbler, juice; crystal, footed, 5-oz, 5" **15.00**

Golf Ball, wine, green, 3-oz, 4¾" . **20.00**

Queen Louise, plate, salad; crystal w/pink **135.00**

Queen Louise, tumbler, crystal w/ pink, footed, 9-oz **395.00**

Queen Louise, wine, crystal w/pink, 2½-oz **400.00**

Sunrise Medallion, cup, pink or green **80.00**

Sunrise Medallion, plate, blue, 8⅜" **22.00**

Sunrise Medallion, vase, bud; crystal, slender, 10" **75.00**

Tinkerbell, plate, finger bowl liner; azure or green **30.00**

Tinkerbell, sherbet, azure or green, 5½-oz **90.00**

Tinkerbell, tumbler, azure or green, footed, 9-oz **90.00**

New Martinsville

Janice, bowl, red or blue, flared, 9½" **65.00**

Janice, creamer, crystal, 6-oz. **12.00**

Janice, salt & pepper shakers, crystal, pr **40.00**

Meadow Wreath, bowl, punch; crystal, #4221/26, 5-qt **140.00**

Meadow Wreath, cheese & cracker, crystal, #42/26, 11" **40.00**

Meadow Wreath, salver, crystal, footed, #42/26, 12" **40.00**

Paden City

Black Forest, bowl, fruit; black, 11" **150.00**

Black Forest, cake stand, green, footed, 2" **125.00**

Black Forest, mayonnaise, pink, w/ liner **125.00**

Black Forest, server, amber, center handle **50.00**

Black Forest, tumbler, crystal, footed, 3-oz, 3½" **50.00**

Gazebo, bowl, blue, bead handles, 9" **70.00**

Gazebo, candy dish, crystal, lg, footed, w/lid, 11" **75.00**

Gazebo, relish, blue, 3-part, #555, 9¾" **65.00**

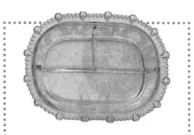

Gazebo, relish, crystal, three-part $30.00. (Photo courtesy Gene and Cathy Florence)

Gazebo, sugar bowl, crystal... **15.00**

Tiffin

Cadena, finger bowl, pink or yellow, footed, #401 .... **45.00**

Cadena, pitcher, crystal, footed, #194 .... **200.00**

Cadena, plate, pink or yellow, 9¼" **75.00**

Cadena, water, crystal, stemmed, #065, 7½" **30.00**

Cherokee Rose, bowl, crimped, crystal, #5902, 12" 65.00

Cherokee Rose, plate, luncheon; crystal, beaded rim, #5902, 8" 15.00

Cherokee Rose, vase, bud; crystal, #14185, 6" 25.00

Classic, creamer, crystal, #5931, $33.00. (Photo courtesy Gene and Cathy Florence

Classic, tumbler, tea; crystal, handled, #14185 .... 35.00

Classic, water, pink, stemmed, 9-oz, 7¼" 70.00

Flanders, bowl, cream soup; crystal, w/handles 60.00

Flanders, candy jar, yellow, footed, w/lid 185.00

Flanders, tray, sandwich; pink, octagon, center handle, #337 . 165.00

Fontaine, candlestick, Twilight, low, #9758, ea 75.00

Fontaine, champagne saucer, amber, green or pink, #033 .... 30.00

Fontaine, vase, amber, green or pink, bowed top, #7, 9¼" 125.00

Fuchsia, bowl, salad; crystal, #5902, 7¼" 35.00

Fuchsia, compote, crystal, #5831, 6¼" 30.00

Fuchsia, lamp, hurricane; crystal, Chinese syle, 12" 250.00

Julia, plate, dessert; amber, #8814 .... 12.00

Julia, sugar bowl, amber, #6 . 35.00

Julia, sundae, crystal w/amber, stemmed, #15011 .... 16.00

June Night, mayonnaise, crystal, w/liner & ladle 45.00

June Night, relish, crystal, 3-part, 6½" 35.00

June Night, salt & pepper shakers, crystal, #2, pr 200.00

Jungle Assortment, basket, #151 .... 100.00

Jungle Assortment, decanter, w/ stopper 125.00

Jungle Assortment, puff box . 40.00

Psyche, bowl, centerpiece; crystal w/green, 13" 125.00

Psyche, plate, crystal, 8" 28.00

Psyche, tumbler, water; crystal w/ green 35.00

Elvis Presley

The king of rock 'n roll, the greatest entertainer of all time (and not many would disagree with that), Elvis remains just as popular today as he was in the height of his career. Over the past few years, values for Elvis collectibles have skyrocketed. The early items marked 'Elvis Presley Enterprises' bearing a 1956 or 1957 date are the most valuable. Paper goods such as magazines, menus from Las Vegas hotels, and ticket stubs make up a large part of any Elvis collection and are much less expensive. His 45s were sold in abundance, so unless you find an original Sun label, a colored vinyl or a promotional cut, or EPs in wonderful condition, don't pay much. The picture sleeves are usually worth much more than the record itself. Albums are very collectible, and even though you see some stiff prices on them at antique malls, there aren't many you can't buy for well under $25.00 at any Elvis convention.

Remember, the early mark is 'Elvis Presley Enterprises' (EP Ent in our description lines); the 'Boxcar' mark was used from 1974 to 1977, and the 'Boxcar/Factors' mark from then until 1981. In 1982 the trademark reverted back to Graceland.

For more information, we recommend *Elvis Presley Memorabilia* by Sean O'Neal (Schiffer). In the following listings, values are for items in near-mint to mint condition unless otherwise noted.

Belt buckle, promotional item for Guitar Man LP record, RCA, 1981, MIP, $60.00.

Book, Private Elvis, from Germany, 200-pg, ca 1969, 11x8½", EX 60.00
Bracelet, dog tag, EP Ent, 1950s, MOC (beware of repros). 150.00
Cookie jar, Elvis in pink Cadillac convertible, Vandor, 1997, MIB 175.00
Decanter, Elvis '77 Mini, plays Love Me Tender, 1979, 50 ml .. 55.00
Decanter, Elvis & Gates of Graceland, musical, McCormick, 1986, 750 ml 175.00

Decanter, Elvis Designer II white, It's Now or Never, McCormick, 1982 .... 125.00
Decanter, Elvis Hound Dog, plays Hound Dog, McCormick, 1986, 750 ml 650.00
Decanter, Elvis Silver Mini, plays How Great Thou Art, McCormick, 1983 .... 110.00
Doll, Aloha From Hawaii, white outfit w/rhinestones, Danbury Mint, 18" 75.00
Doll, Supergold Elvis, #1 in Celebrity Collection, vinyl, 21", MIB 75.00
Doll, white jumpsuit, guitar & microphone, Eugene Dolls, 1984, MIB 55.00
Guitar, toy; Lapin, 1984, MOC (sealed) 75.00
Hat, beach; 1956, EX 140.00
Lobby card, King Creole, 1958, #8, 14x11", EX 110.00

Magazine, Movieland and TV Time, September 1958, EX $50.00. (Photo courtesy gasolineal leyantiques.com)

Menu, Elvis at Summer Festival Sahara Tahoe, 1971, 2-pg, 12x9" 165.00
Menu, Las Vegas International Hotel, 1970 .... 125.00
Photo, promotional; 1956, 10x8", EX 65.00
Plate, Looking at a Legend, EPE/ Delphi, 8½", MIB............. 30.00

Poster, Paradise Hawaiian Style, 1-sheet, 1966, 41x27", EX. **60.00**

Program, Grand Ole Opry, 1955, 18-pg, 11x8½", EX **70.00**

Purse, blue fold-over, image of Elvis & guitar, EP Ent, 1956. **700.00**

Radio, Elvis dressed in white, AM, 1970s **40.00**

Ring, flasher; 1957, EX, minimum value **100.00**

Snow globe, Elvis seated w/guitar, MIB **25.00**

Songbook, Album of Juke Box Favorites, Hill & Range, 1956, 12" **100.00**

Stamps, postage; full sheet of 29¢ stamps (40 total) **25.00**

Teapot, Elvis & motorcycle, guitar is lid, Silver Crane, 8x13½" . **65.00**

Ticket, Alabama & Mississippi Fair & Dairy Show, 1956, EX. **80.00**

Ticket, Chicago May 2, 1977, unused **75.00**

Trading card, Go Go Go Elvis, #1 of 66, Bubbles Inc, 1956, EX. **30.00**

Enesco

Enesco is an importing company based in Elk Grove, Illinois. They're distributors of ceramic novelties made for them in Japan. There are several lines styled around a particular character or group, and with the emphasis collectors currently place on figural pieces, they're finding these especially fascinating. During the 1960s, they sold a line of novelties originally called Mother-in-the Kitchen. Today's collectors refer to them as 'Kitchen Prayer Ladies.' Ranging from large items such as canisters and cookie jars to toothpick holders and small picture frames, the line was fairly extensive. Some of the pieces are very hard to find, and those with blue dresses are much scarcer than those in pink. Where we've given ranges, pink is represented by the lower end, blue by the high side. If you find a white piece with blue trim, add another 10% to 20% to the high end.

Another Enesco line that has become very collectible is called Lucy and Me. These teddy bear figures are designed by Lucy Rigg and range in size from 2½" to 3". All are marked and dated. See also Cookie Jars.

Bank, Human Bean Santa and Baby Bean, 5", $20.00. (Photo courtesy Jim and Beverly Mangus)

Bell, Kitchen Prayer Lady, #E-2825, 4½" **80.00**

Creamer, Kitchen Prayer Lady, pink, 4" **65.00**

Figurine, baby in highchair, Lucy & Me series, 1986, 2½" **6.50**

Figurine, carpenter holding hammer & saw, Lucy & Me series, 1984, 3" **8.50**

Figurine, clown in polka-dot outfit, Lucy & Me series, 1985, 3¼" . **6.50**

Figurine, Hung Out to Dry, cats on clothesline, 7½", MIB **93.00**

Figurine, Magic Is Everywhere, Mickey Mouse, 25¾", MIB. **255.00**

Figurine, mermaid w/coral, shimmer stone **110.00**

Figurine, policeman directing traffic, Lucy & Me series, 1984, 3¼" **8.50**

Figurine, Smokey, elf w/train, North Pole Village, #871524, 1986, NMIB **105.00**

Figurine, St Francis Statue & Birdbath, Jim Shore, #4005182, 29" **180.00**

Instant Coffee jar, Kitchen Prayer Lady, blue, rare, 6", from $110.00 to $135.00.

Music box, Colossal Coaster, multi-action, lights-up, MIB... **370.00**

Music box, Enchanted Clocktower, multi-action, NMIB **233.00**

Music box, Mary Poppins figural teapot, musical, 1960s, 6" **165.00**

Music box, mice playing on payphone, animated, plays I Just Called............................ **110.00**

Music box, Peter Pan, plays I Can Fly, Lucy & Me series, 1990 ...... **82.00**

Napkin holder, Kitchen Prayer Lady, #E-2826, blue, 6¼". **20.00**

Salt & pepper shakers, Kitchen Prayer Lady, blue, pr **15.00**

Scouring pad/soap dish, Kitchen Prayer Lady, #E-4246, pink, 5½" **45.00**

Spoon rest, Kitchen Prayer Lady, #E-3347, pink, 5¾" **20.00**

Toothpick holder, Kitchen Prayer Lady, #E-5199, blue, 4½". **18.00**

Wall plaque, Kitchen Prayer Lady, #E-3349, full figure, 7½". **70.00**

Fenton

The Fenton glass company, organized in 1906 in Martin's Ferry, Ohio, is noted for their fine art glass. Over 130 patterns of carnival glass were made in the earlier years, but even their newer glass is considered collectible. Only since 1970 have some of the pieces carried a molded-in logo; before then paper labels were used. For more information we recommend *Fenton Art Glass, 1907 to 1939*; *Fenton Art Glass Patterns, 1939 to 1980*; *Fenton Art Glass Colors and Hand-Decorated Patterns, 1939 – 1980*; and *Fenton Art Glass Hobnail Pattern*; all are by Margaret and Kenn Whitmyer. Two of Fenton's later lines, Hobnail and Silver Crest, are shown in Gene and Cathy Florence's book called *Collectible Glassware from the 40s, 50s, and 60s*. All are published by Collector Books. See also Glass Animals; Glass, Porcelain, and Pottery shoes. For information on Fenton Art Glass Collectors of America, see Clubs and Newsletters.

Apple Blossom, bowl, relish; heart shape, #7333................... **90.00**

Apple Blossom, vase, double-crimped, 1960-61, 8", from $80 to **90.00**

Aqua Crest, basket, #192, 7". **125.00**

Aqua Crest, puff box, #192-A, 1942, from $65 to **75.00**

Big Cookies, basket, amber, #1681, 1933, 10½", from $90 to. **110.00**

Black Crest, ashtray, #7377 .. **45.00**

Black Crest, plate, early 1970s, 6", from $14 to **16.00**

Blue Crest, bonbon, #7428, 8". **55.00**

Blue Crest, candleholder, #7474-BC, 1963, ea from $55 to **65.00**

Blue Ridge, hurricane lamp, w/ base, #170, ca 1939, from $190 to **220.00**

Blue Ridge, vase, flared, #188-7 .... **70.00**

Cactus, vase, bud; milk glass, #3450, 1959-65, 8", from $10 to **15.00**

Coin Dot, basket, cranberry opal, #1437, 1947-64, 7"........... **95.00**

Coin Dot, candy jar, French opal, dome lid, #93, 1948-50, $200 to **250.00**

Crystal Crest, vase, double-crimped, sq, #1924, 1942, 5", from $50 to **60.00**

Daisy & Button, ashtray, ruby, #1900, 1937-39, from $9 to **11.00**

Daisy & Button, bell, carnival, #1966-CN, 1971-76, from $27 to **35.00**

Daisy & Button, vase, fan; turquoise, footed, #1959-TU, 1955-56, 9".................................. **60.00**

Diamond Optic, basket, aquamarine, #1502, from $175 to **200.00**

Diamond Optic, mayonnaise & ladle, green, from $35 to.. **40.00**

Emerald Crest, bowl, dessert; #680................................ **25.00**

Emerald Crest, nut dish, footed, #680, 1949-56, from $35 to **40.00**

Flame Crest, candleholder, #7474, ea...................................... **60.00**

Gold Crest, jug, #192, 1943-44, 6", from $45 to **55.00**

Gold Crest, plate, #680, 6½".. **10.00**

Hobnail, apothecary jar, Colonial Amber **50.00**

Hobnail, basket, blue opalescent, 7x4½", from $28.00 to $42.00.

Hobnail, bell, milk glass, 1991, from $18 to **20.00**

Hobnail, bowl, banana; milk glass, #3720, 1959-84, from $25 to **35.00**

Hobnail, candleholder, milk glass, #3745, 1973-76, ea from $28 to **32.00**

Hobnail, compote, milk glass, #3825, 1954-68, from $7 to **9.00**

Hobnail, cruet, cranberry opalescent, #3863 .... **90.00**

Hobnail, honey jar, milk glass, #3886, 1953-60, from $95 to............................. **120.00**

Hobnail, nut dish, milk glass, #3631, 1962-68, from $15 to............................... **18.00**

Hobnail, relish dish, 3-part, milk glass, #3822, 1956-73, from $18 to **20.00**

Hobnail, vase, orchid opalescent, 1940s, 6" **75.00**

Ivory Crest, basket, #1523, 1940-42, 13", from $250 to..... **275.00**

Plum Crest, bell, Paisley, hand-painted lilacs on milk glass, #2746 .... 35.00

Rose Burmese, basket, deep, #7238, 1973-75, 7" 250.00

Silver Crest, bowl, soup; #680/#7320, 1949-56, 5½", from $30 to .35.00

Silver Crest, candleholder, #680, 1949-52, ea from $35 to .. 45.00

Silver Crest, creamer, #680/#7261, 1948-67, 3¼" 35.00

Silver Crest, planter, 2-tier, #680, 1950-52, from $55 to 65.00

Silver Crest, plate, #681, 1943-49, 9", from $25 to 30.00

Silver Turquoise, plate, #7217-ST, 1956-57, 8½", from $25 to .35.00

Spiral Optic, basket, blue opalescent, #3137-BO, 1979-80, from $55 to 65.00

Thumbprint, vase, Colonial Blue, #4454-CB, 1964-74, 8", from $20 to 25.00

Thumbprint, water pitcher, Colonial Amber, #4466 CA, 60-ounce, from $65.00 to $85.00. (Photo courtesy Margaret and Kenn Whitmyer)

Fiesta

Since it was discontinued by Homer Laughlin in 1973, Fiesta has become one of the most popular collectibles on the market. Values have continued to climb until some of the more hard-to-find items now sell for several hundred dollars each. In 1986 HLC reintroduced a line of new Fiesta. To date these colors have been used: cobalt (darker than the original), rose (a strong pink), black, white, apricot (very pale), yellow (a light creamy tone), turquoise, sea mist (a light mint green), lilac, persimmon, periwinkle (country blue), sapphire blue (very close to the original cobalt), chartreuse (brighter), gray, juniper (teal), cinnabar (maroon), sunflower (yellow), plum (dark bluish-purple), shamrock (similar to the coveted medium green), tangerine, scarlet, peacock, and evergreen. There is a strong secondary market for limited edition and discontinued pieces and colors of the post-86 Fiesta as well. When old molds were used, the mark will be the same, if it is a molded-in mark such as on pitchers, sugar bowls, etc. The ink stamp differs from the old — now all the letters are upper case.

Our suggested values are for examples in mint condition, with good, even glazing and no distracting factory flaws. Adjust prices sharply downward to evalate items of lesser quality. The listing that follows is incomplete due to space restrictions; refer to *The Collector's Encyclopedia of Fiesta, Tenth Edition*, by Sharon and Bob Huxford (Collector Books) for more information. See also Clubs and Newsletters for information on *Fiesta Collector's Quarterly*.

Ashtray, red, cobalt or ivory, from $45 to **60.00**

Bowl, covered onion soup; red, from $625 to **700.00**

Bowl, cream soup; yellow, light green, or turquoise, from $30 to **45.00**

Bowl, dessert; '50s colors, 6", from $35 to **45.00**

Bowl, fruit; medium green, 4¾", minimum value **550.00**

Bowl, fruit; yellow, turquoise or light green, 5½", from $20 to **25.00**

Bowl, nappy; '50s colors, 8½", from $50 to **60.00**

Bowl, nappy; red, cobalt, ivory or turquoise, 9½", from $60 to **70.00**

Candleholders, bulb; red, cobalt, ivory or turquoise, pr from $120 to **130.00**

Carafe, red, cobalt, ivory or turquoise, from $275 to **300.00**

Casserole, red, cobalt or ivory, from $180 to **200.00**

Coffeepot, demitasse; yellow or light green, from $350 to **400.00**

Coffeepot, regular, '50s colors, from $300 to **350.00**

Compote, yellow or light green, 12", from $160 to **175.00**

Creamer, individual; yellow, from $60 to **80.00**

Creamer, stick handle, yellow or turquoise, from $45 to **60.00**

Cup, demitasse; red, cobalt or ivory, from $80 to **100.00**

Egg cup, yellow, light green or turquoise, from $55 to **65.00**

Marmalade, yellow or light green, from $350 to **375.00**

Mixing bowl, #1, yellow or light green, from $220 to **250.00**

Mixing bowl, #2, red, cobalt, ivory or turquoise, from $125 to . **150.00**

Mixing bowl, #3, yellow or light green, from $110 to **140.00**

Mixing bowl, #4, yellow or light green, from $110 to **145.00**

Mixing bowl, #5, red, cobalt, ivory or turquoise, from $190 to . **235.00**

Mixing bowl, #7, yellow or light green, from $325 to **450.00**

Mug, Tom & Jerry; red, cobalt or ivory, from $70 to **80.00**

Mustard, yellow or light green, from $240 to **275.00**

Pitcher, disk juice; red, from $550.00 to $650.00 (yellow, from $45.00 to $50.00).

Pitcher, disk water; '50s colors, from $200 to **275.00**

Pitcher, ice; red, cobalt, ivory or turquoise, from $130 to. **145.00**

Pitcher, jug, 2-pt; red, cobalt or ivory, from $95 to **105.00**

Plate, '50s colors, 6", from $7 to. **10.00**

Plate, cake; yellow or light green **1,000.00**

Plate, calendar; 1955, 9", from $45 to **55.00**

Plate, chop; red, cobalt or ivory, 15", from $90 to **100.00**

Plate, compartment; yellow, light green or turquoise, 10½", $35 to **40.00**

Plate, deep; red, cobalt or ivory, from $50 to **60.00**

Plate, medium green, 7", from $30 to **45.00**

Plate, yellow, light green or turquoise, 10", from $30 to..**40.00**

Platter, '50s colors, from $50 to.**60.00**

Relish tray, gold decor, complete, from $220 to **250.00**

Relish tray side insert, yellow or light green, from $45 to..**55.00**

Salt & pepper shakers, red, cobalt or ivory, pr, from $25 to..**30.00**

Sauceboat, original colors, from $40.00 to $70.00.

Saucer, demitasse; yellow, light green or turquoise, from $15 to **20.00**

Saucer, regular, medium green, from $10 to **15.00**

Sugar bowl, '50s colors, w/lid, from $70 to **80.00**

Sugar bowl, individual; turquoise, from $400 to **500.00**

Sugar bowl, yellow, light green or turquoise, w/lid, from $50 to **60.00**

Syrup, red, cobalt, ivory or turquoise, from $400 to **425.00**

Teacup, '50s colors, from $35 to.**40.00**

Teacup, yellow, light green or turquoise, from $15 to **20.00**

Teapot, medium; '50s colors, from $250 to **300.00**

Tray, figure-8; cobalt, from $90 to **100.00**

Tray, figure-8; turquoise, from $350 to **400.00**

Tray, utility; yellow or light green, from $40 to **45.00**

Tumbler, juice; red, cobalt or ivory, from $45 to **50.00**

Tumbler, juice; rose, from $55 to **60.00**

Tumbler, water; yellow or light green, from $70 to..........**80.00**

Vase, bud; red, cobalt, ivory or turquoise, from $100 to **125.00**

Vase, red, cobalt, ivory or turquoise, 12", from $1,400 to.....**1,900.00**

Vase, yellow or light green, 8", from $600 to **700.00**

Kitchen Kraft

Bowl, mixing; 6" **60.00**

Bowl, mixing; 8" **80.00**

Casserole, 8½" **85.00**

Covered jar, lg, from $350 to.**375.00**

Covered jar, med, from $275 to.**300.00**

Covered jug, red, large, from $275.00 to $300.00.

Covered jug, sm, from $300 to .**320.00**

Metal frame for platter..........**15.00**

Pie plate, spruce green **150.00**

Pie plate, 10" **40.00**

Platter, spruce green............**150.00**

Shakers, pr from $120 to **150.00**
Spoon, ivory, 12", from $400 to.**500.00**
Stacking refrigerator lid, ivory, from $200 to **225.00**
Stacking refrigerator unit, from $50 to **60.00**
Stacking refrigerator unit, ivory, from $200 to **210.00**

Post '86 Line

Tripod candleholders, lilac, from $550.00 to $600.00 for the pair.

Bowl, chili; apricot, 18-oz, from $40 to **50.00**
Bowl, pasta; lilac, 12", from $75 to **90.00**
Butter dish, chartreuse, from $25 to **32.00**
Carafe, apricot, from $40 to .. **50.00**
Casserole w/lid, lilac, from $125 to **140.00**
Coffee server, apricot, 36-oz, from $50 to **60.00**
Creamer, individual; chartreuse, 7-oz, from $25 to **30.00**
Cup, jumbo, sapphire, 18-oz, from $22 to **28.00**
Cup & saucer, AD; lilac, from $45 to **55.00**
Cup & saucer, Holiday, from $12 to **15.00**
Mug, chartruese, 10-oz, from $40 to **55.00**
Mug, Holiday, from $9 to **12.00**
Place setting, apricot, 5-pc, from $60 to **85.00**
Place setting, Holiday, from $40 to.................................... **50.00**
Plate, luncheon; lilac, 9", from $65 to **75.00**
Platter, Holiday #8, from $15 to. **18.00**
Sugar caddy, apricot, from $12 to. **18.00**
Tray, serving; Holiday, round, w/ handles, 11", from $20 to. **25.00**

Tumbler, sapphire, from $25 to .**30.00**
Vase, bud; chartreuse, 6", from $18 to **22.00**

Fishbowl Ornaments

Mermaids, divers, and all sorts of castles have been devised to add interest to fishbowls and aquariums, and today they're starting to attract the interest of collectors. Many were made in Japan and imported decades ago to be sold in 5-&-10¢ stores along with the millions of other figural novelties that flooded the market after the war. The condition of the glaze is very important; for more information we recommend *Collector's Encyclopedia of Made in Japan Ceramics* by Carole Bess White (Collector Books). Unless noted otherwise, the examples in the listing that follows were produced in Japan.

Bathing beauty on turtle, red, tan & green on white, 2½", from $20 to **30.00**
Castle, multicolored, glossy, 4½", from $20 to **32.00**
Castle towers w/3 arches, tan lustre towers w/red arches, 5¼". **22.00**

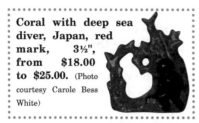

Coral with deep sea diver, Japan, red mark, 3½", from $18.00 to $25.00. (Photo courtesy Carole Bess White)

Diver holding dagger, white suit & helmet, blue gloves, 4¾" . **22.00**

Doorway, stone entry w/open aqua wood-look door, 2" **15.00**

Frogs on lily pad before sign, Welcome to Our Pad, 3¾x5 .... **16.00**

Lighthouse, tan, black, brown & green, 6½x4" **26.00**

Mermaid, sitting w/shell in hand, multicolored, 4½" **30.00**

Mermaid on 2 seashells, multicolored matt, 3½", from $30 to **40.00**

Nude on starfish, painted bisque, 4½", from $75 to **125.00**

Pagoda, triple roof, blue, green & maroon, 5½x3¼" **20.00**

Sign on tree trunk, No Fishing, brown, black & white, 2¼x4" **12.00**

Torii gate, multicolored, 3¾".. **22.00**

Fisher-Price

Since about 1930, the Fisher-Price Company has produced distinctive wooden toys covered with brightly colored lithographed paper. Plastic parts were first added in 1949. The most valuable Fisher-Price toys are those modeled after well-known Disney characters and having the Disney logo. A little edge wear and some paint dulling are normal to these well-loved toys and to be expected; our prices are for toys in very good played-with condition. Mint-in-box examples are extremely scarce and worth from 40% to 60% more. For further information we recommend *A Pictorial Guide to the More Popular Toys, Fisher-Price Toys, 1931 – 1990*, by Gary Combs and Brad Cassity; *Fisher-Price, A Historical Rarity Value Guide*, by John J. Murray and Bruce R. Fox (Books Americana); and *Schroeder's Collectible Toys, Antique to Modern* (Collector Books). See also Dolls, Fisher-Price. See Clubs and Newsletters for information on the Fisher-Price Collectors Club.

#100 Dr Doodle, 1931 .... **700.00**

#100 Musical Sweeper, 1950-52, plays Whistle While You Work **60.00**

#103 Barky Puppy, 1931-33 . **700.00**

#107 Music Box Clock Radio, plays Hickory Dickory Dock, 1971. **1.00**

#110 Puppy Playhouse, 1978-80. **10.00**

#111 Play Family Merry-Go-Round, plays Skater's Waltz, 1972-77 .... **30.00**

#117 Play Family Barnyard, 1972-74, complete **5.00**

#120 Cackling Hen, 1958-66, white **35.00**

#123 Roller Chime, 1953-60 & Easter 1961 .... **30.00**

#125 Music Box Iron, white w/red handle, 1966-69............... **30.00**

#125 Uncle Timmy Turtle, red shell, 1956-58 .... **75.00**

#136 Play Family Lacing Shoe, 1965-69, complete **60.00**

#138 Jack-in-the-Box Puppet, 1970-73 .... **20.00**

#145 Humpty Dump Truck, 1963-64 & Easter 1965 .... **30.00**

#148 Jack & Jill TV Radio, 1959 & Easter 1960, wood & plastic. **55.00**

#150 Pop-Up-Pal Chime Phone, 1968-78 .... **15.00**

#151 Goldilocks & the Three Bears Playhouse, 1967-71 .... **60.00**

#156 Circus Wagon, bandleader in wagon, 1942-44 .... **400.00**

#158 Katie Kangaroo, squeeze bulb & she hops, 1976-77 .... **15.00**

#161 Creative Block Wagon, building blocks & dowels in wagon, 1961-64 .... **60.00**

#166 Bucky Burro, 1955-57... **20.00**

#168 Magnetic Chug-Chug, 1964-69 .... **35.00**

#171 Toy Wagon, 1942-47 .... **250.00**

#180 Snoopy Sniffer, 1938-55. **50.00**

#191 Golden Gulch Express, 1961-Easter 1962 .... **100.00**

#195, Teddy Bear Parade, 1938, 14", $825.00. (Photo courtesy Morphy Auctions)

#196 Peek-A-Boo Screen Music Box, plays Hey Diddle Diddle, 1964 .... **45.00**

#234 Nifty Station Wagon, 1960-62 & Easter 1963 .... **250.00**

#300 Scoop Loader, 1975-77 .. **10.00**

#302 Chick Basket Cart, 1957-59 .... **40.00**

#304 Adventure People Wild Safari Set, 1975-78 .... **50.00**

#305 Walking Duck Cart, 1957-64 .... **40.00**

#310 Adventure People Sea Explorer, 1975-80 .... **20.00**

#310 Mickey Mouse Puddle Jumper, 1953-54 & Easter 1956. **100.00**

#312, Adventure People Northwoods Trail Blazer, 1977 – 1982, $20.00. (Photo courtesy Brad Cassity)

#314 Husky Boom Crane, 1978-82 .... **25.00**

#328 Husky Highway Dump Truck, 1980-84 .... **20.00**

#333 Butch the Pup, 1951-53 & Easter 1954 .... **55.00**

#337 Husky Rescue Rig, 1982-83 .... **20.00**

#339 Husky Power & Light Service Rig, 1983-84 .... **30.00**

#350 Adventure People Rescue Team, 1976-79 .... **15.00**

#353 Adventure People Scuba Divers, 1976-81 .... **15.00**

#400 Donald Duck Drum Major Cart, 1946 only **250.00**

#402 Duck Cart, 1943 .... **250.00**

#407 Chick Cart, 1950-53 ...... **50.00**

#420 Sunny Fish, 1955 .... **150.00**

#444 Puffy Engine, 1951-54 .. **50.00**

#445 Hot Dog Wagon, 1940-41. **200.00**

#447 Woofy Wagger, 1947-48. **75.00**

#450 Donald Duck Choo-Choo, 1941, 8½" **400.00**

#454 Donald Duck Drummer, 1949-50 .... **250.00**

#473 Merry Mutt, 1949-54 & Easter 1955 .... **50.00**

#476 Cookie Pig, 1966-70 ..... **40.00**

#479 Donald Duck & Nephews, 1941-42 .... **400.00**

#488 Popeye Spinach Eater, 1939-40 .... **600.00**

#505 Bunny Drummer, bell on front, 1946 .... **225.00**

#549 Toy Lunch Kit, red w/barn lithograph, w/Thermos, 1962-79 .... **25.00**

#569 Basic Hardboard Puzzle, Airport, 1975 .... **10.00**

#606 Woodsey Bramble Beaver & Book, 1981-82, 32-pg **15.00**

#621 Suzie Seal, 1965-66, ball on nose **30.00**

#657 Crazy Clown Fire Brigade, 1983-84 .... **45.00**

#663 Play Family, 1966-70, tan dog, MIP **170.00**

#674 Sports Car, 1958-60 ...... **75.00**

#686, Play Family Car and Camper, 1968 – 1970, $65.00. (Photo courtesy Brad Cassity)

#695 Pinky Pig, 1958, lithograph eyes **75.00**

#705 Mini Snowmobile, 1971-73 ..**40.00**

#711 Cry Baby Bear, 1967-69 . **15.00**

#712 Fred Flintstone Xylophone, Sears only, 1962 .... **250.00**

#718 Tow Truck & Car, wood & plastic, 1969-70 .... **45.00**

#720 Pinnochio Express, 1939-40 .... **500.00**

#724 Ding-Dong Ducky, 1949-50............................ **200.00**

#845 Farm Truck, w/booklet, 1954-55 .... **250.00**

Fishing Collectibles

Very much in evidence at flea markets these days, old fishing gear has become very collectible. Early twentieth century plugs were almost entirely carved from wood, sprayed with several layers of enamel, and finished off with glass eyes. Molded plastics were of a later origin. Some of the more collectible manufacturers are James Heddon, Shakespeare, Rhodes, and Pflueger. Rods, reels, old advertising calendars, and company catalogs are also worth your attention. For more information we recommend *Fishing Lure Collectibles, Volume One,* by Dudley Murphy and Rick Edmiston; *Fishing Lure Collectibles, Volume Two* by Dudley and Deanie Murphy; *The Pflueger Heritage, Lures and Reels 1881 – 1952* by Wayne Ruby; *The Fred Arbogast® Story, A Fishing Lure Collector's Guide* by Scott Heston; *Modern Fishing Lure Collectibles, Volumes 1 – 5,* by Russell E. Lewis; *Spring-Loaded Fish Hooks, Traps & Lures* by William Blouser and Timothy Mierzqa; and *Captain*

John's Fishing Tackle Price Guide by John Kolbeck. All are published by Collector Books.

Values are for items in good average condition. Mint-in-box lures are worth about twice as much.

Lures

CA Clark Bait, Water Scout #300, 2 trebles, ca 1938, 2⅛".......**35.00**
Creek Chub, Dinger #5600, 1 treble, ca 1939, 2"...............**50.00**
Creek Chub, Dive Bomber, 2 trebles, ca 1942, 2⅞"...........**40.00**
Creek Chub, Jointed Pikie Minnow #2600DD, 3 trebles, ca 1950, 4¼"..................................**40.00**
Creek Chub, Salt Water Pikie #700SW, 2 trebles, 1956, 4¼"............................**100.00**
Heddon, Dowagiac Minnow #00, 5 trebles, ca 1930, 3¾".....**250.00**
Heddon, Dowagiac Surface Lure #200, 3 trebles, ca 1933, 4⅞".......**150.00**
Heddon, Flaptail Jr #7110, 2 trebles, ca 1935, 2½"...........**40.00**
Heddon, Lucky 13 #2500, 3 trebles, ca 1938, 3¾"....................**40.00**
Heddon, Tad Polly #5100, 2 trebles, 1938, 3"...........................**75.00**
Heddon, Weedless Super Surface #210, 2 double, ca 1936, 3¼"............................**50.00**
Jamison, Musky Wig-Wag, 2 trebles, ca 1934, 6"...........**100.00**
Keeling, Spinnered Suface Lure, 2 trebles, ca 1930, 3¾".......**75.00**
Keeling, Tom Thumb, 1 treble, 1 single, ca 1920, 2"...........**40.00**
Paw Paw, Crawfish, 1 treble, ca 1940, 2¾"........................**50.00**

Paw Paw, Croaker Frog, 2 trebles, ca 1940, 3"......................**50.00**
Paw Paw, Moonlight Bass Seeker Jr, 2 trebles, ca 1930, 4⅛"......**50.00**
Paw Paw, Musky Deer Hair Mouse, 1 treble, ca 1935, 4¾"....**150.00**
Paw Paw, Musky Pike Bait, 3 trebles, ca 1946, 6½"...........**50.00**
Paw Paw, Pike Caster, 3 trebles, ca 1940, 4"............................**50.00**

Paw Paw, #71 Croaker, ca. 1940, flyrod version, 1½", from $60.00 to $75.00. (Photo courtesy Dudley Murphy and Deanie Murphy)

Pflueger, Flocked Mouse, 2 trebles, ca 1950, 2¾"...................**150.00**
Pflueger, Neverfail Minnow, 5 trebles, ca 1930, 3¾"..........**150.00**
Shakespeare, Slim Jim #43, 3 trebles, ca 1930, 3¾"............**75.00**
Shakespeare, Swimming Mouse Jr #6580, 2 trebles, ca 1930, 2¾"................................**50.00**

South Bend, Bass-Oreno #973, 1916 – 1964, from $5.00 to $10.00. (Photo courtesy Dudley Murphy and Deanie Murphy)

South Bend, Plunk-Oreno #929, 1 single, ca 1939, 2"...........**20.00**

South Bend, Spin-Oreno, 2 trebles, ca 1950, 2".............. 10.00

Wilson, Grass Widow, 1 double, ca 1919, 2¼"................ 50.00

Winchester Model 2740, gutta percha end, nickel plated center section, wooden crank handle, 3¼" diameter, EX, $175.00. (Photo courtesy James D. Julia Inc.)

Reels

Ballen, Model 50 Click Trout, raised pillars, in bag, 2⅝" dia, NM.............. 200.00

BF Meek #3, #3122, fancy click & drag switches, 2" dia 275.00

Blue Grass #4, #14584, jeweled end cap, front click & drag switches...................... 385.00

Hardy, LRH Lightweight Trout, grooved aluminum foot, 3⅛" dia.................. 100.00

Hardy, Orvis CFO Trout, spool, drag lever, 2⅞" dia 100.00

Heddon, Silver Level Wind Bait, #6736, front click switch, dual handle........................ 192.00

JA Coxe, #15 Level Wind Bait, silver w/aluminum spool, strong click.............................. 165.00

Pflueger, Medalist Trout #1392, metal spool release, 2⅞" dia............................ 10.00

Miscellaneous

Decoy, rainbow trout w/metal fins, Bud Stewart, colorful paint, 12" L................................ 22.00

Minnow bucket, Eclipse Floater #12, green w/gold stenciling, 9" dia................................ 385.00

Minnow bucket, Falls City Expert, oval, green paint, G...... 140.00

Rod holder, iron, C clamp, stamped Pat Aug 28.88, G............. 30.00

Tackle box, wood, flat w/sections, lift-out tray, handle, 13x22x3", VG................................ 90.00

Trap, fish; woven, thin reeds over flat spints, round, 8½x29"...... 110.00

Trap, minnow; glass, embossed CF Orvis Maker..., w/wire harness & lid............................ 220.00

Flashlights

The flashlight was invented in 1898 and has been produced by the Eveready Company for the past 96 years. Eveready dominated the flashlight market for most of this period, but more than 125 other U.S. flashlight companies have come and gone, providing competition along the way. Add to that number 35 known foreign flashlight manufacturers, and you end up with over 1,000 different models of flashlights to collect. They come in a wide variety of styles, shapes, and sizes. The flashlight field includes tubular, lanterns, figural, novelty, litho, etc. At present, over 45 different categories of flashlights have been identified as collectible. Our values are for examples in excellent to near mint condition unless noted otherwise.

Adams Model #1520-A, Self-Contained Flashlight Pointer, black, EXIB 25.00

Bell System, black, angle style, pocket clip, 7½" 30.00

Bond #1658189, brass & chrome, w/belt holder, EX 31.00

Britian #780366, silver metal coating over brass, 1930s, 6¾" 50.00

Burgess, adjustable head, clip on side & bottom, 1940s, 8". 70.00

Challenger, copper, Made in USA, VG 25.00

Dive Bright 500B, painted yellow, Allan Engineering, VG ... 30.00

Eveready, round chrome base, handle lights up for nightlight, 3½" 40.00

Eveready #2631, chrome, 6½". 25.00

Franco 3 in 1 #1051, clear, red & green bulbs, MonoCell 62.00

Hipco, fiberboard w/chrome, wall-eye lens, early 1900s 83.00

Magna-Lux, The Electric Lighter & Complete Service Kit, chrome, MIB 45.00

Niagara Junior Guide, red, 4x3½" 25.00

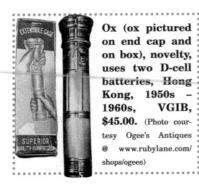

Ox (ox pictured on end cap and on box), novelty, uses two D-cell batteries, Hong Kong, 1950s – 1960s, VGIB, $45.00. (Photo courtesy Ogee's Antiques @ www.rubylane.com/shops/ogees)

Philco Penlight, blue & chrome, promotional Christmas gift, 1960s, MIB 45.00

Stewart R Browne, mine-rated Model F-81X, Class I, Group D, Bakelite 30.00

Teledyne Big Beam #287EX, brass, 2 6-volt batteries, NMIB. 55.00

USALite #TL-122-A, angle style, US Electric Mfg Corp, 1940s, VG 55.00

Winchester, Hi-Power Search Light, chrome, 10", MIB 65.00

Winchester #0181, solid 22k copper, slide switch w/instant button............................. 40.00

Winchester #1511, chrome w/red plastic lens cover, 7¼" 40.00

Winchester A-3400, chrome-plated brass, 3-cell, MIB 35.00

Yale Electric Co, Use Cell No 102, w/colored bulbs............... 30.00

Flower Frogs

Nearly every pottery company and glasshouse in America produced their share of figural flower 'frogs,' and many were imported from Japan as well. They were probably most popular from about 1910 through the 1940s, coinciding not only with the heyday of American glass and ceramics, but with the gracious, much less hectic style of living the times allowed. Way before a silk flower or styrofoam block was ever dreamed of, there were fresh cut flowers on many a dining room sideboard or table, arranged in shallow console bowls with matching frogs such as we've described in the following listings. For further information see *Collector's Encyclopedia of Made in Japan Ceramics* by Carole Bess White (Collector Books). See also specific pottery and glass companies.

Ballerina, pastels w/gold, ceramic, US Zone Germany, 8½"...**80.00**
Bashful Charlotte, crystal glass, Cambridge, 11½"...........**150.00**
Bird, orange & green on blue lustre base w/6 openings, ceramic, Japan...............................**18.00**

Crab, Muskota, pottery, naturalistic matt colors, Weller, 2x5x4"..........................**265.00**
Deer, white matt, pottery, Red Wing, 10½"........................**40.00**
Draped lady, glass, light emerald, Cambridge, 8½".............**125.00**
Lady in skimpy dress w/flowing skirt, glossy white ceramic, #8577, 6"...........................**80.00**
Mandolin lady, crystal glass, Cambridge.....................**200.00**
Nude Deco lady w/curving drape, white ceramic, Germany, 1930s, 6¼"......................**95.00**
Nude lady w/3 openings behind her, white ceramic, Metlox, 1940s-50s...................................**75.00**

Nude sitting on base, ceramic, Yanko Ware Made in Japan, 7x5x4½".............................**30.00**
Parakeet on stump, multicolor on ceramic, Made in Czechoslovakia, 5"..........**30.00**
Ruby glass, domed top, 8 holes, Fenton, 1¾x3"................**135.00**
Snail w/openings on back, ivory ceramic, Shawnee, 4x5"..**27.50**
White metal w/brown enameling, 15 holes, Made in Japan, 4"..**20.00**
White plastic grid, marked Golden Gate Manufacturing...Calif N 43......................................**6.00**

'40s, '50s, and '60s Glassware

Remember the lovely dishes mother used back when you were a child? Many collectors do. With scarcity of the older Depression glassware items that used to be found in every garage sale or flea market, glass collectors have refocused their interests and altered buying habits to include equally interesting glassware from more recent years, often choosing patterns that bring back warm childhood memories.

For more information, see *Collectible Glassware from the 40s, 50s, and 60s;* and *The Hazel-Atlas Glass Identification and Value,* by Gene and Cathy Florence (Collector Books). See also Anchor Hocking; Elegant Glass; Indiana Carnival Glass; King's Crown.

Cambridge

Cascade, ashtray, crystal, 6".**10.00**

Cascade, candy dish, green, w/ lid **75.00**

Cascade, creamer, crystal **8.50**

Cascade, plate, bread & butter; crystal **5.50**

Cascade, plate, crystal, 21" ... **65.00**

Cascade, sugar bowl, green or yellow **20.00**

Cascade, vase, green, 9½" **75.00**

Cascade, water goblet, crystal. **15.00**

Cascade #400 Line, celery dish, crystal, three-part, $20.00.

Square, bonbon, crystal **24.00**

Square, bowl, oval, crystal, 12".. **32.00**

Square, punch bowl, crystal .. **75.00**

Colony

Colony is a trade name of the Lancaster Colony Corporation, who first marketed handmade milk glass items utilizing the same Harvest molds (with some modification) Indiana Glass used for some of the carnival glass they made during the 1970s. In fact, it was Indiana Glass that actually made the early milk glass line, but it was never sold under their name. The line became very popular, and to keep up with demand, the molds were adapted to machine production. Colony Harvest was made until sometime in the 1960s.

Harvest, cake stand, milk glass, 12" **18.00**

Harvest, candleholder (sherbet design), milk glass, footed, ea **10.00**

Harvest, candy dish, milk glass, w/ lid **25.00**

Harvest, console bowl, milk glass, footed, 10", $18.00. (Photo courtesy Gene and Cathy Florence)

Harvest, creamer, milk glass, footed **5.00**

Harvest, cup, milk glass **4.50**

Harvest, goblet, milk glass **6.00**

Harvest, pitcher, milk glass, 40-oz **20.00**

Harvest, pitcher, milk glass, 65-oz **25.00**

Harvest, plate, milk glass, 8".. **3.00**

Harvest, plate, milk glass, 14½". **14.00**

Harvest, platter, milk glass, 14½".. **14.00**

Harvest, punch bowl, milk glass, 8-qt **20.00**

Harvest, punch/snack cup, milk glass, footed **2.50**

Harvest, salt & pepper shakers, milk glass, footed, pr **12.50**

Harvest, sherbet, milk glass, footed **5.00**

Harvest, snack tray, milk glass, oval **4.50**

Harvest, sugar bowl, milk glass, no handles, footed **5.00**

Harvest, tray for creamer & sugar bowl, milk glass, w/handles. **4.00**

Harvest, tumbler, milk glass, 10-oz......................................**5.00**
Harvest, tumbler, milk glass, 14-oz...............................**8.00**

Duncan and Miller

Festive, buffet plate, aqua, 16", $90.00. (Photo courtesy Gene and Cathy Florence)

Festive, candlestick, aqua, 5½", ea..................................**37.50**
Festive, comport, aqua, 9".....**60.00**
Festive, cruet, aqua, 8"..........**45.00**
Festive, gravy boat, honey, w/ ladle..............................**45.00**
Festive, twin server, honey, w/handle, 9½"...........................**38.00**

Federal Glass Co

Clover Blossom, bowl, rim soup; milk glass w/pink & gray decoration................................**10.00**
Clover Blossom, cup, milk glass w/ pink & gray decoration.....**3.00**
Clover Blossom, plate, chop; milk glass w/pink & gray decoration, 11"..............................**10.00**
Clover Blossom, plate, coupe; milk glass w/pink & gray decor, 7⅜".......**5.50**
Golden Glory, bowl, soup; white w/22k gold trim, 6⅜".........**9.00**
Golden Glory, mug, white w/22k gold trim..........................**15.00**

Golden Glory, plate, dinner; white w/22k gold trim, 9⅛".........**5.00**
Golden Glory, platter, white w/22k gold trim, round, 11¼"....**15.00**
Golden Glory, saucer, white w/22k gold trim...............................**.50**
Heritage, bowl, blue or green, 5"..**90.00**
Heritage, bowl, pink, lg, 8½"..**225.00**
Heritage, plate, sandwich; crystal, 12"...................................**15.00**
Heritage, sugar bowl, crystal, open, footed...............................**20.00**

Fostoria

Argus, compote, cobalt or ruby, w/ lid, 8"...............................**100.00**
Argus, creamer, crystal, olive or smoke, 6".........................**20.00**
Argus, sugar bowl, crystal, olive or smoke, w/lid....................**45.00**
Argus, tumbler, juice; cobalt or ruby, 4½-oz, 2⅞"...............**22.50**
Argus, wine, cobalt or ruby, 4-oz, 5"......................................**22.00**
Bouquet, bowl, serving; crystal, w/ handles, 9".......................**35.00**
Bouquet, butter dish, w/lid, crystal, ¼-lb **40.00**
Bouquet, pitcher, crystal, 1-pt, 6⅛"..................................**80.00**
Bouquet, vase, crystal, oval, 8¼"....................................**90.00**
Buttercup, bowl, salad; crystal, #2364, 9"..........................**50.00**
Buttercup, mayonnaise, crystal, #2364, 5".........................**25.00**
Buttercup, plate, cracker; crystal, #2364, 11¼".....................**32.50**
Buttercup, stem, cordial; crystal, #6030, 1-oz, 3⅞".............**42.50**
Buttercup, tumbler, ice tea; crystal, #6030, footed, 12-oz, 6"...**26.00**

Camellia, bowl, cereal; crystal, 6".................................30.00

Camellia, cup, crystal, footed, 6-oz............................... 17.00

Camellia, ice bucket, crystal . 75.00

Camellia, plate, party; crystal, w/ indent for cup, 8"........... 25.00

Camellia, relish dish, crystal, 2-part, 7⅜"...................... 18.00

Camellia, tray, utility; crystal, w/ handles, 9⅛".................... 30.00

Century, bottle, oil; crystal, w/stopper, 5-oz........................... 38.00

Century, bowl, crystal, flared, 8".................................25.00

Century, mustard, crystal, w/spoon & lid............................... 27.50

Century, oyster cocktail, crystal, 4½-oz, 3¾"........................ 16.00

Century, plate, dinner; crystal, 10½"................................. 28.00

Century, salt & pepper shakers, crystal, 3⅛", pr................. 20.00

Century, sugar bowl, crystal, footed, 4"................................... 7.00

Century, tray, crystal, center handle, 11½"............................ 30.00

Chintz, bottle, salad dressing; crystal, #2083, 6½"............... 450.00

Chintz, bowl, vegetable; crystal, #2496, 9½"...................... 75.00

Chintz, candlestick, crystal, #2496, 5½", ea.............................. 32.00

Chintz, pickle dish, crystal, #2496, 8"................................... 32.00

Chintz, vase, crystal, #4108 or #4128, 5"........................ 110.00

Corsage, bowl, crystal, w/handles, #2536, 9".......................... 65.00

Corsage, candelabra, crystal, 2-light w/prisms, #2527............ 120.00

Corsage, candy dish, crystal, 3-part, w/lid, #2496................... 115.00

Corsage, cordial, crystal, #6014, 1-oz, 3¾"......................... 45.00

Corsage, creamer, crystal, #2440.........................15.00

Corsage, mayonnaise, crystal, 2-part, #2440................. 25.00

Corsage, plate, cake; crystal, w/ handles, #2440, 10½"...... 38.00

Corsage, relish dish, crystal, 2-part, #2496............................. 20.00

Corsage, relish dish, crystal, 5-part, #2419............................. 55.00

Corsage, tumbler, crystal, #6014, 5-oz, 4¾"........................ 18.00

Corsage, vase, crystal, footed, #2470, 10"..................... 150.00

Corsage, water, crystal, stemmed, #6014, 9-oz, 7⅜"............. 26.00

Cut Rose, cup, crystal........... 20.00

Cut Rose, finger bowl, crystal. 25.00

Cut Rose, partait, crystal, 5½-oz, 5⅞"................................. 16.00

Cut Rose, plate, crystal, 14".. 45.00

Cut Rose, salt & pepper shakers, crystal, pr........................ 50.00

Cut Rose, saucer, crystal......... 6.00

Cut Rose, sugar bowl, individual; crystal............................. 20.00

Cut Rose, tumbler, crystal, footed, 5-oz, 4⅝"........................ 14.00

Heather, basket, crystal w/wicker handle, 10¼x6½"............. 95.00

Heather, butter dish, crystal, ¼-lb.............................. 75.00

Heather, compote, crystal, 4⅜". 30.00

Heather, plate, torte; crystal, 14"................................. 65.00

Heather, tray, crystal, center handle, 11½"............................ 37.50

Heather, tray, tidbit; crystal, upturned edge, 3-footed, 8⅛". 30.00

Heather, vase, bud; crystal, footed, #5092, 8".................... 85.00

Heirloom, bowl, crinkle; all colors, 6½"...............38.00

Heirloom, candlestick, all colors, 3½", ea..............25.00

Heirloom, plate, all colors, 11". 55.00

Heirloom, vase, all colors, 18". 150.00

Holly, ashtray, crystal, #2364, 2⅝"...............20.00

Holly, pitcher, crystal, #2666, 32-oz...............85.00

Holly, plate, crystal, #2337, 7½".10.00

Holly, plate, crystal, #2364, 11".30.00

Holly, salt & pepper shakers, crystal, #2364, 3¼", pr..........45.00

Holly, tray, celery; crystal, #2364, 11"...............25.00

Holly, vase, crystal, #2619½, 9½"..............125.00

Horizon, coaster, all colors.......9.00

Horizon, plate, all colors, 10".20.00

Horizon, tumbler, all colors, #5650, 5"...............10.00

Jamestown, bowl, serving; blue, pink or ruby, handles, #2719/648, 10"...............70.00

Jamestown, cake salver, green, 7x10", $250.00.

Jamestown, pickle dish, amethyst, crystal or green, #2719/540, 8¾"...............40.00

Jamestown, sherbet, blue, pink or ruby, #2719/7, 7-oz, 4⅛"..15.00

Jamestown, tray, muffin; amber or brown, handle, #2719/726, 9⅜"...............26.00

Jamestown, tumbler, amethyst, crystal or green, #2719/73, 9-oz, 4¼"...............20.00

Jamestown, wine, amber or brown, #2719/26, 4-oz, 4¼".........10.00

Lido, bonbon, crystal, 3-footed, 7⅜"...............17.00

Lido, bottle, oil; crystal, w/stopper, 3½-oz...............95.00

Lido, candlestick, crystal, 5½", ea .22.00

Lido, claret, crystal, #6017, 4-oz, 5⅞"...............24.00

Lido, cup, crystal, footed........15.00

Lido, plate, crystal, 9½".........35.00

Lido, tumbler, crystal, footed, #6017, 9-oz, 5½"..............18.00

Mayflower, bowl, fruit; crystal, #2560, 13"...............60.00

Mayflower, finger bowl, crystal, #869 ....35.00

Mayflower, olive dish, crystal, #2560, 6¾"...............20.00

Mayflower, plate, crystal, #2560, 14"...............65.00

Mayflower, vase, crystal, #2430, 3¾"...............65.00

Meadow Rose, bowl, crystal, w/ handle, 8½"...............45.00

Meadow Rose, ice bucket, crystal, 4⅜"...............100.00

Meadow Rose, mayonnaise, crystal, 3-pc, #2375 or #2496½ 55.00

Meadow Rose, relish dish, crystal, 3-part, 10x7½"...............40.00

Meadow Rose, vase, crystal, #4121, 5"...............85.00

Navarre, candy dish, crystal, 3-part, w/lid, #2496 ....130.00

Navarre, compote, crystal, #2400, 4½"...............35.00

Navarre, continental champagne, blue or pink, #6106, 5-oz, 8".....**195.00**

Navarre, dinner bell, blue or pink..............**95.00**

Navarre, pitcher, crystal, #2666, 32-oz..............**265.00**

Navarre, saucer, crystal, #2440. **4.00**

Navarre, tray, tidbit; crystal, turned-up edge, 3-footed, #2496, 8"..............**28.00**

Navarre, tumbler, crystal, #6106, 13-oz, 3⅝"..............**120.00**

Hazel Atlas

Beehive, bowl, utility; crystal, 19½-oz..............**12.00**

Beehive, butter dish, crystal, 6".**25.00**

Beehive, sherbet, pink, 3¾".....**8.00**

Beehive, tray, serving; pink, 12¼"..............**18.00**

Capri, ashtray, blue, triangular, 6⅝"..............**12.00**

Capri, bowl, blue, swirled, 8¾".**12.00**

Capri, coaster, blue..............**5.00**

Capri, creamer, blue, round...**12.50**

Capri, plate, sq, 8"..............**8.00**

Capri, tumbler, blue, pentagonal, 5-oz, 3⅛"..............**7.00**

Capri, vase, blue, ruffled, 8½".**35.00**

Colonial Couple, pitcher, milk glass w/black decor & red trim, 16-oz..............**40.00**

Colonial Couple, tumbler, milk glass w/black decor & red trim, 8-oz..............**20.00**

Gothic, cup, crystal..............**6.00**

Gothic, goblet, crystal, 7-oz, 5¼".**20.00**

Gothic, plate, crystal, 8"..........**7.50**

Gothic, saucer, crystal..............**2.00**

Gothic, sherbet, crystal, 8-oz, 3⅝"..**3.00**

Gothic, tumbler, crystal, footed, 10-oz, 5¾"..............**6.00**

Moderntone Platonite, bowl, deep cereal, white w/stripes, 5".**9.00**

Moderntone Platonite, bowl, pink, no rim, 8"..............**9.00**

Moderntone Platonite, cup, red or blue Willow decor..........**25.00**

Moderntone Platonite, plate, dinner; pastel colors, 8⅞".......**6.00**

Moderntone Platonite, platter, oval, white w/stripes, 12"........**25.00**

Moroccan Amethyst, bowl, 6".**10.00**

Moroccan Amethyst, chip & dip, bowls in metal holder, 10¾" & 5¾"..............**35.00**

Moroccan Amethyst, ice bucket, 6"..............**38.00**

Moroccan Amethyst, salt & pepper shakers, pr..............**40.00**

Newport, bowl, berry; fired-on colors, 4¾"..............**7.50**

Newport, creamer, fired-on colors..............**7.50**

Newport, plate, white, 8½"......**3.00**

Newport, platter, white, oval, 11¾"..............**10.00**

Newport, sugar bowl, fired-on colors..............**7.50**

Heisey

Cabochon, bottle, oil; crystal, w/#101 stopper, #1951....**60.00**

Cabochon, butter dish, Dawn, #1951, ¼-lb..............**200.00**

Cabochon, cocktail, crystal, #6091, 4-oz..............**5.00**

Cabochon, mayonnaise, crystal, 3-pc w/plate, bowl & ladle, #1951..............**35.00**

Cabochon, relish dish, crystal, 3-part, oblong, #1951, 9".**22.00**

Cabochon, tumbler, crystal, footed, #6091, 5-oz..............**10.00**

Cabochon, vase, crystal, flared, #1951, 3½" **24.00**

Lodestar, bowl, Dawn, #1565, 6¾" **60.00**

Lodestar, candy dish, w/lid, Dawn, 5" **240.00**

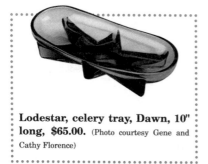

Lodestar, celery tray, Dawn, 10" long, $65.00. (Photo courtesy Gene and Cathy Florence)

Lodestar, plate, Dawn, 14" **90.00**

Lodestar, vase, Dawn, #1626, 8" **200.00**

New Era, ashtray, crystal **40.00**

New Era, plate, crystal, 5½x4½". **15.00**

New Era, relish dish, crystal, 3-part **25.00**

New Era, tray, celery; crystal, 13" **30.00**

New Era, wine, crystal, 3-oz . **25.00**

Imperial

Atterbury Scroll, bowl, salad; crystal **20.00**

Atterbury Scroll, candlestick, crystal, ea **22.00**

Atterbury Scroll, pitcher, jade. **90.00**

Atterbury Scroll, salt & pepper shakers, crystal, pr **30.00**

Atterbury Scroll, tumbler, water; jade **22.00**

Chroma, compote, all colors .. **20.00**

Chroma, goblet, all colors, 8-oz **22.00**

Chroma, sherbet, all colors, 6-oz **16.00**

Chroma, tumbler, all colors, 8-oz **22.50**

Crocheted Crystal, basket, 12". **85.00**

Crocheted Crystal, cake stand, footed, 12" **40.00**

Crocheted Crystal, lamp, hurricane; 11" **75.00**

Crocheted Crystal, plate, cheese & cracker; footed, 12" **40.00**

Crocheted Crystal, tumbler, footed, 6-oz, 6" **25.00**

Crocheted Crystal, vase, 8" ... **35.00**

Indiana Glass Co

Banana Fruit, plate, crystal w/ flashed colors, 7½" **15.00**

Christmas Candy, bowl, crystal, 5¾" **4.50**

Christmas Candy, creamer, teal **30.00**

Christmas Candy, plate, crystal, 6" **3.50**

Christmas Candy, plate, teal, 6" **11.00**

Christmas Candy, tray, tidbit; crystal, 2-tier **17.50**

Constellation, bowl, jumbo salad; crystal **25.00**

Constellation, bowl, nut; crystal, cupped, 6" **10.00**

Constellation, candy dish, colors, 3-toe, w/lid, 5½" **18.00**

Constellation, cookie jar, crystal or colors, 9" **30.00**

Constellation, mayonnaise, crystal, w/ladle **25.00**

Constellation, mug, crystal ... **12.50**

Constellation, plate, crystal, 18". **32.00**

Constellation, tumbler, crystal, 8-oz **12.50**

Daisy, bowl, red or amber, 6". **25.00**

Daisy, creamer, crystal, footed. **6.00**

Daisy, plate, green, 7⅜" **3.50**

Daisy, plate, red or amber, 9⅜". **8.00**

Daisy, plate, sandwich; crystal, 11½"................................ **10.00**

Daisy, saucer, crystal or green. **1.00**

Daisy, tumbler, green, footed, 9-oz **9.00**

Daisy, tumbler, red or amber, footed, 9-oz............................ **18.00**

Diamond Point (ruby band), bowl, flat rim, 6", from $5 to...... **7.00**

Diamond Point (ruby band), bowl, footed/scalloped, 11½", from $15 to **20.00**

Diamond Point (ruby band), cake stand, 10", from $25 to ... **28.00**

Diamond Point (ruby band), compote, flat rim, 7¼", from $12.50 to **17.50**

Diamond Point (ruby band), creamer, footed, from $4 to......... **6.00**

Diamond Point (ruby band), pitcher, water; from $25.00 to $30.00.

Diamond Point (ruby band), salt & pepper shakers, pr from $35 to....................................... **40.00**

Diamond Point (ruby band), sherbet, footed, from $5 to....... **7.00**

Diamond Point (ruby band), vase, footed, from $12 to.......... **15.00**

Diamond Point (ruby band), water tumbler, footed, from $6 to. **8.00**

Diamond Point (ruby band), water tumbler, 9-oz, from $4 to.. **6.00**

Lily Pons, bowl, nappy, green, deep, 7"...................................... **25.00**

Lily Pons, creamer, green...... **25.00**

Lily Pons, pickle dish, colors other than green, 8½"................ **6.00**

Lily Pons, plate, colors other than green, 8"............................ **6.00**

Lily Pons, sherbet, green....... **14.00**

Jeannette

Anniversary, bowl, fruit; crystal, 9"..................................... **12.00**

Anniversary, butter dish, pink **60.00**

Anniversary, candlesticks, iridescent, 4⅞", pr..................... **25.00**

Anniversary, plate, crystal, 10". **6.00**

Anniversary, wine goblet, pink, 2½-oz **18.00**

Camellia, bowl, vegetable; crystal, 8⅞" **12.50**

Camellia, cup, crystal **2.00**

Camellia, plate, crystal, 8" **6.00**

Camellia, tray, crystal, 2-handled **16.00**

Dewdrop, bowl, crystal, 8½" .. **17.50**

Dewdrop, candy dish, crystal, round, w/lid, 7"................ **22.00**

Dewdrop, pitcher, crystal, footed, ½-gal.................................. **22.00**

Dewdrop, punch bowl, crystal, 6-qt................................... **30.00**

Dewdrop, punch bowl base, crystal **10.00**

Dewdrop, sugar bowl, crystal, w/ lid...................................... **13.00**

Floragold, bowl, iridescent, ruffled, 9½" **8.00**

Floragold, candy dish, pink, 4-footed, 5¼" **20.00**

Floragold, coaster, iridescent, 4" **5.50**

Floragold, salt & pepper shakers, iridescent, plastic tops, pr .**55.00**

Floragold, sherbet, iridescent, low, footed **16.00**

Floragold, tray, serving; iridescent, 13½" **25.00**

Floragold, tray, tidbit; iridescent, wooden post **45.00**

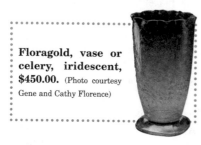

Floragold, vase or celery, iridescent, $450.00. (Photo courtesy Gene and Cathy Florence)

Harp, cake stand, pink, 9" **45.00**

Harp, cup, crystal **32.50**

Harp, saucer, crystal **10.00**

Harp, tray, crystal, rectangular, w/ handles **42.00**

Holiday, bowl, pink, 5⅛" **12.50**

Holiday, bowl, vegetable; pink, oval, 9½" **30.00**

Holiday, pitcher, crystal, 16-oz, 4¾" **15.00**

Holiday, plate, pink, 13¾" **135.00**

Holiday, platter, iridescent, oval, 11⅜" **20.00**

Holiday, tumbler, iridescent, footed, 5-oz, 4" **55.00**

Holiday, tumbler, pink, 10-oz, 4" **23.00**

Iris & Herringbone, bowl, soup; iridescent, 7½" **65.00**

Iris & Herringbone, creamer, green or pink, footed **150.00**

Iris & Herringbone, plate, crystal, 8" **100.00**

National, lazy Susan, crystal . **45.00**

National, relish dish, crystal, 6-part, 13" **18.00**

National, tray, celery; crystal, 9½" **15.00**

National, vase, crystal, 9" **20.00**

Morgantown

Crinkle, pitcher, all colors, sq base **135.00**

Crinkle, plate, all colors, 7½" . **14.00**

Crinkle, tumbler, all colors, footed, 13-oz **22.00**

Crinkle, vase, all colors, 5" or 7". **50.00**

Paden City

Emerald Glo, bottle, oil; **25.00**

Emerald Glo, cocktail shaker, 26-oz, 10" **65.00**

Emerald Glo, ice bucket, w/metal holder & tongs **75.00**

Emerald Glo, relish dish, heart shaped **35.00**

Emerald Glo, sugar bowl, w/lid & liner **25.00**

Emerald Glo, syrup, w/lid & liner **45.00**

Emerald Glo, tumbler, 1-oz, 2⅝". **10.00**

U.S. Glass

Manhattan, bowl, crystal, 6". **10.00**

Manhattan, bowl, crystal, 7". **10.00**

Manhattan, compote, crystal, 9½" **12.00**

Manhattan, compote, crystal, 10½" **15.00**

Manhattan, cup, punch; crystal. **3.00**

Manhattan, goblet, crystal, 4-oz..**8.00**

Manhattan, goblet, crystal, 10-oz **10.00**

Manhattan, plate, crystal, 6".. **5.00**
Manhattan, punch bowl, crystal. **50.00**
Manhattan, saucer, crystal...... **2.00**
Manhattan, tumbler, crystal, 8-oz **16.00**

Viking

Prelude, bonbon, crystal, 3-footed, 6" **22.00**
Prelude, bowl, crystal, 3-footed, 11" **55.00**
Prelude, candlesticks, crystal, 4½", pr...................................... **20.00**
Prelude, compote, crystal, 6". **22.00**
Prelude, creamer, crystal, 4-footed **15.00**
Prelude, platter, crystal, 14½". **65.00**
Prelude, tray, crystal, w/center handle, 11"...................... **35.00**

P r e l u d e , water pitcher, crystal with etching, 7 8 - o u n c e , $265.00. (Photo courtesy Gene and Cathy Florence)

Prelude, wine, crystal, 3-oz ... **22.00**
Prelude, wine carafe, crystal. **50.00**

Franciscan

When most people think of the Franciscan name, their Apple or Desert Rose patterns come to mind immediately, and without a doubt these are the most collectible of the hundreds of lines produced by Gladding McBean.

Located in Los Angeles, they produced quality dinnerware under the trade name Franciscan from the mid-1930s until 1984, when they were bought out by a company from England. Many marks were used; most included the Franciscan name. An 'F' in a square with 'Made in USA' below it dates from 1938, and a double-line script 'F' was used later. Some of this dinnerware is still being produced in England, so be sure to look for the USA mark. For an expanded listing, see *Schroeder's Antiques Price Guide* (Collector Books).

Apple, ashtray, oval **100.00**
Apple, bowl, mixing; sm **170.00**
Apple, box, round **180.00**
Apple, ginger jar **250.00**
Apple, mug, 7-oz.................... **38.00**
Apple, teapot **140.00**
Coronado, bowl, fruit; from $6 to **12.00**
Coronado, butter dish, from $25 to **35.00**
Coronado, platter, oval, 15½", from $25 to **45.00**
Coronado, teapot, from $75 to . **95.00**
Desert Rose, bell, Danbury Mint............................ **95.00**
Desert Rose, bowl, salad; 10".. **95.00**
Desert Rose, candy dish, oval, from $150 to **225.00**
Desert Rose, cup & saucer, demitasse................................ **25.00**
Desert Rose, gravy boat......... **38.00**
Desert Rose, plate, chop; 14". **75.00**
Desert Rose, platter, 12¾" **35.00**
Desert Rose, thimble............. **75.00**
Desert Rose, tumbler, 10-oz... **35.00**
Ivy, butter dish **49.50**

Ivy, mug, barrel shape, 12-oz. **50.00**
Ivy, pitcher, syrup **82.50**
Ivy, plate, chop; 14" **115.00**
Ivy, platter, turkey; 19" **325.00**
Ivy, relish dish, 3-part **72.00**
Ivy, soup ladle......................... **85.00**
Ivy, tile, in frame.................... **60.00**
Starburst, ashtray, oval, lg, from
    $50 to **75.00**
Starburst, bowl, fruit; individual .**15.00**
Starburst, bowl, oval, 8" **35.00**
Starburst, candlesticks, pr from
    $175 to **225.00**
Starburst, casserole, 8½", from
    $100 to **120.00**
Starburst, cruet, vinegar/oil, ea
    from $80 to **110.00**

Starburst, gravy boat with attached tray, from $35.00 to $40.00; Ladle, from $35.00 to $40.00.

Starburst, pepper mill **150.00**
Starburst, plate, dinner; from $15
    to **20.00**
Starburst, platter, 15"........... **65.00**
Starburst, tumbler, 6-oz, from $40
    to **50.00**

Frankoma

Since 1933 the Frankoma Pottery Company has been producing dinnerware, novelty items, vases, etc. In 1965 they became the first American company to produce a line of collector plates. The body of the ware prior to 1954 was a honey tan that collectors refer to as 'Ada clay.' A brick red clay (called 'Sapulpa') was used from then on, and this and the colors of the glazes help determine the period of production. For more information refer to *Frankoma and Other Oklahoma Potteries* by Phyllis and Tom Bess (Schiffer), and *Frankoma Pottery, Value Guide and More*, by Susan N. Cox. See Clubs and Newsletters for information on the Frankoma Family Collectors Association.

Ashtray, arrowhead shape, Desert
    Gold w/brown rim, 1950s,
    1¼x4x2".......................... **15.00**
Bowl, black, Sapulpa clay, 1" ribbed
    pedestal foot, #235, 5x6¼". **12.00**
Bowl, dessert; Wagon Wheel,
    Prairie Green, #94XO, 1942,
    6-oz, 2x4" **17.50**
Bowl, Plainsman, Desert Gold,
    Sapulpa clay, #5XL, 20-oz,
    2⅜x6¼"............................ **15.00**
Candleholder, Desert Gold, Christ
    the Light..., Oral Roberts, 2x6",
    ea...................................... **15.00**
Christmas card, Year of the Potter,
    1975, 3⅛" **25.00**
Creamer & sugar bowl, Plainsman,
    Desert Gold, Frankoma #5DA
    & #5DB............................ **30.00**
Dish, Oklahoma state shape, Clay
    Blue, 10".......................... **25.00**
Figurine, mallard duck, 2-tone
    brown, #208A, 5x10"....... **45.00**
Mug, brown, #26-DC, 6" **30.00**
Mug, elephant; White Sand, Republican Party 1968, 4"............. **45.00**

Novelty, cowboy boot, black, Sapulpa clay, 4½" **30.00**

Pitcher, Mayan Aztec, Prairie Green, Ada clay, #72 .... **60.00**

Planter, cactus shape, Red Bud glaze, Ada clay, #5, 7x5¾" **70.00**

Planter, Prairie Green, 4-footed, #39, 5x6" **30.00**

Plate, Aztec, brown, #7FL, 10½" **8.00**

Plate, Plainsman, Desert Gold, 4-petal rim, 7¾" **8.00**

Plate, Texas w/scenes, White Sand, w/state facts, 8½" **25.00**

Salt & pepper shakers, Wagon Wheel, Prairie Green, Ada clay, 2½", pr **35.00**

Sculpture, elephant, #160, from $125.00 to $150.00.

Stein, Lazybones, Prairie Green, Sapulpa clay, #M2, 18-oz, 6" **20.00**

Trivet, America's Stars & Stripes, Frankoma FL TR w/verse on back, 6" **35.00**

Tumbler, Wagon Wheel, Prairie Green, Ada clay, #80C, 1942-54, 5" **30.00**

Vase, collector; V-02, 1970, 12", from $80 to **90.00**

Vase, collector; V-05, 1973, 13". **85.00**

Vase, collector; V-07, 13" **80.00**

Vase, collector; V-09, w/stopper, 13" **65.00**

Vase, collector; V-12, 13" **65.00**

Vase, cornucopia; Dusty Rose, Ada clay, #159, 7¾x8" **60.00**

Vase, crocus bud; White Sand, Ada clay, #43, 8" **50.00**

Wall pocket, Phoebe, Desert Gold, #730PM, 7x5x3" **125.00**

Fruit Jars

Some of the earliest glass jars used for food preservation were blown, and corks were used for seals. During the nineteenth century, hundreds of manufacturers designed over 4,000 styles of fruit jars. Lids were held in place either by a wax seal, wire bail, or the later screw-on band. Jars were usually made in aqua or clear, though other colors were also used. Amber jars are popular with collectors, milk glass jars are rare, and cobalt and black glass jars often bring $3,000.00 and up, if they can be found! Condition, age, scarcity, and unusual features are also to be considered when evaluating old fruit jars. Color is a major factor.

Atlas, E-Z Seal, amber, qt **55.00**

Atlas Mason (dropped A), 2 lines, clear, zinc Atlas lid, ½-pt .. **6.00**

Atlas Special Mason, aqua, ½-gal **20.00**

Ball Perfect Mason, blue, sq, ½-gal **25.00**

Ball Perfect Mason, green, qt. **70.00**

Ball 3 Tapered Mason, clear, pt **39.00**

Burlington BG Co R'D 1876, clear, ½-gal **75.00**

Cohansey Glass MF'G Co Pat Mar 20 77, aqua, barrel shape..... **175.00**

Dexter, circled by fruit & vegtables, aqua, qt...............150.00

EGCO (Mono) Imperial, aqua, midget..............................55.00

Egco Mono Imperial, aqua, qt.55.00

Electric World Globe, aqua, pt.350.00

Electric World Globe, aqua, ½-gal........................150.00

Fruit Commonwealth Jar, clear, ½-gal..............................100.00

Fruit Keeper GC Co, aqua, ½-gal......................... 100.00

Gem, aqua, 24-oz....................75.00

Globe, aqua, qt.....................200.00

Globe, aqua, wide mouth, pt.500.00

J&B (in octagon) Fruit Jar Pat'd June 14th 1898, aqua, pt, repro lid......................................70.00

Kerr Self Sealing Trademark Reg Patent Mason, blue, qt.100.00

Knowlton Vacuum (star) Fruit Jar, blue, original, pt..............75.00

Mason's CFJCo Patent Nov 30th 1858, sky blue, qt..........250.00

Mason's Patent Nov 30th 1858, early repro, amber, ½-gal..........100.00

Mason's Patent Nov 30th 58, Christmas Mason, aqua, pt.........125.00

Mason's 20 (underlined) Patent Nov 30th 1858, aqua, ½-gal.....30.00

Misson (Bell) Mason Made in California, aqua, ½-pt...125.00

Perfection, clear, qt..................85.00

Pine (P in sq) Mason, clear, ½-pt...........................150.00

Protector Arched, aqua, qt.....50.00

Same Ball, blue, ½-gal.........150.00

Star (above star), aqua, repro closure, ½-gal 200.00

Swayzees (fleur-de-lis) Improved Mason, aqua, ½-gal.........20.00

TM Lightning, aqua, base marked HWP, aqua, ½-gal.............40.00

Trademark Lightning, amber, Putnam base, qt.............68.00

Trademark Lightning Putnam (base), aqua, regular, ½-pt.35.00

Trademark Mason's CFJ Improved, aqua, midget....................40.00

Victory (in shield), Victory Jar on lid, clear, pt 75.00

Wan-Eta Cocoa Boston, amber, original lid, ½-pt...............35.00

Western Pride Patented June 22 1855, aqua, ½-gal.........350.00

Yeoman's Fruit Bottle, aqua, whittled, no stopper, ½-gal.....75.00

Games

The ideal collectible game is one that combines playability (i.e., good strategy, interaction, surprise, etc.) with interesting graphics and unique components. Especially desirable are the very old games from the nineteenth and early twentieth centuries as well as those relating to early or popular TV shows and movies. As always, value depends on rarity and condition of the box and playing pieces. For a greatly expanded list and more information, see *Schroeder's Collectible Toys, Antique to Modern* (Collector Books).

Addams Family, Ideal, 1965, EXIB 50.00

Advance to Boardwalk, Parker Bros, 1985, NMIB...........15.00

Amazing Chan & the Chan Clan, Whitman, 1973, NMIB...20.00

Annie Oakley Game, Milton Bradley, 1950s, lg size, NMIB........................... 45.00

As the World Turns, Parker Bros, 1966, NMIB 30.00

Babes in Toyland, Whitman, 1961, EXIB 25.00

Barbie's Little Sister Skipper Game, Mattel, 1964, NMIB 45.00

Bat Masterson, Lowell, 1958, NMIB 65.00

Battlestar Galactica, Parker Bros, 1978, NMIB 20.00

Betsy Ross Flag Game, 1960s, NMIB 30.00

Big Game, National, 1930s-40s, EXIB 20.00

Bionic Woman, Parker Brothers, 1976, MIB, $18.00.

Black Ball Express, Schaper, 1957, NMIB 30.00

Bonanza Michigan Rummy Game, Parker Bros, 1964, EXIB. 25.00

Bozo the Clown in Circus Land, Transogram, 1960s, NMIB 25.00

Buccaneers, Transogram, 1957, NMIB 45.00

Bullwinkle & Rocky Magic Dot Game, Transogram, 1962, NMIB 100.00

Cabbage Patch Kids, Parker Bros, 1984, EXIB 8.00

Captain Kangaroo, Milton Bradley, 1956, NMIB 50.00

Casey Jones, Saalfield, 1959, NMIB 50.00

Challenge the Chief, Ideal, 1973, NMIB 25.00

Charlie's Angels (Farrah on box), NMIB 25.00

Cinderella, Parker Bros, 1964, EXIB 50.00

Conflict, Parker Bros, 1960, EXIB 50.00

Crusader Rabbit TV Game, Tryne, 1960s, NMIB 125.00

Dark Tower, Milton Bradley, 1981, NMIB 150.00

Dennis the Menace Baseball Game, MTP, 1960, NMIB 45.00

Dick Tracy Card Game, Whitman, 1934, EXIB 75.00

Dogfight, Milton Bradley, 1962, EXIB 85.00

Electric Sports Car Race, Tudor, 1959, NMIB 75.00

Farmer Jones Pigs, McLoughlin Bros, VGIB 130.00

Flintstones Brake Ball, Whitman, 1962, EXIB 85.00

Fugitive Game, Ideal, 1966, VGIB 80.00

Game of Flags, McLoughlin Bros, VGIB 75.00

Game of Golf, JH Singer, VGIB .550.00

Gee-Wiz Horse Race, Wolverine, EX 100.00

Gidget, Standard Toykraft, 1965, MIB, from $75 to.......... 100.00

Gray Ghost, Transogram, 1958, NMIB 90.00

Hardy Boys Treasure, Parker Bros, 1960, VGIB 45.00

Hopalong Canasta Card Game, Pacific, 1950, NM 200.00

Hoppity Hooper Pinball Game, Lidu, 1965, NMIB 100.00

Identipops, Playvalue, 1969, VGIB 200.00

Jack & Jill, Milton Bradley, VGIB 100.00

James Bond Secret Agent 007, Milton Bradley, 1964, NMIB 45.00

Jan Murray's Treasure Hunt, Gardner, 1950s, NMIB ... 30.00

Jerome Park Steeple Chase, McLoughlin Bros, EXIB . 400.00

Jetson's Fun Pad, Milton Bradley, 1963, NMIB 80.00

Kojak Stake Out Detective Game, Milton Bradley, 1975, MIB . 40.00

Legend of Jesse James, Milton Bradley, 1965, NMIB 85.00

Let's Face It, Hasbro, 1950s, NMIB 35.00

Little Rascals Clubhouse Bingo, Gabriel, 1958, EXIB 50.00

Lone Ranger Silver Bullets, Whiting, 1956, MIB 150.00

Lucy Tea Party Game, Milton Bradley, 1971, EXIB 45.00

Matchbox Traffic Game, Bronner, 1960s, MIB 60.00

Merry Milkman, Hasbro, 1955, EXIB 95.00

Mervin Pervis' 'G'-Man Detective Game, Parker Bros, 1936, board only 50.00

Mighty Hercules Game, Hasbro, 1960s, NMIB 325.00

Mighty Mouse, Milton Bradley, 1978, NMIB 30.00

Monkees Game, Transogram, 1968, EXIB 115.00

Monster Old Maid, Card Game, Milton Bradley, 1964, EXIB 50.00

Movie-Land Keeno, EXIB 75.00

Moving Picture Game, Milton Bradley, EXIB 125.00

Mr Magoo's Maddening Mis- adventures, Transogram, 1970, NMIB 70.00

Mystic Skull, The Game of Voodoo, Ideal, 1964, NMIB 50.00

Nancy Drew Mystery Game, Parker Bros, 1957, NMIB 160.00

Newport Yacht Race, McLoughlin Bros, GIB 450.00

Oh Magoo, Warren, 1960s, NMIB 30.00

Overland Trail, Transogram, 1960, NMIB 90.00

Parlor Croquet, Bliss, GIB .. 150.00

Peter Gunn Detective Game, Lowell, 1960, NMIB 55.00

Peter Potamus Game, Ideal, 1964, NMIB 70.00

Pirates of the Caribbean, Parker Bros, 1967, EXIB 25.00

Pokey the Clown Target Game, Wyandotte, 1950s, EXIB . 75.00

Popeye Clobber Cans, Gardner, NMIB 150.00

Price Is Right, 1958, 1st Edition, EXIB 25.00

Rebel, Ideal, 1961, NMIB 75.00

Restless Gun, Milton Bradley, 1950s, EXIB 50.00

Rip Van Winkle, Parker Bros, VGIB 125.00

Robin Hood (Adventures of), Betty-B, 1956, EXIB 65.00

Roulette Wheel, Marx, NMIB . 50.00

Scores & Stripes Bagatelle Game, Marx, 1949, NMIB 125.00

Shenanigans, Milton Bradley, 1964, EXIB 50.00

Slap Stick, Milton Bradley, MIB 25.00

Smokey Bear Forest Prevention Bear, Ideal, 1961, NMIB . 95.00

Snoopy & the Red Baron, Milton Bradley, 1970, MIB 55.00

Snow White & the Seven Dwarfs, Cadaco, 1970s, EXIB 12.00

Spear's Quick Change Comic Pictures, VGIB 65.00

Star Trek Game, Milton Bradley, 1979, EXIB 40.00

Submarine Search, Milton Bradley, 1977, EXIB 60.00

That Girl, Remco, 1969, EXIB. 70.00

Tim Holt Rodeo Dart Games, American Toys, unused, NMIB 100.00

To Tell the Truth, Lowell, 1957, EXIB 20.00

Tom Sawyer & Huck Finn, (Adventures of), Stoll & Edwards, VGIB 125.00

Town & Country Traffic, Ranger Steel, 1940s, EXIB 50.00

Untouchables Target Game, Marx, 1950s, NM 350.00

Walt Disney's Fantasyland, Parker Bros, 1950, MIB 50.00

Wide World Travel Game, Parker Bros, 1957, NMIB 25.00

Wink Tennis, Transogram, 1956, NMIB 15.00

Wow Pillow Fight Game, Milton Bradley, 1964, NMIB 25.00

Yogi Bear Rummy ED-U Cards, 1961, MIB (sealed) 15.00

Young America Target, Parker Bros, VGIB 275.00

Zamboola, Norstar, VGIB 85.00

77 Sunset Strip, Lowell, 1960, EXIB 30.00

Gas Station Collectibles

From the invention of the automobile came the need for gas service stations, who sought to attract customers through a wide variety of advertising methods. Gas and oil companies issued thermometers, signs, calendars, clocks, banks, and scores of other items emblazoned with their logos and catchy slogans. Though a rather specialized area, gas station collectibles encompass a wide variety of items that appeal to automobilia and advertising collectors as well. For further information we recommend *Value Guide to Gas Station Memorabilia* by B.J. Summers and Wayne Priddy (Collector Books).

Badge, hat; Union Oil, cloisonné metal, shield shape, 1¾x1¾", EX 275.00

Bank, Atlas battery, metal, black & red, 3", VG 35.00

Bank, Johnson Motor Oil can, metal, orange, black & white, 3½", EX 120.00

Bank, man figure, Phillips 66, plastic, wearing uniform, 5", EX.....40.00

Blotter, Oilzum, cardboard, 1951 Champions, 3½x6¼", EX. 35.00

Booklet, Standard Oil of Indiana Automobile Lubrication, VG.............................. 35.00

Bottle, Mobil window spray, glass, paper label, G.................. 25.00

Bottle rack, Mobiloil, Authorized Service, porcelain, 25x30", EX............................. 1,700.00

Calendar, 1947, Sinclair Gasoline, pinup girl, 33½x16", EX.. 65.00

Clock, Evinrude, Authorized Parts..., metal & glass, 15" dia, EX 800.00

Clock, Fire Ring Spark Plugs, plastic, light-up, 16½" dia, EX 350.00

Clock, Krome-Oil, American Hammered Piston..., light-up, 15" dia, EX 170.00

Clock, Michelin, plastic, logo in yellow sq, light-up, 25x24", EX......**50.00**

Doll, Phillips 66 Buddy Lee, 13", $300.00. (Photo courtesy Morphy Auctions)

Gas globe, Champion Ethyl, glass, 3-pc, 13½", EX..............**275.00**

Gas globe, Cities Service, glass & plastic, 3-pc, 1950s, 13½", EX..............**350.00**

Gas globe, Clark, glass, 3-pc, 13½", EX..............**300.00**

Gas globe, CO-OP, glass w/gill band, metal screw-on base, 13½", EX..............**400.00**

Gas Globe, Essolene, low profile with metal band and glass lens, 16½", from $400.00 to $500.00. (Photo courtesy B. J. Summers and Wayne Priddy)

Gas globe, Farmers Union, glass & plastic, 13½", EX..........**275.00**

Gas globe, Genoco, glass & metal, 3-pc, 15", EX..................**500.00**

Gas globe, Phillips 66, glass & plastic, 3-pc, 13½", VG........**275.00**

Grease can, Allerton's Axle Grease, 4¼" dia, EX......................**35.00**

Grease can, Scholl's Axle Grease, 6½x5¾" dia, EX **30.00**

Hat, Pennzoil, black cloth w/lg yellow logo, EX..................**20.00**

Hat, Texaco, black cloth, w/bill, EX **125.00**

License plate attachment, M&H Gasoline, metal & celluloid, 5x4", EX........................**125.00**

License plate attachment, 400 Service Station, We Doze..., 6x6", NM......................**175.00**

Mileage card, Gilmore Lion Head, cardboard, 2½x4", EX **35.00**

Nodder, K-C piston, composition, Let Casey..., yellow & black, 7", EX **140.00**

Oil bottle, Texaco Home Lubricant, 3-oz, EX **50.00**

Oil can, Air Race Motor Oil, ca 1935-45, 1-qt, VG.........**110.00**

Oil can, Americo Motor Oil, 1-gal, EX **30.00**

Oil can, Cities Service Oil, 1-gal, EX **35.00**

Oil can, Liberty Motor Oil, 1-qt, EX **255.00**

Oil can, Nourse Oil Co, Viking logo, 1-gal, EX......................**90.00**

Oil can, Pennsylvania 100% Pure Motor Oil, 1-qt, EX.......**130.00**

Oil can, Shell Motor Oil, shell logo on yellow, 1-gal, VG......**155.00**

Oil can, Supreme Auto Oil, 1-gal, 8½x5½", G........................**65.00**

Oil rack, Ford Motor Company, metal, black & white, 25x18", EX **65.00**

Paperweight mirror, Phillips 66, black & white, 1950s, 3½" dia, EX **120.00**

Pocket mirror, glass, Cranepenn Motor Oil, logo on black, red trim, EX........................**75.00**

Sign, Automotive Maintenance Association, porcelain, 20x18", EX **300.00**

Sign, Barnsdall Super-Gas, porcelain, 2-sided, 30" dia, VG......... **150.00**

Sign, Champion, Dependable Spark Plug Service, metal, 18x12", EX **135.00**

Sign, Cooper Tires, metal, oval, 32½x12", EX **200.00**

Thermometer, Atlas Wiper Blades, metal, white & red, 8x14", EX................................ **100.00**

Thermometer, Auto-Lite, metal, yellow, blue & red, 25x8", EX **100.00**

Thermometer, En-Ar-Co Motor Oil, metal, red, white & black, 39x8", EX....................... **325.00**

Thermometer, Mobil, die-cut plastic, white, red & blue, 6¾", EX................................. **175.00**

Thermometer, Willard, Prevent Battery..., glass & metal, 16" dia, EX........................... **55.00**

Tie bar, Union Oil, metal, shield logo in center, 2¼" L, EX. **50.00**

Toy service station, tin, Roadside Rest, Marx, battery-op, 14" L, EX **1,200.00**

Toy truck, Cities Service wrecker, metal, green & white, EX.**275.00**

Travel pack, Union 76, cardboard, w/products, EX **30.00**

Upholstery brush, Dietrich Motor Car, celluloid, 3½" dia, EX.........**140.00**

Gay Fad Glassware

Here's another new area of collecting that's just now taking off. The company started out on a very small scale in the late 1930s, but before long, business was booming! Their first products were hand-decorated kitchenware, but it's their frosted tumblers, trays, pitchers, and decanters that are being sought today. In addition to souvenir items and lines with a holiday theme, they made glassware to coordinate with Royal China's popular dinnerware, Currier and Ives. They're also known for their 'bentware' — quirky cocktail glasses with stems that were actually bent. Look for an interlocking 'G' and 'F' or the name 'Gay Fad,' the latter mark indicating pieces from the late 1950s to the early 1960s. Gay Fad is mentioned in *The Hazel-Atlas Glass Identification and Value Guide* by Gene and Cathy Florence (Collector Books). See also Anchor Hocking.

Bent trays, classic design, paper label, 2 sq trays in metal frame....................... **22.00**

Beverage set, Apple, frosted, 86-oz ball pitcher & 6 13-oz tumblers **130.00**

Beverage set, Magnolia, clear, 86-oz pitcher & 6 13-oz tumblers.**75.00**

Bowl, chili; Fruits, 2¼x5" **12.00**

Bowl, mixing; Poinsettia, red w/ green leaves on Fire-King Ivory Swirl **45.00**

Bowl, splash-proof; Fruits, Fire-King, 4¼x6½"................... **55.00**

Bowls, nesting; Fruits, Fire-King, 6", 7½, 8¾", set of 3 .... **45.00**

Casserole, Apple, open, oval, Fire-King Ivory, 1-qt **45.00**

Casserole, Fruits, divided, oval, Fire King, 11¾" **40.00**

Casserole, Rosemaling (tulips) on lid, clear, 2-qt, w/black wire rack **30.00**

Chip & dip, Horace the Horse w/ cart, knife, 3 bowls, glass as head **45.00**

Cocktail shaker, full-figured ballerina, frosted, 28-oz, 9".. **35.00**

Decanter set, Gay '90s, Scotch, Rye, Gin & Bourbon, frosted inside **85.00**

Ice tub, Gay '90s, frosted **20.00**

Juice set, oranges and leaves, frosted, ribbed lid, with six tumblers, $68.00. (Photo courtesy Donna McGrady)

Juice set, Tommy Tomato, frosted, 36-oz pitcher & 6 4-oz tumblers **40.00**

Loaf pan, Apple, Fire-King Ivory .**35.00**

Martini mixer, A Jug of Wine..., w/glass stirring rod, clear, 10⅝" **25.00**

Mix-A-Salad set, Ivy, 22-oz shaker w/plastic top, press/spoon/recipes **75.00**

Mug, Fruits, stackable, Fire-King, 3" **12.00**

Mug, Notre Dame, frosted, 16-oz **15.00**

Mug set, Here's How in different language on ea, frosted, 12-pc **68.00**

Pitcher, juice; Ada Orange, frosted, 36-oz................................. **20.00**

Plate, Fruits, lace edge, Hazel Atlas, 8½"........................ **17.50**

Range set, Rooster, salt, pepper, sugar & flour shakers, metal lids **120.00**

Refrigerator container, Distlefink on white, Fire-King, w/lid, 4x8" **50.00**

Stem, bent cocktail, Beau Brummel, clear, signed Gay Fad, 3½-oz..................... **10.00**

Tea & Toast, Magnolia, sq plate w/ cup indent & cup, clear .. **15.00**

Tumbler, Bob White, brown, turquoise & gold on clear, 10-oz..........**12.00**

Tumbler, Kentucky state map (1 of 48), yellow or lime, frosted, 10-oz................................. **8.00**

Tumbler, Oregon state map on pink picket fence, clear, marked GF..................................... **8.00**

Tumbler, Say When, frosted, 4-oz............................. **8.00**

Tumbler, Zombie, flamingo, frosted, marked GF, 14-oz............. **20.00**

Waffle set, Blue Willow, 48-oz batter jug & syrup jug, 2-pc **125.00**

Waffle set, Peach Blossoms, 48-oz batter jug & syrup jug, 2-pc.....**52.00**

Geisha Girl Porcelain

More than 65 different patterns of tea services were exported from Japan around the turn of the century, each depicting geishas going about the everyday activities of Japanese life. Mt. Fuji is often featured in the background. Geisha Girl Porcelain is a generic term collectors use to identify them all. Many of our lines contain reference to the color of the rim bands, which many collectors use to tentatively date the ware.

Ashtray, Temple A, multicolored, spade shape **25.00**

Berry set, Dragon Boat, cobalt w/ gold, master & 5 individual bowls **85.00**

Biscuit jar, Lady in Rickshaw, melon-ribbed, red-orange w/gold, footed **55.00**

Bowl, Dragon Boat, 6-lobed, blue w/ gold, 7" **35.00**

Bowl, Footbridge B, red w/yellow, 8" **35.00**

Bowl, Porcelain Bench, 8", $22.00. (Photo courtesy Elyce Litts)

Box, trinket; Koto, club shaped .**28.00**

Butter pat, Flower Gathering B, red-orange, 3¼" **12.00**

Compote, Boat Festival, river scene, footed, #4, 6" **55.00**

Creamer, Boy w/Scythe, cobalt w/ gold **15.00**

Cup & saucer, Geisha Band, cobalt border, Made in Japan.... **15.00**

Dresser box, Garden Bench B, cobalt w/gold, 6" dia **38.00**

Hair receiver, Battledore, grass green, melon-ribbed **24.00**

Hatpin holder, hand-painted Garden Bench pattern, multicolored border, 4" **60.00**

Jar, Lantern B, relief molded, red border w/gold buds, 3x3". **14.00**

Jar, water; Meeting A, red border, mini, 2⅜" **14.00**

Jug, Cherry Blossom, red-orange edge, 6½" **40.00**

Lemonade set, Bellflower, brown w/trim, pitcher & 5 matching mugs **125.00**

Marmalade, Cloud A, red-orange w/ yellow, ribs, w/tray, 5"..... **45.00**

Napkin ring, Rivers Edge, red, triangular **35.00**

Nut dish, Duck Watching A, red w/ gold, footed, individual size..**8.00**

Plate, Basket, swirl fluted, scalloped edge, dark apple green, 8½" **30.00**

Plate, Lady in Rickshaw B, gold/ red/beaded border, scalloped, 5" **14.00**

Plate, Water Boy, pine green, 7".**14.00**

Platter, Ikebana Party, red border w/gold lacing, Kutani, 9½", NM **38.00**

Puff box, Flower Gathering, ribbed, black stencil/red edge, 3½" dia **18.00**

Ring tree, Temple A Nippon .. **75.00**

Shakers, Blind Man's Bluff, swirl-fluted body, light apple green, pr...................................... **22.00**

Tea set, River's Edge, green 3-banded border w/gold, 15-pc. **125.00**

Teapot, So Big, multicolored border, 3-footed, Kutani mark, 5½".**55.00**

Toothpick holder, In a Hurry, blue scalloped border w/gold, 2¼"......**22.00**

Vase, Bamboo Trellis, red-orange, #14, 4½", pr.................... **30.00**

GI Joe

Introduced by Hasbro in 1964, 12" GI Joe dolls were offered in four basic packages: Action Soldier, Action Sailor, Action Marine, and Action Pilot. A Black figure was included in the line, and there were representatives of many nations as well. Talking dolls followed a few years later, and scores of accessory items such as vehicles, guns, uniforms, etc., were made to go with them all. Even though the line was discontinued in 1976, it was evident the market was still there, and kids were clamoring for more. So in 1982, Hasbro brought out the 'little' 3¾" GI Joe's, each with his own descriptive name. Sales were unprecedented. The small figures are easy to find, but most of them are 'loose' and played with. Collectors prefer old store stock still in the original packaging; such examples are worth from two to four times more than those without the package, sometimes even more. For more information we recommend *Schroeder's Collectible Toys, Antique to Modern*, published by Collector Books.

3¾" GI Joe Figures, Sets, and Vehicles

Accessory, Cobra Condor Z25, 1989, w/Aero-Viper Pilot, MIP . **75.00**
Accessory, Hovercraft Killer WHALE, 1984, #6005, MIP **150.00**
Accessory, LCV Recon Sled, 1986, #6067, EX **14.00**
Accessory, Mountain Howitzer, 1984, #6125, EX **8.00**
Accessory, Swamp Skier w/Zartan, 1984, MOC **130.00**
Accessory, Transportable Tactical Battle Platform, 1985, NM. **30.00**
Accessory, USS Flag Aircraft Carrier, 1986, #6001, EX **160.00**
Figure, Airborne, 1983, MOC . **65.00**

Figure, Barbecue, 1985, EX .. **25.00**
Figure, Baroness, 1984, MOC .. **160.00**
Figure, Battle Force 2000 Dodger, 1987, NM **18.00**
Figure, Blowtorch, 1984, MOC .. **55.00**
Figure, Buzzer, 1985, MOC ... **70.00**
Figure, Chuckles, 1987, NM.. **15.00**
Figure, Crimson Guard, 1985, MOC **100.00**
Figure, Dr Mindbender, 1986, MOC **35.00**
Figure, Eels, 1985, NM **28.00**
Figure, Frostbite, 1985, MOC . **18.00**
Figure, Lady Jaye, 1985, MOC .**90.00**
Figure, Major Bludd, 1983, MIP.. **55.00**
Figure, Mutt & Junkyard, 1984, MOC **60.00**
Figure, Psyche-Out, 1987, MOC.. **25.00**
Figure, Quick Kick, 1985, MOC. **100.00**
Figure, Recondo, 1984, MOC . **70.00**
Figure, Scarlett, 1982, MOC . **140.00**

Figure, Sci-fi, 1986, MOC, $32.00.

Figure, Scrap Iron Cobra, 1984, NM **27.00**
Figure, Snake Eyes, w/Timer (wolf), 1985, MOC **160.00**
Figure, Stalker, 1982, MOC . **125.00**
Figure, Tiger Force Road Block, 1988, NM **20.00**
Figure, Zap, 1982, MOC **90.00**
Figure, Zarana, 1986, w/earring, MOC **115.00**
MMS Mobile Missile System, 1982, #6054, MIP **65.00**

12" GI Joe Figures, Sets, and Vehicles

Accessory, Armored Suit, Demolition, EX **15.00**

Accessory, Binoculars, Hurricane Spotter, gray, EX **7.00**

Accessory, Boots, Flying Space Adventure, yellow, EX **32.00**

Accessory, Canteen & Cover, British, EX **35.00**

Accessory, Carrying Case/Play Set, Takara, VG+ **100.00**

Accessory, Case & Map, Sandstorm Survival, silver, EX **7.00**

Accessory, Cobra, Search for the Golden Idol, EX **15.00**

Accessory, Fatigue Pants, Action Soldier, #7504, green, NMOC **250.00**

Accessory, First Aid Pouch, green cloth, w/snap closure, EX. **50.00**

Accessory, Grenade Launcher, Action Man, EX **15.00**

Accessory, Handgun (.45), Action Man, EX **5.00**

Accessory, Helmet Set, #7507, MOC **110.00**

Accessory, Iron Knight Tank, M. **135.00**

Accessory, Life Vest, orange, padded, 1960s **29.00**

Accessory, Parachute Pack, Sky Dive to Danger, EX+ **125.00**

Accessory, Radio, Airborne MP, black, marked Hong Kong, G+ .. **245.00**

Accessory, Sandstorm Jeep, green, EXIB **275.00**

Accessory, Scuba Gear, orange suit, tanks & tins, NM **150.00**

Accessory, Space Capsule Collar, inflatable, Sears, EX **115.00**

Accessory, Volcano Jumper, Adventure Team, #7349 . **50.00**

Figure, Action Marine, Medic, #7720, NM **50.00**

Figure, Action Pilot, Crash Crew Set, #7820, NM **225.00**

Figure, Action Sailor, Navy Attack Set, #7607, NM **150.00**

Figure, Action Soldier, Military Police Helmet & Small Arms, #7526, NM **80.00**

Figure, Adventure Team, Adventurer, Black, Kung Fu Grip, #7823, EX **80.00**

Figure, Adventure Team, Adventurer, Hidden Treasure, #7308-1, EX **20.00**

Figure, Adventure Team, Desert Explorer, #7209-5, NM ... **45.00**

Figure, Adventure Team, Jungle Survival, #7373, MIP **50.00**

Figure, Adventure Team, Man of Action, Talking, #7590, NM **130.00**

Figure, Adventure Team, Winter Rescue, #7309-4, NM **80.00**

Figure, Adventures of GI Joe, Astronaut, Talking, #7615, EX **100.00**

Figure, Adventures of GI Joe, Mysterious Explosion Set, #7921, EX **70.00**

Figure, Air Adventurer, Kung-Fu Grip, NM in VG+ box (Canadian), $275.00. (Photo courtesy Cotswold Collectibles, Inc.)

Figure, French Resistance Fighter, #8203, NM **230.00**

Glass Animals and Figurines

Nearly every glasshouse of note has at some point over the years produced these beautiful models, some of which double for vases, bookends, and flower frogs. Many were made during the 1930s through the 1950s and 1960s, and these are the most collectible. But you'll also be seeing brand new examples, and you need to study to know the difference. A good reference to help you sort them all out is *Glass Animals, Including Animal & Figural Related Items*, by Pat and Dick Spencer. See also Fenton; Flower Frogs.

Airdale, Imperial, Ultra Blue..**70.00**
Bird, Cambridge, crystal satin, 2¾"
   L **25.00**
Bird, Viking, Moss Green, tail up,
   12" **45.00**
Bird, Viking, Orchid, 9½" **100.00**
Bird in flight, Westmoreland, Amber Marigold, wings out, 5"
   L **45.00**
Bird on stump, Cambridge, green, 5¼", minimum value **400.00**

Bird With Cherry Salt Dip, amber, Kanawha, 3½" long, 1970s – 1980s, from $8.00 to $12.00.
(Photo courtesy Pat and Dick Spencer)

Bunny, Fenton, light blue, #5162, 3" **22.00**
Camel, LE Smith, crystal **50.00**
Cat, Tiffin, Sassy Suzie, black satin w/paint decoration, #9448, 11" **175.00**
Colt, Heisey, amber, kicking .**650.00**
Colt, Imperial, amber, balking .**100.00**
Deer, Fostoria, blue, sitting or standing **40.00**
Dolphin candlesticks, Heisey, crystal, #110, pr **400.00**
Duck, Heisey, crystal **140.00**
Duck ashtray, Duncan Miller, crystal, 4" **20.00**
Eagle bookend, Cambridge, crystal, 5½x4x4", ea.....................**90.00**
Elephant, LE Smith, crystal, 1¾"..**8.00**
Fish, Fenton, red w/amberina tail & fins, 2½" **65.00**
Fish, Tiffin, crystal, solid, 8¾x9".**350.00**
Fish, Tropical; ashtray, pink opalescent, 3½" **65.00**
Gazelle, New Martinsville, crystal w/ frosted base, leaping, 8¼"..**50.00**
Heron, Duncan Miller, crystal satin, 7" **125.00**
Horse jumping, American Glass Co, crystal **40.00**
Irish setter ashtray, Heisey, crystal **30.00**
Mallard, Heisey, crystal, wings up **200.00**
Owl, Imperial, milk glass **45.00**
Pelican, Fostoria, amber, 1987 commemorative **65.00**
Penguin, Viking, crystal, 7"...**25.00**
Pheasant, Paden City, crystal, head back, 12" **100.00**
Robin, Westmoreland, pink, 5⅛" **25.00**
Rooster w/crooked tail, New Martinville, crystal, 7½" .**60.00**

Seagull, Cambridge, crystal, 9 holes in base, 9½x6" **75.00**

Seal, Fostoria, topaz, 4" **75.00**

Squirrel on curved log, Paden City, crystal, 5½" **50.00**

Swan, Cambridge, ebony, 3".. **85.00**

Swan nut dish, individual; Heisey, crystal, #1503 .... **20.00**

Two Kids, Cambridge, amber satin, 9¼" **350.00**

Wren on perch, Westmoreland, light blue on white, 2-pc. **45.00**

Glass and Ceramic Shoes

While many miniature shoes were made simply as whimsies, you'll also find thimble holders, perfumes, inkwells, salts, candy containers, and bottles made to resemble shoes of many types. See also Degenhart.

Ceramic

Boot, porcelain, butterflies/floral decoration, 2 bows, Germany, 4" **35.00**

Bootie, openings for laces, silver bow on vamp, white, 1¾x2" **20.00**

Bootie, white bow on vamp, openings for laces, white, 2x3½" **25.00**

Brogan shoe, white w/colonial scene, Old Foley..., 3¾x5¼" **45.00**

Dutch shoe, white porcelain, handpainted flowers, gilded, Limoges, 1" **40.00**

High heel, porcelain, white w/gold ball on toe, Limoges-France, 1x2" **25.00**

High heel, pottery, floral decoration, turquoise, USA, 1950, 3¼" **45.00**

Man's shoe, fine details & laces, black, ca 1930 .... **75.00**

Shoe, flowers on vamp & trim, yellow, Germany, ca 1950, 2½x6" **45.00**

Shoe, pointed toe, cat on buttons, blue, Germany, 2½x4" **50.00**

Slipper, brown, blue & green stripes, 2¼x4" **45.00**

Slipper, Daisy & Button, decal on toe, lace on top, white, 1¼x2" **35.00**

Slipper, emblem on toe, gilded, B Hancock & Sons..., 2¼x3". **65.00**

Slipper, flower on side, ...Jersey City NJ on side, pink, Germany, 2" **65.00**

Slipper, hand-painted flowers on toe & sides, James Kent, 3" **40.00**

Slipper, open-sided, trimed w/white bow & lace, green, 2¼x4½". **30.00**

Slipper, porcelain, white w/gold trim, 1" **20.00**

Slipper, 22k gold w/pale blue lining, Dixon Art Studio, 1¾x4¼" **35.00**

Glass

Boot, band of ribs above instep, amber, 3¼x2" **60.00**

Boot, cuffed, w/defined spur, purple slag, 3¼x4" **85.00**

Boot, cuffed, w/defined spur, solid sole, black, 3¼x4" **85.00**

Boot, plain, yellow, ca 1970, 6½x4" **25.00**

Boot, rigaree at top, leaf on vamp, yellow, red & green spatter, 4" **150.00**

Boot, Santa style, black, M Dawson, 3⅛x4" **185.00**

Boot, w/embossed lid, amber, 2x3¾".................65.00

Boot, Western decoration, applied handle, green, 10x7".......45.00

Boot, wrinkled, crystal on frosted oval base, 3¾"................100.00

Boot, wrinkled, star under heel, Los Angeles, green, 2¾"..40.00

Bootie, crystal w/slight tint, hollow sole, laces close shoe, 3"..50.00

Booties, attached, King Glass Co, crystal, 3⅛x2"................145.00

Chinese style, cane pattern, crystal or amber, 1¾x4¾", $75 to.90.00

High-button shoe, scalloped top, fine cut, blue, HT, 4½"..125.00

Sandal, Daisy & Button, vaseline, 1½x4½"............................85.00

Shoe on skates, Daisy and Square, amber, L. E. Smith, ca. 1978, from $10.00 to $15.00. (Photo courtesy Earlene Wheatley)

Slipper, pointed toe, pink & green ribbons w/latticino, Murano, 2x6"................................85.00

Slipper, pointed toe, white lattice, yellow, pink, & blue, 4x1½".....90.00

Slipper, poppy decoration on sides, opaque blue, gilded, 2x4¾".70.00

Slipper, ribbed vamps w/2 flowers, hollow toe, green, 4x2½".82.00

Slipper, skate; blue w/fine-cut pattern, eyelets to lace up, 3x5½"...........................95.00

Slipper, sq toe, frosted, solid heel, Gillinder & Sons, 2¾x5".100.00

Golden Foliage

If you can remember when this glassware came packed in boxes of laundry soap, you're telling your age. Along with 'white' margarine, Golden Foliage was a product of the 1950s. It was made by the Libbey Glass Company, and the line was rather limited; as far as we know, we've listed the entire assortment here. The glassware featues a satin band with various leaves and gold trim. (It also came in silver.)

Bowl, 2x3¾"............................5.00

Creamer & sugar bowl..........12.50

Goblet, cocktail; 4-oz...............6.00

Goblet, cordial; 1-oz................8.50

Goblet, pilsner; 11-oz..............9.00

Goblet, sherbet; 6½-oz.............5.00

Ice tub, in metal 3-footed frame.19.50

Pitcher, w/metal frame, 5¼"..16.50

Salad dressing set, includes 3 bowls (4") & brass-finished caddy.19.50

Tumbler, beverage; 12½-oz......8.50

Tumbler, juice; 6-oz.................5.00

Tumbler, old-fashioned; 9-oz....6.00

Tumbler, shot glass, 2-oz.........6.50

Tumbler, water; 10-oz..............8.50

Tumbler set, set of 8 (12½-oz) in metal frame....................60.00

Graniteware

Graniteware is actually a base metal with a coating of enamel. It was first made in the 1870s, but graniteware of all sorts was made well into the 1950s. In fact, some of what you'll find today is brand new. But new pieces are much lighter in weight than the old ones. Look for seamed construction, metal handles, and graniteware lids on such things as tea- and coffeepots. All these are indicators of age. Colors are another, and swirled pieces — cobalt blue and white, green and white, brown and white, and red and white — are generally older, harder to find, and therefore more expensive.

Bowl, mixing; apple green w/tangerine inside, 4½x8¾", NM **25.00**
Bowl, vegetable; red w/black trim, 1⅞x8⅝x6½", NM **50.00**
Candlestick, yellow/black ring handle & trim, 1¾x5¾", G, ea **65.00**
Canisters, white w/dark blue trim & lettering, 7½x5", M, ea ... **110.00**
Coffee biggin, solid red w/black trim & handle, squatty, 10½x4", NM **155.00**
Coffeepot, blue & white swirl, white inside, black trim/handle, 7", NM **160.00**
Coffeepot, solid aqua, white inside, black trim, Pyrex insert, 9", NM **85.00**
Colander, solid yellow, blue trim, w/handles, footed, 1970s, 10", EX **30.00**
Cuspidor, white w/blue trim, marked Sweden, 2-pc, 2½x7" dia, NM **95.00**
Custard cup, cream w/green trim, 2¼x3⅜", NM **55.00**
Double boiler, gray med mottle, bail handles, w/insert, 11¾x9", G+ **115.00**

Egg plate, blue & white lg swirl, blue trim, w/handles, 1¾x9", G+ **210.00**
Fudge pan, lavender cobalt & white lg swirl, ¾x6½x9½", G+ .. **195.00**
Grater, red, flat handle, 10x3⅝", G+ **125.00**
Jelly roll pan, blue & white med mottle, white inside, 10¼" dia, NM **85.00**
Ladle, soup; blue & white med swirl, black handle, 13½x3⅝", M **95.00**

Measuring pitcher, blue and white large swirl, 9", NM, $395.00. (Photo courtesy Helen Greguire)

Melon mold, solid blue, tin lid embossed No 50, 3⅝x5¾x7¾", NM **155.00**
Muffin pan, gray lg mottle, 12-cup, Agate Seconds, 12½" L, G+.**295.00**
Mug, cobalt blue & white swirl, cobalt riveted handle, seamed, G+ **95.00**
Pan, solid red-orange, lid w/black knob, handles, ca 1980, 6x7½", M **20.00**
Pie plate, cobalt & white lg swirl, black trim, deep dish, NM **115.00**
Pitcher, white w/blue, black trim, Bakelite-type handle, 6½", G+ **70.00**
Plate, light blue & white med swirl inside & out, ¾x10", G+ ... **95.00**
Pudding pan, blue & white lg swirl, black trim, 3¼x9⅝", G+ ... **195.00**

Roaster, gray sm mottle, seamless, 5x7" dia, NM 110.00

Saucepan, red & white lg mottle, handle, 1960s, 3x4⅝" dia, NM 75.00

Skimmer, solid red inside & out, black handle, Made in Poland, 14½" 45.00

Teakettle, white w/black trim & handle, Special Enameled Ware, 5", M 70.00

Teapot, solid red, black trim & knob, squatty, seamless, 6x6", NM 95.00

Tray, yellow & white lg swirl, black trim, round, 1950s, 1⅝x18", M 95.00

Urinal, gray lg mottle, seamed, riveted handle, 4½x6x10⅛", NM 95.00

Washbowl, dark gray lg mottle, Hoosier... label, 11" dia, M..85.00

Griswold

Cast-iron cooking ware was used extensively in the nineteenth century, and even today lots of folks think no other type of cookware can measure up. But whether they buy it to use or are strictly collectors, Griswold is the name they hold in highest regard. During the latter part of the nineteenth century the Griswold company began to manufacture the finest cast-iron kitchenware items available at that time. Soon after they became established, they introduced a line of lightweight, cast-aluminum ware that revolutionized the industry. The company enjoyed many prosperous years until its closing in the late 1950s. You'll recognize most items by the marks, which generally will include the Griswold name; for instance, 'Seldon Griswold' and 'Griswold Mfg. Co.' But don't overlook the 'Erie' mark, which the company used as well. See Clubs and Newsletters for information on the Griswold and Cast Iron Cookware Association.

Cake pan, Danish; #31, full writing 150.00

Deep fat fryer, w/basket 45.00

Dutch oven, #8, early Tite-Top, block trademark, full writing on lid 50.00

Dutch oven, #9, round bottom, from $50 to 75.00

Gem pan, #1, marked No 1 & 940, 11 round cups, from $75 to . 100.00

Gem pan, #8, EPU slant trademark 250.00

Gem pan, #9, Brownie Cake Pan, #947, from $125 to 150.00

Heat regulator, #300, double-sided 325.00

Kettle, #7, low, EPU trademark, from $50 to 75.00

Lemon squeezer, #2, cast iron. 125.00

Muffin pan, #273, cornstick, 7 cups, from $15 to 25.00

Rack, skillet display; all metal, from $200 to 300.00

Roaster, #5, block trademarks, full writing on lid, from $200 to 350.00

Scotch bowl, #5, block trademark 60.00

Skillet, #5, sm trademark, grooved handle, from $10 to 15.00

Skillet, #6, sq fry, from $75 to ... 125.00

Skillet, #12, sm trademark.... 65.00

Skillet, #15, oval, from $250 to . 300.00

Skillet, egg; #129, sq w/handle on corner **40.00**

Skillet, 5-in-1 Breakfast, from $140 to **160.00**

Skillet grill, #299 .... **100.00**

Skillet lid, #3, high smooth dome, from $150 to **200.00**

Skillet lid, #6, high smooth dome, block trademark, from $50 to **75.00**

Teakettle, toy; Use Erie Ware the Best, from $300 to **325.00**

Trivet, Family Tree, #1726, lg/decorative, from $10 to **20.00**

Trivet, Old Lace (coffeepot), #1739, lg, from $75 to **125.00**

Vienna roll pan, #6, fully marked .**250.00**

Waffle iron, #7, finger ring, low-handle base, from $100 to **125.00**

Waffle iron, #11, sq, high base .. **100.00**

Waffle iron, #11, sq, low bailed base, ball hinge, $175 to **225.00**

Wax ladle, #964, EPU trademark, from $125 to **150.00**

Wheat stick pan, #27, PIN 638, from $250.00 to $275.00. (Photo courtesy Sharon and Charly Harvey/sandcea)

Guardian Ware

The Guardian Service company was in business from 1935 until 1955. They produced a very successful line of hammered aluminum that's just as popular today as it ever was. Sold through the home party plan, special hostess gifts were offered as incentives. Until 1940 metal lids were used, but during the war when the government restricted the supply of available aluminum, glass lids were introduced.

Be sure to judge condition when evaluating Guardian Service. Wear, baked-on grease, scratches, and obvious signs of use devaluate its worth. Our prices range from pieces in excellent to exceptional condition. To be graded exceptional, the interior of the pan must have no pitting and the surface must be bright and clean. An item with a metal lid is worth 25% more than the same piece with a glass lid.

Beverage urn, w/lid (no screen or dripper), common, from $15 to **20.00**

Can of cleaner, unopened **15.00**

Condiment bowl, glass lid, Deco handles, 1 from condiment set, from $40 to **50.00**

Cookbook, Century Metal Crafts, 1st edition, metal lids shown . **35.00**

Double boiler, 2 pcs w/handles, glass lid, 12x9¾" overall . **75.00**

Fryer, chicken; glass lid, 12", from $60 to **80.00**

Griddle broiler, octagonal, w/ handles, polished center, 16½" dia **35.00**

Handle, clamp-on style, from $15 to **20.00**

Kettle oven, glass lid, bail handle, w/rack, 8x12" dia, from $100 to **125.00**

Lid, glass, triangular, from $15 to **20.00**

Lid, glass, 8½" dia, from $20 to .. **25.00**

Lid, glass, 12" dia **35.00**

Pitcher, metal, bulb jug w/recessed disk in sides, hostess gift, 8x10" **275.00**

Pot, triangular, w/glass lid, 7" to top of finial, 11" L, $30 to **40.00**

Roaster, turkey; glass lid, no rack, 16½" L, from $100 to **125.00**

Roaster, turkey; metal lid, w/rack, 16½" L, from $125 to **150.00**

Salt & pepper shakers, teapot forms, metal tops, glass bottoms, pr **45.00**

Tray, serving; hammered center, w/ handles, 13" dia, from $20 to . **30.00**

Tray/platter, w/handles, hammered surface, also roaster cover, 15" L **30.00**

Trivet, expanding, chrome-plated, adjusts from 10⅜" L to 13½x8" **80.00**

Trivet, for Economy Trio set, 11¾" dia, from $35 to **45.00**

Tumblers, glassware, knight & shield in silver, 4 w/coasters & rack **80.00**

Tureen, bottom; glass lid, from $40 to **65.00**

Tureen, top; glass lid, from $30 to **45.00**

Gurley Candle Company

Santas, choir boys, turkeys, and eagles are among the figural candles made by this company from the 1940s until as late as the 1960s, possibly even longer. They range in size from 2½" to nearly 9", and they're marked 'Gurley' on the bottom. Because they were so appealing, people were reluctant to burn them and instead stored them away and used them again and again. You can still find them today, especially at flea markets and garage sales. Tavern candles (they're marked as well) were made by a company owned by Gurley; they're also collectible.

Bride & groom, 4½" ea **12.50**

Christmas, angel, marked Gurley, 5" **7.00**

Christmas, baby angel on half moon, marked Gurley, 2½" **6.00**

Christmas, Black caroler man w/ red clothes, 3" **9.50**

Christmas, caroler set; lamppost, girl & boy carolers w/books & cello **35.00**

Christmas, grotto w/sheperd & sheep **14.50**

Christmas, Santa, 6¼" **12.00**

Christmas, white church w/choir boy inside, 6" **14.50**

Easter, duck, yellow w/purple bow, 5" **9.50**

Easter, pink egg w/squirrel inside, 3" **12.00**

Eskimo & igloo, marked Tavern, 2-pc **12.50**

Halloween, black owl on orange stump, 3½" **10.00**

Halloween, Frankenstein Glow in the Dark, later issue but hard to find, MIB, $24.00.

Halloween, pumpkin-face scarecrow, 5" 12.00

Halloween, skeleton, 8½" 35.00

Halloween, witch, black, 8" ... 22.50

Halloween, 4" cut-out orange owl w/7½" black candle behind it 24.00

Thanksgiving, acorns & leaves, 3½" 5.00

Thanksgiving, Indian boy & girl, brown & green clothes, 5", pr 30.00

Thanksgiving, turkey, 5¾" 10.00

Western girl or boy, 3", ea 8.00

Hagen-Renaker

This California company has been producing quality ceramics since the mid-1940s — mostly detailed, lifelike figurines of animals, though they've made other decorative items as well. Their Designers Workshop line was primarily horses, larger than most of their other figures. Their portrayal of Disney charcters is superb. Other lines collectors seek are their Millesan Drews Pixies, Rock Wall Plaques and Trays (decorated with primitive animals similar to cave drawings), Black Bisque animals, and Little Horribles (grotesque miniature figures). In the late 1980s, they introduced Stoneware and Specialty lines, larger than the miniatures but smaller than the Designers Workshop line. They continue to make the Specialties yet today.

Black bisque, cat, blue-green enameling, 1959, 4" 50.00

Black bisque, horse, 1959 only, 5⅜" 200.00

Black bisque, skunk, 1959, 3". 45.00

Designer's Workshop, Benny, (basset hound), 1965-68, 4½" . 50.00

Designer's Workshop, Calypso Tom, (Siamese cat), 1957-64, 5". 45.00

Designer's Workshop, elephant baby, gray w/pink, 1952-53, 3" 45.00

Designer's Workshop, Jill (duck), 1st version, 1960-72, 2¾". 35.00

Designer's Workshop, mule, 1984-86, 8" 400.00

Designer's Workshop, pig baby, brown, 1970 only, 2x3" .. 270.00

Designer's Workshop, zebra mama and baby, 1952, $300.00.
(Photo courtesy Ed and Sheri Alcorn)

Disney miniature, Chip & Dale chipmunks, 1956, 1¼", ea 85.00

Disney miniature, Dumbo flying, 1956-57, 1⅜" 125.00

Disney miniature, Peg, pekingese dog (Lady & Tramp), 1959, 1¾" 120.00

Disney miniature, Scooter, cocker pup (Lady & the Tramp), 1955-59, 1" 40.00

Little Horribles, Ashes to Ashes, 1959, 1¾" 100.00

Little Horribles, Bag in a Sack, 1959, 2¼" 60.00

Little Horribles, Pruneface, yellow/ green clothes, 1958, 2".... **40.00**

Miniature, Bloodhound, head down sniffing, 1989-92, 1⅜" **25.00**

Miniature, Clydesdale horse, special run of 200 for club, 1997, 2¾" **150.00**

Miniature, crow on rock, 1987 only, 1⅛" **35.00**

Miniature, Fluffy, papa cat on pillow, 1968, 2¼" **85.00**

Miniature, giraffe baby, 1981, 1¾" **40.00**

Miniature, half hippo swimming, 1976-77,½" **10.00**

Miniature, horse rearing, white, A-234, 1958, 3½" **125.00**

Miniature, monkey seated, A-414, 1959 only, 1¼" **55.00**

Miniature, pelican flying w/wire, A-810, 1982, 4" **30.00**

Miniature, Tramp-type terrier, tricolor (rare), 1960s, 2¼" . **120.00**

Plaque, buck, faux AZ flagstone, 1959, 16" **250.00**

Specialty figurine, cat lying w/ball, A-2047, 1989, 2½" **35.00**

Specialty figurine, pelican stoneware, 1989, 2" **65.00**

Wall plaque, double horse rock plaque, 1959-60, 15x21½" **250.00**

Hall

Most famous for their extensive lines of teapots and colorful dinnerwares, the Hall China Company still operates in East Liverpool, Ohio, where they were established in 1903. Refer to *Collector's Encyclopedia of Hall China* by Margaret and Kenn Whitmyer (Collector Books) for more information. See Clubs and Newsletters for information on the Hall China Collector's Club. For listings of Hall's most popular dinnerware line, see Autumn Leaf.

Blue Bouquet, casserole, Radiance **45.00**

Blue Bouquet, gravy boat **65.00**

Blue Bouquet, platter, oval, 11¼".**30.00**

Blue Bouquet, soup tureen.. **320.00**

Cameo Rose, bowl, oval **25.00**

Cameo Rose, salt & pepper shakers, pr............................. **45.00**

Cameo Rose, tidbit, 3-tier...... **75.00**

Christmas Tree & Holly, cookie jar, Zeisel............................. **350.00**

Christmas Tree & Holly, sugar bowl, from coffee set **45.00**

Crocus, bowl, vegetable; 9¼" . **45.00**

Crocus, cup **15.00**

Crocus, pretzel jar............... **200.00**

Crocus, salt shaker, Teardrop, ea................................. **25.00**

Crocus, soap dispenser, metal..**135.00**

Crocus, square leftover, from $100.00 to $120.00. (Photo courtesy Margaret and Kenn Whitmyer)

Fern, ashtray, Century **8.00**

Fern, butter dish, Century .. **125.00**

Fern, ladle, Century **22.00**

Gaillardia, bowl, soup; flat, 8½".**14.00**

Gaillardia, leftover, sq **125.00**

Gaillardia, plate, 9"............... **15.00**

Game Bird, bowl, Thick Rim, 6". **30.00**

Game Bird, mug, Tom & Jerry..**27.00**

Game Bird, platter, oval, 13¼". **75.00**

Golden Oak, ball jug, #3 ...... **125.00**

Golden Oak, creamer, Modern. **12.00**

Golden Oak, salt shaker, handled, ea.................................. **18.00**

Heather Rose, coffeepot, Terrace.**45.00**

Heather Rose, gravy boat & under-plate **32.00**

Heather Rose, pickle dish, 9". **11.00**

Homewood, bowl, fruit; 5½"..... **6.00**

Homewood, bowl, soup; flat, 8½"..**14.00**

Mums, baker, French............. **40.00**

Mums, bowl, Radiance, 6" **22.00**

Mums, creamer, Art Deco...... **25.00**

Mums, jug, Simplicity.......... **220.00**

Mums, mug, beverage............ **60.00**

Mums, stack set, Radiance..**150.00**

No 488, bowl, Thin Rim, 8½".**50.00**

No 488, casserole, Five Band.**75.00**

No 488, platter, oval, 13¼" **50.00**

No 488, saucer........................ **2.50**

No 488, soup tureen............. **350.00**

Orange Poppy, bowl, cereal; 6".**25.00**

Orange Poppy, bread box, metal.**150.00**

Orange Poppy, canister, Radiance **500.00**

Orange Poppy, soap dispenser, metal.............................. **185.00**

Orange Poppy, wastebasket, metal **100.00**

Pastel Morning Glory, bean pot, New England, #4 .... **220.00**

Pastel Morning Glory, cake plate.**45.00**

Pastel Morning Glory, sugar bowl, Modern, w/lid **35.00**

Pastel Morning Glory, tea tile. **120.00**

Prairie Grass, bowl, oval, 9¼".**25.00**

Prairie Grass, cup **8.00**

Primrose, ashtray **10.00**

Primrose, creamer.................... **9.00**

Primrose, jug, Rayed............. **22.00**

Primrose, sugar bowl w/lid.... **16.00**

Red Poppy, ball jug, #3 .... **120.00**

Red Poppy, cake safe, metal ..**55.00**

Red Poppy, cup **14.00**

Red Poppy, gravy boat **40.00**

Red Poppy, plate, 10" **85.00**

Red Poppy, recipe box, metal.**90.00**

Sears' Arlington, sugar bowl w/lid.**16.00**

Sears' Fairfax, bowl, cereal; 6¼"..**8.00**

Sears' Fairfax, platter, oval, 11¼".**16.00**

Sears' Monticello, bowl, cream soup; 5"..................................... **90.00**

Sears' Monticello, saucer **1.50**

Sears' Mount Vernon, casserole & lid................................... **42.00**

Sears' Mount Vernon, coffeepot, all china **225.00**

Serenade, fork **125.00**

Serenade, platter, 13¼".......... **25.00**

Serenade, teapot, Aladdin shape, from $250.00 to $300.00. (Photo courtesy Margaret and Kenn Whitmyer)

Silhouette, bread box **85.00**

Silhouette, casserole, Radiance.**45.00**

Silhouette, jug, #4, Medallion.**30.00**

Silhouette, sifter..................... **60.00**

Springtime, bowl, oval **22.00**

Springtime, custard **14.00**

Springtime, platter, oval, 11¼".**35.00**

Tulip, casserole, Thick Rim ...**45.00**

Tulip, cup, St Denis **35.00**

Tulip, tidbit, 3-tier **65.00**

Wildfire, baker, French, fluted.**22.00**

Wildfire, coffeepot, 5-lid, glass drip-per.................................. **125.00**

Wildfire, jug, Sani-Grid, 7½" . **90.00**
Yellow Rose, bowl, soup; flat 8½"..**18.00**
Yellow Rose, custard **16.00**
Yellow Rose, saucer **2.00**

Teapots

Adele, green **200.00**
Aladdin, Canary, solid color .. **60.00**
Aladdin, Pastel Morning
Glory **700.00**
Albany, Cobalt, gold special... **90.00**
Baltimore, black, standard gold. **55.00**
Boston, Cobalt, old gold design, 1-
to 3-cup **125.00**
Cleveland, turquoise, standard
gold **85.00**
Danielle, blue **185.00**
Fern, Century, 6-cup **185.00**
French, Marine, standard gold, 1-
to 3-cup **55.00**
Globe, Cadet, standard gold. **125.00**
Hollywood, Christmas decals. **225.00**
Illinois, pink, solid color **175.00**
Los Angeles, black, solid color. **45.00**
Musical, Canary **170.00**
New York, Chartreuse, solid color,
1- to 4-cup **30.00**
New York, Heather Rose...... **135.00**
New York, No 488 .... **300.00**
Parade, French Flower, solid
color **200.00**

**Plume, pink with gold floral
decoration, from $50.00 to
$70.00.** (Photo courtesy Margaret and Kenn
Whitmyer)

Streamline, Cadet, solid color. **65.00**
Surfside, turquoise, standard
gold **220.00**

Hallmark

Since 1973, the Hallmark
Company has made Christmas ornaments, some of which are today worth
many times their original price.

American Drum, QX4881, 1988,
tin, MIB **15.00**
Angel Bellringer, QX4556, 1982,
M **45.00**
Animal House, QX149-6, 1978,
handcrafted, MIB......... **125.00**
Bell, Colors of Christmas, QX2002,
1977, glass-look acrylic, M .**17.50**
Betsy Clark, QX2494, 1984, #12 in
series, glass ball, MIB **27.50**
Bicentennial Charmers, 1976, blue
glass ball, M **65.00**
Cardinals, QX2051, glass ball,
M **25.00**
Carousel Reindeer, QXC5817, 1987,
Collector's Club, MIB **20.00**
Christmas Is Sharing, QX4071,
1988, handpainted china,
MIB **20.00**
Christmas Treat, QX1347, 1979,
bear w/candy cane, MIB.**40.00**
Clothespin Drummer Boy, QX408-2,
1981, handcrafted, MIB..**35.00**
Currier & Ives, The Road - Winter,
QX2013, 1982, glass ball,
MIB **15.00**
Della Robia Wreath, QX1935, 1977,
twirl-about, MIB **45.00**
Disney, QX1335, 1977, satin ball,
M **20.00**
Divine Miss Piggy (as angel),
QX4255, 1981, MIB **45.00**

Dove, QX3103, 1978, frosted & clear acrylic, M **50.00**

First Christmas Together, QX2703, 1986, glass ball, MIB **20.00**

First Christmas Together, QX7062, 1981, glass ball, MIB **30.00**

First Christmas Together (doves), QX3705, 1985, MIB **18.00**

Frosty Friends, QX1347, 1980, #1 in series, MIB **350.00**

Frosty Friends, QX4396, 1990, #11 in series, MIB **27.50**

Grandma Moses, QX1502, glass ball, rare, M **55.00**

Locomotive, Nostalgia, QX2221, 1976, (reissued from 1975), M **70.00**

Love, Holiday Highlights, QX3047, 1979, acrylic heart, M..... **30.00**

Mom and Dad 1990, Keepsake Ornament, #459-3, 1990, $12.50.

Mother, QX2663, 1978, glass ball, MIB **30.00**

Mouse, QX5082, 1981, frosted, M **25.00**

Mr & Mrs Santa - The Kringles, QLX705-2, 1985, MIB **70.00**

Norman Rockwell, Santa, QX1661, 1975, satin ball, MIB **22.50**

Peanuts, Peanuts Gang, QX2056, 1978, Linus w/wreath, others sing, M **45.00**

Praying Angel, Little Trimmer, QX1343, 1978, M **25.00**

Raggedy Ann, Keepsake ornament, QX1591, 1975, MIB **170.00**

Santa, Holiday Highlights, QX307-6, 1978, acrylic, MIB **70.00**

Santa Motorcar, QX155-9, 1979, #1 in series, MIB **235.00**

Seashore, QX1602, glass ball, M **30.00**

Skating Snowman, QX1399, 1980, metal skates, felt hat/scarf, MIB **45.00**

Snowflake Chimes, QX165-4, 1980, metal, MIB **15.00**

Soldier, XHD1021, 1974, yarn, M **18.50**

Star Trek Shuttlecraft Galileo, with voice and light, 1992, MIB, $15.00.

Train, QX1811-N, 1976, wood-look, M **40.00**

Train, Yesteryears, #QX1811, 1976, MIB **120.00**

Halloween

Halloween items are fast becoming the most popular holiday-related collectibles on the market today. Although originally linked to pagan rituals and superstitions, Halloween has long since evolved into a fun-filled event; and the masks, noisemakers, and jack-o'-lanterns of earlier years are great fun to look for.

Pamela E. Apkarian-Russell (the Halloween Queen) has written several books on the subject: *Collectible Halloween; Salem Witchcraft and Souvenirs; More Halloween Collectibles; Halloween: Decorations and Games; Anthropomorphic Beings of Halloween;* and *The Tastes and Smells of Halloween.* She is listed in the Directory under New Hampshire. See Clubs and Newsletters for information concerning *The Trick or Treat Trader.*

Bank, Snoopy & Woodstock on jack-o'-lantern, Whitman's Candies, EX 10.00

Book, Peter Pumpkin in Wonderland, Huntington, color illustrations, EX............ 125.00

Candy container, black & yellow owl, composition, EX....... 85.00

Candy container, cat, composition, Germany, 3-5", EX 175.00

Candy container, cat pushing jack-o'-lantern, plastic, 1950s, 5", EX 140.00

Candy container, pumpkin w/ witch's head & cat, hard plastic, 3", EX 45.00

Candy tin, girl dressed as witch, Tindeco, 4" dia, EX 75.00

Cookie cutter, ghost, white plastic, marked Hallmark Cards, 3", EX 5.00

Costume, Atom Ant, Hanna-Barbera, 1965, EX 40.00

Costume, Dr Dolittle, Collegeville, 1966, EX+IB 80.00

Costume, Dr Zaius, Planet of the Apes, Ben Cooper, 1974, NMIB 35.00

Costume, Lily Munster, Ben Cooper, 1964, EXIB 265.00

Costume, Spider-Man, Ben Cooper, 1965, EXIB 45.00

Die-cut, bat, embossed cardboard, Germany, EX 100.00

Die-cut, cat (dressed), embossed cardboard, Germany, EX 150.00

Die-cut, devil, embossed cardboard, Germany, EX 120.00

Die-cut, pumpkin man or lady, embossed cardboard, Germany, 7½", EX 125.00

Figurine, owl, celluloid, plain, M 85.00

Figurine, pumpkin-head baker, composition, Germany, 4¾", EX 400.00

Figurine, scarecrow, celluloid, M 200.00

Figurine, Smurf holding jack-o'-lantern, celluloid, EX........ 8.00

Figurine, witch sitting on pumpkin, celluloid, M 350.00

Figurine, witch w/broom, bisque, Made in Japan, 1940s, 3", EX 30.00

Figurine, witch w/broom, light-up, Empire Plastic, ca 1965, 40", EX 55.00

Jack-o'-lantern, pulp, American, 1940 – 1950s, 8", EX, from $175.00 to $190.00. (Photo courtesy Morphy Auctions)

antern, cat, cardboard, simple round style, Germany, EX **225.00**

Lantern, cat, pressed cardboard w/original face, 1940-50s, EX **175.00**

Lantern, milk glass skeleton head w/black features, battery-op, 5", EX **60.00**

Magazine, Child Life, children carving pumpkin on cover, 1938, EX **10.00**

Magazine, Nabisco, sm boy looking into jack-o'-lantern, 1959, EX **10.00**

Mask, Moon Mullins, paper, Famous Artists Syndicate, 1933, EX . **12.00**

Mask, Raggedy Ann, cloth w/yarn hair, 15", M **25.00**

Noisemaker, bell type, tin, EX . **35.00**

Noisemaker, clicker type, bats/cats/ jack-o'-lanterns, Kirchof, 2", EX **25.00**

Noisemaker, horn type, witches/ bats/cats, Made in USA, 10½", EX **35.00**

Noisemaker, ratchet type, witch/ cat/bat/jack-o'-lantern, Kirchof, EX **45.00**

Noisemaker, spinner, tin, sq, EX.. **35.00**

Noisemaker, tambourine type, tin, Ohio Art, 1930s, 6" dia, EX. **75.00**

Party Game Board, punchboard w/ witch, skeleton, cat, etc, 1960s, MIP **25.00**

Pull toys, plastic, Rosen USA, from $70.00 to $85.00 each. (Photo courtesy Pamela Apkarian-Russel, The Halloween Queen)

Sparkler, jack-o'-lantern, tin lithograph, Chein, 4¾x2½", EX. **300.00**

Toy car, plastic, 1940-50s, EX... **250.00**

Handkerchiefs

Lovely to behold, handkerchiefs remain as feminine keepsakes of a time past. Largely replaced by disposable tissues of more modern times, handkerchiefs found today are often those that had special meaning, keepsakes of special occasions, or souvenirs. Many collectible handkerchiefs were never meant for everyday use, but intended to be a feminine addition to the lady's total ensemble. Made in a wide variety of styles and tucked away in grandmother's dresser, handkerchiefs are now being brought out and displayed for their dainty loveliness and fine craftsmanship. For further information we recommend *Ladies' Vintage Accessories, Identification & Value Guide,* by LaRee Johnson Bruton, and *Handkerchiefs, A Collector's Guide, Volumes I* and *II,* by Helene Guarnaccia and Barbara Guggenheim (Collector Books).

Betsy McCall's cut-out dolls w/toys on yellow, McCall Corp, from $20 to **25.00**

Blondie & Dagwood w/sailboat in heart, yellow border, from $50 to **60.00**

Cats & butterflies, 3 fluffy cats on blue, yellow & orange butterflies................................. **20.00**

Chinatown, blue & white polka-dot border, Keefe, paper label, $70 to **80.00**

Cigarettes, multicolored pastiche, thin red border, from $25 to 30.00

Clarabell, clown on blue, w/yellow balloon, from $40 to 50.00

Dear Damsel, rhyming dating advice, multicolored, paper label, $30 to 35.00

Eggs, green on white, chicken in corner, Kit Ann, paper label, from $20 to 25.00

Girl Scouts, Girl Scouts Have Fun, bright multicolors, from $25 to 30.00

Hangers, red, black, white & tan on brown, Jeanne Miller, from $40 to 45.00

Howdy Doody, blue, red & white, from $35 to 40.00

Jack & Jill, pastel pink, green & yellow on white, from $15 to 20.00

Lilacs in bloom, flowers form wide border on white, from $3 to 5.00

Litter of kitties, multicolored w/ orange & white border, Keefe, from $25 to 30.00

Little Scottie, black, Scottie on diagonal red band in corner, from $8 to 12.00

Magic carpet ride, grey & orange on white, Peg Thomas, from $20 to 25.00

Maple leaves, blue leaves on dark blue, scalloped edge, paper label 10.00

Matchbooks on pink, Jeanne Miller, from $30 to 35.00

Menu, Italian; shaped like pizza on orange, from $15 to 20.00

Oak leaves w/acorns, gray on red, from $5 to 8.00

Primping Pooches, 5 fancy dogs w/ hats on white, from $8 to . 12.00

Professor frog & student duck, blue border, Tom Lamb, from $15 to 20.00

Pussy willows, half gray/half pink, flower in center & on 2 sides, from $7 .... 9.00

Raining cats & dogs, umbrellas in center, on yellow, Pritchard, from $25 to 30.00

Rose (orange/yellow) in full bloom, leaves & buds form edge, from $6 to 9.00

Safety pins form stripe pattern on brown, from $30 to 35.00

Scarecrow w/leaves & woodland animals on blue, Carl Tait, from $25 to 30.00

Squirrels w/nuts, green, acorns & leaves make border, Anderson, from $15 to 20.00

Violets, circle shape, scalloped edge, from $8 to 10.00

White cotton with embroidered rose in corner, in gift box with tag and ribbon still attached, from $12.00 to $18.00. (Photo courtesy LaRee Johnson Bruton)

7 Day Miracle Diet, drawings on calendar, multicolored, from $35 to 40.00

Harker

One of the oldest potteries in the East Liverpool, Ohio, area, the Harker company produced many lines of dinnerware from the late 1920s until it closed around 1970.

Amy, pie lifter/cake slice, 9"..**20.00**
Bamboo, bowl, vegetable; round, from $20 to **22.00**
Bouquet, plate, bread & butter; 6¼" **12.50**
Cameo Rose, batter jug, blue, w/lid, lg, from $35 to **45.00**
Cameo Rose, syrup jug, blue, w/ lid **25.00**
Chesterton, plate, dinner.......**12.00**
Corinthian, plate, salad; 8¼".**10.00**
Corinthian, snack cup & plate, 8¼" **10.00**
Dogwood, platter, 11½x10¾"..**15.00**
Fruit (apple & pear), casserole, red, w/lid **50.00**
Fruit (apple & pear), shakers, Skyscraper, red, pr..........**50.00**
Heritage, plate, luncheon; 8".**20.00**
Intaglio Wheat, cup & saucer..**8.00**
Ivy, bowl, soup........................**12.00**
Ivy, teapot..............................**75.00**
Jewel Weed, canister, 5x6½", EX.................................**42.50**
Laurelton, sauceboat, 6½" **10.00**
Mallow, bowl, cereal; 6½".......**18.00**
Mallow, drippings jar, Lard, w/ lid..................................**75.00**
Mallow, rolling pin................**100.00**
Modern Tulip, cookie jar, oval.**68.00**
Olympic, coffeepot..................**35.00**
Pate Sur Pate, platter, 13½"..**20.00**
Persian Key, bowl, fruit...........**9.00**
Petit Fleurs, platter, 13¼x11⅜"..**27.00**

Petit Point, pie baker, 9" **30.00**
Pine Cone, sugar bowl, w/lid.**18.00**

Red Fireplace, teapot, from $35.00 to $40.00.

Rockingham, pitcher, round handle, 8"......................................**35.00**
Rockinham, mug, Daniel Boone, 4½" **25.00**
Ruffled Tulip, platter, 10⅝" ...**75.00**
Ruffled Tulip, rolling pin, 15".**210.00**
Snowleaf, bowl, soup................**6.00**
Wild Rose, bowl, fruit **12.00**

Hartland

Hartland Plastics Inc. of Hartland, Wisconsin, produced a line of Western and Historic Horseman and Standing Gunfighter figures during the 1950s, which are now very collectible. Using a material called virgin acetate, they molded such well-known characters as Annie Oakley, Bret Maverick, Matt Dillon, and many others, which they painted with highest attention to detail. In addition to these, they made a line of sports greats as well as one featuring religious figures.

Gunfighter, Bret Maverick, NM.**350.00**
Gunfighter, Chris Colt, NM.**150.00**
Gunfighter, Clay Holister, NM..**200.00**
Gunfighter, Dan Troop, NM.**600.00**

Gunfighter, Jim Hardy, NM..**150.00**
Gunfighter, Paladin, NM..... **400.00**
Gunfighter, Wyatt Earp, NM.**150.00**
Horseman, Brave Eagle, NM.**200.00**
Horseman, Bret Maverick, NMIB **600.00**
Horseman, Buffalo Bill, NM.**300.00**
Horseman, Cactus Pete, NM.**150.00**
Horseman, Cheyenne, w/tag, NM **200.00**
Horseman, Commanche Kid, NM **150.00**
Horseman, General George Washington, NMIB **175.00**
Horseman, General Robert E Lee, NM **175.00**
Horseman, Jim Bowie, w/tag, NM **250.00**
Horseman, Lone Ranger, miniature series, NM **75.00**

Horseman, The Rifleman, Lucas McCain, all original, NMIB, $350.00.

Horseman, Roy Rogers, semi-rearing, NMIB...................... **600.00**
Horseman, Sgt Preston, NM.**650.00**
Horseman, Tom Jeffords, NM..**175.00**
Horseman, Tonto, miniature series, NM **75.00**

Hawaiian Shirts

Vintage shirts made in Hawaii are just one of many retro fads finding favor on today's market. Those with the tag of a top designer can bring hefty prices — the more colorful, the better. Shirts of this type were made in the states as well. Look for grapics that shout 'Hawaii'! Fabrics are typically cotton, rayon or polyester. Our values are for shirts that are not faded and show very little wear.

Airman, ocean life print on red rayon.............................. **115.00**
Alfred Shaheen, pacific blue print of Hawaiian village scenes.**135.00**
AMC Sportswear, watercolor print of national parks on white cotton **80.00**

Batik print, heavy cotton, 1960s, $65.00.
(Photo courtesy Vintage Martini)

Bud Burma, Asian print of fish & people, green, red, yellow & white **140.00**
Canoes, Hawaiian maiden w/leis print on white rayon **36.00**
Hallmark, white floral print on brown rayon, pearl buttons, 1940s............................... **75.00**
Kabe, turquoise & gold print w/ lg white birds on white crepe silk **120.00**
Kahanamoku, print w/multicolored vertical stripes down front, 1950s............................... **82.00**
Kuhio, Oriental print in 13 different colors on white rayon **80.00**

Malihini, muliticolored sayings & pictures on khaki **42.00**

Penney's, blue, orange & red island-scene print on white rayon **60.00**

Sun Surf, floral fisherman print, coconut buttons **63.00**

Sun Surf, green cowboy print on white rayon **65.00**

Surf Line, tribal print in turquoise, orange & white............... **23.00**

Surfriders, birds & feathers print in shades of red, yellow & white............................ **290.00**

Unknown label, hisbicus, leaves & diamond tiki print, 1960s. **50.00**

Unknown label, lg red & yellow tiki gods on bottom, metal buttons **40.00**

Head Vases

Many being Japanese imports, head vases were made primarily for the florist trade. They were styled as children, teenagers, clowns, and famous people. There are heads of religious figures, Blacks, Asians, and even some animals. One of the most common types are ladies wearing pearl earrings and necklaces. Refer to *Collecting Head Vases* by David Barron (Collector Books) for more information. See Clubs and Newsletters for information concerning the *Head Hunter's Newsletter.*

Angel, child praying in blue, blond hair, Lefton label, #7341, 7" **160.00**

Baby girl w/blue bow, brown hair, pink outfit, unmarked, 6".**110.00**

Child, in ruffled bonnet, blond hair, pink bow & trim, art mark, 6" **137.50**

Girl w/blond hair, leaf-like hat, black lashes, Velco #6990, 5".... **185.00**

Girl w/umbrella, brown hair, green plaid, 5", 8" overall **215.00**

Lady, blond frosted hair, pearl necklace, scalloped bodice, Enesco, 6" **215.00**

Lady, blue hat & matching bodice, pearls, Made in Japan sticker, 7" **290.00**

Lady, eyes closed, gloved hand to cheek, flip hairdo, #C6428, 6" **215.00**

Lady, hands crossed at chin, earrings, red bodice, #434, 4½" **195.00**

Lady, Lady Aileen, blond curls w/tiara & necklace, #E1756, 5½" **95.00**

Lady, streaked short hair, shoulder bow, #C7294, 8" **320.00**

Lady in hat w/bow, long blond hair, pearl earrings, Lefton #3515, 8" **315.00**

Lady w/black gloved hand to face, pearl bracelet, #C2589B, 5½" **245.00**

Lady w/blond curly updo, hand to face, pearls, Ardco, 7½". **325.00**

Lady w/blond hair, hand to face, green hat, Lee Woods, Japan, 5" **195.00**

Lady w/blue-gloved hand to face, earrings, Napcoware #26429, 7½" **290.00**

Lady w/flower in blond hair, hand to face, Inarco #E-778, 6"...**245.00**

Lady w/frosted hair, green striped bodice, pearls, Relpo #K1633, 7" **315.00**

Lady with hand to face, black hat and bodice, pearl earrings and necklace, Inarco, E-190/L, 9", $350.00. (Photo courtesy David Barron)

Holly Hobbie and Friends

Around 1970 a young home-maker and mother, Holly Hobbie, approached the American Greeting Company with some charming country-styled drawings of children. Since that time, hundreds items have been made. Most items are marked HH, H. Hobbie, or Holly Hobbie.

Lady w/hand to face, blond hair, flat hat w/feathers, Japan #2359, 7" **325.00**

Lady w/hand to throat, blond updo, pearls, blue bodice, Enesco, 8" **380.00**

Lady w/white-gloved hand up, white hair & hat, #C5047, 6½" **275.00**

Newborn baby on pillow, white w/blue trim, Hull, 92-USA, 5¾"............................. **72.50**

Teen girl w/blond hair, flower on bodice, pearls, Ardco label, 6" **180.00**

Teen girl w/blond hair, pearls, black bodice, Napcoware #C7313, 4½" **150.00**

Teen girl w/blond hair, white collar, #D-3220, 6" **215.00**

Teen girl w/brown hair, pearl earrings, #C5939, Japan, 6". **215.00**

Teen girl w/frosted flip, black lashes, Napcoware #C5675, 6".... **225.00**

Teen girl w/frosted hair, tam cap, #P-629, 6" **215.00**

Teen girl w/lg red bow in blond hair, pearls, Japan #T-1576, 6" .**235.00**

Umbrella girl, blond hair, in aqua plaid, 3½", + umbrella ..**245.00**

Umbrella girl, brown hair, lavender bows, Made in Japan, 8".**214.00**

Bed, doll; white-painted wood w/ blue trim, NM **35.00**

Box, trinket; porcelain, miniature figure on lid, 3 different, ea **20.00**

Bubble bath container, plastic, Benjamin Ansehl, 1980s. **20.00**

Colorforms, Holly Hobbie Magic Glow Dollhouse, MIB...... **15.00**

Doll, Holly Hobbie, 27", MIB. **25.00**

Doll, Holly Hobbie Bicentennial, Knickerbocker, 12", MIB.. **25.00**

Doll, scented, clear oranment around neck, 1988, 18", NRFB **30.00**

Doll, 25th Anniversary Collector's Edition, Meritus, 1994, 26", MIB................................ **55.00**

Drinking glass, Christmas Is..., American Greetings/Coca-Cola, 1980....................... **5.00**

Figurine, Friendship Bouquet, 1983, $85.00.

Figurine, porcelain, series of 6, 1973, 8", ea **100.00**

Lunch box, metal, any version, 1970s **35.00**

Lunch box, plastic, 1989 .... **25.00**

Ornament, Holly Hobbie on satin ball **8.00**

Ornament, porcelain, Holly Hobbie, flat disk, For Sister, 3" **8.00**

Pendant, charm & earrings, Sterling Silver by Lang, ea **20.00**

Plate, Holly Hobbie, Sterling Silver, 1973, 10", MIB **550.00**

Plate, Start Each Day in a Happy Way, American Greetings, 10½" **25.00**

Sand pail, Chein, 1974, 6", EX ..**25.00**

Sewing machine, plastic & metal, battery-op, Durham, 1975, 5x9", EX **25.00**

Sing-A-Long Electric Parlor Player, Vanity Fair, 1970s, scarce, NMIB **45.00**

Valentine Activity Book, 1978, 5x8", unused, EX **10.00**

Vase, boy with American flag, 8", from $15.00 to $20.00.

Holt Howard

This company was an importer of Japanese-made ceramics. From the late 1950s, collectors search for their pixie kitchenware items such as condiments, all with flat, disk-like pixie heads for stoppers. In the '60s the company designed and distributed a line of roosters — egg cups, napkin holders, salt and pepper shakers, etc. Items with a Christmas theme were distributed in the '70s, and you'll also find a white cat collectors call Kozy Kitten. These are only a sampling of the wonderful novelties by this company. Most are not only marked but dated as well.

Blue Willow, mugs, set of 4 ... **45.00**

Christmas, boot, white w/holly, elf on side, 1959, 5x4" dia **40.00**

Christmas, candleholder, Santa w/ wreath for O in NOEL, '58, 4½x10" **55.00**

Christmas, candleholder/bell, 3 Kings, ea w/gift, 1960, 3", set of 3 .... **50.00**

Christmas, candy container, w/pop-up Santa, 4¼" **50.00**

Christmas, candy/cookie jar, Santa w/Candy on hat, Cookies on belly **100.00**

Christmas, cheese crock, white w/ holly, Cheese on lid w/Mr & Mrs Santa **40.00**

Christmas, mug, Christmas tree w/ Santa handle **10.00**

Christmas, planter, angel w/hands in muff, spaghetti trim at hem, 4" **25.00**

Christmas, punch bowl, Santa's head, 6x9" dia **50.00**

Christmas, salt & pepper shakers, Holly Girls, 4", pr **30.00**

Christmas, salt & pepper shakers, Santa w/gifts, 2¼" & 2¾", pr **15.00**

Christmas, Santa cookies/candy jar, three-piece, from $50.00 to $65.00.

Jeeves (Butler), ashtray, 1960 .... **45.00**

Jeeves (Butler), jars, Onions, Cherries, Olives, ea from $175 to **185.00**

Kozy Kitten, ashtray, cat on sq plaid base, 4 corner rests **85.00**

Kozy Kitten, cheese crock, Stinky Cheese on side, cats kissing on lid **60.00**

Kozy Kitten, cleanser shaker, full figure, 1958, rare, 6½", $140 to **165.00**

Kozy Kitten, cookie jar, Cat head **40.00**

Kozy Kitten, creamer & sugar bowl, stackable, creamer w/tail handle **135.00**

Kozy Kitten, letter holder, wire spring on cat back, w/pen holder, 6" **55.00**

Kozy Kitten, match holder, Match Dandy, 1959, 6", from $85 to **110.00**

Kozy Kitten, pin box, plaid, cat finial w/tape-measure tongue, 1958 .... **50.00**

Kozy Kitten, pitcher, white w/kitten, 1960, 7½" **120.00**

Kozy Kitten, salt & pepper shakers, cats in basket, 3", pr, $75 to **95.00**

Kozy Kitten, spice set, stacking, from $150 to **175.00**

Kozy Kitten, spoon rest/recipe holder, fish decor on bowl, 2½x8" **80.00**

Kozy Kitten, sugar shaker, cat in apron holding can w/cork stopper **85.00**

Kozy Kitten, wall pocket, cat w/hook tail, 7x3", from $45 to **60.00**

Pajama Kids, salt & pepper shakers, boy & girl seated & kissing, pr **40.00**

Pixie Ware, bottle stopper, 300 Proof **300.00**

Pixie Ware, chili sauce jar, 1958, minimum value **450.00**

Pixie Ware, honey jar, very rare, minimum value **500.00**

Pixie Ware, hors d'ouvres, Pixie w/tall green hat in center, 7½x6" **125.00**

Pixie Ware, instant coffee jar, blond's head w/blue ribbon finial **220.00**

Pixie Ware, ketchup jar, tomato-face finial, 6", from $60 to **85.00**

Pixie Ware, mayonnaise jar, winking brunette finial, from $200 to **235.00**

Pixie Ware, nut dish, whimsical head w/body as tray, Nuts on bow tie **125.00**

Pixie Ware, relish jar, green head as finial **200.00**

Pixie Ware, towel hook, orange-haired Pixie **165.00**

Ponytail Princess, candleholder, girl on figure-8 platform . **35.00**

Ponytail Princess, lipstick holder . **35.00**

Ponytail Princess, tray, girl between 2 joined flower cups **38.00**

Rooster, bowl, 6" **6.00**

Rooster, butter dish, 1961, ¼-lb, from $35 to **45.00**

Rooster, chocolate pot, embossed rooster, plain handle, from $40 to **50.00**

Rooster, cigarette holder, wooden w/ rooster decoration, wall hanging **30.00**

Rooster, coffeepot, electric, from $40.00 to $50.00.

Rooster, cup & saucer, from $9 to **12.00**

Rooster, pitcher, milk; embossed rooster, slim, plain handle, 7" **20.00**

Rooster, salt & pepper shakers, figural, 4¾", pr **25.00**

Rooster, sugar bowl, white w/red bottom, rooster finial, 5x4", $25 to **35.00**

Rooster, vase, figural, 6", from $25 to **35.00**

Homco (Home Interiors)

For years, Home Interiors have been possibly the largest direct seller of home assessories in North America. Their wares have always been easily accessible and moderately priced, and as a result, you'll find many on the secondary market. These items were sold through the hostess party plan, and large pieces such as mirrors, wall shelves, framed prints, and throws were offered as well as smaller items including figurines, candleholders, and candy boxes. Some pieces were produced in Japan, while others originated in Mexico, Thailand, Sri Lanka, and the USA. Their Masterpiece collection included figures of lovely Victorian ladies, wildlife, farm animals, representations of the life of Jesus, and virtually countless other themes. But by far their most popular series was called Denim Days. Each issue represented a day at the farm with Danny, Debbie, and their extended family. Some were quite involved, and many depicted two or more people, perhaps with a cow, an angel, Santa, or whatever props might best represent the featured senario. Denim Days were first produced in the mid-1980s, and after 20 years they were finally retired with a '50th Anniversary Celebration' piece that marked not only Grandma and Grandpa's fiftieth wedding anniversary but 50 years for the company as well. Many pieces will carry the HOMCO gold label, while others are marked with an ink stamp.

Figurine, Bobbing for Apples, Denim Days, #1527 ...... **42.50**

Figurine, Camille, lady in blue & pink, #14039-03, 2003, 9" **50.00**

Figurine, Come Unto Me, Jesus w/children, Masterpiece, 1989, 7¼" **120.00**

Figurine, eagle w/wings up, Masterpiece, 1979, 11¾x7", MIB **55.00**

Figurine, Every Good & Perfect Gift..., Circle of Friends, 1991 .... **20.00**

Figurine, foal lies by fence, studies squirrel, #1461, 3x4x3" ... **30.00**

Figurine, Guardian Angel, Denim Days, #8822, 1997 .... **55.00**

Figurine, Horseshoes, Danny w/ smithy, Denim Days, #8808, 1992 .... **36.00**

Figurine, kitten, white w/pink bow, #1428, 3" **12.50**

Figurine, mallard duck taking flight, Masterpiece, 1984, 11" **45.00**

Figurine, Our Snowman, kids build snowman, Denim Days, #1508, 1985 .... **45.00**

Figurine, Santa's Visit, Denim Days, #8925, 1985, w/tag **65.00**

Figurine, Siberian tigers (2), Endangered Species, 1996, 5½", MIB **55.00**

Figurine, Victoria, peach & ivory, Masterpiece, 1991, 9½", from $45 to **55.00**

Figurine, 50th Celebration, Denim Days final edition **85.00**

Figurines, Gathering Eggs, Denim Days, #1509, 1990, pr **36.00**

Figurines, Let Us Give Thanks, Debbie & Danny, Denim Days, #1502, pr **48.00**

Plaques, clowns in funny poses, plastic, multicolor, 11½", 12", pr **15.00**

Print, Denim Days boy & girl, oval reserve ea side, framed, 14x22" **52.50**

Print, Shepherd's Daughter, girl w/ lamb, in frame, 31x25" ... **55.00**

Prints, roses in vase on table w/crocheted piece, gold-trim frames, pr **60.00**

Homer Laughlin

The Homer Laughlin China Company has produced millions of pieces of dinnerware, toiletry items, art china, children's dishes, and hotel ware since its inception in 1874. On most pieces the back-stamp includes company name, date, and plant where the piece was produced, and nearly always the shape name is included. We have listed samples from many of the decaled lines; some of the more desirable patterns will go considerably higher. Refer to *Homer Laughlin China Company, A Giant Among Dishes,* by Jo Cunningham; and *The Collector's Encyclopedia of Fiesta* by Sharon and Bob Huxford. See Clubs and Newsletters for information concerning *The Laughlin Eagle,* a newsletter for collectors of Homer Laughlin dinnerware. See also Fiesta.

Century

Bowl, baker	**20.00**
Cup	**10.00**
Gravy boat	**20.00**
Plate, dinner	**12.00**
Platter, lg	**15.00**
Sugar bowl	**10.00**
Sugar bowl, w/lid	**18.00**
Teapot	**35.00**
Water jug, 2-qt	**125.00**

Eggshell Nautilus

Bowl, rim soup; deep	**12.00**
Creamer	**15.00**
Cup & saucer	**13.00**

Egg cup, double (Swing) 12.00
Plate, dinner 9.00
Sugar bowl, w/lid 20.00

Empress

Butter dish, w/lid 50.00
Casserole, w/lid 30.00
Celery tray 20.00
Creamer 10.00
Platter 18.00
Sugar bowl, w/lid 18.00
Tureen, sauce 45.00
Vegetable dish, w/handles & lid.30.00
Water jug 40.00

Georgian Eggshell Shape (available in Belmont, Chateau, Greenbriar, and Cashmere)

Bowl, baker 16.00
Bowl, cream soup 22.00
Creamer 12.00
Cup & saucer 14.00
Plate, dinner 6.00
Sugar bowl 25.00
Teapot 65.00

Marigold

Bowl, flat soup 12.00
Casserole, w/lid 32.00
Creamer 10.00
Cup & saucer 8.00
Plate, dinner 8.00
Platter, lg 20.00

Nautilus

Bowl, baker 22.00
Bowl, soup 6.00
Bowl, vegetable; oval 18.00
Casserole, w/lid 20.00

Creamer 10.00
Mug, coffee; Baltimore 15.00

Plate, dark green border around red rose center, from $8.00 to $10.00.

Plate, dinner 7.00
Platter, lg 15.00
Teacup 4.00

Republic Shape (available in Jean, Calais, Priscilla, and Wayside)

Bone dish 15.00
Bowl, fruit 5.00
Bowl, soup 8.00
Butter dish 30.00
Casserole, w/handles & lid 25.00
Creamer 12.00
Cup & saucer 10.00
Platter 12.00
Sauceboat 15.00
Teapot 40.00

Rhythm

Bowl, cereal 12.00
Bowl, fruit 10.00
Bowl, vegetable 12.00
Creamer 8.00
Cup & saucer 12.00
Sauceboat 25.00

Spoon rest 100.00
Sugar bowl, w/lid 20.00
Teapot 40.00

Swing

Bowl, serving 20.00
Casserole, w/lid 35.00
Creamer 18.00
Cup & saucer 15.00
Egg cup, double 12.00
Plate, dinner 10.00
Platter, lg 25.00
Sugar bowl, w/lid 20.00
Teapot 70.00

Virginia Rose

Values are for Moss Rose (JJ59) and Fluffy Rose (VR128); for other patterns, deduct 35%.

Bowl, coupe soup 20.00
Bowl, nappy 24.00
Creamer 15.00
Plate, bread & butter; rare.... 20.00
Platter, lg 24.00
Salt & pepper shakers, regular, scarce, pr 125.00
Sauceboat 12.00
Saucer 5.00
Water jug 65.00

Wells

Casserole, footed, w/handles & lid 65.00
Creamer 20.00
Cup & saucer 18.00
Egg cup 20.00
Pitcher 100.00
Platter, oval 14.00
Sauceboat 15.00

Sauceboat liner 10.00
Teapot, individual 35.00

Hot Wheels

An instant success in 1968, Hot Wheels are known for their fastest model cars on the market. Keeping up with new trends in the big car industry, Hot Wheels also included futuristic vehicles, muscle cars, trucks, hot rods, racers, and some military vehicles. A lot of these can be found for very little, but if you want to buy the older models (collectors call them 'redlines' because of their red sidewall tires), it's going to cost you a little more, though many can still be found under $25.00. By 1971, earlier on some models, black-wall tires had become the standard.

Though recent re-releases have dampened the collector market somewhat, cars mint in the original packages are holding their values and still moving well. Near-mint examples (no package) are worth about 50% to 60% less than those mint and still in their original package, excellent condition about 65% to 75% less. For further information we recommend *Hot Wheels, The Ultimate Redline Guide* and *Hot Wheels, The Ultimate Redline Guide Companion, 1968 – 1977,* by Jack Clark and Robert P. Wicker (Collector Books).

'32 Ford Delivery, 1989, black walls, yellow w/orange/magenta tampo, M 10.00

'57 Chevy, yellow w/flame accents, 1984, MIP **20.00**

'65 Mustang Convertible, 1980s, black walls, blue, black interior, MIP **30.00**

Aeroflash, 1990s, black walls, purple, Gleam Team edition, MIP **12.00**

Alive '55 Chevrolet Station Wagon, 1973, redline, plum, EX+ ..**200.00**

Angeleno, 1970, redline, Sizzler, M-70, M, $35.00; MIB, $45.00. (Photo courtesy Jack Clark and Robert P. Wicker)

AW Shoot, 1976, redline, olive, NM+ **40.00**

Baja Bruiser, 1974, redline, orange, metal base, NM **55.00**

Beatnik Bandit, 1968, redline, ice blue w/white interior, NM. **95.00**

Bone Shaker, 1973, redline, white, original yellow driver, rare, M . **400.00**

Boss Hoss, 1971, redline, olive w/ black roof, NM **200.00**

Bugeye, 1971, redline, light metallic green w/cream interior, EX+ **24.00**

Cement Mixer, 1970, redline, metallic olive w/cream interior, NM **35.00**

Chevy Stocker, metal-flake red, MIP **15.00**

Choppin' Chariot, 1972, orange, original blue driver w/face mask, NM **50.00**

Classic '35 Caddy, 1989, white walls, silver w/beige interior, NM **25.00**

Classic '57 T-Bird, 1969, redline, metallic red w/cream interior, EX+ **35.00**

Cockney Cab, 1971, redline, blue, NM+ **120.00**

Custom Baracuda, 1968, redline, metallic aqua, NM **100.00**

Custom Charger, 1969, redline, red, MIP **650.00**

Custom Cougar, 1968, redline, metallic orange, MIP **400.00**

Custom Fleetside, 1968, redline, light purple, NM+ **125.00**

Custom Mustang, 1968, redline, red w/red interior, NM+ **135.00**

Custom Police Cruiser, 1969, redline, rare prototype w/black fenders **300.00**

Custom Volkswagen, 1968, redline, blue, M **60.00**

Demon, 1970, redline, olive w/white interior, NM+ **45.00**

Dump Truck, 1970, redline, metallic blue w/brown bed & yellow dump, EX **25.00**

El Rey Special, 1974, redline, green w/yellow & orange #1 tampo, NM+ **55.00**

Evil Weevil, 1971, redline, red, #6 tampo, NM **110.00**

Ferarri 512S, 1972, redline gold, NM+ **125.00**

Ferrari 312P, 1974, redline, red, blue & white tampo, w/card, M **100.00**

Fire Eater, 1977, redline, red w/yellow & black tampo, EX+. **15.00**

Formula Fever, 1983, black walls, yellow, MIP **8.00**

Formula PACK, 1976, redline, black w/ orange & yellow tampo, M .. **60.00**

Funny Money, 1974, redline, plum, M **80.00**

Grass Hopper, 1971, redline, metallic green, scarce color, NM+ ... **60.00**

Gremlin Grinder, 1975, redline, green, NM+ **45.00**

Gulch Stepper, 1985, black walls, yellow w/tan roof, MIP **6.00**

Hairy Hauler, 1971, redline, light green, NM+ **40.00**

Heavy Chevy, 1974, redline, yellow, NM+ **110.00**

Heavyweight Dump Truck, 1970, redline, blue, M **50.00**

Heavyweight Snorkle, 1971, redline, purple, NM+ **125.00**

Ice T, 1971, redline, light yellow, M **50.00**

Incredible Hulk, black walls, yellow w/multicolored tampo, 1979, NM **22.00**

Inferno, 1976, redline, yellow, M..**60.00**

King Kuda, 1970, redline, Club Car, chrome, complete, NM **72.00**

Lotus Turbine, 1969, redline, orange, NM+ **27.00**

McClaren M6A, 1969, redline, antifreeze, M **60.00**

Mod Quad, 1970, redline, metallic yellow w/black interior, M. **40.00**

Moving Van, 1970, redline, metallic green w/gray trailer, NM. **55.00**

Neet Streeter, 1977, black walls, light blue, multicolored tampo, M **30.00**

Old Number 5, 1982, black walls, red w/louvers, NM+ **5.00**

Open Fire, 1972, redline, magenta, NM+ **225.00**

Peeping Bomb, 1970, redline tires, metallic orange, M **50.00**

Poison Pinto, 1976, redline, green w/yellow, black & white tampo, NM **30.00**

Porsche 911, 1976, redline, Super Chromes, M **35.00**

Red Baron, 1970, redline, metallic red, sharp point, EX **24.00**

Rock Buster, 1976, redline, yellow w/ multicolored tampo, NM .. **35.00**

Rocket Bye Baby, 1973, redline, red, Shell promotion, MIB **125.00**

Sand Drifter, 1975, redline, yellow w/orange & magenta tampo, EX **45.00**

Short Order, 1971, redline, blue (rare color), MIP, minimum value **250.00**

Six Shooter, 1971, redline, magenta, EX **125.00**

Mean Machine, 1970, Rumblers, MOC, $110.00. (Photo courtesy www.serious toyz.com)

Slingin' Thing, redline, fluorescent lime green, Revvers, M, $60.00; MIB, $130.00. (Photo courtesy Jack Clark and Robert P. Wicker)

Snorkel, 1971, redline, white w/ black interior, M **250.00**

Splittin' Image, 1969, redline, metallic green, M **30.00**

Spoiler Sport, 1977, redline, green w/black, yellow & red tampo, M **50.00**

Street Beast, 1988, black walls, red, MIP **8.00**

Sugar Caddy, 1971, redline, metallic green, complete, NM.. **70.00**

Sweet 16, 1973, redline, fluorescent lime green, M **225.00**

T-4-2, 1971, redline, magenta, EX **95.00**

Team Trailer, 1971, metallic red w/ cream interior, NM **90.00**

Thunderbird Stocker, 1984, black walls, white, MIP **35.00**

Torero, 1969, redline, metallic aqua w/cream interior, NM **24.00**

Turbofire, 1970, redline, metallic red w/cream interior, NM **25.00**

Twin Mill, 1973, redline, fluorescent pink, Shell promotion, MIB **175.00**

Volkswagon Bug, 1974, redline, orange w/black, yellow & green tampo, M **80.00**

Whip Creamer, 1970, redline, metallic pink w/black interior, NM **80.00**

Winnipeg, 1974, redline, yellow w/ blue & orange tampo, M. **130.00**

Hull

Established in Zanesville, Ohio, in 1905, Hull manufactured stoneware, florist ware, art pottery, and tile until about 1935, when they began to produce lines of pastel matt-glazed art-ware which are today very collectible. The pottery was destroyed by flood and fire in 1950. The factory was rebuilt and equipped with the most modern machinery which they soon discovered was not geared to duplicate the matt glazes. As a result, new lines — Parchment and Pine and Ebb Tide, for example — were introduced in a glossy finish. During the '40s and into the '50s their kitchenware and novelty lines were very successful. Refer to *Robert's Ultimate Encyclopedia of Hull Pottery* and *The Companion Guide,* both by Brenda Roberts (Walsworth Publishing), for more information. Brenda also has authored *The Collector's Encyclopedia of Hull Pottery* and *The Collector's Ultimate Encyclopedia of Hull Pottery,* both of which are published by Collector Books.

Blossom Flite, basket, #T-2, 6", from $65 to **105.00**

Bow-Knot, ewer, #B-1, 5½", from $210 to **270.00**

Bow-Knot, sugar bowl, w/lid, #B-22, 4", from $200 to **225.00**

Butterfly, ashtray, heart shape, #B-3, 7", from $40 to **50.00**

Butterfly, vase, #B-10, 7", from $55 to **85.00**

Calla Lily, bowl, #500/32, 10", from $215 to **260.00**

Calla Lily, candleholder, green, unmarked, 2¼", ea from $100 to **130.00**

Cinderella Kitchenware, creamer, Blossom, #28, 4½", from $45 to **70.00**

Cinderella Kitchenware, grease jar, Bouquet, #24, 32-oz, from $50 to **75.00**

Classic, vase, #5, 6", from $25 to **35.00**

Iris, bowl, console; #409, 12", from $310 to **375.00**

Iris, rose bowl, #412, 4", from $120 to **145.00**

Magnolia, candleholder, gloss, #H-24, 4", ea from $50 to **65.00**

Magnolia, double cornucopia, matt, #6, 12", from $205 to..... **255.00**

Magnolia, lamp base, matt, 12½", from $350 to **450.00**

Magnolia, teapot, gloss, #H-20, 6½", from $175 to **225.00**

Magnolia, vase, matt, #20, 15", from $475 to **600.00**

Mardi Gras/Granada, ewer, #66, 10", from $150 to........... **185.00**

Novelty, baby w/pillow planter, #92, 1951, 5½", from $25 to.... **35.00**

Novelty, dancing girl, #955, 1940s, 7", from $60 to................. **85.00**

Novelty, French poodle planter, #114, 8", from $50 to....... **75.00**

Novelty, Old Spice Shaving Mug, 1937-44, 3", from $22 to . **30.00**

Novelty, twin deer vase, #62, 1953, 11½", from $60 to **80.00**

Novelty, wall pocket, dark green & maroon blend, #112, 10½", from $55 to **75.00**

Open Rose, creamer, #111, 5", from $125 to **150.00**

Open Rose, sugar bowl, open, #112, 6¼", from $125 to **150.00**

Orchid, bowl, low, #312, 7", from $170 to **210.00**

Orchid, vase, #303, 4¾", from $120 to.................................. **145.00**

Poppy, bowl, low, #602, 6½", from $225 to **275.00**

Poppy, vase, #607, 6½", from $125 to **160.00**

Rosella, ewer, coral, #R-9, 6½", from $75 to **125.00**

Rosella, vase, ivory, #R-1, 5", from $70 to **95.00**

Serenade, creamer, Regency Blue, #S-18, 3¼", from $75 to. **100.00**

Serenade, fruit bowl, blue w/yellow interior, #S-15, from $140 to................................. **180.00**

Serenade, teapot, Sunlight Yellow, #S-17, 5", from $175 to. **235.00**

Sunglow, basket, hanging; #99, 6", from $85 to **120.00**

Sunglow, casserole, yellow flowers on pink, w/lid, #51, 7½", from $60 to **85.00**

Sunglow, jardiniere, #97, USA, 5½", from $40 to **55.00**

Sunglow, tea bell, 6½", from $100.00 to $125.00.

Sunglow, vase, yellow flowers on pink, #94, 8", from $75 to............................. **110.00**

Tulip, vase, #100/33, 4", from $60 to **90.00**

Water Lily, sugar bowl, tan, #L-20, 5", from $80 to............... **110.00**

Water Lily, teapot, #L-18, 6", from $245 to **300.00**

Water Lily, vase, pink to cream, #L-8, 8½", from $170 to. **200.00**

Water Lily, vase, L-13, 10½", from $250.00 to $330.00.

Mirror Brown, casserole, hen on nest, 8½x8½", from $60.00 to $80.00.

Wildflower, vase, pink to yellow, #W-8, 7½", from $90 to . **125.00**

Woodland, basket, #W-22, 10½", from $250 to **310.00**

Woodland, window box, #W-14, 10", from $60 to **90.00**

Dinnerware

Avocado, bean pot, w/lid, 2-qt, from $22 to **28.00**

Avocado, beer stein, 16-oz, from $6 to **10.00**

Avocado, bowl, fruit; 5¼".......... **5.00**

Avocado, teapot, w/lid, 5-cup, from $20 to **25.00**

Centennial Brown, creamer, unmarked, 4½", from $40 to............................... **50.00**

Centennial Brown, pitcher, milk; unmarked, 7½", from $90 to...................... **110.00**

Heartland, coffeepot, from $40 to **50.00**

Heartland, creamer, from $10 to **15.00**

Heartland, pitcher, 36-oz, from $35 to....................................... **40.00**

Mirror Brown, bean pot, w/lid, 2-qt, from $15 to **20.00**

Mirror Brown, canister, sugar; 8", from $100 to **150.00**

Mirror Brown, canister, tea; from $45 to **60.00**

Mirror Brown, cruet, vinegar; 6½", from $30 to **40.00**

Mirror Brown, custard cup, 8-oz, from $5 to **7.00**

Mirror Brown, leaf dish, 7½", from $15 to **20.00**

Mirror Brown, pie plate, 9¼", from $22 to **32.00**

Mirror Brown, platter, w/chicken lid, from $90 to............. **110.00**

Mirror Brown, spoon rest, 6½", from $40 to **50.00**

Provincial, beer stein, 16-oz, from $15 to **22.00**

Provincial, bowl, mixing; 6¾", from $15 to **20.00**

Provincial, ice jug, 2-qt, from $25 to **35.00**

Rainbow, pitcher, 9", from $40 to **60.00**

Rainbow, plate, luncheon; 8½", from $6 to **8.00**

Ring, creamer, from $10 to **15.00**

Ring, platter, oval, from $15 to..**22.00**

Tangerine, ashtray, 8", from $25 to **35.00**

Tangerine, beer stein, 16-oz, from $8 to **10.00**

Tangerine, bowl, spaghetti/salad; 10¼", from $23 to **27.00**

Tangerine, ice jug, 2-qt, from $25 to **28.00**

Tangerine, plate, dinner; 10¼", from $7 to **9.00**

Tangerine, shaker, 4", ea from $8 to **12.00**

Tangerine, tray (for snack set). **5.00**

Tangerine, vase, bud; 9", from $20 to **30.00**

Utility, bean pot, turquoise, w/lid, #219, 6", from $40 to **55.00**

Utility, bowl, rust color, unmarked, 8", from $35 to **24.00**

Utility, cookie jar, tan, #D-20, 2-qt, 8", from $150 to **200.00**

Indiana Carnival Glass

Though this glass looks old, it really isn't. It's very reminiscent of old Northwood carnival glass with its grape clusters and detailed leaves and vines, but this line was actually introduced in 1972! Made by the Indiana Glass Company, Harvest (the pattern name assigned by the company) was produced in blue, lime green, and marigold. Although they made a few other carnival patterns in addition to this one, none are as collectible or as easy to recognize. (You'll find an identical line in milk glass, and though it was produced by Indiana, it was never marketed in their catalogs. Instead it was sold through the parent company, Colony.)

This glassware is a little difficult to evaluate as there seems to be a wide range of 'asking' prices simply because some dealers are unsure of its age and therefore its value. If you like it, now is the time to buy it! Harvest values given below are based on items in blue. Adjust them downward a price point or two for lime green and even a little more so for marigold. For further information we recommend *Garage Sale and Flea Market Annual* (Collector Books).

Iridescent Amethyst (Heritage)

Basket, footed, 9x5x7", from $60 to **75.00**

Butter dish, 5x7½" dia, from $50 to **65.00**

Candleholders, Harvest, compote style, embossed grapes, 4", pr, $22 to **28.00**

Candleholders, 5½", pr from $45 to **60.00**

Center bowl, 4¾x8½", from $50 to **60.00**

Goblet, 8-oz, from $15 to **22.00**

Pitcher, 8¼", from $50 to **70.00**

Punch set, 10" bowl, 8-cups, no pedestal, from $150 to **185.00**

Punch set, 10" bowl & pedestal, 8-cups, ladle, 11-pc, from $200 to **235.00**

Swung vase, slender & footed w/ irregular rim, 11x3", from $50 to **60.00**

Iridescent Blue

Basket, Monticello, faceted embossed diamonds, 7x6" sq, from $25 to **35.00**

Butter dish, Harvest, embossed grapes, 8" L, from $25 to. **35.00**

Candleholders, Harvest, embossed grapes, compote shape, 4", pr **25.00**

Candy dish, embossed ribs, rectangle w/lacy edge, footed, w/ lid, 7" L **35.00**

Candy dish, Harvest, embossed grapes, lace edge, w/lid, 6½", $35 to **45.00**

Canister/Cookie jar, Harvest, embossed grapes, 9", from $125 to **175.00**

Canister/Snack jar, Harvest, embossed grapes, 8", from $120 to **150.00**

Cooler (iced tea tumbler), Harvest, embossed grapes, 14-oz, 5⅞". **10.50**

Creamer & sugar bowl on tray, Harvest, embossed grapes, 3-pc, $30 to **35.00**

Egg/Hors d'oeuvres tray, sections, off-side holder for 8-eggs, 13" dia **42.00**

Garland bowl (comport), paneled, 7½x8½" dia, from $15 to . **20.00**

Goblet, Harvest, embossed grapes, 9-oz, from $9 to **12.00**

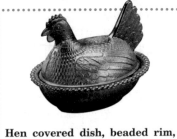

Hen covered dish, beaded rim, from $15.00 to $20.00.

Hen on nest, from $18 to **25.00**

Plate, hostess; Canterbury, diamond facets, flared crimped rim, 10" **20.00**

Punch set, Princess, complete w/ ladle & hooks, 26-pc, from $95 to **115.00**

Punch set, Princess, 12-cups, no ladle or hooks, from $65 to **85.00**

Tidbit, embossed diamond points, shallow w/flared sides, 6½". **12.00**

Wedding bowl (sm compote), Thumbprint, footed, 5x5", from $10 to **12.00**

Iridescent Gold

Basket, Monticello, lg faceted diamonds, sq, 7x6", from $25 to .**30.00**

Cooler (ice tea tumbler), Harvest, embossed grapes, 14-oz, from $8 to **12.00**

Goblet, Harvest, embossed grapes, 9-oz, from $10 to **14.00**

Pitcher, 10½", from $30.00 to $35.00; Tumbler, 5½", from $9.00 to $12.00.

Punch bowl, Princess, w/12-cups & ladle (no hooks) **55.00**

Punch set, Princess, complete w/ladle & hooks, 26-pc, from $100 to.. **125.00**

Snack plate, 8x10", w/2⅞" cup, from $20 to **25.00**

Tumbler, Harvest, embossed grapes, 4", from $7 to **10.00**

Wedding bowl (sm compote), 5x5", from $9 to **12.00**

Iridescent Lime

Candy dish, Harvest, embossed grapes, lace edge, w/lid, 6½", from $25 to **30.00**

Canister/Cookie jar, Harvest, embossed grapes, 9", from $75 to **90.00**

Compote, Harvest, embossed grapes, 7x6", from $15 to **20.00**

Console set, Harvest, 10" bowl w/ compote-shaped candleholders, 3-pc **65.00**

Egg plate, 11", from $18 to **25.00**

Goblet, Harvest, embossed grapes, 9-oz, from $10 to **12.00**

Salad set, Vintage, apple shape, 3-pc w/spoon & fork, 13", from $18 to **25.00**

Iridescent Sunset (Amberina)

Basket, 9½x7½" sq, from $40 to .**55.00**

Bowl, 3½x8½", from $25 to **30.00**

Butter dish, 5x7½" dia, from $40 to **50.00**

Center bowl, 4¾x8½", from $30 to **40.00**

Goblet, 8-oz, from $35 to **40.00**

Pitcher, 7¼", from $35 to **45.00**

Plate, 14", from $40 to **50.00**

Punch set, 10" bowl, pedestal, 8-cups & ladle, 11-pc, from $125 to **175.00**

Swung vase, slender, footed, w/ irregular rim, 11x3", from $50 to **60.00**

Japan Ceramics

Though Japanese ceramics marked Nippon, Noritake, and Occupied Japan have long been collected, some of the newest fun-type collectibles on today's market are the figural ashtrays, pincushions, wall pockets, toothbrush holders, etc., that are marked 'Made in Japan' or simply 'Japan.' In her books called *Collector's Encyclopedia of Made in Japan Ceramics*, Carole Bess White explains the pitfalls you will encounter when you try to determine production dates. Collectors refer to anything produced before WWII as 'old' and anything made after 1952 as 'new.' You'll find all you need to know to be a wise shopper in her books. See also Black Cats; Blue Willow; Egg Timers; Enesco; Fishbowl Ornaments; Flower Frogs; Geisha Girl; Head Vases; Holt Howard; Lefton; Moss Rose; Nippon; Noritake; Occupied Japan; Rooster and Roses; Sewing Items; Toothbrush Holders; Wall Pockets.

Ashtray, camel figure, opening in back, multicolor lustre, 4¼" L................................**27.00**

Ashtray, hand figure, shiny white, 2¾" **18.00**

Ashtray, skull figure, gray stain, red mark, 4¾" **25.00**

Basket, flowers at ends of handle, multicolor lustre, black mark, 4" **25.00**

Bell, girl w/sunbonnet, multicolored, shiny, inscribed Portland Ore **20.00**

Bell, multicolored design on shiny orange, black mark, 3".... **18.00**

Biscuit jar, pink floral & green leaves w/gold, 3 jewels, 4-legged, 6" **40.00**

Bookends, golfer swinging, standing on & beside books, gold mark, 6" **35.00**

Bookends, Indian shooting bow & arrow, multicolor, red mark, 4¼" **45.00**

Bookends, poodle seated on book, pencil holder on back, 6⅛"..**28.00**

Butter dish, tomato form, red-orange on green base, black mark, 3¼" **38.00**

Cache pot, bunny & cart, multicolor lustre, red mark, 3½"......**15.00**

Cache pot, dogs in car, multicolor, black mark, 5¾" **15.00**

Cache pot, horse pulling covered wagon, shiny green, black mark, 9"...........................**12.00**

Candy dish, bellhop standing beside box, Deco style, multicolor, 5" **25.00**

Cigarette box, Scottie dog standing on lid, red mark, 4½" **30.00**

Coffeepot, platinum wheat on white w/gold trim, Fine China Japan, 8".....................................**40.00**

Condiment set, multicolor floral on cream, oil and vinegar on 9" long tray, red mark, from $20.00 to $35.00. (Photo courtesy Carole Bess White)

Condiment set, 3 ducks on water (tray), black mark, 8¾"...**46.00**

Cracker jar, Little Bo Peep figure, Napco, 1957, NM **50.00**

Creamer & sugar bowl, floral on cream, w/lid, Mahuron Ware..., 3", 5" **25.00**

Cruets, anthropomorphic lemons, conjoined w/branch sprouts, PY, 4½"...............................**45.00**

Decanter, elephant, multicolor lustre, black mark, 7¾"......**100.00**

Decoration, bluebird w/metal clip, Vcago, 6x2½" **18.00**

Demitasse set, floral, tan & multicolor lustre, 8¾" pot, 12-pc...........................**155.00**

Figurine, bride (groom kissing), Napco S488A & S488B, 5½", NM, pr **42.50**

Figurine, colonial man w/dog (lady w/bird & cage), Napco C6639, 8", pr **50.00**

Figurine, dachshund pup seated, brown & white, Napco #C6537, 2¾x4" **20.00**

Figurine, foo dog, blue on gray base, Andrea by Sadek, 7½x4x3", pr.................... **90.00**

Figurine, girl w/duck, Hummel-like, red mark, 3"............**12.50**

Figurine, lady devil in dance pose, red feather skirt, Empress..., 6" **70.00**

Figurine, lady's bust, multicolor, red mark, 6¾"..................**18.00**

Figurine, pelican w/mouth open, multicolor lustre, red mark, 4½" **15.00**

Figurine, pixie w/legs in air, chartreuse, red mark, 4½" **10.00**

Figurine, rooster sitting, yellow/green/brown/red, #W587D, 7x7" **50.00**

Flower bowl, elephant figure in center, multicolor crackle, red mark **50.00**

Flower frog, bird perched on stump, multicolor lustre, black mark, 4"....................................**20.00**

Honey pot, hive form w/Deco triangles, multicolor lustre, 4x3½" **55.00**

Incense burner, Maruyama castle & scenery, multicolor lustre, red mark........................ **20.00**

Mug, Miss Cutie Pie, Japan A3511/ YP mark, 4"...................... **40.00**

Nodder, hula girl w/swinging grass skirt, Aloha on base, KN mark, 7".................................... **55.00**

Nodder, Scotsman, Chance It Girls (kilt lifts up), multicolor, 4"......................... **78.00**

Pincushion, shoe, multicolor lustre, red mark, 4¼"................. **18.00**

Pitcher, frog figural, green & white, oval label, 7½"................. **25.00**

Pitcher, pony's head, pink & blue details, Hand Painted mark, 4".................................... **35.00**

Planter, collie seated before container marked Buddy, brown tones, 6"........................... **25.00**

Planter, girl w/poodle, spaghetti trim, AX2752B mark, 7x5x3½"....................... **60.00**

Planter, horse & foal, naturalistic colors, Relpo, 6x5½"........ **35.00**

Planter, Indian boy beside tepee, Napco, 5½"...................... **15.00**

Planter, Mary Had a Little Lamb, Napco S1493B, 4¼"......... **55.00**

Planter, squirrel sitting by tree stump, browns & greens, 3¼x4¼"............................ **20.00**

Plate, anthropomorphic lady apple, PY, 9⅜", NM.................... **45.00**

Shakers, space-like figures, multicolor lustre, pr................. **50.00**

Teapot, camel w/ornate howdah on back, floral decor w/gold, 8½" L..................................... **65.00**

Teapot, swirling design, opal lustre w/silver trim, black mark, 5½"................................. **32.00**

Vase, blue drips on yellow, classic form, Jwaji mark, 7", $40 to............................... **50.00**

Vase, clown figural, green/white lustre, multicolor dots, red mark, 3"........................... **18.00**

Vase, facing hands w/painted nails, pink roses along wrist, 5x3x2"......................... **30.00**

Vase, running gray/orange/brown, gourd-shape, handles, 12", $80 to................................ **120.00**

Vase, Tokanabe style with birds and flowers, multicolor on black, blind mark, 10", from $45.00 to $65.00. (Photo courtesy Carole Bess White)

Wall pocket/planter, Santa's face, Napco, 6x5"...................... **72.50**

Jewelry

Anyone interested in buying jewelry will soon find out that antique gems are the best values. Not only are prices from one-third to one-half less than on comparable new jewelry, but the older pieces display a degree of craftsmanship and and styling seldom seen in modern-day jewelry. Costume jewelry from all periods is popular, especially Art Nouveau and Art Deco examples. Signed pieces are particularly good, such as those by Miriam Haskell, Eisenberg, Trifari, Hollycraft, and Weiss, among others.

There are some excellent reference books available if you'd like more information. Marcia 'Sparkles' Brown has written *Unsigned Beauties of Costume Jewelry; Signed Beauties of Costume Jewelry, Volumes I* and *II; Rhinestone Jewerly: Figurals, Animals, and Whimsicals;* and *Coro Jewelry.* Lillian Baker has written *Fifty Years of Collectible Fashion Jewelry* and *100 Years of Collectible Jewelry.* Books by other authors include *Costume Jewelry* and *Collectible Silver Jewelry* by Fred Rezazadeh; *Collectible Costume Jewelry* by Cherri Simonds; *Collecting Costume Jewelry 101* and *Collecting Costume Jewelery 202* by Julia C. Carroll; *Inside the Jewelry Box Vols. 1* and *2* by Ann Mitchell Pitman; and *Brilliant Rhinestones* and *20th Century Costume Jewelry,* both by Ronna Lee Aikins. All of these books are published by Collector Books. See Clubs and Newsletters for information on the *Vintage Fashion & Costume Jewelry* newsletter and club.

Bracelet, black plastic rhinestone-studded segments, elastic. **75.00**

Bracelet, charm; Cupid's bow, arrow, caged lovebirds, etc, gold-tone **30.00**

Bracelet, Emmons, molded thermoset plastic links w/gold-tone backing **30.00**

Bracelet, hand-set clear rhinestones in single row, dainty **18.00**

Bracelet, Ledesma, hinged cuff, sterling silver abstract design **200.00**

Bracelet, multi-shaped lavender rhinestones on gold-plated cuff **75.00**

Bracelet, Napier, silver blue w/ sky blue crystals, 8 repeating links **65.00**

Bracelet, Sarah Coventry, ocean theme in gold-tone, faux pearls & stones **48.00**

Brooch, Avon, Nouveau dragonfly w/pink glass body, 7-strand pearl tail **68.00**

Brooch, black Bakelite lady's riding boot, ca 1935 .... **115.00**

Brooch, C Dior, gold-plated rose w/ textured petals **180.00**

Brooch, Capri, japanned poodle w/ red rhinestones **48.00**

Brooch, Capri, silver-plated leaf covered w/diamanté rhinestones **55.00**

Brooch, Hollycraft, faux turquoise oval w/blue rhinestones .. **88.00**

Brooch, JJ, elephant w/pewter finish & faux turquoise details **45.00**

Brooch, JJ, gold-plated crescent w/ studded rhinestones **30.00**

Brooch, Lisner, bunch of grapes, lg green rhinestones **65.00**

Brooch, Lucite, orange-yellow orchid **85.00**

Brooch, Marvella, gold-tone peace dove w/olive branch tipped in pearls **58.00**

Brooch, Mazer Bros, gold plated w/clear rhinestones & faux pearls **90.00**

Brooch, pink flamingo, pot metal w/ lg pink stones, lg **90.00**

Brooch, Sarah Coventry, red enameled apple on gold-tone stem, 1" **30.00**

Brooch, sea horse, plastic w/lavender stones 36.00

Brooch, stag, enameled & japanned, green eye, rhinestones on back 55.00

Brooch, Trifari, enameled lizard. 50.00

Brooch, unmarked Austrian, lavender & purple chatons form circle 65.00

Brooch, VB Sterling Denmark, silver & enamel leaf 90.00

Brooch, Weiss, topaz & orange rhinestone flower 55.00

Brooch & earrings, Capri, blue & aurora borealis rhinestones 78.00

Brooch & earrings, enameled pansies w/pearl centers 25.00

Brooch & earrings, Judy Lee, lg blue rhinestone amid faux pearls 55.00

Brooch & earrings, Judy Lee, pink rhinestone flowers 65.00

Brooch & earrings, Sarah Coventry, dogwood flower 75.00

Earrings, aurora borealis rhinestone cluster, pr 38.00

Earrings, Hollycraft, pink rhinestones & pearls 80.00

Earrings, Lucite, lg green buttons w/rhinestones, 1950s 41.00

Earrings, pearls w/rhinestone accents, dainty, pr 15.00

Earrings, Vogue, crystal beads, wire-wrapped clear rhinestones 35.00

Earrings, yellow plastic flower w/ rhinestone center, pr 14.00

Necklace, Barclay, gold plated w/2 pastel rhinestone circles. 90.00

Necklace, cameo framed by faux pearls & black beads, gold-tone chain 38.00

Necklace, Encore, Lucite, clear round & sq beads, ca 1970 .... 75.00

Necklace, Monet, double strand of gold beads 55.00

Necklace, pink celluloid floral dangles on pink chain, 1950s. 75.00

Necklace & earrings, Lisner, silver leaves, aurora borealis stones 65.00

Necklace and earrings, unsigned, pearl and crystal beaded strands with rhinestones, earrings include a hanging rhinestone ball, $65.00 for the set. (Photo courtesy Marcia Brown)

Necklace & earrings, white enamel flowers w/pastel rhinestone centers 55.00

Pendant, laminated celluloid w/applied brass Egyptian design 85.00

Ring, gold-plated sq filled w/opaline chatons 38.00

Ring, Lucite, black w/clear rhinestones 50.00

Ring, metallic cabochon w/2 rows of iridescent chatons 18.00

Ring, opaline clusters on gold-plated finish 45.00

Johnson Brothers

Dinnerware marked Johnson Brothers, Staffordshire, is bought and sold with considerable fervor on today's market, and for good reason. They made many lovely patterns, some scenic and some florals. Most are decorated with multicolor transfer designs, though you'll see blue or red transferware as well. Some, such as Friendly Village (one of their most popular lines), are still being produced, but the lines are much less extensive now, so the secondary market is being tapped to replace broken items that are no longer available anywhere else.

Some lines are more valuable than others. Unless a pattern is included in the following two categories, use the base values below as a guide. (Some of the most popular base-value lines are Bird of Paradise, Mount Vernon, Castle on the Lake, Old Bradury, Day in June, Nordic, Devon Sprays, Old Mill, Empire Grape, Pastorale, Haddon Hall, Pomona, Harvest Time, Road Home, Indian Tree, Vintage [older version], Melody, and Windsor Fruit.) One-Star patterns are basically 10% to 20% higher and include Autumn's Delight, Coaching Scenes, Devonshire, Fish, Friendly Village, Gamebirds, Garden Bouquet, Hearts and Flowers, Heritage Hall, Indies, Millstream, Olde English Countryside, Rose Bouquet, Sheraton, Tulip Time, and Winchester. Two-Star lines include Barnyard King, Century of Progress, Chintz – Victorian, Dorchester, English Chippendale, Harvest Fruit, His Majesty, Historical America, Merry Christmas, Old Britain Castles, Persian Tulip, Rose Chintz, Strawberry Fair, Tally Ho,

Twelve Days of Christmas, and Wild Turkeys. These patterns are from 25% to 35% higher than our base values. For more information refer to *Johnson Brothers Dinnerware* by Mary J. Finegan.

Bowl, berry/fruit...................... **8.00**
Bowl, rimmed soup **14.00**
Bowl, soup; 7"...................... **25.00**
Bowl, vegetable; oval, from $30 to upwards of...................... **50.00**
Butter dish, from $50 to **80.00**
Coaster.................................... **8.00**
Coffee mug, minimum value . **20.00**
Creamer.................................. **30.00**
Cup & saucer, jumbo.............. **30.00**
Egg cup **15.00**
Pitcher/jug, minimum value.. **45.00**
Plate, bread & butter.............. **6.00**
Plate, dinner........................ **14.00**

Plate, dinner; Barnyard King, 10½", $35.00.

Plate, salad; sq or round, from $10 to **18.00**
Platter, turkey; 20½", from $200 to upwards of.................... **300.00**
Platter, 12-14", minimum value . **45.00**
Salt & pepper shakers, pr **48.00**
Sauceboat **48.00**
Sugar bowl, open.................... **40.00**

Sugar bowl, w/lid **48.00**
Teacup & saucer, from $15 to
upwards of **30.00**
Tureen **200.00**

Kentucky Derby Glasses

Kentucky Derby glasses are the official souvenir glasses that are filled with mint juleps and sold on Derby Day. The first glass (1938), picturing a black horse within a black and white rose garland and the Churchill Downs stadium in the background, is said to have either been given away as a souvenir or used for drinks among the elite at the Downs. This glass, the 1939, and two glasses said to have been used in 1940 are worth thousands and are nearly impossible to find at any price.

1938 .... **4,000.00**
1940, aluminum **1,000.00**
1940, glass tumbler, 2 styles, ea,
minimum value **10,000.00**
1941-44, plastic, Beetleware, ea
from $2,500 to **4,000.00**
1945, tall, green horse head facing
right, horseshoe **450.00**
1946-47, clear frosted w/frosted
bottom, L in circle, ea ... **100.00**
1948, clear bottom, green horsehead in horseshoe & horse on
reverse **225.00**
1948, frosted bottom, green horse
head in horseshoe & horse on
reverse **250.00**
1949, He Has Seen Them All, Matt
Winn, green on frost **225.00**
1951, green winner's circle,
Where Turf Champions Are
Crowned **650.00**

1952, Gold Derby Trophy, Kentucky
Derby Gold Cup **225.00**
1953, black horse facing left, rose
garland **200.00**
1954, green twin spires **225.00**
1955, green & yellow horses, The
Fastest Runners, scarce . **200.00**
1956, 1 star, 2 tails, brown horses,
twin spires **275.00**
1956, 2 stars, 2 tails, brown horses,
twin spires **200.00**
1957, gold & black on frost, horse &
jockey facing right **125.00**
1958, Iron Leige, same as 1957
w/'Iron Leige' added **225.00**
1959, gold & black on frost .. **100.00**
1961, black horses on track, jockey
in red, gold winners **110.00**
1962, Churchill Downs, red, gold &
black on clear **70.00**
1963, brown horse, jockey #7, gold
lettering **70.00**
1965, brown twin spires & horses,
red lettering **85.00**
1966-68, black, black & blue respectively, ea **65.00**

1969, $65.00.

1970, green shield, gold lettering **70.00**
1972, 2 black horses, orange &
green print **55.00**
1973, white, black twin spires, red
& green lettering **60.00**
1974, Federal, regular or mistake,
brown & gold, ea **200.00**

1974, regular, Canonero II in 1971 listing on back 16.00
1976, plastic tumbler or regular glass, ea 16.00
1977 .... 14.00
1980 .... 22.00
1981-82, ea 15.00
1983-85, ea 12.00
1986 .... 14.00
1987-89, ea 12.00
1990-92, ea 10.00
1996-98 .... 8.00
1999-2000, ea 6.00
2001-03, ea 5.00
2004-07, ea 4.00

King's Crown, Thumbprint

This pattern has quite a history, having been made first by U. S. Glass and Tiffin (who was part of the U. S. conglomerate) from late in the 1890s through the 1940s, then again by Tiffin when it reopened in 1963, and finally by Indiana Glass during the 1970s. Though the thumbprints were originally oval, Indiana changed theirs to circles. Tiffin's tumblers were flared out at the top, while Indiana's were straight. Our values are for the ruby-flashed issues made by both companies ca. 1960s and 1970s. The darker ruby flashing is preferred. Some pieces were made in crystal with gold trim and our prices apply to them as well. For more information we recommend *Collectible Glassware from the 40s, 50s, and 60s* by Gene and Cathy Florence (Collector Books).

Ashtray, sq, 5¼" 35.00

Bowl, crimped bonbon, handles, 8¾" 100.00
Bowl, crimped rim, 4½x11½". 135.00
Bowl, flower floater, 12½" 85.00
Bowl, straight edge 80.00
Bowl, 5¾" 22.00
Bud vase, 12¼" 135.00
Candleholder, sherbet type, ea ..30.00
Cheese stand 35.00
Compote, flat, sm 28.00
Cup 8.00
Oyster cocktail, 4-oz 14.00
Pitcher 215.00
Plate, salad; 7⅜" 14.00
Punch bowl foot 185.00
Relish, 5-part, 14" 125.00
Tumbler, iced tea, flat, 11-oz . 14.00
Tumbler, juice; footed, 4-oz 12.00

Kitchen Collectibles

From the early patented apple peelers, cherry pitters, and food hoppers to the gadgets of the '20s through the '40s, many collectors find special appeal in kitchen tools. Refer to *Kitchen Glassware of the Depression Years* by Gene and Cathy Florence for more information. It is published by Collector Books.

See also Aluminum; Clothes Sprinkler Bottles; Cookie Cutters; Egg Timers; Enesco; Graniteware; Griswold.

Apothecary jar, pink, from $30 to 35.00
Apple peeler, Reading, cast iron, 1978 reproduction, EXIB 50.00
Baster, Pyrex, dated 1946, EXIB 35.00

Batter jug, amber, Paden City, from $50 to **60.00**

Beater jars: Evenfull, from $65.00 to $75.00; Crystal, from $28.00 to $30.00. (Photo courtesy Gene and Cathy Florence)

Bottle, water; green, Anchor Hocking, from $50 to **60.00**

Bowl, blue, Pyrex, sq base, 12", from $35 to **38.00**

Bowl, Delphite Blue, LE Smith, 7", from $65 to **75.00**

Bowl, mixing; black, 9⅜", from $50 to **60.00**

Bowl, mixing; Jade-ite, Anchor Hocking, 8", from $25 to. **28.00**

Bowl, yellow opaque, ribbed, McKee, 6½", from $25 to. **30.00**

Butter dish, Delphite, McKee, from $400 to **425.00**

Butter dish, pink, bow finial, from $65 to **75.00**

Cake server/Carrier, West Bend, stainless steel, black handle, 1960s **35.00**

Canister, clear glass w/rooster head finial, lg, from $45 to **50.00**

Canister, tea; fired-on green, Anchor Hocking, from $25 to **30.00**

Casserole, crystal, Fry, sq, in frame, w/lid, 7", from $85 to **95.00**

Casserole, Fruits, milk glass, Anchor Hocking, 2-qt, from $30 to **35.00**

Chopper, Foley Food Chopper, 1964 .... **45.00**

Clock, Westclox, turquoise & white, sq, wall mount, 1950s..... **45.00**

Coffeepot, crystal w/pastel-colored rings, McKee, from $25 to..**30.00**

Condiment set, Emerald-Glo, from $60 to **65.00**

Cruet, frosted white clambroth w/ chicken decal, from $15 to..**18.00**

Drawer pulls, green, lg, ea from $6 to **8.00**

Egg beater, Androck, rotary type, red Bakelite bullet handle **40.00**

Egg beater, KC Soap Bubble, metal w/red wooden handles **45.00**

Egg beater, Sears, stainless rotary type, turquoise plastic handle........................... **15.00**

Food mill, Foley #101, metal w/red wooden handles, 7¼" dia, $25 to **35.00**

Funnel, Tufglas, from $75 to. **85.00**

Grater, cabbage; wooden w/3 cutting blades, 1950s **15.00**

Grater, green-painted metal, 2 cutting plates, Kitchenmaster........................... **30.00**

Grater, vegetable; Schroeter No 10 Made in USA, crank handle, 12" **22.50**

Gravy boat, amber, Cambridge, 2-spout, from $45 to........ **55.00**

Grease strainer, Foley, metal w/turquoise wooden handle...... **15.00**

Ice chisel, Gilchrist #50, 6-tine, wooden handle, 9" **30.00**

Ice tub, Emerald-Glo, w/tongs, from $65 to **70.00**

Juicer, Atlas, 1950s-60s **65.00**

Knife sharpener, rasp type w/red Bakelite handle, 12" **35.00**

Ladle, pink, Cambridge, from $25 to **28.00**

Measuring cup, crystal, Glasbake, McKee, 1-cup, from $20 to .**25.00**

Measuring cup, green, Paden City, from $135 to **150.00**

Measuring cup, red, Pyrex, 16-oz, from $100 to **125.00**

Measuring cup, yellow opaque, footed, w/handle, McKee, 4-cup, $125 to **140.00**

Measuring pitcher, pink, ribbed, Anchor Hocking, 2-cup, from $50 to **55.00**

Melon baller, metal w/green wooden handle **7.50**

Mixer, Hamilton Beach, with Seville Yellow bowls, $200.00.
(Photo courtesy Gene and Cathy Florence)

Mug, green, Jeannette, #516, from $40 to **45.00**

Napkin holder, crystal, Paden City, Party Line, from $60 to .. **70.00**

Noodle cutter, metal blades, green wooden handle, 7" L, EX . **40.00**

Nut grinder, Hazel-Atlas, yellow top w/flower decal, glass jar.... **30.00**

Pie plate, Sapphire Blue, Anchor Hocking, 9" **10.00**

Pitcher, milk; cobalt, Hazel-Atlas, from $85 to **100.00**

Platter, fish; crystal, Fry, engraved, 17", from $70 to **75.00**

Potato masher, wire ware w/blue wooden handle **15.00**

Relish, double; Emerald-Glo, w/ holder, from $60 to.......... **70.00**

Rolling pin, milk glass, cold water hole in 1 end, handblown, 13½" **60.00**

Salt & pepper shakers, Chalaine Blue, pr from $125 to.... **135.00**

Scale, Way Rite, cream & green, weighs up to 25 lbs, 1930-40s **50.00**

Scoop, Androck, red Bakelite handle **50.00**

Sifter, Bromwell, apples on cream, 3-cup **25.00**

Sifter, metal w/Magpie embossed on front, 6x5¾" **25.00**

Sifter, mother in kitchen, NM, from $45.00 to $60.00.

Skillet, Ranger-Tec, McKee, from $12 to **15.00**

Spoon, slotted; Cutco #13, rosewood handle, 1960s **15.00**

Sugar shaker, fire-on red, metal top, Gemco....................... **27.00**

Teapot, multicolored enameled rings on clear, Glasbake, from $30 to **35.00**

Timer, Rubershaw Lux Minute Minder, yellow plastic case, 1½x4x3".............................**25.00**

Tumbler, ultramarine, Jeannette, 8-oz, from $50 to **55.00**

Kreiss

These novelties were imported from Japan during the 1950s. There are several lines. One is a totally off-the-wall group of caricatures called Psycho Ceramics. There's a Beatnik series, Bums, and Cave People (all of which are strange little creatures), as well as some that are very well done and tasteful. Others you find will be inset with colored 'jewels.' Many are marked either with an ink stamp or an in-mold trademark (some are dated).

Values are lower than we reported in the last edition; this is only one of many collectibles that has been affected by the internet.

Ashtray, Psycho Ceramics, $50.00.

Bank, blue guy w/black hair & Put Your Money Where My Mouth Is, 5½" **35.00**

Bank, pink guy w/If I'm Empty Headed It's Your Fault on tummy, 5½".......................**50.00**

Bank, Poodle, cold-paint decoration on pink & white poodle, 7½" **45.00**

Bell, choir girl w/'spagetti' decor on dress, 4½".........................**15.00**

Candleholder, boy & girl angels w/ Noel banner, 3x6", ea......**25.00**

Egg cups, Santa & Mrs Claus, 2¼", pr...................................**20.00**

Figurine, Beatnik in blue hat & coat w/black pants, I'm Ready..., 6" L.....................................**40.00**

Figurine, bunny, gray w/white chest & around eyes, pink nose, 3½".........................**15.00**

Figurine, drunk by barber pole, 5"...................................**35.00**

Figurine, horse running, brown w/ white legs, 6¼" **30.00**

Figurine, Little Champ, gold trim, 5", NM...........................**12.00**

Figurine, monkey seated, brown & white, 2¾".........................**22.00**

Figurine, Old Gray Mare, seated w/ red & white plaid hat, 5¼".**40.00**

Figurine, pink guy w/lg white 'ears,' 5⅛" **55.00**

Figurine, poodle, black, 'spaghetti' hair, necklace & tiara, 9"..**110.00**

Figurines, King of Clubs & Queen of Hearts, 7", 6½", pr **60.00**

Figurines, Oriental man (& woman) carrying jug, red w/gold, 10", pr.....................................**40.00**

Mug, pink guy w/toothy grin & You're the Greatest below mouth, 4½".......................**30.00**

Mug, Santa w/rhinestone eyes, 2½"...................................**10.00**

Ornament, elephant in Santa Claus suit, 3⅞"...........................**15.00**

Salt & pepper shakers, cuckoo clock shape, green & red, 2¾", pr.**20.00**

Salt & pepper shakers, horse, light blue w/black mane/tail/hooves, pr.....................................**20.00**

Salt & pepper shakers, monk, pepper sneezing, pr **20.00**

Salt & pepper shakers, penguin, gray w/white bellies, 4½", pr **20.00**

Salt & pepper shakers, rooster (& hen), black/white/red/yellow, 4", 3" **15.00**

Lava Lamps

These were totally cool in the '60s — no self-respecting love child was without one. Like so many good ideas, this one's been revived and is popular again today. In fact, more are being sold this time around than were sold 40 years ago. We've listed only vintage examples.

Aladdin-lamp style, red liquid, 1977 .... **155.00**

Cone style w/flared aluminum base, Aristocat #1122, yellow w/red lava **52.00**

Consort, sq wood base, Lava Manufacturing Corp, ca 1968 .... **68.00**

Enchantress Planter, holds flowers, rocks, etc on base, 1960s, 17" **58.00**

Lantern type, all copper, blueish-green liquid w/green lava, NM **100.00**

Rocket ship, blue liquid, Haggerty Enterprises #5424, MIB. **100.00**

Rocket ship, Mathmos, purple top & base, clear purple w/white lava **160.00**

Lefton China

Since 1940 the Lefton China Co. has been importing and producing ceramic giftware which may be found in shops throughout the world. Because of the quality of the workmanship and the beauty of these items, they are eagerly sought by collectors of today. Lefton pieces are usually marked with a fired-on trademark or a paper label. See Clubs and Newsletters for information concerning the National Society of Lefton Collectors.

Ashtray, Miss Priss, #1524, 6", from $50 to **60.00**

Bank, Devil, Root of All Evil, #4923, 8", from $45 to **65.00**

Bank, Miss Pimples, pig, #9635, 5½", from $35 to **40.00**

Bell, Christmas girl, #8250 ... **40.00**

Bowl, salad; Sweet Violets, #2870, 10", from $50 to **60.00**

Butter dish, Americana, #958, from $55 to **65.00**

Cake plate, Green Heritage, #719, from $38 to **42.00**

Candleholders, Americana, #949, pr from $75 to **80.00**

Candy box, White Christmas, #1342, from $20 to **30.00**

Cheese dish, bluebirds, #437, from $275 to **325.00**

Coffeepot, Yuletide Holly, #7802, from $110 to **135.00**

Cookie jar, Bossie Cow, #6594, from $125 to **150.00**

Cookie jar, Dutch Girl, #2697, from $35 to **40.00**

Cookie jar, Pear 'n Apple, #4335, from $35 to **45.00**

Creamer & sugar bowl, Floral Chintz, #8034, from $45 to **65.00**

Creamer & sugar bowl, Fruit Delight, #3132, from $12 to.............. **18.00**

Creamer & sugar bowl, Misty Rose, #5537, from $45 to 50.00

Cup & saucer, tea; floral design, #976, from $25 to 35.00

Egg cup, Miss Priss, #1510, from $55 to 65.00

Figurine, A Stitch at a Time, #5592, 7½", from $55 to 60.00

Figurine, angel w/animals, #544, 4¼", from $50 to 55.00

Figurine, bluegill, #1072, 4½", from $38 to 42.00

Figurine, child, #3544, 5¼", from $35 to 40.00

Figurine, colonial man (& woman), #568, 8", pr from $140 to. 160.00

Figurine, Marilyn Monroe, #411, 6½", from $175 to 225.00

Figurine, Mr (& Mrs) Claus dancing, #02139, 3½", pr from $20 to 30.00

Figurine, peacock, 6", $25.00.

Figurine, red squirrel, #4492, 8", from $85 to 95.00

Figurine, Valentine girl, #7173, 4", from $12 to 15.00

Gravy boat, Pink Clover, #2505, 8½", from $18 to 28.00

Jam jar, Festival, w/tray & spoon, #2617, from $35 to 45.00

Mug, beer; Paul Bunyan, #609, from $18 to 22.00

Mug, Robert E. Lee, #2365, 4¼", from $35.00 to $45.00. (Photo courtesy Loretta DeLozier)

Mug, Stonewall Jackson, #1112, from $40 to 45.00

Mug, White Holly, #6066, from $8 to 12.00

Music box, carolers, Silent Night, #454, 6¾", from $75 to 85.00

Nightlight, mouse w/mushroom, #7920, 6", from $22 to 28.00

Nightlight, Raggedy Andy, #7090, 6", from $35 to 45.00

Pitcher, milk; Miss Priss, #1504, from $125 to 155.00

Planter, angelfish, #3174, 7½", from $38 to 42.00

Planter, French lady, #50482, 8½", from $55 to 65.00

Planter, heart shape w/Cupid, #2995, 4", from $18 to 22.00

Planter, sprinkler can, Floral Bisque Bouquet, #6968, 6", from $22 to 28.00

Punch bowl, Green Holly, #1367, from $40 to 50.00

Salt & pepper shakers, Mr (& Mrs) Claus in rocking chairs, #8139, pr...................................... 25.00

Salt & pepper shakers, puppy w/ roses, #1726, 3½", pr from $18 to 22.00

Soap dish, Pink Clover, #2504, 7¼", from $8 to 12.00

Teapot, Cuddles, #1448, from $85 to 95.00

Teapot, honey bee, #1278, from $85
to **110.00**
Teapot, Yellow Tulip, #6735, from
$75 to **95.00**
Vase, Brown Heritage Fruit, #3117,
8¾", from $55 to **75.00**
Vase, bud; Rose Chintz, #679, 6¼",
from $28 to **32.00**
Vase, hand w/rose holding urn,
#929, 5", from $65 to **75.00**
Wall pocket, Miss Priss, #1509,
from $125 to **150.00**

L.G. Wright

The L.G. Wright Glass Company
began operations as a glass jobber
and then began buying molds from
other glassworks as they closed.
Wright reproduced many of these
molds as they originally were but
slightly altered others to better suit
his needs. He never actually made
his own glass, instead many companies pressed his wares, among
them Fenton, Imperial, Viking,
and Westmoreland. The company
flourished during the 1960s and
1970s, but closed its doors in the
mid-'90s. For more information we
recommend *Fenton Glass Made for
Other Companies Volumes I* and
II by Carrie and Gerald Domitz
(Collector Books).

Barber bottle, Stars & Stripes,
blue opalescent, bulbous, $175
to **200.00**
Basket, blue overlay w/hand-paint-
ed decor, metal frame, 13", $65
to **75.00**
Bell candy dish, Daisy & Button, amber,
bell is lid, from $75 to **95.00**

Bowl, blue overlay, ruffled &
crimped rim, 13", from $65
to **75.00**
Candleholder, Daisy & Button,
topaz opalescent, 4-toed, 5",
ea, from $50 to **55.00**
Canister, Daisy & Fern, cranberry,
from $300 to **350.00**
Canister, ruby overlay, straight
sided, footed, sm, from $75
to **85.00**
Canoe, Daisy & Button, amber,
11½", from $50 to **60.00**
Compote, Paneled Grape, ruby, footed, w/lid, from $75 to **85.00**
Compote, Priscilla, green, footed,
w/lid, from $75 to **85.00**
Covered dish, Atterbury Duck,
Colonial Blue, from $65 to .**75.00**
Covered dish, Bird & berry, purple
slag, 5", from $35 to **45.00**
Covered dish, cow on nest, amber,
5", from $30 to **45.00**
Covered dish, hen on nest, blue
satin, from $50 to **65.00**
Covered dish, hen on nest, topaz opal-
escent, 7", from $75 to **85.00**
Covered dish, lamb, milk glass, 5",
from $25 to **35.00**
Cruet, light blue satin overlay w/
hand-painted flowers, from
$125 to **150.00**
Cruet, Paneled Sprig, gold overlay,
paneled, from $85 to **100.00**
Fairy lamp, Embossed Rose, ruby,
from $85 to **100.00**
Fairy lamp, Eye Winker, blue, from
$55 to **65.00**
Fairy lamp, Hobnail, green, from
$75 to **85.00**
Lamp, miniature; Beaded Curtain,
light blue overlay, from $250
to **275.00**

Lamp, miniature; Cranberry Spiral half shade, oval base, from $150 to **175.00**

Plate, Thistle, crystal, 7½", from $20 to **25.00**

Liberty Blue

'Take home a piece of American history!,' stated an ad from the 1970s for this dinnerware made in Staffordshire, England. Blue and white depictions of George Washington at Valley Forge, Paul Revere, Independence Hall — 14 historic scenes in all — were offered on different pieces. The ad goes on to describe this 'unique...truly unusual...museum-quality...future family heirloom.'

For every five dollars spent on groceries you could purchase a basic piece (dinner plate, bread and butter plate, cup, saucer, or dessert dish) for 59 cents on alternate weeks of the promotion. During the promotion, completer pieces could also be purchased. The soup tureen was the most expensive item, originally selling for $24.99. Nineteen completer pieces in all were offered along with a five-year open stock guarantee. For more information we recommend Jo Cunningham's book, *The Best of Collectible Dinnerware.*

Bowl, cereal; 6½" **10.00**

Bowl, flat soup; 8¾", from $18 to **20.00**

Bowl, fruit; 5" **2.50**

Bowl, vegetable; oval, from $30 to.................................. **35.00**

Bowl, vegetable; round **30.00**

Butter dish, ¼-lb **45.00**

Casserole, w/lid, from $115 to. **135.00**

Coaster (4 in set, ea w/different scene), ea **8.50**

Creamer, from $15 to **18.00**

Creamer & sugar bowl, w/lid, original box **60.00**

Cup & saucer...................... **3.50**

Gravy boat............................. **40.00**

Gravy boat liner **18.00**

Mug **9.50**

Pitcher, 7½", from $85.00 to $95.00.

Plate, bread & butter, 6" **2.00**

Plate, dinner; 10", from $5 to .. **7.00**

Plate, luncheon; scarce, 8¾" .. **20.00**

Plate, 7" **9.00**

Platter, 12", from $35 to **45.00**

Salt & pepper shakers, pr **35.00**

Soup tureen, w/lid **245.00**

Sugar bowl, w/lid **24.00**

Teapot, w/lid, from $85 to **95.00**

License Plates

Early porcelain license plates are treasured by collectors and often sell for more than $500.00 per pair when found in excellent condition. The best examples are first-year plates from each state, but some of the more modern plates with special graphics are collectible too. Prices given below are for plates in good or better condition.

Alaska, 1962 .... 16.50
Arizona, 1948 .... 44.00
Arkansas, 1941 .... 24.00
California, 1959 .... 17.00
Connecticut, 1990 .... 16.50
Delaware, 1973 .... 9.50
Florida, New Panther 29.00
Georgia, 1990, Olympic 24.00
Hawaii, 1969 .... 12.50
Idaho, 1935 .... 24.00
Illinois, 1948, soybean 20.50
Indiana, 1948 .... 13.50
Iowa, 1941 .... 12.50
Kansas, 1954 .... 10.50
Kentucky, 1961 .... 14.50
Louisiana, 1986 .... 14.50
Maine, 1941 .... 29.00
Maryland, 1941 .... 29.00
Michigan, 1954 .... 16.50
Minnesota, 1954 .... 12.50
Mississippi, 1983 .... 7.50
Montana, 1977-86 .... 7.50
Nebraska, 1941 .... 39.00
Nevada, 1979 .... 9.50
New Hampshire, 1941 .... 19.50

New Jersey, 1913, VG, $10.00;
Pennsylvania Tractor, 1915, VG,
$120.00.

New Jersey, 1956 .... 11.50
New Mexico, 1941 .... 44.00
New York, 1961, tab 7.00
North Carolina, 1975, First in
Freedom 14.50

North Dakota, 1987, teddy 13.50
Oklahoma, 1976, Bicentennial. 14.50
Pennsylvania, 1948 .... 12.50
Rhode Island, 1947 .... 14.50
South Carolina, 1968 .... 9.50
Texas, 1972 .... 7.50
Utah, 1960 .... 16.50
Vermont, 1941 .... 9.50
Washington, 1933 .... 30.00
Wisconsin, 1973-79 .... 7.00
Wyoming, 1958 .... 12.50

Little Red Riding Hood

This line of novelties and kitchenware has always commanded good prices on the collectibles market. In fact, it became valuable enough to make it attractive to counterfeiters, and now you'll see reproductions everywhere. They're easy to spot, though, watch for one-color eyes. Though there are other differences, you should be able to identify the imposters armed with this information alone.

Little Red Riding Hood was produced from 1943 to 1957. The Regal China Company was by far the major manufacturer of this line, though a rather insignificant number of items were made by the Hull Pottery of Crooksville, Ohio, who sent their whiteware to the Royal China and Novelty Company (a division of Regal China) of Chicago, Illinois, to be decorated. For further information we recommend *The Ultimate Collector's Encyclopedia of Cookie Jars* by Joyce and Fred Roerig; and *The Collector's Encyclopedia of Hull Pottery* and *The Collector's*

Ultimate Encyclopedia of Hull Pottery, both by Brenda Roberts. All these books are published by Collector Books.

Bank, standing, 7", from $900 to **1,350.00**
Butter dish, 5½", from $350 to **400.00**
Canister, Cereal, 10" **1,375.00**
Canister, Flour or Sugar, 10", ea from $600 to **700.00**
Casserole, red w/embossed wolf, Grandma, etc, 11¾", from $1,800 to **2,500.00**
Cookie jar, closed basket, from $450 to **650.00**
Cookie jar, full skirt, from $750 to **850.00**
Cracker jar, unmarked, from $600 to **750.00**
Creamer, side pour, from $150 to **225.00**
Creamer, top pour, no tab handle, from $400 to **425.00**
Creamer, top pour, tab handle, from $350 to **375.00**
Dresser jar, 8¾", from $450 to **575.00**
Lamp, from $2,000 to **2,650.00**

Match holder, wall hanging, from $400.00 to $650.00.

Mustard jar, w/spoon, 5¼", from $375 to **460.00**
Pitcher, 7", from $450 to **675.00**

Pitcher, 8", from $550 to **850.00**
Planter, wall-mount, 9", from $400 to **500.00**
Salt & pepper shakers, Pat design 135889, med size, pr (+), from $800 to **900.00**
Salt & pepper shakers, 5½", pr from from $185 to **225.00**
Spice jar, sq base, from $650 to. **750.00**
String holder, from $1,800 to. **25.00**
Sugar bowl, crawling, no lid, from $300 to **450.00**
Sugar bowl, w/lid, from $350 to.. **425.00**
Sugar bowl lid, minimum value. **175.00**
Wolf jar, yellow base, from $750 to................................. **850.00**

Lu-Ray Pastels

Introduced in 1938 by Taylor, Smith, and Taylor of East Liverpool, Ohio, Lu-Ray Pastels is today a very sought-after line of collectible American dinnerware. It was first made in these solid colors: Windsor Blue, Surf Green, Persian Cream, and Sharon Pink. Chatham Gray was introduced in 1948 and is today priced higher than the other colors.

Bowl, cream soup **70.00**
Bowl, fruit, 5" **6.00**
Bowl, lug soup; tab handles .. **24.00**
Bowl, mixing; 5½", 7", or 8¾", ea. **125.00**
Bowl, mixing; 10¼" **150.00**
Bowl, salad; colors other than yellow **65.00**
Bowl, salad; yellow **55.00**
Bud vase **400.00**
Casserole **140.00**
Chocolate cup, after dinner; straight sides **80.00**

Chocolate pot, after dinner; straight sides 400.00
Coaster/nut dish 65.00
Coffeepot, after dinner 200.00
Creamer 10.00
Egg cup, double 30.00
Epergne 125.00
Jug, footed 150.00
Muffin cover w/8" underplate. 165.00
Nappy, vegetable; round, 8½". 25.00
Pickle tray 28.00
Pitcher, bulbous w/flat bottom, colors other than yellow.... 125.00
Pitcher, bulbous w/flat bottom, yellow 95.00
Plate, cake 70.00
Plate, Chatham Gray, rare color, 7" 16.00
Plate, grill; 3-part 35.00
Plate, 6" 3.00
Plate, 7" 12.00
Plate, 8" 25.00
Plate, 9" 10.00
Plate, 10" 25.00
Platter, 11½" 20.00
Platter, 13" 24.00

Relish dish, four-part, $125.00.

Salt & pepper shakers, pr 18.00
Sauceboat 28.00
Saucer 2.00
Saucer, coffee/chocolate 30.00
Sugar bowl, after dinner; w/lid..40.00
Sugar bowl, w/lid 15.00
Teacup 8.00

Teapot, curved spout 125.00
Teapot, flat spout 160.00
Tumbler, juice 50.00
Tumbler, water 80.00

Lunch Boxes

In the early years of this century, tobacco companies often packaged their products in tins that could later be used for lunch boxes. By the 1930s oval lunch boxes designed to appeal to school children were being produced. The rectangular shape that is now popular was preferred in the 1950s. Character lunch boxes decorated with the faces of TV personalities, super heroes, Disney, and cartoon characters are especially sought after by collectors today. The ranges in our listings represent values for examples in excellent to near-mint condition. Metal boxes are priced without their vacuum bottle; those are listed separately. For vinyl and plastic boxes, however, values are given for the box complete with the bottle. Refer to *Pictorial Price Guide to Vinyl and Plastic Lunch Boxes and Thermoses* and *Pictorial Price Guide to Metal Lunch Boxes and Thermoses* by Larry Aikens (L-W Book Sales) for more information. For an expanded listing, see *Schroeder's Collectible Toys, Antique to Modern* (Collector Books).

A-Team, metal, 1980s, from $25 to 40.00
Addams Family, metal, 1970s, from $75 to 125.00

Aladdin Cable Car, steel, 1962, EX, $120.00. (Photo courtesy Morphy Auctions)

America on Parade, metal, 1970s, from $25 to **50.00**

Annie, metal, 1980s, from $30 to **40.00**

Apple's Way, metal, 1970s, from $50 to **75.00**

Astronauts, metal, dome, 1960, from $85 to **150.00**

Atom Ant, metal bottle, 1960s, from $35 to **65.00**

Barbie Lunch Kit, plastic, 1960s, from $300 to **400.00**

Barbie Lunch Kit, vinyl, 1960s, from $300 to **400.00**

Battle of the Planets, plastic bottle, 1970s, from $15 to **20.00**

Beatles, metal bottle, 1960s, from $125 to **225.00**

Bees Gees, plastic bottle, 1970s, from $15 to **20.00**

Benji, plastic, 1970s, from $20 to **30.00**

Betsy Clark, metal, 1970s, from $35 to **55.00**

Beverly Hillbillies, metal, 1960s, from $100 to **150.00**

Black Hole, metal, 1970s, from $30 to **60.00**

Bonanza, metal bottle, 1960s, 3 versions, ea from $50 to . **75.00**

Brave Eagle, metal, 1950s, from $150 to **200.00**

Buck Rogers, metal, 1970s, from $25 to **50.00**

Bullwinkle & Rocky, metal bottle, 1960s, from $175 to **275.00**

Cabbage Patch Kids, metal, 1980s, from $15 to **30.00**

Campbell Kids, metal bottle, 1970s, from $30 to **60.00**

Casey Jones, metal bottle, 1960s, from $100 to **150.00**

Casper the Friendly Ghost, vinyl, 1960s, from $400 to **500.00**

Cracker Jack, metal, 1970s, from $30 to **60.00**

Crest Toothpaste, plastic, tubular, 1980s, from $50 to **75.00**

Daniel Boone, Aladdin, metal, 1960s, from $125 to **175.00**

Davy Crockett, metal, green rim, 1955, from $150 to **200.00**

Dick Tracy, metal bottle, 1960s, from $25 to **50.00**

Disney on Parade, metal, 1970s, from $30 to **60.00**

Disney World, metal, 1970s, 50th Anniversary, from $30 to **50.00**

Donny & Marie, vinyl, 1970s, from $80 to **120.00**

Double-Deckers, metal, 1970s, from $50 to **75.00**

Dr Suess, plastic, 1990s, from $20 to **25.00**

Evel Knievel, metal, 1970s, from $50 to **100.00**

Family Affair, metal, 1960s, from $45 to **90.00**

Flinstones, metal, 1970s, from $100 .... **150.00**

Flipper, metal bottle, 1960s, from $20 to **40.00**

Grizzly Adams, metal, dome, 1970s, from $50 to **75.00**

Gunsmoke, metal, 1962, from $175 to **225.00**

Happy Days, metal, 1970s, 2 versions, ea from $50 to **75.00**

Happy Days, plastic, dome, Canada, 1970s, from $30 to **50.00**

Highway Signs, metal, 1960s or 1970s, 2 versions, ea from $30 to **75.00**

Hopalong Cassidy, metal bottle, 1954, from $85 to **150.00**

Jabberjaw, plastic, 1970s, from $30 to **40.00**

Jungle Book, metal, 1960s, from $45 to **90.00**

Keebler Cookies, plastic, 1980s, from $30 to **50.00**

Kung Fu, metal, 1970s, from $40 to **80.00**

Laugh-In, metal, 1971, from $75 to **150.00**

Little Old Schoolhouse, vinyl, 1970s, from $50 to **75.00**

Little Orphan Annie, plastic, dome, 1970s, from $35 to **45.00**

Lost in Space, metal, 1967, EX/NM, from $350.00 to $450.00; bottle, EX/NM, from $30.00 to $60.00.

Mardi Gras, vinyl, 1970s, from $50 to **110.00**

Marvel Super Heroes, metal, 1970s, from $25 to **50.00**

Mary Poppins, vinyl, 1970s, from $75 to **100.00**

Miss America, metal, 1970s, from $50 to **100.00**

Muppet Babies, plastic, 1980s, from $15 to **25.00**

Peanuts, metal, 1976, from $20 to **35.00**

Pee Wee Herman, plastic, 1980s, from $20 to **30.00**

Pepsi-Cola, vinyl, yellow, 1980s, from $50 to **75.00**

Popeye, metal, 1964, from $100 to. **150.00**

Porky Pig's Lunch Box, steel, 1959, EX, $120.00. (Photo courtesy Morphy Auctions)

Ringling Bros & Barnum & Bailey Circus, vinyl, 1970s, from $125 to **175.00**

Ronald McDonald, metal, 1980s, from $15 to **30.00**

Six Million Dollar Man, metal, 1970s, any from $35 to ... **55.00**

Snoopy at Mailbox, vinyl, red, 1969, from $65 to **85.00**

Soupy Sales, vinyl, 1960s, from $300 to **375.00**

Star Wars Ewoks, plastic, 1980s, from $20 to **30.00**

Steve Canyon, metal, 1959, from $150 to **250.00**

Sunnie Miss, plastic, 1970s, from $50 to **75.00**

Tarzan, metal, 1960s, from $100
to **150.00**

Underdog, metal bottle, 1970s,
from $150 to **250.00**

Winnie the Pooh, metal, 1970s,
from $150 to **200.00**

World of Barbie, vinyl, 1971, EX,
from $50 to **75.00**

Yogi Bear & Friends, metal, 1960s,
from $85 to **135.00**

Young Astronauts, plastic, 1980s,
from $20 to **30.00**

240 Robert, plasic bottle, 1970s,
from $350 to **450.00**

Magazines

Some of the most collectible
magazines are *Life* (because of the
celebrities and important events they
feature on their covers), *Saturday
Evening Post* and *Ladies' Home
Journal* (especially those featuring
the work of famous illustrators such
as Parrish, Rockwell, and Wyeth),
and *National Geographics* (with particularly newsworthy features). As
is true with any type of ephemera,
condition and value are closely related. Unless they're in fine condition
(clean, no missing or clipped pages,
and very little other damage), they're
worth very little; and cover interest
and content are far more important than age. For more information
we recommend *Old Magazines* by
Richard E. Clear (Collector Books).

American Heritage, 1989, February,
front cover, NM **6.00**

Atlantic Monthly, 1973, August,
black & white cover & article,
NM **12.00**

Automobile Digest, 1942-50,
EX **15.00**

Better Living, 1955, July, advertising, NM **11.00**

Brides Magazine, 1970 to present,
EX **10.00**

Cars, 1964, October, EX.........**22.00**

Cinema, Italy, 1955, November,
Marilyn Monroe on cover,
EX **180.00**

Collier's, 1953, June 24, NM.**21.00**

Construction Methods & Equipment, 1961, December, EX.**40.00**

Cosmopolitan, 1936, April, EX.**26.00**

Country Life, 1922, August,
VG..............................**20.00**

Cue, 1953, June 27, front cover &
article, NM **20.00**

Diver Below, 1961, November,
EX **110.00**

Dog Fancy, 1993, November, EX.**5.00**

Down Beat, 1934-59, EX........**20.00**

Ebony, 1948, December, EX...**26.00**

Esquire, 1960s-70s, EX..........**25.00**

Exhibitor, 1952, July 9, front cover,
NM **60.00**

Fabulous Las Vegas, 1955, July,
EX **30.00**

Field & Stream, 1921, October,
EX **45.00**

Field & Stream, 1949, February,
features Roy Rogers & Dale
Evans, EX **25.00**

Fortune, 1933, February, NM.**50.00**

Fotoparade, 1949, December, front
cover & article, NM **125.00**

Frontier Stories, 1940-50s, EX,
ea **20.00**

Glamour, 1972, July, how-to-issue,
EX **18.00**

GQ, 1965, December, Barbara
Striesand cover, Woody Allen
article, EX **105.00**

Harley-Davidson Enthusiast, 1944, May, VG 38.00

Harper's Bazaar, 1938, September, EX 20.00

Harper's Bazaar, 1970, September, EX 29.00

Hollywood Detective, 1943-50, EX, ea 40.00

Hot Rod, 1948, May, EX 225.00

Hunting & Fishing, 1932, November, VG 23.00

Jem, 1959, June, EX 25.00

Judge, 1934, January, VG 30.00

Ladies' Home Journal, 1930-39, EX, ea 15.00

Life, 1961, January 13, Clark Gable cover, EX, from $10.00 to $15.00.

Life, 1966, March 11, Batman cover, EX 25.00

Life, 1969, September, Special Edition, Woodstock, NM . 15.00

Master Detective, 1940-50, NM, ea 10.00

Mickey Mouse Magazine, 1937, August, EX 50.00

Modern Bride, 1954, spring, EX 25.00

Morris Owner, 1935, July, EX 46.00

Motion Picture, 1955, March, Grace Kelly cover, EX............... 20.00

Motorcross Action, 1975, September, VG+ 20.00

Movie Mirror, 1943, EX 20.00

Movieland, 1953, January, Marilyn Monroe cover 155.00

National Geographic, 1939-49, EX, from $3 to 6.00

National Geographic, 1950 to present, from $1 to 2.00

Newsweek, 1975, October, Bruce Springsteen, EX 5.00

Outdoor Life, 1933, January . 28.00

Pageant, 1946, June, Marilyn Monroe, EX 115.00

Petersen's Surfing, 1964, March/ April/May, VG 34.00

Photoplay, 1935, February, Myrna Loy cover, EX 40.00

Playboy, 1954, April, EX 350.00

Playboy, 1954, February, EX+ ..450.00

Playboy, 1954, March, w/centerfold, EX 400.00

Playboy, 1954, October, NM .. 25.00

Playboy, 1955, January, Betty Paige issue, EX 250.00

Playboy, 1957, April, NM 30.00

Playboy, 1958, January, EX... 20.00

Playboy, 1960, August, Sophia Loren pictorial, NM 35.00

Playboy, 1977, February, EX ... 9.00

Popular Mechanics, 1940-59, EX, ea 3.00

Quick, 1952, October, Lucille Ball & Desi Arnaz cover, NM . 15.00

Race & Rally, 1976, December, Dave Thompson cover 42.00

Radio Mirror, 1948, EX............ 3.00

Rolling Stone, 1969, January, EX 45.00

Rolling Stone, 1971, featuring Jim Morrison eulogy, EX 70.00

Salute, 1946, August, NM ... 175.00

Saturday Evening Post, 1938, EX 15.00

Saturday Evening Post, 1952, July 12, picture, NM 10.00

Saturday Evening Post, 1956, May, article & pictures, NM.... 12.00

Saturday Evening Post, 1960 to present, EX, ea 2.00
Screen Guide, 1936, Ginger Rogers, EX 20.00
Screen Romances, 1936, October, EX 30.00
See, 1952, July, NM 20.00
See, 1954, November, NM 18.00
Seventeen, 1950, NM 10.00
Seventeen, 1959, April, EX 28.00
Seventeen, 1960, EX 5.00
Skin Diver, 1953, October, M. 200.00
SnowGoer, 1967, January, EX.. 108.00
Song of the Month, 1954, July, NM 10.00
Sports Album, 1948, Joe DiMaggio cover, EX 125.00

Sports Illustrated, Muhammad Ali, Sportsman of the Year, EX, $10.00.

Sports Illustrated, 1965, EX ... 7.00
Stocking Parade, 1942, NM ... 30.00
Surfer Magazine, 1961, VG ... 75.00
Throttle, 1941, May, EX 10.00
Time, 1937, December, Walt Disney w/7 Dwarfs, EX 18.00
Time, 1939, February, Picasso, EX 12.00
Time, 1947, September, CS Lewis, EX 6.00
Time, 1953, November, NM 7.00
Time, 1956, May, NM 10.00
Time, 1973, June, Secretariat, EX 8.00
Today, 1961, February, NM ... 11.00
Travel, 1958, EX 9.00

TV Guide, December 10 – 16, 1955, Lucille Ball, EX, from $100.00 to $125.00.

US, 1946, May, NM 125.00
USA 1, 1962, July, NM 4.00
Vanity Fair, 1960, March, VG. 18.00
Variety, 1940-49, EX, ea 5.00
Vibe, 2001, November, Aaliyah tribute, EX 2.00
Vim & Vigor, 1986, Fall, John Denver, EX 7.00
Vogue, 1934, May, Summer Travel, NM 45.00
Vogue, 1965, September, EX . 65.00
Vogue, 1966, August, Patti Boyd cover, EX 106.00
Vogue, 1967, July, Twiggy, EX. 10.00
Western Flying, 1938, August, EX 25.00
Why, 1953, June, NM 35.00
Winchester Life, 1949, November, cover by Lynn Bogue Hunt, EX 110.00
Woman's Home Companion, 1947, NM 7.00
World of Barbie, 1964, 1st issue, EX 35.00
You, 1940, Fall, VG 25.00
Young Physique, 1963, May, EX. 100.00
Your Money Maker, 1951, September, NM 196.00
Zoom, 1989, August, NM 10.00

Marbles

Because there are so many kinds of marbles that interest

today's collectors, we suggest you study a book that covers each type. Everett Grist (see Directory, Tennessee) has written several. In addition to his earlier work, *Antique and Collectible Marbles*, he has also written *Machine-Made and Contemporary Marbles*. His latest title is *Everett Grist's Big Book of Marbles*, which includes both antique and modern varieties. All are published by Collector Books.

Remember that condition is extremely important. Naturally, chips occurred; and though some may be ground down and polished, the values of badly chipped and repolished marbles are low. In our listings, values are for marbles in the standard small size and in excellent to near-mint condition unless noted otherwise. Watch for reproductions of the comic character marbles. Repros have the design printed on a large area of plain white glass with color swirled through the back and sides. While common sulfides may run as low as $100.00, those with a more unusual subject or made of colored glass are considerably higher, sometimes as much as $1,000.00 or more. See Clubs and Newsletters for information concerning the Marble Collectors' Society of America.

Agate, contemporary, carnelian, 1¾" **20.00**
Akro Agate, carnelian oxblood..**175.00**
Akro Agate, translucent oxblood swirl, from $75 to **250.00**
Akro Agate, 3-colored corkscrew. **25.00**

China, decorated, glazed, apple or rose, 1¾" **750.00**
China, design hand-painted over glaze prior to 2nd firing. **100.00**
Christensen Agate, clear Cobra, NM **145.00**
Christensen Agate, green slag . **10.00**
Christensen Agate, orange & yellow swirl **25.00**
Christensen Agate, royal blue slag **10.00**
Clambroth, opaque, blue & white **200.00**
Clear w/goldstone flakes, white & yellow spiral bands **50.00**
Comic, Andy Gump, M **85.00**
Comic, Betty Boop, M **275.00**
Comic, Little Orphan Annie, M..**100.00**
Indian swirl, black glass w/colored swirls in earth tones **150.00**
Jackson, 3-color swirl, M **25.00**
Limeade corkscrew **30.00**
Lutz type, blue opaque, gold swirl w/white borders & thin swirls **350.00**
Lutz type, clear w/gold-color swirls, blue & white borders **125.00**
Marble King, Cub Scout blue & yellow **6.00**
Marble King, multicolor Rainbow **4.00**
Marble King, watermelon.... **400.00**

Mesh bags of marbles, commonly made after WWII, $40.00 each.

Mica, blue **30.00**

Onionskin, w/mica **110.00**
Opaque swirl Lutz-type, blue, yellow & green **325.00**
Peltier Glass, slag **15.00**
Peltier Glass, 3-color Rainbow w/ rose & yellow base **200.00**
Peppermint swirl, red, white & blue **100.00**
Sulfide, boar, 1⅞" **165.00**
Sulfide, eagle, 1¾" **200.00**
Sulfide, gnome, 1½" **615.00**
Sulfide, owl w/spread wings, detailed feathers, 1¾" ... **350.00**

Sulfide, squirrel standing, 1¾".**170.00**
Transitional, Leighton, 1", M.**1,000.00**
Transparent swirl, double-swirl ribbon core, multicolor..**200.00**
Transparent swirl, yellow latticino core, red & white bands.**325.00**
Transparent swirl w/red core, blue & white lines, yellow threads..........................**60.00**
Vitro Agate, prominent V, ea from $2 to **10.00**
Vitro Agate, red, white & blue swirls, faded-looking colors .... **.50**

Mar-Crest Stoneware

This is a line of old-fashioned, ovenproof stoneware made by The Western Stoneware Company of Monmouth, Illinois. It was sold through Marshall Burns, a Division of Technicolor, a distributor from Chicago. The most collectible of these wares is a pattern called Daisy and Dot (aka Pennsylvania Dutch) in the Warm Colorado Brown glaze. Pieces from this line are listed below.

Bean pot, shouldered, w/handles, lg, from $20 to **30.00**
Bowl, cereal; from $5 to **7.00**
Bowl, lug soup; 2¼x4¾"+handle. **8.00**
Bowl, 10" **17.50**
Carafe, from $20 to **25.00**
Casserole, w/lid, 9", +warming stand, from $40 to **45.00**
Cookie jar, 7½x6", from $22 to.**30.00**
Creamer & sugar bowl, w/lid, from $25 to **38.00**
Mug, 3½" **5.00**

Plate, 3-compartment, 11" **35.00**
Plate, 9½", from $7 to **12.00**
Salt & pepper shakers, pr from $15 to **20.00**

Matchbox Cars

Introduced in 1953, the Matchbox Miniatures series has always been the mainstay of the company. There were 75 models in all but with enough variations to make collecting them a real challenge. Larger, more detailed models were introduced in 1957. This series, called Major Pack, was replaced a few years later by a similar line called King Size. To compete with Hot Wheels, Matchbox converted most models over to a line called SuperFast that sported thinner, low-friction axles and wheels. (These are much more readily available from the original 'regular wheels,' the last of which was made in 1959.) At about the same time, the King Size series became known as Speed Kings; in 1977 the line was reintroduced under the name Super Kings.

Another line that's become very popular is their Models of Yesteryear. These are slightly larger replicas of antique and vintage vehicles. Values of $20.00 to $60.00 for mint-in-box examples are average, though a few sell for even more.

Sky Busters, introduced in 1973, are small-scale aircraft measuring an average of 3½" in length. Models currently being produced sell for about $4.00 each.

To learn more, we recommend *Matchbox Toys, 1947 to 2003; The Other Matchbox Toys, 1947 to 2004;* and *Toy Car Collector's Guide,* all by Dana Johnson. There is also a series of books by Charlie Mack (there are three): *Lesney's Matchbox Toys Regular Wheels, SuperFast Years,* and *Universal Years.* To determine values of examples in conditions other than given in our listings, based on MIB or MOC prices, deduct a minimum of 10% if the original container is missing, 30% if the condition is excellent, and as much as 70% for a toy graded only very good.

King Size, Speed Kings, and Super Kings

Allis-Chalmers Earth Scraper, #K-006, 1961, MIP, from $45 to **60.00**

Articulated Horse Box, #K-018, 1967, complete, NM+, from $45 to **60.00**

Baracuda Custom Racer, #K-051, 1973, MIP, from $20 to ...**25.00**

Cargo Hauler, #K-033, 1978, MIP, from $25 to **35.00**

Dodge Charger, #K-022, 1969, MIP, from $24 to **32.00**

Fire Tender, #K-009, 1973, MIP, from $12 to **16.00**

Javelin Drag Racing Set, #K-057, 1975, MIP, from $30 to ...**40.00**

Lamborghini Miura, #K-24, 1969, bronze, mag wheels, NM+, from $20 to **30.00**

Matra Rancho, #K-090, 1982, MIP, from $18 to **24.00**

Mercury Cougar, #K-021, 1968, red interior, MIP, from $40 to.**55.00**

Road Construction Set, #K-137, 1986, MIP, from $35 to ...**50.00**

Scammel Tipper Truck, #K-19, 1967, MIP, from $40 to ...**55.00**

Shovel Nose Custom Car, #K-32, 1972, MIP, from $20 to ...**30.00**

Weather Hydraulic Shovel, #K-001, 1960, MIP, from $70 to ...**90.00**

Models of Yesteryear

Atkinson Blue Circle Portland Cement Steam Wagon, #Y-1, yellow, MIP.....................**20.00**

Busch Steam Fire Engine (1905), #Y-43, 1991, MIP, from $65 to **80.00**

Crossly Beer Lorry, #Y-26, 1984, any color/decal, MIP, ea from $20 to **30.00**

Ford Model A Woody Wagon, #Y-21, 1981, yellow/brown, MIP, from $24 to **32.00**

Ford Model T Truck, #Y-12, 1979, cream w/black roof, Coca-Cola, MIP **85.00**

Grand Prix Mercedes (1908), #Y-10, 1958, cream, MIP, from $125 to **175.00**

Lagonda Drophead Coupe, #Y-11, 1973, plum w/black interior, from $28 to **34.00**

Matchbox Collectibles Fire Engine Collection, YFE-03, introduced in 1994, MIP, from $25.00 to $30.00. (Photo courtesy Dana Johnson)

Mercedes Benz SS Coupe, #Y-16, 1972, metallic gray w/red chassis, MIP **85.00**

Peugeot, #Y-5, 1969, yellow w/clear windows, black roof, MIP, from $80 to **100.00**

Riley MPH, #Y-3, 1974, metallic red w/red 12-spoke wheels, from $40 to **50.00**

Rolls Royce Silver Ghost, #Y-15, 1960, silver-gray w/gray tires, MIP **75.00**

Sentinel Steam Wagon, #Y-4, 1956, unpainted metal wheels, MIP, from $45 to **60.00**

Stutz Bearcat, #Y-14, 1974, cream & red w/red wheels, MIP, from $35 to **50.00**

1911 Renault 2-seater, #Y-002, 1963, silver-plated, MIP, from $70 to **85.00**

Skybusters

Alpha Jet, #SB-011, 1973, blue & red, MIP, from $10 to **15.00**

Army Helicopter, #SB-020, 1977, olive, MIP, from $10 to ... **15.00**

Cessna 210, #SB-014, 1973, orange-yellow & white, MIP, from $9 to **12.00**

Corsair A7D, #SB-002, 1973, khaki & white w/camouflage, MIP, from $8 to **10.00**

Heinz 57 SST Super Sonic Transport, #SB-023, 1979, white, MIP, from $24 to .. **32.00**

Lightning, #SB-0212, 1977, olive or silver-gray, MIP, ea from $8 to **12.00**

MiL M24 Hind-D Chopper, #SB-035, 1990, any, MIP, ea from $6 to **8.00**

Military Helicopter, avocado green and bright purple, 2003, MIP, from $4.00 to $5.00. (Photo courtesy Dana Johnson)

Mirage F1, #SB-004, 1973, red w/ bull's-eye on wings, MIP, from $12 to **16.00**

Piper Comanche, #SB-19, 1977, beige & blue, Macau cast, MIP, from $7 to **10.00**

Pitts Special Biplane, #SB-012, 1980, any, MIP, from $16 to **20.00**

Spitfire, #SB-008, 1973, dark brown & gold, MIP, from $18 to **24.00**

Starfighter F104, #SB-005, 1973, red & white w/maple leaf labels, MIP **10.50**

Tornado, #SB-022, 1978, light gray & white, MIP, from $9 to. **12.00**

USAF Lockheed SR-71 Blackbird, #SB-29, 1989, black, MIP, from $4 to **6.00**

007 Rescue Helicopter, #SB-025, 1979, red & white, MIP, from $10 to **15.00**

1 – 75 Series

AMC Javelin AMX, #9, 1971, red w/black hood scoop, MIP, from $40 to **50.00**

Aston Martin DB2 Saloon, #53, 1958, light green, plastic wheels, MIP **75.00**

Aston Martin Racer, #19, 1961, gray or white driver, MIP, from $60 to **80.00**

Atlantic Trailer, #16, 1957, tan w/ tan towbar, plastic wheels, MIP **75.00**

Baja Dune Buggy, #13, 1971, green w/police shields decal, MIP, from $35 to **50.00**

Bedford 'Matchbox Removal' Van, #17, 1956, maroon body, MIP, from $425 to **475.00**

Berkley Cavalier Travel Trailer, #23, 1956, lime green, MIP, from $100 to **125.00**

Caterpillar Bulldozer, #18, 1961, silver plastic rollers, MIP, from $175 to **225.00**

Caterpillar Tractor #8, 1955, orange w/orange driver, no blade, MIP **200.00**

Commer Pickup, #50, 1958, tan w/metal or plastic wheels, MIP **87.00**

Corvette Convertible, #14, 1987, purple w/orange interior, 3", MIP **3.00**

DAF Girder Truck, #58, 1970, cream, SuperFast Wheels, MIP, from $75 to **90.00**

DAF Tipper Truck, #47, 1970, SuperFast Wheels, silver & yellow, M **40.00**

Datson 280ZX, #24, 1983, white w/ red & blue Turbo 33 tampo, MIP, from $6 to **8.00**

Dennis Fire Escape, #9, 1955, no front bumper, no number cast, MIP **55.00**

Dennis Refuse Truck, #15, 1963, blue w/gray container, MIP, from $45 to **60.00**

Dodge BP Wreck Truck, #13, 1970, SuperFast Wheels, MIP, from $65 to **85.00**

Dodge Crane Truck, #63, 1968, yellow, M, from $12 to **16.00**

Dumper, #2, 1953, unpainted metal wheels, MIP, from $65 to **90.00**

Eight-Wheel Tipper Truck, #51, 1969, Pointer decal, MIP, from $30 to **50.00**

Ergomatic Horse Box (AEC), #17, 1970, SuperFast Wheels, MIP, from $25 to **40.00**

Ferrari F1 Racer, #73, 1962, w/ driver, MIP, from $20 to . **30.00**

Ferret Scout Car, #61, 1959, olive green w/black plastic wheels, MIP 20.00

Fiat 1500 w/Luggage on Roof, #56, 1965, red, MIP, from $85 to 100.00

Flying Bug, #11, 1972, MIP, from $15 to 20.00

Foden Concrete Truck, #21, 1970, SuperFast Wheels, MIP, from $25 to 40.00

Ford Esso Wreck Truck, #71, 1968, amber windows, MIP, from $200 to 300.00

Ford Galaxie Police Car, #55, 1966, red dome light, MIP, from $16 to 24.00

Ford Mustang Wildcat Dragster, #8, 1970, MIP, from $25 to 40.00

Ford T-Bird, #75, 1960, cream & pink w/black plastic wheels, MIP 275.00

Ford Thames Trader Wreck Truck, #13, 1961, gray wheels, from $115 to 140.00

Ford Tractor, #39, 1967, yellow & blue, MIP, from $15 to 20.00

GMC Refrigerator Truck, #44, 1967, MIP, from $12 to 16.00

Gruesome Twosome, #4, 1971, gold w/amber windows, MIP, from $12 to 16.00

Honda ATC, #23, 1985, red, MIP, from $10 to 12.00

Jaguar XKE, #32, 1961, red w/gray plastic wheels, clear windows, MIP 110.00

Lincoln Continental, #31, 1970, SuperFast Wheels, green-gold, MIP 57.00

Lotus Racing Car, #19, 1970, SuperFast Wheels, MIP, from $45 to 60.00

Maserati 4CL T/1948 Racer, #52, 1958, yellow w/black tires, MIP 120.00

Mechanical Horse & Trailer, #10, 1955, red & gray, metal wheels, MIP 90.00

Mercedes Trailer, #2, 1969, SuperFast Wheels, gold, orange canopy, MIP 30.00

Mercury Cougar, #62, 1970, SuperFast Wheels, doors open, MIP, from $30 to 45.00

Nissan Fairlady Z, #5, 1981, red, MIP, from $18 to 24.00

Peterbilt Wrecker, #61, 1982, blue w/amber windows, black boom, MIP 66.00

Pickford Removal Van, #46, 1960, dark blue w/gray plastic wheels, MIP 73.00

Pontiac Grand Prix, #22, 1964, black plastic wheels, MIP, from $24 to 28.00

Porsche 911 Turbo, #3, 1978, metallic brown w/unpainted base, MIP 53.00

Prime Mover Truck Tractor, #15, 1956, yellow w/metal wheels, MIP 1,000.00

Racing Mini, #26, 1970, orange, MIP, from $12 to 16.00

Road Tanker, #11, 1955, red w/gold trim, metal wheels, Esso decal, MIP 68.00

Road Tanker, #11, 1955, yellow w/ metal wheels, MIP, from $125 to 150.00

Seasprite Helicopter, #74, regular, 1977, dark green, MIP, from $285 to 340.00

Volkswagen Camper, #23, 1970, turquoise, opening roof, M, from $20 to 30.00

Wells Fargo Armored Truck, #69, 1978, red w/clear windows, MIP, from $35 to **50.00**

McCoy

A popular collectible with flea market goers, McCoy pottery was made in Roseville, Ohio, from 1910 until the late 1980s. They are most famous for their extensive line of figural cookie jars, more than 200 in all. They also made amusing figural planters, as well as dinnerware, and vases and pots for the florist trade. Though some pieces are unmarked, most bear one of several McCoy trademarks. Beware of reproductions made by a company in Tennessee who at one time used a very close facsimile of the old McCoy mark. They made several cookie jars once produced by McCoy as well as other now defunct potteries. Some of these (but by no means all) were dated with the number '93' below the mark. (Values for cookie jars are listed in the Cookie Jar category.) For more information refer to *McCoy Pottery, Collector's Reference & Value Guide, Volumes I, II,* and *III,* by Bob Hanson, Craig Nissen, and Margaret Hanson. All are published by Collector Books. See Clubs and Newsletters for information concerning the newsletter *NM (Nelson McCoy) Xpress.*

Ashtray, bird at side of flower, yellow & green, 1951, 5¼", from $40 to **50.00**

Bank, cats at the barrel, red, white, blue or yellow, NCP mark, from $70 to **90.00**

Bank, Metz Premium Beer, barrel form, 6¼", from $35 to **45.00**

Birdbath, blue or white speckled, 3 metal legs, 1950-60s, 18x13" **180.00**

Bookend/planter, naturalistic dog, from $150.00 to $200.00 for the pair. (Photo courtesy Margaret Hanson, Craig Nissen, and Bob Hanson)

Console set, Starburst Line, bowl & candleholders, MCP mark, '72, 3-pc **90.00**

Flower bowl ornament, peacock, white, 4¾", from $100 to. **125.00**

Flower holder, pelican, white or yellow, 1940s, 3", from $250 to.................................. **350.00**

Flower holder, sea horse, white or green, 1940s, 6", from $600 to **800.00**

Flowerpot, embossed ribs, attached base, NM mark, 1940s, 3¾" **30.00**

Jardiniere, Acorn, matt color, unmarked, 1935, 4½", from $35 to **50.00**

Jardiniere, Holly, brown onyx, 1930s, 10½", from $100 to **150.00**

Jardiniere, swallows in relief on brown gloss, 7", from $90 to **125.00**

Lamp base, Blossomtime, pink flowers w/leaves on white, handles, 7"......................200.00

Lazy Susan, green & brown glazes, 1970s, 12".................40.00

Oil jar, cobalt, NM mark, 1930s, 12", from $125 to...........200.00

Pitcher, bird figural, green, 1940s, 32-oz, 6", from $40 to......60.00

Pitcher, Butterfly, embossed decor on yellow, NM mark, 10", from $125 to...........................200.00

Pitcher, pig, green, 1940s, 5", from $700 to.............................800.00

Planter, baby crib, pink or blue, 1954, from $60 to............75.00

Planter, Basketweave, lime green, 1956, 7½" L, from $12 to..15.00

Planter, bird dog pointing, white w/black spray, 1959, 7¼", from $135 to............................185.00

Planter, duck w/egg, yellow w/decor, 1940s, 3¼x7", from $30 to.......................................35.00

Planter, Dutch shoe, bird on branches, Floraline, 8" L, from $18 to................................25.00

Planter, Dutch shoe, blue, 1940s, 5" L, from $20 to.................30.00

Planter, fawn among foliage, light blue, NM mark, 1940s, 4½x5".............................66.00

Planter, frog w/umbrella, 1954, from $125 to..................175.00

Planter, kitten w/ball of yarn, #3026, 7x5½", from $80 to.........100.00

Planter, Mammy sitting on scoop, 1953, 7½", from $150 to.200.00

Planter, Mary Ann shoe, pink pastel, NM mark, 1940s, 5" L, from $25 to......................40.00

Planter, panther, chartreuse, 1950, from $70 to.....................90.00

Planter, rabbit, white w/cold paint, scarce, 7½", from $100 to.125.00

Planter, swan, Antique Rose, brown on white, 7½", from $50 to..60.00

Planter, yellow ball shape w/Garden Club sticker, 1950s-60s, 6x5"........................30.00

Planter, zebra & baby, black & white stripes, 1956, 6½x8"......725.00

Planters, Spinning Wheel, green, 7¼x7¼", hand-decorated white dog, 1953, from $30.00 to $40.00; Wishing Well, green, 6¾", from $30.00 to $40.00. (Photo courtesy Margaret Hanson, Craig Nissen, and Bob Hanson)

Porch jar, Butterfly, white, unmarked, 11", from $150 to.............300.00

Salt & pepper shakers, cucumber & bell peppers, 1954, pr from $75 to.....................................100.00

Spoon rest, penguin figural, yellow w/decor, 1953, 7x5", $100 to.150.00

Stretch animal, goat (ramming/butting), pastel, 1940s, 3¼x5½".............................250.00

TV lamp/planter, rocking chair, green, 8½x5½", from $60 to..........80.00

Umbrella stand, blended glaze, 18", from $300 to..................350.00

Vase, chrysanthemum, pink or yellow, 1950, 8", from $110 to........140.00

Vase, double tulips, yellow w/green leaves, late 1940s, 8", from $75 to.....................................100.00

Vase, embossed sailboat, blue matt, NM mark, 1942, 9", from $50 to **70.00**

Vase, flared cylinder w/embossed ribs, green or white, 1950s, 10" **65.00**

Vase, hand in glove, white, NM mark, 1940s, 8¼", from $250 to **350.00**

Vase, Hobnail, green, V-shaped rim, NM mark, 9", from $125 to **150.00**

Vase, ivy, green & brown on cream, twig handles, 1953, 9" .. **125.00**

Vase, ivy, green on yellow, 1950s, 6", from $400 to **500.00**

Vase, ram's head, burgundy (rare color), 1950s, 9½", from $130 to **200.00**

Vase, Sunburst Gold, ornate handles, flared foot, 6", from $30 to **40.00**

Vase, Uncle Sam, bright yellow, 1940s, 7½", from $50 to .. **60.00**

Vase, yellow waisted form w/low handles, USA, 1940s, 10", from $90 to **110.00**

Violet pot, Tudor Rose, 1965, 2½", from $10 to **15.00**

Wall pocket, bellows, black w/blue spray, 1950s, 9½x4½", from $700 to **800.00**

Wall pocket, lady w/bonnet, standard decoration, 1940s, 8", from $200 to **350.00**

Wall pocket, lily bud, lavender matt, 6", from $200 to... **250.00**

Wall pocket, Mexican man, pastel, 7½", from $50 to **90.00**

Melmac Dinnerware

Melmac was a product of the postwar era, a thermoplastic material formed by the interaction of melamine and formaldehyde. It was popular because of its attractive colors and patterns, and it was practically indestructible. But eventually it faded, became scratched or burned, and housewives tired of it. By the late '60s and early '70s, it fell from favor.

Collectors, however, are finding its mid-century colors and shapes appealing again, and they're beginning to reassemble melmac table services when well-designed items can be found. Condition, as is true with any collectible, is a very important worth-assessing factor; our values are for examples in fine original condition with minimal scratching (NM to EX) unless noted otherwise. Texasware or any other of the confetti (mixed color) lines often go for very high prices. We have listed a few confetti items in this section. For more information we recommend *Melmac Dinnerware* by Alvin Daigle Jr. and Gregg Zimmer (see the Directory under Minnesota).

Bowl, cereal; Prolon, green w/multicolor confetti, 4 for **20.00**

Bowl, divided vegetable; Branchell Color-Flyte, gray, 2¼x10½x8" **22.50**

Bowl, mixing; Brookpark, multicolor confetti on tan, nesting set of 3 .... **55.00**

Bowl, mixing; Texas Ware, light blue w/multicolor confetti, #3125, 11" **45.00**

Bowl, salad; Boonton, orange w/multicolor confetti, 5", 8 for **80.00**

Bowl, Texas Ware, charcoal gray w/ multicolor confetti, 2½x8". **38.00**

Butterdish, Burrite, aqua & yellow, ¼-lb **22.50**

Coasters, Imperial Ware, pastels, 6 for **18.00**

Creamer & sugar bowl, Residential, yellow, w/lid **30.00**

Cup, Royalon, avocado green w/ white interior, 8 for **16.00**

Dinnerware set, Blue Hawaii, Oneida, service for 8, 45 pcs, MIB **125.00**

Dinnerware set, Libbey, apple green & white, service for 4, 20 pcs **42.50**

Lunch tray, Silite, 6-compartment, pink w/multicolor confetti, 10x14" **6.00**

Mug, Raffia Ware, pastels w/clear handle, set of 8 .... **20.00**

Pitcher, Raffia Ware, brown on white, ice lip, water size. **15.00**

Platter, Branchell Color-Flyte, gray, 12" L **12.00**

Salt & pepper shakers, Boonton, yellow, pr **12.00**

Sugar bowl, Brookpark, orange, w/ lid **10.00**

Water set, Watertown Lifetime Ware, heavy weight, 7¼" pitcher, 3¾" tumblers, M, from $35.00 to $45.00. (Photo courtesy Lori Kalal)

Metlox

Since the 1940s, the Metlox company of California has been producing dinnerware, cookie jars, novelties, and decorative items, and their earlier wares have become very collectible. Some of their best-known dinnerware patterns are California Provincial (the dark green and burgundy rooster), Red Rooster (in red, orange, and brown), Homestead Provincial (dark green and burgundy farm scenes), and Colonial Homestead (farm scenes done in red, orange, and brown).

Carl Gibbs is listed in the Directory under Texas; he is the author of *Collector's Encyclopedia of Metlox Potteries*. His book is highly recommended if you'd like to learn more about this company. See also Cookie Jars.

California Aztec, celery dish, from $60 to **75.00**

California Aztec, coffee carafe, w/ stopper, 8", from $150 to. **175.00**

California Aztec, pitcher, water; from $225 to **275.00**

California Ivy, butter dish, from $40 to **60.00**

California Ivy, egg cup, from $25 to **35.00**

California Ivy, salt & pepper shakers, sm, pr from $22 to ... **28.00**

California Ivy, tray, 2-tier, from $40 to **50.00**

California Peach Blossom, gravy boat, from $45 to **50.00**

California Peach Blossom, saucer, from $4 to **5.00**

California Provincial, bowl, vegetable; 10", from $55 to .. **60.00**

California Provincial, bread server, 9½", from $75 to **80.00**

California Provincial, cruet set, 5-pc, from $185 to **200.00**

California Provincial, saucer, 6⅛", from $4 to **5.00**

California Strawberry, bowl, fruit; 5⅜", from $10 to **12.00**

California Strawberry, buffet server, round, 13½", from $50 to **55.00**

California Strawberry, mug, 8-oz, from $19 to **22.00**

Colorstax, cup, lg, 16-oz, from $18 to **22.00**

Colorstax, flowerpot, 7", from $30 to **35.00**

Colorstax, salt & pepper shakers, sm, pr from $24 to **26.00**

Homestead Provincial, casserole, kettle; w/lid, 2-qt, 12-oz, from $130 to **140.00**

Homestead Provincial, cup & saucer, 6-oz, 6½", from $16 to **18.00**

Homestead Provincial, gravy boat, 1-pt, from $40 to **45.00**

Homestead Provincial, pepper mill, from $50 to **55.00**

Homestead Provincial, platter, 13½", from $40.00 to $50.00. (Photo courtesy Carl Gibbs Jr.)

Homestead Provincial, soup tureen, w/lid, from $450 to **475.00**

Homestead Provincial, teapot, 7-cup, from $125 to **135.00**

La Mancha, bowl, cereal; 6⅝", from $12 to **13.00**

La Mancha, coffeepot, 8-cup, from $70 to **80.00**

La Mancha, gravy boat, 12-oz, from $22 to **25.00**

Lotus, banana leaf, 24", from $70 to **75.00**

Lotus, cup, demitasse; from $18 to **20.00**

Lotus, gravy boat, from $36 to . **38.00**

Lotus, tray, 2-tiered, from $45 to **50.00**

Provincial Blue, butter dish, from $70 to **75.00**

Provincial Blue, pitcher, 1-qt, from $65 to **75.00**

Provincial Blue, plate, dinner; 10", from $16 to **18.00**

Provincial Blue, tumbler, 11-oz, from $40 to **45.00**

Provincial Blue, turkey platter, 22½", from $275 to **300.00**

Red Rooster, bowl, salad; 11⅛", from $75 to **80.00**

Red Rooster, buffet server, 12½", from $60 to **65.00**

Red Rooster, coffee server, 11", from $105 to **115.00**

Red Rooster, cookie jar, from $90 to **100.00**

Red Rooster, pepper mill, from $35 to **40.00**

Red Rooster, pitcher, 1½-pt, from $30 to **40.00**

Sculptured Grape, compote, footed, 8½", from $70 to **75.00**

Sculptured Grape, creamer, 10-oz, from $26 to **28.00**

Sculptured Grape, sugar bowl, w/ lid, from $29 to **32.00**

Sculptured Grape, tumbler, 12-oz, from $32 to **35.00**

Sculptured Zinnia, bowl, fruit; 6", from $10 to **12.00**

Sculptured Zinnia, butter dish, from $50 to **55.00**

Sculptured Zinnia, sugar bowl, w/ lid, 10-oz, from $28 to **30.00**

Vineyard, creamer, 8-oz, from $22 to **25.00**

Vineyard, jam & jelly, 8¼", from $40 to **50.00**

Vineyard, teapot, 6-cup, from $90 to **95.00**

Woodland Gold, baker, oval, 11", from $40 to **45.00**

Woodland Gold, bowl, fruit; 5⅜", from $10 to **12.00**

Woodland Gold, plate, salad; 8", from $8 to **9.00**

Woodland Gold, platter, oval, 11", from $30 to **35.00**

Woodland Gold, tumbler, 12-oz, from $26 to **28.00**

Yorkshire, cup, from $8 to **10.00**

Yorkshire, gravy boat, from $22 to **25.00**

Yorkshire, salt & pepper shakers, pr from $20 to **24.00**

Poppets

Angelina, angel, 7⅝", from $75 to **85.00**

Charlie, seated man, 5⅞" **60.00**

Chimney Sweep, 7¾", from $55 to **65.00**

Florence, nurse, w/4" bowl, from $60 to **70.00**

Mickey, choir boy #1, from $40 to . **50.00**

Minnie, mermaid, from $55 to . **65.00**

Nellie, 8⅝", from $55.00 to $65.00.

Ralph, bather man, 11¾", from $45 to **55.00**

Sally, w/4" bowl, from $50 to . **60.00**

Sarah, choral lady #1, 7¾", from $75 to **85.00**

Tina, costumed girl, 8½", from $55 to **65.00**

Miller Studio

Brightly painted chalkware plaques, bookends, thermometers, and hot pad holders modeled with subjects that range from Raggedy Ann and angels to bluebirds and sunfish were the rage during '50s and '60s, and even into the early '70s you could buy them from the five-&-dime store to decorate your kitchen and bathroom walls with style and flair. Collectors who like this 'kitschy' ambience are snapping them up and using them in the vintage rooms they're re-creating with period appliances, furniture, and accessories. They're especially fond of the items marked Miller Studio, a manufacturing firm located in New Philadelphia, Pennsylvania. Most but not all of their pieces are marked and carry a copyright date. If you find an unmarked item with small holes on the back where stapled-on cardboard packaging has been torn away, chances are very good it's Miller Studio as well. Miller Studio is still in business and is today the only American firm that continues to produce hand-finished wall plaques. (Mr. Miller tells us that although they had over 300 employees back in the 1960s and 1970s, they presently have approximately 75.)

Unless noted otherwise, our values are for examples in near mint to mint condition.

Basket of daisies plaques, brown/ yellow/green, 5½x5½" **15.00**

Bluebird plaques, blue & yellow, 1960, 4½x3", 3-pc set **25.00**

Boy (& girl) holding ear of corn plaques, 1955, 5x5¾" **25.00**

Boy in pajamas/kneeling in prayer plaque, 1984, 6x2½" **12.50**

Chef head plaques, bond hair & white hats, 1964, pr........ **21.50**

Cockatoo on branch plaques, 1968, 11x4", pr **40.00**

Dachshund head plaques, brown tones, 1961, 4x4", pr **17.50**

Duck w/umbrella thermometer, 9x6", sm duck, 4x2½", pr. **15.00**

Fish bathometer, green w/pink face & red lips, 1977.............. **12.50**

Fish plaque, 1971, 9x8" **18.00**

Fruit plaques, 8x11½", 6x6", 5x6", 3-pc set............................ **25.00**

Goldfish plaques, pink, 1954, 5½x5½", pr **12.50**

Kitten plaques, pink & gray w/lg black eyes, 6x4", pr **20.00**

Mermaid plaques, 1 w/shell, other w/shell & starfish, 1968, 6", pr **23.50**

Owl memo holder w/note pad & pencil, 7x6¾" **10.00**

Palomino horse head plaques, black background, 4½x8½", pr.. **28.00**

Parrot on branch plaques, bold multicolors, 1974, 14", 13", pr **150.00**

Poodle in tub bathometer, 1973. **10.00**

Recipes plaque, brown box among vegetables & wooden spoon, 1981 .... **17.50**

Rooster plaques, ornate tail feathers, 1965, 12x6", 10x7½", pr..... **15.00**

Rooster weathervane thermometer, coppery brown tones, 1969. **22.50**

Sea horse plaque, bright yellow & dark green, 8½x4¾"......... **15.00**

Skunk bathometer, 1954, 6½x8". **30.00**

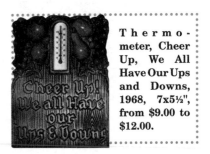

Thermometer, Cheer Up, We All Have Our Ups and Downs, 1968, 7x5½", from $9.00 to $12.00.

Wine jug & fruit plaques, 1967, 5½x5½", pr **17.50**

Model Kits

The best-known producer of model kits today is Aurora. Collectors often pay astronomical prices for some of the character kits from the 1960s. Made popular by all the monster movies of that decade, ghouls like Vampirella, Frankenstein, and the Wolfman were eagerly built up by kids everywhere. But the majority of all model kits were vehicles, ranging from 3" up to 24" long. Some of the larger model vehicle makers were AMT, MPC, and IMC. Condition is very important in assessing the value of a kit, with other things factoring into pricing as well — who is selling, who is buying and how badly they want it, locality, supply, and demand. For additional listings we recommend *Schroeder's Collectible Toys, Antique to Modern* (Collector Books).

Condition is very important in assessing the value of a kit, with built-ups priced at about 50% lower than one still in the box. Unless noted otherwise, our values are for examples mint an in the original box. If the box is still sealed, add 20% to our prices.

Adams, Hawk Missile Battery, 1958 .... 70.00
Addar, Planet of the Apes, Gen Ursus, 1973-74 .... 40.00
Addar, Super Scenes, 1975, Jaws in a Bottle 60.00
Airfix, Corythosaus, 1970, NRFB 30.00
Airfix, 2001: A Space Odyssey, 1970, Orion 75.00
AMT, Flintstones, 1974 .... 75.00
AMT, KISS Custom Chevy Van, 1977 .... 75.00
AMT, Star Trek, USS Enterprise Command Bridge, 1975 .. 80.00
Arii, Regult Missile Carrier .. 25.00
Aurora, Addams Family Haunted House, 1964 .... 850.00
Aurora, Captain Action, 1966. 300.00

Aurora, Dick Tracy in Action, 1968 .... 350.00
Aurora, Frankenstein, 1975, Monsters of the Movies .. 325.00
Aurora, Gold Knight of Nice, 1965 .... 275.00
Aurora, Guys & Gals, 1957, Indian Chief 125.00
Aurora, Hunchback of Notre Dame, 1969, glow-in-the-dark . 150.00
Aurora, John F Kennedy, 1965. 150.00
Aurora, Lone Ranger, 1967 . 175.00
Aurora, Mummy, 1963 .... 325.00
Aurora, Phantom of the Opera, 1969, glow-in-the-dark . 175.00
Aurora, Rat Patrol, 1967 ..... 115.00

Aurora, Robin the Boy Wonder, 1966, $125.00.

Aurora, Rodan, 1975, Monsters of the Movies, rare 375.00
Aurora, Spider-Man, 1966 ... 300.00
Aurora, Steve Canyon, 1958, Famous Fighters 200.00
Aurora, Superboy, 1974, Comic Scenes 100.00
Aurora, Tonto, 1967 .... 250.00
Aurora, Voyage to the Bottom of the Sea, 1966, Seaview. 325.00
Aurora, Witch, 1969, glow-in-the-dark 200.00
Bandai, Kinggidrah, 1984 ..... 50.00
Billiken, Frankenstein, 1988. 150.00
Eldon, Pink Panther, 1970s, MIB 75.00

Geometric Design, Boris Karloff as the Mummy, MIB **50.00**

Hawk, Cherokee Sports Roadster, 1962, MIB **35.00**

Hawk, Francis the Foul, 1963, MIB **60.00**

Hawk, Monte Carlo Sports Roadster, 1962, MIB **75.00**

Horizon, Frankenstein, MIB. **100.00**

Horizon, Marvel Universe, 1988, Punisher, MIB **50.00**

Imai, Batman Boat, 1960s, MIB (box in Japanese) **300.00**

ITC, Neanderthal Man, 1959, MIB **50.00**

Life-Like, Roman Chariot, 1970s, MIB **20.00**

Lindberg, Flying Saucer, 1952, MIB **200.00**

Lindberg, SST Continental, 1958, MIB **175.00**

Monogram, Barnabas, 1968, Dark Shadows **400.00**

Monogram, Buck Rogers, 1970, Marauder **70.00**

Monogram, Fred Flypogger as Flip Out! the Beachcomber, 1965, $160.00.

Monogram, Giraffes, 1961 ..... **50.00**

Monogram, Sand Crab, 1969. **50.00**

MPC, Beverly Hillbillies Truck, 1968 .... **200.00**

MPC, Dukes of Hazzard, 1982, Sheriff Rosco's Police Car. **40.00**

MPC, Road Runner & the Beep Beep T, 1972 .... **75.00**

MPC, Star Wars, 1978, Darth Vader TIE Fighter **35.00**

Pyro, Indian Warrior, 1960s .. **60.00**

Pyro, Surf's Up!, 1970 .... **40.00**

Revell, Apollo Astronaut on Moon, 1970 .... **125.00**

Revell, Beatles, 1965, Paul McCartney **200.00**

Revell, CHiPs, 1980, Jon's Chevy 4x4 .... **35.00**

Revell, Disney's Love Bug Rides Again, 1974 .... **100.00**

Revell, Dune, 1985, Ornithopter, NRFB **60.00**

Revell, Ed 'Big Daddy' Roth, 1965, Fink-Eliminator **125.00**

Revell, Peter Pan Pirate Ship, 1960, #377 .... **100.00**

Screamin', Mars Attacks, Target Earth, assembled, NM.... **30.00**

Tsukuda, Ghostbusters Terror Dog. **125.00**

Tsukuda, Mummy **100.00**

Mood Indigo

Quite an extensive line, this ware was imported from Japan during the 1960s. It was evidently quite successful, judging from the amount of it still around today. It's inexpensive, and if you're into blue, this is for you! It's a deep, very electric shade, and each piece is modeled to represent stacks of various fruits, with handles and spouts sometimes turned out as vines. All pieces carry a stamped number on the bottom which identifies the shape. There are more than 30 known items to look for, more than likely others will surface.

Ashtray, rest in ea corner, E-4283, 9".. **25.00**

Bell, 5"...................................... **15.00**

Bud vase, E-3096, 8", from $20 to.................................... **22.50**

Cake plate, footed, E-3462, 2¾x9⅜"............................ **50.00**

Candleholders, owl figure, E-4612, 6", pr................................ **20.00**

Candy jar, cylindrical, footed, w/lid, 9½"...................................... **45.00**

Coffee cup, E-2431, 4", from $4 to...................................... **6.00**

Cruet, E-3098, 7½"................ **28.00**

Dish, oval, E-2376, 8½x5¾"... **18.00**

Figurine, E-2883, cat seated, rare, 14½"................................ **75.00**

Gravy boat, E-2373, 6½"........ **15.00**

Jar, cylindrical, w/lid, 6½"..... **15.00**

Ladle, 9¾"................................ **25.00**

Lavabo, 2-pc: handled covered vase (11") over ½-bowl shape, 5x9"................................ **40.00**

Mug, E-4489, 5"...................... **12.00**

Oil lamp, E-3267, frosted shade, 9½"...................................... **25.00**

Pitcher, E-2853, footed, 6"..... **15.00**

Pitcher, E-5240, 4", w/saucer under-tray.................................. **15.00**

Pitcher, footed, E-2429, 6½"... **18.00**

Planter, donkey pulling cart, 6x7¾"................................ **18.00**

Plate, allover fruit, E-2432, 10"...................................... **30.00**

Platter, 15x10"....................... **45.00**

Salt & pepper shakers, E-2371, 3½", pr............................... **12.00**

Salt & pepper shakers, E-2371, 3½", pr............................... **12.00**

Soap dish, cherub sits on side of shell, E-4656, 4¾"........... **22.00**

Teapot, E-2430, 8"................. **22.00**

Tray, divided, E-2728, 12x6".. **30.00**

Tray, shell shape, 3-compartment, E-4555............................ **40.00**

Trivet, 6" dia........................ **10.00**

Tureen, E-3379, $30.00.

Moon and Star

A reissue of Palace, an early pattern glass line, Moon and Star was developed for the market in the 1960s by Joseph Weishar of Island Mould and Machine Company (Wheeling, West Virginia). It was made by several companies. One of the largest producers was L.E. Smith of Mt. Pleasant, Pennsylvania, and L.G. Wright (who had their glassware made by Fostoria and Fenton, perhaps others as well) carried a wide assortment in their catalogs for many years. It is still being made on a very limited basis, but the most collectible pieces are those in red, blue, amber, and green — colors that are no longer in production. The values listed here are for pieces in red or blue. Amber, green, and crystal prices should be 30% lower.

Ashtray, allover pattern, scalloped rim, 4 rests, 8" dia, from $16 to...................................... **25.00**

Ashtray, moons at rim, star in base, 6-sided, 5½", from $18 to. **28.00**

Ashtray, moons at rim, star in base, 6-sided, 8½", from $24 to . **32.00**

Banana boat, allover pattern, scalloped rim, 12", from $30 to **45.00**

Basket, allover pattern, moons form scalloped rim, split handle, 9x6" **110.00**

Basket, allover pattern, moons form scalloped rim, 5", from $30 to **45.00**

Basket, allover pattern, scalloped rim, solid handle, 6", from $30 to **40.00**

Basket, allover pattern, scalloped rim, solid handle, 9", from $40 to **55.00**

Bowl, allover pattern, crimped rim, footed, 7½", from $20 to .. **30.00**

Bowl, allover pattern, footed, scalloped rim, 3x5", from $18 to **25.00**

Bowl, allover pattern, scalloped rim, footed, 5x9½", from $30 to **45.00**

Butter dish, allover pattern, scalloped base rim, star finial, 8½" **65.00**

Butter/cheese dish, round, patterned lid, plain base, 7" dia, $45 to **65.00**

Cake salver, allover pattern w/scalloped rim, raised foot, 5x12" dia **55.00**

Cake stand, allover pattern, removable plate, 2-pc, 11" dia, $70 to **90.00**

Candle lamp, patterned shade, clear base & cup, 7¾x4½", $30 to **45.00**

Candle lamp, patterned shade & base, plain insert, 9", from $45 to **60.00**

Candleholders, allover pattern, flared base, 4½", pr from $20 to **35.00**

Candy dish, allover pattern, ball shape, footed, 6" **35.00**

Candy dish with lid, 7", $35.00.

Canister, allover pattern, 1-lb or 2-lb, from $10 to **20.00**

Canister, allover pattern, 3½-lb or 5-lb, from $30 to **40.00**

Chandelier, ruffled dome shape w/ allover pattern, amber, 10", from $60 to **70.00**

Compote, allover pattern, raised foot, w/lid, 7½x6", from $25 to **35.00**

Compote, allover pattern, scalloped rim, footed, 7x10, from $25 to **40.00**

Compote, allover pattern, w/lid, 8x4", from $25 to **38.00**

Console bowl, allover pattern, scalloped rim, flared foot, 8", from $20 to **35.00**

Cruet, vinegar; 6¾", from $50 to. **65.00**

Egg plate, from $35 to **55.00**

Epergne, allover pattern, 2-pc, 9", from $75 to **120.00**

Fairy lamp, cylindrical dome-top shade, 6" **25.00**

Goblet, water; plain rim & foot, 6", from $12 to **16.00**

Jardiniere/cracker jar, allover pattern, w/lid, 7¼".............100.00

Jelly dish, patterned body & lid, plain flat rim, dish foot, 7x3½"............................30.00

Lamp, miniature; blue, from $165 to....................................190.00

Lamp, oil or electric; allover pattern, red or blue, 24", minimum..............................300.00

Lamp, oil; patterned hurricane shade, oval base w/handle, 12", from $45 to......................65.00

Nappy, allover pattern, crimped rim, 2¾x6", from $18 to..28.00

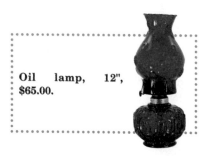

Oil lamp, 12", $65.00.

Plate, patterned body & center, smooth rim, 8", from $30 to...............................60.00

Relish bowl, 6 lg scallops form allover pattern, 1½x8", from $25 to....................................40.00

Rose bowl, allover pattern, scalloped incurvate rim, 3x4½", from $35 to......................50.00

Soap dish, allover pattern, oval, 2x6", from $9 to..............12.00

Sugar bowl, allover pattern, straight sides, scalloped foot, 8x4½"..............................43.00

Sugar/cheese shaker, allover pattern, chrome lid, 4½", from $30 to...............................45.00

Syrup pitcher, allover pattern, metal lid, 4½x3½", from $45 to...................................65.00

Tumbler, plain rim & disk foot, 6", from $22 to......................30.00

Vase, pattern near top, ruffled rim, dish foot, 6", from $20 to.22.00

Mortens Studios

Animal models sold by Mortens Studios of Arizona during the 1940s are some of today's most interesting collectibles, especially among animal lovers. Hundreds of breeds of dogs, cats, and horses were produced from a plaster-type composition material constructed over a wire framework. They range in size from 2" up to about 7", and most are marked. Crazing and flaking are nearly always present to some degree. Our values are for animals in excellent to near-mint condition, allowing for only minor crazing. Heavily crazed examples will be worth much less.

Beagle sitting, 3¼"................65.00

Bedlington terrier standing, 3½x5"...........................165.00

Black Labrador retriever standing, 6¾", from $70 to..............85.00

Boxer (male) dog standing, 5½".85.00

Bulldog puppy sitting, brown & white, 3"...........................65.00

Cocker spaniel standing, light brown, 5½x7"...................65.00

Collie puppy sitting, 3¼x3½".35.00

English bulldog standing, 3½x6", from $65 to......................75.00

German shepherd puppy seated, 3½x2¼"...............................75.00

German shepherd rolling, 2⅛x3¾".............................**80.00**
Horse, wild stallion on base, #718, 9½", from $95 to **110.00**
Lion, striding 12" L, from $95 to **120.00**
Panther slightly rearing, 12½" L, from $120 to **145.00**

Pekingese standing, 3x4½", $60.00.

Pointer dog standing, black & white, 5x6¾".....................**85.00**
Pomeranian standing w/head up, 2x2¾" **55.00**
Russian wolfhound standing, black & white, w/label, 6".........**45.00**
Saint Bernard standing, 6¾".**75.00**
Wirehaired terrier begging, brown, black & white, 3".............**60.00**
Wirehaired terrier sitting, light brown w/black, 4¼x3¾"...**65.00**

Moss Rose

Though the Moss Rose pattern has been produced by Staffordshire and American pottery companies alike since the mid-1800s, the lines we're dealing with here are all from the twentieth century. Much was made from the late 1950s into the 1970s by Japanese manufacturers. Even today you'll occasionally see a tea set or a small candy dish for sale in some of the chain stores. (The collectors who are already picking this line up refer to it as Moss Rose, but we've seen it advertised as Victorian Rose, and some companies called their lines Chintz Rose or French Rose; but for now, Moss Rose seems to be the accepted terminology.

Rosenthal made an identical pattern, and prices are generally higher for examples that carry the mark of that company. The pattern consists of a briar rose with dark green mossy leaves on stark white glaze. Occasionally, an item is trimmed in gold. In addition to dinnerware, many accessories and novelties were made as well. Refer to *Garage Sale and Flea Market Annual* for more a more extensive listing.

Bell, heart finial w/gold trim, Golden Crown, Made in England.**15.00**
Bottle, perfume; w/stopper & tray, Made in Japan, 5½" dia..**30.00**
Bowl, dessert; Royal Rose, 5½".**5.00**
Bowl, Johann Haviland, 3x8½" **40.00**
Bowl, soup; Johann Haviland, 7½", set of 4, MIB....................**27.50**
Bowl, vegetable; w/lid, Pompadour, Rosenthal, 1-qt...............**70.00**
Butter dish, rectangular, gold trim, 2½x6x3"............................**22.50**
Candy dish, 2-part, tab handles, gold trim, unmarked Japan, 7½" **18.00**
Coffeepot, demitasse; silver base, Rosenthal........................**65.00**

Condiment dish, w/lid, spoon & underplate, Japan mark, 4½", 5" dia................................45.00

Creamer & sugar bowl, gold trim, ornate handles, unmarked, 5¼", 5"...............................18.00

Creamer & sugar bowl, w/lid, Ucagco.............................15.00

Cup & saucer, demitasse; gold trim, ornate handle, unmarked......................12.50

Egg coddler, w/lid, unmarked Japan, 4"...........................20.00

Egg cup, gold scalloped edge, footed, unmarked, 1960s, 2¼".......9.00

Gravy boat, attached underplate, Pompadour, Rosenthal, 5x9"............................30.00

Oil lamp, Aladdin style, gold trim, Japan, 8", w/glass shade...........................35.00

Plate, dinner; gold trim, Sango Japan, 10".........................15.00

Platter, Johann Haviland, 12¾x9½".............................27.50

Powder box, rectangular, gold trim, unmarked Japan, 4½" L.20.00

Relish tray, 3-part w/center handle, Gold Castle, 1950s, 7" dia.................................. 80.00

Salt cellar, silver foot, Rosenthal, 1¾", w/3" spoon...............40.00

Smoke set, plate w/indent & cup, gold trim, Ucagco Japan, 8", 2x3½"...............................15.00

Tea service, Gold Coast China Japan, serves 6, 46-pc set.............65.00

Teapot, electric, Japan, 1960s, 7"..................................25.00

Teapot, pearl lustre w/gold trim, individual........................15.00

Teapot, Royal Sealy, 8½".........20.00

Teapot, Ucagco, 7½"...............24.00

Teapot, no mark, 6½", from $15.00 to $18.00.

Teapot bag holder, I'll Hold the Bag on teapot shape, Japan, 8 for...............................30.00

Tidbit tray, 2-tier, Johann Haviland, 6¼" & 10" plates...............35.00

Vase, ruffled rim w/gold trim, handles, sm foot, 5¾x5¼"......45.00

Niloak

Produced in Arkansas by Charles Dean Hyten from the early 1900s until the mid-1940s, Niloak (the backward spelling of kaolin, a type of clay) takes many forms — figural planters, vases in both matt and glossy glazes, and novelty items of various types. The company's most famous product and the most collectible is their Swirl or Mission Ware line. Clay in colors of brown, blue, cream, red, and buff are swirled within the mold, the finished product left unglazed on the outside to preserve the natural hues. Small vases are common; large pieces or unusual shapes and those with exceptional coloration are the most valuable. Refer to *Collector's Encyclopedia of Niloak, A Reference and Value*

Guide, by David Edwin Gifford for more information.

Note: The terms '1st' and '2nd art mark' used in the listings refer to specific die-stamped trademarks. The earlier mark was used from 1910 to 1924, followed by the second, very similar mark used from then until the end of Mission Ware production. Letters with curving raised outlines were characteristic of both; the most obvious difference between the two was that on the first, the final upright line of the 'N' was thin with a solid club-like terminal.

Ashtray, frog figure w/open mouth, block letters, 3½"............ **36.00**
Bowl, flower; Mission, inverted rim, 2nd art mark, 1½x6½" **88.00**
Bowl, Peter Pan on edge, impressed mark, 7½", from $25 to ... **30.00**
Candlestick, Mission, attached self-liner, 2nd art mark, 4", ea.**165.00**
Carafe, Mission, slim neck, bulbous body, cork-wrapped stopper, 8"............................ **485.00**
Cookie jar, tab handles, matt, impressed mark, 11".....**125.00**
Cup, punch; Mission, 2½"...... **90.00**
Figure, Trojan horse, matt, 2nd art mark, 8½" **180.00**
Jug, whiskey; Mission, stamped Pensacola Golden Corn, unmarked, 3½".............. **460.00**
Mug, Bouquet dinnerware line, impressed mark, 3½", from $5 to **10.00**
Mug, Mission, vivid colors, outside glaze, 1st art mark, 4¼".**515.00**
Pitcher, maroon, graceful handle, straight sides, 2nd art mark, 3"..................................... **20.00**

Planter, kangaroo boxing, matt, block letters, 5½"............. **38.00**
Planter, pouter pigeon, ivory, impressed mark, 9"....... **185.00**
Planter, rocking horse, Ozark Blue, block mark, 6½"............. **110.00**
Powder jar, Mission, knob finial, 2nd art mark, 3x5"........ **385.00**
Shot glass, Mission, 2nd art mark, 2", from $65 to............... **110.00**

Strawberry jar, brown, 7¼", **$35.00.** (Photo courtesy David Edwin Gifford)

Teapot, Fox Red, Aladdin lamp style, unmarked, 6½" **95.00**
Tumbler, Mission, shot-glass size, 2" **110.00**
Vase, flamingo & palm trees, rope-like handles, marked, 7½"........**130.00**
Vase, Mission, classic shape w/ flared rim, 1st art mark, 5½"............................... **95.00**
Vase, Mission, fan form w/flared pedestal foot, 2nd art mark, 6¾" **195.00**
Vase, Mission, squat, ball shape, 1st art mark, 7x7"........... **30.00**
Vase, Winged Victory handles, Ozark Dawn, 4½-6", from $15 to **30.00**
Wall pocket, half pitcher, Tobacco Spit, low relief mark, 5½". **55.00**
Wall pocket, rolled rim, browns & blues, unmarked, 9"...... **310.00**

Nippon

In complying with American importation regulations, from 1891 to 1921, Japanese manufacturers marked their wares 'Nippon,' meaning Japan, to indicate country of origin. The term is today used to refer to the highly decorated porcelain vases, bowls, chocolate pots, etc., that bear this term within their trademark. Many variations were used. Refer to *Van Patten's ABC's of Collecting Nippon Porcelain* by Joan Van Patten (Collector Books) for more information. See Clubs and Newsletters for information concerning the International Nippon Collectors Club.

Ashtray, Mexican cowboy, 3 rests, Imperial mark, 6½".......320.00
Bowl, floral, golden eagle on cobalt border, M-in-wreath mark, 8½"...............200.00
Cake plate, roses w/jewel butterfly, handle, Maple Leaf mark, 10½"............... 750.00
Chocolate pot, floral w/gold beading, waisted, Royal Kinran, 9½"...............800.00
Cigarette box, Howo bird on lid, M-in-wreath mark 340.00
Dutch shoe, Sunbonnet Babies in postoral scene, M-in-wreath mark, 3"........................200.00
Ewer, irises w/coralene, ruffled rim/slim neck, Patent mark, 10½"..1,300.00
Ginger jar, blue cloud, Lego Made in Japan, 5".................... 55.00
Humidor, Black man w/banjo on cream, green M-in-wreath mark, 5¼"...............900.00

Matchbox holder, owl on branch, green M-in-wreath mark, 3½".............................375.00
Plaque, buffalo scene in relief, green M-in-wreath mark, 10½"............................. 880.00
Plaque, Chief Sitting Bull, blue M-in-wreath mark, 10½".......2,600.00
Plate, roses, gold & jewels on cobalt rim, Maple Leaf mark, 10¼"............................. 800.00
Stein, hunt scene reserve on green, M-in-wreath mark, 7¼".975.00

Tankard, roses and gold beading, maple leaf mark, 13¾", from $500.00 to $650.00.

Trivet, Dutch girl w/umbrella, 8-sided, green M-in-wreath mark, 5¾"......................225.00
Vase, bleeding hearts w/coralene, handles, 3-footed, Patent mark, 7"................................1,000.00
Vase, clipper ship at sunset, gold handles, M-in-wreath mark, 10"............................. 780.00
Vase, floral cloisonné, trumpet neck, M-in-wreath mark, 10"..800.00
Vase, floral reserves, moriage trim, handles, unmarked, 7"..650.00
Vase, gold overlay mums on cobalt, handles, M-in-wreath mark, 12¼" 1,500.00
Vase, irises in shaded brown tones, floral handles, Royal Kinran, 9"................................. 425.00

Vase, moriage dragons, integral handle, Maple Leaf mark, 4¾" **275.00**

Vase, moriage swans in sunset scene, M-in-wreath mark, 8". **11,250.00**

Whiskey jug, Rodney Stone (bulldog), green M-in-wreath mark, 6¾" **1,200.00**

Noritake

Since the early 1900s, the Noritake China Company has been producing fine dinnerware, occasional pieces, and figural items decorated by hand in delicate florals, scenics, and wildlife studies. Azalea and Tree in the Meadow are two very collectible lines of dinnerware. We've listed several examples. Note: Tree in the Meadow is only one variant of the Scenic pattern. It depicts a thatched-roof cottage with a tree growing behind it, surrounded by a meadow and some water. Other variants that include features such as swans, bridges, dogs, and windmills are not Tree in the Meadow.

Azalea

Bonbon, #184, 6¼" **60.00**
Bowl, fruit; #9, 5¼" **8.00**
Butter tub, w/insert, #54 .... **30.00**
Candleholders, glass, 3½", pr. **100.00**
Cheese/cracker, glass **110.00**
Coffeepot, demitasse; #182 .. **595.00**
Compote, glass **95.00**
Condiment set, #14, 5-pc **52.00**
Creamer & sugar bowl, #7..... **38.00**
Creamer & sugar bowl, scalloped, individual, #449 .... **395.00**

Cruet, #190 .... **180.00**
Cup & saucer, bouillon; #124, 3½" **26.00**
Egg cup, #120 .... **60.00**
Gravy boat, #40 .... **40.00**
Mustard jar, #191, 3-pc.......... **48.00**
Olive dish, #194 .... **25.00**
Plate, breakfast/luncheon; #98 .. **18.00**
Plate, salad; sq, 7⅝" **65.00**
Platter, #17, 14" **60.00**
Relish, 2-part, loop handle, #450.. **295.00**
Salt & pepper shakers, bell form, #11, pr.............................. **35.00**
Spoon holder, #189, 8" **120.00**
Toothpick holder, #192......... **120.00**

Vase, fan form, #187, $210.00. (Photo courtesy Linda Williams)

Whipped cream/mayonnaise set, #3, 3-pc **38.50**

Tree in the Meadow

Basket, Dolly Varden **95.00**
Bowl, oval, 9½" **48.00**
Bowl, vegetable; 9".................. **35.00**
Butter tub, open, w/drainer... **35.00**
Candy dish, octagonal, w/lid, 5½"............................. **395.00**
Cheese dish............................. **95.00**
Creamer & sugar bowl, berry .. **110.00**
Cruets, vinegar & oil; conjoined, #319 .... **210.00**
Egg cup **30.00**
Jam jar/dish, cherries on lid, 4-pc **95.00**

Plate, dinner; 9¾" 75.00

Plate, 8" 12.00

Platter, 10" 110.00

Relish, divided 30.00

Teapot 75.00

Miscellaneous

Basket vase, gold overlay on cobalt, 8¾" 350.00

Bowl, parrot on branch, black rim, M-in-wreath mark, 10" ... 85.00

Candlesticks, floral/exotic bird reserve on lustre, 9", pr . 240.00

Celery set, celery on shaded brown, handles, 12", +6¾" salts . 140.00

Humidor, lion killing python in relief on red, M-in-wreath mark, 7" 850.00

Humidor, owl on branch in relief, M-in-wreath mark, 7" ... 850.00

Lemon dish, lemons & leaves, tan lustre rim, M-in-wreath mark, 5¾" 40.00

Match holder, horses heads on bell shape, M-in-wreath mark, 3½" 150.00

Napkin ring, multicolor roses, M-in-wreath mark, 2¼" L 45.00

Nappy, floral on white w/gold, gold handle, M-in-wreath mark, 6½" 45.00

Shaving mug, river scenic, earth tones w/gold, M-in-wreath mark, 4" 120.00

Toast rack, blue lustre w/bird finial, M-in-wreath mark, 5½" L . 125.00

Vase, jack-in-pulpit; river scenic, M-in-wreath mark, 7¾" . 200.00

Vase, peacock feather on tan, ruffled rim, slim, 8", pr 180.00

Vase, tulip form, purple & green, M-in-wreath mark, 5¼" . 300.00

Novelty Telephones

Novelty telephones representing well-known advertising or cartoon characters are proving to be the focus of lots of collector activity — the more recognizable the character, the better. Telephones modeled after product containers are collectible as well. For more information refer to *Schroeder's Collectible Toys, Antique to Modern* (Collector Books).

Beetle Bailey, plastic figure, white base, 1982, 10", MIB 65.00

Cabbage Patch Girl, 1980s, M . 75.00

Charlie the Tuna, eyes blink when number dialed, 1988, MIB . 50.00

Crest Sparkle, MIB 75.00

Garfield, lift reciever & eyes open, Tele Concept, 1981, EX ... 50.00

Ghostbusters, white ghost inside red circle, Remco, 1987, EX 20.00

Keebler Elf, NM 65.00

Kermit the Frog, AT&T/Henson, 1980s, EXIB 100.00

Little Orphan Annie & Sandy, Columbia Pictures, 1982, 11", EX 100.00

Love Bus, 1960s, MIB 40.00

M&M Candy, talking w/figures sitting by M&M dial, yellow receiver, MIB 50.00

Mickey Mouse, American Telecommunications Corp, 1976, VG+ 75.00

Mickey Mouse, Western Electric, 1976, EX 175.00

Oscar Mayer Wiener, EX 65.00

Power Rangers, NM 25.00

Roy Rogers, plastic wall-type, 1950s, 9x9", EX 50.00

R2-D2 (Star Wars), top spins when phone rings, 12" **35.00**

Snoopy & Woodstock, Am Telephone Corp, touch-tone, 1976, EX **100.00**

Spider-Man, climbing down chimney, $135.00.

Strawberry Shortcake, M **55.00**

Superman, ATE, 1979, MIB . **950.00**

Ziggy, 1989, MIB **75.00**

Occupied Japan

Items with the 'Occupied Japan' mark were made during the period from the end of World War II until April 1952. Porcelains, novelties, paper items, lamps, silver plate, lacquer ware, and dolls are some of the areas of exported goods that may bear this stamp. Because the Japanese were naturally resentful of the occupation, it is felt that only a small percentage of their wares were thus marked. Although you may find identical items marked simply 'Japan,' only those with the 'Occupied Japan' stamp command values such as we have suggested below. Items in our listings are ceramic unless noted otherwise, and figurines are of average, small size. See Clubs and Newsletters for information concerning The Occupied Japan Club.

Ashtray, baseball glove, metal. **15.00**

Ashtray, peacock decor in center, metal **10.00**

Bank, elephant trumpeting, white w/floral decor **35.00**

Bell, chef w/rolling pin, 3" **35.00**

Book, printed in Occupied Japan. **25.00**

Bowl, oval w/open latticework, floral center, gold trim **15.00**

Box, dragon (ornate) decor, metal, w/lid, crown mark, 4x7".. **27.50**

Box, piano form, silver-tone metal w/red velvet liner **25.00**

Butter dish, basket weave, rectangular, ¼-lb **20.00**

Cigarette box, pagoda scene.. **30.00**

Clock, birdcage design, impressed mark **250.00**

Cookie jar, cottage shape, T-in-circle mark **75.00**

Cup & saucer, chintz-like floral on white, Merit **20.00**

Cup & saucer, house scene, lustre **15.00**

Dinnerware, set for 4 w/3 plate sizes +creamer & sugar, soup bowls **200.00**

Dinnerware, set for 6, w/3 plate sizes +gravy boat & platter..... **250.00**

Doll, baby in snowsuit, celluloid w/ paint detail **50.00**

Doll, Betty Boop type, celluloid, under 8" **50.00**

Egg cup, plain white w/gold middle & rim band **12.50**

Figurine, angelic trio in robes playing instruments, 5¾", ea. **30.00**

Figurine, ballerina in net dress, 5¾" **40.00**

Figurine, boy & girl tending sunflower, bisque, 5½" **60.00**

Figurine, bride & groom on base, bisque, 6" **50.00**

Figurine, colonial couple at piano, 4" **22.50**

Figurine, fisher boy w/basket & pole, Ucagco, 7" **40.00**

Figurine, girl w/teddy bear in basket, 5½" **25.00**

Figurine, horses jumping, brown pr on base, 5" **40.00**

Figurine, man beside lady playing cello, Maruyama, 3½" **25.00**

Figurine, spaniel-type dog, seated, 4½" **25.00**

Figurine, villain in black w/captive lady, blue mark, 7½" **65.00**

Ice bucket, lacquerwware, 7½". **55.00**

Lamp base, colonial couple, Chikuoa, 10¼" to top of socket **40.00**

Pencil holder, dog figure **10.00**

Planter, duck w/cart, 3x5" **7.00**

Planter, elf w/tulip pot **20.00**

Old MacDonald's Farm

Made by the Regal China Co., items from this novelty ware line were designed around characters and animals from Old MacDonald's farm. Recently prices have softened somewhat for all but the harder-to-find items, but due to the good quality of the ware and its unique styling, it's still very collectible.

Butter dish, cow's head, $150.00.

P l a q u e, Colonial couple, marked Paulux, 6x6½", $45.00. (Photo courtesy Gene and Cathy Florence)

Plaque, mallard in flight, wings wide, 6½" **25.00**

Salt & pepper shakers, penguin figural, metal, pr **20.00**

Shelf sitter, boy w/horn, 3¾".. **15.00**

Teapot, ribbed stoneware ball form w/bamboo handle **30.00**

Tray, lobster in center, 3-part . **40.00**

Vase, snake charmer couple stands before vase, 5½" **30.00**

Vase, urn; embossed grapes, embossed mark **15.00**

Wall pocket, peacock on branch . **30.00**

Canister, flour, cereal or coffee; med, ea from $225 to **245.00**

Canister, pretzels, peanuts, popcorn, chips or tidbits; lg, ea from $270 to **315.00**

Canister, salt, sugar or tea; med, ea from $110 to **135.00**

Canister, soap or cookies; lg, ea from $315 to **375.00**

Cookie jar, barn **175.00**

Grease jar, pig, from $110 to . **135.00**

Pitcher, milk; from $180 to .. **200.00**

Salt & pepper shakers, boy & girl, pr **75.00**

Salt & pepper shakers, churn, gold trim, pr **80.00**

Salt & pepper shakers, feed sacks w/sheep, pr from $80 to . **110.00**

Spice jar, assorted lids, sm, ea from $110 to **135.00**

Teapot, duck's head **200.00**

Paint-By-Number

If you were an aspiring artist back in the 1950s, you probably remember paint-by-number kits. Even a person with no talent could turn out masterpieces with the help of the canvas boards with numbered shapes and the odoriferous oil paints that were included in each kit. Whether landscapes, wildlife, florals, or portraits, there were countless subjects to choose from, and somehow just by filling in the lines, there would emerge a work of art with shadows, details, and shadings worthy of being framed and hung on display. Today these are sought out and displayed again in the homes of collectors who appreciate all things vintage. The larger ones are perhaps the most valuable, but don't overlook the smaller ones altogether — those with horses, dogs of specific breeds, cats, etc., are crossover collectibles, appreciated for their subject matter. Our values are framed paintings unless noted otherwise. Those rated excellent will have very minor scuffs or soil. See also Character Collectibles.

Asian man kneels w/parasols & bamboo background, no frame, 16x20", pr **115.00**

Birch trees w/Autumn foliage, mountains beyond, 13x13", EX **50.00**

Bullfighter, red cape furled, 12x6", pr, EX.............................. **35.00**

Caballero, senorita, adobe mission, set of 3, no frames, 16x18", EX **50.00**

Collie, recumbent/posing, 16x20".**110.00**

Cowboys on horseback mountain ranges, new frames, 10x14", pr .. **50.00**

Geisha standing w/open parasol behind her, 29x13" **80.00**

Horse (head in profile), heavy oak frames, 14x10", pr.......... **65.00**

Hunting dogs (pr in ea), heavy frames w/gilt liner, 12x15", pr....... **45.00**

Lighthouse scene, wide frames, 8x10", pr **45.00**

Mountain Road, scene w/black bear, Series C No 82, 12x16" ... **80.00**

Mountains, palm trees, ocean, sailboat in 1, 2nd w/hut, 15x19", pr.................................... **115.00**

Ocean view, lg waves, rocks, hills beyond, 16x20" **35.00**

Pansy bouquet, blowing drapery behind, 12x15"................. **45.00**

Parakeet prs on flowering branches, unframed, 8x10", pr, EX. **135.00**

Paris street scene w/Arc de Triomphe, 12x16" **45.00**

Pink flamingos in swamp w/lily pads & flowers, unframed, 112x17" **60.00**

Pomeranian (chest-up view), 8x12", pr..................................... **32.00**

Portrait of blonde girl holding pink rose (waist up), 12x9" **38.00**

Running Stallions: 2 w/several more in background, 18x24", EX **50.00**

Virgin Mary, Jesus on back (unpainted), Palmer-Pann, unframed, 14x10"........... **38.00**

Paper Dolls

Though the history of paper dolls can be traced even farther back, by the late 1700s they were being mass produced. A century later, paper dolls were being used as an advertising medium by retail companies wishing to promote sales. But today the type most often encountered are in book form — the dolls on the cardboard covers, their wardrobe on the inside pages. These have been published since the 1920s. Celebrity and character-related dolls are the most popular with collectors, and condition is very important. If they have been cut out, even if they are still in fine condition and have all their original accessories, they're worth only about half as much as an uncut doll. In our listings, if no condition is given, values are for mint, uncut paper dolls. For more information, we recommend *Price Guide to Lowe and Whitman Paper Dolls* and *20th Century Paper Dolls*, both by Mary Young (see the Directory under Ohio); and *Paper Dolls of the 1960s, 1970s, and 1980s* by Carol Nichols. For an expanded listing of values, see *Schroeder's Collectible Toys, Antique to Modern* (Collector Books). See Clubs and Newsletters for information concerning the *Paper Doll News*.

Angel Face, Gabriel #293, 1950s..**20.00**
Baby Brother & Sister, Whitman #1956, 1961 .... **50.00**
Baby Kim, Whitman #1969, 1960-62 .... **25.00**
Betsey McCall, Avalon/Standard Toykraft #85, 1960 .... **35.00**
Betty & Barbara, Milton Bradley #4382, 1934 .... **50.00**
Bobby & Betty, Burton #550, 1934 .... **75.00**

Century Dolls, Platt & Munk Co #243, 1960 .... **65.00**
Chatty Cathy, Whitman/Mattel #1961, 1963 .... **55.00**
Cindy & Mindy, Whitman #1974, 1960 .... **35.00**
Cleopatra, Blaise #1000, 1963. **25.00**
Country Weekend w/Kathy & Jill, Reuben H Lilja #913, ca 1950 ....**20.00**
Cutie Paper Dolls, Milton Bradley #4053, 1940s.................. **40.00**
Dolly Dingle's Travels, John H Eggers series 2, 1921 ...... **75.00**
Dozen Cousins, Whitman #2090, 1960 .... **50.00**
Earnest & Justin Tubb, Jenson, 1946 .... **60.00**
Elizabeth Taylor, Whitman #2057, 1957 .... **150.00**
I'm Debra Dee the Bride, Lisbeth Whiting #189, 1963......... **25.00**
It's a Date, Whitman #1976, 1956 ....**40.00**
Jackie & Caroline, Magic Wand #107, early 1960s **50.00**
Johnny Jones, Goldsmith #2005, 1930 .... **30.00**
Little Ballerina, Whitman #1963, 1961 .... **25.00**
Little Folks Crepe Paper Doll Oufit, American Toy Works #902, 1930s.................................... **50.00**

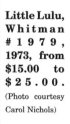

Little Lulu, Whitman #1979, 1973, from $15.00 to $25.00. (Photo courtesy Carol Nichols)

Little Red School House Kindergarten, McLoughlin #549, 1940 .... **100.00**
Little Women, Artcraft #5127. **35.00**
Mickey & Minnie Steppin' Out, Whitman #1979, 1977 .... **25.00**
Miss America, Reuben H Lilja #900, 1941 .... **75.00**
Modern Dolls a Plenty, Gabriel #895, ca 1933 .... **90.00**
Modern Girls Sewing Set, American Toy Works #400, 1930s ... **35.00**
My Fair Lady, Avalon/Standard Toykraft #401, 1960s **50.00**
Patsy, Childrens Press #3002, 1946 .... **30.00**

Patty Duke, Whitman #1991, from $25.00 to $45.00. (Photo courtesy Carol Nichols)

Peg, Nan, Kay & Sue, Whitman/Western #1995, 1966 ...... **40.00**
Round About Dolls on Parade, McLouglin Bros #2992, 1941 .... **80.00**
Santa's Workshop, Whitman #1989, 1960 .... **75.00**
Sapphire, Queen of Night Clubs, Rueben H Lilja #907, 1940s **100.00**
Shirley Temple, Gabriel #303, ca 1961 .... **60.00**
Sonny & Sue, Lowe #522, 1940 . **35.00**
Tina & Trudy, Whitman #1952, 1967 .... **40.00**
Toni, Merry Manufacturing Co #6501, 1960s **30.00**

Town & Country, Gabriel #894, 1930s **90.00**
Umbrella Girls, Merrill #2562, 1956 .... **75.00**
Waltons, Whitman #4334, 1974, boxed set **30.00**

Pennsbury Pottery

From the 1950s through the 1970s, dinnerware and novelty ware produced by the Pennsbury company was sold through tourist gift shops along the Pennsylvania turnpike. Much of their ware was decorated in an Amish theme. A group of barbershop singers was another popular design, and they made a line of bird figures that were very similar to Stangl's, though today much harder to find.

Ashtray, Don's Be So Doppich, 5" **20.00**
Bowl, Amish, motto, 9" **60.00**
Bowl, divided vegetable; Rooster, 9½x6¼" **50.00**
Bowl, pretzel; Amish Couple . **85.00**
Bowl, pretzel; Eagle, 12x8".... **85.00**
Bowl, pretzel; Gay Ninety, 12x8" .**95.00**
Bread plate, Sheaves of Wheat, oval or round **40.00**
Butter dish, Rooster, ¼-lb, from $45 to **50.00**
Cake stand, Amish, 4½x11½". **85.00**
Cake stand, Harvest or Hex, 4½x11½" **80.00**
Candy dish, Hex, heart shape . **35.00**
Canister, Rooster, Sugar, 7½". **110.00**
Chip 'n dip, Folkart **80.00**
Coaster, Fisherman, 4½", set of 4 .... **80.00**
Compote, holly & berries, 5" . **25.00**

Creamer & sugar bowl, Amish ..30.00
Cruets, rooster finials, pr 50.00
Egg cup, Folkart.................... 16.00
Figurine, Magnolia Warbler. 150.00
Mug, beer; eagle & flag......... 20.00
Mug, Irish coffee; horse w/gold
trim 40.00
Pie plate, Amish boy & girl, roman-
tic verse, 9" 88.00
Pitcher, Delft Toleware, blue,
5" 55.00
Pitcher, E Pluribus Unum & eagle
in blue, 6¼"...................... 45.00
Pitcher, Gay Ninety, 7¼"...... 125.00
Pitcher, Hex, 6¼".................... 65.00
Pitcher, Tulip, 3-qt, 9¾" 45.00
Plaque, Amish sayings, 7x5" . 25.00
Plaque, Baltimore & Ohio Rail-
road, Lafayette (train), rec-
tangular........................ 45.00
Plaque, horse & carriage, 6"..50.00
Plaque, It Is Whole Empty, 4"
dia.............................35.00
Plaque, Outen the Light, 4¼".24.00
Plaque, Pea Hen, 6" dia......... 40.00
Plaque, River Steamboat,
13½x10¼"...................... 160.00
Plate, Amish, 11¼" 65.00

Plate, Amish cou-
ple, he with
mug, 8",
$35.00.

Plate, Family Wagon, 8" 30.00
Plate, Red Rooster, dinner size..32.00
Plate, Treetops Christmas, 1961..25.00
Platter, fish, 17x10¼"........... 225.00
Platter, Rooster, 11" 48.00
Relish tray, Rooster, 14½x11½"..85.00

Snack tray & cup, Folkart or
Hex...............................20.00
Tea tile, skunk, Why Be
Disagreeable, 6".............. 40.00
Tureen, Rooster, w/ladle nook. 120.00
Wall pocket, cowboy............... 85.00

PEZ Collectibles

Originally a breath mint tar-
geted for smokers, by the '50s PEZ
had been diverted toward the kid's
candy market, and to make sure
the kids found them appealing,
the company designed dispensers
they'd be sure to like — many of
them characters the kids could easily recognize. On today's collectible
market, some of those dispensers
bring astonishing prices!

Though early on collectors preferred the dispensers with no feet,
today they concentrate primarily
on the character heads. Feet were
added in 1987, so if you want your
collection to be complete, you'll
need to buy both styles. For further information and more listings, see *Schroeder's Collectible
Toys, Antique to Modern* (Collector
Books). Our values are for mint
dispensers. Very few are worth
collecting if they are damaged or
have missing parts. See Clubs and
Newsletters for information concerning *PEZ Collector News*.

Angel, no feet 75.00
Baloo, w/feet 20.00
Bambi, no feet 50.00
Batgirl, no feet, soft head 150.00
Bugs Bunny, no feet............... 15.00
Captain America, no feet....... 90.00

Clown w/Collar, no feet......... **60.00**
Dalmatian Pup, w/feet........... **50.00**
Dumbo, w/feet, blue head...... **25.00**
Football Player..................... **175.00**
Frog, w/feet, whistle head..... **40.00**
Garfield, w/feet, orange w/green hat...................................... **3.00**
Gorilla, no feet, black head ... **80.00**
Henry Hawk, no feet.............. **75.00**
Indian, w/feet, whistle head.. **20.00**
Inspector Clouseau, w/feet...... **5.00**
Jiminy Cricket, no feet........ **175.00**
Lion w/Crown, no feet.......... **100.00**
Merlin Mouse, w/feet............. **15.00**
Monkey Sailor, no feet, w/white cap..................................... **50.00**
Octopus, no feet, black........... **85.00**
Odie, w/feet.............................. **5.00**
Olive Oyl, no feet **200.00**
Papa Smurf, w/feet, red........... **6.00**
Pilgrim, no feet..................... **125.00**
Raven, no feet, yellow beak... **70.00**
Rhino, w/feet, whistle head..... **6.00**

Road Runner, purple body, $25.00; Uncle Sam, $175.00.

Rooster, w/feet, whistle head. **35.00**
Sheik, no feet......................... **55.00**
Snow White, no feet............. **225.00**
Thumper, w/feet, no copyright. **45.00**
Tweety Bird, no feet.............. **15.00**
Wile E Coyote, w/feet............. **60.00**
Wonder Woman, w/feet........... **3.00**
Yappy Dog, no feet, orange or green, ea..................................... **80.00**
Yosemite Sam, w/feet............. **3.00**

Pfaltzgraff Pottery

Since early in the seventeenth century, pottery has been produced in York County, Pennsylvania. The Pfaltzgraff Company that operated there until 2007 was the outgrowth of several of these small potteries. A changeover made in 1940 redirected their efforts toward making the dinnerware lines for which they became best known. Their earliest line, a glossy brown with a white frothy drip glaze around the rim, was called Gourmet Royale. Today collectors find an abundance of good examples and are working toward reassembling sets of their own. Village, another very successful line, is tan with a stenciled Pennsylvania Dutch-type floral design in brown. Many other patterns were produced and became very good sellers, and since the factory is no longer in operation, collectors are turning toward the secondary market for replacement pieces.

Giftware consisting of ashtrays, mugs, bottle stoppers, a cookie jar, etc., all with comic character faces were made in the 1940s. This line was called Muggsy, and it is also very collectible, with the more common mugs starting at about $35.00 each. For more information refer to *The Collector's Encyclopedia of American Dinnerware* by Jo Cunningham (Collector Books) and *Pfaltzgraff, America's Potter*, by David A. Walsh and Polly Stetler, published in conjunction with the Historical Society of York County, York, Pennsylvania.

Christmas Heritage, bowl, vegetable; 12-sided oval, 11x8¼"........ **15.00**

Christmas Heritage, cheese tray, #533, 10½x7½".................. **9.00**

Christmas Heritage, coffee carafe, thermal, 13"..................... **22.50**

Christmas Heritage, coffee cup, 4".....................................**5.00**

Christmas Heritage, cookie jar..**35.00**

Christmas Heritage, dish, oblong w/lobed rim, 8¼x6"......... **20.00**

Christmas Heritage, lamp, green shade, 14"........................ **30.00**

Christmas Heritage, ornament, angel, 1987, MIB, from $22 to......**30.00**

Christmas Heritage, pie plate, 9"............................... **22.00**

Christmas Heritage, pitcher, 5¾".............................. **20.00**

Christmas Heritage, teapot, lighthouse shape, 8½"............. **15.00**

Gourmet Royale, baker, #321, oval, 7½", from $8 to................ **10.00**

Gourmet Royale, baking dish, 12x7".............................. **35.00**

Gourmet Royale, bean pot, #11-1, 1-qt, from $10 to **12.00**

Gourmet Royale, bean pot, #11-3, 3-qt..................................**25.00**

Gourmet Royale, bean pot warming stand............................... **10.00**

Gourmet Royale, bowl, mixing; 14".............................. **70.00**

Gourmet Royale, bowl, oval, #241, 7x10", from $10 to........... **12.00**

Gourmet Royale, bowl, salad; tapered sides, 10", from $10 to **14.00**

Gourmet Royale, bowl, spaghetti; shallow, #219, 14", from $15 to **20.00**

Gourmet Royale, butter dish, #394, ¼-lb, from $9 to **12.00**

Gourmet Royale, butter warmer & stand, stick handle, 2-spout, 9-oz..................................... **13.00**

Gourmet Royale, candleholders, saucer type w/finger ring, pr.. **20.00**

Gourmet Royale, casserole, hen on nest, 2-qt, from $50 to **60.00**

Gourmet Royale, casserole, stick handle, 4-qt, from $25 to . **35.00**

Gourmet Royale, casserole warming stand........................... **7.00**

Gourmet Royale, cheese shaker, bulbous, 5¾", from $12 to **15.00**

Gourmet Royale, chip and dip set, $30.00.

Gourmet Royale, coffeepot, 9". **25.00**

Gourmet Royale, cup & saucer, demitasse.......................... **18.00**

Gourmet Royale, lazy Susan, 3 sections w/center bowl, #308, 14" **23.00**

Gourmet Royale, plate, bread; #528, 12" L.................................. **20.00**

Gourmet Royale, plate, luncheon; 8½" **12.00**

Gourmet Royale, salt & pepper shakers, bell shape, pr from $15 to **20.00**

Gourmet Royale, soup & sandwich, rectangular 12" tray & cup, $12 to **18.00**

Gourmet Royale, toby mug, 6¼", from $22 to **28.00**

Gourmet Royale, tray, serving; round, 4-section, center handle, $15 to **18.00**

Gourmet Royale, trivet, round, w/ handles, 6½" **28.00**

Heritage, bowl, soup; wide rim, 8½" **8.00**

Heritage, cake plate, pedestal foot, 6½x12½" **75.00**

Heritage, coffee/teapot, 13½". **40.00**

Heritage, condiment server, 3 cups in wood wire stand **30.00**

Heritage, gravy boat, w/under-tray **22.00**

Heritage, honey pot, w/lid & drizzler **40.00**

Heritage, napkin rings, set of 4, MIB **22.00**

Heritage, pitcher, 5", w/#772 bowl **30.00**

Heritage, plate, egg; holds 12, 12½" L **35.00**

Heritage, punch bowl, 6 cups & ladle **75.00**

Heritage, salt & pepper shakers, w/ handle, 5", pr from $20 to . **30.00**

Heritage, salt crock jar, #560. **35.00**

Heritage, soup tureen, w/ladle & underplate, 3½-qt, $35 to. **40.00**

Heritage, tidbit, 3-tier **35.00**

Heritage, vase, bud; 6½" **18.00**

Muggsy, bottle stopper, head, ball shape **85.00**

Muggsy, canape holder, lift-off head pierced for toothpicks, from $125 to **150.00**

Muggsy, cigarette server **95.00**

Muggsy, clothes sprinkler bottle, Myrtle, white, from $250 to **295.00**

Muggsy, clothes sprinkler bottle, Mytrle, Black, from $275 to **375.00**

Muggsy, mug, Black action figure **125.00**

Muggsy, shot mug, character face, ea from $40 to **50.00**

Muggsy, utility jar, Handy Harry, hat w/short bill as flat lid **150.00**

Village, bowl, batter; w/spout & handle, 8", from $32 to ... **40.00**

Village, bowl, onion soup; stick handle **8.00**

Village, bread tray, 12" **15.00**

Village, colander, enamel on metal, footed **30.00**

Village, cooler/drink dispenser, spigot on front, 10x7", from $60 to **75.00**

Village, lazy Susan, 5-pc **45.00**

Village, measuring cups, ceramic, 4 on hanging rack **40.00**

Village, pie plate, 9½", $15.00.

Village, potpourri jar, 4¾", from $10 to **12.00**

Village, seafood baker, fish shape, 10½" **45.00**

Village, soap dish **42.00**

Village, soap dispenser, 6" **28.00**

Village, soup tureen, #160, w/lid & ladle, 3½-qt, from $40 to. **45.00**

Village, tape dispenser **85.00**

Village, teakettle, 3-qt **35.00**

Village, teapot, individual, 16-oz. **10.00**

Village, vase, cylindrical, 7½".. **45.00**

Village, welcome plaque, oval, 4¾x6¾" **30.00**

Pie Birds

What is a pie bird? It is a functional and decorative kitchen tool most commonly found in the shape of a bird, designed to vent steam through the top crust of a pie to prevent the juices from spilling over into the oven. Other popular designs were elephants and black-faced bakers. The original vents that were used in England and Wales in the 1800s were simply shaped like funnels.

From the 1980s to the present, many novelty pie vents have been added to the market for the baker and the collector. Some of these could be obtained from Far East Imports; others have been made in England and the US (by commercial and/or local enterprises). Examples can be found in the shapes of animals (dogs, frogs, elephants, cats, goats, and dragons), people (policemen, chefs with and without pies, pilgrims, and carolers), or whimsical figures (clowns, leprechauns, and teddy bears). A line of holiday-related pie vents were made in the 1990s. Consequently, a collector must be on guard and aware that these new pie vents are being sold by dealers (knowingly in many instances) as old or rare, often at double or triple the original cost (which is usually under $10.00). Though most of the new ones can't really be called reproductions since they never existed before, there's a black bird that is a remake, and you'll see them everywhere. Here's how you can spot them: They'll have yellow beaks and protruding white-dotted eyes. If they're on a white base and

have an orange beak, they are the older ones. Another basic tip that should help you distinguish old from new: Older pie vents are air-brushed versus being hand painted. Please note that incense burners, one-hole pepper shakers, dated brass toy bird whistles, and ring holders (for instance, the elephant with a clover on his tummy) should not be mistaken for pie vents. See Clubs and Newsletters for information concerning *Pie Birds Unlimited Newsletter*.

Bird, blue w/pink eyes & wing-tips, Shawnee for Pillsbury, 5½" **50.00**
Bird, thin neck, Scotland, 1972, 4¼", from $75 to **90.00**
Black clown holding pie, embossed England on pants, 4½".... **45.00**
Bugs Bunny, California, 4".... **27.00**
Bumble bee, multicolored, California, 5" **35.00**

Chick, yellow with black eyes and red beak, Josef Originals, 3", $55.00.

Cutie Pie, Josef (or Lorrie Design), hen in bonnet, from $125 to **150.00**
Donald Duck, identified on side, c Walt Disney **825.00**
Duck, long neck, maroon, 5".. **75.00**
Dutch girl, multipurpose kitchen tool, from $150 to **195.00**
Eagle, golden color, Sunglow, from $75 to **85.00**

Elephant, Nutbrown Pie Funnel, Made in England, 3½" **55.00**

Funnel, pagoda, Gourmet Pie Cup, Reg No 369793 .... **75.00**

Funnel, terra cotta, Wales **35.00**

Granny w/mixing bowl, Josef, 3¼", from $100 to **125.00**

Great Blue Heron, Carmack, 4". **40.00**

Half-bird, black, w/scalloped or triangular bottom, from $100 to **125.00**

Mammy, multipurpose kitchen tool, outstretched arms, from $125 to **150.00**

Rooster, multicolored, Cleminson. **50.00**

Rooster, white w/black, red & yellow details, Marion Drake, 5" **125.00**

Rowland's Hygienic Patent, England **90.00**

Songbird, cream (or black) w/gold, Chic Pottery **200.00**

Songbird, cream w/flowers, Chic Pottery **250.00**

Songbird, Kansas in brown lettering, sunflower on ea shoulder, 4" **30.00**

Train engine, black, Boyd Special, Boyd Glass, 3½x3¾" **25.00**

Yankee Blackbird, Made in England, 1950-60s, 4¼" .. **55.00**

Pin-Back Buttons

Because most of the pin-backs prior to the 1920s were made of celluloid, collectors refer to them as 'cellos.' Many were issued in sets on related topics. Some advertising buttons had paper inserts on the back that identified the company or the product they were advertising. After the 1920s, lithographed metal buttons were produced; they're now called 'lithos.'

In the late '40s and into the '50s, some cereal companies packed a pin-back button in each box of their product. Quaker Puffed Oats offered a series of movie star pin-backs, but Kellogg's Pep Pins are probably the best known of all. There were 86 different Pep pins. They came in five sets — the first in 1945, three more in 1946, and the last in 1947. See also The Beatles; Elvis Presley; Political.

Amazing Spider-Man, in black suit on yellow, 1987, 2¼", EX. **15.00**

American Legion Baseball Booster, red, white & blue, 1955, 1¾", EX............... **135.00**

Bozo the Clown, portrait, multicolor, Chicago, 1979, 2", EX........ **15.00**

Buster Brown Jr Business Club Member, multicolored, 1", EX.............................**50.00**

Charles Berry, portrait in baseball uniform on yellow, ¾" dia, EX.........................**30.00**

Cleanup Week, Symbol of Healthful..., Dutch girl, 1", EX................................. **20.00**

Cycle Trades Safety League, yellow bicycle, red border, ⅞", NM.**60.00**

Deanna Durbin Doll, portrait, black & white, 1", EX **85.00**

Ducks Unlimited 1948, duck on water, 1¼", EX................. **40.00**

Flatten the Falcons (Penn State), Central Counties Bank, 1973, EX **180.00**

Hopalong Cassidy, Mary Jane Bread, black & white closeup on red, NM **42.00**

I (heart) Scandinavia, multicolor, 2½", M............................. **12.00**

Joe Louis standing in boxing pose, black & white, 1930-40s, 1¾", EX **27.50**

Ko Ko (Taylor), Black lady singing w/microphone, black on yellow, EX **20.00**

Lion Coffee, Millions Drink It, steaming cup, celluliod, ⅞", EX **18.00**

Michigan State...Student Tour, Rose Bowl Jan 1 1966, multi-colored, EX **15.00**

Pep pin, Andy Gump, EX **12.00**

Pep pin, BO Plenty, NM **30.00**

Pep pin, Corky, NM **16.00**

Pep pin, Dick Tracy, NM **30.00**

Pep pin, Don Winslow, MIP... **20.00**

Pep pin, Smokey Stover, EX.. **10.00**

Pep pin, Uncle Avery, EX **20.00**

Pep pin, Wimpy, NM **20.00**

Roberto Clemente, black & white pic on red, white & blue, '69, 4", NM **105.00**

Shrine Circus in green, multicolor clown on white, 1940s, 1¾", NM **8.00**

Smokey Bear, Prevent...Fires, brown, yellow & red, Green Duck Co, M **15.00**

Speedway Stamina Skyway Style, Studebaker..., Green Duck Co, 1", VG **22.50**

To Hell w/the Beatles, red, white & blue, lg, NM **60.00**

Vote Betty Crocker, red, white & blue, General Mills, 1945, 1", EX **10.00**

Worchester Salt, celluloid over metal, blue, cream & black, 1½", EX **30.00**

Yankees, We're No 1, baseball & Uncle Sam hat, 1970s, 3½", EX **12.50**

Pinup Art

Collectors of pinup art look for blotters, calendars, prints, playing cards, etc., with illustrations of sexy girls by artists who are famous for their work in this venue: Vargas, Petty, DeVorss, Elvgren, Moran, Mozert, Ballantyne, Armstrong, and Davis among them. Though not all items will be signed, most of these artists have a distinctive style that is easy to recognize.

Blotter, All American, blond on back w/ball, Enoch Bolles, ca 1939, M **50.00**

Book, Playboy's Vargas Girls, 1972, EX **90.00**

Calendar, A Pleasing Discovery, girl on scale w/dog, Elvgren, 1946, NM **25.00**

Calendar, different girl ea month, Layne art, complete, '50, 15x7", VG **100.00**

Calendar, different girl ea month, Vargas, Esquire, '46, 12x8½", NM **145.00**

Calendar, Enchantment, Zoe Mozert, complete, 1952, 14x11", EX **185.00**

Calendar, Goodness Skates, Moran, partial pad, 1936, 10x5", EX **25.00**

Calendar, Let's Be Friends, girl w/back exposed, Armstrong, 1949, EX **55.00**

Calendar, Miss Advertising, Armstrong, 1941, full pad, 23x11", EX **70.00**

Calendar, Pepsi-Cola, redhead in yellow swimsuit, complete, 1944, EX **50.00**

Calendar print, Elvgren girl w/ skirt in ringer, LF Dow, '46, 9x7½" **35.00**

Calendar print, girl with Scottie dogs, Elvgren, 1930s, from $20.00 to $30.00. (Photo courtesy Candace Sten Davis and Patricia J. Baugh)

Calendar print, lady holding orchids, DeVorss, 1930s, 9½x8", EX (+).............................. **70.00**

Centerfold, girl in swimsuit, 4-fold pull-out, Vargas, Esquire, EX.................. **80.00**

Cigarette lighter, girl in black on telephone, Petty, Zippo, 1999............................ **30.00**

Clock, Sundrop Golden Cola, girl in cup, light-up, sq, Pam, 15", EX **100.00**

Hot water bottle, girl figure, plastic, Poiynter Products...1957, EX **65.00**

Lithograph, girl in short overalls w/fishing pole, 26x18", +frame, NM **150.00**

Movie poster, Behave Yourself, Vargas image of Shelly Winters, '51, EX **125.00**

Painting, nude girl in landscape, Paint-By-Numbers, 1950s, 24x18", VG...................... **60.00**

Photo, Mamie Van Doren, in shorts, w/dog, black & white, 10x13", EX **115.00**

Photo, Natalie Wood in corset w/ garters, black & white glossy, 10x8"............................ **100.00**

Playing cards, Anything Goes, various pinups, 1 per card, Vargas, EXIB **110.00**

Playing cards, Top Hat, pinup girls, Elvgren, EXIB................. **60.00**

Playing cards, Western World..., 53 pinups, Vargas, poker size, MIB.............................. **100.00**

Print, Alluring, full-figured nude, signed Earl Moran, 25x20½", NM **100.00**

Print, Good Pikins, girl in red lingerie picks apples, L Dow, '40s, NM **10.00**

Print, Happy Landing, blonde skiing, DeVorss, 15½x11", EX **40.00**

Print, Pistol Packin' Mama, Vargas, 1944, 17½x13", EX **40.00**

Print, Temptation, brunette reclining, Vargas, American Classics, NM **45.00**

Print, Youthful Charm, blond w/ fringed shaw, DeVorss, '40s, 21x16", NM.................. **110.00**

Playing Cards

Here is another field of collectibles that is inexpensive, easy to display (especially single cards), and very diversified. Variations are endless. Some backs are printed with reproductions of famous paintings or pinup art. Others carry advertising messages, picture tourist attractions, or commemorate a world's fair. Early decks are scarce, but those from the 1940s on are usually more attractive anyway, so pick an area that interests you most and have fun! Though they're usually not dated, you may find some clues that will help you to determine an approximate date. Telephone numbers, zip codes, advertising slogans, and patriotic messages are always helpful. See also Pinup Art.

Air Force One, Ronald Reagan, blue backs, double deck, MIB, (sealed) 80.00

American Saddlebred Stars of the Past, Congress, NM in hinged box.................................. 28.00

The Best of Betty Boop, $7.50.
(Photo courtesy Mark Pickvet)

Catalina Island Steamship Line, Congress, 1940s, EXIB ... 45.00

Chippendales, sexy men backs, 1982, MIP........................ 27.50

Eden big-eyed girl (2 different) backs, double deck, MIB (sealed) 55.00

Famous Cities, Happy Families Game, Piatnik, ca 1952, complete, EX........................... 40.00

Golden Lights Quality Playing Cards, like cigarette package, 1975, MIP........................ 16.00

Great Northern Railway, Indian girl w/doll, Brown & Bigelow, EXIB 130.00

Greyhound Scenicruiser Service, bus on blue backs, M (sealed).. 40.00

Hillbilly backs, Highland Builders Supply, Paul Webb art, 1950s, EXIB 12.50

Historical Facts About Texas, mid-1960s, complete, M (sealed)......................... 25.00

Jeep w/3 soldiers wearing M-17A1 helmets, Congress Hamilton Card, MIB........................ 38.00

KEM, Arrow Poker design, all plastic, regular, 2 decks, MIB. 25.00

Lady w/dogs, double deck, Congress, 54 cards, MIB w/ instructions 27.50

Luxus Salon Kort, Handa No 99, 1950s, MIB (sealed)........ 50.00

Marlboro Texan #45 Poker Cards, star backs, copyright 1984, MIB.............................. 48.00

Mobil Oil, Pegasus flying before full moon backs, complete, EXIB 30.00

No 20 American Rover, blue backs, MIB.............................. 125.00

Oliver Finest in Farm Machinery, 2 decks, red & green backs, NMIB.............................. 180.00

Port scenes by Lionel Barrymore, double deck, Brown & Bigelow, 1965, M............................ 45.00

Sailing ships in oval on red or blue, 2 decks, Kem, MIB.......... 60.00

Siamese kittens (2) on grass, all plastic, 2 decks, Astor, M (sealed) 67.50

Space Shuttle, Kennedy Space Center souvenir, 1980s, EXIB 8.00

Springer spaniel & Irish setter backs, double deck w/4 jokers, EXIB 32.50

Trip or Trap, drug info, WR Spence MD, Spenco, 1960, 54 cards, MIB.............................. 35.00

US Capitol building, linen, 10¢ tax stamp, 53 cards, EXIB.... 25.00

Political Collectibles

Pennants, posters, badges, pamphlets — in general, anything related to a presidential campaign or politicians — are being sought by collectors who have an interest in the political history of our country. Most valued are items from a particularly eventful period or those things having to do with an especially colorful personality.

Celluloid pin-back buttons ('cellos') were first widely used in the 1896 presidential campaign; before that time medals, ribbons, and badges of various kinds predominated. Prices for political pin-backs have increased considerably in the last few years, more due to speculative buying and selling rather than inherent scarcity or unusual demand. It is still possible, however, to find quality collectible items at reasonable prices. In flea markets, recent buttons tend to be overpriced; the goal, as always, is to look for less familiar items that may be priced more reasonably. Most buttons issued since the 1964 campaign, with a few notable exceptions, should be in the range of $2.00 to $10.00. Condition is critical: cracks, scratches, spots, and brown stains ('foxing') seriously reduce the value of a button.

Unless otherwise noted, prices are for items in excellent condition. Reproductions are common; many are marked as such, but it takes some experience to tell the difference. For more information we recommend Edmund Sullivan's *Collecting Political Americana, 2nd Edition*. See Clubs and Newsletters for information concerning Political Collectors of Indiana.

Apron, Kennedy Is the Remedy, red, white & blue vest, 1960s **165.00**
Badge, Democratic Convention Delegate, Chicago, 1932 . **45.00**
Binoculars, view of Grover Cleveland & Lady Liberty inside, 1885,¾" **215.00**
Cap, Harding & Coolidge, red & white cloth, 1920 .... **200.00**
Cigarettes, Campaign '72 I'm 1000% for McGovern, 3x3½", G **20.00**
Hat, Kennedy Will Win, band on molded plastic, 1968 .... **50.00**
Lapel pin, IKE, metal letters, 1953,¾x¾", MOC **12.00**
License plate, Reagan Inaugural, 1981, NM **30.00**

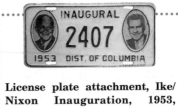

License plate attachment, Ike/ Nixon Inauguration, 1953, $150.00. (Photo courtesy Michael McQuillen)

Mug, Vote 72, Uncle Sam pointing finger, milk glass, Federal Glass **35.00**
Pennant, Our 36th President Lyndon B Johnson, portrait on shield, NM **15.00**
Pin-back button, Ford for President, black & white portrait, sm, M **4.00**

Pin-back button, I Like Bobby Kennedy Yeah! Yeah! Yeah!, 3½"............145.00

Pin-back button, I'm for Nixon, portrait flasher, 2¼"............10.00

Pin-back button, If I Were 21 I'd Vote for Bobby Kennedy, 3½"....15.00

Pin-back button, Independent FDR Voter, red, white & blue..15.00

Pin-back button, McGovern, orange & yellow, 1972, M............4.00

Pin-back button, Robert F Kennedy for US Senate................60.00

Pin-back button, Roosevelt for Humanity, red, white & blue, sm, VG............10.00

Pin-back button, Wings for Willkie America, plane, multicolor.28.00

Poster, Back Ike's Team, red & blue on white, 1946, 44x28"...55.00

Poster, LBJ for the USA, portrait & map, vinyl, 24x17½"........27.50

Poster, Nixon & Agnew as cartoon bikers, black & white, 22x34"......................100.00

Poster, Reagan-Bush '84, Bringing America Back, portraits on white..............................32.50

Poster, Robert Kennedy portrait, black & white, 1968, 19x12", M......................42.50

Poster, Vermont Republican Rally, 1956, black print on yellow, 22x14"..............................25.00

Poster, Vice President Spiro Agnew dressed as Hippie, 30x21", VG..................................30.00

Record, Richard M Nixon, vinyl on paper, 33 1/3 rpm............15.00

Record album, JF Kennedy on civil rights, 7 speeches............35.00

Ribbon, B Harrison Our President 1892, black & white, 2½", VG........100.00

Sheet music, Hail Prosperity, FD Roosevelt portrait cover, 1936............................40.00

Tapestry, Martin L King, John & Robert Kennedy, late 1960s, 19x37"............................40.00

Thermometer, Richard J Daley for Mayor, tin litho, 1955, 6⅜".50.00

Thomas E Dewey for President, portrait, black & white, 1944, 2½"................................20.00

Tray, McKinley portrait, tin litho, 16x13"..........................125.00

Wristwatch, Jimmy Carter w/ peanut face, legs tell time, 1976............................75.00

Wristwatch, Spiro Agnew, copyright Sheffield Watch, leather band............................25.00

Wristwatch, You're Pardoned, Nixon playing football, Honest Time, M..........................85.00

Princess House Glassware

The home party plan of Princess House was started in Massachusetts in 1963 by Charlie Collis. His idea was to give women an opportunity to have their own business by being a princess in their house, thus the name for this company. Though many changes have been made since the 1960s, the main goal of this company is to better focus on the home party plan.

Most Princess House pieces are not marked in the glass — they carry a paper label. Heritage is a crystal cut floral pattern, introduced not long after the company started in business. Fantasia is a crystal pressed floral pattern, introduced about 1980.

Both lines continue today; new pieces are being added, and old items are continually discontinued.

Baker, Fantasia, #588, 3¼x12¾x8¾", MIB, from $35 to **45.00**

Basket, Heritage, #33, hostess booking gift, 10x7¾" **45.00**

Bowl, salad; Fantasia, #567, 10¾".**24.50**

Bowl, trifle; Heritage, #21, MIB.**40.00**

Butter dish, Heritage, #461, domed lid, 4¾x4½" **9.50**

Cake pan, Heritage, #6127, sculptured tube, hostess gift, 10" **45.00**

Casserole, Fantasia, #529, w/lid, 3-qt, 5x11x8¼" **30.00**

Chip & dip, Heritage, #41, 11¼".**19.50**

Cookie jar, Fantasia, #569, 10"..**30.00**

Cup & saucer, Fantasia, #515.**5.00**

Dish, lasagna; Fantasia, crystal handles, #535, 3½x12½x8¼".... **50.00**

Egg plate, Fantasia, #591, 10".**24.00**

Figurine, Bull, #770, Wonders of the Wild **60.00**

Figurine, Kitten, Katrina, #811, Pets collection, 3¼" **12.00**

Figurine, Moose, Wonders of the Wild, 7½x7½" **55.00**

Figurine, Wild Mustang, recumbent, #935, Wonders of the Wild, 7½" **58.00**

Goblet, bridal flute; Heritage, #431, 7½-oz, 10" **12.50**

Goblet, martini; Heritage, #435, 7-oz **10.00**

Goblet, water; Heritage, #418, 11-oz **8.50**

Hurricane lamp, Heritage, #428, 2-pc, 11¾" **12.50**

Mayonnaise, Heritage, 2½x5", +6" underplate **10.00**

Mug, coffee; Heritage, #504, 10-oz, 5½" **7.50**

Mug, Fantasia, #516, 4", $6.00.
(Photo courtesy Debbie and Randy Coe)

Mug, Fantasia, #523 .... **8.00**

Pie plate, Fantasia, 9" **18.00**

Plate, Fantasia, #437, 8" **8.00**

Plate, Fantasia, #512, 6" **4.50**

Relish, Fantasia, 3-part, #534, 12¼x7" **18.00**

Roaster, Heritage, #41, w/lid, 13½" L, from $60 to **75.00**

Salt & pepper shakers, Fantasia, #542, 4", pr **12.50**

Salt & pepper shakers, Heritage, #471, 4", pr **9.50**

Straw dispenser, Heritage, metal lid, 10½" **70.00**

Tray, Heritage, #292, hostess gift, 15x12½" **45.00**

Tumbler, cooler; Heritage, #4672, 6¼" **10.00**

Tumbler, Heritage, roly poly, 2¼".**6.00**

Vase, bud; Heritage, 4", from $5 to **7.00**

Vase, Heritage, #475, 11½" **19.50**

Purinton

Popular among collectors due to its 'country' look, Purinton Pottery's dinnerware and kitchen items are easy to learn to recognize due to their bold yet simple designs, many of them of fruit and flowers, created with basic hand-applied colors on a creamy white gloss.

Apple, baker, 7" **30.00**

Apple, bottles, oil & vinegar; 1-pt, 9½", pr................................75.00
Apple, candy dish, divided, w/pottery handle, 6¼"................50.00
Apple, coffeepot, 8-cup, 8".....90.00
Apple, honey jug, 6¼"...........150.00
Apple, mug, beer; 16-oz, 4¾".55.00
Apple, plate, dinner; 9¾".......15.00
Apple, platter, meat; 12"........45.00
Cactus Flower, teapot, 2-cup.125.00
Chartreuse, bowl, vegetable; 8½".30.00
Chartreuse, juice mug, 6-oz, 2½"..25.00
Crescent, jug, Oasis; rare, minimum value....................750.00
Crescent, teapot, 2-cup..........50.00
Crescent Flower, coaster, 3½" dia................................75.00
Fruit, bowl, range; red trim, w/lid, 5½"......................45.00
Fruit, cookie jar, red trim, oval, 9".60.00
Fruit, jug, Dutch, 5-pt...........25.00
Fruit, plate, lap; 8½"..............30.00
Fruit, plate, 12"......................35.00
Fruit, salt & peppers shakers, mini jug, pr................................10.00
Fruit, sugar bowl, w/lid, 4"....25.00
Fruit, tumbler, 12-oz, 5"........20.00
Grapes, bowl, range; w/lid, 5½".45.00
Heather Plaid, jug, 5-pt, 8"...75.00
Heather Plaid, mug, beer......40.00
Heather Plaid, teapot, 6-cup, 6".65.00
Intaglio, bean pot, w/lid, 3¾".50.00
Intaglio, butter dish, 6½".......35.00
Intaglio, cookie jar, oval, 9½".75.00
Intaglio, jam & jelly dish, 5½".25.00
Intaglio, jug, 5-pt, 8".............75.00
Intaglio, plate, 9¾"..................15.00
Intaglio, teapot, 6-cup, 6½"....65.00
Intaglio, tidbit, 2-tier, metal handle, 10"..............................25.00
Ivy (red), cornucopia vase, 6".25.00
Ivy (red), salt & pepper shakers, jug style, 2½", pr.............20.00

Ivy (yellow), jug, honey; 6¼"..18.00
Leaves, jardiniere, 5"............25.00
Maywood, bowl, vegetable; w/lid..35.00
Maywood, cup & saucer, 2½" & 5½"......................................15.00
Maywood, teapot, 6-cup, 6½".45.00
Ming Tree, cup & saucer.......30.00
Ming Tree, planter, 5"...........25.00
Ming Tree, plate, 12"...........125.00
Mountain Rose, bean pot, 4½".65.00
Mountain Rose, decanter, 5".45.00
Mountain Rose, jug, Kent; 1-pt, 4½"......................................45.00
Mountain Rose, plate, 12".....95.00
Mountain Rose, wall pocket, 3½".65.00
Normandy Plaid, bowl, fruit; 12".35.00
Normandy Plaid, cookie jar, oval, 9½"......................................60.00

Normandy Plaid, grease jar, 5½", $60.00. (Photo courtesy Susan Morris-Snyder)

Palm Tree, basket planter, 6¼".100.00
Palm Tree, plate, 10"..........125.00
Palm Tree, vase, 5"...............75.00
Peasant Lady, candleholder, signed William Blair, minimum value, ea....................................500.00
Pennsylvania Dutch, salt & pepper shakers, Pour & Shake, pr.75.00
Petals, coffeepot, 8-cup, 8".....75.00
Petals, teapot, 8-cup, 8".........75.00
Provincial Fruit, plate, 9½"...35.00
Saraband, beer mug..............45.00
Saraband, cookie jar, oval, w/lid, 9½"......................................100.00
Saraband, teapot, 6-cup, 6½".25.00

295

Seafoam, salt & pepper shakers, 3",
pr..................................... 55.00
Tea Rose, bowl, vegetable; open,
8½"..................................... 40.00
Tea Rose, creamer & sugar bowl, w/
lid..................................... 95.00
Tea Rose, platter, meat; 12" .. 50.00
Woodflowers, pitcher, 6½"...... 65.00

Puzzles

Of most interest to collectors of vintage puzzles are those made of wood or plywood, especially the early hand-cut examples. Character-related examples and those representing a well-known personality or show from the early days of television are coming on strong right now, and values are steadily climbing in these areas. For an expanded listing, see *Schroeder's Collectible Toys, Antique to Modern.*

Aquaman, jigsaw, Whitman, 1968,
100 pcs, EXIB................... 30.00
Archie, jigsaw, Jaymar, 1960s, malt
shop scene, 60 pcs, NMIB. 75.00
Batman, frame-tray, Batman &
Robin fighting Joker, Whitman,
'66, EX+........................... 25.00
Captain Kangaroo, jigsaw, Fairchild
#1560, 1960s, EXIB........ 20.00
Charlie's Angels, jigsaw, Farrah w/
flower, Pro Arts, '77, 11x17",
EXIB............................... 18.00
Cinderella, frame-tray, 1960s,
EX...................................8.00
Dukes of Hazzard, frame-tray, plastic, 1980s, 4x4", EX........... 6.00
Flintstones, jigsaw, Bedrock Postal
Service, 1975, EXIB........ 15.00

Flip the Frog, jigsaw, Saalfield/
Celebrity Prod, '32, boxed set
of 4..................................... 75.00
Goldfinger/James Bond 007, jigsaw,
Milton Bradley, 1965, 600 pcs,
NMIB.............................. 50.00
Gulliver's Travels, jigsaw, Saalfield,
1930s, set of 3, EXIB.... 125.00
Howdy Doody, frame-tray, Whitman,
1952, EX......................... 45.00
Incredible Hulk, frame-tray,
Whitman, 1954, EX+...... 25.00
Jungle Book, frame-tray, Golden,
8x11", EX.......................... 5.00
Katzenjammer Kids, jigsaw,
Featured Funnies, 1930s,
14x10", EXIB.................. 80.00
Lady & the Tramp, frame-tray,
Whitman, 1954, EX+...... 25.00
Land of the Giants, jigsaw,
Whitman, 1969, NMIB... 40.00
Marvel Superheroes, jigsaw, Milton
Bradley, 1967, 100 pcs, EXIB. 50.00
Mary Poppins, frame-tray, Jaymar,
1964, NM+...................... 25.00
Monkees Greatest Hits, jigsaw,
Sunsout Inc, 500 pcs, 19x19",
MIB................................ 15.00
My Little Pony, jigsaw, Milton
Bradley #4576-10, 1989,
EXIB................................ 8.00
Peter Pan, frame-tray, Whitman,
1952, EX......................... 30.00
Pink Panter, jigsaw, Whitman, 100
pcs, EXIB........................ 25.00
Pinocchio Picture Puzzles,
Whitman, 1939, set of 2,
10x8½", NMIB 50.00
Popeye in 4 Picture Puzzles, jigsaw,
Saalfield/KFS #908, VGIB .65.00
Raggedy Ann & Andy Picture
Puzzles, Milton Bradley, '44,
set of 3, MIB.................. 80.00

Rescuers, jigsaw, Golden, 200 pcs, NMIB **6.00**

Rin-Tin-Tin, jigsaw, Jaymar, 1957, NMIB **25.00**

Robert Louis Stevenson Puzzle Box, Saalfield #575, set of 7, EXIB **65.00**

Rootie (Kazootie) Wins the Soap..., frame-tray, Fairchild, 10x14", EX **30.00**

Sky Hawks, frame-tray, Whitman, 1970, NM **20.00**

Smokey Bear, jigsaw, Whitman #4610, 1971, 100 pcs, EXIB **15.00**

Smurfs, jigsaw, beach scene, Milton Bradley #4278-2, 1982, NMIB **10.00**

Superman, frame-tray, various scenes, Whitman, 1966, EX+, ea............................. **30.00**

Superman Saves a Life, jigsaw, Saalfield, 1940s, 500 pcs, EX+IB **300.00**

Thunderball/James Bond 007, jigsaw, Milton Bradley, 600+ pcs, NMIB **50.00**

Top Cat, frame-tray, Whitman, 1961, NM **25.00**

Wagon Train, frame-tray, Whitman, #4427, ca. 1958, VG, $35.00. (Photo courtesy gasoline alleyantiques.com)

Wizard of Oz, frame-tray, Jaymar, 1960s, NM+ **25.00**

Wizard of Oz, frame-tray, Whitman, 1976, NM+ **10.00**

Woody Woodpecker, jigsaw, w/ shark, 1970s, VG+IB **10.00**

Zorro, frame-tray, Whitman, Zorro by tree, 1957, 15x11½", NM **40.00**

Radios

Novelty radios are those that carry an advertising message or are shaped like a product bottle, can, or carton; others may be modeled after the likeness of a well-known cartoon character or disguised as anything but a radio — a shoe or a car, for instance. It's sometimes hard to recognize the fact that they're actually radios.

Transistor radios are collectible as well. First introduced in 1954, many feature space-age names and futuristic designs. Prices here are for complete, undamaged examples in excellent to near mint condition unless noted otherwise. If you have vintage radios you need to evaluate, see *Collector's Guide to Antique Radios* by John Slusser and the Staff of Radio Daze (Collector Books).

Novelty Radios

Batman & Robin, clips to belt, FM only, DC Comics, Kenner, 1997, MIP **60.00**

Big Bird on nest, transistors, Seasame Street, Concept 2000, NMIB **15.00**

Bullwinkle, 1969, 12" **150.00**

Casper the Friendly Ghost, Harvey Cartoons/Sutton, 1972 .... **50.00**

Champion Spark Plug, gray & white, 15x5".................... **65.00**

Dick Tracy, Creative Creations, wristband type, 1970s, AM...... **225.00**

Globe, hard plastic, 6 transistors, Peerless, 1970s, 8½"........ **55.00**

Hopalong Cassidy, red plastic case, lasso antenna, 4½x8x4".**995.00**

Huckeberry Hound, blue plastic w/ enameling, British Hong Kong, ca 1960............................ **32.50**

Incredible Hulk, Marvel Comics, 1978, 7"............................ **75.00**

King Kong, Amico, 1986, 13".**35.00**

Knight standing & holding sword, plastic, transistors.......... **25.00**

Ladybug, Sonnet, AM, Made in Hong Kong, 1960-70s, 5¾x3¼", MIB................................. **55.00**

Masters of the Universe, mouth moves w/music, 5½"........ **50.00**

Mickey Mouse in red car, AM only, Concept 2000, Walt Disney #181................................. **40.00**

Oatmeal Creme Pies, story of founder on back............... **55.00**

Owl, figural, cream & gold plastic, knobs are eyes, transistors, 7"..................................... **75.00**

Panapet R-60S ball on chain, Panasonic, 1970s............. **50.00**

Pinocchio, AM only, Walt Disney, Philgee International, 6¾x6".....**35.00**

Radio Shack, red plastic lettering, AM, Tandy Corp, 1979, 4x7x2"............................ **38.00**

Rolls Royce car, plastic, spare tires are on/off switch & dial ..**28.00**

Santory Whisky bottle, AM, transistors, Japan, 1960, MIB....**35.00**

Sinclair Dino Supreme gas pump, 6 transistors, w/case & earphones............................ **50.00**

Sinclair Gas Pump, Dino logo, AM only, 1960s........................ **40.00**

Snoopy Doghouse, Determined, 1970s, 6x4", NMIB.......... **55.00**

Soft drink shape, McDonald's 30th Anniversary, transistors, 1985.............................. **125.00**

Sputnick shape, red & white plastic, Japan, 1950s, 4½x2".**45.00**

Superman Exiting Phone Booth, Vanity Fair, AM, 1970s...**50.00**

TAZ, AM/FM radio/alarm clock, Toshiba, MIB................... **35.00**

Wilson Official Football With Kicking Tee, made in Hong Kong, 10" long, from $20.00 to $30.00.

Winnie the Pooh's head, yellow plastic, transistors, 6x5x1", MIB................................. **45.00**

Zany perfume bottle, AM, Avon, Hong Kong, 1979 .... **40.00**

Transistor Radios

Admiral, Y2023, Super 7, horizontal, AM, 7 transistors, 1960............................. **25.00**

Admiral, 7M14, horizontal, 7 transistors, AM, 1958 .... **50.00**

Admiral, 717, Imperial 8, horizontal, AM, 8 transistors, 1959............................. **30.00**

Ambassador, A-1064, horizontal, AM, 10 transistors, 1965.**15.00**

Arvin, 62R48, vertical, AM, 8 transistors, 1962 .... **25.00**

Bell Kamra, KTC-62, horizontal, camera radio, AM, 6 transistors **100.00**

Bulova, 620, horizontal, AM .. **85.00**

Bulova Super Transistor 7, Japan, 1962, 4¾" L **35.00**

Cameo, 64N06-03, vertical, AM, 6 transistors, 1964 ....**15.00**

Channel Master, 6503, vertical, AM, 5 transistors, 1960 .. **30.00**

Crosley, JM-8BK, Enchantment, book shape, 2 transistors, 1956 ....**150.00**

Delmonico, 6TRS, horizontal, AM **25.00**

Dewald, K-544, horizontal, leather, AM, 4 transistors, 1957 .. **125.00**

Emerson, 849, horizontal, AM, 1955 ....**150.00**

Everplay, PR-1266, rechargeable, vertical, AM, 6 transistors **35.00**

GE, P715-D, vertical, AM, 6 transistors, 1958 ....**35.00**

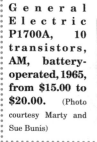

General Electric P1700A, 10 transistors, AM, battery-operated, 1965, from $15.00 to $20.00. (Photo courtesy Marty and Sue Bunis)

Golden Shield, 7186, vertical, AM, 6 transistors **20.00**

Hitachi, TH-831, vertical, AM, solid state **20.00**

Holiday, HS921, Super DX, vertical, AM, 9 transistors **20.00**

ITT, 628, horizontal, leatherette, AM, 6 transistors, 1963 .. **35.00**

Lincoln, L640, vertical, AM, 6 transistors, 1963 ....**125.00**

Matsushita, T-7, vertical, AM, 7 transistors **30.00**

Motorola, X31N, Ranger, horizontal, leather, AM, 1962 .....**20.00**

Motorola, 7X25W, Power 9, vertical, AM, 7 transistors, 1959 ... **40.00**

Motorola, 8X26S, vertical, AM, 8 transistors **30.00**

NEC, NT-6B, horizontal, AM . **30.00**

Olympic, 447, horizontal, AM, 4 transistors, 1957 ....**135.00**

Panasonic, T-7, vertical, AM, 7 transistors, 1964 ....**30.00**

Philco, T-20-124, vertical, AM, 7 transistors **35.00**

Philips, L1X75T, Fanette, horizontal, AM, 7 transistors, Germany, 1958 ....**45.00**

RCA, T-150-4, horizontal, AM, 1956 ....**200.00**

RCA, 1-RG-11, vertical, AM, 6 transistors **20.00**

Realistic, Hi-Fiver, horizontal, AM **40.00**

Realtone, TR-1843, vertical, AM, 8 transistors **40.00**

Realtone, TR-1859, vertical, AM, 8 transistors, 1964 ....**15.00**

Regency, TR-99, World Wide, vertical, AM, 7 transistors, 1960 .....**90.00**

Seminole, 1205, horizontal, AM/FM, 12 transistors, 1964 ....**20.00**

Silvertone, 5210, vertical, AM, 8 transistors, 1964 ....**20.00**

Sony, TR-714, horizontal, AM, 7 transistors, short wave, 1961 ....**65.00**

Standard, SR-F25, horizontal, AM, 6 transistors **95.00**

Star-Lite, DE-62, HIFI Deluxe, vertical, AM, 6 transistors ... **20.00**

Toshiba, 6P-15, horizontal, AM, 6 transistors, 1962 .... **30.00**

Toshiba, 6TP-394, vertical, AM, 6 transistors **45.00**

Trutone, DC3270, horizontal, AM, 9 transistors, USA **40.00**

Vista, 833, horizontal, AM, 8 transistors, short wave **35.00**

York, TR-121, horizontal, leather, AM, 12 transistors, 1965 . **20.00**

Zenith, Royal 130, vertical, AM **35.00**

Zenith, Royal 500D, vertical, AM, 8 transistors, 1959 .... **75.00**

Ramp Walkers

Ramp walkers date back to at least 1873 when Ives produced a cast-iron elephant walker. Wood and composite ramp walkers were made in Czechoslovakia and the USA from the 1920s through the 1940s. The most common were made by John Wilson of Watsontown, Pennsylvania. These sold worldwide and became known as 'Wilson Walkies.' Most are two-legged and stand approximately 4½" tall.

Plastic ramp walkers were manufactured primarily by the Louis Marx Co. from the 1950s through the early 1960s. The majority were produced in Hong Kong, but some were made in the USA and sold under the Marx logo or by the Charmore Co., a subsidiary of Marx.

The three common sizes are: small premiums about 1½" x 2"; the more common medium size, 2¾" x 3"; and large, approximately 4" x 5". Most of the smaller

walkers were unpainted, while the medium and large sizes were hand or spray painted. Several of the walking types were sold with wooden or colorful tin lithographed ramps. For more extensive listings and further information, see *Schroeder's Collectible Toys, Antique to Modern* (Collector Books).

Ankylosaurus w/Clown, Marx . **40.00**

Astro, Marx **150.00**

Big Bad Wolf & Three Little Pigs, Marx **150.00**

Bonnie Braids' Nursemaid, Marx .. **50.00**

Bunny on Back of Dog, Marx . **50.00**

Clown, Wilson **30.00**

Cow, Czechoslovakian **35.00**

Cowboy on Horse w/metal legs, sm, Marx **30.00**

Donald Duck & Goofy Riding Go-Cart, Marx **40.00**

Fidler & Fifer Pigs, Marx **50.00**

Fred Flintstone & Barney Rubble, Marx **40.00**

Frontiersman w/Dog, Marx ... **95.00**

Hap and Hop soldiers, Marx, $25.00. (Photo courtesy Randy Welch)

Indian Chief, Wilson **70.00**

Little King & Guard, Marx ... **60.00**

Little Red Riding Hood, Wilson . **40.00**

Mad Hatter w/March Hare,
Marx.............................. **50.00**
Mickey Mouse & Pluto Hunting,
Marx **40.00**
Monkey, Czechoslovakian...... **45.00**
Monkeys Carrying Bananas,
Marx............................... **60.00**
Olive Oyl, Wilson **175.00**
Pebbles on Dino, Marx........... **75.00**
Pluto, plastic w/metal legs, sm,
Marx **35.00**
Popeye, Wilson **200.00**
Popeye & Wimpy, heads on springs,
Marx, MIB........................ **85.00**
Reindeer, Marx........................ **45.00**
Santa & Mrs Claus, faces on both
sides, Marx........................ **50.00**
Santa w/white sack, Marx..... **40.00**
Slugger the Walking Bat Boy, w/
ramp & box, Marx......... **250.00**
Soldier, Wilson........................ **30.00**
Spark Plug, Marx................. **200.00**
Stegosaurus w/Black Caveman,
Marx **40.00**
Walking Baby, in Canadian Mountie
uniform, lg, Marx............. **50.00**

Records

Records that made it to the 'top ten' in their day are not always the records that are prized most highly by today's collectors, though they treasure those which best represent specific types of music: jazz, rhythm and blues, country and western, rock 'n roll, etc. Many search for those cut very early in the career of artists who later became superstars, records cut on rare or interesting labels, or those aimed at ethnic groups. A fast-growing area of related interest is picture sleeves for 45s. These are often worth more than the record itself, especially if they feature superstars from the '50s or early '60s.

Condition is very important. Record collectors tend to be very critical, so learn to watch for loss of gloss, holes, writing on the label, warping, and scratches. In the following listings, the first condition code describes the record and the second condition code describes the jacket. So NM/EX means near mint record with excellent jacket.

The American Premium Record Guide by Les Docks is a great source for more information. We also recommend *The Complete Guide to Vintage Children's Records* by Peter Muldavin, published by Collecor Books.

Children's Records

ABCs, 45 rpm, Peter Pan, w/full-color book, 24 pgs, 1974, NM/
NM **10.00**
Alice in Wonderland, Toy Toon, picture disk, 1952, NM/NM . **15.00**
Animal Supermarket, Children's Record Guild 9004, 78 rpm,
'50s, EX/EX....................... **9.00**
Birthday Song to You, Voco 35215, picture disk, 1948, 5" sq, NM/
NM **40.00**
Blue-Tail Fly, 78 rpm, 1953, EX/
EX **30.00**
Bugs Bunny & the Tortoise, 78 rpm, Capitol, 1949, EX/NM...... **35.00**
Cinderella, 78 rpm, Golden, 1950s, EX/EX **10.00**
Dennis the Menace, 78 rpm, Playtime, 1954, NM/NM . **15.00**

Dracula, 45 rpm, Peter Pan, 1970s, EX/EX **5.00**

Felix the Cat, 45 rpm, Cricket Records, 1958, EX **5.00**

Fred Flintstone, The Magician, 45 rpm, w/book, EX/EX **7.00**

Indiana Jones & the Temple of Doom, 33⅓ rpm, 1984, NM **15.00**

Jetsons New Songs of the TV Family..., 33⅓ rpm, Golden, '60s, EX/EX **85.00**

Lady & the Tramp, 33⅓ rpm, Decca, 1955, w/book, EX/EX **40.00**

Little Orley, told by Uncle Lumpy, Decca, ca. 1948, 78 rpm, EX+, from $12.00 to $15.00. (Photo courtesy Peter Muldavin)

Lionel Train Sound Effects, picture disk, 1951, NM/NM **50.00**

Mary Poppins, Happy Time Records, 33⅓ rpm, EX/EX **4.00**

Mister Ed, 33⅓ rpm, soundtrack, 1962, EX/EX **40.00**

Pedro in Argentina, Children's Record Guild 5035, 78 rpm, '50s, EX/EX **7.50**

Robin Hood, 45 rpm, Disneyland, 1973, w/book, EX **12.00**

Sgt Bilko's March Time, Peter Pan, 78 rpm, 1958, EX/EX **6.00**

Space: 1999, 33⅓ rpm, 3 stories, 1975, EX **25.00**

Strawberry Shortcake, Let's Dance, 33⅓ rpm, 1982, NM **20.00**

Superman, Power Records, 33 rpm, 1970s, EX/EX **3.00**

The Bug That Tried..., Johnny Cash, Columbia, 33 rpm, w/ book, 1970, EX **30.00**

The Fox, Talking Book Corp, picture disk, 78 rpm, 1917, rare, NM/M **150.00**

The Milk's Journey, Children's Record Guild 5029, 78 rpm, '50s, EX/EX **8.50**

Winnie the Pooh & Heffalumps, 45 rpm, 1968, w/book, EX/ EX **15.00**

LP Albums

AC/DC, Dirty Deeds Done Dirt Cheap, APLP-020, imported, 1976, EX/EX **110.00**

Alice Cooper, From the Inside, Warner Bros 3263, 1978, sealed, M/M **70.00**

Beatles, Abbey Road, MFSL 1-023, 1970s, M/NM **135.00**

Beatles, Yesterday & Today, Capitol, EX/EX **135.00**

Beowulf, Test Pressing, speed metal, NM/EX **200.00**

Beverley Kenney, Like Yesterday, Decca 78948, EX/EX **100.00**

Blind Willie Johnson, self-titled, Folkways 3585, EX/EX ... **80.00**

Bob Dylan, Clean Cuts, picture disc, M **160.00**

Commander Venus, The Uneventful Vacation, NM/NM **90.00**

Dave Ray, Fine Soft Land, Elektra 319, NM/VG **35.00**

David Bowie, Ziggy Stardust, MFSL 1-064, 1970s, M/M **65.00**

Elvis, King Creole, RCA Victor LPM-1884, EX/EX, $75.00.

Fabulous Cadillacs, self-titled, Jubilee 1045, EX/VG....... **65.00**

Fleetwood Mac, Mirage, MFSL 1-119, 1980s, M/NM...... **135.00**

Foreigner, Double Vision, MFSL 1-052, 1970s, M/M **45.00**

Frank Sinatra, In the Wee Small Hours, Capitol, SM-581, sealed, M/M................................. **60.00**

Hell's Angels '69, soundtrack, Capitol Records, VG/VG . **45.00**

James Brown, The Always Amazing; VG/VG............................. **95.00**

Jimi Hendrix, Axis Bold as Love!, Reprise Records, EX/EX. **110.00**

John Coltrane, Giant Steps, Atlantic 1311, NM/NM ... **88.00**

Johnny Griffin Quartet, Way Out, Riverside 12-274, NM/NM .**70.00**

Kiss, debut w/o song Kissin' Time, NB 9001 on blue label, '74, EX/EX **100.00**

Macpherson Singers & Dancers of Scotland, Caledoni, EX/VG **115.00**

Perfect Circles, Mer De Noms, 2 records, M/M **130.00**

Ricky Nelson, Teen Time, MG V-2083, 1957, EX/NM ... **110.00**

Rolling Stones, December's Children, LL 3451, NM/EX.............. **85.00**

Rolling Stones, Song of the Rolling Stones, ABKCO MPD 1, NM/NM................................ **380.00**

Roy Meriwether, Live, Stinger 1001, 1975, NM/EX......... **80.00**

Sam Cooke, Night Beat, VG/VG............................**70.00**

Shelley Fabares, Gold Colpix 426, M/M.............................. **300.00**

Steve Miller Band, Fly Like an Eagle, MFSL 1-021, 1978, M/M............................... **60.00**

The Stone Killer, soundtrack, Fonit-Centra ILS 9032, 1974, NM/NM.......................... **320.00**

The Who, My Generation, Decca 4664, NM/EX................... **65.00**

Traffic, self-titled, United Artist Records #6676, sealed, M/M. **60.00**

Troggs, Wild Thing, ATCO 33-193, 1966, EX/NM................... **35.00**

Yardbirds, Little Games, Epic LN 24313, M/M **90.00**

Yes, Close to the Edge, MFSL 1-077, 1970s, M/NM................... **90.00**

Yoni Nameri, Silence From the Other World, CBS-463260-1, 1980s, M/M................... **235.00**

45 rpms

Aladdins, I Had a Dream Last Night, Aladdin 3298, M .. **30.00**

Beach Boys, Surfin', Candix 331, M..................................... **45.00**

Beatles, Let It Be/You Know My Name, Apple 2764, EX.... **15.00**

Bee Gees, You Should Be Dancing (1-sided), RSO 853, NM.. **10.00**

Belmonts, Walk on By, Sabina 517, EX **15.00**

Belvederes, Pepper Hot Baby, Baton 217, EX **15.00**

Blenders, Tell Me What's on Your Mind, Decca 31284, NM . **15.00**

Bobby Bare, That's Where I Want To Be, Fraternity 861, M .. **8.00**

Buddy Holly, Peggy Sue, Coral 61885, EX **10.00**

Cadillacs, Speedo, Josie 785, EX. **8.00**

Capitols, Day by Day, Getaway 721, EX **20.00**

Cashmeres, Little Dream Girl, Herald 474, NM **12.00**

Chuck Berry, Maybellene, Chess 1604, EX **15.00**

Debonaires, As Others Are, Combo 129, NM/EX **45.00**

Dion, The Majestic/The Wanderer, Laurie 3115, NM **8.00**

Eagles, Please Please, Mercury 70391, EX **12.00**

Elvis Presley, That's All Right, RCA 6380, EX **20.00**

Heartbreakers, My Love, Vik 0299, M **30.00**

Hornets, Crying Over You, Flash 125, NM **15.00**

Jack & Jill, Party Time, Caddy 110, EX **10.00**

Jan & Dean, There's a Girl, Dore 531, EX **12.00**

Johnny Mathis, It's Not for Me to Say, Columbia 40851, M ... **6.00**

Johnny Tillotson, Earth Angel, Cadence 1377, EX **8.00**

Loretta Lynn, I'm a Honky Tonk Girl, Zero 107, M **50.00**

Lynn Pratt, Tom Cat Boogie, Hornet 1000, EX **60.00**

Majestics, Searching for a New Love, Pixie 6901, NM **12.00**

Mickey Gilley, Valley of Tears, Sabra 518, NM **11.00**

Platters, My Prayer, Mercury 70893, maroon label, EX **10.00**

Platters, The Great Pretender, Mercury 70753, maroon label, M **10.00**

Ravens, White Christmas, Mercury 70505, NM **20.00**

Ricky Nelson, Fools Rush In, Decca 31533, M **12.00**

Rolling Stones, Time Is on My Side, London 9708, M **10.00**

Sam the Sham & the Pharaohs, Wooly Bully, XL 906, EX. **20.00**

Squires, Dreamy Eyes, Aladdin 3360, NM **15.00**

Vince Everett, Buttercup, Towne 1964, NM **12.00**

78 rpms

Ada Jones & American Quartet, Come Josephine..., Victor 16844, VG **37.00**

Andrews Sisters, Boogie Woogie Bugle Boy, Decca 3598, EX **40.00**

Bell Hops, For The Rest of My Life, Decca 48208, EX **20.00**

Bill Haley, Burn That Candle, Decca 29713, VG **24.00**

Billie Holiday, Strange Fruit, Commodore 526, EX **33.00**

Buell Kazee, The Ship That's Sailing High, Brunswick 155, 1927, EX **40.00**

Carl Perkins, Blue Suede Shoes, Sun 234, EX **55.00**

Clarence Williams, The Right Key but the Wrong..., Vocalion 2563, EX **32.00**

Dean Martin, Memories Are Made of This, Capitol 3295, NM **26.00**

Dixie Washboard Band, Wait Till You See My Baby..., Columbia 14128, EX 21.00

Earl Oliver's Jazz Babies, Show That Fellow the..., Edison 51745, EX 37.00

Edna Hicks, Oh Daddy Blues, Gennett 5234, EX 20.00

Elvis Prestley, Hard Headed Woman, RCA 20-7280, EX 29.00

Everly Brothers, Bye Bye Love, Apex 76152, EX/EX 73.00

Frankie Avalon, Venus, REO 8335, EX 38.00

Hank Williams, Faded Love & Winter Roses, MGM 11928, EX 30.00

Jerry Lee Lewis, Great Balls of Fire, Sun 277, VG 55.00

Jimmy Braken's Toe Ticklers, Shirt Tail Stomp, Domino 4274, VG 33.00

Joe Stafford, You Belong to Me, Columbia C-2000, NM 60.00

Johnny Cash & Tennessee Two, I Walk the Line, Sun 241, VG 35.00

Leroy Carr, Christmas in Jail - Ain't That a Pain, Vocalion 1432, EX 37.00

Louis Armstrong & His Savoy Ballroom Five, Save It..., Okeh 41180, EX 37.00

Muddy Waters, Just Make Love to Me, Chess 1571, EX 31.00

Mystics, Hushabye, Quality 1915, EX 36.00

Nic Nacs, Gonna Have a Merry Christmas?, RPM 342, EX .60.00

Patsy Montana, ...I Get to Where I'm Goin', R 721, picture record, EX 64.00

Paul Anka, You Are My Destiny, Sparton 529, NM 60.00

Ray Charles, Rock House, Atlantic 2006, EX 42.00

Richie Valens, Come On Let's Go, Apex Specialty 76369, EX 120.00

Ricky Nelson, Poor Little Fool, Imperial 5528, EX 15.00

Royal Teens, Short Shorts, ABC-Paramount 78-9882, VG. 22.00

Rudi Richardson, Fool's Hall of Fame, Sun 271, EX 58.00

Vladimir de Pachmann, Spring Song, Victrola 1110, EX .. 37.00

Red Glass

Ever popular with collectors, red glass has been used to create decorative items such as one might find in gift shops, utilitarian bottles and kitchenware, figurines, and dinnerware lines such as were popular during the Depression era. For further information and study, we recommend *Ruby Glass of the 20th Century* by Naomi Over.

Barware shakers: Barbell, attributed to New Martinsville, from $125.00 to $135.00; Duncan and Miller, from $70.00 to $80.00.
(Photo courtesy Gene and Cathy Florence)

Basket, Hobnail, Fenton, ca 1985-86, 7".............................. **30.00**

Basket, Inverted Thistle, Mosser, crystal handle, 1980, 5½".................. **30.00**

Bell, rose decoration, Westmoreland, 1980s, 7"......................... **25.00**

Bowl, Bambu, Imperial, ca 1960-72, 11"............................. **65.00**

Bowl, Paden City, silver overlay, 4 legs, ca 1920-51, 9¼"....... **95.00**

Candleholders, bell shaped, satin, 4¼", pr............................. **20.00**

Chocolate box, Maple Leaf, Westmoreland, 1989, 6½"....................... **50.00**

Coaster, silver casing w/Park Sherman, 3¾"................. **20.00**

Creamer, Argus, Fostoria, 1967, 6-oz................................... **30.00**

Pitcher, English Hobnail, footed, sm lip, Westmoreland, 1982, 38-oz.............................. **150.00**

Plate, American, Fostoria, ca 1980, 14"..................................... **75.00**

Plate, Diamond, Imperial, ca 1920-30, 8".............................. **15.00**

Plate, Epic, Viking, 17".......... **55.00**

Platter, Simplicity, Paden City, 1930s, oval....................... **45.00**

Powder box, lady cover, Mosser, 1980, 5½"......................... **20.00**

Salt & pepper shakers, LG Wright, 1970s, 3½", pr.................. **40.00**

Sherbet, crystal stem w/knob, Cambridge, ca 1949-53, 7-oz **20.00**

Spooner, Eyewinker, 3 footed, LG Wright, 1960s, 5½".......... **50.00**

Tray, Regina, Paden City, 1936, 13¼x7¾"............................ **45.00**

Wine, crystal stem, Paden City, 1932, 2-oz....................... **25.00**

Red Wing

Taking their name from the location in Minnesota where they located in the late 1870s, the Red Wing Company produced a variety of wares, all of which are today considered noteworthy by pottery and dinnerware collectors. Their early stoneware lines, Cherry Band and Sponge Band (Gray Line), are especially valuable and often fetch prices of several hundred dollars per piece on today's market. Production of dinnerware began in the '30s and continued until the pottery closed in 1967. Some of their more popular lines — all of which were hand painted — were Bob White, Lexington, Tampico, Normandie, Capistrano, and Random Harvest. Commercial artware was also produced. Perhaps the ware most easily associated with Red Wing is their Brushware line, unique in its appearance and decoration. Cattails, rushes, florals, and similar nature subjects are 'carved' in relief on a stoneware-type body with a matt green wash its only finish. For more information we recommend *Red Wing Stoneware* and *Red Wing Collectibles,* both by Dan DePasquale, Gail Peck, and Larry Peterson (Collector Books).

Art Ware

Bowl, brown w/orange interior, flat, #414, 7"............................ **38.00**

Bowl, bulb; leaves embossed on dark green, low, 1920-30s, 9½"............................... **135.00**

Bowl, Mandarin style, green matt, #331, 11" L **60.00**

Bowl, shell; Blue Nile Fleck, #M1567, 9" **50.00**

Candleholder, English Garden, ivory/brown wipe, #1190, 6", ea. **26.00**

Compote, white, brass handles, #M1598, 8" **55.00**

Jardiniere, flecked pink, scalloped top, #M1610, 6" **22.00**

Juicer, yellow, footed, #256 .. **150.00**

Pitcher, urn; Vintage, semi-matt ivory w/brown wipe, #616, 11" **90.00**

Planter, gray w/coral interior, sq, #1378, 5½" **40.00**

Planter, violin shape, black semi-matt, #1484, 1950-60s, 13". **53.00**

Teapot, yellow, chicken shape, #257 .... **125.00**

Vase, cattails on dark green, cylindrical, 1920-30s, 7" **100.00**

Vase, fan; ivory w/green interior, #982, 1940s, 7½" **40.00**

Vase, gloss gray w/coral interior, #B1397, 7" **35.00**

Vase, green w/lion motif, 7½". **200.00**

Vase, oil-lamp form, maroon w/gray interior, #1377, 10" **95.00**

Vase, swirl, yellow gloss, #1590, 10" **50.00**

Vase, swirl blue gloss, #952, 1940s, 6" **55.00**

Vase, Tropicana line, Shell Ginger, EB2007, 12", $42.00. (Photo courtesy Brenda Dollen)

Anniversary, bowl, salad; 5½". **10.00**

Anniversary, bowl, salad; 10½"..**28.00**

Blossom Time, bowl, cream soup; w/lid **12.00**

Blossom Time, relish dish **18.00**

Bob White, casserole, w/handles & lid, 13" L **50.00**

Bob White, gravy boat, stick handle, w/lid **38.00**

Bob White, pitcher, slim, 7"... **35.00**

Bob White, platter, 19½" L **72.00**

Brittany, beverage server, w/lid .**70.00**

Brittany, teapot, from $35.00 to $40.00.

Capistrano, bowl, cereal **14.00**

Capistrano, nappy.................. **18.00**

Capistrano, tureen, soup; w/lid. **110.00**

Chrysanthemum, plate, dinner; 10½" **18.00**

Crazy Rhythm, plate, dinner; 10½".**18.00**

Crocus, bowl, vegetable **24.00**

Desert Sun, bean pot, w/lid, 1½-qt.**40.00**

Desert Sun, bread tray **50.00**

Desert Sun, platter, 13" **20.00**

Driftwood, platter, 15" **36.00**

Iris, celery dish...................... **18.00**

Iris, cup & saucer................... **25.00**

Iris, spoon rest **50.00**

Lexington, coffee cup **10.00**

Lexington, dinner plate **12.00**

Lexington, teapot, 11" L **55.00**

Lotus, creamer **10.00**

Lotus, dish, sauce/fruit **6.00**
Lotus, plate, dinner; 10½" **12.00**
Lute Song, bread tray **28.00**
Lute Song, platter, sm **24.00**
Lute Song, teapot **135.00**
Magnolia, bowl, berry; sm **5.00**
Magnolia, celery dish **16.00**
Magnolia, gravy boat, w/tray . **22.00**
Merrileaf, cup & saucer **12.00**
Merrileaf, plate, dinner; 10" .. **25.00**
Morning Glory, plate, dinner; 10½" **22.00**
Orleans, plate, 7" **12.00**
Pepe, creamer, 5" **10.00**
Pepe, dish, vegetable; divided, 12½" L **45.00**
Pepe, pitcher, 13" **115.00**
Pepe, platter, 15" **65.00**
Plain, cruet, oil; 4" **35.00**
Plain, salt & pepper shakers, 3", pr **25.00**
Plum Blossom, bowl, cereal ... **12.00**
Plum Blossom, plate, 6½" **8.00**
Random Harvest, bowl, serving; 9x8" **38.00**
Random Harvest, chip & dip. **30.00**
Random Harvest, creamer **38.00**
Random Harvest, plate, dinner. **12.00**
Smart Set, casserole, tab handles, 15" **55.00**
Smart Set, tray, 24" L **50.00**
Tampico, coffeepot **75.00**
Tampico, nappy **22.00**

Tampico, trivet, 4 sm feet, 8¾" **65.00**
Tip Toe, nappy **15.00**
Tip Toe, plate, dinner; 10½"... **10.00**
Town & Country, bowl, mixing; spout & handle, 6x12" .. **165.00**
Town & Country, creamer, 4¾"..**75.00**
Town & Country, cup & saucer .**23.00**
Town & Country, mustard jar. **175.00**
Town & Country, platter, 11x7½".**72.00**
Town & Country, sugar bowl, w/ lid **80.00**
Town & Country, syrup........ **125.00**
Zinnia, teapot **85.00**

Restaurant China

Restaurant china is specifically designed for use in commercial food service. Not limited to restaurants, this dinnerware is used on planes, ships, and trains as well as hotel, railroad, and airport dining rooms. Churches, clubs, department stores, and drug stores also put it to good use.

The popularity of good quality American-made heavy gauge vitrified china with traditional styling is very popular today. Some collectors look for transportation system top-marked pieces, others may prefer those with military logos, etc. It is currently considered fashionable to serve home-cooked meals on mismatched top-marked hotel ware, adding a touch of nostalgia and remembrances of elegant times past. For a more thorough study of the subject, we recommend *Restaurant China, Identification & Value Guide for Restaurant, Airline, Ship &*

Tampico, plate, 7", $8.00.

Railroad Dinnerware, Volume 1 and *Volume 2,* by Barbara Conroy. She is listed in the Directory under California.

Ashtray, Buffalo, Western New York Restaurant Association Show, 1962....................... **15.00**

Ashtray, Fraunfelter, Book Cadillac Hotel (Detroit), 1924....... **40.00**

Ashtray, Largenthal, Trans-Europe Express, Inverted TEE pattern, 1976 .... **30.00**

Bowl, bouillon; Walker, Ocean Spray Cranberry House, 1965 date code.......................... **15.00**

Cake plate, Syracuse, New Ebbitt Hotel, Mayflower shape, 1906, 10¼" **125.00**

Casserole, Pfaltzgraff, BWIA International Airways, Golden Abis w/logo **12.00**

Coffeepot, Syracuse, blue glaze, Doric shape, 1950s.......... **30.00**

Creamer, McNicol, blue, Paragon back stamp, 1940-60s **8.00**

Cup, Buffalo, Mister Donut, 1970s (logo designed in 1964)... **40.00**

Cup, Wallace, Sambo's, late 1950s **80.00**

Cup & saucer, Racket, Alaska Airlines Gold Coast pattern, 1980s............................... **22.00**

Cup & saucer, Shenango, Palace Hotel (San Francisco CA), 1945 & 1952 .... **25.00**

Flagon, Hall, Clearman's North Woods Inn, 1980s, 12-oz . **24.00**

Match holder, black glaze, Coors, Chefsware backstamp, 1950s. **22.00**

Mug, Hall #1272 back stamp, Hobo Joe's Family Restaurant, 1960s, 8-oz....................... **28.00**

Mug, Irish coffee; Hall #1272, Court of Two Sisters, 1960s, 8-oz . **15.00**

Mug, Jackson, Tony's restaurant (Redondo Beach CA), 1981 date code.......................... **18.00**

Mug, Shenango, Walgreens, 1975 date code.......................... **30.00**

Mug, Sterling, Burger Pit (sm CA chain), 1968 date code.... **40.00**

Mug, Veteran Administration, Inter-American Brasil back stamp, 1980.................... **15.00**

Pitcher, cream; Royal China, US Army Medical Department, early 1940s **20.00**

Pitcher, milk; Hacienda Hotel & Casino, Las Vegas, 1957 – present, McNicol, from $60.00 to $80.00. (Photo courtesy Barbara Conroy)

Cup and saucer, Borshtch 'N' Tears (restaurant), Steelite backstamp, Royal Doulton, early 1980s, from $20.00 to $25.00. (Photo courtesy Barbara Conroy)

Plate, Bauscher Bros, Reefs Hotel (Bermuda), 1950s, 10½".. **40.00**

Plate, butter; Wedgwood, Quantas Alice Springs pattern, 1960-1985 .... **22.00**

Plate, Iroquois, Surfside Hotel (Miami FL), ca 1935, 10¾".**50.00**

Plate, Iroquois, tan, New Parker House (Boston MA), stamped, 1950s, 5" **16.00**

Plate, Jackson, pine cone transfer w/green & brown bands, 1930s, 9" **20.00**

Plate, Laughlin, The Dog House, 1964 date code, 6½" **30.00**

Plate, Maddock, Bowater Steamship Co Alice Bowater pattern, 1940s, 8" **50.00**

Plate, Mayer, Howard Johnson Ice Cream Shoppes & Restaurants, '51, 9" **42.00**

Plate, Mayer, Villa Chartier (San Mateo CA), 1957 date code, 5½" **18.00**

Plate, Scammell's Trenton, New Britain Masonic Hall Association, 9" **18.00**

Plate, Shenago, Golfcrest Country Club (TX), 1981, 10½" **24.00**

Plate, Shenango, Standard Sandwich Shop, 1930s, 8" **65.00**

Plate, Syracuse, Casa Montero, 1977 date code, 6½" **12.50**

Plate, Warwick, Liggetts (East Coast drugstore chain), 1920-40s, 7" **30.00**

Platter, Tepco, Burger Pit (sm CA chain), 1950s-early 60s, 13" L...................................**40.00**

Platter, Wallace, Antola's, 1960s, 11½" **25.00**

Sugar bowl, Hall, Plaza, w/knob lid, 1950s-60s **25.00**

Teapot, Sterling, Red Coach Inn, 1952 date code **65.00**

Tray, Alverez, Hotel Alhambra, Santa Clara back stamp, 1950s, 4¼" **10.00**

Tray, celery; Haviland, New York Central, Depew pattern, stamped, 1900 .... **200.00**

Tray, Maastricht, Westbury Hotel (Brussels Germany), 1960s, 4¼" **6.50**

Rock 'n Roll Collectibles

Concert posters, tour books, magazines, sheet music, and other items featuring rock 'n roll stars from the '50s up to the present are today being sought out by collectors who appreciate this type of music and like having these mementos of their favorite performers around to enjoy. See also Elvis Presley; Records.

Aerosmith, belt buckle, red & blue on gold metal, Pacifica, 1976, EX **35.00**

Aerosmith, T-shirt, 1984-85 Back in the Saddle Tour, gray w/ black, EX **40.00**

Alice Cooper, concert poster, black on pink, 1969, M **150.00**

Andy Gibb, doll, Ideal, 1979, 7½", MIB **85.00**

Beatles, bookbinder, gray cloth cover, UK, 1964, M **375.00**

Beatles, drum, Ringo graphics, New Beat, 14" dia, EX.. **675.00**

Beatles, game board, Flip Your Wig, Milton Bradley, 1960s, EX+ **150.00**

Beatles, magazine, Newsweek, Bugs About Beatles, 1964, M **35.00**

Beatles, sheet music, various songs, 1960s, M, ea **20.00**

Bobby Darin, sheet music, Dream Lover, EX **20.00**

Chubby Checker, Limbo Under the Bar Game, Wham-O, 1961, complete, NM **100.00**

Culture Club, T-shirt, Boy George in V Westwood squiggle shirt, '83, M **20.00**

David Cassidy, guitar, Carnival Toys, 1970s, from $75.00 to $100.00.
(Photo courtesy Joe Hilton and Greg Moore)

David Cassidy, slide-tile puzzle, 1970s, M **35.00**

Eagles, program, Farwell I Tour, M **25.00**

Frank Zappa, comic book, 1970s, EX **20.00**

Greatful Dead, cloth patch, skull logo, 3", M, $15.00.
(Photo courtesy gaso linealley.com)

Grateful Dead, concert poster, Winterland, 1978, NM .. **160.00**

Joey Romone, bobblehead, w/micro-phone, NECA, NMIB **20.00**

Jon Bon Jovi, calendar, Official, 1991, unused, M **25.00**

KISS, game, KISS on Tour, late 1970s, EXIB **60.00**

KISS, model kit, KISS Custom Chevy Van, AMT, 1977, MIB (sealed) **170.00**

KISS, pencils, set of 4, Wallace Pencil Company, 1978, MIP **75.00**

KISS, songbook, Double Platinum, EX **30.00**

Madonna, stationery, Dream Idol, Star Stationery, 1986, M (sealed) **50.00**

Michael Jackson, magazine, Michael, souvenir edition, Vol 1, 1984, NM **17.50**

Monkees, Paint-By-Number set, unused, complete, EX ... **140.00**

Pink Floyd, concert program, The Wall, 1980 American Tour, EX **45.00**

Queen, song book, 12 songs for piano, vocals & guitar, EX **20.00**

Ricky Nelson, sheet music, Hello Mary Lou, photo cover, ca 1961, EX **10.00**

Rolling Stones, pin-back, tongue logo, gold glitter, MIP **15.00**

Rolling Stones, program, 1972 tour, Jagger w/arms raised, EX..**35.00**

Shaun Cassidy, record case, card-board, Vanity Fair, 1978, EX **35.00**

Supremes, tour program, Japan, 1974, EX **25.00**

Ted Nugent, tour program, sus-penders, 1979-1980, M ... **20.00**

ZZ Top, mirror, 1980s, 6x6", M. **10.00**

Rooster and Roses

Rooster and Roses is a quaint and provincial line of dinnerware made in Japan from the '40s and

'50s. The rooster has a yellow breast with black crosshatching, a brown head, and a red crest and waddle. There are full-blown roses, and the borders are yellow with groups of brown diagonals. Several companies seem to have made the line, which is very extensive — more than 75 shapes are known. For a complete listing of the line, see *Garage Sale and Flea Market Annual* (Collector Books).

Ashtray, rectangular, part of set, 3x2"............................ **9.50**
Ashtray, sq, lg, from $35 to ... **45.00**
Bell, rooster & chicken on opposing sides, rare, from $95 to.**125.00**
Bowl, 8", from $45 to **55.00**
Box, trinket; w/lid, round, from $25 to **35.00**
Candle warmer (for tea & coffee-pots), from $25 to **35.00**
Castor set, mini; 2 cruets, shakers, mustard jar on tray, from $50 to **75.00**
Castor set in wire rack, 2 cruets, mustard & shakers, rare, $125 to **150.00**
Chamberstick, saucer base, ring handle, 3x6" dia, from $35 to **50.00**
Cigarette box w/2 trays, scarce, from $60 to **70.00**
Coaster, ceramic disk embedded in round tray, rare, minimum value **45.00**
Coffeepot, new tankard shape, 8"................................. **50.00**
Coffeepot, w/creamer & sugar, all w/labeled neck bands, 3 pcs, from $75 to **85.00**

Cookie/cracker jar, cylindrical w/ rattan handle, 5x6", from $55 to **75.00**
Creamer & sugar bowl, w/lid, 4", from $40 to **50.00**
Creamer & sugar bowl on rectangular tray, from $55 to.... **70.00**
Cruets, conjoined w/twisted necks, sm **45.00**
Cruets, oil & vinegar, flared bases, pr from $50 to **60.00**
Cruets, oil & vinegar, w/salt & pepper shakers in shadow box, from $55 to **75.00**
Demitasse pot, elongated ovoid, long handle & spout, 7½", minimum..................................**90.00**
Demitasse pot, w/4 cups & saucers, minimum value............. **150.00**
Deviled egg plate, 12 indents, patterned center, 10", from $35 to **50.00**
Eggcup on tray, from $35 to ..**45.00**
Flowerpot, buttress handles, 5", from $35 to **45.00**
Hamburger press, wood-embedded ceramic tray, round, minimum value **24.00**
Jam & jelly containers, conjoined, w/ lids & spoons, loop handle..**85.00**
Jam jar, attached underplate, from $35 to **45.00**
Lamp, pinup; made from either a match holder or pin box, from $75 to **100.00**
Marmalade, round base w/tab handles, w/lid & spoon, from $35 to **50.00**
Measuring spoons on 8" ceramic spoon-shaped rack, from $40 to **55.00**
Mug, rounded bottom, med, from $25 to **30.00**

Pitcher, lettered Milk on neck band, 8", from $28 to 35.00

Pitcher, syrup; w/2 sm graduated pitchers on tray, minimum.75.00

Pitcher, tankard shape, 3".....28.00

Plate, luncheon; from $15 to .25.00

Platter, 12", from $55.00 to $60.00.
(Photo courtesy Jacki Elliott)

Recipe box, w/salt & pepper shakers; part of shadow box set, from $40 to 50.00

Relish tray, 3 wells w/center handle, from $55 to 65.00

Salt & pepper shakers, drum shape w/long ceramic handle, lg, pr from $30 to 40.00

Salt & pepper shakers, w/handle, pr from $15 to 20.00

Salt & pepper shakers, w/lettered neck band, pr 25.00

Salt canister, sq, 6x4" 50.00

Shaker, cheese or sugar; 4" ...35.00

Snack tray w/cup, rectangular, 2-pc, from $50 to 60.00

Spice rack, 2 rows of 3 curved-front containers, flat back, $75 to .85.00

Spice set, 9 sq containers in frame, pull-out tray in base, $75 to .95.00

Spoon holder, w/lg salt shaker in well on side extension, from $20 to 25.00

Stacking tea set w/ teapot, creamer & sugar bowl 125.00

Tea bag jar, bulbous w/lettering, no crosshatching, w/lid, 6"...60.00

Tumbler 18.00

Roselane Sparklers

A line of small figures with a soft shaded finish and luminous jewel eyes was produced during the late 1950s by the Roselane Pottery Company who operated in Pasadena, California, from the late 1930s until possibly the 1970s. The line was a huge success. Twenty-nine different models were made, including elephants, burros, raccoons, fawns, dogs, cats, and fish. Not all pieces are marked, but some carry an incised 'Roselane Pasadena, Calif.,' or 'Calif. U.S.A'; others may have a paper label.

Angelfish, 4½", from $20 to....25.00

Basset hound sitting, 4", from $15 to 18.00

Bulldog looking up, jeweled collar, 3½", from $22 to 25.00

Cat, Siamese lying down, head on paw, jeweled collar, 5½" L 45.00

Cat, Siamese mother & 2 babies, blue eyes, 9½", 3¾".........75.00

Cat, Siamese sitting, 4".........30.00

Cat sitting, head turned, tail out behind 25.00

Cocker spaniel, 4½", from $15 to 20.00

Deer standing, w/antlers, jeweled collar, 4½", from $22 to ...28.00

Donkey standing, lg ears, pink eyes 35.00

Elephant sitting on hind quarters, 6", from $35 to 40.00

Elephant striding, trunk raised, jeweled headpiece, 6", from $35 to **40.00**

Fawn, legs folded under body, 4x3½" **25.00**

Fawn, upturned head, 4x3½" . **20.00**

Kangaroo mother and babies, 4½", from $40.00 to $45.00.

Kitten, sitting, 1¾" **12.00**

Owl, very stylized, teardrop-shaped body w/lg round eyes, lg . **25.00**

Owl, 3½" **15.00**

Owl, 5¼" **25.00**

Owl, 7" **30.00**

Pheasants (2) looking back, pink & blue, 3¾" & 5", pr from $30 to **35.00**

Pig, lg **25.00**

Pouter pigeon, 3½" **20.00**

Raccoon standing, 4½", from $20 to **25.00**

Roadrunner, 8½" L, from $30 to . **45.00**

Squirrel eating a nut, lg bushy tail, blue & brown highlights, 4" . **30.00**

Whippet sitting, 7½" **28.00**

Rosemeade

Novelty items made by the Wapheton Pottery Company of North Dakota from 1941 to 1960 are beginning to attract collectors of American pottery. Though smaller items (salt and pepper shakers, figurines, trays, etc.) are read-

ily found, the larger examples are scarce and can be very expensive. The name of the novelty ware, 'Rosemeade,' is indicated on the paper labels (many of which are still intact) or by the ink stamp.

Ashtray, fish, pink, 6¼", from $100 to **125.00**

Ashtray, w/white turkey figure, 7", from $375 to **425.00**

Basket, blue, twisted handle, 3x2¾", from $100 to **125.00**

Basket, white w/rose handle, 5x5¼", from $100 to **125.00**

Bowl, swirl cloverleaf, 1½x3½", minimum value **200.00**

Butter dish, pink w/blue & red rooster head, w/lid, ¼-lb, $200 to **225.00**

Candleholders, pink w/white, heart shape, 3", pr from $100 to . **125.00**

Creamer & sugar bowl, ducks, white, from $125 to **150.00**

Creamer & sugar bowl, grapes, white, 3½", 3", from $50 to . **75.00**

Figurine, circus horse, red & yellow, solid, 4¼x4¼", $350 to ... **400.00**

Figurine, coyote howling, $195.00. (Photo courtesy Darlene Hurst Dommel)

Figurine, deer standing in grass, 7¾x7¾", from $100 to **125.00**

Figurine, frog, green w/black spots, 1¼", from $100 to **125.00**

Figurine, puppy begging, blue, solid, 3x3", from $75 to ... **85.00**

Jam jar, white w/pear finial, 5", from $125 to **150.00**

Mug, pheasant decal, Hausauer Beverages, 4¼", from $150 to **175.00**

Mug, Prairie Rose, 3¾", from $65 to **85.00**

Pitcher, Prairie Rose, 6", from $75 to **100.00**

Planter, sleigh, pink, 4x5¼", from $75 to **125.00**

Plaque, walleye decal on round tile, 6", from $75 to.............. **125.00**

Plate, Garden Spot, 6¾", from $250 to **30.00**

Plate, red & yellow leaves, rare, 4½", minimum **250.00**

Salt & pepper shakers, black Angus, 1¾", pr from $300 to **350.00**

Salt & pepper shakers, black ducklings, 2½", 2¼", pr from $75 to **100.00**

Salt & pepper shakers, hen & rooster, 2", 3¼", pr from $85 to..... **100.00**

Salt & pepper shakers, red potato, w/ tray,¾", 1½", set $400 to .. **450.00**

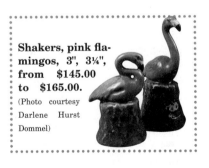

Shakers, pink flamingos, 3", 3¼", from $145.00 to $165.00.
(Photo courtesy Darlene Hurst Dommel)

Spoon rest, sunflower, 5", from $125 to **150.00**

Spoon rest, white dogwood, rare, 3½", minimum value **300.00**

Toothpick holder, rooster strutting, 3¾x2¾", from $100 to.... **125.00**

Tray, snack; w/4" pheasant pick holder, 9¼", from $100 to **125.00**

Vase, black & blue crackle, hand thrown, 5", from $150 to. **200.00**

Vase, blue & tan gloss, 4¾", minimum value.................... **250.00**

Vase, Chinese jade, Rosemeade No Dak mark, 5", from $100 to........ **125.00**

Vase, wheat on green, 6", from $65 to **85.00**

Vases, horses running (3), Harvest Gold, rare, 7", minimum value............................. **350.00**

Wall pocket, brown kitten in black stocking, rare, 6½", minimum **850.00**

Roseville Pottery

This company took its name from the city in Ohio where they operated for a few years before moving to Zanesville in the late 1890s. They are recognized as one of the giants in the industry, having produced many lines in art pottery from the beginning to the end of their production. Even when machinery took over many of the procedures once carefully done by hand, the pottery they produced continued the fine artistry and standards of quality the company had always insisted upon.

Several marks were used along with paper labels. The very early art lines often carried an applied ceramic seal with the name of the line under a circle containing the words Rozane Ware. From 1910 until 1928 an Rv mark was used.

Paper labels were common from 1914 until 1937. From 1932 until closure in 1952, the mark was Roseville in script or R USA. Pieces marked RRP Co Roseville, Ohio, were not made by Roseville Pottery but by Robinson Ransbottom of Roseville, Ohio. Don't be confused. There are many jardinieres and pedestals in a brown and green blended glaze that are being sold at flea markets and antique malls as Roseville that were actually made by Robinson Ransbottom as late as the 1970s and 1980s. That isn't to say they don't have some worth of their own, but don't buy them for old Roseville.

If you'd like to learn more about the subject, we recommend *The Collector's Encyclopedia of Roseville Pottery Revised Edition, Vols. 1* and *2*, by Sharon and Bob Huxford and Mike Nickel. Mr. Nickel is listed in the Directory under Michigan.

Note: Watch for reproductions! They've flooded the market! Be especially wary at flea markets and auctions. These pieces are usually marked only Roseville (no USA), though there are exceptions. These have a 'paint by number' style of decoration with little if any attempt at blending. See Clubs and Newsletters for information concerning *Rosevilles of the Past* newsletter.

Apple Blossom, basket, #309, green or pink, 8", from $275 to **325.00**
Apple Blossom, bud vase, #379, blue, 7", from $175 to ... **200.00**

Artcraft, jardiniere, 6", from $450 to **500.00**
Artwood, planter, #1054, 6½x8½", from $85 to **95.00**
Artwood, vase, #1057-8, 8", from $85 to **95.00**
Aztec, vase, waisted, floral, 9", from $400 to **500.00**
Baneda, candleholders, #1088, green, 4½", pr from $850 to **950.00**
Baneda, center bowl, #237, pink, 13", from $750 to **900.00**
Bittersweet, basket, #810, 10", from $250 to **300.00**
Bittersweet, cornucopia, #857-4, 4½", from $100 to **125.00**
Bittersweet, ewer, #816, 8", from $100 to **125.00**
Bleeding Heart, basket, #360, blue, 10", from $375 to **425.00**
Bleeding Heart, vase, #968-9, green or pink, 8½", from $325 to **350.00**
Bushberry, jardiniere, #657, orange, 3", from $80 to **90.00**
Cameo II, flowerpot, 5½", from $350 to **450.00**
Cameo II, wall pocket, from $500 to **600.00**
Capri, leaf, #532, 15", from $65 to **75.00**
Capri, shell dish, from $50 to . **60.00**
Carnelian I, console bowl, 14", from $150 to **200.00**
Carnelian I, ewer, 15", from $400 to **500.00**
Carnelian II, planter, handles, 3x8", from $125 to **150.00**
Carnelian II, vase, 6½", from $400 to **450.00**
Clemana, candleholders, #388, brown or green, 8", pr from $300 to **325.00**

Clemana, vase, #123, tan, 7", from $250 to **300.00**

Clematis, center bowl, #456-6, brown or green, 9", from $125 to **150.00**

Clematis, cookie jar, #3, brown or green, 10", from $350 to. **400.00**

Clematis, vase, #112, blue, from $175.00 to $225.00. (Photo courtesy David Rago Auctions)

Columbine, bookend planters, #8, blue or tan, 5", pr from $350 to **400.00**

Columbine, vase, #20, pink, 8", from $250 to **300.00**

Corinthian, ashtray, 2", from $175 to **200.00**

Corinthian, compote, 10x5", from $150 to **175.00**

Corinthian, hanging basket, 8", from $200 to **250.00**

Cosmos, flower frog, #39, blue, 3½", from $200 to **250.00**

Cremora, bowl, sq, 9", from $125 to **150.00**

Cremora, candleholder, 4", ea from $75 to **85.00**

Cremora, fan vase, 5", from $125 to **150.00**

Cremora, vase, 10½", from $250 to **300.00**

Dahlrose, bud vase, 8", from $400 to **450.00**

Dahlrose, center bowl, oval, 10", from $175 to **200.00**

Dahlrose, window box, #377, 6x12½", from $450 to **500.00**

Dawn, vase, #826, green or pink, 6", from $200 to **250.00**

Dogwood I, basket, 8", from $200 to **250.00**

Dogwood II, wall pocket, from $375 to **425.00**

Donatello, basket, 15", from $600 to **750.00**

Donatello, bowl, 3", from $75 to. **95.00**

Donatello, compote, 4", from $125 to **150.00**

Donatello, pitcher, 6½", from $375 to **425.00**

Dutch, pitcher, 7½", from $225 to **275.00**

Dutch, tankard, 11½", from $175 to **200.00**

Earlam, candlesticks, #1080, 4", pr from $600 to **650.00**

Earlam, vase, #521-7, 7", from $450 to **500.00**

Falline, center bowl, #244, blue, 11", from $500 to **600.00**

Ferella, bowl, #212, red, 12", from $1,100 to **1,300.00**

Ferella, vase, #498, red, 4", from $550 to **600.00**

Florane, basket, 8½", from $300 to **350.00**

Florane, bud vase, 7", from $30 to **35.00**

Florentine, basket, 8", from $200 to **250.00**

Florentine, bowl, 9", from $75 to **100.00**

Freesia, bookends, #15, tangerine, from $350 to **375.00**

Freesia, ewer, #19, tangerine, 6", from $225 to **250.00**

Fuchsia, candlesticks, #1132, blue, 2", pr from $175 to **200.00**

Fuchsia, pitcher, #1322, green, 8", from $550 to **625.00**

Fuchsia, vase, #987-8, brown & tan, 8", from $300 to **350.00**

Futura, planter, #191, 7", from $600 to **650.00**

Futura, vase, #431, 10", from $1,500 to **1,750.00**

Gardenia, basket, #609, 10", from $300 to **350.00**

Gardenia, bowl, #641-5, 5", from $125 to **150.00**

Imperial I, basket, 06", from $150 to **175.00**

Imperial I, basket, 13", from $350 to **400.00**

Imperial I, triple bud vase, 8", from $150 to **175.00**

Imperial II, bowl, 4½", from $300 to **350.00**

Iris, bowl, #360, pink or tan, 6", from $175 to **225.00**

Iris, pillow vase, #922-8, blue, 8½", from $325 to **375.00**

Iris, wall shelf, #2, blue, 8", from $500 to **550.00**

Ivory II, bowl vase, #259, Russco shape, 6", from $75 to **95.00**

Ixia, basket, #346, 10", from $300 to **350.00**

Ixia, rose bowl, #326, 4", from $150 to **175.00**

Ixia, vase, #853, 6", from $150 to **175.00**

Jonquil, basket, #328, 10", from $1,000 to **1,100.00**

Jonquil, vase, #539, 4", from $175 to **225.00**

Juvenile, cake plate, chicks, 9½", from $700 to **800.00**

Juvenile, egg cup, rabbit, footed, 3", from $1,500 to **2,000.00**

La Rose, bowl, 6", from $100 to. **125.00**

La Rose, candleholders, 4", pr from $250 to **275.00**

Laurel, bowl, #251, russet, 7", from $275 to **300.00**

Lotus, vase, #668, green, 6", from $300 to **325.00**

Luffa, jardiniere, #631, 4", from $400 to **450.00**

Luffa, vase, #685, 7", from $550 to................................. **650.00**

Lustre, basket, 10", from $200 to **250.00**

Magnolia, mug, #3, brown & green, 3", from $125 to **135.00**

Magnolia, pitcher, #1327, 7", from $300 to **350.00**

Mayfair, planter, #113-8, 3½x8½", from $70 to **85.00**

Ming Tree, center bowl, #528, 10", from $125.00 to $150.00.

Ming Tree, ewer, #516, 10", from $150 to **175.00**

Mock Orange, basket, #909, 8", from $250 to **300.00**

Mock Orange, jardiniere, #900, 4", from $75 to **100.00**

Mock Orange, planter, #981, 7", from $150 to **175.00**

Moderne, compote, #295, 5", from $250 to **275.00**

Morning Glory, bowl vase, #268, ivory, 4", from $350 to... **400.00**

Morning Glory, vase, #730, ivory, 10", from $650 to........... **700.00**

Moss, center bowl, #294, blue, 12", from $225 to **250.00**

Mostique, jardiniere, 10", from $300 to 400.00

Orian, bowl vase, #274, tan, 6", from $400 to 450.00

Orian, vase, #742, tan, 12", from $400 to 450.00

Peony, basket, #379-12, 11", from $250 to 275.00

Peony, wall pocket, #1293, 8", from $250 to 300.00

Persian, bowl, 3 handles, 3½", from $175 to 200.00

Pine Cone, cornucopia vase, #126, blue, 6", from $350 to 400.00

Pine Cone, pitcher, #425, brown, 9", from $750 to 850.00

Poppy, basket, #347, pink, 10", from $450 to 550.00

Poppy, basket, #348-12, pink, from $650 to 750.00

Poppy, ewer, #876, gray or green, 10", from $375 to 450.00

Raymor, butter dish, #181, from $75 to 100.00

Raymor, casserole, #183, med, 11", from $75 to 85.00

Raymor, pitcher, #189, 10", from $100 to 150.00

Rosecraft Hexagon, bowl vase, green, 4", from $500 to . 550.00

Rozane, letter holder, floral, C Neff, 3½", from $275 to 325.00

Rozane Light, bud vase, #831, 6", from $125 to 150.00

Rozane Pattern, bud vase, #2, 6", from $125 to 150.00

Russco, bud vase, #695, 8", from $175 to 200.00

Russco, triple cornucopia, 8x12½", from $300 to 350.00

Russco, vase, #259, heavy crystals, 6", from $300 to 350.00

Silhouette, cigarette box, #740, from $150 to 175.00

Silhouette, ewer, #717, 10", from $175 to 200.00

Silhouette, wall pocket, #766, 8", from $225 to 275.00

Snowberry, ashtray, #1AT, blue or pink, from $150 to 175.00

Snowberry, ewer, #1TK, blue or pink, 6", from $150 to ...175.00

Sunflower, candlesticks, 4", pr from $1,000 to 1,200.00

Teasel, ewer, #890, dark blue or rust, 18", from $850 to .. 950.00

Thorn Apple, vase, #808, 4", from $150 to 175.00

Topeo, center bowl, red, 3x11½", from $100 to 125.00

Topeo, vase, blue, 9", from $600 to.. 700.00

Tourmaline, cornucopia, 7", from $75 to 100.00

Tourmaline, ginger jar, 9", from $450 to 500.00

Tourmaline, pillow vase, 6", from $100 to 125.00

Tuscany, candleholders, pink, 3", pr from $125 to 150.00

Tuscany, console bowl, pink, 11", from $150 to 175.00

Velmoss, bowl, #266, blue, 3x11", from $225 to 275.00

Velmoss Scroll, compote, 9x4" dia, from $200 to 250.00

Velmoss Scroll, vase, 12", from $450 to 500.00

Water Lily, basket, #382, brown, 12", from $450 to..........500.00

Water Lily, cookie jar, #1, brown, 10", from $400 to..........500.00

Water Lily, ewer, #10, brown, 6", from $150 to 175.00

White Rose, double candlesticks, #1143, 4", pr from $200 to. 250.00

White Rose, pitcher, #1324, from
$225 to **250.00**
Wincraft, basket, #210-12, 12",
from $500 to **600.00**

**Wincraft, vase, #284, 10", from
$225.00 to $250.00; Vase, #290,
10", from $900.00 to $1,000.00.**

Wisteria, vase, blue, #682, 10", from
$1,750 to **2,000.00**
Woodland, bud vase, floral, 4-sided,
7", from $550 to **650.00**
Zephyr Lily, basket, #393, brown,
7", from $150 to **175.00**
Zephyr Lily, ewer, #24, blue, 15",
from $750 to **850.00**

Royal China

Several lines of the dinnerware
made by Royal China (Sebring,
Ohio) are very collectible. Their
Currier and Ives pattern (decorated with scenes of early American
life in blue on a white background)
and the Blue Willow line are well
known, but many of their others
are starting to take off as well.
Since the same blanks were used
for all patterns, shapes and sizes
will all be the same from line to
line. Both Currier and Ives and
Willow were made in pink as well

as the more familiar blue, but pink
is hard to find and not especially
collectible in either pattern. See
Clubs and Newsletters for information on Currier & Ives Dinnerware
Collectors Club.

Blue Heaven, bowl, vegetable;
10" **22.00**
Blue Heaven, butter dish, ¼-lb .. **22.00**
Blue Heaven, cake plate, w/han-
dles, 11½" **15.00**
Blue Heaven, cup & saucer **5.00**
Blue Heaven, pitcher, ice lip,
8½" **30.00**
Blue Heaven, platter, tab handles,
10½" **20.00**
Blue Willow, ashtray, 5½" **10.00**
Blue Willow, bowl, fruit nappy,
5½" **6.50**
Blue Willow, bowl, vegetable;
10" **28.00**
Blue Willow, gravy boat, double-
spout **28.00**
Blue Willow, platter, serving; tab
handles, 10½" **20.00**
Blue Willow, tray, tidbit; 2-tier. **95.00**
Buck's County, ashtray, 5½" .. **15.00**
Buck's County, bowl, vegetable;
10" **28.00**
Buck's County, creamer **8.00**
Buck's County, cup & saucer ... **8.00**
Buck's County, gravy boat, double-
spout **35.00**
Buck's County, platter, oval, 13". **45.00**
Buck's County, sugar bowl, w/
lid **18.00**
Colonial Homestead, bowl, cereal;
6¼" **15.00**
Colonial Homestead, bowl, soup;
8¼" **12.00**
Colonial Homestead, casserole,
angled handles, w/lid **75.00**

Colonial Homestead, creamer . **5.00**

Colonial Homestead, cup & saucer **5.00**

Colonial Homestead, pie plate. **25.00**

Colonial Homestead, plate, 12".**18.00**

Colonial Homestead, teapot .. **95.00**

Currier & Ives, bowl, cereal; round.............................. **15.00**

Currier & Ives, bowl, dip; from Hostess set, 4⅜" **40.00**

Currier & Ives, bowl, soup; 8½".**10.00**

Currier & Ives, bowl, vegetable; 9"..................................... **20.00**

Currier & Ives, candy dish, 7¾".**40.00**

Currier & Ives, casserole, angle handles, $100.00. (Photo courtesy Jack and Treva Hamblin)

Currier & Ives, deviled egg tray, from Hostess set............ **250.00**

Currier & Ives, gravy boat, double spout **20.00**

Currier & Ives, gravy ladle, 3 styles, ea..................................... **50.00**

Currier & Ives, lamp, candle; w/ globe................................. **375.00**

Currier & Ives, pie baker, 10", (depending on print) from $25 to **45.00**

Currier & Ives, platter, oval, 13"..**35.00**

Currier & Ives, platter, Rocky Mountains, tab handles, 10½" dia **20.00**

Currier & Ives, sugar bowl, no handles, flare top, w/lid .. **65.00**

Currier & Ives, tidbit tray, 3-tier..**30.00**

Currier & Ives, tumbler, glass, 5-oz, 3½" **15.00**

Fair Oaks, bowl, soup **15.00**

Fair Oaks, butter dish **45.00**

Fair Oaks, casserole, w/lid **95.00**

Fair Oaks, gravy boat, w/under-plate **25.00**

Fair Oaks, platter, tab handles, 10½" **25.00**

Fair Oaks, platter, 13" L........ **20.00**

Fair Oaks, salt & pepper shakers, pr...................................... **25.00**

Fair Oaks, teapot **145.00**

Memory Lane, bowl, cereal; 6¼".**15.00**

Memory Lane, bowl, fruit nappy, 5½" **6.00**

Memory Lane, casserole, w/lid. **85.00**

Memory Lane, cup & saucer ... **5.00**

Memory Lane, gravy boat, double-spout **24.00**

Memory Lane, gravy boat liner .**13.50**

Memory Lane, gravy ladle, plain, white, for all sets, from $35 to **50.00**

Memory Lane, plate, bread & but-ter; 6½"............................... **3.00**

Memory Lane, plate, 12" **25.00**

Memory Lane, plate, 13" **35.00**

Memory Lane, platter, tab handles, 10½" **22.00**

Memory Lane, salt & pepper shak-ers, pr............................... **25.00**

Memory Lane, tumbler, iced tea; glass **18.00**

Old Curiosity Shop, ashtray, 5½" dia **15.00**

Old Curiosity Shop, bowl, fruit nappy, 5½" **5.00**

Old Curiosity Shop, butter dish, ¼-lb **45.00**

Old Curiosity Shop, casserole, w/ lid **90.00**

Old Curiosity Shop, creamer... **8.00**

Old Curiosity Shop, pie plate, 10".................................**32.00**

Old Curiosity Shop, platter, oval, 13"...................................**35.00**

Old Curiosity Shop, salt & pepper shakers, pr.......................**22.00**

Old Curiosity Shop, teapot.. **115.00**

Old Curiosity Shop, tidbit tray, 3-tier, center handle........ **40.00**

Royal Copley

Produced by the Spaulding China Company of Sebring, Ohio, Royal Copley is a line of novelty planters, vases, ashtrays, and wall pockets modeled after appealing puppy dogs, lovely birds, innocent-eyed children, etc. The decoration is airbrushed and underglazed; the line is of good quality and is well received by today's pottery collectors. For more information we recommend *Collecting Royal Copley Plus Royal Windsor & Spaulding* by Joe Devine; he is listed in the Directory under Iowa. See Clubs and Newsletters for information concerning *The Copley Currier*.

Ashtray, bird on perch, embossed inside, USA mark, 5½x6". **40.00**

Ashtray, straw hat w/bow, 5". **30.00**

Creamer, leaf handles............ **35.00**

Figurine, bluebird, 5"............. **45.00**

Figurine, canary, paper label, scarce, 5½" **70.00**

Figurine, dog, brown tones w/dark ears, paper label, 8"........ **30.00**

Figurine, flycatcher, tail down, paper label, 8" **42.00**

Figurine, gull, wing molded to base, paper label only, 8" **42.00**

Figurine, lark, paper label, 5". **18.00**

Figurine, mallard duck, head erect, paper label, 9¼"............... **45.00**

Figurine, titmouse, 8" **25.00**

Figurines, hen and rooster, Royal Windsor, 10", 10½", from $225.00 to $250.00 each. (Photo courtesy Joe Devine)

Lamp, child praying, paper label, 7¾" **80.00**

Pitcher, Daffodil, green stamp, 8"................................... **55.00**

Planter, barefoot boy or girl, paper label, 7½", ea **45.00**

Planter, coach, green stamp or embossed mark, 3¼x6", from $20 to **30.00**

Planter, cockatiel, paper label, 8½" **50.00**

Planter, colonial old man, 8". **55.00**

Planter, dog in picnic basket, paper label, scarce, 7¾"............. **95.00**

Planter, dogwood w/verse, Home Is Where the Heart Is, 4½". **30.00**

Planter, Dutch boy (or girl) w/bucket, paper label, 6"............ **30.00**

Planter, Hildegard, rose & ivory, 2½x7¼"............................. **20.00**

Planter, horse running, paper label, 6"................................... **18.00**

Planter, Laura's Twigs, 5" **20.00**

Planter, Madonna praying, Royal Windsor, embossed mark, 8½" **42.00**

Planter, Oriental boy w/arms around lg vase, 4¾" **15.00**

Planter, pirate head, embossed letters, 8" **45.00**

Planter, poodle, 7" long, from $32.00 to $38.00.

Planter, poodles resting, 6½". **75.00**

Planter, ram's head, paper label, 6½" **27.00**

Planter, Siamese cats (2), 8". **125.00**

Plaque/planter, Fruit Plate, embossed mark, 6¾" **35.00**

Vase, bud; warbler on stump, green stamp or embossed mark, 5" **22.00**

Vase, Carol's Corsage, 7" **18.00**

Vase, embossed stylized leaf, 8¼".**15.00**

Vase, fish shape, tan w/red striped fins, rare, 6" **125.00**

Vase, floral decal, handles, gold stamp, 6¼" **12.00**

Vase, Joyce decal, tab handles, 4" **15.00**

Vase, planter, nuthatch on stump, paper label, 5½" **32.00**

Vase, rooster, paper label, 7⅛". **45.00**

Wall pocket, cocker spaniel head, 5" **30.00**

Wall pocket, girl w/wide brim hat, 7½" **45.00**

Window box, Harmony, 4½"... **20.00**

Royal Haeger, Haeger

Manufactured in Dundee, Illinois, Haeger produced some very interesting lines of artware, figural pieces, and planters. They're animal figures designed by Royal Hickman are well known. These were produced from 1938 through the 1950s and are recognized by their strong lines and distinctive glazes. For more information we recommend *Haeger Potteries Through the Years* by David Dilley (L-W Books); he is listed in the Directory under Indiana.

Ashtray, Douglas, R-106, 7"... **15.00**

Ashtray, Green Agate, freeform, R-873 USA, minimum value **15.00**

Ashtray, panther in center, brown mottle, R-632, $45.00.

Basket, Rose of Sharon, chartreuse w/ red flowers, R-575, 7" dia ...**75.00**

Basket, wicker; R-1375, 12½". **25.00**

Bowl, cloudy blue w/applied white flowers, R-373, 6½x19x6", minimum **75.00**

Bowl, Daisy, chartreuse, R-224, 2x11¾" **40.00**

Bowl, Modern, chartreuse & ebony, R-1338, 3½x13x6½", minimum **20.00**

Bowl, peasant, Gold Tweed, #329-H, 21¼" L **40.00**

Candleholder, Peach Agate, twisted stem, #243, 7½x4", ea, minimum **50.00**

Candleholders, blue crackle, #004, 1½x6x3", pr, minimum value **15.00**

Candy box, Hawaiian, round, 2-pc, R-590, 8" **50.00**

Candy dish, triple shell w/fish finial, blue, R-459, 8½" L **50.00**

Figurine, baby booties on sq base, light blue, 75th Anniversary, 3" **10.00**

Figurine, fighting cock, left, R-790, 11½" **75.00**

Figurine, lady with two baskets, 17", from $75.00 to $85.00.

Figurine, pheasant hen, R-164, 6" **85.00**

Figurine, tigress, amber, R-314, 11x10x4", minimum value . **75.00**

Flower frog, nude bathing, white, #77, 7x5" dia, minimum value **75.00**

Flowerpot, double tulip, R-525, 10" **16.00**

Planter, colonial girl, chartruese, #3318, 9" **20.00**

Planter, gondolier, Green Agate, R-657, 19" L **75.00**

Planter, oblong, w/stand, R-1416, 14" **40.00**

Triple candleholder dish, brown w/white accents, #3068, 12" dia **45.00**

Vase, butterfly, R-1221, 7½"... **24.00**

Vase, pillow; chartruese & Silver Spray, R-476, 15" L **25.00**

Vase, sailfish, Mauve Agate, 9x13", $85.00.

Vase, relief design, Briar Agate, #257, 9¼" **15.00**

Russel Wright Dinnerware

Dinnerware with a mid-century flair was designed by Russel Wright, who was at one time one of America's top industrial engineers. His most successful lines are American Modern, manufactured by the Steubenville Pottery Company (1939 – 1959) and Casual by Iroquois, introduced in 1944. He also introduced several patterns of melmac dinnerware and an interesting assortment of spun aluminum serving and decorative items such as candleholders, ice buckets, vases, and bowls.

To calculate values for items in American Modern, at least double the low values listed for these colors: Canteloupe, Glacier

Blue, Bean Brown, and White. Chartreuse is representd by the low end of our range; Cedar, Black Chutney, and Seafoam by the high end; and Coral and Gray near the middle. To price Casual, use the high end for Sugar White, Charcoal, and Oyster. Avocado, Yellow, Nutmeg Brown, and Ripe Apricot fall to the low side. Canteloupe commands premium prices, and Brick Red is even more valuable. Glassware prices are given for Flair in Crystal and Pink; other colors are higher. Add 100% for Imperial Pinch in Cantaloupe. Ruby is very rare, and market value has not yet been established.

Ashtray, Clover decorated, from $40 to **45.00**

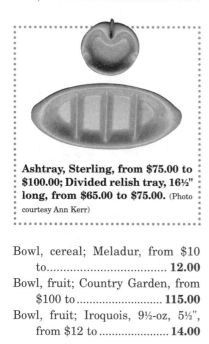

Ashtray, Sterling, from $75.00 to $100.00; Divided relish tray, 16½" long, from $65.00 to $75.00. (Photo courtesy Ann Kerr)

Bowl, cereal; Meladur, from $10 to **12.00**
Bowl, fruit; Country Garden, from $100 to **115.00**
Bowl, fruit; Iroquois, 9½-oz, 5½", from $12 to **14.00**

Bowl, salad; American Modern, from $100 to **115.00**
Bowl, soup; Theme Informal, from $75 to **100.00**
Bowl, Spun Aluminum, from $75 to **95.00**
Bowl, vegetable; American Modern, 36-oz, 8⅛", from $20 to ... **25.00**
Bowl, vegetable; Black Velvet, divided **37.50**
Bowl, vegetable; Knowles, divided, from $55 to **75.00**
Bun warmer, Spun Aluminum, 10" **75.00**
Casserole, Iroquois, 2-qt, 8", from $35 to **45.00**
Celery dish, American Modern, from $38 to **45.00**
Creamer, American Modern, from $15 to **20.00**
Creamer, Knowles, from $35 to. **45.00**
Cup, Clover, from $12 to........ **15.00**
Cup, Highlight, from $40 to .. **55.00**
Cup, Home Decorator **6.00**
Cup, White Clover, from $12 to. **15.00**
Cup & saucer, coffee; Iroquois, from $18 to **22.00**
Gravy boat, White Clover decorated, from $40 to **60.00**

Hostess/party plate, Casual, from $70.00 to $80.00. (Photo courtesy Ann Kerr)

Ice bucket, Spun Aluminum, from $75 to **100.00**

Ladle, Country Garden, from $125 to **175.00**

Pitcher, water; Sterling, 2-qt, from $125 to **150.00**

Plate, American Modern, 10", from $18 to **20.00**

Plate, Sterling, 7½", from $10 to. **12.00**

Plate, Theme Formal, 7½", from $75 to **100.00**

Platter, Copper Penny **42.00**

Platter, Highlight, sm, oval, from $50 to **75.00**

Platter, Knowles, oval, 13", from $45 to **55.00**

Platter, Theme Informal, oval, from $150 to **175.00**

Salt & pepper shakers, Clover, either size, pr from $30 to **35.00**

Salt & pepper shakers, Iroquois, stacking, pr from $30 to. **40.00**

Saucer, Meladur, from $4 to **5.00**

Spoon, salad; American Modern, from $85 to **95.00**

Sugar bowl, Highlight, from $65 to **75.00**

Sugar bowl, Sterling, w/lid, 10-oz, from $22 to **25.00**

Teapot, Knowles, from $250 to .**300.00**

Tidbit, Spun Aluminum, double, from $150 to **200.00**

Tumbler, Residential Flair **18.00**

Salt Shakers

You'll probably see more salt and pepper shakers during your flea market forays than T-shirts and tube socks! Since the 1920s they've been popular souvenir items, and many have been issued by companies to advertise their products. These advertising shakers are always good, and along with miniature shakers (1½" or under) are some of the more valuable. Of course, those that have a cross-over interest into other categories of collecting — Black Americana, Disney, Rosemeade, Shawnee, Ceramic Arts Studios, etc. — are often expensive as well. There are many good books on the market; among them are *Florences' Big Book of Salt & Pepper Shakers* and *Florences' Glass Kitchen Shakers* by Gene and Cathy Florence. Both are published by Collector Books. See also Advertising Collectibles; Ceramic Arts Studio; Character Collectibles; Disney; Shawnee; Rosemeade.

Only when the molds for both shakers are identical will they be termed a 'pair' — otherwise they will be described as '2-pc' or '3-pc' (as some will include a tray or a complementary third shape).

Alcatraz prison inmate bust, ceramic, Japan, 4½", pr **45.00**

Anthropomorphic with teapot heads, unmarked, 5", from $25.00 to $30.00. (Photo courtesy Gene and Cathy Florence)

Army & Navy men, ceramic, multicolor, 1940-50s, 2¾", 2-pc. **28.00**

Babar Elephant, ceramic, multicolor, Japan, 1950s, 5", stacking 2-pc **70.00**

Baseball batter & catcher, ceramic, cold paint, Japan, 1940s, 4", 2-pc **85.00**

Baseball player, ceramic, Copalis Beach WA, 1950s, 3½", pr. **75.00**

Bass fish, ceramic, Made in Japan label, 2x5½", pr **25.00**

Bellhop w/2 suitcases (shakers), ceramic, Japan, 1950s, 4", 3-pc **55.00**

Betty Boop (head & body), ceramic, Benjamin Medwin, 1955, 5", 2-pc **34.00**

Betty Boop & Bimbo, ceramic, in 3½x5" boat, Vandor, 1981, 3-pc **65.00**

Billy Sykes & Capt Cuttle, ceramic, multicolor, Artone, 2½", 2-pc. **32.00**

Bird & birdhouse, ceramic, Japan, 1950s, 3", 2-pc **20.00**

Black boy w/shoeshine box, ceramic, Japan, he: 3", 2-pc **65.00**

Bluegill fish, ceramic, realistic, Enesco, 2x4", pr **25.00**

Bride & groom, ceramic w/gold, red Japan mark, 1950s, 4⅛", 2-pc **25.00**

Bride & groom (reverses to aged couple), ceramic, 3½", 2-pc **37.50**

Brush w/comb & mirror, ceramic, Arcadia, mini, 2-pc **35.00**

Buddha, ceramic, tan, Japan, 1950s, 3½", pr **30.00**

Cactus, Yuma Arizona, ceramic, green & white, 4⅛", pr **9.00**

Cinderella's slipper on pillow, ceramic, pastels, Applause, 3x3", 2-pc **28.00**

Coffee mill & graniteware coffeepot, ceramic, Arcadia, mini, 2-pc **35.00**

Corn on cob & broccoli people, anthropomorphic, Clay Art, 2-pc. **50.00**

Covered wagon, Abiline Kansas, ceramic, gold trim, Japan, 2", pr **8.00**

Dandy & Preacher Crow from Dumbo, ceramic, 3", 4", 2-pc **80.00**

Dinosaur w/tail up, pottery, plastic stopper, unmarked, 1970s, 3", pr **28.00**

Dog, Bonzo-like, ceramic, Occupied Japan, 2¾", pr **38.00**

Donald Duck, ceramic, multicolor, Brechner, 1961, 4⅞", pr .. **95.00**

Dopey (Snow White's dwarf), ceramic, multicolor, Japan, 4", pr **55.00**

Drunk & lamppost, ceramic, Maruri... Japan, 1950s, 3-pc **22.50**

Eagle (patriotic), chalkware, Denver souvenir sticker, 2⅝", pr **35.00**

Fish, hole in mouth, ceramic, multicolor, Arcadia, mini, 1⅛", pr. **20.00**

Flying saucer, ceramic, white w/red & green, Coventry, 1950s, 2", pr **40.00**

Fork & spoon dancing couple, anthropomorphic, ceramic, 5", 2-pc **45.00**

Frog & water lily, ceramic, Japan, 3", 2-pc **37.50**

Gingham Dog & Cat, ceramic, multicolor, 1950s, 4½", 2-pc .. **30.00**

Goldilocks w/The Three Bears book, ceramic, Relco Japan, 1950s, pr **36.00**

Golf bag & ball, brown & white ceramic, Japan H-151, bag: 3¼", 2-pc **20.00**

Golliwog driving car, ceramic, gold trim, England, 2-pc **110.00**

Gonzo, ceramic, gold trim, 1930s, 3", pr **28.00**

Goose & golden egg, ceramic, c Ballona Star, 5½", 2-pc ... **55.00**

Grandma & Grandpa, ceramic, turnabouts, frowning/smiling, 4¾", 2-pc **15.00**

Hunter & rabbit, ceramic, unmarked, 1950s, 3½", 2-pc **18.00**

Jack & Jill, bone china, mulicolor, mini, 2½", 2-pc.................. **95.00**

Jack Spratt & wife, ceramic, he: 3½", 2-pc **52.50**

Jack-in-the-box, ceramic, multi-color, unmarked, 1950s, 4", pr **28.00**

Jonah & whale, ceramic, unmarked, 2", 2-pc............................. **65.00**

Lady (bare breasted) & naughty man, ceramic, Empress..., 4½", 2-pc **60.00**

Lady w/bonnet, full skirt, orange lustre, Japan, 3½", pr **85.00**

Leopard, ceramic, Victoria Ceramic...Japan, 4", 2½x4¼", pr...................................... **35.00**

Lions on base, nodder heads are shakers, ceramic, 3-pc .. **110.00**

Maid & chef, I'm Salt/I'm Pep on caps, ceramic, Japan, '50s, 3", 2-pc **20.00**

Mammy w/mixing bowl, bisque, LAG NO 1977 Taiwan, pr **32.00**

Man in doghouse & lady w/rolling pin, ceramic, Vallona Star, 2-pc **75.00**

Man in toilet, Good-bye Cruel World, ceramic, Japan, 1950s, 2-pc **35.00**

Matador & bull, ceramic, Japan, 1950s, 4¼", 2-pc............... **24.00**

Miss Muffet & spider, ceramic, Poinsetta Studios, she: 2½", 2-pc **65.00**

Moon & rocket ship, ceramic, Enesco, 1950s, spaceship: 4¼", 2-pc **45.00**

Native, wooden head/wire body, drum shakers, Japan, 1950s, pr...................................... **60.00**

Native on cabbage, ceramic, Japan, 1950s, 2½x3", pr.............. **55.00**

Nude reclining, ceramic, detailed features, 5" L, pr, MIB.... **55.00**

Old Mother Hubbard & dog, ceramic, Poinsettia Studio, she: 3½", 2-p **75.00**

Oswald & Homer, ceramic, Walter Lantz/ Napco, 1958, 4", 2-pc............. **135.00**

Love Bugs, huggers, burgundy, Bendel for Regal, large, from $150.00 to $175.00.

Paul Bunyan and Babe the Blue Ox, from $35.00 to $42.00. (Photo courtesy Helene Guarnaccia)

Pebbles & Bamm-Bamm, ceramic, multicolor, Harry Hames, 4", 2-pc **40.00**

Penguin in formal attire, pottery, ca 1984, 3½", pr **18.00**

Phonograph (crank type), ceramic, multicolor, Napco, 1950s, 3¼", pr **24.00**

Pink Panther, seated & hugging knees, ceramic, pr, minimum value **160.00**

Pipe, ceramic, Wolf Creek Dam KY, 2 rest on base, 2¾", 3-pc ... **8.00**

Pirate & treasure chest, ceramic, green & brown, unmarked, 1950s, 2-pc **22.00**

Pixie & Dixie (mice), ceramic, Japan label, 3¼", 2-pc **55.00**

Pixie on rocket ship, ceramic, multicolor w/gold, 1950s, 3x3½", pr **45.00**

Popeye, ceramic, multicolor, Foreign mark, 1930s, 3", pr **125.00**

Potty & window, ceramic, Colorado souvenir, 1¼", 2¾", 2-pc .. **24.00**

Purple cow, pottery, Made in Japan by Thames, 1950s, 4", pr.. **22.00**

Queen of Hearts & jester, ceramic, Japan #6440, 4⅝", 2-pc ... **45.00**

Raggedy Ann, ceramic, pastels, unmarked vintage import, 4", pr **40.00**

Roast turkey in pan, ceramic, multicolor, unmarked, 2½", 2-pc .**12.00**

Saggy Baggy Elephant, ceramic, multicolor, Japan, 1950s, 2½", pr **45.00**

Santa & Mrs Claus, ceramic, hugging (interlocking), 1965, 3¼", 2-pc **18.00**

Santa on bell, ceramic, multicolor, Napcoware X6047, 1950s, 3½", pr **22.00**

Singing Tower, silver-tone metal, Lake Wales FL, 3½", pr **35.00**

Snails (snuggling), ceramic, Crown Art...Japan, tallest: 4½", pr.........................**40.00**

Stan Laurel & Oliver Hardy faces on tray, ceramic, Dresden, 3-pc **200.00**

Sylvester the Cat, ceramic, Warner Bros, 1970s, 4¼", pr **75.00**

Tropical bird, ceramic, Germany, 1930s, 3½", pr................**28.00**

Tweedle Dee & Tweedle Dum, ceramic, Fitz & Floyd, 1992, 4", 2-pc **45.00**

Winnie the Pooh & Hunny Pot, ceramic, New England..., 3", 2-pc **40.00**

Wizard of Oz, ceramic, Clay Art, 1990s, 3½", pr.................**30.00**

Yoda, ceramic, Sigma, 1983, 4", pr **195.00**

Zodiac boy & girl, ceramic, red Japan mark, 4½", 2-pc **35.00**

Scottie Dogs

An amazing array of Scottie dog collectibles can be found in a wide range of prices. Collectors might choose to specialize in a particular area, or they may enjoy looking for everything from bridge tallies to original portraits or paintings. Most of the items are from the 1930s and 1940s. Many were used for advertising purposes; others are simply novelties. Values in the listings that follow are for items in excellent to near mint condition unless noted otherwise.

Bracelet, white celluloid, 2 dogs side by side, Occupied Japan, 2" **68.00**

Charm, sterling silver, dog by lamp-post w/bead at top, ⅝x¼". **80.00**

Compact, metal, leather, and composition, Pilcher, 1940 – 1950s, from $65.00 to $85.00. (Photo courtesy Candace Sten Davis and Patricia Baugh)

Compact, yellow leather bottom, yellow top w/brown dog, 2½" dia **53.00**

Doorstop, cast iron, black w/red collar, Hubley, 3x3½" **42.00**

Figurine, painted ceramic, dog w/ pup, 1950s, 4¾x5¾" **47.00**

Figurine, painted metal, sitting dog w/collar, 1½x2" **40.00**

Fork & spoon, childs, red Bakelite handle w/orange dog, 5" L **120.00**

Ice bucket, fired-on decoration, $32.50.

Napkin ring, Bakelite, marbled yellow & brown w/red accents, 3" **35.00**

Paperweight, painted composition, 2 dogs sitting side by side, 2", VG **63.00**

Pin, celluloid, white dog on red suitcase, Made in Germany, 1½" **61.00**

Pin, pink Bakelite, rhinestone eye & collar, 1950s................ **23.00**

Playing cards, 2 pups by doghouse, gold trim, Finesse, VGIB **24.00**

Powder jar, clear patterned glass, 3 dog figures on lid, 5x4¼". **27.00**

Wall plaque, ceramic, head/neck, shiny black w/red collar, 9½" **55.00**

Scouting Collectibles

Founded in England in 1907 by Major General Lord Baden-Powell, scouting remains an important institution in the life of young boys and girls everywhere. Recently scouting-related memorabilia has attracted a following, and values of many items have escalated dramatically in the last few years. Early first edition handbooks often bring prices of $100.00 and more. Vintage uniforms are scarce and highly valued, and one of the rarer medals, the Life Saving Honor Medal, is worth several hundred dollars to collectors. For more information we recommend *A Complete Guide to Scouting Collectibles* by Rolland J. Sayers; he is listed in the Directory under North Carolina. Our values are for items in excellent to near mint condition unless noted otherwise.

Boy Scouts

Award, Silver Beaver sterling pendant on blue & white ribbon, 1968 .... 125.00

Belt buckle, Daniel Webster Council, bronze, Max Sibler, 1950s 190.00

Book, Handbook for Boys, paperback, 568-pg, 1948 .... 20.00

Bookends, logo w/Be Prepared banner, cast iron, 1940s, 6x4x6", pr 70.00

Bugle, Rexcraft Official, brass & chrome, chain on mouthpiece 90.00

Cap gun, ca. 1930, $200.00. (Photo courtesy Don and Carol Raycraft)

Cuff links, yellow emblem w/black ribbon w/Be Prepared, enameled 20.00

Firemaking equipment, Official; complete, EXIB 45.00

Flagpole finial, emblem on ball, brass & aluminum 25.00

Hat, Scout Master campaign; w/logo on band, 1958, EXIB 85.00

Patch, Achievement; 2nd Canadian BS Jamboree, Ottawa, 1953, 5" dia 25.00

Patch, Fall Fellowship, Canyon Camp, Order of the Arrow, 1967 .... 25.00

Patch, Miami Valley Council, 1916-1991, 75 Years...Service, 4½". 20.00

Patch, 1979 Pow Wow, Alaska Royal Rangers 25.00

Pin, Sea Scouts emblem in silver w/ blue enameled ring, ¾" 50.00

Pocketknife, Leader's, #1043, bone handle, 2 blades, NM (plastic case) 50.00

Utensil set, fork, spoon & knife, logo on leather pouch 45.00

Whistle, Acme, brass, 1940-50s, 2½" 80.00

Girl Scouts

Book, Junior, GS Handbook, original plastic cover, 1963 .... 15.00

Bracelet, emblem w/sq chain links, 1950s, 6" 25.00

Camera, Imperial Mark XII, w/ flash, EXIB 40.00

Catalog, GS Equipment, Fall 1967-Spring 1968, 23 pg 20.00

Compass, green plastic case, Taylor #11-358, EXIB 30.00

Doll, complete, Terri Lee Sales Corp #11-955, MIB 165.00

Doll, Official Cadette, Effanbee, vinyl, 11", MIB 200.00

Doll, Patsy Ann, Brownie dress/ pantaloons/cap, Effanbee, 1959, 15" 60.00

Hat, Beanie w/2 original bows, #2-153, 1950s, EX+ (G box) 15.00

Mess kit, plate, skillet, cup, & pot w/lid, plaid bag, 1950s, EXIB 20.00

Patch, Central Maryland Council, state image w/trees, round. 10.00

Patch, Whispering Oaks GSC, The Beginning, 1986, acorn center 10.00

Pin, green trefoil w/white Girl Scouts, Bakelite, 1⅛x1" .. **50.00**

Pin, GS Volunteer, 15-year pin, 1960s, 1x1½".................... **20.00**

Poster, It's Girl Scout Cookie Time, Scouts hanging banner, 1963 .... **35.00**

Sewing kit, complete w/needle & spools, case w/gold emblem, 1960s................................ **30.00**

Utensil set, 3-pcs flatware & can opener, leather pouch, Schrade.......................... **70.00**

Wristwatch, GS emblem on face, blue plastic band, Timex . **25.00**

Sears Kitchenware

During the 1970s the Sears Company sold several lines of novelty kitchen ware, including Country Kitchen, Merry Mushrooms, and Neil the Frog. These lines, especially Merry Mushrooms, are coming on strong as the collectibles of tomorrow. There's lots of it around and unless you're buying it from someone who's already aware of its potential value, you can get it at very low prices. It was made in Japan. Besides the ceramic items, you'll find woodenware, enamelware, linens, and plastics.

Country Kitchen

Bread box, w/drawers, enamelware, 16x12x18" **75.00**

Canister set, 4-pc **40.00**

Creamer.................................. **9.00**

Measuring cups, pitcher form, set of 4 .... **95.00**

Napkin holder, 4½x5¾" **15.00**

Salt and pepper shakers, 4¾", $15.00 for the pair.

Spoon rest, rectangular, 4 rests.**10.00**

Merry Mushrooms

Ashtray, mushroom shape, rest on side, 6x5" **85.00**

Bowl, salad; w/original wooden fork & spoon, rare.................. **60.00**

Canister, mushroom shape, from $10.00 to $12.00.

Canister set, basketweave background, 4-pc..................... **65.00**

Canister set, plastic, brown lids, 4-pc **32.00**

Casserole, Corning Ware, glass lid, 2½-qt **40.00**

Celery set, 4-pc...................... **32.00**

Coffee mug, thermo-plastic ... **16.00**

Coffeepot, Corning ware, 6-cup .**70.00**

Coffeepot, 9½".......................... **25.00**

Cookie jar............................... **18.00**

Corn dishes, mushroom at end of corn tray, set of 4, MIB... **60.00**

Creamer & sugar bowl, w/lid . **35.00**

Curtains, 68x24", pr, MIP...... **45.00**
Fondue set, 2-qt, MIB........... **35.00**
Gravy boat, 5½" L w/7" under-
tray 30.00
Lamp shade, ceiling mount, glass &
metal, hexagonal............. **60.00**
Lazy Susan canister, 4 units fit
together to form lg mushroom,
1 lid................................ **125.00**
Mail holder/letter sorter, wooden,
3-pocket, 8x6x2".............. **40.00**
Mold, 3 mushrooms on white,
2½x9½x7½", from $35 to. **45.00**
Napkin rings, set of 4........... **25.00**
Paper towel holder, wooden, w/shelf
above, 20" L..................... **60.00**
Salt & pepper shakers, 5", pr. **16.00**
Spice rack, 2-tier, 2 drawers in base,
12 spice jars, minimum ... **65.00**
Teapot, 7"............................ **22.50**
Timer, dial in mushroom shape.**35.00**
Toaster cover, vinyl **20.00**
Tureen, w/underplate & ladle,
2½-qt **58.00**
Wall pocket, pitcher & bowl
shape **35.00**

Neil the Frog

Bank, frog leaning on elbow, from
$35 to **45.00**

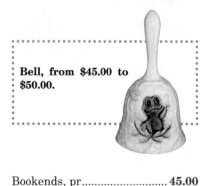

Bell, from $45.00 to $50.00.

Bookends, pr....................... **45.00**

Clock, wall; frog on yellow lily on
white pad......................... **45.00**
Coffee mugs, set of 4 on scrolling
metal tree, from $25 to... **35.00**
Cookie jar, lg seated frog, from $50
to **60.00**
Cruets, oil & vinegar; 5", pr .. **30.00**
Figurines, 1 holding yellow lily, 2nd
w/umbrella, 1¾", 1⅝", pr. **45.00**
Pitcher, frog figure, mouth is spout,
6½", from $45 to **50.00**
Salt & pepper shakers, frog & yellow water lily, 2-pc set.... **20.00**
Salt & pepper shakers, range;
cylindrical w/embossed frog,
5", pr **18.00**
Saucepan, enamelware, green lid,
6½" dia **25.00**
Soap dish, frog w/scrub brush in
hand in tub of white bubbles,
7" L.................................. **75.00**
Spice rack, white painted wood
2-tier shelf w/12 spice shak-
ers.................................... **85.00**
Spoon rest, frog at side of 2 lily
pads.................................. **20.00**
Teapot, 2-cup, 5¾".................. **95.00**
Trivet.................................... **20.00**

Sewing Items

Sewing notions from the
1800s and early twentieth century, such as whimsical figural tape measures, beaded satin
pincushions, blown glass darn-
ing eggs, and silver and gold
thimbles, are pleasant reminders
of a bygone era — ladies' sewing circles, quilting bees, and
beautifully hand-stitched finery.
With the emphasis collectors of
today have put on figural ceramic

items, the pincushions such as we've listed below are coming on strong. Most were made in Japan; some were modeled after the likenesses of Disney characters. For more information we recommend *Sewing Tools & Trinkets, Volume I* and *II,* by Helen Lester Thompson. (Collector Books).

Basket, cords on wood frame, red trim, hinged lid, Sears, '55, 6x10x7" **100.00**

Book, Simplcity Unit of Sewing, softcover, 142-pg, 1957 ..... **7.50**

Book, Singer Sewing Book, Mary Brooks Picken, copyright 1949 .... **35.00**

Box, pin; cube, gold & marbleized paper cover, USA, 2¼" **22.00**

Button, Kutani porcelain, Seven Immortals, Japan, 1950s, set of 7 .... **250.00**

Button, molded blue glass, Little Red Riding Hood **6.00**

Button, red glass w/foil-back glass inlay, 1950s, lg **25.00**

Button, silvered brass, Cupid, lg, 1⅝" **55.00**

Darner, amethyst, pestle shape, USA, 4" **70.00**

Darner, ebony egg w/embossed grapes on silver handle, Sterling, 6¼" **70.00**

Darner, silver glove type w/ repoussé, Sterling, 4" **50.00**

Dress pattern, Vogue, sexy halter dress, 1950s, M in VG package **24.00**

Emery, Miss Dinah, Black lady's head, w/poem on lid of box, MIB **140.00**

Manual, Sears 222K Featherweight sewing machine, VG **40.00**

Pincushion, ceramic, dog w/Bonzo-like appearance by yellow top hat **65.00**

Pincushion, ceramic, German sheperd on velvet pillow, 1930s, 1½x2" **65.00**

Pincushion, ceramic, pelican, multicolor w/lustre, cushion back **40.00**

Pincushion, metal, mouse, cushion back, 3" **50.00**

Pincushion, redware pottery, bulldog, USA, 6" **200.00**

Pincushions, dog and top hat, Japan, from $20.00 to $30.00 each. (Photo courtesy Carole Bess White)

Child's sewing machine, Casige, sheet metal, made in Germany, 6x4½x9½", from $65.00 to $85.00. (Photo courtesy Glenda Thomas/Joe and Evelyn Watkins)

Scissors, lady's leg handles, Capitol Cutlery Co, Germany, 5⅜"..**10.00**

Scissors, stork figural, Rochester Cutlery Co, 3½", from $20 to **35.00**

Tape measure, brass, shoe, Three Feet in One Shoe on front, 1½x2" **95.00**

Tape measure, celluloid, baseball player, Made in Japan .. **250.00**

Tape measure, celluloid, chick on base w/measure, 2⅝" **60.00**

Tape measure, celluloid, deer w/spots on its back, Japan, 1950s **65.00**

Tape measure, celluloid, pig w/red hat, Japan, 1¼x2½" **55.00**

Tape measure, celluloid, ship, red and white, 2x2¼", from $65.00 to $85.00.

Tape measure, gold-tone metal, clamshell, measures inches & metric **25.00**

Tatting shuttle, mother-of-pearl, 2⅝" **35.00**

Thimble, silver, church embossed on border, Sterling **50.00**

Thimble, 14k gold, clamshell design, cartouch w/monogram, lg **150.00**

Shawnee

The novelty planters, vases, cookie jars, salt and pepper shakers, and 'Corn' dinnerware made by the Shawnee Pottery of Ohio are attractive, fun to collect, and still available at reasonable prices. The company operated from 1937 until 1961, marking their wares with 'Shawnee, U.S.A.,' and a number series, or 'Kenwood.' Refer to *Shawnee Pottery, An Identification and Value Guide,* by Jim and Bev Mangus (Collector Books) for more information. See also Cookie Jars. See Clubs and Newsletters for information concerning the Shawnee Pottery Collectors' Club.

Ashtray, Valencia, from $16 to . **18.00**

Bowl, baker; Lobster, open, 917, 7", from $35 to **40.00**

Bowl, cereal; King Corn, Shawnee 94, from $45 to **50.00**

Bowl, vegetable; Queen Corn, Shawnee 95, 9", from $50 to **55.00**

Candleholders, dark blue w/ embossed leaves, 3¼", pr from $22 to **24.00**

Canister, Snowflake, 2-qt, from $45 to **55.00**

Casserole, French; Lobster, 900, 10-oz, from $18 to **21.00**

Casserole, Valencia, 7½", from $55 to **60.00**

Cookie jar, Queen Corn, Shawnee 66, from $300 to **350.00**

Creamer, Lobster, 921, from $45 to **50.00**

Creamer, Puss 'n Boots, USA 85, from $100 to **125.00**

Flowerpot, embossed diamonds, USA 484, 4", from $10 to . **12.00**

Fork, Valencia, from $40 to ... **45.00**

Grease jar, Sahara, Kenwood USA 977, from $50 to **55.00**

Lamp base, ballerina figure (sitting on base), unmarked, from $65 to **75.00**

Mug, King Corn, Shawnee 69, from $45 to **50.00**

Pitcher, Fern, octagonal, 1½-pt, from $60 to **70.00**

Pitcher, Laurel Wreath, USA, from $22 to **24.00**

Pitcher, Stars & Stripes, USA, from $16 to **18.00**

Planter, elephant w/trunk up, gold trim, USA 759, from $24 to. **26.00**

Planter, highchair, USA 727, from $60 to **65.00**

Planter, poodle & carriage, USA 704, from $32 to **35.00**

Plate, compartment; Lobster, claw shape, 912, from $75 to. **100.00**

Plate, Queen Corn, Shawnee 68, 10", from $35 to **40.00**

Plate, Valencia, unmarked, 13", from $20 to **25.00**

Punch bowl, Valencia, 12", from $45 to **55.00**

Relish tray, from $130 to **135.00**

Salt and pepper shakers, 3¼", from $28.00 to $32.00.

Salt & pepper shakers, duck, sm, pr from $25 to **30.00**

Salt & pepper shakers, jug, USA, pr from $100 to **110.00**

Salt & pepper shakers, Smiley & Winnie the Pig, w/gold trim, pr **80.00**

Sugar bowl, Sunflower, w/lid, USA, from $50 to **55.00**

Teapot, Horseshoe, USA, 8-cup, from $40 to **45.00**

Teapot, Paneled, with gold and decals, from $45.00 to $55.00.
(Photo courtesy Bev and Jim Mangus)

Teapot, Valencia, regular, from $55 to **65.00**

Utility jar, basket, all-over gold, oval, w/lid, USA, from $100 to................................... **110.00**

Vase, bud; organic form, USA 705, 5", from $12 to................. **14.00**

Vase, swirled body, USA, 5", from $12 to **14.00**

Sheet Music

The most valuable examples of sheet music are those related to early transportation, ethnic themes, Disney characters, a particularly popular actor, singer, or composer, or with a cover illustration done by a well-known artist. Production of sheet music peaked during the 'Tin Pan Alley Days,' from the 1880s until the 1930s. Covers were made as attractive as possible to lure potential buyers, and today's collectors sometimes frame and hang them as they would a print. Flea markets are a good source for sheet music, and prices are usually very reasonable. Most are available for under $5.00. Some of the better examples are listed here. Refer to *The Sheet Music Reference and Price Guide* by Anna Marie Guiheen and Marie-Reine A. Pafik (Collector Books).

Along the Santa Fe Trail, Dubin, Coolidge & Groz, 1940 ...... **8.00**
America Calling, Meredith Wilson, 1941 .... **5.00**
Bibbidi-Bobbidi-Boo, Mack David, Al Hoffman & Jerry Livingston, 1949 .... **15.00**
Bring Back the Thrill, R Poll & P Rugolo, Eddie Fisher photo, 1950 .... **5.00**
Color My World, James Pankow, 1970 .... **3.00**

Cow Cow Boogie, by Don Raye, GeneDePaul, and Benny Carter, 1942, $15.00. (Photo courtesy Guiheen and Pafik)

Diane, Rapee & Pollack, movie: 7th Heaven, Barbelle cover, 1927 .... **16.00**
Faithful Forever, L Robin & R Rainger, movie: Gulliver's Travels, 1939 .... **8.00**
First Time I Saw Your Face, The; Ewan MacColl, 1972 .... **3.00**
Gigi, Alan J Lerner & Frederick Loewe, movie: Gigi, 1958.. **5.00**

Goodnight My Love, Gordon & Revel, Shirley Temple cover, 1936 .... **25.00**
I Beg of You, Elvis Presley, 1957 .... **20.00**
I'd Like to Teach the World to Sing, Backer, Davis, Cook & Greenway **3.00**
Indiana Moon, Davis & Jones, Perret cover artist, 1923.. **10.00**
Jesse James, Jerry Livingston, Eileen Barton photo, 1954.. **5.00**
Katie, Cole Porter, movie: DuBarry Was a Lady, 1943 .... **10.00**
King's Horses & King's Men, Noel Gay & Harry Graham, 1930 .... **10.00**
Lady Bird Cha Cha Cha, Norman Rockwell cover artist, 1968.**25.00**
Leaving on a Jet Plane, John Denver, Peter, Paul & Mary photo, 1969 .... **5.00**
Let It Snow, Cahn & Styne, Les Brown photo, 1945 .... **4.00**
Love Song From Buccaneer, David & Bernstein, Brenner & Heston photo **6.00**
Malaguena, Banks & LeCuona, Connie Francis photo, 1954 .... **80.00**
May I Never Love Again, Sano Marco & Jack Erickson, 1940 .... **5.00**
Michelle, John Lennon & Paul McCartney, Beatles on cover, 1965 .... **15.00**
Misfits, North, movie: The Misfits, Monroe, Gable, & Clift photo, 1960 .... **10.00**
Moon River, Johnny Mercer & Henry Mancini, Audrey Hepburn photo, 1961 .... **8.00**
Moxie Fox Trot Song, D Shea & E Fitzgerald, 1930 .... **55.00**

Nightingale, Coburn, Fredrick S Manning cover, 1920 .... **15.00**

No Two People, Frank Loesser, movie: Hans Christian Anderson **10.00**

Old Aquaintance, Gannon & Waxman, B Davis & M Hopkins photo, 1943 .... **13.00**

On the Atchinson, Topeka and the Santa Fe, Mercer and Warren, 1934, from the Movie The Harvey Girls, Judy Garland photo, $15.00. (Photo courtesy Guiheen and Pafik)

Poor Butterfly, John Golden & Ray Hubbell, 1916 .... **10.00**

Pretty Kitty Blue Eyes, Mann Curtis & Vic Mizzy, 1944 .. **3.00**

Put Your Head on My Shoulder, Paul Anka, 1958 .... **5.00**

Querida, Edward G Simon & Jose Valdez, 1929 .... **3.00**

Red River Valley, Harold Potter, Gene Autry photo, 1935 .... **6.00**

Rum & Coca Cola, Amsterdam/ Sullivan/Baron, Andrews Sisters photo, 1944 .... **12.00**

Salt Water Cowboys, Redd Evans, 1944 .... **4.00**

Second Hand Rose, G Clarke & J Hanley, Barbra Streisand photo, 1965 .... **14.00**

Sweet & Low, Barnby & Tennyson, Starr Sisters photo, 1935 . **5.00**

Thanks a Million, Johnston & Kahn, Dick Powell photo, 1948 ... **5.00**

Theme From The Monkees, Boyce & Hart, group photo cover, 1966 .... **20.00**

There Goes My Dreams, David Heneker, 1940 .... **5.00**

Valentine Candy, Sherman & Sherman, Leslie Ann Warren photo, 1966 .... **3.00**

Vict'ry Polka, Samuel Cahn & Jule Styne, 1943 .... **11.00**

Vo-Do-De-O, Jack Yellen & Milton Ager, 1927 .... **5.00**

Wait Till Tomorrow, Lloyd & DePaul, D Day & P Graves photo, 1967 .... **5.00**

Wait Until Dark, Livingston, Evans & Mancini, A Hepburn photo, 1967 .... **10.00**

Wedding March, Felix Mendelsohnn, 1935 .... **5.00**

With You in My Arms, BA Dunham & Dan Alexander, 1946 .... **4.00**

Zip-A-Dee-Doo-Dah, Wrubel & Gilbert, movie: Song of the South (Disney) **15.00**

Zoot Suit for My Sunday Gal, Ray Gilbert & Bob O'Brien, 1941 .... **10.00**

Shot Glasses

Shot glasses, old and new, are whetting the interest of today's collectors, and they're relatively easy to find. Basic values are given for various categories of shot glasses in mint condition. These are general prices only. Glasses that are in less-than-mint condition will obviously be worth less than the price given here. Very rare and unique items will be worth more. Sample glasses and other individual one-of-a-kind oddities are a bit harder to classify and really need to be evaluated on an individual basis. For more information we redcommend *Shot Glasses: An American Tradition* by Mark Pickvet; he is listed in the Directory under Michigan. See Clubs and Newsletters for information concerning the Shot Glass Club of America.

Advertising, Hard Rock Cafe, Orlando, Florida, 1990, 4", $35.00.

Black porcelain replica, from $3.50 to 5.00
Carnival colors, plain or fluted, from $100 to 150.00
Carnival colors, w/patterns, from $125 to 175.00
Culver 22k gold, from $6 to 8.00
Depression, colors, from $10 to..12.50
Depression, colors w/patterns or etching, from $17.50 to ... 25.00
Depression, tall, general designs, from $10 to 12.50
Depression, tall, tourist, from $5 to 7.50
European design, rounded w/gold rim, from $4 to 6.00
Frosted w/gold designs, from $6 to...................................... 8.00
General, advertising, from $4 to .6.00

General, enameled design, from $3 to 4.00
General, frosted design, from $3.50 to 5.00
General, gold design, from $6 to 8.00
General, porcelain, from $4 to . 6.00
Inside eyes, from $6 to 8.00
Iridized silver, from $5 to 7.50
Mary Gregory or Anchor Hocking Ships, from $150 to 200.00
Nude, from $25 to 35.00
Plain, w/or w/out flutes, from 50¢ to .... .75
Pop or soda advertising, from $12.50 to 15.00
Ruby flashed, from $35 to 50.00
Sayings & toasts (1940s & 1950s), from $5 to 7.50
Sports (Professional Teams), from $5 to 7.50
Square, general, from $6 to 8.00
Square, w/etching, from $10 to..12.50
Square, w/pewter, from $12.50 to 15.00
Square, w/2-tone bronze & pewter, from $15 to 17.50
Standard glass w/pewter, from $7.50 to 10.00
Steuben or Lalique crystal, from $150 to 200.00
Tourist, colored glass, from $4 to .6.00
Tourist, general, from $3 to 4.00
Tourist, porcelain, from $3.50 to .5.00
Tourist, Taiwan, from $2 to 3.00
Tourist, turquoise or gold, from $6 to 8.00
Whiskey or beer advertising, modern, from $5 to 7.50
Whiskey sample, good condition, from $50 to 100.00
Whiskey samples, mint condition, from $75 to 350.00

19th-century cut patterns, from $35 to **50.00**

Silhouette Pictures

Silhouettes and reverse-paintings-on-glass were commercially produced in the US from the 1920s through the 1950s. Some were hand painted, but most were silkscreened. Artists and companies used either flat or convex glass. Common subjects include romantic couples, children, horses, dogs, and cats. Many different styles, sizes, colors, and materials were used for frames. Backgrounds also vary from textured paper to foils, colorful lithographs, wildflowers, or butterfly wings. Sometimes the backgrounds were painted on the back of the glass in gold or cream color. These inexpensive pictures were usually sold in pairs, except for the advertising kind, which were given by merchants as gifts. For more information we recommend *The Encyclopedia of Silhouette Collectibles on Glass* by Shirley Mace (Shadow Enterprises); she is listed in the Directory under New Mexico.

Art Publishing, flat, boy & girl feeding ducks **40.00**
Art Publishing, flat, windblown lady w/whippet **22.00**
Baco, convex, Snowland Splendor, deer watching man w/sled dogs, 1950 .... **32.00**
Benton, convex, boy stands by girl in pumpkin **50.00**

Benton, convex, couple dancing in interior scene, she in ruffled gown **40.00**
Benton, convex, couple making snowman **45.00**
Benton, convex, lady & child w/cat, dark blue **60.00**
Benton, convex, lady looks upon well on hill **30.00**
Benton, convex, man watching lady shoot bow & arrow **30.00**

Benton, Scottie dog chasing bird, convex glass, ca. 1940, 4x5", from $35.00 to $50.00. (Photo courtesy Candace Sten Davis and Patricia J. Baugh)

Benton, convex, Scottie dog chases butterfly **30.00**
Buckbee Brehm, flat, Happy Bride, lady adjusting veil for bride .. **40.00**
Buckbee Brehm, flat, lady's portrait in profile **15.00**
C&A Richards, flat, Elfin Music. **140.00**
CE Erickson Co, convex, sleigh/cottage scene, advertising & thermeter **30.00**
Fisher, convex, boy & his dog fishing, dried flowers **30.00**
Fisher, flat, My Mother, lady rocking, wildflower background **55.00**
Flowercraft, flat, girl chasing dog w/stolen doll **30.00**
Lee Mero, flat, nude about to dive into water **50.00**
Newton, flat, family scene before fireplace **28.00**
Reliance, flat, Beau Brummel, man in tails w/top hat & cane. **18.00**

Reliance, flat, Courtship **22.00**
Reliance, flat, Swan Pond **30.00**
Reliance, flat, terriers playing tug-
of-war **18.00**
Tinsel Art, flat, girl w/candle &
kitten **20.00**

Snow Domes

Snow domes are water-filled paperweights. The earliest type was made in two pieces with a glass globe on a separate base. First made in the mid-nineteenth century, they were revived during the 1930s and 1940s. The most common snow domes on today's market are the plastic half-moon shapes made as souvenirs or Christmas toys, a style that originated in West Germany during the 1950s. Other types such as round and square bottles, tall and short rectangles, cubes, and other simple shapes are found as well.

Advertising, Texaco tanker truck
against cityscape in round
dome **65.00**
Advertising, 50 Years of Leadership
American Household...,
4x3x3" **85.00**
Character, B Potter's Peter Rabbit,
Schmid 1983, musical, 7". **14.00**

Character, Bugs Bunny 24k Friend, plastic, 1989, 2¾", $13.00.
(Photo courtesy whatacharacter.com)

Character, Charlie Brown & Snoopy
by Christmas tree, musical, 6",
MIB **35.00**
Character, Mickey Mouse seated w/
globe, Walt Disney Productions,
5" **30.00**
Character, Phantom of the Opera,
San Francisco Music...,
China **45.00**
Character, Raggedy Ann & Andy
in sled, Bobbs-Merrill, 1980,
3" **35.00**
Character, Wicked Witch from Oz,
others inside globe, Warner
Bros, 8" **75.00**
Christmas, angel holding wand,
pink dress, German, 1950,
2½" **62.00**
Christmas, bears sliding on snowy
hill, glass, musical, 5½" .. **18.00**
Christmas, ornament, angel w/
instrument, glass, German,
4½" **40.00**
Christmas, ornament, nativity,
glass, West Germany, 3x2¾"
dia **27.00**
Christmas, Rudolph the Red Nosed
Reindeer, black base, Driss,
4" **28.00**
Christmas, Santa & Mrs Claus
on fireplace, plastic, #8827,
5x4" **12.50**
Christmas, Santa w/deer on shoul-
ders, globe in belly, #758,
1960s **18.00**
Christmas, snow scene, light-up,
Silvestri musical, wood base,
8", MIB **18.00**
Disney, Belle from Beauty & the
Beast, Disney store, 7x7". **60.00**
Disney, Goofy riding carousel
horse & playing banjo, musi-
cal **20.00**

341

Disney, Jiminy Cricket, glass w/ wood base, NE The First Limited... ....65.00

Disney, Lion King, lion family & Rafiki in globe, others on base 38.00

Disney, Mickey & Minnie Wedding, glass w/resin base, 9x6", MIB......................70.00

Easter, rabbits in garden, detailed ceramic base, musical, 1970s 17.00

Promotional, Balto animated film, Universal, 1995, MIB 95.00

Souvenir, Boston Bruins, plastic, 1960s, Hong Kong, 4¼x3".16.00

Souvenir, Crystal Cave, PA, plastic, 2¼" 14.00

Souvenir, Dallas landmarks, plays Yellow Rose of Texas, Saks, 6½" 50.00

Souvenir, Hawaii-The 50th State, hula girls on beach, 1960s, 3" L......................28.50

Souvenir, Mexico, 2 men sleeping on seesaw, #354-V, 1970s, 2¾".22.00

Souvenir, New York City skyline, plastic, white base, 2x2½". 30.00

Souvenir, Paris buildings, plastic, Made in France, 2¼x3" ...20.00

Souvenir, Penn's Cave PA, boat in cave scene, purple base, 3".11.50

Souvenir, Yellowstone National Park, brown bear, black base 13.00

Soda Pop Collectibles

Now that vintage Coca-Cola items have become rather expensive, interest is expanding to include some of the less widely known flavors of soda — Dr. Pepper, Nehi, and Orange Crush, for instance. For more informatin we recommend *Collectible Soda Pop Memorabilia* by B.J. Summers (Collector Books).

Dr. Pepper

A young pharmacist, Charles C. Alderton, was hired by W.B. Morrison, owner of Morrison's Old Corner Drug Store in Waco, Texas, around 1884. Alderton, an observant sort, noticed that the drugstore's patrons could never quite make up their minds as to which flavor of extract to order. He concocted a formula that combined many flavors, and Dr. Pepper was born. The name was chosen by Morrison in honor of a beautiful young girl with whom he had once been in love. The girl's father, a Virginia doctor by the name of Pepper, had discouraged the relationship due to their youth, but Morrison had never forgotten her. On December 1, 1885, a U.S. patent was issued to the creators of Dr. Pepper.

Bottle, Desert Storm commemorative, 10-oz, EX...............10.00

Bottle carrier, cardboard, holds 6 16-oz bottles, 1950s, EX . 15.00

Bottle opener, metal wall-mount type, 3x2", VG 62.50

Bottle topper, Cindy Garner, EX+ 165.00

Bullet pencil/bottle opener, EX..65.00

Clock, composition w/glass front, plaid logo, Telechron, 14" dia, EX 300.00

Clock, double bubble, Dr Pepper Co limited edition, 15" dia, NMIB **225.00**

Clock, glass front, diamond shape, Pam, 1950s, 15", EX **215.00**

Cooler, metal w/plastic handles, red lettering, Progress...Company, EX **165.00**

Fan, cardboard w/wooden handle, pretty girl, E Morgan art, EX **75.00**

Ice chest, wood w/rope handles, red lettering, 1885-1985, EX.. **50.00**

Menu board, metal over chalkboard w/plaid logo above, 23x17", VG **150.00**

Mug, Serve Dr Pepper Hot, red lettering on white glass, Fire-King, M **55.00**

Sign, cardboard, phrase/bottle cap/ couple sq dancing, horizontal, EX **425.00**

Sign, cardboard standup, phrase/ plaid logo/girl/football game, EX **250.00**

Sign, porcelain, resembles brick wall, 1940s, 10½x26", EX **215.00**

Sign, tin, Dr Pepper, 7x20", EX **30.00**

Sign, tin litho, bottle, 10-2-4 on yellow, 55x18", G **110.00**

Thermometer, glass front, red & blue on white, Pam, 1960s, 12" dia, NM **285.00**

Thermometer, tin litho, Hot or Cola, red & white, 1970s, 12x7", NM **145.00**

Hires Root Beer

Did you know that Hires Root Beer was first served to fairgoers at the Philadelphia Centennial in 1876? It was developed by Charles E. Hires, a druggist who experimented with roots and herbs to come up with the final recipe. The company originally chose the Hires boy as their logo, and if you'll study his attire, you can sometimes approximate a guess as to when an item he appears on was manufactured. Very early on he appeared in a dress, and from 1906 until 1914 it was a bathrobe. He sported a dinner jacket from 1915 until 1926.

Blotter, Real Root Juices Make...Avoid Imitations, 1920, EX **15.00**

Menu board, cardboard, image of moustached man, 1950s, 28x15", VG+ **75.00**

Menu board, tin litho top, 29x15", EX **175.00**

Sign, tin, More Than Refreshing, self-framed 17x27", EX, from $235.00 to $250.00.

Mug, Mettlach, 4", EX+, $100.00. (Photo courtesy Past Tyme Pleasures)

Pocket mirror, celluloid, Hires boy pointing, 2¼" dia, EX **25.00**

Sign, cardboard, shows Hires w/ food specials, 1950s, 8x24", NM 60.00

Sign, metal, Say! Drink Hires 5¢/It Is Pure, 9½x17", VG 85.00

Sign, tin, Hires R-J Root Beer in Bottles Ice Cold, 10x28", NM 50.00

Sign, tin bottle shape, 1950s, 22", M 200.00

Sign, tin litho, Drink...Bottles on blue & white stripes, 35" dia, NM 285.00

Sign, tin litho, Enjoy...girl in red cap on blue, 1930s, 10x28", NM 220.00

Syrup dispenser, front spout, stainless steel w/tin signs, 8½", NM 135.00

Thermometer, bubble glass front, 2½x12" dia, NM 98.00

Thermometer, tin litho, multicolor on white, 1950s, 27x8¼", EX 225.00

Thermometer, tin litho bottle shape, 28½x7½", NM 85.00

Tray, Drink...Honest Root Beer, 2 girls, Haskell Coffin, 14x10", EX 15.00

Nehi

Banner, paper, NE above bottle/HI below, 1940s, 19x40", VG .. 100.00

Bottle opener, engraved Drink Nehi, Consolidated Cork Co, EX 15.00

Clock, glass front, metal frame, yellow dot, 15" dia, NM 325.00

Menu board, embossed tin litho top, 1950s, 27½x19¾", EX 95.00

Nehi, bottle opener, metal, wall mount, Starr Patd X Reg, early, EX 110.00

Paperweight, glass, pinup-style sailor girl, NM 25.00

Pump, chrome, 19", EX 250.00

Sign, paper litho, girl rowing boat, 1938, 18½x11¼", EX 165.00

Sign, tin litho, Drink Genuine..., bottle by lady's legs, 11x17", EX 35.00

Tray, girl in red swimsuit in ocean wave & bottle, rectangular, VG 110.00

Nesbitt's

Bottle, clear w/white painted label, 9½", EX 10.00

Bottle opener, embossed metal, Drink Nesbitt's, 3¼", EX.. 20.00

Calendar, 1953, complete, EX . 65.00

Clock, fluorescent tube light, Drink Nesbitt's Orange, 26x12x4", EX 50.00

Menu board, tin, 1950s, 20x28", NM 70.00

Picnic cooler, 1950s, EX 65.00

Shot glass, clear w/orange & white painted logo, 2¼", EX 12.00

Sign, cardboard, clown w/2 kids drinking Orange, 16x24", EX 25.00

Sign, die-cut cardboard, lady in hat & gloves w/bottle, 1950s, 21", EX 75.00

Sign, tin, Drink & 5¢ above bottle, 1950s, 49x16", EX 275.00

Sign, tin bottle shape, 84x24", NM+ 850.00

Thermometer, Don't Say Orange Say..., professor & lg bottle, 22", EX 165.00

Thermometer, metal, black & yellow, red & white letters, 1938, 27", NM 200.00

Thermometer, tin, 4-color, 1950s, 24", EX............135.00

Thermometer, tin litho, orange bottle on white (left side), 16x6", EX.............................115.00

Orange-Crush

Bottle, clear w/embossed letters, ribbed, 24-oz, 1920s, EX.25.00

Bottle opener, metal wall mount, Made in USA, Starr, Patd Apr 1925, EX.........................40.00

Calendar, 1946, complete, 31x16", VG..............................125.00

Display with bottle, 1930s, EX+, $425.00.

Menu board, logo & bottle at top, Stout Sign, 1940-50s, 27x19", EX+..............................100.00

Orange-Crush, metal bottle opener, wall mount, Starr, Pat Apr 1925, EX.........................40.00

Sign, cardboard hanger, Have Red Hot...Orange-Crush, 1920s, EX...............................250.00

Sign, celluloid over cardboard orange button, Crushy phrase, 9", EX.............................165.00

Sign, reverse-painted glass, round, Fresh/Drink O-C/Crushy, 9½", EX..............................200.00

Sign, steel & iron, shows ribbed bottle, F Robertson, 1927, 35x9", VG........................275.00

Sign, tin bottle cap form, wall mount, 39" dia, EX........665.00

Thermometer, bubble glass front, Pam, 12" dia, NM..........295.00

Thermometer, metal bottle form, 28"................................185.00

Thermometer, tin litho, bottle cap at top on green, 14½x5½"....135.00

Tray, 6 bottles arranged like spokes of a wheel, 1940s, 10" dia, NM.........................150.00

Pepsi-Cola

Pepsi-Cola has been around about as long as Coca-Cola, but since collectors are just now beginning to discover how fascinating this line of advertising memorabilia can be, it's generally much less expensive. You'll be able to determine the approximate date your items were made by the style of logo they carry. The familiar oval was used in the early 1940s, about the time the two 'dots' (indicated in our listings with '=') between the words were changed to one. But the double dots are used nowadays as well, especially on items designed to be reminiscent of the old ones — beware! The bottle cap logo was used from about 1943 until the early to mid-1960s with variations. For more information refer to *Pepsi-Cola Collectibles* by Bill Vehling and Michael Hunt and *Introduction to Pepsi Collecting* by Bob Stoddard.

Ashtray, chrome bowl w/painted bottle cap, Pepsi-Cola Montreal, EX 90.00

Bottle, double-dot paper label and shoulder ribbon, 12-ounce, VG, $65.00.

Bottle, Iowa Bowl 1978 commemorative, unopened, 16-oz .. **15.00**

Bottle opener, solid brass w/banner logo, Muddler, 1948, 5x2½", EX **42.50**

Carrier, cardboard, blue w/white stripes, w/6 full 12-oz bottles, NM **50.00**

Cigarette lighter, bottle cap & Pepsi on can form, VG **35.00**

Clock, light-up, Be Sociable Have a Pepsi, sq, 15¾", EX **75.00**

Clock, light-up, bottle cap logo, Swihart, 1940s, 15" dia. **450.00**

Clock, light-up, double-bubble, Say Pepsi Please, 1950s **600.00**

Clock, light-up, The Light Refreshment, plastic, 1950s, G.............................. **350.00**

Door push, Drink Pepsi & bottle cap on yellow, wrought-iron look, EX **125.00**

Glass, fountain; red, white, & blue painted-on label, 4½", EX. **15.00**

Menu board, Enjoy..., yellow tin w/blackboard bottom, 27x19", EX **165.00**

Menu board, Have a..., bottle cap logo, tin, 1950s, 30x19½", VG **120.00**

Menu board, plastic light-up, modern logo, 21x54x8", G...... **25.00**

Pitcher, stained-glass window-style logo on clear glass, 8¼", EX. **32.00**

Rack, wire w/die-cut cap logo, 3-tier, 1940s, 42x22", VG........ **185.00**

Sign, bottle cap, painted metal, 1950s, 31" **200.00**

Sign, cardboard die-cut standup, Santa in long johns, 20x16", EX **55.00**

Sign, embossed tin, Say Pepsi Please, bottle & cap on yellow, 47", EX **155.00**

Sign, It's Got a Lot To Give, cardboard, couple w/bottle, 25x37", EX **135.00**

Sign, Listen to Country - Spy..., paper, 8x19"..................... **85.00**

Thermometer, red painted tin, bottle cap at top, 1950s, 27x8½", VG **115.00**

Thermometer, tin litho, Say Pepsi..., scale-like bar, 28x7½", VG **90.00**

Thermometer, yellow painted tin, bottle cap at top, 1950-60s, 27", EX **125.00**

Toy dispenser, white plastic, Pepsi-Cola logo, 10", EXIB **85.00**

Tray, Bigger & Better, stylized flowers, 1940, 11x14", EX...... **50.00**

Royal Crown Cola

Bottle crate, wooden, red w/yellow lettering, EX................... **30.00**

Bottle display, cardboard & foil, pleated fan shape w/button, 1930s, M **135.00**

Bottle opener, wall mount, raised letters in red on silver, Star X, EX **30.00**

Calendar, 1951, Ann Blyth w/dog, complete, 24", EX.......... **160.00**

Clock, convex glass front, Best by Taste Test, 15" dia, EX . **425.00**

Clock, glass front, diamond shape, Pam, 1963, NM **185.00**

Clock, glass front, wooden frame, Drink..., sq, 16x16", EX. **385.00**

Cooler, metal, red letters embossed on yellow, bail handle, 16x18", EX **85.00**

Cooler, painted metal, red lettering on yellow, VG **85.00**

Fan, cardboard, all-American girl, 1950s, EX **30.00**

Menu board, embossed tin top, red, white & blue, 28x19¾", EX. **75.00**

Radio, can shape, GE/Hong Kong, EX **20.00**

Sign, cardboard, image of Barbara Stanwyck, 1940s, 11x28". **75.00**

Sign, metal, Drink..., red & white, 1950s, 17x34", EX **125.00**

Sign, self-framed embossed tin, lg bottle graphic, 36x16", VG...... **175.00**

Sign, tin litho bottle shape, Donaldson, 1953, 58½", G **165.00**

Thermometer, tin litho, Best by Taste-Test, ca 1947, 25½x9½", EX **155.00**

Thermometer, tin litho, bottle at right on yellow, 1935, 13½x6", EX **195.00**

Thermometer, tin litho, Enjoy RC on white, minor rust, 26x10", VG **48.00**

Thermometer, tin litho, red & cream, Donasco, 1957, 25½x10", EX **85.00**

Thermometer, 26x10", EX, from $90.00 to $110.00.

7-Up

Though it was originally touted to have medicinal qualities, by 1930 7-Up had been reformulated and was simply sold as a refreshing drink. The company who first made it was the Howdy Company, who by 1940 had changed its name to 7-Up to correspond with the name of the soft drink. Collectors search for the signs, thermometers, point-of-sale items, etc., that carry the 7-Up slogans.

Ashtray, round glass dish w/logo in center, 1950-60s, 4½" dia, EX+ **25.00**

Bottle topper, Top O' the Mornin', leprechaun & shamrocks, NM **12.00**

Clock, glass front, wooden frame, sq, 4½x16x16", EX........ **175.00**

Clock, glass front on sq oak frame, You Like It..., 1950s, EX. **115.00**

Clock, metal/plastic, neon tube on face, battery, 15" dia, NM **85.00**

Cooler, metal w/embossed logo, swing handles, 1950s, EX. **50.00**

Display bottle, plastic, 1960s, 28", EX **85.00**

Doll, Fresh-Up Freddie, painted rubber, 1959, VG........... **125.00**

Door push, painted aluminum, EX............................... **175.00**

Drinking glass, The Unglass, upside-down bell shape, EX............ **5.00**

Menu board, hand pouring bottle above blackboard, 1950s, 27½", EX **165.00**

Menu board, tin chalkboard, hand-held bottle, 27x19", EX+. **70.00**

347

Sign, cardboard standup, grocer holding case, 1948, 12x10", M...**65.00**

Sign, light-up, Now Fountain, tilted bubbles label on white, EX.**375.00**

Sign, tin, First Against Thirst, 1960s, 20x28", VG...........**40.00**

Sign, tin, Get Real Action, Your Thirst Away, 1963, 43", NM.......**350.00**

Sign, tin flange, 2-sided, bubble logo, 1940s, 10x12½", EX........**300.00**

Sign, tin litho, Fresh Up, 1956, 13x6½", NM...................**200.00**

Sign, tin litho, Fresh Up w/7-Up & bubbles on oval, 40x30", EX.............**300.00**

Sign, tin litho, tilted logo on white, 12x14", EX+..................**165.00**

Sign, tin litho, Uncola & rainbow, 12x24", EX.....................**155.00**

Telephone, Red Spot figure, 7-Up Co, 1990, EX...................**18.00**

Thermometer, dial type, Fresh Clean Taste, 1960s, 12" dia, EX.................**50.00**

Thermometer, dial type, 7-Up Likes You, 10" dia, NM...........**275.00**

Thermometer, porcelain, The Fresh-Up Family Drink/bottle, 15", NM...........**85.00**

Thermometer, tin litho, lg green bottle on right, 15x6", EX....**150.00**

Thermometer, tin litho, logo on black, 20x5", EX............**100.00**

Tie clip, enameled logo on bar, EX................**15.00**

Miscellaneous

A&W Root Beer, sign, porcelain over steel, 12" dia, EX....**35.00**

A&W Root Beer, Snoopy serving mug, glass, United Feature..., 6", EX................**85.00**

Big Red, bottle, clear, 10-oz, NM..**10.00**

Bubble Up, sign, tin litho, green & white, 1960s, 12x30", NM.**130.00**

Bubble Up, thermometer, green painted metal, 17x5", EX.**75.00**

Canada Dry, sign, tin, Drink..., yellow & white lettering, 12x30", EX................**65.00**

Cliquoit Club Pale Ginger Ale, thermometer, tin litho, 1950s, 14", NM..............**140.00**

Dad's Root Beer, wooden crate, metal strapping, 10x18x13", EX................**22.50**

Diet-Rite Cola, sign, tin litho, Enjoy Sugar Free..., 1961, 12x32", EX................**80.00**

Dog 'n Suds Root Beer, clock, convex glass front, dog/hot dog/mug, NM.......................**350.00**

Double Cola, clock, convex glass in black frame, Ingraham, '53, 8" dia...................**95.00**

Frostie, cardboard chalkboard, 18x24", EX, from $20.00 to $25.00.

Frostie Root Beer, mug, lettering on clear glass, 5½".........**18.00**

Frostie Root Beer, plastic sign, figure holding sign, 1955, 12x13", EX................**120.00**

Frostie Root Beer, thermometer, white tin litho, 1950s, 12x3¼", EX.................................145.00

Grapette, bank, clear glass cat figure, clown lid w/slot, 6¼", EX............................... 48.00

Grapette, sidewalk marker, solid brass, 1930s, 4", EX........30.00

Grapette, thermometer, tin litho, Thirsty or Not, 1950s, 15x6", EX.................................100.00

Kist, clock, bubble glass front, It's Kist Time, 16" dia, EX..250.00

Kist, clock, convex glass front, diamond shape, Pam, 1961, 15", EX................................135.00

Kist, mirror, Refreshing Anytime & lips, 12x12"....................65.00

Kist, thermometer, tin litho, multicolor on black, 16x6", EX.90.00

Mountain Dew, soda jerk hat, hillbilly, red, white & green, 1960s, EX.................................30.00

Moxie, hand fan, cardboard litho, boys on rocking horse, 1922, EX.................................40.00

NuGrape, clock, round convex glass face, light-up, bottle & logo, EX...............................150.00

NuGrape, sign, paper die-cut, girl standing in boat, 1935, 31½", EX................................185.00

NuGrape, thermometer, Have Fun..., w/bottle on white, 12" dia, EX............................75.00

NuGrape, tray, tin litho, hand-held bottle on green, American Art, VG.................................45.00

Sprite, thermometer, green plastic, light fading, 18x7", EX...35.00

Squirt, doll, Squirt Boy, vinyl w/cloth outfit, 1960s, 17", VG......................... 200.00

Squirt, menu board, boy/bottle on yellow above blackboard, 24x19", EX......................90.00

Squirt, sign, tin litho, boy w/bottle, multicolor, 1959, G..........75.00

Squirt, thermometer, tin litho, boy/bottle on white, 1965, 13½", EX.................................90.00

Sun Crest, bottle topper, cardboard litho, 1950s, 7½x9½".......37.50

Sun Crest, clock, convex glass, blue, white, & orange, 8" dia, G..60.00

Vernor's, sign, tin litho, man in round reserve, 6x18", EX.70.00

Whistle, door push, painted metal, adjusts from 30" to 36" L, EX....................130.00

Whistle, sign, cardboard die-cut bottle, 1951, 30x11"......250.00

Whistle, sign, metal bottle cap, Thirsty Just Whistle, 3x28" dia, EX..........................150.00

Whistle, sign, tin litho, blue, white & orange, 1948, 4x21½", NM.220.00

Whistle, thermometer, elf w/bottle pushing cart, Pam, 12" dia, EX.................................400.00

Souvenir Glassware

For many years travelers have been returning home with small keepsakes to remind them of the good times shared on their journeys. As a result, tourist shops began stocking small items that could easily be picked up and carried home. Souvenir glassware was a result of that custom. Found in custard, vaseline, pressed patterns, even ruby-stained pieces, collectors are having fun making choices. States tumblers are popular, with prices somewhat higher for Western states, as they are harder to find. Everything from bells to vases can be found, so the possibilities abound. For information on tumblers or mugs, we recommend *The Hazel-Atlas Glass Identification and Value Guide* by Gene and Cathy Florence (Collector Books).

Bell, Harlem Casino NY, flowers & gold on custard, 6¼"........**32.50**

Box, Murdo SD & farm scene on custard, 2¾x4" dia...........**45.00**

Goblet, Bead Swag, Spirit Falls WI & flowers on custard, Heisey, 6".....................................**55.00**

Hat, Green Bay WI, black lettering on vaseline, 2⅛", EX.......**16.00**

Mug, Atlantic City NY, 1898, ruby stained, 3¾", EX..............**40.00**

Mug, KS State Industrial Reformatory... & scene on vaseline, 4"..............................**32.00**

Mug, Stuckey's Coffee Club, red & blue pyro on milk glass, Fire King..................................**85.00**

Pitcher, Gettysburg 1863, red lettering on custard w/gold, 3½"..............................**30.00**

Pitcher, Sabine TX 1904, black lettering on vaseline, worn gold, 3".....................................**40.00**

Salt shaker, Lake Charles LA, ruby stained, EX gold, original lid, ea......................................**32.00**

Sugar bowl, Cut Block, Aurorahville WI, orange on custard, 2½"...................**37.50**

Tumbler, Alabama, Cotton State, black pyro on milk glass, from $6 to...............................**10.00**

Tumbler, Billy the Kid Museum, Ft Sumner New Mexico, blue pyro, 4¾"..........................**12.50**

Tumbler, Georgia the Peach State, yellow, 2-color pyro on white, $6 to................................**8.00**

Tumbler, Land of Lincoln, N Salem State Park, red pyro on blue frost...................................**5.00**

Tumbler, Montana & map, 2-color pyro on frost (Western states rare)...............................**20.00**

Tumbler, Washington DC, Capital building on white frost, from $5 to...................................**7.00**

Vase, Main Street Winfield KS & street scene on custard, 6¼x3"...........................**38.00**

Vase, Rolla ND & pink flower on custard, gold scalloped rim, 6".**55.00**

Wine stem, Bonilla South Dakota, red pyro on custard w/gold, 4¼"......................................**62.50**

Souvenir Spoons

Originating with the Salem Witch spoons designed by Daniel Low, souvenir spoons are generally reasonably priced, easily displayed, and often exhibit fine artwork and craftsmanship. Spoons are found with a wide range of subject matter including advertising, commemorative, historic sites, American Indians, famed personalities, and more. Souvenir spoons continue to capture the imaginations of thousands of collectors with their timeless appeal.

Alaska, sterling, transfer print enamel finial, demi, from $5 to **15.00**

Arkansas, Fairbanks skyline full-figure handle, JB Erd, from $125 to **175.00**

California, bear/poppies figural handle, plain bowl, Shiebler, from $75 to **125.00**

California Mid-Winter Fair, San Francisco, 1984, from $5 to.**15.00**

Colorado embossed on handle, Gateway to Garden on Gods in bowl, from $40 to **75.00**

Columbian Exposition on handle, Ferris wheel embossed in bowl, from $5 to **10.00**

Flatiron Building, New York embossed in bowl, various handles, from $20 to **75.00**

Hershey's, name enameled on handle, silver plate, from $5 to........**10.00**

High Water Mark Gettysburg in bowl, Baronial pattern, Smith, from $40 to **75.00**

Illinois, Morrison Water Works engraved in bowl, Stuart H, from $30 to **50.00**

Japan in open filigree handle, embossed flower in bowl, sheet silver **20.00**

Kenya on finial, elephants in bowl, from $5 to **15.00**

Mardi Gras woman hand-painted in bowl, state handle, from $100 to **200.00**

Michigan, Main St Jackson; various handles, ea from $25 to **50.00**

Monmouth Illinois, Willet's School engraved in bowl, Melrose handle **25.00**

Monte Carlo, mechanical enameled roulette wheel finial, from $40 to **85.00**

New York, Metropolitan Building embossed in bowl, hidden swastika..........................**25.00**

New York stacked skyline full-figure handle, Shepard, from $75 to **150.00**

Ohio, Findlay courthouse in bowl, corn-design handle, from $50 to **75.00**

Paducah & Old Kentucky Home w/ cabin engraved in bowl, from $25 to **50.00**

Queen Wilhelmina of Netherlands handpainted in bowl, crest handle **200.00**

Rome, St Peter's Basilca & Vatican, printed scenes in bowl, from $25 to **65.00**

Salt Lake City, Morman Tabernacle in bowl, elk's tooth finial, from $50 to **150.00**

Spain, dancing senorita on finial, plain bowl, demi, from $10 to **20.00**

Stork handle, engraved bowl, Lunt, from $30 to **60.00**

Thomas Jefferson handpainted in bowl, from $300 to **500.00**

Wai kiki Hawaii, handle w/4 card suits cut-out, city engraved in bowl..................................**80.00**

Wai kiki Hawaii, ornate handle w/ boat scene in long bowl, from $140 to **200.00**

Yellowstone Park, Great Falls image on cut-out handle, Robins, from $15 to......... **30.00**

Sports Collectibles

When sports cards became so widely collectible several years, other types of related memorabilia started to interest sports fans. Now they search for baseball uniforms, autographed baseballs, game-used bats and gloves, and all sorts of ephemera. Although baseball is America's all-time favorite, other sports have their own groups of interested collectors.

Bag, gym; white w/ABA striped basketball logo, 1960s, 12x20", EX................... **382.00**

Bank, Sonics, light skin version, ca. 1970 uniform, 7", from $60.00 to $75.00. (Photo courtesy gasolinealley.com)

Baseball, stamped Official National League Ford C Frick, Spalding, EX................... **112.00**

Baseball glove, Carl Furillo, Dubow 747B, early 1950s, EX.... **78.00**

Baseball jersey, San Diego #22, blue on white, Rawlings 44, EX................... **255.00**

Basketball, 1960 NCAA Championship, 5 signatures on white panel, NM...................... **325.00**

Bat, Lou Gehrig, NM.......... **510.00**

Board game, Vince Lombardi's Game, 1970s, complete, NM......... **47.00**

Book, Lawn Tennis, instruction book, Lieut Peile, 1885, 90-pg.. **134.00**

Bust, Knute Rockne (Notre Dame), cast iron w/silver plate, 1931, 7x7"............................... **100.00**

Football helmet, leather w/original chin strap, Nokona #317, 1930s, EX........................ **99.00**

Football pants, wood slats inside legs, olive green, 1924, 27½" L..**235.00**

Golfball, Old Sport Baby Dimple, original wrapper............. **48.00**

Guide, 1951 College Football, Bobby Reynolds cover, 56-pg, VG..**54.00**

Magazine, Look, Hank Greenberg cover, April 1946, NM..... **70.00**

Magazine, Sports Illustrated, Bear Bryant cover, August 1966, EX.................... **55.00**

Magazine, Sports Illustrated, J Lucas cover, January 1960, EX..................... **32.00**

Magazine, Sports Illustrated, Ohio State National Champion, March '61........................ **25.00**

Media guide, UCLA Basketball 1963-64, soft cover, 36-pg, EX.. **162.00**

Pennant, Cincinnati Reds Champions, white on red, 1961, EX.......................... **67.00**

Pennant, 1973 World Champ... Dolphins, orange & aqua on white, 29", EX................. **57.00**

Pennant, Mickey Mantle, Holiday Inn, Joplin, MO, EX, $175.00. (Photo courtesy Morphy Auctions)

Photo, team; World Champions 1948 Philadelphia Eagles, w/ name list, EX 35.00

Photo, team; 1952 Seattle Rainers, players listed at bottom, 7x11", EX 54.00

Photo, wire; Earl Averill appearing in All-Star game, 1931, 8x6", EX 75.00

Pin, '51 American League Anniversary, eagle/shield on diamond shape, M 50.00

Pin, 1977 NY Yankees 31st World Series, silver-tone, 1½x1", M 140.00

Poster, Jimmy Connors, Sports Illustrated, 1978, 37x24", EX. 32.00

Program, dinner menu; 1916 Chicago Cubs, bear & pennant on front, EX 165.00

Program, Oregon State & Duck at 1942 Rose Bowl, multicolor cover, NM 380.00

Program, tournament; Municipal Auditorium Kansas City, March 1971, EX 25.00

Ring, Homes Jr College National Championship, silver w/enamel, EX 380.00

Sign, Goudey Heads-Up, Brand New..., cardboard, 1938, 7x10½", EX 68.00

Tennis racquet, original stringing, Bridgeport Athletic..., 26" L, VG 25.00

Ticket, Georgia Tech vs Notre Dame, Notre Dame school photo, 1968, M 47.00

Ticket, 1967 All-Star baseball game, played in Anaheim California, NM 58.00

Yearbook, Converse Encyclopedia of 1976-77 basketball season, EX 30.00

Stangl

The Stangl Company of Trenton, New Jersey, produced many striking lines of dinnerware from the 1920s until they closed in the late 1970s. Though white clay was used earlier, the red-clay patterns made from 1942 on are most often encountered and are preferred by collectors. Decorated with both hand painting and sgraffito work (hand carving), Stangl's lines are very distinctive and easily recognized. Virtually all is marked, and most pieces carry the pattern name as well.

In addition to the dinnerware, Stangl is famous for their lovely bird figurines, which they made from 1940 until as late as 1978. Nearly all are marked and carry a four-digit number used to identify the species. For more information we recommend *Collector's Encyclopedia of Stangl Artware, Lamps, and Birds* by Robert C. Runge, Jr. (Collector Books).

Birds

#3250A, Duck standing, 3¼". 100.00

#3274, Penguin, 6" 400.00

#3276D, Bluebirds (pr), 8½".. 150.00

#3286, Hen, 3¼" 50.00

#3402, Oriole, beak down, old style, 3½" 125.00

#3405, Cockatoo, 6" 50.00

#3406, Kingfisher, teal, 3½"... 75.00

#3408, Bird of Paradise, 5½". 80.00

#3444, Cardinal, female 150.00

#3445, Rooster, gray, 10" 175.00

#3449, Paroquet, 5½" **165.00**
#3452, Painted Bunting, 5" ... **85.00**
#3490D, Redstarts (pr), 9" ... **150.00**
#3492, Cock Pheasant **165.00**

**#3518D, White-Crowned Pigeons,
7½x12½", $1,000.00.**

#3582D, Parakeets (pr), blue, 7". **250.00**
#3585, Rufous Hummingbird,
3" **70.00**
#3589, Indigo Bunting, 3½" ... **50.00**
#3592, Titmouse, 3" **45.00**
#3596, Gray Cardinal, 5" **60.00**
#3598, Kentucky Warbler, 3". **45.00**

Dinnerware

Ashtray, Holly #3869, fluted, 5",
from $25 to **35.00**
Baking dish, Town & Country
#5287, blue, 9x14", from $75
to **100.00**
Bowl, mixing; Orchard Song #5110,
12", from $50 to **60.00**
Bowl, salad; Amber-Glo #3899, 12",
from $35 to **50.00**
Bowl, salad; Mediterranean #5186,
11", from $70 to **80.00**
Bowl, sherbet; Provincial #3966,
from $30 to **35.00**
Bowl, vegetable; Festival #5072,
from $35 to **45.00**
Bread tray, Chicory #3809, from
$50 to **60.00**

Bread tray, Windfall #3930, from
$20 to **25.00**
Butter dish, Blueberry #3770, from
$50 to **60.00**
Butter dish, Pink Lily #3888, from
$25 to **30.00**
Cake stand, Garland #4067, from
$20 to **25.00**
Candy jar, Colonial #1388, from
$45 to **55.00**
Casserole, Florette #5073, w/lid, 8",
from $50 to **65.00**
Coffeepot, Provincial #3966, 4-cup,
from $85 to **100.00**
Creamer, Newport #3333, from $35
to **40.00**
Cruet, Windfall #3930, w/stopper,
from $20 to **25.00**
Egg cup, Country Garden #3943,
from $12 to **15.00**
Gravy boat, Chicory #3809, from
$30 to **35.00**
Gravy boat, Orchard Song #5110,
from $20 to **25.00**
Gravy boat, Yellow Tulip #3637,
from $25 to **30.00**
Lazy Susan, Orchard Song #5110,
from $65 to **75.00**
Mug, Amber-Glo #3899, 2-cup, from
$20 to **25.00**
Mug, Holly #3869, 1-cup, from $25
to **35.00**
Mug, Holly #3869, 2-cup **50.00**
Pickle dish, Windfall #3930, from
$10 to **15.00**
Pitcher, Blueberry #3770, 2-qt,
from $90 to **100.00**
Pitcher, Garland #4067, 2-qt, from
$85 to **100.00**
Plate, Amber-Glo #3899, 12½", from
$25 to **35.00**
Plate, Colonial #1388, 10", from
$20 to **25.00**

Plate, Garland #4067, 6", from $10
to **12.00**

Plate, pie; Town & Country #5287,
black or crimson, 10½", from
$40 to **50.00**

Platter, Amber-Glo #3899, 13¾",
from $30 to **40.00**

Platter, Mediterranean #5186,
13¾", from $55 to **65.00**

Platter, Orchard Song #5110, 14¾",
from $35 to **40.00**

Ramekin, Colonial #1388, 4", from
$12 to **15.00**

Relish dish, Festival #5072, from
$20 to **30.00**

Salt & pepper shakers, Florette
#5073, pr from $16 to **20.00**

Soap dish, Town & Country #5287,
brown, from $20 to **25.00**

Teacup, Colonial #1388, from $8
to **10.00**

Teapot, Holly #3869, from $150
to **175.00**

Teapot, Provincial #3966, from $75
to **85.00**

Tidbit, Windfall #3930, 10", from $8
to **10.00**

Tray, Orchard Song #5110, sq, 7",
from $20 to **25.00**

Underplate, gravy; Pink Lily #3888,
from $8 to **10.00**

Star Wars

Capitalizing on the ever-popular space travel theme, the movie *Star Wars* with its fantastic special effects was a mega box office hit of the late 1970s. A sequel called *Empire Strikes Back* (1980) and a third adventure called *Return of the Jedi* (1983) did just as well, and as a result, licensed merchandise flooded the market, much of it produced by the Kenner company. The last three films were *Star Wars Episode I* and, of course, *Episode II* soon followed. *Episode III* was released in 2004.

Original packaging is very important in assessing a toy's worth. As each movie was released, packaging was updated, making approximate dating relatively simple. A figure on an original *Star Wars* card is worth more than the same character on an *Empire Strikes Back* card, etc.; and the same *Star Wars* figure valued at $50.00 in mint-on-card condition might be worth as little as $5.00 'loose.' Especially prized are the original 12-back *Star Wars* cards (meaning 12 figures were shown on the back). Second issue cards showed eight more, and so on. For more information we recommend *Star Wars Super Collector's Wish Book* by Geoffery T. Carlton; and *Schroeder's Collectible Toys, Antique to Modern*. Both are published by Collector Books.

Note: Because space was limited, SW was used in our descriptions for Star Wars, ROTJ was used for Return of the Jedi, ESB for Empire Strikes Back, and POTF for Power of the Force.

Bank, Yoda, SW, Sigma, M **90.00**
Bop Bag, Darth Vader, Kenner,
MIB **125.00**
Doll, Latara the Ewok, plush, 1984,
16", MIB **50.00**
Figure, Admiral Ackbar, ROTJ,
MOC **60.00**

Figure, Anakin Skywalker, M (in sealed mailer bag)...........**40.00**

Figure, AT-ST Driver, POTF, MOC **95.00**

Figure, Ben (Obi-Wan) Kenobi, ESB, white hair, MOC..**175.00**

Figure, Bespin Security Guard, ROTJ, Black, MOC **75.00**

Figure, Boba Fett, SW, M **45.00**

Figure, C-3PO, Droids, MOC.**95.00**

Figure, Chewbacca, ESB, MOC.**275.00**

Figure, Chief Chirpa, ROTJ, MOC **50.00**

Figure, Darth Vader, ROTJ, MOC (light saber drawn)......... **65.00**

Figure, Death Squad Commander, ESB, MOC **140.00**

Figure, Death Star Droid, ROTJ, MOC............................. **125.00**

Figure, Emperor, ROTJ, MOC ..**50.00**

Figure, ESB, Bespin outfit, M.**15.00**

Figure, Hans Solo, ROTJ, MOC (tri-logo)......................... **125.00**

Figure, Imperial Commander, ESB, MOC............................... **85.00**

Figure, Jawa, SW, 12-back, MOC, $200.00.
(Photo courtesy June Moon)

Figure, Luke Skywalker, ESB, Bespin fatigues, blond hair, MOC........................... **150.00**

Figure, Luke Skywalker Jedi, ROTJ, green light saber, MOC **95.00**

Figure, Princess Leia, ROTJ, Boushh outfit, M **26.00**

Figure, Stormtrooper, ROTJ, MOC **65.00**

Figure, Yoda, ROTJ, MOC...**150.00**

Game, Escape From Death Star, Kenner, 1977, NMIB.......**40.00**

Magnets, ROTJ, set of 4, MOC **25.00**

Paint Kit, Luke Skywalker or Han Solo, Craftmaster, MOC, ea **16.00**

Playset, Death Star Space Station, SW, complete, EX.......... **115.00**

Playset, Ewok Village, ROTJ, MIB **225.00**

Playset, Jabba the Hutt Dungeon w/8D8, ROTJ, MIB **145.00**

Playset, Turret & Probot, ESB, MIB................................**160.00**

Playset, Van Set, EX, $125.00.
(Photo courtesy Morphy Auctions)

Puppet, Yoda, hollow vinyl, Kenner, 1981, 10", EX...................**25.00**

Scissors, ROTJ, MOC **10.00**

Stickers, ROTJ, 12 pcs, 1983, MOC...............................**10.00**

Telephone, toy; speaker, Darth Vader, MIB **95.00**

Vehicle, Armored Sentinel Transport, ROTJ, mini-rig, MIB................................**45.00**

Vehicle, Darth Vader's TIE Fighter, SW, MIB **140.00**

Vehicle, Imperial Cruiser, ESB, complete, EX **50.00**

Vehicle, Imperial Troop Transport, SW, MIB 135.00

Vehicle, Jawa Sand Crawler, remote control, all accessories, EX, $175.00.

Vehicle, Multi-Terrain Vehicle (MTV-7), ESB, mini-rig, MIB.............35.00
Vehicle, Speeder Bike, ROTJ, MIB 50.00
Vehicle, Twin-Pod Cloud Car, ESB, complete, EX....................45.00
Vehicle, Y-Wing Fighter, ROTJ, MIB...............................225.00

Swanky Swigs

Swanky Swigs are little decorated glass tumblers that once contained Kraft Cheese Spread. The company has used them since the Depression years of the 1930s up to the present time, and all along, because of their small size, they've been happily recycled as drinking glasses for the kids and juice glasses for adults. Their designs range from brightly colored flowers to animals, sailboats, bands, dots, stars, checkers, etc. There is a combination of 223 verified colors and patterns. In 1933 the original Swanky Swigs came in the Band pattern, and at the present time they can still be found on the grocery shelf, now a clear plain glass with an indented waffle design around the bottom.

They vary in size and fall into one of three groups: the small size sold in Canada, ranging from 3¹⁄₁₆" to 3¼"; the regular size sold in the United States, ranging from 3⅜" to 3⅞"; and the large size also sold in Canada, ranging from 4³⁄₁₆" to 5⅝".

A few of the rare patterns to look for in the three different groups are small group, Band No. 5 (two red and two black bands with the red first); Galleon (two ships on each glass in black, blue, green, red, or yellow); Checkers (in black and red, black and yellow, black and orange, or black and white, with black checkers on the top row); and Fleur-de-lis (black with a bright red filigree design).

In the regular group: Dots Forming Diamonds; Lattice and Vine (white lattice with colored flowers); Texas Centennial (cowboy and horse); Special Issues with dates (1936, 1938, and 1942); and Tulip No. 2 (black, blue, green, or red).

Rare glasses in the larger group are Circles and Dots (black, blue, green, or red); Star No. 1 (small stars scattered over the glass in black, blue, green, or red); Cornflower No. 2 (dark blue, light blue, red, or yellow); Provincial Cress (red and burgundy with maple leaves); and Antique No. 2 (assorted antiques on each glass in lime green, deep red, orange, blue, and black).

Antique #1, any color, 1954, 3¾"..............................**4.00**

Bachelor Button, red, white & green, Canadian, 1955, 4¾".........**15.00**

Band #2, black & red, Canadian, 1933, 4¾"..........................**20.00**

Band #3, white & blue, 1933, 3⅜".................................**3.00**

Blue Hearts & Red Apples, US 2003....................................**5.00**

Blue Tulips, 1937, 4¼"..........**20.00**

Bustlin' Betty, any color, Canadian, 1953, 4¾"..........................**20.00**

Carnival, blue, green, red or yellow, 1939, 3½"..........................**9.00**

Circles & Dot, any color, 1934, 3½".....................................**7.00**

Coin, coin decor around base, 1968, 3¼"......................................**2.00**

Colonial, waffle decor around middle & base, 1976, 3¾"...........**.50**

Cornflower #1, light blue & green, Canadian, 1941, 4⅝".......**20.00**

Cornflower #1, light blue & green, 1941, 3½"..........................**4.00**

Cornflower #2, dk blue, lt blue, red or yellow, Canadian, 1947, 4¼"......................................**30.00**

Crystal Petal, clear & plain w/ fluted base, 1951, 3½".......**2.00**

Ethnic Series, lime green, blue, burgundy, red or yellow, 1974, 4½".....................................**20.00**

Forget-Me-Not, dk blue, lt blue, red or yellow, 1948, 3½"..........**4.00**

Hostess, clear & plain w/indented groove base, 1960, 3¾"......**1.00**

Jonquil (Rosy Pattern), yellow & green, Canadian, 1941, 3¼".**8.00**

Jonquil (Rosy Pattern), yellow & green, 1941, 3½"................**4.00**

Kiddie Kup, any color, Canadian, 1956, 4¾"..........................**20.00**

Kiddie Kup, any color, 1956, 3¾"...............................**3.00**

NASCAR driver, No 3 Kurt Busch #97 or No 4 Michael Waltrip #15....................................**10.00**

Petal Star, clear w/indented star base, Canadian, 1978, 3¼"..**2.00**

Provencial Crest, red & burgundy, Canadian, 1974, 4⅝".......**25.00**

Sailboat #1, blue, 1936, 3½"..**12.00**

Sailboat #2, blue, green, light green or red, 1936, 3½".............**12.00**

Special Issue, Lewis-Pacific Dairyman's..., Kraft Foods, 1947, 3½".....................**100.00**

Sportsman Series, red hockey, football or baseball, Canadian, 1976................................**20.00**

Stars #1, any color, Canadian, 1934, 4¾"..................................**20.00**

Stars #1, black, blue, green or red, 1935, 3½"..........................**7.00**

Stars #2, clear w/orange stars, Canadian, 1971, 4⅝".........**5.00**

Train, passenger car, Greetings, blue, 2005.........................**5.00**

Tulip (Posy Pattern), red and green, Canadian, 1941: 3¼", from $7.00 to $8.00; 4½", from $20.00 to $25.00; 3¼", $10.00. (Photo courtesy Gene and Cathy Florence)

Tulip (Posy Pattern), red & green, Canadian, 1941, 4⅝".......**20.00**

Tulip #3, dark blue, light blue, red
or yellow, 1950, 3⅞" **4.00**
Violet (Posy Pattern), blue & green,
Canadian, 4⅝" **20.00**
Violet (Posy Pattern), blue & green,
1941, 3½" **4.00**

Syroco

From the early 1940s until
1962, Syroco items were replicas
of wood carvings cast from wood
fiber, but most that you'll find today
are made of resin. They're not at
all hard to find; and because they
were made in so many shapes and
designs, it's easy and inexpensive
to build an interesting collection.
Some are hand painted, and others are trimmed in gold. You may
also find similar products stamped
'Ornawood,' 'Decor-A-Wood,' and
'Swank.' These items are collectible
as well.

Bookends, eagle in relief, metal
base, 5½x5¼" **30.00**
Bookends, terrier dog, brown stain,
1950s, 7x5⅝" **37.50**
Bottle opener, horse head figural,
4⅛x5x2⅛" **70.00**
Brush holder, dog w/glass eyes, tongue
mechanism, 3½x6" **45.00**
Business card holder, sailing
ships, brown tones, foil label,
3¾x7" **25.00**
Candleholders, flower form, 1¼x4"
dia, pr **30.00**
Candleholders, 2-light, gold swirl-
ing Nouveau design, 19x8",
pr **110.00**
Corkscrew, bulldog figure, walnut
stain, 5¾" **100.00**

Corkscrew, monk standing, brown
tones, 8" **650.00**
Corkscrew, Senator Volstad Codger (aka
Old Codger), 1930s, 8½" **160.00**
Doorstop, bulldog w/glass eyes,
brown w/green collar, 1930-
40s, 6½" **55.00**
Doorstop, cat, recumbent w/curled
tail, white w/yellow eyes,
1970s **25.00**
Figurine, Dagwood Bumstead,
marked 1944 KFS, 5" **35.00**
Ice bucket, grapes in relief, bail
handle, brown stain **30.00**
Mirror, ornate roses & leaves,
beveled glass, easel back,
18x14½" **65.00**
Pipe stand, acorns & leaves,
brown stain, holds 3 pipes,
2½x6¾" **36.00**
Plaque, key, ornate w/rearing
lion on top bar, gold paint,
7½x18" **20.00**
Plaque, lady w/basket on head
stands w/palm tree & cacti, 6"
dia **50.00**
Shelf, rose & flowers w/scrolls,
white w/gold wash, #6202,
1965, 7x19" **40.00**

Wall pocket, marked, ca. 1946, 12", from $20.00 to $22.00. (Photo courtesy Betty and Bill Newound)

Tea Bag Holders

These are fun and inexpensive to collect. They were made,

359

of course, to hold used tea bags, but aside from being functional, many are whimsical and amusing. Though teapots are the most commonly found shape, you can find fruit, bird, and vegetable shapes as well.

Bowl form, yellow roses & laurel rings, Rosenthal Briar Rose, 3" dia **20.00**

Flower form, Desert Rose, Franciscan **18.00**

Flower form, pink w/green center, Stangl, 3¾x4" **20.00**

Leaf form, clear glass, 4x2½"... **9.00**

Lemon form, smiling face, yellow & green, Enesco #307, 3¾" . **15.00**

Plate form, Old England Earl Grey London Tea, gray/navy/red, 7x5" **17.00**

Plate form, white & blue, Langeline #9705/708, Made in Denmark, 3" sq **12.00**

Strawberry form, red & green, ceramic, set of 4 in 5x5x2½" frame................................ **25.00**

Teapot form, butterfly, blue on white w/green trim, Raynaud Limoges **20.00**

Teapot form, floral design, Lefton, #8282, from $5.00 to $8.00. (Photo courtesy Loretta DeLozier)

Teapot form, gray parrot on white, English China, 5⅛" **25.00**

Teapot form, Hawaii the 50th State, hula dancer, ceramic w/gold trim **15.00**

Teapot form, I Will Hold the Teabag, ceramic, set of 4 in frame. **35.00**

Teapot form, Let Me Hold the Bag, Cleminson........................ **15.00**

Teapot form, Miss Cutie Pie, 2 birds on top, Napco, 1950s **35.00**

Teapot form, plant life encased inside, hard plastic, 3½x4½" **11.50**

Teapot form, red & green roses w/ gold, Lefton, 3¼x4¾" **6.00**

Teapot form, roses on white, Lefton #6672, 4½" **10.00**

Teapot form, white w/Eastern Star symbol, ceramic, SM-535.. **12.00**

Teapots

The popularity of teatime and tea-related items continues, and vintage and finer quality teapots have become harder to find. Those from the 1890s and 1920s reflect their age with three and four digit prices. Examples from the 1700s and 1800s are most often found in museums or large auction houses. Teapots listed here represent examples still available at the flea market level. Most collectors begin with a general collection of varied teapots until they decide upon the specific category that appeals to them. Collecting categories include miniatures, doll or toy sets, those made by a certain manufacturer, figurals, or a particular style (such as Art Deco or English floral). Some of the latest trends in collecting are

Chinese Yixing (pronounced yee-shing — teapots from an unglazed earthenware in forms taken from nature), 1950s pink or black teapots, Cottageware teapots, and figural teapots (those shaped like people, animals, or other objects). While teapots made in Japan have waned in collectibility, collectors have begun to realize many detailed or delicate examples are available. Of special interest are Dragonware teapots or sets. Some of these sets have the highly desired lithophane cups — where a Geisha girl is molded in transparent relief in the bottom of the cup. When the cup is held up to the light, the image becomes visible.

Coalport, Indian Tree, gold trim, 1945, 8" W 72.00
Cornishware, cream w/wide blue stripes, Made in England, ca 1950 .... 145.00
Erphila, rabbit form, cream, brown & black, Germany, 1945. 144.00
Fitz & Floyd, kangaroo figure, joey at handle, 7" 51.00
Fitz & Floyd, pig figure, 1976, 4½x8" 20.00
Germany, pink & green flowers w/ gold leaf trim, ornate 60.50
Gold Castle, pastel flowers on white, Made in Japan, 4x7" 100.00
Johnson Brothers, Old English Castle, pink tranfer, 5x10". 66.00
Mexico, man on siesta, cactus, aloe & squirrels, pottery, Mexico VW 148.00
Pasadena, pink & gray rosebuds on white, Noritake China #6311, 7" 115.00

Ridgways, Coaching Days & Coaching Ways, 4¼" 70.00
Royal Albert, Memory Lane, white bone china, ornate handle, 7" 92.00

Royal Albert, Tea Rose, 5¼x8", from $65.00 to $80.00.

Royal Albert, Tenderness, white bone china, ornate gold trim, lg 135.00
Royal Crown Derby, Imari, 1940, 4½" 192.00
Sadler, fox hunting scene, marked STIRRUP CUP, Made in England 90.00
Sadler, merry-go-round, Edwardian Entertainments, Bandstand #2005895 .... 35.00
Sadler, special edition, American Bi-Centenary 1779-1976, 6½". 46.00
Shelley, cream w/gold trim & handle, Fine Bone China..., 5x7½" 160.00
Spode, Mayflower, Federal style, 5½x11"........................... 154.00
Union Pacific, Streamliner, white w/14k gold striping, 5".. 190.00
Wade Heath, Donald Duck figure, hand-painted, 1930s, sm, 4" 266.00

Tiara Exclusives

Collectors are just beginning to take notice of the glassware sold through Tiara in-home parties, their Sandwich line in particular. Several companies were involved in producing the lovely items they've marketed over the years, among them Indiana Glass, Fenton, Dalzell Viking, and L.E. Smith. In the late 1960s Tiara contracted with Indiana to produce their famous line of Sandwich dinnerware (a staple at Indiana Glass since the late 1920s). Their catalogs continue to carry this pattern, and over the years, it has been offered in many colors: ruby, teal, crystal, amber, green, pink, blue, and others in limited amounts. We've listed a few pieces of Tiara's Sandwich below, and though the market is unstable, our values will serve to offer an indication of current values. Unless you're sure of what you're buying, though, don't make the mistake of paying 'old' Sandwich prices for Tiara. To learn more about the two lines, we recommend *Collectible Glassware from the 40s, 50s, and 60s* by Gene and Cathy Florence (Collector Books). Also refer to *Collecting Tiara Amber Sandwich Glass* by Mandi Birkinbine; she is listed in the Directory under Idaho.

Ashtray, Amber, 1¼x7½", from $8 to **10.00**
Basket, Chantilly Green, 7¾x5x6½", from $65 to **85.00**
Bell, dinner; Pink, 6", from $12 to **15.00**
Bowl, Amber, 6-sided, 1¼x6¼", from $8 to **12.00**
Bowl, salad; Amber, crimped, 4¾x10", from $15 to **18.00**

Bowl, salad; Amber, slant sides, 3x8⅜", from $10 to **15.00**
Butter dish, Amber, domed lid, 6", from $20 to **25.00**
Butter dish, Chantilly Green, domed lid, 6", from $20 to **30.00**
Candleholders, Amber, flared foot, 3¾", pr from $10 to **12.00**

Candy dish, Amber, with lid, 7½", from $65.00 to $80.00. (Photo courtesy Mandi Birkinbine)

Canister, Amber, 38-oz, 7½", from $12 to **20.00**
Celery tray/oblong relish, Amber, 10⅜x4⅜", from $16 to **22.00**
Clock, wall hanging, Amber, 16" dia, from $45 to **55.00**
Clock, wall hanging, Spruce, 12" dia, from $12 to **18.00**

Compote, Spruce Green, 8", from $20.00 to $25.00.

Cup, snack/punch; Amber, from $2 to **3.00**
Fairy (Glo) lamp, Amber, egg shape, pedestal foot, 2-pc, 5¾" ... **10.00**
Fairy (Glo) lamp, Horizon Blue, 2-pc, 5¾", from $20 to **25.00**
Goblet, Bicentennial Blue, 8-oz, 5¼", from $10 to **12.00**

Goblet, Spruce Green, 8-oz, 5¼",
from $5 to 7.00

Napkin holder, Amber, 4x7½", from
$15 to 20.00

Pitcher, Amber, 8¼", from $25 to .. 35.00

Plate, dinner; Amber, 10", from $9
to 15.00

Plate, salad; Chantilly Green, 8¼",
from $4 to 8.00

Puff box, Amber, 3⅝" dia, from $10
to 15.00

Saucer, Amber 2.00

Tray, Amber, footed, 1¾x12¾", from
$20 to 35.00

Tray, divided relish; Amber, 4-com-
partment, 10", from $15 to . 20.00

Tray, egg; Peach, 12", from $20
to 35.00

Tumbler, juice; Amber, footed, 3",
from $10 to 12.00

Tobacco Collectibles

Even though the smoking habit
is frowned upon nowadays, related
items still have collector appeal.
The tobacco industry used to widely advertise their products, and
retail companies turned out many
types of smoking accessories, such
as pipes, humidors, lighters, and
ashtrays to accommodate smokers. Vintage tins, store bins, cigarette packs, tobacco pouches, signs,
and thermometers are among the
more sought-after items. Unless
otherwise noted, our values are for
examples in excellent to near mint
condition.

Cigar box, Bances & Suarez La
Carolina, original factory
scene, 1930s.................... 45.00

Cigar box hammer, JA Henckels,
metal w/plastic handle, 6½"
L.................................... 52.00

Cigar cutter, figural grotesque face,
brass, bottom slides out . 145.00

Cigar cutter, 14k gold, scissor-type,
Tiffany & Co, 1920s, 2" L.. 210.00

Cigar cutter (in lion's mouth)
embossed brass, guillotine-
type 90.00

Cigar holder, genuine amber & patterned metal, 1900s, 3¼" L. 60.00

Cigarette box, W Ariel Gray & Co,
lid w/steamship in ocean scene,
tin................................. 115.00

Cigarette cards, Colour in Nature,
complete set of 50, Ogdens,
1952, M........................... 45.00

Cigarette case, tabletop; figural globe
on corner, 1950s, 4x7"...... 280.00

Cigarette dispenser, elephant figure, cast iron, ashtray ring at
base............................... 50.00

Cigarette dispenser, leather, spring
mechanism, round, clock in
lid 40.00

Cigarette holder, brass & bamboo,
1920s, 13½" L 45.00

Cigarette holder, carved white ivory
hand at end holds cigarette, 5"
L.................................... 42.00

Cigarette paper, Top Wheat
Straw, RJ Reynolds, 100 in
package 10.00

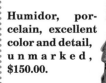

**Humidor, por-
celain, excellent
color and detail,
unmarked,
$150.00.**

Humidor, wood w/felt lining, Decatur Industries, 3x11x7¾" **20.00**

Label, Chief Joseph, portrait & scene, P Schmidt & B Litho, 6x10" **120.00**

Label, crate; Zadie, classical lady w/dove, Petersburg USA, 13¾x7" **40.00**

Match holder, Punch figure, brass, hat tips back, 6x4" **110.00**

Mirror, pocket; HD Soyster Altoona High Grade Cigars..., oval, VG **115.00**

Pack, Home Run Cigarettes, baseball scene, w/1910 tax stamp, unopened **230.00**

Pipe, meerschaum cherub, Bakelite & silver handle, w/leather case **490.00**

Pipe tool, Kleen Reem, WJ Young Co Peabody, M in case **12.00**

Sign, Camel cigarette ad, metal, Where a Man Belongs, man on cycle **163.00**

Sign, RG Sullivans 7-20-4, porcelain, white & red on blue, 12x24" **235.00**

Sign, Viceroy Cigarettes, multicolor on metal, Come In!, 1929, 25x11" **80.00**

Thermometer, Camels Cigarettes, metal, ca. 1950, $75.00. (Photo courtesy B. J. Summers)

Thermometer, Vantage, metal, Buy a Pack Today, triangular, 9", VG **50.00**

Tin, Bagley's Sweet Tips Smoking, black label on gold-tone, oval, 4" **70.00**

Tip card, Lucky Strike Cigarettes, portrait of Dorothy Marshall, 5½x4", EX, $65.00.

Tobacco pack, Good Old Summer-Time Long Cut..., man & woman on beach **28.00**

Tobacco pouch, black leather roll-up, Dunhill, 5 pocket, 9" L ... **120.00**

Tray, La Verdo, painted couple on steps in garden, Meek Co, 14x17" **213.00**

Tools and Farm Implements

Old farm tools and implements have been long sought after by collectors. Some like to decorate their country-inspired rooms with these primitives, while others appreciate them for their enduring quality and the memories they evoke of times gone by. For whatever reason you may be collecting them, flea markets can be a treasure trove of great old tools.

Auger, AA Wood & Sons, adjusts from ¼-1¼" dia, hollow, VG **140.00**

Axe, broad; Powell Tool Co Cleveland O, original handle, 26" **195.00**

Axe, ship builder's, Campbell's, head only, 6", G+ **55.00**

Bee fogger, metal w/wood, working patina, 6½x9"................... **30.00**

Bevel square, Zenith by Disston, 6", VG................................ **20.00**

Carpenter's plumb and level, Stanley #104, hardwood with brass, 1960s – 1970s, worn finish, $45.00.

Chisel, butt; Stanley #750, bevel edge, Made in USA, 9⅜", VG **45.00**

Chisel, butt; 1" bevel edge, 7⅝" L, G...................................... **20.00**

Chisel, firmer; Stanley #720, ½" bevel edge, USA, 12¾", EX **50.00**

Chisel, firmer; Stanley Everlasting #20, bevel edge 12¼", VG..................... **150.00**

Chisel, paring; Buck Bros, CI, VG............................... **25.00**

Chisel, skew; Buck Bros #2, ⅛", G **12.50**

Clam rake, cast-iron curved/cupped tines, 10½" w/51" wooden handle........................... **295.00**

Corn grinder, spiral-feed to series of knives, wood body, crank handle............................ **85.00**

Corn sheller, Black Hawk #1903A, cast iron, crank handle... **65.00**

Corn sheller, Grey Bros, hand-held squeeze type, EX........... **295.00**

Draw knife, Greenlee, laminated blade, 8", G...................... **25.00**

Draw knife, Sargent, patternmaker's w/black handles, 4", G **30.00**

Draw knife, Wilkinson, folding handles, laminated blade, 8", G...................................... **40.00**

Drill, breast; Millers Falls #120B, 2-speed, 3-jaw chuck....... **50.00**

Drill, push; Millers Falls #100, Buck Rogers type, w/8 bits **40.00**

Fodder fork, Z&M Randleman... IA, wood lever, Pat 1888, EX.............................. **95.00**

Funnel, galvanized metal, turns to lock in position, lg........... **25.00**

Gauge, butt; Stearns #85, nickle-plated cast iron, G **15.00**

Gouge, socket; Zenith,¼", 12½" L overall, VG **25.00**

Hammer, hoof-pick; folding type, nickle plated, Stout Pat, 6", VG................................. **115.00**

Hammer, saw setting; unmarked, hand forged, for lg-toothed saws, G **25.00**

Hammer, saw-setting; Simonds, for crosscuts, etc, VG............ **45.00**

Hammer, tack; Stanley #601, magnetic, # on handle, w/decal, NM **35.00**

Hay hook, handmade wood handle, ca 1900, 8" w/7½" hook ... **20.00**

Hay knife, slim saw type, aka Connecticut type, late 1800s, EX **85.00**

Implement seat, Stoddard, cast iron, from $85.00 to $95.00.

Mallet, horse collar; burl head, 7" dia, VG.............................**125.00**

Monkey wrench, H&H Balto MD, wedge at back collar, 6", VG **85.00**

Nippers, W Scollhorn, nickle plated, Bernard's Pat Oct 24 1899, VG...............................**25.00**

Oxen yoke, wood w/3¾" dia iron ring, double, 33", EX.......**65.00**

Pipe wrench, Cook's Pat January 28, 1890, self-adjusting, VG.. **115.00**

Plane, fore; Sargent #418, mahogany handle, ca 1920, VG ..**75.00**

Plane, smooth; Fulton #409 made by Sargent, G+ **50.00**

Planter, hand-operated, American Standard #4...1918, 33x11½".**27.50**

Planter, hand-operated, wood w/2 metal seed containers, 34" L, G..................................**55.00**

Pliers, Vacuum Grip, early snap-on type, 4½", VG...................**20.00**

Plow, Allis Chalmers, 2-bottom, missing coulters.............**125.00**

Pulley, cast-iron frame over wood, Myers OK H-299, 11½", EX..**14.00**

Riveter, leather-working type, Fulton, 6x12½" **25.00**

Rope maker, 3-strand, primitive, unmarked, EX...............**175.00**

Rule, extension; Durall, brass slide, 6", NM............................**15.00**

Saw, crosscut; Disston D23, curved applewood handle, 9 tpi, 1940, 26"....................................**35.00**

Saw, crosscut; Spear & Jackson, Spearior, 8 tpi, 26 L, G ...**40.00**

Saw, hack; Disston & Son #240, 22" blade, 24" overall, NM..**155.00**

Saw, rip; Disston & Sons #12, applewood handle, 1897-1917, 28", VG **115.00**

Saw jointer, Pike Perfect, spring-loaded, NMIB **35.00**

Saw set, Stearns #106, 6-14 gauge, 15", G **30.00**

Saw vise, Disston #1, 9" jaws, VG.**50.00**

Scoop, metal w/iron & wood handle, 9¾x6¼", VG **24.00**

Screwdriver, spiral ratchet; Yankee #1351, inner spring, nickel plated................................**30.00**

Scythe, unmarked, 20" blade, 58" wood handle **40.00**

Shovel, grain; softwood, straight front edge, arched handle, 37x12"...............................**45.00**

Skew, SJ Addis #2, 3/16", G...**15.00**

Spoke pointer, unmarked #2, points up to 2⅝" dia stock, G.....**50.00**

Square, bevel; cast iron w/patented lock on bottom, unmarked 9"................................... **28.00**

Square, take-down; Southington Hardware Co, rafter scales, VG...............................**60.00**

Square set, Brown & Sharp 12" combo, original black crinkle paint.................................**85.00**

Square set, LS Starrett, level bubble & scribe, 12" **40.00**

Tire pump, John Deere, power-take-off driven, replaced hose, VG...............................**60.00**

Wheelbarrow, green painted wood, chamfered slats w/chip-carved ends...............................**100.00**

Wheelbarrow seeder, Star Seeder... NY, wood frame, 16" seed box, EX **95.00**

Toothbrush Holders

Children's ceramic toothbrush holders represent one of today's popular collecting fields, with some of the character-related examples bringing $150.00 and up. Many were made in Japan before WWII. For more information we recommend *A Pictorial Guide to Toothbrush Holders* by Marilyn Cooper; she is listed in the Directory under Texas.

Bellhop w/flowers, 1 hole, Japan, 5¼", from $75 to **85.00**

Boy in knickers, multicolor, 2 holes, stands on tray, 4¾", $75 to..**95.00**

Boy w/cap & tie, 3 holes, Japan, 6¼", from $75 to **85.00**

Bozo, multicolor lustre, 2 holes, Japan, 5¾", from $75 to.. **85.00**

Calico cat, tray at feet, 2 holes, Japan, 5½", from $100 to **120.00**

Clown, multicolor paint on cast iron, arms hold brush, 3¾", from $225 to **250.00**

Cowboy standing by cactus, opening in hat, Japan, 5½", from $90 to **95.00**

Doc Says Brush Your Teeth 'Snow White,' Walt Disney Productions, #42, from $95.00 to $110.00.

Dog w/basket, multicolor, hole in basket, tray at feet, Japan, 5¾" **95.00**

Donald Duck, bisque, 2 holes, tray at feet, WDE, 5¼", from $285 to **315.00**

Duckling, painted chalkware, 2 holes, no tray, 4¾", from $40 to **50.00**

Ducky Dandy, multicolor, 2 holes, tray at feet, Japan, 4¼", from $175 to **200.00**

Dutch boy w/hands on hips, 3 holes (2 at pockets), tray at feet, 5".......................... **70.00**

Elephant w/tusk (facing right), multicolor, 1-hole, w/tray, 5½" **85.00**

Giraffe, 3 holes, tray at feet, Japan, 6", from $130 to **145.00**

Girl w/umbrella, multicolor, 2 holes, tray at feet, Japan, 4½" .. **80.00**

Halloween policeman, 1 hole, tray at feet, Japan, 5", from $100 to **115.00**

Indian chief, multicolor, 2 holes, tray across chest, Japan, 4½" **275.00**

Mary Poppins w/purse & umbrella, multicolor, 2 holes, w/tray, 5¾" **175.00**

Mother Hubbard, dog at her feet, Germany, 6¼", from $400 to..**430.00**

Orphan Annie, 2 holes, tray at feet, Japan, 5¼", from $110 to. **150.00**

Peter Rabbit, name on overalls, 2 holes, tray at feet, 5½", from $100 to **135.00**

Popeye, multicolor paint on bisque, 1 hole, stands, Japan, 5", from $525 to **575.00**

Three Bears, multicolor, 2 holes, tray at feet, Japan, 5", from $85 to **100.00**

Uncle Willie, multicolor, 2 holes, tray at feet, FAS Japan, 5⅛" .. **110.00**

Toys

Toy collecting remains a very popular hobby, and though some areas of the market may have softened to some extent over the past two years, classic toys remain a good investment. Especially strong are the tin windups made by such renowned companies as Strauss, Marx, Lehmann, and Chein, and the battery-operated toys made from the '40s through the '60s in Japan. Because of their complex mechanisms, few survive.

Toys from the 1800s are rarely if ever found in mint condition but should at least be working and have all their original parts. Toys manufactured in the twentieth century are evaluated more critically. Compared to one in mint condition, original box intact, even a slightly worn toy with no box may be worth only about half as much. Character-related toys, space toys, toy trains, and toys from the '60s are very desirable.

Several good books are available, if you want more information: *Matchbox Toys, 1947 – 2003, The Other Matchbox Toys, 1947 – 2004,* and *Toy Car Collector's Guide* by Dana Johnson; *Collecting Disneyana* and *Collector's Toy Yearbook* by David Longest; *Star Wars Super Collector's Wish Book* by Geoffrey T. Carlton; *Big Book of Toy Airplanes* by W. Tom Miller; and *Schroeder's Collectible Toys, Antique to Modern.* (All are published by Collector Books.) See also Action Figures; Breyer Horses; Hartland; Character Collectibles; Ramp Walkers; Star Wars; Western Heroes; Clubs and Newsletters.

Battery-Operated

Barney Bear the Drumming Boy, remote control, 1950s, 11", NMIB **200.00**
Bubble Lion, litho tin, MT, 1950s, 7", EXIB **125.00**
Crowing Rooster, plush, white, yellow & orange, Y, 1950s, 9", EXIB **75.00**
Dragster Racer (Bump & Go Action), Sears, 13", EXIB **220.00**
Dune Buggy (w/Surf Board), tin & plastic, w/driver, TPS, 10" L, EXIB **100.00**
Electronic Periscope-Firing Range, Cragston, 1950s, VGIB. **100.00**
Ford GT, Bandai, 11", NMIB. **110.00**
French Cat, Alps, 1950s, 10" L, MIB **125.00**
Genie Bottle, plastic, Hobby Craft/ Hong Kong, 12", MIB **65.00**

Good Time Charlie, MT/Japan, 13", EXIB, $150.00.

Hamburger Chef, K, 1960s, 8", MIB **250.00**
Happy Singing Bird, MY, 1950s, 3" L, M **75.00**

Hooty the Happy Owl, Alps, 1960s, 9", MIB **200.00**

James Bond 007 Aston Martin, Gilbert, 11½", NM **175.00**

King Size Fire Engine, Bandai, 1960s, 13", M.................**150.00**

Linemar Hauler, Linemar, 1950s, 14", MIB **250.00**

Magic Snow Man, holding broom, MT, 1950s, 11", EXIB....**140.00**

Marching Bear, plush, w/drums & cymbals, Alps, 1960s, 10", EXIB **250.00**

Mickey Mouse Locomotive, MT, 1960s, 9", NM.................**175.00**

Monkee-Mobile, ASC, 1960s, 12", EX **325.00**

Mother Goose, plush, Cragstan, 10", VGIB **75.00**

Mr McPooch Taking a Walk & Smoking..., plush, remote control, 8", EXIB.................**150.00**

Musical Jolly Chimp, C-K, 1960s, 10", EXIB........................**80.00**

Mystery Police Car, TN, 1960s, 10", NM **150.00**

Nutty Nibs, Linemar, 12½", EXIB, $950.00.
(Photo courtesy Randy Inman Auctions Inc.)

Old Fashioned Bus, MT, 13", NMIB **85.00**

Overland Stage Coach, litho tin, MT, 1950s, 15" L, EXIB.**175.00**

Peppermint Twist Doll, Haji, 1950s, 12", EXIB.......................**245.00**

Picnic Bear (It Drinks), plush, Alps, 1950s, 12", EXIB...........**100.00**

Pioneer Covered Wagon, litho tin & vinyl, Ichida, '60s, 15" L, EXIB **120.00**

Playful Puppy w/Caterpillar, litho tin base, MT, 7½", EXIB.**130.00**

Police Cadillac, MIB **250.00**

Police DP 35, litho tin, flashing light, Japan, 8", EXIB ..**175.00**

Popeye & Olive Oyl Tumbling Buggy, Hong Kong, 1981, 7", NMIB **60.00**

Porsche 911R, plastic, Schuco, 10", NMIB **150.00**

Quick Draw McGraw Target Car w/ Baba Looie, EXIB **200.00**

Rambling Ladybug, MT, 1960s, 8", EX **100.00**

Rex Doghouse, Tel-E-Toy, 1950s, 5", M.....................................**130.00**

Roaring Gorilla Shooting Gallery, MT, 1950s, 9", EXIB **125.00**

Rooster, litho tin, black & white horizontal stripes, 7", EXIB...**115.00**

Santa Bank, Trim-A-Tree/Noel..., plush figure on house, 11", EXIB **150.00**

Showdown Sam Robot Target Game, figure w/pistol in ea hand, 10", EXIB **115.00**

Singing Circus Truck, Tomy, 1960s, 10½", VG.........................**75.00**

Skipping Monkey, plush, in outfit w/rope, TN, 1960s, 10", EXIB **65.00**

Smoking Pa Pa Bear, plush, standing, remote control, SAN, 8", VGIB..............................**90.00**

Space Patrol, litho tin, Snoopy in rocket ship, MT, 11½" L, EXIB............................**200.00**

Squirmy Hermy the Snake, tin, remote control, 12", NMIB **225.00**

Super Control Anti-Aircraft Jeep, tin, S&, 9", NMIB 100.00

Super Susie, Linemar, 1950s, 8x6", NMIB 525.00

Suzette the Eating Monkey, plush & tin, Linemar, 1950s, 9", G.150.00

Taxi, remote control, light-up sign on top, Linemar, 7½", NMIB . 85.00

Tin Man Robot (Wizard of Oz), plastic, Remco, 1969, 21", MIB 200.00

Tractor T-27, Amico, 1950s, rare, 12", M 125.00

Traveler Bear, plush, 1950s, w/tin suitcase, remote control, 8", NMIB 375.00

Trumpet Monkey, plush & tin, Alps, 1950s, 10", EXIB 160.00

Tumbling Bozo the Clown, Sonsco, 1970s, 8", M...................... 75.00

Union Mountain Monorail, TN, 1950s, MIB 225.00

Wagon Master, MT, 1960s, 18" L, NM 150.00

Walking Donkey, plush, Linemar, 1950s, remote control, 9", VGIB 140.00

Wee Little Baby Bear, plush, reading/lighted eyes, Alps, 10", EXIB 375.00

Whistling Hobo, Waco, 1960s, 13", EXIB 100.00

Worried Mother Duck & Baby, TN, 1950s, 7", MIB............... 250.00

X-1018 Tank, MT, 9", NMIB . 125.00

Yo-Yo Clown, S&E, 1960s, rare, 10", MIB.............................. 425.00

Train Sets

American Flyer, engine, tender, baggage car & 2 passenger cars, #12, G 130.00

American Flyer, Golden State, loco & 3 cars, VGIB.............. 575.00

American Flyer, Reliable Freight w/loco & 3 cars, #30705, EXIB............................ 150.00

Carette, loco w/cowcatcher, tender & coaches, black w/red, steam-powered 900.00

Ernst Plank, Vulkan dribbler loco, tender & baggage car, repainted 925.00

Gilbert, Pennsylvania steam freight/tender/3 cars/track/manual, NMIB 300.00

Hafner, loco, 4 cars & tracks, EXIB 130.00

Hafner, Overland Flyer, cast iron & litho tin, windup, EX.... 200.00

Ives, Blue Vagabond, w/loco, tender & 3 cars, G 225.00

Lionel, Hiawatha, #1000, MIB.825.00

Lionel, loco (#402E) & 3 cars, restored, EX 600.00

Lionel, loco & 3 cars, #254, olive green w/red trim, NM... 525.00

Lionel, Santa Fe Alco, #1649, MIB.......................... 1,950.00

Lionel, Southern Pacific FM Trainmaster, #8951, NMIB 500.00

Lionel, standard gauge trolley #110, G, $2,015.00 at auction. (Photo courtesy James D. Julia Inc.)

Lionel, Western Maryland, MIB........................ 500.00

Marklin, painted litho tin, loco, tender, 3 cars & track, EXIB .**850.00**

Marx, NY Central Passenger, #35250, 5-pc, VGIB **200.00**

Vehicles

Arcade, Fire Chief Car, cast iron with red paint, Chief on doors, rubber tires, 5", EX, $1,045.00.
(Photo courtesy Bertoia Auctions)

Bandai, Cadillac (1960 Gold), remote control, 17", NM **225.00**

Bandai, Chevy Sedan (1963), friction, 11", NM **150.00**

Buddy L, Emergency Auto Wrecker, red & white, 1950s, 17", VG **130.00**

Buddy L, Farm Supplies Dump Truck, 2-color diagonal paint, 1940s, G **110.00**

Buddy L, Pickup Truck, light blue, 1960s, VG **22.00**

Buddy L, Super Market Delivery Truck, white, 1940s, 13", VGIB **130.00**

Corgi, Ford Thunderbird, #214s, w/ suspension, from $95 to . **120.00**

Corgi, Jaguar 2.4 Saloon, no suspension, from $120 to ... **140.00**

Corgi, Plymouth Suburban, #219, from $90 to **110.00**

Dinky, Armoured Car, #670, from $200 to **225.00**

Dinky, Parsley's Car, #477, from $170 to **195.00**

Etrl, 1967 Corvette L-71 Roadster, Sunfire Yellow, die-cast ... **36.00**

Hubley, Bell Telephone Truck w/ Pole Trailer, die-cast, 24", from $175 to **200.00**

Hubley, Packard Sedan (1939-40), die-cast, 5½", from $75 to . **90.00**

Johnny Lightning, Custom Eldorado, die-cast, 1969 . **125.00**

Johnny Lightning, Sand Stormer, die-cast, roof & body same color, 1970 .... **150.00**

Kenton, Double-Decker Bus, cast iron, long nose, 6½", EX . **600.00**

Keystone, Dump Truck, open cab, side crank, 27", G **420.00**

Keystone, US Mail Truck, #45, screened van, restored, 26" **410.00**

Kingsbury, Dump Truck, black & orange, windup, 11", VG. **385.00**

Majorette, Mercedes-Benz 280SE, die-cast, from $12 to **16.00**

Marx, Dump Truck, DUMP on side of bed, 12", EX **90.00**

Marx, Fire Chief Car, red, windup, w/siren, 14", EX **190.00**

Marx, Reversible Coupe, heavy tin, windup, 15½", EX **500.00**

Marx, Sinclair Tanker, tin, green w/red & white, 10 wheels, 18", G **175.00**

Metalcraft, Heinz Delivery Truck, battery-operated headlights, 12", G **300.00**

Ny-Lint, Payloader, rubber treads, 1950s, 17", EX **120.00**

Ny-Lint, Telescoping Crane, red & yellow, 4 wheels, 1950s, 22", G **45.00**

Ny-Lint, U-Haul Pickup Truck & Trailer, 1960s, 21", VG ... **75.00**

Smith-Miller, Bank of America Truck, 1940s, 14", G **175.00**

Smith-Miller, Kraft Foods Delivery Truck, box van, yellow, 14", EX **250.00**

Smith-Miller, Silver Streak Semi, GMC, 1940s, 24", EX **200.00**

Tonka, Construction Utility Tractor w/Tandem Trailers, 3-pc, 24", EX **75.00**

Tonka, Grain Hauler, 1940s, 22", VG **120.00**

Tonka, Pickup Truck, dark blue w/ oval decal on door, 1950s, 13", G.................................... **110.00**

Tonka, Steam Shovel on Lowboy Truck, red & blue, 1950s, 25½", G..................................... **130.00**

Tootsie Toy, Sky Fleet Set, 1920s, 5-pc, EXOC **75.00**

Turner, Steam Shovel, 4-wheeled platform, 1930s, 15", G... **55.00**

Wind-Ups, Friction, and Other Mechanicals

All State Express Bus, litho tin, open windows, Masudaya, 8½", EXIB **150.00**

Bulldozer w/Plow & Rock Cart, litho tin, Ranger Steel, w/driver, EXIB **100.00**

Cadillac Convertible, tin, nickel-plated trim, driver & lady, 13", EX **550.00**

Capitol Hill Racer, litho tin, Unique Art, 11" L, EXIB............ **135.00**

Chrysler Airflow Sedan, tin, nickel-plated grill/bumpers/spare, 5", VG.................................. **165.00**

Chrysler Convertible (1950s), litho tin, w/driver, Hadson, 10", NMIB **800.00**

Circus Car w/Performing Seal, litho tin, 8", EX **100.00**

Circus Jeep, litho tin, w/clown & elephant on globe, Excelo, 6", NMIB **200.00**

Circus Truck, red & yellow litho tin cage truck w/animals, 10" L, EXIB **125.00**

Convertible, litho tin, w/retractable roof, Wyandotte, 1950s, 13", VG................................ **175.00**

Convertible Car Pulling House Trailer, tin, Haji, 16" overall, EXIB **250.00**

Diamond Racer, litho tin, flashing lights, w/driver, 15½", NMIB **1,260.00**

Dick Tracy Police Station, w/car, Marx, 9" L, EX **250.00**

Donald Duck Hand Car, figure w/Pluto figure & doghouse, Lionel, 11" L **425.00**

Donkey Truck, litho tin, donkey playing drum, Japan, 8" L, G **75.00**

Dream Car, plastic, clear top, Mattel, 1950s, 10½", EXIB........... **200.00**

Dump Truck, litho tin, lever-op bed, Bonnet, NMIB............... **425.00**

Farm Truck, tin, stake bed w/2 horses, opening rear gate, 5" L, NMIB **65.00**

Ferris Wheel Truck, litho tin, Japan, 8", EXIB **300.00**

GI Joe & His Jouncing Jeep, litho tin, Unique Art, 7", VG. **150.00**

Go-Round Tram Car, litho tin, Yonezawa, 5½" sq, NMIB.. **150.00**

Graham Paige Sedan (1933), litho tin, nickel-plated detail, Kosuge, G **400.00**

Greyhound Bus, litho tin, white, blue, & silver, Japan, 10", VG.... **55.00**

Hokey & Poky Handcar, litho tin, Wyandotte, 6½" L, EXIB. **300.00**

Humphery Mobile, litho tin, Wyandotte, 9", G **200.00**

Land Rover, green tin, Cragstan, NMIB **350.00**

Merry-Go-Round Truck, litho tin, Japan, 8" L, EX **150.00**

Mickey's Delivery, litho tin, Linemar, 5½" L, EX **300.00**

Police Chief Car, litho tin, battery-operated headlights, Hoge, 14", G **650.00**

Popeye the Champ, Marx, EX (in poor box), $1,300.00. (Photo courtesy Bertoia Auctions)

Skeeter-Bug Bumper Car, couple in pressed steel car, Lindstrom, 9½" **425.00**

Street Sweeper, litho tin, w/plastic driver, Ny-lint, 8" L, EXIB. **300.00**

TC 600 Custom Cruiser, plastic, w/ rear luggage deck, Sears, '50s, NMIB **125.00**

Trolls

The first trolls to come to the United States were molded after a 1952 design by Marti and Helena Kuuskoski of Tampere, Finland. The first to be mass produced in America were molded from wood carvings made by Thomas Dam of Denmark. They were made of vinyl, and the orignal issue carried the mark 'Dam Things Originals copyright 1964 – 1965 Dam Things Est.; m.f.g. by Royalty Designs of Fla. Inc.' (Other marks were used as well; look on the troll's back or the bottom of his feet for Dam trademarks.) As the demand for these trolls increased, several US manufacturers became licensed to produce them. The most noteworthy of these were Uneeda doll company's Wishnik line and Inga Dykin's Scandia House True Trolls. Thomas Dam continued to import his Dam Things line.

The troll craze from the '60s spawned many items other than dolls such as wall plaques, salt and pepper shakers, pins, squirt guns, rings, clay trolls, lamps, Halloween costumes, animals, lawn ornaments, coat racks, notebooks, folders, and even a car.

In the '70s, '80s, and '90s, more new trolls were produced. While these trolls are collectible to some, the avid troll collector still prefers those produced in the '60s. Condition is a very important worth-assessing factor; our values are for examples in EX/NM condition. To evaluate trolls in only G/VG condition, decrease these numbers by half or more.

Beatle, JN Reisler, blue jumpsuit, w/guitar, 3", VG............... **70.00**

Bo Peep, Storybook Collection, Norfin, 1977, 9" **35.00**

Born to Ski, Russ, 3½" **12.00**

Boy, Dam, long yellow hair, felt outfit, 1960s, 2½"............30.00

Bride & Groom, Uneeda Wishnik, 1970s, pr............35.00

Cow, Dam, white hair & brown eyes, 3½"............55.00

Dr Olav, Dam/Norfin #6058, green surgeon's outfit, 1977, 9½"..30.00

Elvis, Norfin, white satin outfit w/ gold trim, guitar, 1977, 9".25.00

Eskimo Boy, Scandia House (unmarked), 6", VG........90.00

Fire Chief, Treasure Trolls, blue hair & eyes, 4"............12.00

Giraffe, Dam (European), seated, 11"............95.00

Girl, Dam, 1979, seated, 18".65.00

Girl, Scandia, purple hair, blue spiral eyes, tutu, 1960s, 2¾"......110.00

Girl Scout, Dam Things, 1960s, 12", VG............55.00

Green Monster, L Khem, pink hair, white robe, 1964, 3½"......60.00

Hanna Elf, Norfin, white hair, blue & yellow outfit, 1980.......35.00

Hobo Clown, Russ #18716, 6".70.00

Hunt-Nik, Totsy Wishnik, w/rifle, from $20 to............25.00

Iggy, Dam, blond hair, green eyes (rare), street clothes, 11".125.00

Iggy, Dam, in leopard skin, 1960s, 13"............65.00

Lion, Dam, 1968-72, 6¾x8¼".60.00

Lion, keychain, rare, sm........15.00

Little Red Riding Hood, Russ Storybook, 4½"............14.00

Mermaid, Russ, iridescent hair & outfit, 5"............25.00

Owl, Gonk #953577/England, all-over red animal fur, w/hang cord, sm............20.00

Petal People, Wishnik, 1964, 7"............10.00

Prisoner #51538, Dam/Norfin, purple hair, prison outfit, 1977, 9"............22.00

Redhead, Dam Things, green jumper w/lime green shirt, 1960s, 12"............95.00

Santa, Wishnik, 7"............35.00

Seal, Norfin Pets/Dam, 1984, 6½"............50.00

Snorkler, Russ, w/goggles & swim fins, 4"............15.00

Sock-It-To-Me, Uneeda Wishnik, 6"............50.00

Squeek Mouse, Norfin/Dam, troll in mouse costume, 1985, 3½"..15.00

St Louis Cardinals, nodder, Russ, 1992............14.00

Teenage Mutant Ninja Turtles, 1992, 7", MIB............8.00

Troll Lying on Log, Nyform, 5x5"............75.00

Turtle, Nofrin/Dam, amber eyes, 1984, 4"............50.00

Two-Headed Troll, Uneeda, nude, 1965, 3"............35.00

Universal Potteries

Located in Cambridge, Ohio, Universal Potteries Incorporated produced various lines of dinnerware from 1934 to the late 1950s, several of which are very attractive, readily available, and therefore quite collectible. Refer to *Collector's Encyclopedia of American Dinnerware* by Jo Cunningham (Collector Books) for more information. See also Cat-Tail Dinnerware.

Ballerina, bowl, mixing; 4½x6"..10.00

Ballerina, coffee/teapot, slim, 11¼", from $30 to............40.00

Ballerina, plate, chop; 10½x11" .18.00

Ballerina, sugar bowl, w/lid, from $18 to 22.00

Bittersweet, casserole, w/lid, 2½-qt, 4¼x8¾" 65.00

Bittersweet, drippings jar, w/lid, from $30 to 35.00

Bittersweet, salt & pepper shakers, egg shape, pr 25.00

Blue & White, canteen jug, from $35 to 40.00

Blue & White, syrup pitcher, God Bless America, from $55 to.60.00

Blue & White, teapot, from $35 to 45.00

Calico Fruit, casserole, w/lid, 4x8", from $20 to 25.00

Calico Fruit, pie plate, 10"....40.00

Calico Fruit, pitcher, milk; 4⅞"..25.00

Calico Fruit, plate, dinner; 10", from $12 to 18.00

Calico Fruit, plate, 7", from $12 to 14.00

Calico Fruit, saucer, from $4 to. 6.00

Calico Fruit, syrup pitcher, w/lid, 5¼", from $55 to 60.00

Circus, spoon, from $30 to.....35.00

Holland Rose, bowl, fruit/sauce; 4", from $4 to 6.00

Holland Rose, pitcher, cylindrical, 6⅛x4½" 20.00

Hollyhocks, canteen jug.........30.00

Iris, bowl, deep, 4", from $15 to..............................18.00

Iris, bowl, vegetable; oval, 9⅛". 27.50

Iris, gravy boat, from $25 to.. 32.00

Iris, jug, from $40 to 45.00

Iris, plate, luncheon; 9", from $7 to 10.00

Iris, platter, sq w/rounded corners, 11½"..................................25.00

Mod Flower, cookie jar, from $55 to 60.00

Poppy, cup & saucer, flat, from $12 to 15.00

Poppy, plate, utility; 11½", from $12 to 15.00

Poppy, platter, oval, 13½", from $30 to 38.00

Red & White, bean pot, w/lid, from $35 to 40.00

Rodeo, bowl, cereal; 6"..........10.00

Rodeo, cake plate, rope edge, tab handles 23.00

Rodeo, plate, dinner..............14.00

Rose, bowl, coupe soup; 7¾" .. 10.00

Rose, cup & saucer, flat..........12.50

Rose, plate, bread & butter; 6¼".4.00

Rose, plate, luncheon; 9" 8.00

Shasta Daisy, creamer...........15.00

Shasta Daisy, cup & saucer...12.50

Shasta Daisy, plate, dinner; 10"................................12.50

Shasta Daisy, sugar bowl, w/lid.17.50

Thistle, bowl, fruit/dessert; 5⅜". 7.50

Thistle, cup & saucer.............15.00

Thistle, plate, salad; 7½" 6.00

Woodvine, bowl, salad; 9¾"....45.00

Woodvine, cup & saucer, flat.12.50

Woodvine, gravy boat.............45.00

Woodvine, plate, chop; 13½", from $30.00 to $35.00; Pitcher, 7", $20.00.

Woodvine, plate, dinner; 10½".16.00

Woodvine, plate, luncheon; 9⅜". 7.50

Valentines

Remember the valentines that years ago you gave to fellow students, and the boxes you used to put them in? Baby boomers are now starting to search for memorabilia from their childhood days, and that includes valentines. How about 'for the teacher' cards or those with trolls or Disney characters? All are unique in their own special way.

There are many styles of cards to look for: dimensional (when counting the dimensions on a card, the background is included in the count), mechanical-flat, mechanical, novelty, flat, folded-flat, hold-to-light, and greeting cards. Whatever else you collect, chances are good there will be a valentine that relates to it, whether it be antique lamps, Black Americana, record players, dolls, track and field, dogs, cat, sewing machines, etc. Remember to keep these seven factors in mind before purchasing a card: condition, size, manufacturer, category, scarcity, artist signature, and age. For more information we recommend *Valentines with Values, One Hundred Years of Valentines,* and *Valentines for the Eclectic Collector,* all by Katherine Kreider.

Key:

D — dimensional

HCPP — honeycomb paper puff

PIG — Printed in Germany

Dimensional, Black children/blackboard, 2-D, Tuck, early 1900s, 5x6" **45.00**

Dimensional, cherub fishing, 1-D, Germany, early 1900s, 5x4x4" **5.00**

Dimensional, costumed couple, 3-D, PIG, early 1900s, 6x4x2".. **25.00**

Dimensional, dirigible w/jumping rope, 1-D, Germany, 1940s, 6x4x1½" **25.00**

Dimensional, longhorn steer, 2-D, PIG, 5½x3x½" **15.00**

Dimensional, train, 1-D, American Greetings, 1950s, 6x7x5".. **10.00**

Flat, Army man w/bullet, 1940s, 3½x2½" **3.00**

Flat, Art Deco Father card, 1920s, 4x6" **15.00**

Flat, crossword puzzle, USA, 1950s, 6¾x2½" **6.00**

Flat, picketer, USA, 1940s, 4½x2" **10.00**

Flat, Russian officer, USA, 1940s, 6x5" **15.00**

Flat, Tin Man, Wizard of Oz, 1960s, 3½x2½" **3.00**

Flat, Yogi Bear, 1960s, 3½x5".. **4.00**

Folded-flat, girl w/ruler, 1940s, 5x2½" **2.00**

Folded-flat, hanging heart/train, Raphael Tuck & Sons, 8x8". **75.00**

Folded-flat, roller coaster, USA, 1940s, 4x6", EX, $15.00. (Photo courtesy Katherine Kreider)

Folded-flat, walnut & nutcracker, 1940s, 5x3½" **10.00**

HCPP, big-eyed kid tea party, PIG, 1920s, 7½x6x3"............... **75.00**

HCPP, embossed alligator briefcase, PIG, 1920s, 4½x3x2"........ **50.00**

HCPP, lamp, PIG, 1930s, 8x5x2¾"..........................**20.00**

HCPP, pedestal w/clown, 1920s, 5x5".................................. **3.00**

Mechanical-flat, Art Deco airplane, Carrington Co, 1940s, 3½x5½"........................... **6.00**

Mechanical-flat, children reading books, Katz, USA, 1920s, 6¾x7"................................. **5.00**

Mechanical-flat, crying baby, PIG, early 1900s, 6½x6"..........**15.00**

Mechanical-flat, delivery man, by Edwin Boese, USA, 7x4"..**35.00**

Mechanical-flat, drummer, by Edwin Boese, USA, 7x4", EX.............................. **35.00**

Mechanical-flat, girl on dresser, Twelvetrees, PIG, 1940s, 6¾x5"................................. **5.00**

Mechanical-flat, St Bernard, PIG, 1920s, 5x4"........................ **4.00**

Mechanical-flat, tennis player, PIG, 1920s, 7½x3½"................... **5.00**

Novelty, banjo, Proxylin, early 1900s, 19x8½x2"............. **500.00**

Novelty, bookmark, wood, cameo-embossed paper, 7x2½". **350.00**

Novelty, button boy, easel back, 1920s, 3½x3½".................. **25.00**

Novelty, candy container w/dimensional top, Philadelphia, 1925,½x2".........................**15.00**

Novelty, elephant, w/metal cymbals, PIG, 7x3¾".............. **45.00**

Novelty, Fuller Brush bottle attached to sports card, 1950s, 5x2"................................ **125.00**

Novelty, gift giving, pup w/hankie in original box, 1940s, 8x5½".......................... **25.00**

Novelty, HCPP basket, Beistle, USA, 1920s, 4x4", EX....... **2.00**

Penny Dreadful, Big Business, USA, 1932, 5x6"............... **2.00**

Penny Dreadful, Lawyer, USA, 1930s, 9½x6"..................... **5.00**

Van Briggle

The Van Briggle Pottery of Colorado Springs, Colorado, was established in 1901 by Artus Van Briggle upon the completion of his quest to perfect a completely flat matt glaze. His wife, Ann, worked with him and they, along with George Young, were responsible for the modeling of the wares. Known for their flowing Art Nouveau shapes, much of the ware was eventually made from molds with each piece carefully trimmed and refined before the glaze was sprayed on. Their most popular colors were Persian Rose, Ming Blue, and Mustard Yellow.

Van Briggle died in 1904, but the work was continued by his wife. With new facilities built in 1908, tiles, gardenware, and commercial lines were added to the earlier artware lines. Reproductions of some early designs continue to be made, The Double AA mark has always been in use, but after 1920 the dates and/or shape numbers were dropped. The Anna Van Briggle glaze was developed for a later line that was made between 1956 and 1968.

Bottle, broad leaves, green to blue, 1920s, 10½x5"............... **365.00**

Bowl, curved shoulder, dark mulberry, late 1910s, 4"...... **160.00**

Bowl, leaves & tendrils, aqua, globular, 2¼x3¼"................. **200.00**

Ewer, Persian Rose, catalog #322, ca 1978, 9"....................... **90.00**

Lamp, Damsel of Damascus, black matt, 10½", +replaced shade. **80.00**

Paperweight, rabbit figural, blue-green, gold label, 2½"...... **90.00**

Vase, deep blue, #747, ca 1922-26, 4½x5¼"........................... **245.00**

Vase, dragonfly, maroon & blue matt, #792, 6½x3"......... **345.00**

Vase, floral, dark blue with maroon highlights, 1916, 7", $600.00; Vase, floral, tobacco brown with black specks, 1907 – 1912, 4", $475.00. (Photo courtesy Treadway Galleries)

Vase, flowerheads to shoulder/curving stems, maroon, dirty bottom, 5"............................ **135.00**

Vase, green to blue, bulbous base, 1920s, 7x4½"................. **325.00**

Vase, ivory & lavender, artist mark, #325, 1906, 5¾x4"......... **600.00**

Vase, lavender gloss, blue interior, #681, 1920s, 2x3½"........ **425.00**

Vase, leaves repeating, blue matt, #730, 1915, 5¼x4"......... **500.00**

Vase, leaves/buds, Mountain Craig Brown, 4¼"................... **100.00**

Vase, maroon & blue matt, #824, 1920, 7x3"..................... **350.00**

Vase, mulberry, #310, late 1910s, 3½x3¼"........................... **195.00**

Vase, ribs, green to blue, ca 1922-26, 17¼x6¼"................... **595.00**

Vase, spade leaves form 4 panels, green, #465, 1910, restored, 5"................................... **500.00**

Vase, spade leaves in geometric panels, steel blue, #640, 6½x6"............................... **495.00**

Vase, yucca leaves, dark mulberry w/green overspray base, #747, 4x5"............................... **365.00**

Vernon Kilns

From 1931 until 1958, Vernon Kilns produced hundreds of patterns of fine dinnerware that today's collectors enjoy reassembling. They retained the services of famous artists and designers such as Rockwell Kent and Walt Disney, who designed both dinnerware lines and novelty items. Examples of their work are at a premium. Nearly all artist-designed lines utilized the Ultra Shape. To evaluate the work of Blanding, use 200% of the high range of our suggested Ultra prices; for Disney lines, 700% to 800%;

Kent – Moby Dick and Our America 250%; for Salamina, 500% to 700%. For other patterns on the shapes we have listed below, use the higher end for the more elaborate lines and the lower side of the range if the pattern is relatively simple.

Anytime, casserole, w/lid, 8", from $30 to **50.00**

Anytime, mug, 12-oz, from $15 to **25.00**

Anytime, pitcher, 1-qt, 8", from $20 to **30.00**

Anytime, plate, salad; 7½", from $7 to **10.00**

Anytime, syrup, Drip-cut top, from $45 to **65.00**

Anytime, tray, oval, ring handle, 6", from $40 to **50.00**

Chatelaine, bowl, salad; topaz or bronze, 12", from $45 to . **55.00**

Chatelaine, creamer, decorated platinum or jade, from $30 to .. **35.00**

Chatelaine, plate, decorated platinum, leaf on 4 corners, 10½" **27.00**

Chatelaine, salt & pepper shakers, decorated jade, pr from $25 to **30.00**

Chatelaine, teacup & saucer, pedestal foot, decorated jade, $22 to **25.00**

Harvest, teapot, six-cup, from $50.00 to $60.00.

Lotus, bowl, fruit; 5½", from $6 to **10.00**

Lotus, bowl, salad; 12½", from $30 to **45.00**

Lotus, teacup & saucer, from $10 to **15.00**

Lotus, tumbler, #5, 14-oz, from $18 to **20.00**

Melinda, butter dish, oblong, from $35 to **75.00**

Melinda, jam jar, from $65 to.. **75.00**

Melinda, plate, bread & butter; 6½", from $6 to **10.00**

Melinda, platter, 12", from $20 to **30.00**

Montecito, ashtray, round, 5½", from $12 to **20.00**

Montecito, buffet server, trio, from $50 to **80.00**

Montecito, flowerpot, w/saucer, 3", from $35 to **45.00**

Montecito, platter, 12", from $20 to **30.00**

Montecito, spoon holder, angular, from $45 to **65.00**

Montecito, tumbler, #1, banded rim & base, 4½", from $20 to . **25.00**

Pan American Lei, bowl, mixing; 5", from $20 to **30.00**

Pan American Lei, bowl, soup; coupe, 8½", from $18 to... **25.00**

Pan American Lei, butter dish, oblong, from $60 to **65.00**

Pan American Lei, teapot, 8-cup, from $85 to **95.00**

San Marino, bowl, chowder; 6", from $10 to **15.00**

San Marino, eggcup, double, from $15 to **22.00**

San Marino, pitcher, 1-qt, from $25 to **32.00**

San Marino, spoon holder, from $30 to **45.00**

Souvenir plate, Hollywood, blue transfer on white, ca. 1940, 10½", $45.00. (Photo courtesy Maxine Nelson)

Transitional (Year 'Round), bowl, fruit; 5½", from $5 to......... **7.00**

Transitional (Year 'Round), casserole, w/lid, 8", from $25 to **45.00**

Transitional (Year 'Round), mug, 12-oz, from $12 to **20.00**

Transitional (Year 'Round), salt & pepper shakers, pr from $12 to **15.00**

Transitional (Year 'Round), sugar bowl, w/lid, from $10 to .. **15.00**

Ultra, bowl, mixing; 5", from $15 to **25.00**

Ultra, bowl, serving; 9", from $18 to **30.00**

Ultra, bowl, soup; coupe, 8¼", from $12 to **20.00**

Ultra, compote, from $50 to .. **75.00**

Ultra, eggcup, from $18 to..... **25.00**

Ultra, pitcher, 2-qt, from $45 to.**75.00**

Ultra, plate, salad; 7½", from $8 to **12.00**

Ultra, salt & pepper shakers, pr from $20 to **30.00**

Ultra, sauceboat, from $20 to.. **25.00**

Ultra, teapot, 6-cup, from $45 to **100.00**

Vietnam War Collectibles

There was confict in Vietnam for many years before the United States was drawn into it during the Eisenhower years, and fighting raged until well into 1975 when communist forces invaded Saigon and crushed the South Vietnamese government there. Today items from the 1960s and early 1970s are becoming collectible. Pins, booklets, uniforms, patches, and the like reflect these troubled times when anti-war demonstrations raged and unsound political policies cost the lives of many brave young men. Unless noted otherwise, values are for examples in excellent to near mint condition.

Battle pack, M79 grenade; 6 in pouch, inert, w/plastic inserts........................ **120.00**

Belt, pistol; officer's NVA type, olive green & silver metal..... **100.00**

Beret, RVN Marine, bright green wool w/insignia, vinyl edge..........................**200.00**

Binoculars, Bell & Howell, BMCLR M19 7x50" on hinge pin, w/ case **138.00**

Bomb, practice; US Navy, blue, Dell Industries MOD 4, 42" . **230.00**

Book, First Infantry Division in Vietnam, Vol 3, 1969, 300+ pgs................................... **110.00**

Cap badge, silver wings, red & blue enamel shield, Air America, 2" **345.00**

Combat boots, black leather, Goodyear w/wing foot logo on sole, pr **97.00**

Compass, US Army, Jay Bee Corp, 1966 Field Gear **90.00**

Dress uniform, Army Airborne Special Forces Class A.. **150.00**

Field pack, combat; M-1956, complete w/accessories, 1964 .... **162.00**

Game, Grunt; Tactical Combat in Vietnam, Simulations, 1965, MIB **110.00**

Hat, Navy pilot; leather w/silver eagle & gold-plated brass emblem **78.50**

Hat badge, gold and silver metal, 1⅜", $70.00. (Photo courtesy Michael Dougerty)

Helmet, helicopter pilot; olive, dated 5/67, w/accessories & case **315.00**

Jacket, flak; Army issue, zippered, DSA-100-67-C-3077, 1967. **165.00**

Jacket, G-1 flight; brown leather, zippered **505.00**

Jacket, jungle; 1st pattern, buttons, shoulder & back tabs, 1964.. **305.00**

Knife, De Leon Vietnam Model A, 7" blade, w/leather scabbard, M **400.00**

Pants, tiger stripe, size US-M, 1968, MIP **360.00**

Parachute, non-auto chest; August 1965, w/log book, 15 lbs. **130.00**

Patch, ARVN Special Forces, tiger/ parachute/lightning on blue, 1969, M **140.00**

Patch, MACV SOG NHA TRANG, skull w/green beret on red, 5x3½" **210.00**

Radios, Hallicrafters HT-1A, #B-6373 & B-6343, w/manual & storage box **525.00**

Ring, Special Forces Airborne Army Beret, silver 925 .... **175.00**

Rucksack, tropical; Army, olive green nylon, 1968, 16x11" **191.00**

Sign, USMC Recruiting; metal, Pride in America Ask..., '66, 39½x30" **230.00**

Survival vest, SV-1 Navy, w/radio & snake bite kit, nearly complete **268.00**

Wristwatch, Breitling, manual-wind, olive green nylon band ... **460.00**

Viking

Formed during the 1950s, Viking Glass (West Virginia) made glassware innovative in design as well as color. They are perhaps most famous for their Epic line (1950s – 1960s) which was made in vibrant reds, amethyst, brilliant blues, strong greens, black, amber, and amberina. They produced many glass animals and birds which are treasured by today's collectors. During the 1980s the company was known as Dalzell-Viking; by 1998 they were out of business. See also Glass Animals and Birds

Ashtray, amber butterfly shape, 1950s, 4¼x5½" **30.00**

Ashtray, orange-red alligator figural, 11¼" **70.00**

Ashtray, Orb, peacock blue, single rest, 4" dia **36.00**

Candleholders, amethyst, triangular base w/3 curved arms, 6¼", pr **70.00**

Console set, Epic, amethyst, 3x16x12" bowl & 1¾" candleholders **50.00**

Decanter, ruby teardrop shape w/ crystal stopper, 13" **30.00**

Fairy lamp, Diamond Point, blue, 7" **35.00**

Fairy lamp, Georgian, ruby red, w/ original label, 4¾" **45.00**

Fairy lamp, owl figure, vaseline, 7¼" **110.00**

Paperweight, mushroom, amber, 3x4" **30.00**

Paperweight, mushroom, cobalt, 2⅝x3" **35.00**

Rose bowl, amethyst w/clear flower frog, footed, 7" **85.00**

Vase, green, handkerchief rim, melon ribs, 22" **130.00**

Vase, med blue, handkerchief rim, melon ribs, 22" **140.00**

Vase, orange, handkerchief rim, melon ribs, 20" **130.00**

Vase, swung; gold-red, footed, 24", from $40 to **50.00**

Votive candleholder, Bull's-Eye, cobalt, 3½" block, ea **70.00**

Votive candleholder, Bull's-Eye, red, 3½" block, ea **50.00**

Wall Pockets

Wall pockets are collectibles that are easily found, relatively inexpensive, and very diversified. They were made in Japan, Czechoslovakia, and by many, many companies in the United States. Those made by companies best known for their art pottery (Weller, Roseville, etc.) are in a class of their own, but the novelty, just-for-fun wall pockets stand on their own merits. Examples with large, colorful birds or those with unusual modeling are usually the more

desirable. For more information we recommend *Collector's Encyclopedia Made of Japan Ceramics* by Carole Bess White, who is listed in the Directory under Oregon. (Collector Books). See also California Pottery, Cleminson; McCoy; Shawnee; other specific manufacturers.

Bird on branch, Czechoslovakia, 5½", pr **85.00**

Bird w/wings spread, cranberry, Albaware, 7¼x11" **50.00**

Cat peeking in red & white checked golf bag, Japan, 5¾x3" **60.00**

Cherub holding vase on head, bisque, ArtMart #7942, 9½x5", pr **55.00**

Fish, yellow & black, Tropic Treasures by Ceramicraft..., 7x9" **40.00**

Floriform, orange to green bottom, Rosecraft, 9x5" **170.00**

Flower, closed, yellow pottery, 7" L, VG **50.00**

Girl dancing, pink dress/hair bow, white apron, P-392, 1945, 6½" **45.00**

G o u d a (Holland), 8¾", **$125.00.** (Photo courtesy Fredda Perkins)

Horse head, brown, black & white, 7¼x3" **40.00**

Koi fish, orange & white, 1950s, 10x3¼" **35.00**

Lady in long gown holding skirt wide, white, 1935, 8" L ... **35.00**

Lily w/girl in red dress, bright colors, 6¼x3¾".....................**30.00**

Noel, red w/choir children, Christmas decor, Inarco E-1019, pr, MIB **60.00**

Oriole bird w/chick on leaves, ceramic pastels, Japan, 6x4" **35.00**

Parrot, multicolored bird on branch w/pink flower, Japan, 6x4½" **45.00**

Pheasants in rose medallion design, bright multicolor enamel, 7".....................**52.00**

Rooster, multicolored painted pottery, 10x8"........................**48.00**

Scalloped cone form, white, Trenton Potteries, 6x5", pr **75.00**

Strawberries on cutting board w/ basket, chalkware, 1975, 10x4½" **70.00**

Teen girl, pink hat & dress, w/original orange flowers, 6¾x5".**85.00**

Violin, white w/hand-painted floral decoration, Italy, 18", VG..**45.00**

Weeping Gold

Weeping gold was produced by many American potteries during the 1950s. It is characterized by the irregular droplets of lustrous gold that covers its surface. On some items the gold may be heavy; sometimes it is applied in random swirls. Real gold was actually used, and some examples will be stamped '22k (or 24k) gold.' You may see silver used in this manner as well. Figural items, larger vases, and serving pieces are most marketable. Cups and saucers are scarce, so they often sell in the higher ranges as well.

Ashtray, w/metal frame, shiny black interior, 6½" dia.....**16.00**

Basket, flared rim, marked Swetye 22k gold Salem O, 7½"....**20.00**

Box, vanity; w/lid, 3".............**30.00**

Decanter, ornate, Jim Bean label, w/stopper, 10"..................**13.00**

Dish (elm-leaf), 5¼x4¼".........**15.00**

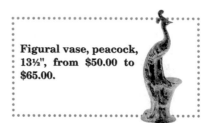

Figural vase, peacock, 13½", from $50.00 to $65.00.

Figurine, panther, 6x11", from $35 to **40.00**

Pitcher, bulbous, signed Peg Johnston, 6"....................**45.00**

Pitcher, ewer form, gold drips on black, 7"............................**12.00**

Plate, 50th Anniversary, 1950s bride & groom, gold rim, 9¼" dia **75.00**

Salt & pepper shakers, white w/ gold ring handles in sq gold base, pr **10.00**

Tidbit, 3-compartment w/center handle, 8" dia, from $15 to **20.00**

Vase, bud; slim Deco style, 9"..**15.00**

Western Heroes

As children, Baby Boomers often spent Saturday mornings watching television shows featuring Roy Rogers, Sky King, and The Lone Ranger, to name only a few. Davy Crockett and Daniel Boone were regulars on Wonderful World of Disney on Sunday nights. One western hero after another struggled with the 'bad guys' every day of the week on radio. As a result of all those popular TV and radio shows, vast amounts of merchandise and premiums were sold or given away to ardent fans. Many of those fans (all grown up) are on the hunt today for items relating to their favorite western heroes. For more information, we recommend *Schroeder's Collectible Toys, Antique to Modern,* published by Collector books. See also Character and Promotional Drinking Glasses; Children's Books; Coloring Books; Comic Books; Games; Puzzles.

Davy Crockett

Davy Crockett had long been a favorite in fact and folklore. Then with the opening of Disney's Frontierland and his continuing adventures on 1950s television came a surge of interest in all sorts of items featuring the likeness of Fess Parker in a coonskin cap. Millions were drawn to the mystic excitement surrounding the settlement of our great country. Due to demand, there were many types of items produced for eager fans ready to role play their favorite adventures.

Binoculars, plastic, Harrison, MIB **175.00**
Dart Gun Target, Knickerbocker, unused, MIB **80.00**
Guitar, w/yarn strap, windup mechanism plays music, Mattel, 14", EX **50.00**

Lamp, chalkware figural base w/ mountain scene on shade, 18", VG **100.00**
Marionette, talker, Hazelle's, 15", MIB **350.00**
Napkins, Beach Prod, 1950s, 30-count, 5" sq, MIP **40.00**
Pin, metal rectangle w/scalloped border, swords on front, NMOC **65.00**
Play horse, Pied Piper Toys, MIB **125.00**
Tie clip, sq copper-tone metal, embossed musket, powder horn w/name, M **18.00**
Towel, white terry w/image of Davy/ Fess Parker, Cannon/WDP, 37x20", NM **40.00**
Tray, litho tin w/image of Davy fighting Indian, 1955, 13x17", VG **75.00**
Wallet, brown vinyl w/Davy profile, Walt Disney..., 1955, 5x4", EXIB **75.00**

Gene Autry

First breaking into show business as a recording star with Columbia Records, Gene went on to become one of Hollywood's most famous singing cowboys. From the late '30s until the mid-'50s, he rode his wonder horse Champion through almost 90 feature films. He did radio and TV as well, and naturally his fame spawned a wealth of memorabilia originally aimed at his young audiences, now grabbed up just as quickly by collectors.

Doll, composition, cloth outfit w/felt hat, Terry Lee, 16", NM+ ...**500.00**

Figure, caricature-style, ceramic, on horseshoe base, 8½", EX **400.00**

Figure, painted composition, name on chaps, wood base, 12", EX **275.00**

Flashlight, Cowboy Lariat, EXIB **100.00**

Guitar, plastic, Emenee, 32", NMIB **225.00**

Pistol horn, Metal Products, 6½", NMIB **175.00**

Record player, plastic, 'Flying A' decal, Columbia, 13" L, VG **250.00**

Rug, tan chenille w/name & Champ, image of horse's head, 37x25", EX+ **75.00**

Spurs, Official Cowboy..., Leslie-Henry, EXIB **100.00**

Wallet, leather w/zipper, Gene & Champion, Aristocrat, 1950s, VGIB **75.00**

Hopalong Cassidy

One of the most popular western heroes of all time, Hoppy was the epitome of the highly moral, role-model cowboys of radio and the silver screen that many of us grew up with in the '40s and '50s. He was portrayed by Bill Boyd who personally endorsed more than 2,200 items targeting Hoppy's loyal followers.

Boots, 3-color leather, Acme, child's, EXIB **800.00**

Coin, emb Hoppy front w/Good Luck From Hoppy on back, 1¼" dia, VG **15.00**

Drinking straws, cut-out photo of Hoppy on back of box, 1950s, MIB **75.00**

Figure & Paint Set, Laurel Ann, complete, used, EXIB ... **250.00**

Lamp, rotating cylinder, Econolite, 10", NM **500.00**

Pants, black cloth, chaps-style, Hoppy/Topper/wagons/steer heads, VG **50.00**

Playhouse, 4 lithoed panels, William Boyd/Charcook, 1950, NM **650.00**

Spurs, silver-tone & brass w/leather straps, NM **200.00**

Stagecoach Toss, Beanbag Target Game, Transogram, 1950s, 24x18", EX **75.00**

Stationery folio, complete w/paper & envelopes, EX **50.00**

Sweater, tan w/color graphics, Hoppy w/image, 1950s, child-sz, EX **100.00**

TV set, plastic, Automatic Toy, 5x5", EXIB **250.00**

Wallet, vinyl w/images of stagecoach & Hoppy on Topper, 3x7½", EX **60.00**

Western Frontier Set, Milton Bradley, 1950s, complete, NMIB **300.00**

Woodburning Set, American Toy, 1950s, unused, EXIB **100.00**

The Lone Ranger

Recalling 'those thrilling days of yesteryear,' we can't help but remember the adventures of our hero, The Lone Ranger. He's been admired since that first radio show in 1933, and today's collectors seek a wide variety of his memorabilia; premiums, cereal boxes, and even carnival chalkware prizes are a few examples. See Clubs and

Newsletters for information on *The Silver Bullet.*

Binoculars, plastic, Harrison, EX+IB **135.00**
Doll, stuffed w/composition head, Dollcraft Novelty, 15", EX+ **600.00**

First Aid Kit, empty tin, American Can Co., dated 1938, 4x4x1½", NM, $55.00. (Photo courtesy Past Tyme Pleasures)

Guitar, cardboard w/wooden neck, Jefferson, 1950s, 28½", EX **100.00**
Hi-Yo Silver the Lone Ranger Target Game, Marx, EXIB **65.00**
Horseshoe set, rubber, Gardner, NMIB **85.00**
Neck scarf & concho slide, purple cloth, Lone Ranger & Silver images **50.00**
Official outfit, w/chaps, vest, hat, mask, shirt, etc, Henry, NMIB **480.00**
Puppet, push-button, Long Ranger on Silver, Press Action Toys, MIB **175.00**
Ring-Toss, die-cut cardboard, Rosebud Art, MIB **250.00**
School bag, canvas w/plastic handle, image on side pocket, 1950s, EX **100.00**

Snow dome, Lone Ranger Round Up, plastic base, Driss/TLR, 1954, 4", EX **50.00**
Soap figure set, Lone Ranger, Tonto & Silver, Kerk, 1939, 4", VG **50.00**
Target, litho tin w/metal support, Marx, TLR Inc, 1930s, 9½" sq, EX **50.00**

Roy Rogers

Growing up during the Great Depression, Leonard Frank Sly was determined to make his mark in the entertainment industry. In 1938 after landing small roles in films featuring Gene Autry and others, Republic Studios (recognizing his talents) renamed their singing cowboy Roy Rogers and placed him in his first leading role in *Under Western Stars.* By 1943 he had become America's 'King of the Cowboys.' And his beloved wife Dale Evans and his horse Trigger were at the top with him. See Clubs and Newsletters for information on the Roy Rogers — Dale Evans Collectors Association.

Archery set, Ben Pearson, 37", scarce, NMOC **185.00**
Bank, metal boot form w/copper finish, Almar Metal Arts Co, 5½", EX **75.00**
Branding Set/Ink Pad, tin container, 1950s, ½x2", EX **65.00**
Flashlight, Signal Siren, tin, Usalite, 7", MIB **150.00**
Fountain pen, name on black plastic barrel, gold trim, 1950s, 5", VG **50.00**

Guitar, wood, red w/wht sihouette images, Range Rhythm/Rich Toys, NMIB **200.00**

Hand puppet, cloth w/vinyl head & hat, 1950s, 7", NM **75.00**

Lantern, litho tin, 8" w/handle up, EX **50.00**

Lucky Horseshoe Game, Ohio Art, 1950s, EX **75.00**

Modeling clay set, in box w/Roy on rearing Trigger, NMIB .. **150.00**

Paint-By-Number paint set, RRE set C/Post Sugar Crisp, unused, MIB **75.00**

Paint-by-Number paint set, RRE Set C/Post Sugar Crisp, used, EXIB **40.00**

Pencil case, vinyl, Roy & Trigger, flap top w/snap closure, 8", EX **50.00**

Pony Contest entry form, Hudson's Bay Co, 1950s, 12x9", unused, NM **50.00**

Postcard, image of Roy on rearing Trigger, Quaker Oats, 1948, NM **50.00**

Pull toy, horse-drawn covered wagon, NN Hill, 20", EX **250.00**

Rodeo program, Chicago Stadium, 1946, 20-pg, EX **75.00**

Scarf, red & gold w/vignette graphics, King of the Cowboys, 25x25", EX **75.00**

School bag, brown textured vinyl w/ leather strap, badge on pocket, EX **100.00**

School tablet, Roy Rogers & Dale Evans, Frontiers, 10x8", unused, EX **25.00**

Telescope, plastic, H George, 9", MIB **200.00**

Trick Lasso, Classy Products, 1950s, complete, EXIP.... **75.00**

Miscellaneous

Andy Devine, hand puppet, cloth w/ vinyl head, 1950s, EX... **100.00**

Annie Oakley & Tag, belt, tooled leather w/name & rope design, MOC................................. **85.00**

Bat Masterson, cane, chrome-covered plastic handle, name on top, EX+.......................... **35.00**

Buffalo Bill, Jr., belt buckle, aluminum and plastic, Flying A Productions, EX, $45.00.

Cisco Kid, belt, black leather w/ brown embellishments, 1950s, NM **55.00**

Daniel Boone, coonskin cap, vinyl & fur, American Tradition, 1960s, EX **75.00**

Daniel Boone, Woodland Whistle, Autolite premium, EXIB. **100.00**

Gabby Hayes, Champion Shooting Target, Hacker/Ind, 1950s, NMIB **225.00**

Gabby Hayes, Fishing Outfit, steel 2-part rod & reel, tin container, G................................. **170.00**

Gabby Hayes, hand puppet, cloth w/ vinyl head, JVZ, 1949, EX. **200.00**

Gunsmoke, cowboy hat, brown felt w/vinyl trim, tie string, 1950s, EX **65.00**

Kit Karson, 3-Powered Binoculars, 1950s, EXIB **150.00**

Maverick, Eras-O-Picture Book, Hasbro, 1958, complete, EX **40.00**

Rin-Tin-Tin, figure, Rinny, painted plaster, rhinestone eyes, 11", EX **75.00**

Rin-Tin-Tin, outfit, Fighting Blue Devil 101st..., w/accessories, NMIB **185.00**

Tales of Wells Fargo, Paint-by-Number, 1959, partially used, EX **55.00**

Tonto, soap figure, Kerk, 1939, 4", EXIB (unopened) **50.00**

Tonto, stuffed, w/composition head, outfit, guns & holster, 20", EX **500.00**

Virginian, Movie Viewer, Chemtoy, 1956, MOC (sealed) **45.00**

Zorro, accessory set w/mask, Williams photo on card, Shimmel/Disney, M **150.00**

Zorro, bolo tie, metal medallion w/plastic inset, Zorro on red, NM **50.00**

Zorro, bowl & plate, Sun-Valley Melmac, 1955, 5" dia & 7" dia, EX, set **40.00**

Zorro, Oil-Painting-By-Number, Hassenfeld Bros, complete, 1960s, VGIB **65.00**

Zorro, Target Shoot, Lido/Walt Disney Productions, MIB. **225.00**

Zorro, tote bag, red vinyl, EX. **275.00**

Westmoreland

Originally an Ohio company, Westmoreland relocated in Grapesville, Pennsylvania, where by the 1920s they had became known as one of the country's largest manufacturers of carnival glass. They are best known today for the high quality milk glass which accounted for 90% of their production. For further information we recommend *Westmoreland Glass, The Popular Years,* by Lorraine Kovar (Collector Books); see the Directory for information on the Westmoreland Glass Society, Inc., listed in Clubs and Newsletters. See also Glass Animals and Birds.

Ashtray, American Hobnail, olive green, 4½" dia **7.50**

Ashtray, English Hobnail, green or pink, round, 4½" **35.00**

Ashtray, Old Quilt, milk glass w/ Forget-Me-Not, sq, 4½" ... **25.00**

Basket, American Hobnail, lilac opalescent, double crimped, 6" **45.00**

Basket, English Hobnail, cobalt, tall, rare, 9" **100.00**

Basket, Lotus, pink opalescent, star, footed, 8" **35.00**

Bonbon, English Hobnail, pastel pink, sq, flat, 6½" **15.00**

Bowl, Doric, cupped, three-part stem, 10" diameter, $27.50. (Photo courtesy Ruth Grizel)

Bowl, fruit; Colonial, Bermuda Blue, lipped, footed, 11".. **55.00**

Bowl, Lotus, Flame, cupped, 9"............................. **50.00**

Bowl, Paneled Grape, milk glass, shallow, 2x9".................... **45.00**

Bowl, Princess Feather, Golden Sunset, flat, 12".............. **50.00**

Butter dish, Sawtooth, Lilac, 5x6½"............................. **50.00**

Candle lamp, dark blue with Mary Gregory-type decoration, 7½", $65.00. (Photo courtesy Ruth Grizel)

Candleholders, Cherry, milk glass, 4", pr............................... **65.00**

Candleholders, Lotus, black, 3½", pr...................................... **35.00**

Candleholders, Paneled Grape, milk glass, skirted, 4", pr......... **50.00**

Candy dish, Dolphin & Shell, amber, 3-footed, 6".......... **40.00**

Cigarette box, Beaded Grape, milk glass w/painted decoration............................... **95.00**

Cocktail, Paneled Grape, milk glass, 3-oz, 4".................... **35.00**

Compote, Lotus, Flame, pointed rim, 6"............................. **35.00**

Compote, mint; Della Robbia, crystal w/any stain, footed, 6½"................................... **35.00**

Compote, Old Quilt, milk glass, cupped rim, octagon foot, 6".............................. **30.00**

Compote, Sawtooth, Bermuda, w/ lid, 14x9"...................... **120.00**

Cordial, American Hobnail, crystal, 3⅜".................................. **22.50**

Covered animal dish, camel, emerald green or turquoise carnival................................. **175.00**

Covered animal dish, camel, lilac mist................................. **150.00**

Covered animal dish, cat in boot, black............................... **35.00**

Covered animal dish, cat on ribbed base, milk glass, 5½"............................. **40.00**

Covered animal dish, chick on eggs, basketweave nest, milk glass, 6".................................. **95.00**

Covered animal dish, dog on vertical-rib base, milk glass, 5½".... **75.00**

Covered animal dish, dove & hand on rectangular lacy base, milk glass............................. **175.00**

Covered animal dish, duck on oval basketweave base, ruby carnival, 5"............................. **80.00**

Covered animal dish, eagle & babies on basketweave, milk glass, 8" **125.00**

Covered animal dish, eagle & babies on basketweave base, Chocolate, 8".................. **250.00**

Covered animal dish, fox on oval lacy base, milk glass, 7½" L...................... **125.00**

Covered animal dish, Hen on basketweave nest, black carnival, 5½" **100.00**

Covered animal dish, hen on basketweave base, green, painted accents **30.00**

Covered animal dish, hen on diamond base, black carnival, 5½".................. **100.00**

Covered animal dish, lamb on picket fence, milk glass, 5½" L ... **50.00**

Covered animal dish, lamb on picket-fence base, Antique Blue, 5½"..................... **90.00**

Covered animal dish, lion on diamond base, milk glass, 8".......... **135.00**

Covered animal dish, lovebirds, almond or mint green, 5¼x6½"........................... **85.00**

Covered animal dish, rabbit on oval vertical-rib vase, milk glass............................. **50.00**

Covered animal dish, rabbit on picket-fence base, milk glass, 5½"....................... **60.00**

Covered animal dish, rabbit w/ eggs on oval base, milk glass, 8".................................. **80.00**

Covered animal dish, rabbit w/ eggs on oval base, Ruby Marble, 8".................... **180.00**

Covered animal dish, robin on twig nest base, Apricot Mist, 6¼"................................ **70.00**

Covered animal dish, rooster on diamond base, purple marble, 8"...................................**150.00**

Covered animal dish, rooster on lacy base, milk glass, 8".**45.00**

Covered animal dish, swan on diamond base, ruby carnival, 5½"............................... **75.00**

Creamer, Beaded Edge, #4 floral decor on milk glass..........**30.00**

Creamer, Paneled Grape, crystal w/ruby stain, footed, individual **20.00**

Cruet, English Hobnail, milk glass, 2-oz, 5"...........................**22.00**

Cruet, English Hobnail, Pink Pastel, handled, 2-oz, 5".**20.00**

Decanter, Thousand Eye, crystal w/ stain...............................**175.00**

Figurine, butterfly, Purple Marble, 2½".....................................**30.00**

Figurine, owl on tree stump, milk glass mother-of-pearl, 5½"..............................**35.00**

Figurine, penguin on ice floe, Crystal Mist or milk glass.............**80.00**

Figurine, Porky Pig, milk glass, late 1970s, 3" L, from $15 to **20.00**

Figurine, pouter pigeon, Lilac Mist................................. **40.00**

Figurine, swallow, Green or Yellow Mist, solid.......................**25.00**

Finger bowl, Waterford, crystal, flat, 2¼x4¾"......................**20.00**

Goblet, water; American Hobnail, Bradywine Blue, 8-oz......**35.00**

Goblet, water; Colonial, crystal or brown, footed...................**10.00**

Goblet, wine; Della Robbia, milk glass, 3-oz, 4⅝"................**18.50**

Jardiniere, Paneled Grape, Mint Green, straight, footed, 5".**30.00**

Lamp, Americana, pink floral, smooth brass base, 13½".**80.00**

Lamp, boudoir; English Hobnail/#555, milk glass, stick type, flat base..................**45.00**

Lamp, mini-lite, Crystal Mist w/ child's decal, w/shade......**65.00**

Marmalade, Crystal Velvet, w/lid & spoon..............................**75.00**

Napkin ring, milk glass w/pink flower..............................**35.00**

Paperweight, turtle, Lilac or Green Mist, no holes..................**50.00**

Parfait, Beaded Grape, milk glass, ftd....................................**40.00**

Pickle dish, Paneled Grape, milk
glass, oval 32.50
Pitcher, English Hobnail, crystal,
bulbous, 38-oz 150.00
Plate, bread & butter; Old Quilt,
milk glass, 6" 25.00
Plate, dinner; Beaded Grape, milk
glass, 10½" 55.00
Plate, luncheon; American Hobnail,
Brandywine Blue, 8½" 22.50
Plate, luncheon; Della Robbia, green
w/frosted accents, 9" 35.00
Plate, salad; Paneled Grape, Laurel
Green, 8½" 35.00
Platter, Beaded Edge, milk glass,
handles, 11¾" 65.00
Relish, Thousand Eye, crystal w/
stain, 6-part, 10" 25.00
Salt & pepper shakers, Colonial,
Laurel Green, pr 40.00
Salt & pepper shakers, Della Robbia,
milk glass, ftd, pr 40.00
Saucer, Beaded Edge, milk glass w/
floral decor 10.00
Sherbet, Princess Feather, Roselin,
low foot 18.50
Tray, canape; Beaded Grape,
milk glass, center handle,
7¼" 45.00
Trinket box, heart-shape w/lid,
Lilac Mist w/daisy 35.00
Tumbler, Colonial, crystal, flat,
8-oz, 4" 12.50
Tumbler, English Hobnail, milk
glass, footed, 9-oz, 6" 10.00
Tumbler, gingerale; English
Hobnail, pink, flat, 5-oz,
3¾" 20.00
Tumbler, iced tea; Waterford,
crystal w/ruby stain, footed,
12½-oz 30.00
Tumbler, Princess Feather, crystal,
footed 25.00

Vase, daisy decal on Green Mist,
12", $45.00. (Photo courtesy Lorraine
Kovar)

Vase, Old Quilt, milk glass, flat,
straight 85.00

Willow Tree

Susan Lordi was already well
known as a textile artist, and in
2000 she introduced a line of collectible angels, figurines, Keepsake
boxes, and plaques. Some have
already been retired, and collectors are beginning to search for
earlier examples. Susan carved the
original models from wood; the production figures are resin. Angels
have wirework wings. Most of these
figures are a few inches tall, but
much larger ones were made as
well. Behind each there is a theme
— love, prayer, rememberance, etc.
Each figure is signed, dated, and
marked Demdaco.

Angel of Comfort, #26062, retired,
3¾", MIB 25.00
Angel of Grace, 326067, retired,
4½", MIB 25.00
Angel of Joy, #26004, retired in
2001, 8", MIB 42.50

Angel of Song, #26047, retired, MIB **40.00**

Brothers, retired, 5", MIB **25.00**

Child's Touch, retired, MIB ... **30.00**

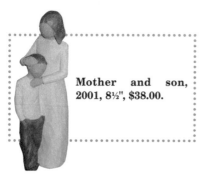

Mother and son, 2001, 8½", $38.00.

Sister & Brother, #26057, retired, 3¼", MIB **36.00**

Wilton Pans

Wilton started mass merchandising the shaped pans in the early 1960s, and the company has been careful to keep up with trends since then. Thus, many of the pans are limited production which adds to the collectible factor. You've probably seen several of these as you made your flea-market rounds. Especially good are the pans that depict cartoon, story book, or movie characters. Of course, condition is vital, and examples with the paper inserts/instructions, and accessory pieces bring the highest prices.

As with any collectible, future demand is impossible to predict, but since many Wilton pans can be found at garage sales, thrift stores, and flea markets for just a few dollars, right now it doesn't take a lot of money to start a collection.

Ariel (Little Mermaid), instructions & new face plate, used, EX **55.00**

Ballet slippers, #2105-2065, w/ insert & instructions, unused, M **30.00**

Baseball glove, 1987, pan only, used, EX **30.00**

Batman oval emblem, 1964, pan only, used, EX.................. **30.00**

Beer mug, 1984, pan only, used, EX **35.00**

Bob the Builder, #2105-5025, w/ insert & icing kit, unused, M **35.00**

Boba Fett (Star Wars), w/insert, 1983, used, EX **65.00**

Bowling a Strike!, 1990, w/insert & instructions, unused, M.. **40.00**

Cabbage Patch Kids, #2105-1988, 2-pc, stand, clips & instructions, MIB........................ **30.00**

Care Bear, 2-pc pan, stand, 6 clips & instructions, NMIB..... **45.00**

Cathy, 1983, M, $18.00. (Photo courtesy whatacharacter.com)

Cookie Monster, 1982, w/instructions, used, EX **35.00**

Cowboy boot, 1995, w/insert, used, EX **40.00**

Cuddles the Cow, 1988, w/reprinted instructions, used, EX **30.00**

C3PO (Star Wars), 1983, #502-2197, pan only, used, EX **45.00**

Darth Vader (Star Wars), 1980, pan only, used, EX **65.00**

Elmo (Sesame Street), holding ice cream cone, w/insert, used, EX **30.00**

Flowerpot, #2105-2030, w/instructions, used, EX **65.00**

Golf bag, 1987, pan only, used, EX **30.00**

Goofy head, 1976, #515-1104, pan only, used, EX **40.00**

Grand piano set, 6-pc, w/instructions, 1965, complete, unused, M **65.00**

Hockey player, 1998, w/instructions, unused, NM **35.00**

Jeep (Trail Rider), 1984, pan only, used, EX **40.00**

Lamb, 2-pc, w/instructions, used, EX **30.00**

Minnie Mouse head, #515-809, pan only, used, EX **35.00**

Motorcycle, w/insert & instructions, used, EX **60.00**

My Little Pony, 1986, pan only, used, EX **70.00**

Mystical Dragon, 1984, pan only, used, EX **75.00**

Nintendo Super Mario Brothers, w/ instructions, used, EX **30.00**

Pinocchio, mini, 1976, pan only, used, EX **33.00**

Playboy Bunny head, #2105-3025, pan only, used, EX **50.00**

Pokemon Pikachu, 1995, w/insert, used, EX **30.00**

Power Ranger, 1994, #2105-5975, w/instructions, used, EX............................. **40.00**

Precious Moments, #2105-9365, w/ instructions, used, EX **35.00**

R2-D2, 1980, with insert, unused, M, from $50.00 to $60.00.

Sailboat, w/instructions, used, EX **30.00**

Semi-tractor & trailer, 1986, #2105-0018, used, EX **30.00**

Spaceship, w/rare plastic topper & insert, used, EX **30.00**

Teenage Mutant Ninja Turtle, 1989, w/insert, unused, NM **30.00**

Thomas the Tank Engine, 1998, w/ insert, unused, M **40.00**

Winnie the Pooh, w/heating core, 6 clips & instructions, used, EX **60.00**

Winnie the Pooh holding #1, w/ insert, used, NM **45.00**

Wizard, 1984, w/insert, used, EX............................. **55.00**

World's Fairs and Expositions

Souvenir items have been issued since the mid-1800s for every world's fair and exposition. Few fairgoers have left the grounds without purchasing at least one. Some of the older items were often manufactured right on the fairgrounds by glass or pottery companies who erected working kilns and furnaces just for the duration of the fair. Of course, the older items are usually more valuable, but even souvenirs from the past 50 years are worth hanging on to. See Clubs and Newsletters for information concerning the World's Fair Collectors' Society, Inc. Unless noted otherwise, values are for examples in excellent to near mint condition.

Paperweight, 1933 Chicago, paper under glass, 4" long, $40.00. (Photo courtesy Buffalo Bay Auction Company)

1939 New York

Ashtray, metal with glass balls inset around rim, from $45.00 to $50.00.

Badge, NYWF Safety Team, enameled logo in gold horseshoe, 1½" **70.00**

Cup & saucer, Trylon & Perisphere w/rainbow-colored background, Japan **75.00**

Dresser carpet, Trylon & Perisphere scene, w/fringe, Italy, 18x8" **75.00**

Paint book, Bag Full...Pictures, suitcase shape, Whitman, 32-pg **120.00**

Pin-back, G Washington Bridge w/ skyline, metal, ¾x1¾" **35.00**

Salt & pepper shakers, Trylon & Perisphere in tray, Japan, 3-pc **45.00**

Spoon set, fair buildings, Rogers Mfg Co, 6", set of 12, M (EX boxes) **90.00**

Toy trolley, Greyhound Lines NY Worlds Fair, Arcade Toy, CI **210.00**

1939 San Francisco

Booklet, World's Fair Pictorial Panorama, 24-pg, 11x8½". **12.00**

Cigarette snuffer, Space Needle shape, Vica Novelty, 3½", EXIB **30.00**

Dish, Monorail, glass, 4x4¾". **20.00**

Paperweight, Space Needle shape, CI w/silver finish, 6½"..... **35.00**

Pillow, San Francisco scenes, fringe, 10½x10½" **17.50**

Social Security card, brass, stamped at fair **40.00**

1964 New York

Badge, Ford Motors Pavillion, NY, plastic **15.00**

Bank, mechanical, rocket shoots coin into globe, silvered metal, 9".................................... **45.00**

Bank, Persistance of Vision, Disney's involvement, 144-pg........ **30.00**

Cooler, Pepsi Cola, Disneyland Fun, red, white & blue w/strap. **85.00**

Cup, folding; swirled pink plastic, gold logo on lid................ **20.00**

Decanter, Jim Beam, 11½"..... **60.00**

Hat, Adam Burmuda, NMIB (fair logo on lid)...................... **25.00**

Lighter, copper w/raised fair scenes, chrome top, Japan.......... **25.00**

Map, Official Souvenir.......... **25.00**

Model kit, Santa Maria - Ship in a Bottle, Multistate Toy, EXIB **100.00**

Paperweight, Unisphere, silvered metal, 3" dia on base **140.00**

Slide set, 64 color scenes, 2" sq, EXIB **40.00**

Toy, Karosel Kitchen, Marx for Sears, 12", EXIB **50.00**

1982 Knoxville

Coin, commemorative; logo/aerial view, gold-tone, ½" dia **10.00**

Guide book, Official, 200+ pgs w/ fair map **8.00**

Pin-back, We're Going to...w/ Greyhound........................ **6.50**

Pocketknife, white Bakelite w/red Coca-Cola logo, 2-blade... **10.00**

Postcard, US Pavilion.............. **2.50**

Shell tray, 4", from $10.00 to $12.00.

Spoon, Sunsphere finial, engraved bowl, 5" **10.00**

Directory

The editors and staff take this opportunity to express our sincere gratitude and appreciation to each person who has in any way contributed to the preparation of this guide. We believe the credibility of our book is greatly enhanced through their participation. Check these listings for information concerning their specific areas of expertise.

If you care to correspond with anyone listed here in our Directory, you must send a SASE with your letter. If you are among those listed, please advise us of any changes in your address, phone number, or e-mail.

Alabama
Cataldo, C.E.
4726 Panorama Dr. SE
Huntsville, 35801
256-536-6893
genecams@aol.com.
Specializing in classic and used cameras

California
Conroy, Barbara J.
P.O. Box 2369
Santa Clara, CA 95055-2369
Author of *Restaurant China, Restaurant, Airline, Ship & Railroad Dinnerware, Vols. I* and *II* (Collector Books)

Elliott, Jacki
9790 Twin Cities Rd.
Galt, 95632
209-745-3860
Specializing in Rooster and Roses

Harrison, Gwynneth
11566 River Heights Drive
Riverside, 92505
951-343-0414
morgan27@sbcglobal.net
Buys and appraises Autumn Leaf; edits newsletter

Hibbard, Suzi
Dragon_Ware@hotmail.com
Specializing in Dragonware and 1000 Faces china, other Orientalia

Needham, Leonard
screensider@sbcglobal.net
Specializing in automobilia, advertising

Utley, Bill; Editor
Flashlight Collectors of America
P.O. Box 40945
Tustin, 92781
714-730-1252 or fax 714-505-4067
flashlights1@cox.net
Specializing in flashlights

Colorado
Diehl, Richard
5965 W Colgate Pl.
Denver, 80227
Specializing in license plates

Connecticut
Sabulis, Cindy
P.O. Box 642
Shelton, 06484
203-926-0176
www.dollsntoys.com

Specializing in dolls from the '60s – '70s (Liddle Kiddles, Barbie, Tammy, Tressy, etc.); co-author of *The Collector's Guide to Tammy, The Ideal Teen*, and author of *Collector's Guide to Dolls of the 1960s & 1970s* (Collector Books)

Florida
Kuritzky, Lewis
4510 NW 17th Pl.
Gainesville, 32605
352-377-3193
lkuritzky@aol.com
Author of *Collector's Guide to Bookends*

Posner, Judy
P.O. Box 2194
Englewood, 34295
judyposner@yahoo.com
Specializing in figural pottery, cookie jars, salt and pepper shakers, Black memorabilia, and Disneyana; sale lists available; fee charged for appraisals

Idaho
McVey, Jeff
1810 W State St. #427
Boise, 83702-3955
Author of *Tire Ashtray Collector's Guide;* available from the author

Illinois
Garmon, Lee
1529 Whittier St.
Springfield, 62704
217-789-9574
Specializing in Elvis Presley

Jungnickel, Eric
P.O. Box 4674

Naperville, 60567-4674
630-983-8339
Specializing in Indy 500 memorabilia

Kadet, Jeff
TV Guide Specialists
P.O. Box 20
Macomb, 61455
Buying and selling *TV Guide* from 1948 through the 1990s

Karman, Lauri and Rich
Editors of *The Fenton Flyer*
815 S. Douglas
Springfield, 62704
Specializing in Fenton art glass

Klompus, Eugene R.
Just Cuff Links
P.O. Box 5970
Vernon Hills, 60061
847-816-0035
genek@cufflinksrus.com
www.justcufflinks.com
Specializing in cuff links and men's accessories

Indiana
McGrady, Donna
P.O. Box 14
Waynetown, IN 47990
765-234-2187

McQuillen, Michael and Polly
P.O. Box 50022
Indianapolis, 46250-0022
317-845-1721
michael@politicalparade.com
www.politicalparade.com
Specializing in political memorabilia

Sanders, Lisa
8900 Old State Rd.
Evansville, 47111
1dlk@insightbb.com
Specializing in M. A. Hadley

Iowa
Devine, Joe
D&D Antique Mall
1411 South 3rd St.
Council Bluffs, 51503
712-328-7305
Author of *Collecting Royal Copley Plus Royal Windsor & Spaulding*

Kentucky
Florence, Gene and Cathy
Box 22186
Lexington, 40522
Authors (Collector Books) on Depression glass, Occupied Japan, Elegant glass, and kitchen glassware

Hornback, Betty
707 Sunrise Ln.
Elizabethtown, 42701
Specializing in Kentucky Derby and horse racing memorabilia; send for informative booklet, $15 ppd.

Louisiana
Langford, Paris
415 Dodge Ave.
Jefferson, 70121-3311
504-733-0067
bbean415@aol.com.
Author of *Liddle Kiddles*; specializing in dolls of the 1960s – 1970s

Maine
Hathaway, John
Hathaway's Antiques

3 Mills Rd.
Bryant Pond, 04219
207-665-2214
Specializing in fruit jars, mail-order a specialty

Massachusetts
Porter, Richard T.
Porter Thermometer Museum
Box 944
Onset 02558
thermometerman@aol.com
Specializing in thermometers

White, Larry
108 Central St.
Rowley, 01969-1317
978-948-8187
larrydw@erols.com
Specializing in Cracker Jack; author of books; has newsletter

Michigan
Nickel, Mike; and Cindy Horvath
P.O. Box 456
Portland, 48875-0456
517-647-7646
mandc@voyager.net
Specializing in Ohio art pottery, Kay Finch, author of *Kay Finch Ceramics, Her Enchanted World*, available from the authors; co-author of *Collector's Encyclopedia of Roseville Pottery Revised Edition, Vol I* and *Vol II* (Collector Books)

Pickvet, Mark
5071 Watson Dr.
Flint, 48506
Author of *Shot Glasses: An American Tradition*, available for $12.95 plus $2.50 postage and han-

398

dling from Antique Publications
P.O. Box 553
Marietta, OH 45750

Nebraska
Johnson, Donald-Brian
3329 S 56th St. #611
Omaha, 68106
donaldbrian@webtv.net
Specializing in Ceramic Arts
Studio, Higgins glass, Moss lamps,
vintage eyeware, and Whiting and
Davis purses

New Hampshire
Holt, Jane
P.O. Box 115
Derry, 03038
Specializing in Annalee dolls

New Jersey
Litts, Elyce
P.O. Box 394
Morris Plains, 07950
973-361-4087
happy.memories@worldnet.att.net
www.happy-memories.com
Specializing in Geisha Girl (author
of book); also ladies' compacts

Palmieri, Jo Ann
27 Pepper Rd.
Towaco, 07082-1357
201-334-5829
Specializing in Skookum Indian dolls

Perzel, Robert and Nancy
Popkorn
P.O. Box 1057
Flemington, 08822
Specializing in Stangl dinnerware,
birds and artware; American pot-
tery and dinnerware

New Mexico
Mace, Shirley
Shadow Enterprises
P.O. Box 1602
Mesilla Park, 88047
505-524-6717; fax 505-523-0940
silhouettes-us@yahoo.com
www.geocities.com/Madison
Avenue/Boardroom/1631
Author of *Encyclopedia of Silhouette
Collectibles on Glass* (available
from the author)

New York
Beegle, Gary
92 River St.
Montgomery, 12549
845-457-3623
Liberty Blue dinnerware, also
most lines of collectible modern
American dinnerware as well as
character glasses

Weitman, Stan and Arlene
P.O. Box 1186
Massapequa Park, 11758
scrackled @earthlink.net
www.tias.com/stores/crackleking/
Authors of *Crackle Glass,
Identification and Value Guide,
Volumes I* and *II* (Collector Books)

North Carolina
Brooks, Ken and Barbara
4121 Gladstone Ln.
Charlotte, 28205
Specializing in Cat-Tail Dinnerware

Newbound, Betty
2206 Nob Hill Dr.
Sanford, 27330
Author (Collector Books) on Blue
Ridge dinnerware, milk glass,

wall pockets, figural planters, and vases; Specializing in collectible china and glass

North Dakota
Farnsworth, Bryce L.
1334 14½ St.
S Fargo, 58103
701-237-3597
Specializing in Rosemeade

Ohio
Benjamin, Scott
P.O. Box 556
LaGrange, 44050-0556
440-355-6608
www.oilcollectibles.com
Specializing in automobilia, gas globes

China Specialties, Inc.
Box 471
Valley City, 44280
Specializing in high-quality reproductions of Homer Laughlin and Hall china, including Autumn Leaf

Graff, Shirley
4515 Grafton Rd.
Brunswick, 44212-2005
Specializing in Pennsbury

Mangus, Beverly and Jim
5147 Broadway NE
Louisville, 44641-8869
Authors (Collector Books) specializing in Shawnee pottery

Whitmyer, Margaret and Kenn
P.O. Box 30806
Gahana, 43230-2704
Authors (Collector Books) specializing in children's dishes, Christmas

collectibles, Hall china, and Fenton glass

Young, Mary
P.O. Box 9244
Wright Bros. Branch
Dayton, 45409
937-298-4838
Author of books; specializing in paper dolls

Oklahoma
Boone, Phyllis
14535 E 13th St.
Tulsa, 74108-4527
918-437-7776
Specializing in Frankoma pottery

Ivers, Terri
Terri's Toys and Nostalgia
114 Whitworth Ave.
Ponca City, 74601-3438
580-762-1122
toylady@cableone.net
Specializing in character collectibles, lunch boxes, advertising items, Breyer and Hartland figures

Moore, Shirley and Art
4423 E. 31st St.
Tulsa, 74135
918-747-4164
Specializing in Lu-Ray Pastels and Depression glass

Oregon
Brown, Marcia 'Sparkles'
P.O. Box 2314
White City 97503
541-826-3039
Collector Books author specializing in jewelry

Coe, Debbie and Randy
Coes Mercantile
P.O. Box 173
Hillsboro, 97123
Specializing in Elegant and Depression glass, art pottery, Cape Cod by Avon, Golden Foliage by Libbey Glass Company, Gurley candles, and Liberty Blue dinnerware

White, Carole Bess
2225 NE 33rd Ave.
Portland, 97207-5116
Specializing in Japan ceramics; author of books

Pennsylvania
BOJO/Bob Gottuso
P.O. Box 1403
Cranberry Twp., 16066-0403
Phone or fax 724-776-0621
www.bojoonline.com
Specializing in the Beatles and rock 'n roll memorabilia

Greenfield, Jeannie
310 Parker Rd.
Stoneboro, 16153-2810
724-376-2584
dlg3684@yahoo.com
Specializing in cake toppers and egg timers

Kreider, Katherine
P.O. Box 7957
Lancaster, 19604-7957
717-892-3001
katherinekreider@valentinesdirect.com
Specializing in valentines

South Carolina
Belyski, Richard
P.O. Box 14956
Surfside Beach, 29587
Specializing in PEZ

Greguire, Helen
79 Lake Lyman Heights
Lyman, 29365
864-848-0408
Author (Collector Books) specializing in Graniteware

Tennessee
Fields, Linda
230 Beech Lane
Buchanon, 38222
731-644-2244
Fpiebird@compu.net
Specializing in pie birds

Texas
Docks, L. R. 'Les'
Shellac Shack; Discollector
Box 691035
San Antonio, 78269-1035
docks@texas.net
Author of *American Premium Record Guide;* Specializing in vintage records

Gibbs, Carl, Jr.
1716 Westheimer Rd
Houston, 77098
Author of *Collector's Encyclopedia of Metlox Potteries* (Collector Books); specializing in American dinnerware

Jackson, Joyce
900 Jenkins Rd.
Aledo, 76008-2410
817-441-8864

jjpick@earthlink.net
Specializing in Swanky Swigs

Nossaman, Darlene
5419 Lake Charles
Waco, 76710
Specializing in Homer Laughlin China information and Horton Ceramics

Pogue, Larry
L and J Antiques & Collectibles
8142 Ivan Ct.
Terrell, 75161-6921
972-551-0221
L&JAntiques@direcway.com
www.LandJAntiques.com
Specializing in head vases, string holders, general line

Woodard, Dannie
P.O. Box 1346
Weatherford, 76086
817-594-4680
Author of *Hammered Aluminum, Hand Wrought Collectibles*

Utah
Spencer, Rick
Salt Lake City
801-973-0805
Specializing in Shawnee, Roseville, Weller, Van Tellingen, Regal, Bendel, Coors, Rookwood, Watt; also salt and pepper shakers, cookie jars, cut glass, radios, and silver flatware

Vermont
Dinner, Craig
P.O. Box 184
Townshend VT 05353
718-729-3850
Specializing in figural cast-iron items (door knockers, lawn sprinklers, doorstops, windmill weights)

Wisconsin
Helley, Phil
629 Indiana Ave.
Wisconsin Dells, 53965
608-254-8659
Specializing in Cracker Jack items, radio premiums, dexterity games, toys (especially Japanese wind-up toys), banks, and old Dells souvenir items marked Kilbourn

West Virginia
Apkarian-Russell, Pamela
Castle Halloween
577 Boggs Run Rd.
Benwood 26031-1001
304-233-1031
Specializing in Halloween collectibles, postcards of all kinds, and Joe Camel

Clubs and Newsletters

Akro Agate Collectors Club
Clarksburg Crow
Roger Hardy
10 Bailey St.
Clarksburg, WV 26301-2524
304-624-4523
rhardy0424@wirefire.com
Annual membership fee: $25

Antiques Coast to Coast
Mark Chervenka, Editor
P.O. Box 12130
Des Moines, IA 50312-9403
acrn@repronews.com
800-227-5531 (subscriptions only)
or 515-274-5886
12 monthly issues: $32 US, $41
Canada, $59 foreign

The Antique Trader Weekly
Nancy Crowley, Editor
P.O. Box 1050
Dubuque, IA 52004-1050
collect@krause.com
www.antiquetrader.com
Subscription: $38 (52 issues) per
year; sample: $1

Autographs of America
Tim Anderson
P.O. Box 461
Provo, UT 84603
801-226-1787 (afternoons, please)
www.AutographsOfAmerica.com
Free sample catalog of hundreds of
autographs for sale

Autumn Leaf
Glen Karlgaard, Editor
13800 Fernando Ave.
Apple Valley, MN 55124

952-431-1814
www.nalcc.org

Avon Times
c/o Dwight or Vera Young
P.O. Box 9868, Dept. P.
Kansas City, MO 64134
AvonTimes@aol.com
Send SASE for information

Bookend Collector Club
Louis Kuritzky, M.D.
4510 NW 17th Place
Gainsville, FL 32650
352-377-3193
lkuritzky@aol.com
Membership (includes newsletter):
$25 per year

Candy Container Collectors of
America
c/o Jim Olean
115 Mac Beth Dr.
Lower Burrel, PA 15068-2628
www.candycontainer.org

CAS Collector's
206 Grove St.
Rockton, IL 61072
www.cascollectors.com
Ceramic Arts Studio history website: www.ceramicartsstudio.org; Established in 1994 as the Ceramic Arts Studio Collectors Association, CAS Collectors welcomes all with a common interest in the work of Ceramic Arts Studio of Madison, Wisconsin. The club publishes a quarterly newsletter and hosts an annual convention in Madison each

August in conjunction with the Wisconsin Pottery Association Show & Sale. Family membership: $25 per year. Information about the club and its activities, as well as a complete illustrated CAS history, is included in the book *Ceramic Arts Studio: The Legacy of Betty Harrington* by Donald-Brian Johnson, Timothy J. Holthaus, and James E. Petzold (Schiffer Publishing, 2003).

CC International, Ltd.
A Collectors' Club of Campbell
  Soup Memorabilia
Glenn Fahey
806 Hile Lane
Englewood, OH 45322
www.soupclan.com
Membership: $30 per year, includes quarterly issues of the club's newsletter, annual memento, and access to club's website

Cookie Crumbs
Ruth Capper, Secretary/Treasurer
PO Box 245
Cannon Falls, MN 55009
www.cookiecuttercollectorsclub.com
Subscription $20 per year (4 issues, payable to CCCC)

Currier & Ives Dinnerware
  Collectors
Royal China Collectors Club
Edward Michniewicz, Treasurer
7022 Shaker Rd.
Louden, NH 03307-1130
603-783-4023
royalchinaclub.com
Membership: $15

Czechoslovakian Collectors Guild
  International
Alan Badia, Membership Chairman
15006 Meadowlake St.
Odessa, FL 33556-3126
www.czechartglass.com/ccgi

Doll News Magazine
United Federation of Doll Clubs
10900 N. Pomona Ave.
Kansas City, MO 64153
816-891-7040
www.ufdc.org

Doorstop Collectors of America
Jeanie Bertoia
2413 Madison Ave.
Vineland, NJ 08630
609-692-4092
Membership: $20 per year, includes 2 newsletters and convention; send 2-stamp SASE for sample

Dragonware Club
c/o Suzi Hibbard
849 Vintage Ave.
Fairfield, CA 94585
Dragon_Ware@hotmail.com

FBOC (Figural Bottle Opener
  Collectors)
FBOC (Figural Bottle Opener
  Club)
Lyle Moreland
864 Jeannette Ave.
Baltimore, MD 21222

Fenton Art Glass Collectors of
  America, Inc.
Butterfly Net newsletter
P.O. Box 384
702 W. 5th St.
Williamstown, WV 26187

faqcainc@wirefire.com
Membership: $20; Associate member: $5

Fiesta Collector's Quarterly
P.O. Box 471
Valley City, OH 44280
www.chinaspecialties.com
Subscription: $12 per year

Fisher-Price Collector's Club
Jacquie Hamblin
38 Main St.
Oneonta, NY 12820-2519
www.fpclub.org
Monthly newsletter with information and ads; send SASE for more information

Flashlight Collectors of America Newsletter
Bill Utley
P.O. Box 4095
Tustin, CA 92781
714-730-1252
flashlight@worldnet.att.net
Flashlights, Early Flashlight Makers of the 1st 100 Years of Eveready, full color, 320 pages, now available; quarterly flashlight newsletter, $12 per year

Frankoma Family Collectors Association
c/o Nancy Littrell
P.O. Box 32571
Oklahoma City, OK 73123-0771
www.frankoma.org
Membership dues: $35 (includes quarterly newsletter and annual convention)

The Front Striker Bulletin
Bill Retskin
P.O. Box 18481
Asheville, NC 28814-0481
704-254-4487 or fax 704-254-1066
bill@matchcovers.com
www.matchcovers.com
Membership: $10 per year

Griswold & Cast Iron Cookware Association
G&CICA Secretary
223 Summit Circle
Lakeville, PA 18438
Membership: $20 per individual or $25 per family (2 members per address) payable to club

Hall China Collectors' Club Newsletter
Virginia Lee
P.O. Box 360488
Cleveland, OH 44136

Head Hunters Newsletter
c/o Maddy Gordon
P.O. Box 83 H
Scarsdale, NY 10583
For collectors of head vases; subscription: $26 yearly for 4 quarterly issues; Ads free to subscribers

International Nippon Collectors Club (INCC)
Dick Bittner, Membership Chairperson
8 Geoley Court
Thurmont MD 21788
www.nipponcollectorsclub.com
Publishes newsletter 6 times a year; Holds annual convention; Membership: $30

International Perfume and Scent Bottle Collectors Association
c/o Randall B. Monsen
P.O. Box 529
Vienna, VA 22183
fax 703-242-1357
www.perfumebottles.org

Just Cuff Links
Eugene R. Klompus
PO Box 5970
Vernon Hills, IL 60061
847-816-0035; fax: 847-816-7466
genek@cufflinksrus.com

Knife Rests of Yesterday and Today
Marble Collectors' Society of
    America
51 Johnson St.
Trumbull, CT 06611
blockschip@aol.com
www.blocksite.com

McDonald's© Collector Club
PMB 200
1153 S. Lee St.
Des Plains, IL 60016-6503
www.mcdclub.com
Membership: $25 individual per year; $30 family

National Assoc. of Avon Collectors
c/o Connie Clark
6100 Walnut, Dept. P
Kansas City, MO 64113
Information requires LSASE

National Depression Glass
    Association
P.O. Box 8264
Wichita, KS 67208-0264
Membership: $20 per year
www.ndga.net

National Fenton Glass Society
Laurie & Rich Karman, Editors
815 S. Douglas
Springfield, IL 62704
Membership: $20; includes *The Fenton Flyer* newsletter

National Graniteware Society
P.O. Box 9248
Cedar Rapids, IA 52409-9248
www.graniteware.org
Membership: $20 per year

National Imperial Glass Collectors'
    Society, Inc.
P.O. Box 534
Bellaire, OH 43906
www.imperialglass.org
Membership: $18 per year (+$3 for each associate member), quarterly newsletter

National Milk Glass Collectors'
    Society and *Opaque News,* quarterly newsletter
Barb Pinkston, Membership
    Chairman
1306 Stowe St.
Inverfness, FL 34450-6853
membership@nmgsc.org
www.nmgcs.org
Please include SASE

National Reamer Association
c/o Wayne Adickes
408 E. Reuss
Cuero, TX 77954
adickes@sbcglobal.net
www.reamers.org
Membership: $25 per household

National Society of Lefton
    Collectors

The Lefton Collector Newsletter
National Valentine Collectors
Association
Nancy Rosen
P.O. Box 1404
Santa Ana, CA 92702
714-547-1355
Membership: $16

NM (Nelson McCoy) Xpress
Carol Seman, Editor
8934 Brecksville Rd., Suite 406
Brecksville, OH 44141-2318
McCjs@aol.com
www.nmxpress.com
Subscription: $26 per year

The Occupied Japan Club
c/o Florence Archambault
29 Freeborn St.
Newport, RI 02840-1821
florence@aiconnect.com
Publishes *The Upside Down World of an O.J. Collector*, a bimonthly newsletter; Information requires SASE

On the LIGHTER Side
International Lighter Collectors
Judith Sanders, Editor
136 Circle Dr.
Quitman, TX 75783
903-763-2795 or fax 703-763-4953
Annual convention held in different cities in the US; send SASE when requesting information

Paden City Glass Collectors Guild
Paul Torsiello, Editor
42 Aldine Road
Parsippany, NJ, 07054
pcguild@yahoo.com

Paper & Advertising Collectors' Marketplace
PO Box 128
Scandinavia, WI 54977-0128
715-467-2379 or fax 715-467-2243
pacpcm@engleonline.com
www.paperandadvertisingcollector.com
Subscription: $19.95 in US (12 issues)

Paper Doll News
Emma Terry
P.O. Box 807
Vivian, LA 71082
Subscription: $12 per year

Pez Collector's News
Richard Belyski, Editor
P.O. Box 14956
Surfside Beach, SC 29587
peznews@juno.com
www.pezcollectorsnews.com

Pie Birds Unlimited Newsletter
Rita Reedy
1039 NW Hwy. 101
Lincoln City, OR 97367
ritazart@lycol.com

Political Collectors of Indiana
Michael McQuillen
P.O. Box 50022
Indianapolis, IN 46250-0022
317-845-1721
michael@politicalparade.com
www.politicalparade.com
Official APIC (American Political Items Collectors) Chapter comprised of over 100 collectors of presidential and local political items

The Prize Insider Newsletter for
Cracker Jack Collectors
Larry White
108 Central St.
Rowley, MA 01969
978-948-8187
larrydw@erols.com

Rosevilles of the Past Newsletter
Nancy Bomm, Editor
P.O. Box 656
Clarcona, FL 32710-0656
407-294-3980
rosepast@worldnet.att.net
Send $19.95 per year for 6 to 12
newsletters

Roy Rogers – Dale Evans
Collectors Association
Nancy Horsley, Exec. Secretary
P.O. Box 1166
Portsmouth, OH 45662-1166
www.royrogersfestival.org

Shawnee Pottery Collectors' Club
c/o Pamela Curran
P.O. Box 713
New Smyrna Beach, FL 32170-0713
Send $3 for sample copy

The Shot Glass Club of America
Mark Pickvet, Editor
P.O. Box 90404
Flint, MI 48509

The Silver Bullet
Lone Ranger Fan Club
P.O. Box 9561
Longmont, CO 80502
806-373-3969
www.lonerangerfanclub.com
Membership: $36

Stretch Glass Society
P.O. Box 3305 Society
Quartz Hill, CA 93586
www.stretchglasssociety.org
Membership: $22 (US); $24 (International); holds annual convention

The TeaTime Gazette
P.O. Box 40276
St. Paul, MN 55104
612-227-7415
info@teatimegazette.com

Tiffin Glass Collectors
P.O. Box 554
Tiffin, OH 44883
Membership: $15
www.tiffinglass.org

Toy Shop
700 E State St.
Iola, WI 54990-0001
715-445-2214
www.toyshopmag.com
Subscription (3rd class) $33.98 (US)
for 26 issues

The Trick or Treat Trader
Pamela E. Apkarian-Russell
C.J. Russell and The Halloween
Queen
577 Boggs Run Rd
Benwood, WV 26031-1002
halloweenqueen@cheshire.net
www.castlehalloween.com
Subscription: $15 (4 issues)

*Vintage Fashion & Costume
Jewelry* Newsletter/Club
P.O. Box 265
Glen Oaks, NY 11004
718-969-2320 or 718-939-3095

www.lizjewel.com/vf
Yearly subscription: $20 (US) for 4 issues; sample copy available by sending $5

Westmoreland Glass Society
Steve Jensen
P.O. Box 2883
Iowa City, IA 52240-2883
www.westmorelandglassclubs.org/wgsi_mem.html
Membership: $15 single or $25 household

The Willow Review
P.O. Box 41312
Nashville, TN 37204
Send SASE for information

World's Fair Collectors' Society, Inc.
Fair News newsletter
Michael R. Pender, Editor
P.O. Box 20806
Sarasota, FL 34276-3806
941-923-2590
wfcs@aol.com
Dues: $20 (US), $25 (Canada), $30 (overseas)

Index

Index